WAR IN THE SHADOWS

The Guerrilla in History

By Robert B. Asprey

Volume I

DOUBLEDAY & COMPANY, INC.
GARDEN CITY, NEW YORK

This book is dedicated to Arthur Wittenstein—
loyal friend, wise and patient counselor

Grateful acknowledgment is made for permission to use excerpts from the following copyrighted material:

Dean Acheson, *Present at the Creation*, copyright © 1969 by Dean Acheson. Reprinted by permission of W. W. Norton & Company, Inc. and Hamish Hamilton Ltd.
Loeb Appian, *Appian's Roman History*, copyright 1912 by The Loeb Classical Library. Reprinted by permission of The Loeb Classical Library. (Harvard University Press and William Heinemann.)
Ronald Atkin, *Revolution! Mexico 1910–1920*, copyright © 1969 by Ronald Atkin. Reprinted by permission of The John Day Company.
John A. Armstrong, editor, *Soviet Partisans In World War II*, copyright © 1964 by the Regents of the University of Wisconsin. Reprinted by permission of The University of Wisconsin Press.
Donald L. Barnett and Karari Njama, *Mau Mau From Within*, copyright © 1966 by Donald L. Barnett and Karari Njama. Reprinted by permission of Monthly Review Press and Granada Publishing Limited.
Edward Behr, *The Algerian Problem*, copyright © 1961 by Edward Behr. Reprinted by permission of Hodder and Stoughton, Limited.
C. N. M. Blair, *Guerrilla Warfare*, copyright © 1957 by United Kingdom Ministry of Defence. Reprinted by permission of Ministry of Defence.
W. C. Bullitt, "A Report to the American People on China," October 13, 1947 issue of *Life*. Copyright © 1947 by Time Inc. Reprinted by permission of Time/Life Syndication Service.
Joseph Buttinger, *Vietnam: A Dragon Embattled*, copyright © 1967 by Joseph Buttinger. Reprinted by permission of Praeger Publishers, Inc. and Phaidon Press, Limited.
Bernard Callinan, *Independent Company*, copyright 1953 by Bernard Callinan. Reprinted by permission of William Heinemann, Ltd.
C. E. Callwell, *Small Wars and Their Practice*. Reprinted by permission of Her Majesty's Stationery Office.
F. Spencer Chapman, *The Jungle Is Neutral*, copyright 1949 by F. Spencer Chapman. Reprinted by permission of Chatto and Windus and the Author's Literary Estate.
Winston S. Churchill, *World Crisis*, copyright 1923, 1927 by Charles Scribner's Sons. Reprinted by permission of Charles Scribner's Sons and The Hamlyn Publishing Group, Limited.
Clark M. Clifford, "A Viet Nam Reappraisal," July 1969. Copyright © 1969 by Council on Foreign Relations, Inc. Reprinted by permission from *Foreign Affairs*.
Richard Clutterbuck, *The Long Long War*, copyright © 1966 by Richard Clutter-

. . . There are fearful excitements on any side.
Any side can accuse the other
And feel virtuous without the hardships of virtue.
When pride of race has been pent up
In a tyrannous disregard, and valued liberties
Have been lost for long enough, what comes in the way
Of dignity's free and natural flowing
Is nothing but rocks to be blasted. I envy them
Their certainty. Each private man
Has a public cause to elucidate him,
And a reasonable sense of having been wronged.
If you like you can call this man your enemy;
It's what he expects.

CHRISTOPHER FRY
The Dark Is Light Enough

Apologia

PERHAPS UNFORTUNATELY, the modern writer has slipped away from the habit of justifying a work of non-fiction to the reader. While some books require none, others do and this is one.

War in the Shadows is an attempt to explain the Vietnam conflict in the historical terms of guerrilla warfare. It is not a history of guerrilla war—that would be a multivolume effort. It is an attempt to place the role of guerrilla warfare in history in order to give the interested reader a perspective heretofore denied him, and one I believe essential to an understanding of the conflict that has so confused, embittered, and divided intelligent people not only in America, but throughout the world.

What is guerrilla warfare?

It is a type of warfare characterized by irregular forces fighting small-scale, limited actions, generally in conjunction with a larger political-military strategy, against orthodox military forces. The word *guerrilla* means little war, and its use stems from the duke of Wellington's Iberian campaigns (1809–13), when Spanish-Portuguese irregulars, or *guerrilleros* (also referred to at the time as partisans and insurgents), helped drive the French from the peninsula.

In its simplest form, it is primitive people dressed in skins and armed with sticks and stones fighting in defense of home and country. It is traditionally a method of protest employed to rectify real or imagined wrongs levied on a people either by a foreign invader or a ruler. Most of the great conquests of history included guerrilla actions; many were in large part pacification campaigns. Darius, Alexander, and Hannibal all fought guerrilla warfare. This was both rude, as against the Scythians, and sophisticated, as when Hannibal unsuccessfully tried to bring the Roman general Quintus Fabius Maximus to battle—thus the birth of Fabian tactics. The Romans fought guerrilla warfare for over two hundred years in Spain before the birth of Christ (a crisis in this campaign is the reason our calendar year commences on the first of January). Norman crusaders came up against quasi-guerrilla opposition from the Seljuk Turks in Syria; Edward I fought what were essentially pacification campaigns in Wales and Scotland.

In time, guerrilla warfare became a useful adjunct to a larger, political-military strategy—a role in which it complemented orthodox military operations, real or intended, either inside enemy territory or in areas seized and occupied by an enemy. Early classic examples of this role occurred in the Silesian wars (1741–45); in the American revolution, in which southern irregulars (relying heavily on terrorist tactics) helped drive Cornwallis from the Carolinas to defeat at Yorktown; and in Spain and Russia, where guerrillas helped to defeat Napoleon's armies.

But guerrilla and quasi-guerrilla tactics have also been used traditionally in a third role, an aggressive role, as witness such predatory barbarians as the Goths and Huns, who began the destruction of the Western Roman Empire; or the later Magyars, who conquered Hungary; or the Vikings, who overran Ireland, England, and France; or the Mongols, who won China and terrified central Europe.

While certain details of these various campaigns are lacking, ancient chroniclers have described barbarian organization and tactics and, most important, the development of countertactics. Byzantine writings, in particular, show a firm grasp of the subject, including political implications.

The ancient record is valuable on three counts. First, it is interesting in its own right as establishing the thread of guerrilla and quasi-guerrilla tactics and even strategy in the history of warfare. Second, the tactical record suggests that orthodox generals who adapted conventional tactics to meet the guerrilla challenge usually prospered while those who failed to do so suffered defeat. From Darius onward, we find commanders cursed with an arrogance of ignorance often compounded by arrogance of power—terms we shall use again—and we find their soldiers and peoples paying a heavy cost in consequence.

Third, the political record suggests that even the most valid counterguerrilla tactics provided transitory victory that gained meaning only when exploited politically by the ruler's putting his own house in order. Here again we find plentiful examples of an arrogance of ignorance compounded by arrogance of power, with resulting misery and frequently loss of kingdom and even empire.

The reader will be surprised, I believe, to learn the historical progression of guerrilla warfare in more recent times to its exalted state as the major instrument in today's revolutionary wars. Tactically, the record is as impressive as it is tragic, and generally repeats the trend set in ancient campaigns despite the earnest writings of a few to educate the many.

The political element is even more important. Ancient campaigns never entirely lacked a political consideration (except on the part of barbarians, who were generally more interested in booty than conquest), but only in the nineteenth century did it become intrusive and only in the twentieth century predominant over military action. Primitive peoples, and some not so primitive such as the Boers, still fought guerrilla wars for traditional reasons. But, slowly, guerrilla warfare evolved into an instrument to achieve specific, usually revolutionary political goals, as witness the Mexican revolution. Lenin clearly recognized guerrilla warfare as a military means to a political end, and Mao Tse-tung further defined its role in an agrarian context. Ho Chi Minh successfully synthesized this thinking to fit his particular situation, and he was fortunate enough to have a military genius, Vo Nguyen Giap, translate desire to deed. Yet it would be wrong to grant Communists a monopoly on guerrilla warfare. Kenya Mau Maus, Greek Cypriotes, and Algerians were free of Communist connections, yet all used revolutionary war to gain political ends.

For a very long time Western statesmen and military leaders have over-looked the significance of this predominant political element. The late Bernard Fall, an expert on Southeast Asia who was killed in Vietnam, aptly wrote in a preface to Roger Trinquier's frightening book on revolutionary warfare[1]:

American readers—particularly those who are concerned with today's operations in South Vietnam—will find to their surprise that their various seemingly "new" counter-insurgency gambits, from strategic hamlets to large-scale pacification, are mere rehashes of old tactics to which helicopters, weed killers, and rapid-firing rifles merely add a new dimension of speed and bloodiness without basically changing the character of the struggle—nor its outcome, if the same *political* errors that the French have made are repeated.

Dr. Fall failed to add that the final French effort in Vietnam repeated not only many of the tactical "gambits" of history, but also many of its *political* errors.

A historical sampling of guerrilla warfare, then, should claim more than academic interest, for within the context of our day a knowledge of this history, even if sharply abridged, is vital to the understanding and further study of a disturbing fact: For a number of reasons, guerrilla warfare has evolved into an ideal instrument for the realization of social-political-economic aspirations of underprivileged peoples. This is so patently true as to allow one to suggest that we may be witnessing a transition to a new era in warfare, an era as radically different as those which followed the writings of Sun Tzu, Machiavelli, Clausewitz, and Mahan.

This particular development, however, is more difficult to grasp, partly because of the dichotomy in political thought nurtured by a vast economic gulf between have and have-not countries, and partly because of incredible technological advances which have resulted in such sophisticated and awesome weapons as the H-bomb—thus creating the military paradox of destructive impotence.

A part of the total impact of today's "people's war" or "wars of national liberation" may be explained by the frustration of rich and powerful nations possessing highly scientific weapons systems which either cannot be employed because of moral-political considerations or are technically unsuitable for fighting in a particular environment. So long as conventional commanders fail to adapt organization, techniques, and tactics to meet the guerrilla challenge instead of trying to convert it to orthodox challenge, these revolutionary campaigns will prosper. Even when properly challenged, however, they do not lend themselves to an exclusive military "solution," which at best is ephemeral. The words "winning" and "victory" diminish in meaning as we face the awesome political-economic challenge that, to date, many of our leaders, particularly military commanders, seem unable to comprehend—despite manifold lessons of history.

I hope this book will bring home those lessons and will help the readers to grasp more fully the ramifications of a complex subject, and thus enable him to question more intelligently the qualifications and attitudes of his future elected representatives. The pages that follow emphasize the cost to any coun-

1. Roger Trinquier, *Modern Warfare—A French View of Counter-Insurgency* (New York: Frederick A. Praeger, 1964).

try when its civil and military leaders fail to consider yesterday while dealing with tomorrow. In this sense, the book is also a warning: America can afford one Vietnam, but not another.

Apology is sometimes part of justification, and I want to apologize on several counts. The reader will not find a study of recent Middle East or African guerrilla campaigns or the present Ulster insurgency—none of these influenced the Vietnam war.

I also regret the amount of blood splashed on the following narrative. In writing these chapters, I sometimes thought of Julia A. Moore, "The Sweet Singer of Michigan," whose tragedy-ridden ballads caused Mark Twain to remark that, in each, she killed more people than a Gatling gun. I will ask the sensitive reader to keep in mind Henry James's reply to John Buchan, who expressed nausea over some lust-ridden Byronic correspondence: "Nauseating, perhaps, but how quite inexpressibly significant."

If I seem harsh on the subject of British and French (and other) colonialism and the subsequent insurgencies caused thereby, it is not a condemnation of peoples, but rather a regret of a social-historical-economic condition that allowed shortsighted and greedy persons and governments an exploitive hand against peoples lacking but slight recourse. My British and French friends know my pride in our friendship and my respect for the noble institutions bequeathed to civilization by their countries. My criticism centers on those tragic colonizing periods when civilization was momentarily suppressed—and I have been as hard on my own country's record in Vietnam despite its different motivations.

I must briefly mention sources and treatment. I have quoted from a good many works, not from laziness but from unwillingness to deprive either the reader or myself of the added enjoyment of an apt phrase or description contemporary to the period, or to deprive the author of a measure of appreciation for a well-expressed thought often derived from a lifetime of specialized study. I have listed my sources in case the reader wishes to pursue further one or more of the highly abridged accounts of guerrilla campaigns. I would like the reader to remember that my spelling of place names is arbitrary—he will frequently find variations, particularly in Arabic and oriental areas; I have tried to use the most convenient version. Similarly, the sketch maps are intended primarily for orientation purposes. I should stress that the selection of sources is curtailed—most of the standard works, however, contain pertinent bibliographies and detailed maps.

Contemporary sources, particularly those concerning Vietnam, are limited. Dangers await any writer who attempts at this early date to analyze America's role in this area. Vietnam is not an isolated phenomenon, and American interest in Asia did not suddenly develop in 1965 or 1958 or 1950. Some readers will be surprised to learn that the national interest dates from 1833, when America first signed a trade agreement with the kingdom of Siam, and that it demonstrably grew when we acquired the Philippines and thus a stake in the region. Fundamental to any understanding of America's role in Vietnam is her relationship with China and the trauma that followed Chiang

Kai-shek's fall—I have tried to explain this, albeit from the standpoint of guerrilla warfare.

But definitive historical appreciation, particularly from 1950 to the present, will depend in part on documents not likely to become available for a long time. On the other hand, the divisive nature of this war has caused a number of concerned principals to speak out on some important aspects, and the publication of the Pentagon Papers has also yielded valuable if somewhat lopsided historical evidence. In certain instances, particularly those concerning secret high-level official debates, these sources permit educated guessing—at all times identified as such.

The final point is more personal. Certain of my conclusions conflict with stated professional opinions of some old and valued friends, including diplomats, military analysts, and senior military commanders. Such is the emotional reaction evoked by the expensive failure of American arms in Vietnam —a reaction really of fear—that a critical writer, no matter his objectivity, will reap "establishment" opprobrium comparable to that delivered by an ancient and celebrated Legalist: Han Fei-tzu righteously denounced the criticism of empire offered by double-faced scholars who dwelt in caves, ". . . pursued private studies . . . engaged in intrigues, and elaborated unorthodox views."[2] Excepting the cave and "intrigues," I am guilty; while I regret this conflict of opinion, I think that the issues are sufficiently important to justify a strain on friendship.

I am equally concerned about the feelings of Vietnam veterans—of the wounded, of those who have survived the dead, of all the men and women who did their best when called to their country's service. Those of us who fought in World War II and who shared the Korean experience know something of postwar disillusionment, and it is an obscene feeling. To many of us, the later shattering of some toes, if not both feet, of our idol Mars made us question the worth of sacrifice. That does not negate the *fact* of sacrifice, and the individual rightly can carry this knowledge proudly to his grave. Yet I remain entirely too aware that some of my conclusions will offend today's veterans. While regretting this enormously, I must again plead the overriding importance of the issues to the future of America and the civilized world.

Many knowledgeable people have given generously of talent and time in reading portions of this book or in discussing its various aspects. They have repaired my work a thousandfold, and I am grateful. The faults remain the author's burden.

In England, I wish particularly to thank: Professor M. R. D. Foot, Professor Hugh Thomas, C. M. Woodhouse, Julian Amery, Colonel F. W. Deakin, Professor Maung Htin Aung, the late Colonel F. Spencer-Chapman, Brigadier Sir Bernard Fergusson, Mrs. Joan Saunders, Airey Neave, Eric Christiansen, Major General Richard Clutterbuck, Robert Stephens, Philip Ziegler, Brigadier Frank Kitson, Dr. George Boyce, Arthur Koestler, A. R. Burn, Professor A. Andrewes, Sir Nicolas Cheetham, Adam Roberts, Robin Lane Fox, and Sir Sidney Ridley. In America, Brigadier General Samuel B.

2. S. B. Griffith, *Sun Tzu—The Art of War* (London: Oxford University Press, 1963).

Griffith, Professor D. J. A. Harrison, Joseph Buttinger, Professor Lucian Pye, General Matthew B. Ridgway, Colonel David D. Barrett, Dr. George K. Tanham, Professor John A. Armstrong, Professor Theodore Draper, Professor Peter Paret, Colonel George C. Carrington, Professor Roberta Wohlstetter, Ambassador George Kennan, Professor John Beeler, Professor John R. Alden, Professor Russell Weigley, Professor Roger Hilsman, Robert Shaplen, Brigadier General Don Blackburn, Dr. Ellen Hammer, Brian Jenkins, and Professor Donald Zagoria.

I am further indebted to Mr. D. W. King and the librarians of the Ministry of Defence Library; the London Library; and the Bodleian Library; to Mrs. Pat Brayne for typing the manuscript not once but several times; to Miss Mary Potter, who so diligently and patiently prepared the maps; to Miles Blackwell for logistic services rendered; and to Stewart Richardson and the Doubleday staff for patiently meeting and solving numerous production problems.

Finally, I wish to thank Sam Griffith, to whom I have turned for twenty years in developing and refining my military thinking, and who has read and greatly improved this present work; and Belle Griffith, who has sat quietly and helpfully by. As usual, my parents, Mr. and Mrs. Peter Asprey, and my sister, Professor Winifred Asprey, have provided constant encouragement and support during the lengthy and at times frustrating years involved in researching and writing this book.

ROBERT B. ASPREY

Warwick
Bermuda

New College
Oxford

Contents

PART TWO   Mao and Revolutionary Warfare

shek's "bandit-suppression campaign" fails • Mao's growth in strength • Falkenhausen's counterguerrilla tactics • The Long March to Shensi • Its accomplishments • Mao resumes the offensive • The United Front against the Japanese invaders

Continued in Volume II.

List of Maps

Maps by Mary Potter

Volume I

increasing numbers of men in his search for us and would progressively exhaust his strength."

PART ONE

Lenin's Heritage

No dictatorship of the proletariat is to be thought of without terror and violence.

LENIN

Chapter I

Darius bows to Scythian guerrillas • Alexander the Great's tactics against the Asiatic Scythians • Alexander's later guerrilla wars • Hannibal's victory over Alpine guerrillas • Rome's colonial wars • The war of Spartacus • Pompey's victory over naval guerrillas • Caesar and Cassivellaunus

ANCIENT CHRONICLES offer countless examples of guerrilla actions, usually of an independent type undertaken in self-defense by nomads and peasant bands, and normally resulting in little more than temporary embarrassment to the incumbent ruler or temporary harassment to the invader.

A splendid exception is related by the Greek historian Herodotus. In 512 B.C., the Persian warrior-king, Darius, wanted to secure his northern flank before reducing Thrace and Macedonia. Marching almost due north through today's Bulgaria, his army accepted tribal submissions, bridged the Danube, and crossed to the land of what were then called the Scythians.[1]

1. J. B. Bury, *A History of Greece—To the Death of Alexander the Great* (London: Macmillan, 1959), rev. R. Meiggs. The identity of these tribes is obscure. Professor Bury noted: ". . . North of the Danube, in the lands which are now called Walachia and Moldavia [today's Romania] (between the Danube, the Car-

Here was a bloodthirsty race of altogether unpleasant barbarians for whom Herodotus held little brief except

. . . in one respect . . . the contrivance whereby they make it impossible for the enemy who invades them to escape destruction, while they themselves are entirely out of his reach, unless it please them to engage with him. Having neither cities nor forts, and carrying their dwellings with them wherever they go; accustomed, moreover, one and all of them, to shoot from horseback; and living not by husbandry but on their cattle, their wagons the only houses that they possess, how can they fail of being unconquerable, and unassailable even?[2]

This was a reasonable if rhetorical question, and it may explain why Darius chose to invade their lands, although the gold mines of Dacia possibly attracted him more than the thought of enhancing his already formidable reputation. At this time, Darius ruled the largest empire and commanded the best army in the world. Yet, for all its panoply on the march, for all the efficiency of splendidly organized divisions—a tactical advance considered by Professor Breasted to be ". . . one of the most remarkable achievements in the history of the ancient Orient, if not the world"—the Persians did not subdue the Scythians.[3]

Historians differ as to what happened. Herodotus claimed that the numerically inferior and technically impoverished barbarian army used guerrilla tactics including a scorched-earth policy to force the mighty Darius into retreat: ". . . and as he did so they attacked his rearguard and captured his baggage train." J. B. Bury, on the other hand, judged Darius' adventure a success and pointed out that it led to the eventual submission of Thrace and token submission of Macedonia.[4] A. R. Burn, however, holds that Darius narrowly missed total disaster and at the very least suffered ". . . some temporary loss of prestige."[5] We also know that Darius withdrew across the Bosporus and did not again contest the Scythians.

A few decades later, in northern Greece, some Phocian bands who had escaped the invading Persians found refuge on Mount Parnassus

---

pathians, and the Pruth), lived tribes which were allied in many respects to the tribes south of the river. The Greeks included these tribes under the general name of Scythian, which they applied to the whole series of peoples who dwelled between the Carpathians and the Caucasus. While the most easterly of that series approximated in language to the Persian, the most westerly approximated to the Thracian"; see also A. R. Burn, *Persia and the Greeks* (London: Edward Arnold, 1962).

2. Herodotus, *The History of Herodotus* (London: John Murray, 1897). Vol. 1 (Book IV) of 2 vols. Ed. A. J. Grant, tr. George Rawlinson. Although Herodotus must be read with caution, he can still be read with extreme enjoyment.

3. J. F. C. Fuller, *The Decisive Battles of the Western World* (London: Eyre & Spottiswoode, 1956). Vol. 1 of 3 vols.

4. Bury, op. cit.

5. Burn, op. cit.

and, as Herodotus reported, ". . . made expeditions from thence, whereby they distressed Mardonius . . . and so did good service to the Grecian cause."[6]

In 426 B.C., Demosthenes lost a large number of soldiers in attempting to subdue the ill-armed but very mobile Aetolians, who, Thucydides tells us, ". . . attacked the Athenians and their allies, running down from the hills on every side and showering javelins upon them, then retreating whenever the Athenian army advanced and advancing whenever they retreated." The Athenians soon grew tired, then disorganized:

. . . The Aetolians kept plying their javelins, and being swift of foot and lightly equipped, following at their heels they caught many there in the rout and slew them; but the greater number missed the roads and got into the forest, from which there were no paths out, and the Aetolians brought fire and set the woods ablaze around them. Then every manner of flight was essayed and every manner of destruction befell the army of the Athenians.[7]

Demosthenes himself profited from the experience and later used similar tactics in fighting the Lacedaemonians.

Alexander the Great (356–323 B.C.) encountered serious guerrilla opposition when he campaigned against Bessus, the assassin of Darius III, prior to invading India. This two-year campaign in the Persian satrapies of Bactria and Sogdiana (roughly Afghan Turkestan and Bokhara) tested Alexander to the hilt. In J. F. C. Fuller's words:

. . . In this theater the whole mode of fighting was to differ from what it had been. No great battles awaited Alexander; he was to be faced by a people's war, a war of mounted guerrillas who, when he advanced would suddenly appear in his rear, who entrenched themselves on inaccessible crags, and when pursued vanished into the Turkoman steppes. To overrun such a theater of war and subdue such an enemy demanded generalship of the highest order, much higher than needed against an organized army on the plains. . . .

Unfortunately Arrian and other historians tell us little about the tactical changes Alexander introduced although we may assume that there was a considerable expansion of light troops, both foot and horse; yet all we hear is the introduction of mounted javelin-men and that Alexander lightened the equipment of part of the phalanx. Whatever the changes, one thing is certain, they were based on mobility and flexibility, coupled with the use of a large number of military posts and military colonies that restricted his enemy's mobility while they added to his own.[8]

6. Herodotus, op. cit. (Book IX).
7. Thucydides, *History of the Peloponnesian War* (Cambridge, Mass.: Harvard University Press, 1953). Vol. 2 of 4 vols. Tr. Charles F. Smith.
8. J. F. C. Fuller, *The Generalship of Alexander the Great* (London: Eyre & Spottiswoode, 1958). Hereafter cited as Fuller (*Alexander*).

In the spring of 329 B.C., Alexander crossed the Hindu Kush in pursuit of the Persian leader Bessus. Hoping to halt the pursuer, Bessus had ravaged the countryside, but Alexander led his army despite severe cold and hunger to the Oxus river. Lacking sufficient timber to bridge the fast-flowing river, he ". . . collected the hides the troops used for tent covers and ordered them to be filled with the driest possible chaff, and then to be tied down and stitched neatly together so as to be watertight. When they were filled and stitched together they were efficient enough to take the army across in five days."[9]

Although Bessus was captured, the Sogdians soon rebelled under Spitamenes. North of the Oxus, where Alexander was building a garrisoned city (today's Chodjend) on the Jaxartes River, he launched a punitive campaign during which he systematically destroyed seven major encampments, summarily executing tribesmen and enslaving women and children.[10]

Alexander still had to reckon with the Massagetae, or "Asiatic Scythians," who lived north of the Jaxartes and harassed the Macedonians from the other side of the river. Alexander mounted catapults on the bank, and with the aid of this protective fire crossed the river, his men again using skins stuffed with straw. Landing archers and slingers first, he then brought over the infantry and cavalry. Once his army gained the other bank, he sent a force of spearmen and heavy cavalry against the enemy. Arrian tells us,

. . . the Scythians, who were in strong force, awaited them, and then rode round the smaller party of the enemy, which kept shooting at them, while they themselves easily managed to escape by flight.[11]

While small, Alexander's army was flexibly organized and mobile. Seeing the problem, Alexander massed archers, light infantry, and cavalry and moved against the Scythians. Apparently taken by surprise and definitely outgunned—the foot archer's range due to the size of his bow is greater than the horse archer—the Scythians lost the initiative. Arrian continued:

. . . When they were quite close, he ordered three regiments of the Companions [his elite units] and all the mounted javelin-men to charge them;

9. Arrian, *Anabasis Alexandri* (London: William Heinemann, 1929). Vol. 1 of 2 vols. Tr. E. I. Robson.

10. Ibid; see also A. R. Burn, *Alexander the Great* (New York: Collier, 1947). Hereafter cited as Burn (*Alexander*); Bury, op. cit.; Fuller (*Alexander*), *supra;* W. W. Tarn, *Alexander the Great* (London: Cambridge University Press, 1948), Vol. 1 of 2 vols.; U. Wilcken, *Alexander the Great* (London: Chatto & Windus, 1932). Tr. G. C. Richards; Robin Lane Fox, *Alexander the Great* (London: Allen Lane, 1973).

11. Ibid.

and he himself brought up the rest of the cavalry at full speed and charged with his squadrons in column. . . .[12]

This attack disrupted the enemy's wheeling tactics; when his formations broke, Alexander exploited the disorder by sending forward infantry and light cavalry, which killed about a thousand and captured one hundred fifty of the Scythians. Although he ordered his cavalry in pursuit, he did not regain contact, and a bad case of diarrhea, caused by foul water, prevented him from going farther. The battle was nonetheless notable,

. . . for it shows Alexander, who had never seen desert or "Parthian" tactics before, meeting them with complete confidence and certainty.[13]

The revolt meanwhile had spread to Bactria, where a group of horse archers of the Massagetae, some six hundred men under Spitamenes, laid siege to Maracanda (today's Samarkand). Sent to relieve the garrison, a force under one of Alexander's interpreters, Pharnuches, was teased to pursue into the desert. Suddenly the nomads struck from all sides. Although Pharnuches formed his troops into a square and fought a successful rearguard action back to a river, his troops broke formation in their rush to cross to safety and were virtually annihilated—". . . the bloodiest, and the only serious, defeat ever suffered by one of Alexander's columns."[14]

Upon learning of the disaster, Alexander marched a mixed force of infantry, archers, and cavalry 135 miles in seventy-two hours to fall on the besiegers of Maracanda, who immediately disappeared in the desert waste. Alexander pursued as far as the desert but made no contact. After burying his dead, he ravaged the villages that had supported Spitamenes and then laid waste the valley to deprive him of future food supply.[15]

Alexander was not yet finished, however. After quartering at Zariaspa for the winter, he split his force, leaving a large portion of it in Bactria.[16] With the remainder, he formed five columns, which made a "sweep" against the guerrillas before rejoining at Maracanda. He next sent two of the columns ". . . to raid the independent nomads, among whom Spitamenes was reported, and Hephaistion to unite the villages of Sogdiana into walled towns—i.e., to concentrate the population, so that they could not easily help the guerrillas."[17] Although Alexander

12. Ibid.
13. Fuller (*Alexander*), *supra.*
14. Burn (*Alexander*), *supra.*
15. Arrian, op. cit.; see also Tarn, op. cit.
16. Historians disagree on identity and location of Zariaspa (Balkh), which some maintain was also Bactra. Our map derives in part from those in Professor Bury's excellent work cited above.
17. Burn (*Alexander*), *supra.*

captured a number of enemy strongholds, he could not capture
Spitamenes, who was raiding behind his lines.

To get Spitamenes, Alexander relied on a strong force which he left
to winter in Sogdiana. As he hoped, Spitamenes turned up. But now
the guerrilla force, numbering some three thousand horse, found the
countryside bare, the food guarded in Hephaistion's walled cities. Forced
into a conventional attack, Spitamenes suffered eight hundred killed
against only a few Macedonian dead, a disaster that caused him to retreat. Losing some of his savage hordes by desertion, he yielded control
of the rest. Upon hearing that Alexander was going to pursue, they
turned on Spitamenes, cut off his head, and sent it to the Macedonian
king as a token of full submission.[18]

Alexander faced a final challenge from Oxyartes, a Bactrian baron
who with a small band had holed up in a mountain fortress, the Sogdian
Rock. Oxyartes' envoys refused Alexander's demand to surrender:
". . . they with barbaric laughter bade Alexander find winged soldiers
to capture the height for him, since they cared for [that is, feared] no
other kind of man."[19] They reckoned without Alexander's tactical adaptability: by offering special rewards to volunteers with mountain-
climbing experience, he recruited three hundred men who made a night
ascent of a peak ". . . which was most sheer, and so unguarded." Thirty
men fell to their death, but the survivors had gained the drop on the
enemy camp by dawn. A herald now informed Oxyartes that he must
surrender, for Alexander ". . . had found sure enough the winged
men."[20]

But Alexander did more than adapt his tactics to counter unorthodox
tactics. After subduing the various tribes, he invariably tried to win them
to his side, a move explained, according to Tarn, by an innate belief
in the unity of mankind—the concept of *Homonoia*—but more likely by
shrewd political sense.[21] When a nomad chieftain at Chodjend blamed
resistance on undisciplined youth, Alexander overlooked contrary evidence and said he believed him, a face-saving move that brought peace
and gained him numerous skillful recruits. After capturing Oxyartes, he

18. Arrian, op. cit.
19. Ibid.
20. Ibid.
21. Fuller (*Alexander*), *supra*: ". . . It was this aspiration which he expressed
in his prayer at Opis, and, according to Tarn, it had little to do with his so-
called policy of fusion which was 'a material thing,' but with an idea, 'an imma-
terial thing.' It was firstly, that all men are brothers; and secondly, that he had
'a divine mission to be the harmonizer and reconciler of the world, to bring it
to pass that all men, being brothers, should live together in Homonoia, in unity
of heart and mind. . . . It was and was to remain a dream, but a dream greater
than all his conquests"; see also W. W. Tarn, *Alexander the Great and the Unity
of Mankind* (London: Oxford University Press, 1933); E. Badian, "Alexander
the Great and the Unity of Mankind," *Historia* (Wiesbaden: Franz Steiner Verlag, 1952), Vol. 7, pp. 425–44. Most scholars accept this as refuting Tarn's thesis.

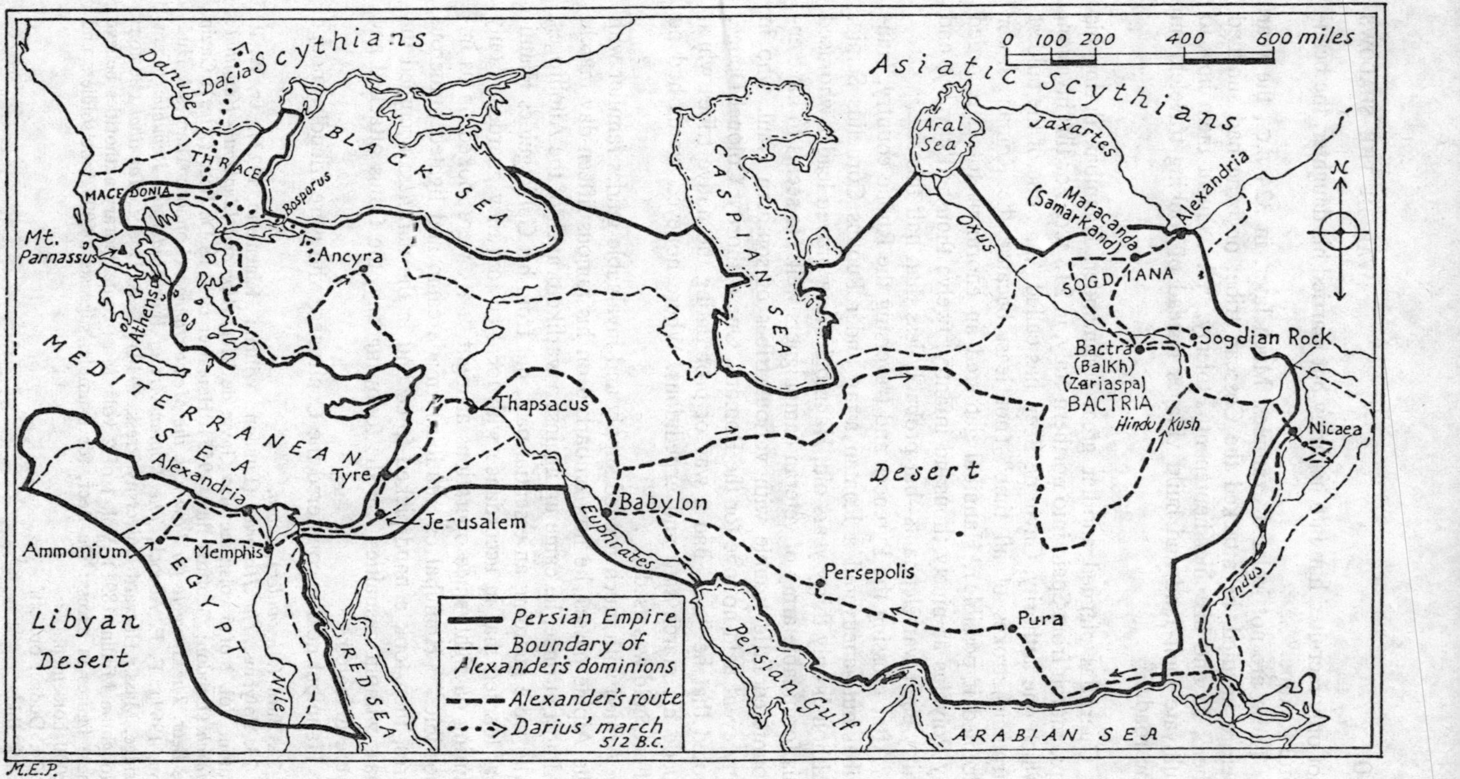

0 100 200 400 600 miles
Scythians
Danube
Dacia
THRACE
MACEDONIA
Mt. Parnassus
Athens
BLACK SEA
Bosporus
Ancyra
CASPIAN SEA
Asiatic Scythians
Aral Sea
Jaxartes
Oxus
Maracanda (Samarkand)
Alexandria
SOGDIANA
Sogdian Rock
Bactra (BalKh) (Zariaspa)
BACTRIA
Hindu Kush
Nicaea
N
MEDITERRANEAN SEA
Alexandria
Thapsacus
Tyre
Jerusalem
Babylon
Euphrates
Desert
Ammonium
Memphis
EGYPT
Libyan Desert
Nile
RED SEA
Persepolis
Pura
Persian Gulf
Indus
ARABIAN SEA
Persian Empire
Boundary of Alexander's dominions
Alexander's route
Darius' march 512 B.C.
M.E.P.

not only recruited him into his army but married his daughter, the beautiful Roxane.

These are not isolated examples. Much later, in 324 B.C., the year before he died, he attacked the Cossean tribe; once he had subdued them, he and his chief lieutenant, Ptolemy, ". . . taught them how to cultivate their land and build villages instead of robbing travelers on the road."[22]

Guerrillas plagued another great commander, Hannibal, during his epic march from Spain into northern Italy, in 218 B.C. For this invasion, which one authority, Gavin de Beer, has called ". . . one of the boldest strategic strokes of all time" (not least because the Romans never deemed it possible), Hannibal gathered an enormous force, recorded by Polybius as ninety thousand infantry, twelve thousand cavalry, and thirty-eight war elephants—but probably less than half this size.[23]

After crossing the Pyrenees and traversing the Rhône country, Hannibal outmaneuvered a Roman army under Publius Cornelius Scipio. Although only thirty years old, Hannibal was a proven leader who used his formidable army of veteran campaigners well. He seems to have encountered little trouble with various tribes of southern Gaul, who in any event held no love for the Romans. One authority, Colonel Dodge, noted that he ". . . had a way of propitiating the native tribes which made his march safe and expeditious. Where honeyed words had no effect, gold was used. . . ."[24]

Armed with much needed supply and invaluable guides familiar with the Alpine passes, he now embarked on his famous fifteen-day march. Almost at once, he came up against a warlike branch of the Allobroges, who were guarding an essential pass, but from his Gallic guides Hannibal learned that in accordance with local custom they guarded it only during daylight, since operations at night ". . . were looked on as impossible."[25] Hannibal ostentatiously made camp and lighted numerous fires, then took a hand-picked force and in the darkness occupied the pass without casualties. On the following day, the Gauls attacked and were defeated.

Hannibal next encountered the Ceutrones, who were friendly enough

22. Burn (*Alexander*), *supra*.
23. Polybius, *The Histories* (London: William Heinemann, 1922). Tr. W. R. Paton. Vol. 2 of 6 vols.; see also Gavin de Beer, *Alps and Elephants—Hannibal's March* (London: Geoffrey Bles, 1955). Hereafter cited as De Beer (*Alps*); Gavin de Beer, *The Struggle for Power in the Mediterranean* (London: Thames & Hudson, 1969); F. E. Adcock, *The Roman Art of War Under the Republic* (Cambridge, Mass.: Harvard University Press, 1940); T. A. Dodge, *Hannibal* (Boston: Houghton Mifflin, 1891), Vol. 1 of 2 vols. Most contemporary authorities believe these figures in excess: De Beer, for example, suggests 38,000 foot soldiers and 8,000 horsemen.
24. Dodge, op. cit.
25. Ibid.

but whom he didn't trust. Pretending to ally with them, he accepted some as guides and continued his march, his route probably leading to the Traversette pass.[26]

Fearful of an ambush in the rugged terrain, Hannibal reversed the order of march, placing ". . . the baggage, elephants and cavalry in front, while with the heavy-armed troops he held the rear."[27] Just what prompted this change is uncertain—it may have been his desire to put his cavalry, which he knew would prove essential in Italy, in the least vulnerable place; perhaps, however, he thought his cavalry could react more effectively to an attack, or perhaps his Gallic guides recommended the formation.

Whatever the case, he seems to have chosen correctly. He was struck by an attack in force as his vanguard was moving through a particularly close ravine. The barbarians, ". . . assembled together in great numbers," lined the heights, from where they rolled down boulders and stones on the surprised column. Although causing losses, they erred in delivering the main attack against Hannibal's rear, precisely where he was strongest. Noting where the enemy's weight lay, Hannibal took up an effective defensive position at the mouth of the defile, sent out flanking forces, and held the enemy until his main force completed its night march through the ravine. This limited the enemy to isolated attacks on his vanguard forces the following day. At the summit of the pass, Hannibal chose another good defensive position and camped for two days while recovering a large number of stragglers and pack animals.

No one can say with certainty how many men Hannibal lost. Whatever his strength upon debouching from the Alps, his army, combined with his brilliant generalship and Roman-army confusions and weaknesses, proved sufficient to put him at the gates of Rome.

Rome followed her victory over the Carthaginians in the Second Punic War with a period of territorial expansion that forced her legions to fight numerous and costly campaigns against such conventionally armed foes as the Macedonians, Sicilians, and Carthaginians, but also against a variety of irregular forces that frequently employed guerrilla tactics.

In colonizing northern Italy, she provoked a general uprising of the Celtic tribes, a campaign lasting over twenty years. To subdue this area, she built strong points such as the burgess colony at Luna (Spezia) and later at Aquileia, which was ". . . brought into being to command the eastern passes and serve as a control point for the northern Adri-

26. Dodge and other older authorities suggest the Little St. Bernard pass, but recent scholarship points to the Traversette. De Beer (*Alps*), *supra*, writes on this in detail.

27. Polybius, op. cit.

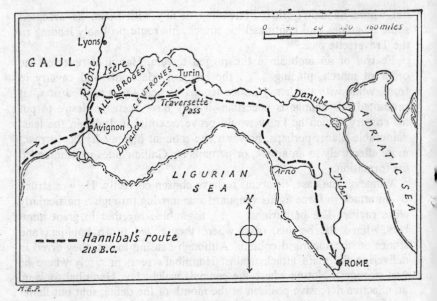

Hannibal's route
218 B.C.

M.E.P.

atic."[28] These proved only partially successful against continued incursions by the Celts, the Istrians, and the Dalmatians, who were not subdued until 156 B.C.

Sicily also proved a hotbed of insurrection. In 139 B.C., the slaves there rebelled:

. . . with a few rags of skins about their nakedness, armed with reap hooks, spits, and stakes pointed and hardened in the fire, they swarmed through the streets, bursting into the houses and massacring all who came in their way, without regard to age or sex. More and more slaves from the surrounding estates crowded in to join Eunus and his earlier followers, and every man's foes were those of his own household. This led to an island-wide insurrection and in 135 B.C. the beginning of a three years' campaign which finally crushed the insurrection.[29]

Another major Sicilian outbreak occurred in 109 B.C. under "Salvius the Soothsayer," whose followers, by using guerrilla tactics, held out for nearly five years. The French historian Mirabeau later wrote of this insurrection: ". . . The misery caused in Sicily by this long war, which ended in 100 B.C., may be estimated by the fact that, whereas Sicily usually supplied Rome with corn, it was now desolated by famine, and its towns had to be supplied with grain from Rome."[30]

28. Reginald Hargreaves, *Beyond the Rubicon* (New York: New American Library, 1966).

29. Ibid.

30. Ibid.

In Italy proper, Rome faced a serious uprising of gladiators led by a Thracian, Spartacus, who used guerrilla tactics while forming an army. The war of Spartacus lasted for two years and cost thousands of Roman lives. Spartacus was finally killed in regular battle by the armies of Crassus and Pompey.[31]

In the east, Rome also had to deal with numerous insurrections and guerrilla raids: ". . . in the Balkan peninsula it demanded all the energies of M. Lucullus to contain the raids of the barbarian tribes, who were not finally brought to interim submission until 73 B.C."[32]

Guerrilla warfare even spread to the sea. Plutarch tells us, probably with exaggeration, that Mediterranean corsairs, the Cilicians, virtually controlled the Mediterranean with a fleet of a thousand galleys based on four hundred cities.

. . . They had in various places arsenals, ports, and watchtowers, all strongly fortified. Their fleets were not only extremely well manned, supplied with skillful pilots, and fitted for their business by their lightness and celerity, but there was a parade of vanity about them more mortifying than their strength, with gilded sterns, purple canopies, and plated oars, as if they took pride and triumphed in their villainy. . . . They not only insulted the Romans at sea, but infested the great roads and plundered the villas near the coast.[33]

After several ineffectual attempts against these seagoing freebooters, the Roman Senate called Pompey to the military command and granted him emergency powers. In two major campaigns, Pompey destroyed 120 bases, killed 10,000 and captured 20,000 of the enemy, sunk 1,300 galleys, and captured 400 more—a welcome victory.[34]

Although evidence is scant, the Roman legions undoubtedly encountered guerrilla tactics in the conquest of central Europe and Britain, as is suggested by the frequent use of the word *latrocinium*—brigandage or banditry. Julius Caesar described the ambush of one of his legions shortly after he landed in Britain. Sent to fetch corn, the soldiers discovered that the fields had been gleaned except in one place:

. . . The enemy, anticipating that the Romans would come here, had lain in wait in the woods during the night; then, when the troops had laid aside their weapons and were dispersed and busy reaping, they had suddenly fallen upon them. A few were killed; the rest, whose ranks were not properly formed, were thrown into confusion; and the enemy's horse and war chariots had at the same time encompassed them.[35]

31. Plutarch, *Lives* (London: Macmillan, 1902), Vol. 3 of 5 vols. Tr. A. H. Clough.
32. Hargreaves, op. cit.
33. Plutarch, op. cit., Vol. 4.
34. Ibid.
35. Julius Caesar, *Commentaries on the Gallic War* (London: Macmillan, 1908), Vol. 1 of 2 vols. Tr. T. Rice Holmes.

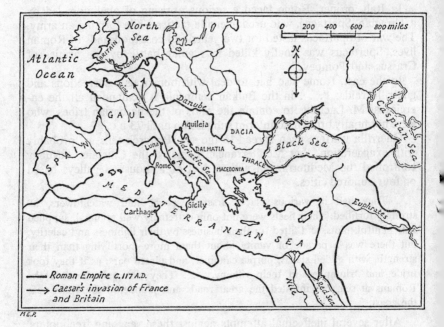

— Roman Empire c. 117 A.D.
—→ Caesar's invasion of France
     and Britain

M.E.P.

The enemy fought in a way unfamiliar to the Romans. Chariots came
onto the field,

. . . the warriors hurling missiles; and generally they throw the enemy's
ranks into confusion by the mere terror inspired by their horses and the clat-
ter of the wheels. As soon as they have penetrated between the troops of
cavalry [their own], the warriors jump off the chariots and fight on foot.
The drivers meanwhile gradually withdraw from the action, and range the
cars in such a position that, if the warriors are hard pressed by the enemy's
numbers, they may easily get back to them. Thus they exhibit in action the
mobility of cavalry combined with the steadiness of infantry; and they become so efficient from constant practice and training that they will drive their
horses at full gallop, keeping them well in hand, down a steep incline, check
and turn them in an instant, run along the pole, stand on the yoke, and step
backwards again to the cars with the greatest nimbleness.

Our men were unnerved by these movements, because the tactics were new
to them. . . .[36]

Fortunately for the beleaguered legion, Caesar led a relief force to their
aid and executed a fighting withdrawal. The initial success of the Britons
made them overconfident, and when they attacked Caesar's camp shortly
after, they were defeated.

36. Ibid.

Upon Caesar's return to Britain a year later, his legions encountered the same tactics employed by a number of tribes that had united under a local leader, Cassivellaunus. By judicious use of cavalry and infantry, Caesar advanced successfully against the Britons until he reached the river Thames. Here he found the enemy deployed in force on the opposite bank:

. . . The bank was fenced by sharp stakes planted along its edge; and similar stakes were fixed under water and concealed by the river.

When Caesar discovered this from prisoners and successfully crossed the river, Cassivellaunus, abandoning "regular" warfare,

. . . disbanded the greater part of his force, retaining only about four thousand charioteers; watched our line of march; and, moving a little away from the track, concealed himself in impenetrable wooded spots, and removed the cattle and inhabitants from the open country into the woods in those districts through which he had learned that we intended to march. Whenever our cavalry made a bold dash into the country to plunder and devastate, he sent his charioteers out of the woods (for he was familiar with every track and path), engaged the cavalry to their great peril, and by the fear which he thus inspired prevented them from moving far afield. Caesar had now no choice but to forbid them to move out of touch with the column of infantry, and, by ravaging the country and burning villages, to injure the enemy as far as the legionaries' power of endurance would allow.[37]

A lack of unity among enemy tribes soon ended resistance. Disloyal chiefs told Caesar the location of Cassivellaunus' headquarters, which he attacked and captured. Shortly thereafter, he forced Cassivellaunus into submission.

37. Ibid.

Chapter 2

The Roman pacification of Spain • Reasons for the Roman presence • Scipio's campaign • The first uprisings • Cato's reply to the guerrillas • Guerrilla strength and weakness • Roman atrocities • The Roman investment • Rome's continued political and military failures • The reforms of Gracchus and Marcellus • The shame of Lucullus and Galba • The rise and fall of brave Viriathus • Scipio Aemilianus' reforms • The extraordinary rebellion of Quintus Sertorius • Final Roman "victory" • The campaign analyzed

Rome's problems in pacifying her northern, eastern, and southern ramparts seem slight when compared to the almost two hundred years of guerrilla warfare she encountered in winning control of Spain.

At one time occupied by numerous tribes, some indigenous and some of African stock, Spain had been overrun in the early Iron Age by Celtic tribes from Gaul. Bypassing the ferocious Basques in the Northwest, the Celts slowly melded with the original Iberians to produce a Celtiberian race of hardy and warlike peoples. Such tribes as the Cantabrians and Asturians in the north and west, the Galicians and Lusitanians in the south, and the Carpetanians, Vettones, and Numantians in the center remained virtually untouched by the coastal colonizing efforts of Phoenicians, Greeks, Carthaginians, and Romans, who impressed themselves on the more sophisticated and generally peaceful coastal tribes.[1]

1. E. S. Bouchier, *Spain Under the Roman Empire* (Oxford: Blackwell, 1914).

Roman control of Spain stemmed from the Second Punic War, when the Romans landed an army in Spain in order to deprive Hannibal of support from this Carthaginian stronghold. The effort did not at first prosper. Gnaeus Scipio, who landed with two legions in 218 B.C. at Emporiae (Ampurias) and was joined a year later by his brother, Publius, fought Hasdrubal and the Carthaginians for several years. By 212 B.C., they had pushed well south of the Ebro to occupy an advanced base at Saguntum, from where they had won submission of many of the local tribes. But now disaster struck. Splitting his forces, Publius was attacked by a Celtiberian force under the guerrilla leader Indibilis, who destroyed the Roman army and killed its commander. Gnaeus was betrayed by local tribes, and he and his army were also destroyed.

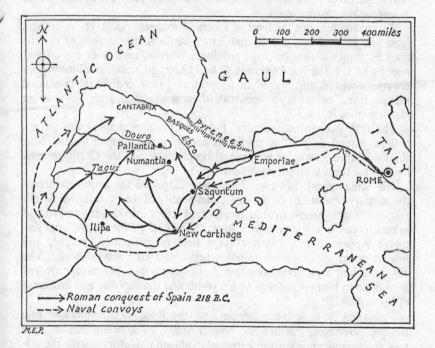

About nine thousand Roman survivors managed to hold the line of the Ebro until late in 211 B.C., when Claudius Nero arrived with reinforcements. The following year, Publius Cornelius Scipio, the twenty-seven-year-old son of the unfortunate Publius, arrived with ten thousand infantry and one thousand cavalry and relieved Claudius Nero. Scipio soon commenced a campaign south of the Ebro that would end Carthaginian rule of this land. Brilliant victories followed one after the other: Cartagena, Baecula, Ilipa—in all, young Scipio defeated four generals in a brilliant campaign well described by, among others, H. H. Scullard in his new book, *Scipio Africanus: Soldier and Politician*.[2]

By 206–205 B.C., Rome had replaced Carthage as the overlord of "civilized" or Nearer Spain, consisting of the coastal areas of Andalusia, Murcia, and Valencia. Her holdings consisted of little more than a series of ports or coastal enclaves with "finger salients" pushing inland, an area occupied both by friendly and by enemy tribes and also subject to raids by the fierce inlanders.

The Romans ran into trouble almost at once. The major reason was their attitude, which was purely exploitive in the worst sense. The praetors and their legionaries arrived as "civilized" conquerors of "barbarian" peoples. Roman arms had theretofore proved victorious over barbarian rabble and the Roman senate saw no reason why this would not prove the case in Spain.

Arrogance was not the least of Roman problems. As C. H. V. Sutherland has pointed out, the Roman army was virtually devoid of experience in administering colonial provinces when it took over the coastal regions of the Iberian Peninsula. The efficacy of ensuing military governments waxed and waned in proportion to the individual talents of the praetors, or governors-general, thenceforth sent with bewildering rapidity from Rome.[3]

The first Roman commander, Publius Cornelius Scipio, was an excellent general despite his youth. In pacifying and forging treaties with the local tribes, many of whom had been allied with the Carthaginians, he blended force with common sense.

His achievement, however, in no way disguised the brutal nature of the military operations or the rapacious quality of the occupation. Scipio frequently slaughtered or sold recalcitrant tribes into slavery and forced others to pay heavy war indemnities. "Scipio sailed for Rome," the historian Appian noted, "with a large fleet magnificently arrayed, and loaded down with captives, money, arms, and all kinds of booty. The city gave him a glorious reception, bestowing noble and unprecedented honors upon him on account of his youth and the rapidity and greatness of his exploits."[4]

Following Scipio's recommendations, the Romans attempted to rule the two provinces, Further and Nearer Spain, by a dual command system (communications being extremely difficult). Unfortunately the ad-

2. H. H. Scullard, *Scipio Africanus: Soldier and Politician* (London: Thames & Hudson, 1970); see also H. M. D. Parker, *The Roman Legions* (Cambridge, England: W. Heffer & Sons, 1958), for the origin and development of the Roman army; Adcock, op. cit.

3. C. H. V. Sutherland, *The Romans in Spain* (London: Methuen, 1939).

4. Appian, *Appian's Roman History* (London: William Heinemann, 1964), Vol. 1 of 4 vols. Tr. Horace White; see also Scullard, op. cit.: Upon Scipio's return to Rome, ". . . he deposited in the Treasury 14,324 lbs. of silver (over a million *denarii*) in addition to coined silver."

ministration proved at once corrupt and oppressive, the praetors possessing all of Scipio's personal cupidity but none of his political acumen. Tribal levies continued with the introduction of the hated *stipendium*, a dual tax paid in money and in bodies for service in the Roman army. The praetors were soon systematically plundering the provinces, rich in metals and wheat, olives and wine. "As early as 203 B.C. great quantities of corn were exported to Rome. . . . In the years 206–197 B.C. alone the quantities of bullion [that were exported to Rome] amounted to 130,000 pounds of silver and 4,000 pounds of gold."[5]

The upshot of the Roman policy was that coastal tribes that had been friendly to Phoenicians, Greeks, and Carthaginians now rebelled. In 197 B.C., the Romans faced a general insurrection in both provinces. In Further Spain this was led by Indibilis, who had defeated Scipio's father and who was finally slain. Appian tells us that ". . . those who were guilty of inciting the revolt were brought to trial, and sentenced to death, and their property was confiscated. The tribes that took sides with Indibilis were fined, deprived of their arms, required to give hostages, and placed under stronger garrisons." But fighting continued in Nearer Spain. By 195 B.C., the Roman army controlled only two interior strongholds and the port of Emporiae. A relief army under M. Porcius Cato enticed the insurgents into formal battle and defeated them to win formal submission of the province.

So dissatisfied were the tribes, however, that rumor of Cato's departure prompted them to a new revolt. Cato answered this insurrection promptly and rigorously: After reducing the dissident communities and selling the people *en masse* into slavery, he ordered every town in the province to tear down its walls (and thus make itself defenseless against his arms).[6] Following his return to Rome in 194 B.C., however, there was ". . . no cessation of guerrilla warfare . . . with its constant drain upon Roman troops; Livy can write that a new governor lost nearly a half of his army in this manner during his years of office."[7]

Thus began a pattern: a revolt put down, "justice" done, treaties signed, exploitation continued, another revolt. Under subsequent praetors, the original *stipendium* gave way to a dual tax on property and persons. Later, provincial quaestors, or financial advisers, fixed grain prices to tribal disadvantage while the army frequently levied extraordinary requisitions of grain with inadequate or no compensation. On occasion, certain excesses proved even too much for Rome: in 171 B.C., the Roman senate's investigation of wholesale graft resulted in the exile of two former governors and some long overdue administrative re-

5. A. Schulten, "The Romans in Spain." In *The Cambridge Ancient History* (London: Cambridge University Press, 1930), Chapter 10 of Vol. 8.
6. Appian, op. cit.
7. Sutherland, op. cit.

forms.[8] By and large, however, the bloodsucking policy continued through the decades and even centuries. In New Carthage (today's Cartagena) Polybius discovered forty thousand slaves, probably Iberian, working in the silver mines, which offered a daily yield of twenty-five thousand *denarii*.[9] A latter-day historian, A. Schulten concluded that ". . . the Iberians were treated little better than cattle."

Wholesale exploitation, unjust taxes and conscriptive levies continued as a matter of course, the Roman senate either not realizing that such a policy could only bring formerly dissident tribes together in mutual indignation—or they realized it, and did not care. The ancient historian Livy later pointed out that, because of the general policy, the Spaniards were for the first time fighting a purely personal war.

The Romans must have realized that the Spanish would fight. Many of the tribes had gained considerable military experience in the Second Punic War, and evidence of military skill and cunning was at hand. As early as 229 B.C., they rid themselves of one Carthaginian menace in the form of Hamilcar: "Taking a number of wagons loaded with wood, they yoked oxen to them, and themselves followed in arms. When the Africans [Carthaginians] saw this they fell to laughing, not perceiving the stratagem. But when they came to close quarters the Spaniards set fire to the wagons, with the oxen still yoked to them, and drove them against the enemy. The fire, being carried in every direction by the fleeing oxen, threw the Africans into confusion. Their ranks being thus broken the Spaniards dashed among them and killed Hamilcar himself and a great many others who came to his aid."[10]

Nor did Iberian tribes lack spirit. A sample of their personal courage and stoicism is found in an incident occurring shortly before Scipio left the country in 205 B.C. One of his generals, Marcius, had surrounded the town of Astapa, which had remained loyal to the Carthaginians. Only too well aware of their fate should they surrender—wholesale reduction to slavery—

They brought all their valuables into the market-place, piled wood around them, and put their wives and children on the heap. They made fifty of their principal men take an oath that whenever they should see that the city must fall, they would kill the women and children, set fire to the pile, and slay themselves thereon. Then calling the gods to witness what they had done, they sallied out against Marcius, who did not anticipate anything of the kind. For this reason, they easily repulsed his light-armed troops and cavalry. When they became engaged with the legionaries, they still had the best of it, because they fought with desperation. But the Romans eventually overpowered them by sheer numbers, for the Astapians certainly were not in-

8. Ibid.
9. Schulten, op. cit.
10. Appian, op. cit.

ferior to them in bravery. When they had all fallen, the fifty who remained behind slew the women and children, kindled the fire, and flung themselves on it, thus leaving the enemy a barren victory. Marcius, in admiration of the bravery of the Astapians, refrained from wantonly injuring their houses.[11]

Such delicacy was rare. The two decades necessary for Romans to gain control of coastal areas were marked by guerrilla wars involving heavy casualties and what today would be called atrocities. A favorite Roman punishment, for example, short of massacring an entire tribe or selling a tribe into slavery or burning tribal crops for miles around or demolishing all tribal villages, was to cut off the hands of the warriors. The insurgents invariably replied *quid pro quo,* usually by torturing or beheading Roman captives, and then fighting all the harder. Not only did dissident tribes willingly fight for their independence, or even for reasonable survival, but they fought exceptionally well. So long as they avoided set-piece battles in favor of the sudden attack or the ambush, they usually claimed the upper hand, although inevitably their guerrillas tired, tribes fell out with one another, and in the long run Roman force of arms told.

But at a tremendous cost to the conquerors, a cost that significantly contributed to the rise of the standing Roman army, to civil strife at home, to civil war, to dictatorship, and finally the monarchy.

From the beginning, the Spanish experience heavily taxed Roman resources. By 205 B.C., ". . . casualties [in the Punic Wars] had wiped out nearly a fourth of the burgess population, the traditional source of the Legions' very best recruits, and suitable replacements to fill the yawning gaps in the ranks were hard to find."[12] Nonetheless, early losses in Spain were extraordinarily heavy. From 206 to 179 B.C. over seventy thousand legionaries and eighty thousand Latin *socii,* or allies, were drafted to the provinces; the two crises of 195 and 187 B.C. account for a proportionately large share of these, ". . . but each province appears to have received fairly regular reinforcements varying from a half-legion, as happened frequently, up to eight or ten thousand men, this incessant drain being caused by the ever-widening area of warfare and partly by the peculiarly wearing and expensive character of guerrilla tactics."[13]

At a time when the Roman army was already spreading thin, the occupation and further conquest of Spain called for four strong legions. This commitment was the more serious, and indeed marks a very significant change in Roman policy, because, as the able historian Mommsen points out, ". . . the old Roman custom of sending troops only where the exigencies of war at the moment required them, and

11. Ibid.
12. Hargreaves, op. cit.
13. Sutherland, op. cit.

of not keeping the man called to serve, except in very serious and important wars, under arms for more than a year, was found incompatible with the retention of the turbulent and remote Spanish provinces beyond the sea; it was absolutely impossible to withdraw the troops from these, and very dangerous even to relieve them extensively. The Roman burgesses began to perceive that dominion over a foreign people is an annoyance not only to the vanquished but the victor, and began to murmur loudly regarding the odious war-service of Spain."[14]

The troops were also murmuring. By the time provincial riches filtered through praetors, quaestors, and other satraps, both military and civil, precious little remained for the ordinary legionnaire, who found himself in a strange and generally hostile land, his day devoted either to tiresome garrison routine or to extended campaigns "up-country." Such campaigns called for hard physical labor expended either in hewing elaborately fortified camps out of unfriendly soil or in chasing elusive guerrillas. Conventionally minded commanders insisted on using "mass" tactics that, inappropriate to the terrain, frequently resulted in dreaded and costly ambush by the lurking enemy. Moreover, the ordinary soldier's pay was frequently delayed; so was his relief. Casualties were high and, even worse, the numerous campaigns seemed never-ending in this land ". . . where large armies starved and small armies got beaten."[15]

These difficulties scarcely deterred either the Roman senate or its praetors in Spain from pursuing an expansionist policy designed to win control of the interior of the country. Before the coastal regions were even pacified, expeditionary forces began probing inland to launch a war that would last, with interruptions, for nearly 150 years—a war marked by all the errors of the earlier fighting.

The most striking characteristic of the Roman conquest is not Spanish successes, but rather Roman political and military failures—the seeming inability to adjust sufficiently to meet what in time must have become an obvious challenge. The lessons of the earlier insurrectionary crises must have struck even the most obtuse governor or dim-witted military commander; yet, with the passing of each crisis, the lessons seemingly vanished into the prevailing morass compounded of imperialistic arrogance, personal greed, and professional ineptness. Although records are somewhat scanty, one reads more often than not of severe setbacks such as that in 191 B.C., when the Lusitanians forced a Roman army, ". . . after heavy loss, to abandon its camp, and to return by forced marches into the more tranquil districts."[16] Time and again, commanders led their bulky columns into costly, often disastrous ambushes. The few successful commanders showed much more respect for the adver-

14. Theodor Mommsen, *The History of Rome* (London: J. S. Dent & Sons, 1911), Vol. 3. Tr. W. P. Dickson.

15. Sutherland, op. cit.

16. Hargreaves, op. cit.

sary, and more than once employed guerrilla tactics in order to gain victory.

But an enlightened commander appeared only occasionally. Tiberius Sempronius Gracchus was one such. After putting down a severe insurrection in Further Spain in 179 B.C. (with the usual harsh methods), he attempted to exploit his victory by extending Roman friendship to various Celtiberian tribes in the form of equitable treaties: in return for annual tribute, he offered tribes certain economic and administrative advantages. Gracchus followed his conquest of Cantabria, for example, by forming the poor ". . . into a part of the community, making them a grant of land, and with all the tribesmen of this district he made clearly defined treaties, by which they were to be friends of Rome; and he exchanged oaths with them to this effect, for which they often yearned in the subsequent wars."[17]

Another moderate and farsighted ruler, Claudius Marcellus, echoed Gracchus' reforms. Marcellus even persuaded major tribes of the interior to send a peace embassy to Rome—an excellent plan voided by the catastrophic refusal of the Roman senate to receive the barbarians.

The progressive reforms of these two rulers soon fell victim to reaction. A series of particularly rapacious praetors abrogated the treaties to start new wars. Seriously alarmed, Rome now took the unusual step of sending out a consul, Lucius Lucullus,[18] but, by the time he arrived, peace had been declared. Unwilling to forsake either fame or booty, Lucullus distinguished himself by attacking and slaughtering some twenty thousand members of a friendly Celtiberian tribe; he followed this with a highlands campaign but, plagued by Pallantian guerrillas, soon retreated south to join forces with the praetor Servius Galba. Soon thereafter, Galba further extended Roman honor by inviting three Lusitanian tribes to the treaty table, then loosing general tribal massacres.[19]

The effect of such perfidy can well be imagined. As is invariably the case, it wrought far more harm than good to the perpetrators: a few years later, in 148 B.C., the wheel of Roman treachery turned full circle. A new governor, Gaius Vetilius, had surrounded a force of some ten thousand Lusitanian rebels. These were about ready to surrender when Viriathus, a minor guerrilla leader who had escaped the earlier Galba

17. Appian, op. cit.

18. To hasten Lucullus' arrival, the senate shifted the normal date of his taking office from March 15 to January 1, which thenceforth marked the beginning of the new calendar year.

19. Mommsen (op. cit.) concluded: ". . . War has hardly ever been waged with so much perfidy, cruelty, and avarice as by these two generals; yet by means of their criminally acquired treasures the one escaped condemnation and the other escaped even impeachment. The veteran Cato, in his eighty-fifth year, a few months before his death, attempted to bring Galba to account before the burgesses; but the weeping children of the general, and the gold which he had brought home with him, demonstrated to the Roman people his innocence."

massacre, rose in assembly to remind the Lusitanians of Roman promises and Roman deeds—and then persuade them to an escape attempt. Appian has left us a detailed account of this experience. Viriathus

. . . drew them all up in line of battle as though he intended to fight, but gave them orders that when he should mount his horse they should scatter in every direction and make their way as best they could by different routes to the city of Tribola and there wait for him. He chose one thousand only whom he commanded to stay with him. These arrangements having been made, they all fled as soon as Viriathus mounted his horse. Vetilius was afraid to pursue those who had scattered in so many different directions but turning towards Viriathus who was standing there and apparently waiting a chance to attack, joined battle with him. Viriathus, having very swift horses, harassed the Romans by attacking, then retreating, again standing still and again attacking, and thus consumed the whole of that day and the next dashing around on the same field. As soon as he conjectured that the others had made good their escape, he hastened away in the night by devious paths and arrived at Tribola with his nimble steeds, the Romans not being able to follow him at an equal pace by reason of the weight of their armor, their ignorance of the roads, and the inferiority of their horses. Thus did Viriathus, in an unexpected way, rescue his army from a desperate situation.

During his retreat, Viriathus set up an ambush in a dense thicket. When these irregulars fell on the pursuing Romans, Viriathus doubled his main force back to the attack: "Vetilius himself was taken prisoner; and the man who captured him not knowing who he was, but seeing that he was old and fat, and considering him worthless, killed him. Of the 10,000 Romans, 6,000 with difficulty made their way to the city of Carpessus on the seashore. . . ."[20] Although casualty figures offered by the ancients are always suspect, there seems little doubt that Viriathus and his guerrillas accounted for thousands of Roman lives in the following virulent decade. During these years of what Viriathus called "fiery war," ". . . legion after legion vanished in the defiles of the mountains, whose heights were crowned with captured trophies of Roman arms."[21]

In desperation, Rome sent her best generals, but although these inflicted an occasional setback on Viriathus, he continued to give far more than he received. In 140 B.C., he surrounded a Roman army and possibly could have ended Roman hegemony in Further Spain by destroying it. Instead, probably because of the fatigue of his own forces, he agreed to a treaty ratified by the Roman senate. But as Sutherland points out, ". . . in neither province was the sanctity of treaties much more, by now, than a diplomatic method for extricating Roman soldiers from

20. Appian, op. cit.
21. Hargreaves, op. cit.

a strategic impasse." With the knowledge of the Roman senate, a local commander soon abrogated the treaty and renewed the war. Adding to perfidy, the Romans now arranged to have Viriathus stabbed to death while he slept. His death severely weakened the insurrection and led to uneasy peace in 137 B.C.

Once again the Romans had won a Pyrrhic victory: ". . . it would be wrong to suppose that . . . [subsequent Roman campaigns] enjoyed any permanence, or that they hastened the pacification of these backward and warlike [Celtiberian] tribes, which still awaited subjection over a century later. . . ."[22]

Nor was there peace in the north, where for twelve years guerrilla bands had held two strongholds and on one occasion had forced the surrender of an entire Roman army. Furious in humiliation, the Roman senate turned to P. Cornelius Scipio Aemilianus Africanus Minor, famed conqueror of Carthage, who reached Spain in 134 B.C.

The incessant wars had left their mark on the Roman army, both in Spain and elsewhere. The military reforms of Gaius Gracchus were not altogether lost and had inspired further reforms by Marius, who attempted to increase the mobility and efficiency of the army. One authority tells us that at the time of Marius ". . . the Roman legionary carried a saw, a basket, a spade, an axe, a leather thong, a sickle, a chain, and three days' rations, not to mention some kit." Marius lightened this load and also is said to have devised a method by which the soldier removed ". . . his pack without interfering with his armor."[23]

In Spain, however, the individual soldier's lot had deteriorated through the decades. Appian has given us a graphic description of one of Lucullus' field camps:

. . . Their soldiers were sick from watching [the enemy] and want of sleep, and because of the unaccustomed food which the country afforded. They had no wine, no salt, no vinegar, no oil, but lived on wheat and barley, and quantities of venison and rabbit's flesh boiled without salt, which caused dysentery, from which many died.[24]

Rear-area duty was as unattractive in a different way, the cities being hotbeds of drunken and licentious behavior. According to Mommsen, by 137 B.C. the army was a shocking mixture of "dissoluteness, insubordination and cowardice," and it was this state of affairs that Scipio Aemilianus tried to put right.

Scipio immediately ". . . expelled all traders and harlots; also the soothsayers and diviners, whom the soldiers were continually consulting because they were demoralized by defeat. . . ." After this breath of

22. Sutherland, op. cit.

23. Parker, op. cit.; see also Graham Webster, *The Roman Imperial Army of the First and Second Centuries A.D.* (London: Adam & Charles Black, 1969).

24. Appian, op. cit.

fresh air, he ". . . ordered all wagons and their superfluous contents to be sold, and all pack animals, except such as he himself permitted to remain. For cooking utensils it was only permitted to have a spit, a brass kettle, and one cup. Their food was limited to plain boiled and roasted meats. They were forbidden to have beds, and Scipio was the first to sleep on straw. He forbade them to ride on mules when on the march; 'for what can you expect in a war,' said he, 'from a man who is not even able to walk?' They had to bathe and anoint themselves without assistance, Scipio saying sarcastically that only mules, having no hands, needed others to rub them. Thus in a short time he brought them back to good order."[25] He then went on to "win" a war against the Numantians, his final "victory" significantly enough involving sixty thousand troops (including forty thousand native auxiliaries) against four thousand enemy.[26] Nonetheless, Scipio ended a black era and in conjunction with a senatorial commission from Rome brought a better day to the peninsula. These reforms helped open the Castiles to the conquerors, who colonized as far north as the Douro River and as far west as the Tagus.

A relatively quiet period now ensued, but was broken by civil strife at home which led to a rebellion by one Quintus Sertorius. A remarkable man, Sertorius. Veteran of Cimbrian, Spanish, and Italian campaigns (he had lost an eye), he had become a democratic revolutionary, a supporter of Marius and Lepidus. Banished to Spain by Sulla, he soon won a considerable following of dissident officers and soldiers, but was now forced to go to Africa, where, according to Mommsen, he led ". . . a restless life of adventure along the Spanish and African coasts, sometimes in league, sometimes at war, with the Cilician pirates who haunted these seas, and with the chieftains of the roving tribes of Libya."

In 81 B.C., the Lusitanians persuaded him to lead them in a revolt against Roman rule, and he returned to Spain, where he commanded a small legion of Romans, mostly deserters and Africans. A brilliant commander and organizer, Sertorius organized and trained this nucleus along formal Roman lines. Supported by guerrilla bands, also under his command, he raised the standard of revolt in the interior, where his small army easily evaded the legions of Quintus Caecilius Metellus. Like Viriathus before him, Sertorius used Spain's vast spaces to lure legions from coastal enclaves and then attack lines of communication and harass at will. Clever Sertorius even made common cause with coastal privateers, who intercepted Roman supply ships. But his real key to success lay in building a strong political base from diverse Celtiberian tribes. In contrast to the average Roman governor, as Mommsen pointed out, Sertorius

25. Ibid.
26. Sutherland, op. cit.

. . . endeavored to attach the provincials to Rome and to himself personally. His chivalrous character rendered it easy for him to enter into Spanish habits, and excited in the Spanish nobility the most ardent enthusiasm for the wonderful foreigner who had a spirit so kindred with their own. . . . Throughout he exercised a just and gentle rule. His troops, at least so far as his eye and his arm reached, had to maintain the strictest discipline . . . he reduced the tribute, and directed the soldiers to construct winter barracks for themselves, so that the oppressive burden of quartering the troops was done away and thus a source of unspeakable mischief and annoyance was stopped. For the children of Spaniards of quality an academy was erected at Osca (Huesca) in which they received the higher instruction usual in Rome. . . . It was the first attempt to accomplish their Romanization not by extirpating the old inhabitants and filling their places with Italian emigrants, but by Romanizing the provincials themselves. . . .

By the end of 77 B.C., the whole of Nearer Spain.had become ". . . by treaty or force dependent on Sertorius, and the district on the upper and middle Ebro thenceforth continued the mainstay of his power."[27]

Pompey arrived with reinforcements the following year. A more skillful tactician than Metellus, Pompey invaded the highlands and slowly forced Sertorius to fragment his forces. Although Sertorius held his own for another few years, Roman weight slowly told, as it had in the case of Viriathus. Loss of his better officers, particularly his chief lieutenant, L. Hirtuleius, hurt him, as did the defection of various tribes. But Pompey had still not won a "decisive" battle against him when a rival, Perperna, murdered Sertorius, in 72 B.C.

Pompey could scarcely claim victory. Sertorius' legion probably never exceeded five thousand troops, but in trying to capture it and subdue the supporting guerrillas, Mommsen tells us that, in all, the Romans employed 120,000 infantry, 2,000 archers and slingers, and 6,000 horse. Mommsen summed up the tragic record:

. . . The [Roman] state suffered from it beyond description. The flower of the Italian youth perished amid the exhausting fatigues of these campaigns. The public treasury was not only deprived of the Spanish revenues, but had annually to send to Spain for the pay and maintenance of the Spanish armies very considerable sums, which the government hardly knew how to raise. Spain was devastated and impoverished, and the Roman civilization, which unfolded so fair a promise there, received a severe shock; as was naturally to be expected in the case of an insurrectionary war waged with so much bitterness, and but too often occasioning the destruction of whole com-

27. Mommsen, op. cit., Vol. 4; see also Sutherland, op. cit.; Adcock, op. cit.: A pupil of Marius, Sertorius ". . . combined skill in the normal tactics of a Roman army with a keen appreciation of the advantages which Spain offers to a nimble army which can make the country and its inhabitants its allies."

munities. . . . The generals had encountered an opponent far superior in talent, a tough and protracted resistance, a warfare of very serious perils and of successes difficult to be attained and far from brilliant.[28]

The final territorial expansion began under Julius Caesar's governorship of Further Spain when, in 61–60 B.C., he extended Roman frontiers to the mouth of the Douro. After the interim of the Caesar-Pompey wars, Augustus continued the task in a series of bloody campaigns that won Rome control of the northwestern corner in the vicinity of the Cantabrian Mountains.

With this conquest, completed in 19 B.C., nearly all of Spain lay subject to Roman control. Sporadic uprisings, however, continued to mar the scene, and Augustus was forced to garrison the newly won areas with three legions—a heavy commitment, considering their material value.

Some authorities suggest that, even with various reforms, the essential ruthlessness of the Roman policy had not really changed at the beginning of the fifth century A.D., when Eastern barbarians crossed the Rhine and flooded Gaul and Spain. According to Salvian, local peoples even preferred barbarians to imperial tax collectors, and big landowners had as much to fear from agrarian insurgents, the Bagandae, as from the barbarians.

The Roman experience in Spain, once the Carthaginians were defeated, is remarkable for several reasons. One is the value of leadership to both sides. Roman fortunes soared under capable leaders such as Scipio Africanus, Cato, Gracchus, and Scipio Aemilianus; they suffered under such incompetents as Lucullus and Galba. In general, Roman leadership was lacking, and not alone in Spain. One authority, F. E. Adcock, noted that ". . . the faults of Roman generals and admirals are sometimes those of inexperience, more commonly the failure to discover new tactics to meet either unfamiliar heresies or some unusual situation. . . . Overconfidence combined with an imperfect intelligence service and bad scouting was a frequent cause of defeat."[29]

A Roman commander in Spain faced three essential challenges. First he had to inspire troops who held little reason for being inspired—leadership had to replace reason. Leadership was greatly aided by tactical victory, but in order to achieve this, the commander had to be sufficiently competent and flexible to respond satisfactorily to the second challenge, his tactical environment. And in order to exploit a tactical victory, he had to meet the challenge of the political environment.

Roman strength lay primarily in organization and force of arms—in the ability to wage sustained war. Although a Roman army might be

28. Ibid.
29. Adcock, op. cit.

tactically defeated—even decimated, as happened more than once—it was replaceable and, just as important, the Roman senate was willing to replace it. So long as communications existed with the home country —so long as Rome controlled the western Mediterranean—the Romans were able to pursue a strategy of attrition or, more simply, exhaustion. In the end, this gained the political-economic goal in Spain—but at a tremendous price. The strategic-economic value of the conquest could not conceivably justify the effect of the prolonged war on domestic politics, while the large garrison forces required to hold the peace were made available only by weakening vulnerable frontiers.

If leadership was important to the Romans, it was vital to the guerrillas, who sadly lacked cohesion and organization. Defense of the homeland is a splendid motivation for militant action, but unless organized, it is virtually useless, a nuisance nagging to nothing.

A Punicus or a Mummius could lead a tribal insurrection; a Viriathus was required to organize and train an intertribal force large enough and good enough to threaten Roman aspirations for a decade. Considering the lack of military organization, training, arms, equipment, supply, and communications, Viriathus' achievements are startling, particularly since part of his army reached paramilitary and even regular military status sufficient to wage limited but successful semiorthodox warfare. In the end, however, organizational and material deficiencies engendered enough fatigue and dissatisfaction to trigger inter- and intra-tribal rivalries (never very quiescent) and forced him to make peace with the Romans at a time when he held an entire Roman army at his mercy. This was a fatal mistake, as it turned out. It was possibly unavoidable: the guerrilla also gets tired.

Rebel strength lay primarily in extreme mobility based on local knowledge of the terrain and aided by minimum logistic requirements. This worked very well for hit-and-run warfare: the ambush, the sudden attack, the isolated assassination. Lacking staying power, however, unable to organize and build a regular military force, the guerrillas remained vulnerable to the tactical extension of Rome's political policy, *divide et impera*—divide and rule. Had the Roman senate decreed a just political-economic policy for prudent commanders to follow, it is conceivable that the conquest of Spain would have taken ten years, not two centuries.

The tactical lessons are manifest. On the Roman side, failure of most commanders to adjust to local challenges wasted thousands of lives. This is in part understandable. It is an uncomfortable paradox that the weight of an organized military force may at times prove a weakness in a campaign against irregulars, but nonetheless this weight is often necessary to win the tactical domination essential to gain and maintain peace. But this weight must be held to an absolute minimum—Scipio Aemilianus, for example, quickly eliminated the numerous camp followers and unnecessarily bulky supply trains. From the beginning in Spain, the situation called for what was eminently possible: a streamlining of standard legion organization and of standard tactics, both developed for a different kind of war. The Spanish experience brought significant changes in organization—it probably helped produce the cohort in place of the manciple—and it also brought changes in weapons, probably accounting for the Romans' adopting the two-edged sword.[30] But such changes came all too slowly, as did tactical modifications.

A few commanders rose to the tactical challenge. Gracchus, Cato, the Scipios, and Pompey each fought noteworthy campaigns. Experienced military commanders, they had learned a great deal from previous wars, and were not above learning from the Spanish enemy. The inability or refusal of other Roman commanders either to respect or learn from this same enemy invariably brought disaster—the inevitable result of the arrogance of ignorance reinforced by the arrogance of power.

30. Parker, op. cit.

Chapter 3

Cyrus' tactical tricks • Hannibal's cunning • Fabian strategy and tactics • Tactical adaptation in Spain • The spear and sword of the West versus the bow and arrow of the East • Warfare in early China • The amazing Sun Tzu: The Art of War • Quasi-guerrilla tactics of Goths and Huns • Fridigern and the battle of Adrianople • Political weaknesses of the barbarians • Rise of the Franks • Attila and the Huns

NEITHER EASTERN TRIBES nor Celtiberians monopolized guerrilla tactics. Persian, Greek, and Roman commanders who assembled forces secretly, marched rapidly, and struck unexpectedly often proved victorious. Nor did early guerrillas monopolize cunning and deception. Orthodox generals of antiquity on occasion produced victory, sometimes against great odds, by introducing unorthodox tactics to the battlefield.

These commanders used a variety of tricks, any one of which would have brought wrathful protest if used by guerrillas. Some stemmed from imagination of individual commanders, some from a boorish technological extension of existing weapons. They are interesting for two reasons: first because they demonstrate the genesis of what too many contemporary strategists and commanders believe is exclusive to our day, the contrasting use of surprise, deception and shock; and second because their circumscribed use in the West indicates a philosophy of warfare that before the birth of Christ was beginning to contrast with that of the East.

Some tricks were basic, even amusing. The Persian king Cyrus, to neutralize the power of Lydian cavalry, ". . . collected together all the camels from his supply train and mounted riders on them then advanced them in front of his other troops . . . the reason being that the horse has a natural dread of the camel and cannot abide either the sight or smell of him. The Lydian warhorses immediately galloped off the field, a great combat ensued and the Persians won the victory. . . ."[1]

Thus wrote Herodotus, who went on to describe another Cyrian ploy, on a slightly higher plane. Frustrated in his siege of Babylon, Cyrus ingeniously diverted the Euphrates in order that his troops could enter the city by means of the dry river bed. Had the Babylonians any notion of what was taking place, ". . . they would never have allowed the Persians to enter the city, but would have destroyed them utterly; for they would have made fast all the street-gates which gave upon the river, and mounting upon the walls along both sides of the stream, would so have caught the enemy as it were in a trap." But not dreaming that Cyrus could or would divert a river, ". . . they were engaged in a festival, continued dancing and revelling until they learnt the capture but too certainly."[2]

The Phocians relied on extreme if cruel cunning in a war against the stronger Thessalians. As a defense against Thessalian cavalry, the Phocians dug a trench in a pass the invaders would have to use, filled it with empty wine jars, then camouflaged it and sat back, weapons on the ready. Seeing the enemy, the Thessalian cavalry ". . . rushed rapidly forward and became entangled in the wine-jars, which broke the legs of their horses." The Phocians later pulled off one of the most successful night attacks of antiquity by whitening their bodies with chalk, which caused the enemy to imagine a supernatural visitation. Completely panicking, the Thessalians were slaughtered.[3]

Darius was not so subtle, but by attaching finely honed scythes to his chariot wheels, he combined shock and terror to gain a far greater tactical advantage than that warranted by the weapon itself.

An even less subtle use of an existing weapon was conceived by an unknown commander who first used catapults to heave decaying animal cadavers into besieged towns in order to cause disease. This was later refined by heaving plague-ridden human corpses over city walls.

On the less violent side are instances of tactical adaptation. In a regular military organization standard tactics are necessary if the commander's will is to be expressed, but an able commander will bend and shape his tactics to an unusual degree if the situation so dictates.

Hannibal's early victories in Italy owe considerable to his having acted

1. Herodotus, op. cit.
2. Ibid.
3. Ibid.

unexpectedly, for example by taking an "impossible" route of march to ambush a Roman army. De Beer offers several instances of the Carthaginian general's cunning. To throw off a Roman army guarding a pass through the Apennines that he needed to use, ". . . Hannibal had lighted torches tied to the horns of a number of cattle and drove them at night in another direction. The Romans mistook the cattle for the Carthaginians, while Hannibal's men were then able to slip through." In De Beer's words: ". . . His ruses were so numerous and his stratagems so subtle that the Romans felt constantly insecure. He became the embodiment of what the Romans called 'Punic faith,' by which they meant treacherousness. When they did the same thing, it was of course no longer treachery. . . ."[4]

Hannibal was stymied, on the other hand, by Quintus Fabius Maximus, who turned the Roman army into virtually a guerrilla force. For months, Fabius shadowed Hannibal's marches, ". . . harassing his foragers, cutting off stragglers, nipping off a stray patrol, but never permitting himself to be drawn into full-scale battle."[5] Impatient Romans derisively called him "the Laggard"; history has treated him more kindly by acknowledging him as the inventor of Fabian tactics.

The most successful Roman commanders in Spain were the most adaptable. When Gracchus was suddenly attacked by twenty thousand "peace petitioners," who had come to his camp bearing olive branches, he ". . . adroitly abandoned his camp to them and simulated flight; then suddenly turning he fell upon them while they were plundering, killed most of them, and made himself master of the Complega . . ." (and, it should be noted, offered an equitable treaty at once accepted).[6] On another occasion, the Roman general M. Fulvius Nobilior was ambushed by a Segedian force under Carus and took a terrible beating with some six thousand casualties. But when Carus ". . . was engaged in a disorderly pursuit after the victory, the Roman horse, who were guarding the baggage, fell upon him, and in their turn killed no less than 6,000 Arevaci, including Carus. . . ."[7] When one of Scipio Aemilianus' tribunes, Rufus, led his cavalry into a Numantian ambush, Scipio followed hard on, divided ". . . his horse into two bodies, and ordered them to charge the enemy on either side alternately, hurling their javelins all together and then retiring, not to the same spot from which they had advanced, but a little farther back each time. In this way the horsemen were brought in safety to the plain"—a neat fighting withdrawal. Scipio now decided to retire across a river. Learning that the enemy had set an ambush around the difficult and muddy ford, he ". . . took a route that was longer and less exposed to ambushes. Here he marched by

4. De Beer (*Alps*), *supra*.
5. Hargreaves, op. cit.
6. Appian, op. cit.
7. Ibid.

night on account of the heat and thirst, and dug wells which yielded for the most part only bitter water. He saved his men with extreme difficulty, but some of his horses and pack animals perished of thirst."[8]

On the part of the Romans, such tactical adaptation was rare, and almost always was forced by the enemy rather than produced voluntarily by a commander trained to think in terms of either the unexpected or the indirect approach based on cunning. As J. F. C. Fuller presciently pointed out, the homeric tradition of warfare stressed the cult of the individual hero: ". . . It is out of valor that European history rises; the spear and sword, and not, as in Asia, the bow and arrow, are its symbols. The bravest and not the most crafty are the leaders of men, and it is their example rather than their skill which dominates battle. . . . Valor disdained inventiveness."[9]

Long before the birth of Christ, valor had embraced inventiveness in the Far East. Until early in the fifth century B.C., Chinese armies conformed to the dynastic tradition of the West. They were invariably commanded by kings or princes or lords, who engaged in frequent "honorable" battles fought ". . . to satisfy a whim, to revenge an insult, or to collect booty . . . primitive melées which usually produced no decisive results."[10]

As specific states grew in size and strength and in turn began nibbling at less powerful neighbors, China, in the mid fifth century B.C., entered a period known as the Warring States. Feudalism declined sharply and warfare became what one ancient Chinese nobleman termed "a fundamental occupation." Powerful rulers now formed standing armies commanded by professional officers who conducted important campaigns far from their home states. Technological advances such as the invention of the crossbow (which did not appear in the West until the fifth century A.D.) and the introduction of iron weapons spelled the decline of primitive chariot warfare. Armies grew increasingly sophisticated, generals employed staff officers, and highly trained, elite units practiced march security and scouting techniques.

One of the more interesting treatises ever written on warfare dates from this period: Sun Tzu's *The Art of War,* written probably around the mid fourth century B.C. In thirteen relatively short chapters, this brilliant philosopher-general displayed a strategic and tactical insight as unorthodox as it was astute, and the work undoubtedly caused neighboring rulers much uneasiness. Often standing at odds with Greco-Roman military doctrines (as we believe we know them), it is essentially a demand for an indirect approach to war at political, strategic, and tactical levels.

8. Ibid.
9. Fuller, op. cit.
10. S. B. Griffith, *Sun Tzu: The Art of War, supra.* This section is taken almost completely from Dr. Griffith's excellent work.

By Sun Tzu's time, war had become ". . . a matter of vital importance to the State; the province of life or death, the road to survival or ruin." Such are disadvantages of war to the state that it should be avoided whenever possible by clever diplomacy (which should utilize high-level espionage). Able statesmanship, by isolating and demoralizing the potential enemy, should defeat him before the combat stage is reached. In Sun Tzu's mind, ". . . to win one hundred victories in one hundred battles is not the acme of skill. To subdue the enemy without fighting is the acme of skill." Sun Tzu recommended that a state go to war only if the diplomatic offensive failed. But a state should do this only after making a careful estimate of the situation to determine if human, physical, and doctrinal factors favored rapid victory, ". . . for there has never been a protracted war from which a country has benefited."

If a state decided on battle, the able general must pay closest attention to such factors as terrain, weather, and enemy plans, ". . . for the crux of military operations lies in the pretence of accommodating one's self to the designs of the enemy." Therefore: ". . . Know the enemy, know yourself; your victory will never be endangered. Know the ground, know the weather; your victory will then be total."

Sun Tzu insisted that both strategy and tactics be fashioned with the knowledge that ". . . all warfare is based on deception": ". . . Therefore, when capable, feign incapacity; when active, inactivity. When near, make it appear that you are far away; when far away, that you are near." The able general must maneuver his army in such a way as ". . . to make the devious route the most direct and to turn misfortune to advantage." The commander who understands the strategy of the indirect approach "will be victorious."

Having "shaped" his enemy by his own foresight, by control of his forces, by extreme mobility (aided by native scouts) and by careful terrain appreciation, the general next deployed two tactical elements: the *cheng,* or orthodox force, normally used to hold the enemy, and the *ch'i,* or unorthodox force, normally used to attack the enemy's flanks and rear. These two forces ". . . are mutually reproductive; their interaction as endless as that of interlocked rings. Who can determine where one ends and the other begins?" The one complements the other, and if the tactical commander correctly employs them, ". . . his potential is that of a fully drawn crossbow; his timing, the release of the trigger."

That Sun Tzu's words were assiduously studied is proved by the careful remarks of "the Commentators"—later analysts such as Tu Yu, Li Ch'üan, Chang Yü, and Tu Mu, who clarified some of Sun Tzu's principles and added contemporary experiences to illustrate them.

These offer an invaluable insight into Chinese military thinking, and Dr. Griffith wisely included a selection of them in his translation of Sun Tzu's work. The oriental mystique is well illustrated in one discussion on terrain. Sun Tzu stated that ". . . in encircled ground I would block the points of access and egress."

Centuries later, a famous scholar named Tu Mu read this sentence. Picture old Tu in a silk robe sipping tea, stroking his wispy beard. Then, suddenly inspired, he puts brush to rice paper, the beautiful Chinese characters reading: ". . . It is military doctrine that an encircling force must leave a gap to show the surrounded troops there is a way out, so that they will not be determined to fight to the death. Then, taking advantage of this, strike."

Tu Mu now finishes his tea, strolls to a pool, feeds an idle carp, relives another campaign or two, and suddenly remembers that one day a general is the encircler, the next day the encircled. He returns to his brush and rice paper and concludes: ". . . Now, if I am in encircled ground, and the enemy opens a road in order to tempt my troops to take it, I close this means of escape so that my officers and men will have a mind to fight to the death."

Just what currency Sun Tzu's work gained outside China is a moot question. Considering the literacy level of the barbarian tribes that invaded the Roman Empire, a tempting answer is, None at all. But this is to disallow that songs, legends, stories, and teachings have always survived primarily by word of mouth. Commercial intercourse by boat also existed among China, Egypt, and Africa; students may have passed on his teachings, probably in mutilated form, to various incursive tribes such as the Hiong Nu, ". . . who attacked the empire of China in the second and first centuries B.C." before turning west.[11]

These tribes practiced a quasi-guerrilla form of warfare remarkably oriental, but part of the reason was the nomadic quality of the central Asian environment—the necessity for tribal mobility and great stealth in hunting and a marked preference for plunder, not conquest.

Supreme among these tribes in the West were the Goths and the Huns, who in the fourth and fifth centuries overran large parts of both the Eastern and the Western Roman empires. No one is certain of their origins. The Goths, originally a Teutonic people, probably migrated from southern Russia, where they had become expert horsemen, to the middle and lower Danube; by A.D. 236, they had penetrated imperial borders. In the next fifteen years, they crossed over the Danube and into the Balkans, overrunning Moesia and Thrace, a campaign culminating in A.D. 251 in the battle of Forum-Trebonii, where they killed Emperor Decius and decimated his army. For some twenty years, they virtually controlled the middle provinces, but, about A.D. 270, the Romans stopped fighting each other long enough to force them from the Balkans

11. C. D. Gordon, *The Age of Attila* (Ann Arbor, Mich.: University of Michigan Press, 1960).

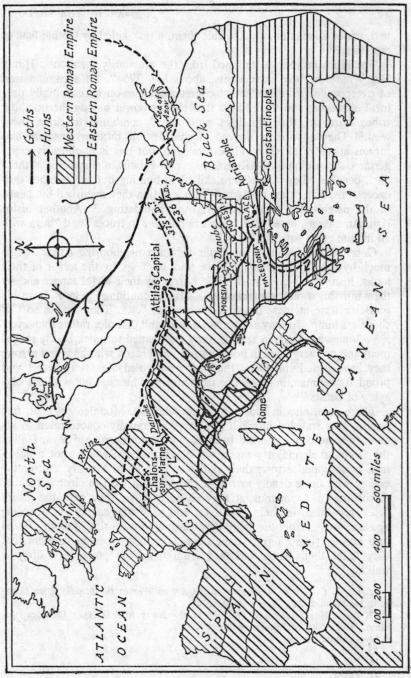

and, under Diocletian, even to rule them, a task aided by Gothic fear of the Huns.[12]

The Huns may have stemmed from the previously mentioned Hiong Nu. Whatever their antecedents, about A.D. 375 ". . . a combination of overpopulation, the effect of climatic changes on an essentially pastoral existence, and the endless struggle for power among the nomadic tribes north of the Himalaya mountains" combined to drive them west.[13] They apparently arrived in considerable numbers; ancient historians speak of seven hundred thousand, but this is doubtlessly exaggerated. According to the Roman historian Priscus, a chronicler of these dark decades, they ". . . were skilled in hunting but in no other task except this. After they had grown into a nation they disturbed the peace of the neighboring races by thefts and plundering."[14] Another historian, Ammianus, noted that "they are faithless in truces" and "burn with an infinite greed for gold."[15]

Once on the Danube, the Huns subdued neighboring tribes not so much by superior numbers, we are told, as ". . . by the terror of their looks, inspiring them with no little horror by their awful aspect and by their horribly swarthy appearance." Priscus continues to look down his patrician nose at these unwonted intruders: ". . . They have a sort of shapeless lump, if I may say so, not a face, and pinholes rather than eyes. . . . Somewhat short in stature, they are trained to quick bodily movement and are very alert in horsemanship and ready with bow and arrow; they have broad shoulders, thick-set necks, and are always erect and proud. These men, in short, live in the form of humans but with the savagery of beasts."[16]

These men, also in short, were fine warriors. Mounted on light, fast ponies, they traveled in small groups which rapidly concentrated to attack, then quickly dispersed to meet again by prearranged plan. Unlike the Goths, their major weapon was the horn bow, which shot a noiseless, bone-tipped arrow; their skill was such as to literally shower the enemy with these deadly arrows if they did not wish to close with him. According to Ammianus, if they chose to close they used the sword ". . . regardless of their own lives; and while the enemy are guarding against wounds from the sabre-thrusts, they throw strips of cloth pleated into nooses (lassos) over their opponents and so entangle them that they fetter their limbs and take from them the power of riding or walking."[17]

12. C. W. C. Oman, *A History of the Art of War in the Middle Ages* (London: Methuen, 1924), Vol. 1 of 2 vols.

13. R. S. Hoyt, *Life and Thought in the Early Middle Ages* (Minneapolis, Minn.: University of Minnesota Press, 1967).

14. Gordon, op. cit.

15. Ibid.

16. Ibid.

17. Fuller, op. cit.

Hun warriors lived on their horses and off the land, their foraging diet supplemented by meat, blood, and milk from extra horses and mares led by each man. The warrior bands preceded women, children, and older warriors, who traveled in wagons. In times of danger, they formed these into a defensive laager, or "wagon-city."

Although the Goths feared the Huns, they nonetheless copied their quasi-guerrilla tactics. Under their great chief Fridigern, the Ostrogoths soon rebelled against restrictive Roman rule in favor of plundering raids through Bulgaria and Macedonia. Adopting the wagon-city tactic, they relied primarily on heavy cavalry for shock power, but also employed infantry armed with pikes and with the long and short sword as well as battle-axes, ". . . which, whether thrown or wielded, would penetrate Roman armor and split the Roman shield."[18]

A major weakness, lack of siege trains, prevented Fridigern from capturing Adrianople in A.D. 378 (as it had prevented Hannibal from capturing Roman cities). Having withdrawn a few miles from this walled bastion, Fridigern was attacked by a large Roman force under command of the eastern emperor, Valens. Hastily summoning his cavalry from a raid, the barbarian leader cunningly gained time first by parley with the enemy, then by firing fields ripe with August harvest in order to delay and confuse deployment of the ponderous Roman legions. When these began to close on him, he held them back by volleys of missiles fired from within the protected laager. And now his cavalry returned to charge and rout the Roman horse and then fall on the exposed Roman flank, in Ammianus' words, ". . . like a thunderbolt which strikes on a mountain top, and dashes away all that stands in its path."[19] The Roman ranks, already confused by heavy missile fire, pressed one onto the other, a chaotic mass so compressed that ". . . men could not raise their arms to strike a blow." At this point, Fridigern loosed his carefully hoarded infantry to deliver the *coup de grâce*. Only a few thousand enemy escaped the slaughter. Ammianus Marcellinus estimated a loss of some forty thousand Roman-allied lives—a disaster to Roman arms comparable only to Cannae (216 B.C.).[20]

18. Oman, op. cit.; see also Hoyt, op. cit.
19. Ibid.
20. Older historians, such as Oman and Fuller, have held that Fridigern's victory foreshadowed a new epoch in the history of war: cavalry would replace infantry as the decisive arm (which it did in the Middle Ages); but see also Lynn White, Jr., *Medieval Technology and Social Change* (London: Oxford University Press, 1962). Professor White argues that, during the battle of Adrianople, an impetuous advance had already confused the Roman army and had made it particularly vulnerable to cavalry action, ". . . not because of superior strength [of Ostrogoth cavalry], but rather by effecting a surprise attack which amounted almost to ambush." The rise of the horseman, the mounted knight, at the expense of the foot soldier depended in large part, Professor White argues, on the adoption of the stirrup, in the eighth century A.D., to give the rider the necessary shock power.

Although Fridigern's quasi-guerrilla tactics are interesting, his victory did not topple the Roman Empire. Along with other barbarians, the Goths wanted booty more than "victory." Lacking specific political goals, Fridigern ". . . spent the next year aimlessly pillaging Greece and the provinces to the north."[21] A new emperor, the Spanish general Theodosius, made peace with the Goths, reorganized the Roman army, raised cavalry units, and ". . . began to enlist wholesale every Teutonic chief whom he could bribe to enter his service."[22] Six years after the Roman defeat, he had brought forty thousand Goths and other Teutons into his army of the east; these became the Teutonic *foederati,* whose dubious loyalty went to the emperor's person rather than to the empire, and which, more than any other influence, explained the eventual disintegration of Roman rule in the West.

The willingness of some barbarian tribes to assimilate with the Romans and fight other barbarian tribes was a major weakness, only slowly overcome by tribal amalgamations and growth culminating in the rise of the Franks. It was not fully repaired until Charlemagne introduced political purpose into tribal conquest to revive the Western Roman Empire. Earlier tribes, loyal to a single chief, interested only in plunder and not territorial conquest and settlement, refused to unite. At a time when the Roman army was overextended and the empire torn with civil war, a tribe would strike here, another there, spaced onslaughts usually contained by the hard-pressed legions. Had the tribes struck simultaneously, they undoubtedly would have overrun the Roman Empire as early as the fourth century.

A large part of this weakness stemmed from the *comitatus* concept, wherein particularly able warriors formed a bodyguard to a chief or supreme warrior: ". . . Everywhere in the Germanic world the ruler, whether king or chief, was attended by a bodyguard of well-born companions."[23] When tribes came together in earlier centuries, as we noted with Attila and the Huns, intense jealousy invariably ensued, with constant bickering and jockeying for favor by the chief lieutenants. Internecine feuds obliterated whole tribes. Leaders could never feel secure. Attila the Hun acceded to power only by murdering his coregent, his brother Bleda. Attila, who forged a number of tribes into a Danubian kingdom of sorts, undoubtedly recognized the tenuous quality of his political structure. He certainly did not shirk from the violence of his environment. His brutal raids up to the gates of Constantinople and later in the West killed and maimed thousands of hapless victims. Attila rather cleverly advertised himself as "the scourge of God"—meaning, as Professor Hoyt has pointed out, ". . . the punishment visited by God's

21. Hoyt, op. cit.
22. Oman, op. cit.
23. F. M. Stenton, *Anglo-Saxon England* (London: Oxford University Press, 1943); see also Hoyt, op. cit.

wrath upon a sinful people. The terror struck into the hearts of his intended victims by this sort of propaganda was a potent 'secret weapon.'"

Attila evidently possessed considerable charisma, as evidenced by his
lengthy reign and by accounts left by various Roman ambassadors. A
later source described him as ". . . short of stature with a broad chest,
massive head and small eyes. His beard was thin and sprinkled with
grey, his nose flat, and his complexion swarthy, showing thus the signs
of his origins." Haughty in carriage, he cast ". . . his eyes about him
on all sides so that the proud man's power was to be seen in the very
movements of his body." But although he was a lover of war, ". . . he
was personally restrained in action, most impressive in counsel, gracious
to suppliants, and generous to those to whom he had once given his
trust."[24] He was also something of a politician, for if on occasion he
led devastating military raids deep into the empire, he was also content
to sit quietly by in his Danubian kingdom receiving tribute from the terrified Romans. (Professor Gordon estimated that, between A.D. 443 and
450, he was paid twenty-two thousand pounds of gold!)

Materially profitable, yes; politically constructive, no. Attila's numerous conquests were no more permanent than those of Fridigern or of
Alaric, who, in A.D. 407, led his Goths to the virtual conquest of Italy,
including the sacking of Rome. And then? Two years later, on his own
volition, he returned to the Rhineland. This was political naïveté in its
extreme form and brings to mind the lament of the cavalry general
Maharbal after the Carthaginian victory at Cannae: "You know how
to gain a victory, Hannibal; you know not how to use one."

Political naïveté helps to explain the military shortcomings of the barbarians. Their daring and skill and cunning were largely neutralized by
a lack of staying power, which in their own minds they did not need.
They wanted to eat, plunder, and move on. They invariably followed
the line of least resistance, as noted by Amédée Thierry: ". . . The nomads, unlike ourselves, do not consider flight a dishonor. Considering
booty of more worth than glory, they fight only when they are certain
of success. When they find their enemy in force, they evade him to return when the occasion is more opportune."[25]

Although, on occasion, Attila used siege engines and was not above
learning from the Romans, for example by replacing his ponies with
horses, he generally avoided attacking defended towns and cities:
". . . operations took the form of whirlwind advances and retirements.
Whole districts were laid waste and entire populations annihilated, not
only in order to establish a heat of terror which would evaporate opposition, but also to leave the rear clear of all hostile manpower and so
to facilitate withdrawals. The tactics may be defined as 'ferocity under

24. Gordon, op. cit.
25. Fuller, op. cit.

authority.' Fury, surprise, elusiveness, cunning and mobility, and not planning, method, drill, and discipline were its elements."[26]

When these guerrilla characteristics were not allowed to assert themselves, the result was usually disastrous. Attila was fought to a standstill by Aëtius at Chalons-sur-Marne in A.D. 451, a victory that depended largely on his Teutonic *foederati* buttressed by Theodoric's heavy Visigothic cavalry—barbarians brought under Roman discipline. Attila did manage, however, to extricate his surviving force and continue plundering tactics until his premature death, possibly the result of a hemorrhage on the night of his wedding to the young and beautiful Kriemhild.[27]

26. Ibid.
27. Hoyt, op. cit.; Gordon, op. cit. Priscus gives the cause as hemorrhage induced by intoxication; other sources state that a woman stabbed him to death.

Chapter 4

Justinian's campaigns • Belisarius: brain versus brawn • Justinian's Long Wall • Belisarius' sad end • Emperor Maurice's defense against guerrilla tactics • Emperor Leo's great work: Tactics • Emperor Nikephoros Phokas: On Shadowing Warfare • The growing difference in warfare between East and West

WE HAVE SEEN how Theodosius adapted his military machine to repair the disaster of the Byzantine defeat at Adrianople in A.D. 378. While the Western Empire, torn by internal dissension, dissolved into a sea of invading Germanic tribes, the Eastern Empire managed to survive by a judicious blending of city fortifications, native armies, privately controlled mercenary cavalry hosts, and outright bribes to deflect such potential predators as the Huns and the Ostrogoths.

The heavy-cavalry units formed by Theodosius more than justified themselves. By Justinian's reign (527–65), the mainstay of the army was the horse archer supported by light cavalry and heavy infantry. The historian Procopius was obviously impressed: ". . . They are expert horsemen, and are able without difficulty to direct their bows to either side while riding at full speed, and to shoot an opponent in pursuit or flight. They draw the bowstring along by the forehead about opposite the right ear, thereby charging an arrow with such impetus as to kill whoever stands in the way, shield and corselet alike having no power to check its force."[1]

By building small, mobile armies around such disciplined barbarians, Belisarius and Narses recovered numerous Roman provinces from the Vandals in Africa and from the Goths in Italy, achievements more remarkable considering Justinian's parsimony in supporting these expeditionary forces. Perhaps because of limited means, Belisarius relied on brain rather than brawn. He saw no dishonor in avoiding battle when he could, a lesson driven home early in his career. At twenty-six years of age he commanded a force that was screening a Persian withdrawal. Opposite Callinicum, his officers and troops urged him to take this last opportunity to strike the enemy. In a public harangue, Belisarius replied: ". . . Whither would you urge me? The most complete and most happy victory is to baffle the force of an enemy without impairing our own, and in this favorable situation we are already placed. Is it not wiser to enjoy the advantages thus easily acquired, than to hazard them in the pursuit of more?" Failing to convince his men, he grudgingly agreed to battle, only to suffer a near-disastrous defeat.[2]

He did not so err again, and in campaigns in Africa, Sicily, and Italy he also displayed political shrewdness. In North Africa, he scourged two of his soldiers who had stolen fruit and emphasized to his troops ". . . the importance of soothing and conciliating the native Africans, and of detaching them from the Vandal cause, to which from religious differences they were already disaffected." A few years later, in Italy, he ordered a lieutenant in a distant province to ". . . avoid all insult or injury to the Italian inhabitants."[3]

Although aware of his tactical superiority over the Goths, who had little knowledge of archery, Belisarius respected their superior numbers as well as the ability of such Gothic leaders as Totila. His polyglot army, which included Isaurian mountaineers and Hunnish and Moorish cavalry, probably numbered only about twelve thousand, and from this he had to garrison cities and strong points, since part of his strategy was to let the enemy wear himself out by siege attacks, whereupon the garrison force would sally forth and attack. In 537, during the siege of Rome, the citizens pressed him to give battle. Belisarius replied:

. . . I well know the character of that senseless monster the people, unable either to support the present or to foresee the future, always desirous of attempting the impossible, and of rushing headlong to its ruin. Yet your unthinking folly shall not induce me to permit your own destruction, nor to betray the trust committed to me by my sovereign and yours. Success in

1. R. A. Preston, and others, *Men in Arms* (London: Thames & Hudson, 1962). Hereafter cited as Preston; see also Fuller, op. cit.

2. Lord Mahon, *The Life of Belisarius* (London: John Murray, 1829).

3. Ibid.

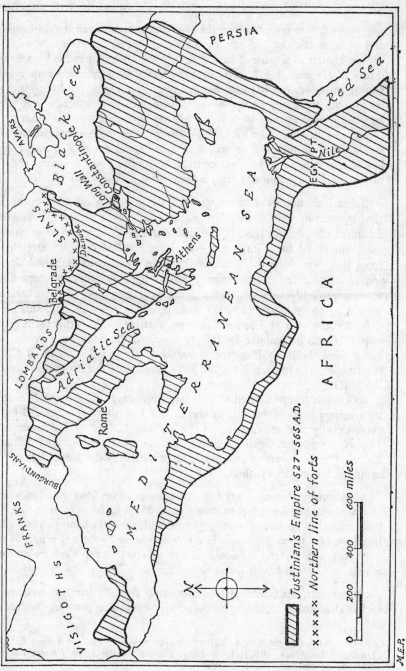

PERSIA

Red Sea

Black Sea

AVARS

Constantinople

Long Wall

SLAVS

Danube

Belgrade

Athens

EGYPT

Nile

MEDITERRANEAN SEA

AFRICA

Adriatic Sea

LOMBARDS

Rome

BURGUNTIANS

FRANKS

VISIGOTHS

N

Justinian's Empire 527–565 A.D.

xxxx Northern line of forts

0   200   400   600 miles

M.E.P.

war depends less on intrepidity than on prudence to await, to distinguish, and to seize the decisive moment of fortune. You appear to regard the present contest as a game of hazard, which you might determine by a single throw of the dice; but I, at least, have learnt from experience to prefer security to speed. But it seems that you offer to reinforce my troops and to march with them against the enemy. Where then have you acquired your knowledge of war? And what true soldier is not aware that the result of a battle must chiefly rest on the skill and discipline of the combatants? Ours is a real enemy in the field; we march to a battle and not to a review. I am, however, willing to praise your courage, to forgive your murmurs, and to prove to you that my present delay is founded on judicious policy.[4]

Belisarius' successful campaign in Italy proved a mixed blessing in that by causing the Goths to withdraw troops from the east, it opened Justinian's borders to fresh barbarian incursions. To hold these in check, Justinian relied on a large and expensive fortified complex stretching from Belgrade along the south bank of the Danube to the Black Sea—some sixty fortresses theoretically linked by five hundred intervening towers, probably used to shelter local peasantry until the barbarians passed by on their way to richer loot. In addition to this line, Justinian defended the pass at Thermopylae and, farther south, fortified the isthmus of Corinth; grander by far, he repaired the *Makron Teichos,* or Long Wall, built by Emperor Anastasius: forty miles north of Constantinople, its ramparts stretched sixty miles from the Propontis east to the Black Sea.

So long as troops existed in sufficient numbers to man these defenses, they helped keep barbarians in check. But Justinian overextended both economically and militarily, and the abilities neither of Belisarius nor Narses, once again fighting in Italy, could repair a paucity of military means. The last years of Justinian's reign marked a decline in Byzantine arms. According to Agathias,

. . . the emperor having entered on the last stage of his life seemed to weary of his labors, and preferred to create discord among his foes or to mollify them with gifts, instead of trusting to arms and facing the dangers of war. So he allowed his troops to decline in numbers because he did not expect to require their services, and the ministers who collected his taxes and maintained armies were affected with the same indifference.[5]

As one result, his border defenses became virtually useless, an unprotected sheepfold, according to Agathias, where the prowling wolf, far

4. Ibid.
5. Oman, op. cit.; see also, J. B. Bury, *A History of the Eastern Roman Empire* (London: Macmillan, 1912); J. B. Bury, *History of the Later Roman Empire* (London: Macmillan, 1923), 2 vols.

from encountering a bite, is not even threatened by a bark; and in 559
Zabergan led his Bulgarians into Thrace seemingly without difficulty.[6]

Belisarius met this new threat, again with careful restraint. When his
soldiers wanted to attack precipitately, he cautioned: ". . . Judgment,
and not headlong courage, is the true arbiter of war."[7]

But even Belisarius could not escape the dissension of Justinian's last
years. In 564, the emperor accused the general of trying to assassinate
him, stripped him of all honors and holdings, and had him blinded. As a
beggar, the victim of Justinian's wrath stood before the gates of the con-
vent of Laurus and pleaded, "Give a penny to Belisarius the General."[8]

When Justinian died, Constantinople faced the threat of the Avars
and Slavs in the north and the Persians in the south. Under Maurice
(582–602), ". . . the empire entered a defensive phase which was to
be its military outlook for the next 500 years."[9]

Maurice and his successors differed radically from Western tradition
in their approach to warfare. Though Hellenistic in outlook in many
respects, they seem to have reverted to the oriental thought of Sun Tzu.
They definitely preferred diplomacy and deception (including bribery)
to battle. Because of limited human resources, war was to be fought
only as a last resort. But since almost constant incursions of Slavs,
Avars, Bulgarians, Persians, Saracens, Franks, Russians, and Turks
meant a good many last resorts, the Eastern Empire attached greatest
importance to its armed forces, many details concerning which have
been preserved in two treatises, Maurice's *Artis Militaris* and Leo VI's
Tactics.

To deal with barbarian hordes, Maurice reduced the standing army
in size and restored it to control of the central government. He fortified his frontiers in depth and defended them in part with local militia.
This system evolved by the end of the seventh century into decentralized
defense, with the empire ultimately divided into military districts, or
themes, each containing ". . . a permanent army corps, bolstered by
local militia and commanded by a *strategos* who was also the head of
the area's civil government."[10] The hub of empire, Constantinople
". . . was surrounded by a sixty-foot moat, guarding a triple ring of
immense walls, each wall studded with towers at frequent intervals, and
the innermost wall reaching a height of thirty feet," a formidable defense, further strengthened by a powerful fleet and by the secret and

6. Mahon, op. cit.
7. Ibid.
8. Ibid.
9. Preston, op. cit.
10. Ibid.; see also Sidney Toy, *A History of Fortifications* (London: William
Heinemann, 1955).

devastating weapon of "Greek fire," which was poured on ships or on scaling parties.[11]

The relatively small professional army was well ahead of its time. Although continuing to rely primarily on mounted bowmen, it also included infantry and artillery units, the whole supported by engineers and quartermasters, even a medical corps. Other innovations included sectionalized boats, which, transported by mules, could be put together for fording purposes, and a series of military textbooks to instruct officers on diverse strategies and tactics ". . . based on the principle that the methods to be employed must be varied according to the people to be fought."[12]

Maurice wrote knowingly of the battle characteristics of the Persian, Lombard, Avar, and Slav enemy, describing tactics that should be used against each. No detail escaped his attention. He noted of the Slavs that ". . . they have abundance of cattle and grain, chiefly millet and rye, but rulers they cannot bear and they live side by side in disunion." But he was also impressed with their guerrilla tactics and their habit, when pursued, of disappearing under water and breathing through a reed until the danger passed.[13]

Sensing the danger of fighting against greatly superior numbers, yet wishing to avoid overdependence on unreliable mercenaries, Maurice favored a nation-in-arms concept: ". . . We wish that every young Roman of free condition should learn the use of the bow, and be constantly provided with that weapon and with two javelins." This ambition apparently came to nothing during the Persian and Saracen onslaughts of the seventh and eighth centuries, which brought the Eastern Empire continuing crisis and cost it Egypt and Syria.

Maurice's thinking was elaborated three hundred years later by Emperor Leo VI (886–912), whose *Tactics* borrowed freely from Maurice's work. For centuries, the Eastern Empire had been pursuing a "no-win" policy in order to survive against hordes of powerful enemies. At Leo's accession, it stood on the permanent defensive. Faced with fighting Franks, Saracens, Slavs, and Turks, the emperor found suitable countertactics prescribed by Maurice, who had written from firsthand experience:

. . . The Franks and Lombards are bold and daring to excess, though the latter are no longer all that they once were: they regard the smallest movement to the rear as a disgrace, and they will fight whenever you offer them battle. When their knights are hard put to it in a cavalry fight, they will turn

    11. Ibid.
    12. Ibid.
    13. F. Schevill, *History of the Balkan Peninsula* (New York: Harcourt, Brace, 1922).

their horses loose, dismount, and stand back to back against very superior numbers rather than fly. So formidable is the charge of the Frankish cavalry with their broadsword, lance, and shield, that it is best to decline a pitched battle with them till you have put all the chances on your own side. You should take advantage of their indiscipline and disorder; whether fighting on foot or on horseback, they charge in dense, unwieldy masses, which cannot maneuver, because they have neither organization nor drill. Tribes and families stand together, or the sworn war bands of chiefs, but there is nothing to compare to our own orderly division into battalions and brigades. Hence they readily fall into confusion if suddenly attacked in flank and rear—a thing easy to accomplish, as they are utterly careless and neglect the use of pickets and vedettes and the proper surveying of the countryside. They encamp, too, confusedly and without fortifying themselves, so that they can be easily cut up by a night attack. Nothing succeeds better against them than a feigned flight, which draws them into an ambush; for they follow hastily, and invariably fall into the snare. But perhaps the best tactics of all are to protract the campaign, and lead them into hills and desolate tracts, for they take no care about their commissariat, and when their stores run low their vigor melts away. They are impatient of hunger and thirst, and after a few days of privation desert their standards and steal away home as best they can. For they are destitute of all respect for their commanders—and they will deliberately disobey orders when they grow discontented. Nor are their chiefs above the temptation of taking bribes; a moderate sum of money will frustrate one of their expeditions. On the whole, therefore, it is easier and less costly to wear out a Frankish army by skirmishes, protracted operations in desolate districts, and the cutting off of its supplies, than to attempt to destroy it at a single blow.[14]

The Turks posed a different problem: innumerable bands of light horsemen armed with javelins and scimitars, but, like the Huns, relying on the bow and arrow, ". . . given to ambushes and stratagems of every sort . . . in battle they advanced not in one mass, but in small scattered bands, which swept along the enemy's front and around his flanks, pouring in flights of arrows, and executing partial charges if they saw a good opportunity." In proper terrain, they could be beaten by heavy cavalry; nor could they subdue trained infantry including foot archers, whose larger bow outranged the horse archers: ". . . The general who had to contend with the Turks, therefore, should endeavor to get to close quarters at once, and fight them at the earliest opportunity. But he should be careful about his flanks, and cover his rear if possible by a river, marsh, or defile. He should place his infantry in the front line, with cavalry on the flanks, and never let the two arms be separated. Heedless pursuit by

14. Oman, op. cit.

the cavalry was especially to be avoided, for the Turks were prompt at rallying, and would turn and rend pursuers who followed in disorder."[15]

The best defense against Eastern predators was a nation-in-arms, once called for by Maurice and echoed now by Leo: ". . . The bow is the easiest of weapons to make, and one of the most effective. We therefore wish that those who dwell in castle, countryside, or town, in short, every one of our subjects, should have a bow of his own. Or if this be impossible, let every household keep a bow and forty arrows, and let practice be made with them in shooting both in the open and in broken ground and in defiles and woods. For if there come a sudden incursion of enemies into the bowels of the land, men using archery from rocky ground or in defiles or in forest paths can do the invader much harm; for the enemy dislikes having to keep sending out detachments to drive them off, and will dread to scatter far abroad after plunder, so that much territory can thus be kept unharmed, since the enemy will not desire to be engaging in a perpetual archery-skirmish."[16] A lack of internal homogeneity apparently extinguished this scheme.

Supreme realists, Maurice and Leo never ignored the enemy but constantly respected and studied him. Few Frankish or Anglo-Saxon commanders would have written of an enemy, as Maurice and Leo did of the early Saracens, that they were ". . . the best advised and most prudent in their military operations." Or counseling that the Oriental did not like ". . . cold and rainy weather . . . at times when it prevailed he did not display his ordinary firmness and daring, and could be attacked with great advantage."[17]

The tenth century also added to Byzantine military literature. Emperor Nikephoros Phokas, around 965, ordered a handbook of defensive warfare prepared to help counter the incursive raids made by a great Moslem general, Sayf al-Dawla. The work, *On Shadowing Warfare,* reflects many of the earlier teachings of Maurice and Leo; according to its author, it was a method ". . . whereby a small army, too weak to engage the enemy in battle, could nevertheless preserve unharmed both itself and the territory of the state." Dr. Howard-Johnston, the translator of this work, concluded that

. . . the particular elements of the method resembled those of modern guerrilla warfare, in that they relied heavily upon the natural advantages offered by terrain, on the willing cooperation of the civilian population, on good intelligence, on interrupting the enemy's line of communication, and

15. Ibid.
16. Ibid.
17. Ibid.

finally on the demoralizing effect of an endless sequence of small, surprise, "carefully planned tactical attacks in a war of strategical defensive."[18]

On Shadowing Warfare evidences sophisticated military thinking produced by almost continuous offensive and defensive wars. Like Sun Tzu's *Art of War,* and like Maurice's and Leo's writings, it forms an interesting contrast to Western thinking of the time.

Oman underlines the vast difference in Eastern and Western military philosophy at this stage:

. . . Of the spirit of chivalry there was not a spark in the Byzantine, though there was a great deal of professional pride, and a not inconsiderable infusion of religious enthusiasm. The East-Roman officer was proud of his courage, strength and skill; he looked upon himself as charged with the high task of saving Christendom from pagan and Saracen, and of preserving the old civilization of the empire from the barbarian. But he was equally remote from the haughty contempt for sleights and tricks which had inspired the ancient Romans, and from the chivalrous ideals which grew to be at once the strength and the weakness of the Teutonic West. Courage was considered at Constantinople as one of the requisites necessary for obtaining success, not as the sole and paramount virtue of the warrior. The generals of the East considered a campaign brought to a successful issue without a great battle as the cheapest and most satisfactory consummation in war. They considered it absurd to expend stores, money, and the valuable lives of veteran soldiers in achieving by force an end that could equally well be obtained by skill. . . . They had a strong predilection for stratagems, ambushes, and simulated retreats. For the officer who fought without having first secured all the advantages for his own side they had the greatest contempt.[19]

The traditional criticism levied on the Byzantines is that, by accepting the strategic defensive, they forfeited initiative and eventually lost the empire. This criticism fails to respect the fact that a defensive strategy demands as competent leadership as an offensive strategy. Byzantine leadership was unfortunately spotty; thus, when the army mutinied and killed Maurice in 602, power went to an imbecile emperor, Phocas, under whom empire fortunes plunged, only to be retrieved by Heraclius' reforms and leadership. Had firm leadership continued, had the nation-in-arms concept worked, the Eastern Empire might have avoided a constant internal weakening by overreliance on quasi-assimilated military mercenaries. Even with these weaknesses, the military disasters against the Seljuk Turks of Arp Arslan, particularly the decisive battle of Manzikert, in 1071, might have been avoided had Romanus respected Leo's and Nikephoros Phokas' tactical instructions instead of yielding

18. James Howard-Johnston, "Studies in the Organization of the Byzantine Army in the Tenth and Eleventh Centuries" (Oxford: Ph.D. thesis, 1971).
19. Oman, op. cit.

to his own rashness.[20] The critic should also remember that, despite
its final fall, the Eastern Empire lasted longer than any in history, nor
did its eclipse in any way diminish the tactical brilliance of some of its
emperor-generals.

20. Ibid. Oman points out that command confusion, specifically alleged treachery
of the cavalry commander, Andronicus, undoubtedly played a major role in the
Byzantine defeat.

Chapter 5

Viking raids and invasions • French and English countertactics • Magyar tactics • Their defeat by Henry the Builder and Otto the Great • The rise of feudal warfare in the West • Knightly warfare: fiction versus fact • Early crusades • Seljuk Turk tactics • Byzantine influence on Frankish crusaders • Battle of Dorylaeum and Bohemond's tactical changes • The Frankish experience • Political failures of Seljuk Turks and Egyptians • The strategy of limited war • Political failure of the Franks

THE BARBARIAN PATTERN of the fourth and fifth centuries was emulated throughout the Middle Ages, notably by the Vikings in Britain, Ireland, and France; the Magyars and later the Mongols in central Europe; and the Persians, Slavs, and Saracens in the Eastern Empire.

Late in the eighth century, sleek Viking warships, their high bows fronted by leering dragon sprites, began to appear off English and Irish coasts. These open, oak-hulled vessels about seventy-five feet long were propelled by sixteen pairs of pine oars ". . . so regulated in length that they struck the water in unison," as well as ". . . a big square sail made of strips of heavy woolen cloth."[1] The shallow-draught vessels were easily beached to disgorge sixty to a hundred fierce warriors—Danes, Swedes, and Norwegians, small ". . . warbands of adventurers enlisted under the banner of some noted leader."[2]

1. Gwyn Jones, *A History of the Vikings* (London: Oxford University Press, 1968). Professor Jones has taken the Gokstad ship as prototype for his interesting and detailed description.

2. Oman, op. cit.; see also J. M. Wallace-Hadrill, *The Barbarian West 400–1000* (London: Hutchinson, 1952).

The intruders at first raided rich monasteries along the coast. They wanted booty, not battle, though they were efficient enough with spear, sword, and ax. But they preferred to rely on surprise and terror:

. . . The unexpectedness, the swiftness, and the savagery of the viking raid on the monastery at Lindisfarne in 793 came as a bolt from the blue not only to the monks surprised and slaughtered there but to Alcuin over in Charlemagne's court, [who wrote]: "It is some 350 years that we and our forefathers have inhabited this lovely land, and never before in Britain has such a terror appeared as this we have now suffered at the hands of the heathen. Nor was it thought possible that such an inroad from the sea could be made."[3]

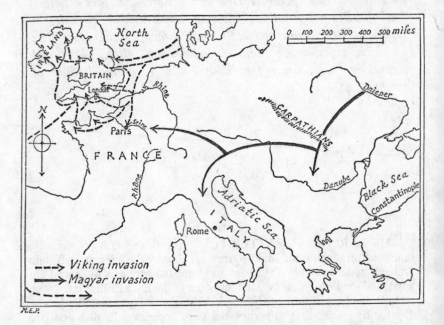

Cruising along a foreign coast, the Vikings might beach to take on food and water, perhaps raiding a herd of cattle; or strike a monastery or town, steal whatever of value they could find, sometimes kidnap the able-bodied to take back as slaves. If contested by arms, they hastily re-embarked to strike in a safer place, but in those early decades they found in their own phrase "little defence for the land."[4]

3. Jones, op. cit.; see also John Beeler, *Warfare in Feudal Europe 730–1200* (Ithaca, N.Y.: Cornell University Press, 1971).
    4. Ibid.

Until about A.D. 825 local lords, magnates, and imperial officials regarded these as little more than nuisance raids—unpleasant, but possible to live with. Charlemagne and Louis the Pious had largely vitiated the Viking threat with able diplomacy including bribery, and also a strong army. But the breakdown of the Carolingian empire into warring factions made the realm much more vulnerable.

From the Viking standpoint, success also bred expansion, a welcome development, considering a swelling population and limited natural resources at home. The sight of stolen gold or husky slaves certainly appealed to those who theretofore had remained behind, tilling the unwilling ground. By 834, the raids had grown larger and were spreading inland to France, Frisia and Aquitaine. The predators boldly sailed up rivers, possibly forming a defensive laager with their boats, rounded up horses and raided sometimes a hundred miles distant, then escaped by water before the local lord could collect a force and attack. Later they established semipermanent island and river bases, some of which withstood lengthy sieges. In 842, a force of no less than ". . . 67 ships appeared off the Loire" to sack Nantes—perhaps at the invitation of an ambitious nobleman. After this brutal but profitable raid, the Northmen withdrew to the island of Noirmoutier to spend the winter.

At the same time, the raids had spread to England and Ireland, and by 850 would even reach North Africa. Thus ". . . the nuisance raids of individual leaders" developed ". . . into big, well-organized expeditions which exploited local divisions and lived off the invaded country for lengthening periods of time." From their bases, the invaders pushed ever farther inland: the Danes plundered Paris on two occasions and in 885–86 held it under siege for eleven months. Prior to this, however, the Viking effort had entered its third phase, ". . . of conquest and residence."[5]

French and English rulers adopted several countermeasures. Whether faced with nuisance raids or the later expeditions, the obvious solution, a well-organized, mobile army, was virtually an impossibility at this time. Professor Gwyn Jones cites the dilemma of Charles the Bald in Aquitaine: ". . . in theory, Charles, like his brothers, could raise armies, build fleets, garrison towns, fortify coasts, bar rivers, and manhandle all vikings out of his realm—and who can doubt that he would have liked to? But theory and fact are different things. Charles had much to contend with: thrusting foreign foes, rivalry and enmity from his brothers, the veiled disaffection of great nobles, and the open rebellion of great provinces. He could be confident neither of the fighting spirit of his soldiers nor the patriotism of the counts who hung back from leading them."[6] To cope, he chose the reasonable alternative of bribery:

5. Ibid.
6. Ibid.

in 845, he paid the Viking chief Ragnar seven thousand pounds of silver to leave Paris. Similar payments followed over the years, the *Danegeld,* or bribe, also becoming familiar to the English, who paid out hundreds of thousands of pounds, at first to the Danes and later, as taxes, to their own kings.

Local rulers also introduced military measures which helped pave the way for the feudal structure that played such an important role in Western civilization. In neither country could local levies deal adequately with the challenge. These gave way to semiregular forces raised by important lords to whom lesser nobles and freemen turned for protection. In England, these were primarily infantry forces which were augmented by a series of fortified towns called *burhs* and also by a navy. The Franks relied on ". . . cavalry, walled towns, and fortified bridgeheads."[7]

When neither bribery nor military forces sufficed, rulers perforce yielded to delaying action and even limited assimilation. Although the Saracens, in 881, destroyed the monastery at Monte Cassino and went on to sack papal possessions, they lacked political cohesion and, cut from reinforcements from home, eventually faded from the picture.[8] But King Alfred's peace with Guthrum in 878 established the Danes on English soil, where in time they themselves became subject to hostile raids and from where they exercised a decisive influence on English arms. In the tenth century, the Franks bribed the Vikings with the gift of the rich province that later bore their name, Normandy, and from where William, Duke of Normandy, sailed to invade England in 1066 to beat Harold Godwineson at the battle of Hastings.[9]

Toward the end of the ninth century, the Magyars struck Europe from the east. From the Bug and the Dnieper, they crossed the Carpathians into the Danube Valley. Once the home of the Avars, this area was peopled by the Slavs, who quickly submitted to the bellicose newcomers. What was to become the kingdom of Hungary was thus born.

The Magyars were no more attractive than the early Huns, described by Priscus, and were just as cruel. But they fought well. Generally mounted, they were masters of reconnaissance; they traveled fast and struck unexpectedly, and in one chronicler's words (Regino), ". . . no man could stand against them if their strength and their perseverance were as great as their audacity." Their weaknesses were traditional among barbarians: no siege engines, slight staying power. Oman wrote that ". . . their tactics . . . were to hover round the enemy in successive swarms and overwhelm him with flights of missiles. When charged by

7. Oman, op. cit.
8. Hoyt, op. cit.
9. C. N. Barclay, *Battle 1066* (London: J. M. Dent & Sons, 1966).

the heavy Frankish horse, they fled, still pouring their arrows behind them."

A few years after claiming Hungary, the Magyars began raiding into Italy and Bavaria, areas torn by civil war. Once again, success bred expansion: By A.D. 924, they had crossed the Rhine, plundering as far as Champagne; thirty years later, they coursed through Burgundy, crossed the Alps into Italy and returned triumphantly to the Danube.

Duke Henry of Saxony began contesting these raids in 924. His means were by now familiar: After a large amount of damage had been done by the invaders, he gained temporary surcease by bribery; he then constructed a series of border strongholds similar to the English *burhs*, a zealous effort which earned him the name Henry the Builder; finally he raised cavalry formations headed by his nobles—in all, an effective defense, as proved by the victory at Merseburg in 933.[10] Henry's son, Otto the Great, carried on this work and, in 955, ended the Magyar threat with his great victory at the Lechfeld—a set-piece battle foolishly accepted by the Magyars, who retired to Hungary and in due time were converted to Christianity.

During the tenth century, the barbarian threat to the West declined while feudal warfare rose in importance. The rise of the mounted knight, who brought a new shock power to battle, and the concomitant development of military feudalism gradually brought imperial and religious wars designed to spread aristocratic authority by conquest and retention of land. Although crusaders would face a new style of warfare in the Middle East and although the Mongols would sweep through central Europe in the thirteenth century—a short-lived incursion we shall discuss in time—warfare in the West was developing in a peculiar fashion. By the time of the First Crusade (1095–99), it was becoming highly stylized, with armies cored by the mounted knight.

This did not mean mass armies of mounted knights. Two important factors checked the growth of knightly warfare. One was the Church, which wanted to limit warfare in order to protect its own holdings. Various popes proscribed from the battlefield such weapons as the crossbow, ". . . a weapon fateful to God and unfit for Christians." Lateran councils forbade employment of Spanish and Netherlandian mercenaries and tried to prevent bloody knightly tourneys by denying Christian burial to those who fell.[11] Neither the man in armor nor priests dependent on lords particularly heeded any of these prohibitions, though in time the tourney became less violent.

Another factor was cost. Horses were expensive, so was armor, and so were education and training required to produce a proficient knight.

10. Beeler, op. cit.
11. R. G. D. Laffan, *Select Documents of European History* (London: Methuen, 1930), Vol. 1 of 2 vols.

A knight was so valuable that an enemy preferred to capture and hold him for ransom rather than kill him. Mounted knights rarely fought alone—they needed servants and foot soldiers—and these men could not accompany expeditions and still work the soil. Most knights owed only so much annual military service to a lord—usually forty days—and this also tended to restrict campaigns.[12]

Although the arrangement at times sorely hindered bellicose desires of a lord or king—no one apparently *ever* had enough knights—it was not without social benefit. For if the Church was interested in maintaining the status quo, so was aristocracy. So long as a lord commanded a loyal force of knights, his authority was not likely to be questioned by bothersome peasant upstarts. The last thing nobles wanted was armed peasants: When a group of peasants in Belgium in 859 bravely took arms against an invading force of Danes, we have reason to believe that their own lords turned on them and killed them!

An important aspect of feudal warfare was a chivalric code that painted practical factors with a romantic veneer not entirely discounted even today. The early-twelfth-century epic poem *La Chanson de Roland* set the tone. *The Song of Roland* treated Charlemagne's invasion of Spain as a Christian crusade against Moslems. Aside from glorifying the campaign, in reality a costly flop, the work not only accepted but glorified war's brutality and cruelty at this time. And it was cruel: On one occasion, Charlemagne murdered forty-five hundred unarmed Saxon captives. On another occasion, a Byzantine emperor, Basil II (976–1025), sent the Bulgarian czar fifteen thousand prisoners, all blinded except for one in every hundred to serve as guide.[13]

The bards who sang and many of the scribes who wrote of the age of chivalry were as blind (intentionally) as Basil's poor prisoners. Arthurian legends have taught generations of youngsters to think of an era of richly armored knights setting forth on elaborately caparisoned steeds to uphold manly honor and maidenly virtue by slaying EVIL, sometimes human, sometimes dragon. Less-golden teachings have concentrated on the physical and awkward bulk of man and horse indulging in meaningless campaigns and melee-type tactics.

Within these terms, the age of chivalry is about the last place to search for military unorthodoxy.

But these terms are too easy.

Knighthood greatly varied in both definition and performance over the centuries and in different Western countries. Oman tells us that

---

12. Hoyt, op. cit.; R. C. Smail, "Art of War." In A. L. Poole (ed.), *Medieval England* (London: Oxford University Press, 1958), Vol. 1 of 2 vols.; Sidney Painter, "Western Europe on the Eve of the Crusades." In Kenneth M. Setton (ed.), *A History of the Crusades* (Madison, Wis.: University of Wisconsin Press, 1969), Vol. 1 of 2 vols.; Beeler, op. cit.

13. Schevill, op. cit.

". . . the original knights of the [Norman] settlement were a mixed multitude of many races drawn from many different stations in life; some were the kinsmen of great Norman barons, others were military adventurers who had drifted in from all parts of the Continent."[14] Two modern historians of this period, Strayer and Munro, concluded:

. . . the modern eye looks past the pageantry of knightly combat to see a record of horror, atrocity, and devastation surpassing that of the barbarian raids of the ninth century. As was usual, in medieval wars, non-combatants suffered more severely than soldiers. . . . Some districts in France lost all their inhabitants and reverted to a state of wilderness; others were so harassed that both religious and secular officials abandoned their posts, while the people became little better than savages. Never was the contrast between the chivalric ideals of the aristocracy and their actual behavior more acute.[15]

The truth seems to be that knightly warfare as many of us envisage it never did exist. Modern medieval historians, for example the late R. Stewart Hoyt, R. C. Smail, and John Beeler, have reinterpreted existing evidence—admittedly in short supply—to contradict the exclusive nature of this warfare and to throw new light on its campaigns and tactics. They have pointed to the important and almost constant role of the foot soldier in feudal combats, and they have also suggested and in many ways proved that, on occasion, good commanders developed effective strategy and adapted tactics in accordance with the combat environment of their day.

The First Crusade is a case in point. As Smail points out in his excellent book *Crusading Warfare,* the relatively small European army that contested Islamic control of Syria had either to adjust tactically or perish.[16] Their enemies, the Seljuk Turks and the Egyptians, were far superior in numbers, they knew the country, and they had positive ties to its diverse peoples.

From the standpoint of quasi-guerrilla tactics, the Egyptians are of little interest: They fought dismounted, using lance and sword, and until Saladin successfully merged an Egyptian army with the Turks, the Europeans, though on occasion losing a battle, defeated them or at least held their own.

The Turks provided a far greater challenge. In addition to bow and arrows, horsemen carried a light lance and shield and also sword and club. Their tactics skillfully blended surprise, mobility and firepower. The crusaders first experienced them in strength at Dorylaeum, where

14. Oman, op. cit.

15. J. R. Strayer and D. C. Munro, *Middle Ages, 395–1500* (New York: Appleton-Century, 1942).

16. R. C. Smail, *Crusading Warfare (1097–1193)* (London: Cambridge University Press, 1956); see also S. Runciman, *A History of the Crusades* (New York: Penguin Books, 1965), 3 vols.; Setton, op. cit.

the local emir, Kilij Arslan, who had abandoned his capital at Nicaea to the invaders, attacked in force. Opening fire from a distance, the Turks caused the knights to charge from the main body, as dictated by Western tactics. But, instead of standing ground, the Turkish horse-

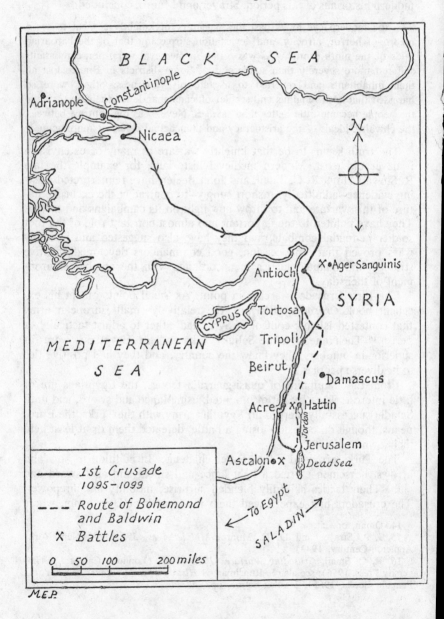

1st Crusade
1095-1099

Route of Bohemond
and Baldwin

X   Battles

0   50 100   200 miles

M.E.P.

men galloped off while others closed in on the main force. Unable to find a target, the knights became confused and fell back on their foot soldiers and pilgrims, while their enemies began moving in for what they imagined would be the kill. Although the Turks were frustrated by a cohesive and determined defense of heavier-armed foot soldiers, the battle was admittedly going badly for the Franks when a second crusader force appeared and chased off Kilij Arslan.[17] Recognizing the superior strength of the Franks, the emir ". . . sent orders out to evacuate the cities along the crusaders' route, and he and his people took to the hills after ravaging the countryside and blocking the wells."[18]

The crusaders soon learned to know and respect Turkish tactics: An anonymous chronicler of the time ". . . declared that, if only they were Christians, they would be the finest of races."[19] In fighting pitched battles and in attacking marching columns, the Turks invariably tried to surprise the Franks and often did. They usually opened arrow fire from a distance, a barrage designed to confuse, demoralize and even break up the Frankish force. In pitched battles, the Turks attempted to draw off Frankish horse while working around the flanks of the foot host; on the march, they attacked front, center and rear, hoping to disable or kill horses by arrow fire and thus sting knights into precipitate charges.

The Turk was a master of feigned retreat. On occasion, he led Frankish horse a chase lasting days; on other occasions, he lured them into prepared ambush. When attacking marching columns, he concentrated on separating the components, usually striking the rear. And, just as disconcerting, if things went wrong for the attackers they did not hesitate in breaking off action and disappearing.

Nearly everything about Turkish fighting methods—from hideous yells to drum signals to surprise and deception—must have upset the newcomers. Yet, from the beginning, the Franks held certain advantages. The diverse columns were fired with a zeal compounded of religious conviction, desire for adventure, and, not least, hunger for land and loot. They had already suffered considerably in the long trek from France and Italy to the Middle East—no easy matter in that day—and they were prepared to suffer in satisfying diverse ambitions.

Their military forces also held certain natural advantages over the enemy. Frankish body armor offered reasonable protection from arrows; more than one account describes foot soldiers after a battle as looking like porcupines from spent arrows protruding from armor. Frankish horse was heavy and the Turkish archer at a disadvantage once contact was achieved. Moreover, if the Turk closed in, he came up

17. Ibid.
18. S. Runciman, "The First Crusade: Constantinople to Antioch." In Setton, *supra*.
19. The work referred to is a pro-Norman chronicle, *Gesta Francorum et aliorum Hierosolymitanorum*.

against tight ranks and heavier-armed foot soldiers, as at Dorylaeum, and in coming to close quarters, he had to fully engage, which made him vulnerable to cavalry action, provided that knights could be restrained until the propitious moment.

This was a matter of good generalship, and here, like most armies, the Franks were not generously endowed. One exception was the stormy Bohemond, who commanded at Dorylaeum. Bohemond was the son of Robert Guiscard, a minor Norman nobleman who had carved out an impressive dukedom in Italy[20]: Emperor Alexius' daughter, Anna Comnena, later wrote that father and son ". . . might rightly be termed 'the caterpillar and the beast'; for whatever escaped Robert . . . his son Bohemond took to him and devoured."[21] Robert and Bohemond had taken an expedition to Albania, from where they hoped to wrest Greece, if not the whole Byzantine Empire, from Alexius, an ambitious project that failed. Bohemond jumped at the material opportunity offered by the First Crusade and quickly raised an army.[22]

Bohemond was an impressive leader. At forty years of age, he was a large, powerful and fiery man who, according to Anna Comnena, ". . . in roguery and courage . . . was far superior to all the Latins who came through [Constantinople] then, as he was inferior to them in forces and money."[23] Undeniably ambitious—he failed to persuade Alexius to appoint him commander-in-chief or Great Domestic of the East—he was also a skillful general who adapted rapidly to the new tactical challenge imposed by the Seljuk Turks.[24]

Just what influence, if any, the Byzantine experience exerted is not clear. Older authorities such as Oman held that the Franks expressed contempt for the Byzantine Greeks, learned nothing from them militarily, and suffered in consequence. This is probably true of some crusader leaders. Frankish knights might not have studied either Maurice's or Leo's tactical treatises—the favored work of the time was Vegetius' *Epitoma rei militaris* (*Summary of the Art of War*)—but some were professional soldiers who had experienced some contact with Byzantine warfare.[25] Moreover, most of them spent some time in Constantinople on their way to Syria. Although Alexius trusted neither Bohemond, his former enemy, nor most crusaders, he still reasoned that if properly controlled, their armies could do him more good than harm by challenging Seljuk Turkish rule in the south. If crusader leaders pledged fealty to Alexius' overlordship, and nearly all did, he helped them. In addition

20. Painter, op. cit.
21. Anna Comnena, *The Alexiad* (London: Routledge & Kegan Paul, 1967). Tr. E. A. S. Dawes.
22. Frederic Duncalf, "The First Crusade: Clermont to Constantinople." In Setton, *supra*.
23. Comnena, op. cit.
24. Runciman ("The First Crusade"), *supra*.
25. Wallace-Hadrill, op. cit.

to rich presents, he supplied their armies with food. According to Anna
Comnena, he also ". . . discoursed of the things likely to befall them
on their journey [to Jerusalem], and gave them useful advice; he also
instructed them in the Turks' usual method of warfare, and suggested
the manner in which they should dispose the army and arrange their
ranks, and advised them not to go far in pursuit of the Turks when they
fled."[26] Alexius also provided a force of infantry including a detachment of engineers, who helped the Franks besiege and capture Nicaea
(which Alexius promptly claimed); he also furnished Byzantine guides
under one Taticius, and it would not be surprising if they advised on enemy tactical habits[27]; in 1101, at the request of Stephen of Blois, who
had brought out a large army, Alexius ". . . gave them Raymond
of Toulouse and the Greek general Tsitas as advisers and a force
of mounted native auxiliaries known as Turcopoles—estimated at 500
strong—to serve as guides."[28]

Bohemond was probably smart enough to respect the value of local
knowledge, but he was also a good enough general to realize that tactical changes were in order. His changes strongly reflected the teachings
of Leo the Wise. First in importance was flank protection, which in
pitched battles meant seeking favorable terrain. Second was the necessity of retaining a mounted tactical reserve, which in subsequent battles
Bohemond personally commanded. This meant placing the foot soldiers
in front of the knights, and this became standard battle order for nearly
a century.

Bohemond and other commanders, such as King Baldwin I, also made
significant changes in marching order, paying particular attention to
front and rear guards when marching in column. In open flat ground,
they assumed a different formation: In 1099, when approaching battle
at Ascalon, ". . . their force was divided into nine squadrons organized
in three ranks of three squadrons, a square formation in which attack
could be met equally well from whatever direction it developed."[29]
This early version of the marching square may have been learned from
Alexius—his daughter described it graphically: ". . . had you seen it,
you would have said a living walled city was marching. . . ." The trick
was to keep closed up and moving. Smail offers a fine illustration during the siege of Acre in 1190, when a Latin column found itself isolated
from the main body:

. . . Saladin ordered his men to hem in the Franks on all sides. His horsemen kept close to the Latin column, and his mounted archers were constantly
reinforced throughout the day. Despite the Muslims' arrows, and the re-

26. Comnena, op. cit.
27. Runciman ("The First Crusade"), *supra*.
28. James L. Cate, "The Crusade of 1101." In Setton, *supra*.
29. Smail, op. cit.

peated short attacks at close quarters to which they were subjected, the Franks, grouped around their standard, marched slowly forward in close order. The foot-soldiers protected the knights like a wall and, together with the archers, especially distinguished themselves in the rear of the column. It was here that the Turks followed their normal practice and developed their heaviest attacks, and often, as at Arsuf in the following year, forced the Christian infantry to face about and to fight while marching backwards. As in 1147 they concealed their losses by carrying their wounded, and by burying their dead as they marched.[30]

None of this was easy, neither in early days nor later, and violations were common. In general, the knights were an impatient and vainglorious lot, a Frankish trait commented on by Emperor Leo two centuries earlier, and one constantly exploited by the Turks. A Frankish commander had a difficult time instilling and maintaining what chroniclers called *disciplina militaris*—particularly cavalry discipline, foreign to knightly concepts of challenge, honor and individual valor. During a Turkish attack in 1111, Roger of Antioch ordered ". . . that no man should accept the enemy's challenge [to battle] under pain of losing his eyes."[31] When knights obeyed, a Frankish force was seldom defeated: harassed and hurt, yes—but not stopped. When commanders neglected either march or battle discipline, they suffered. Bohemond himself fell into a Turkish ambush and spent three years in captivity before being ransomed.[32] In 1119, Roger of Antioch, commanding a force of seven hundred knights and some three thousand foot, was taken by surprise, the enemy approaching by "little-used paths"; he was killed and his army so decimated that Latin writers called the battlefield Ager Sanguinis (Field of Blood). In 1149, Raymond of Antioch met a similar fate.[33] New arrivals did not necessarily benefit from past lessons. As one authority, Professor James Cate, has noted:

. . . The crusades of 1101 had no organization, no system, no luck, and so they set a pattern of failure that was to be followed by those of 1147 and 1190. Of more immediate importance was their failure to reinforce the Latin kingdom. The newly established states of the Crusaders were forced, therefore, to rely largely on their own resources for both defense and administration. These resources were very limited, and therein lies the major problem of the ensuing years.[34]

30. Ibid.
31. Ibid.
32. Harold S. Fink, "The Foundation of the Latin States, 1099–1118." In Setton, *supra:* Bohemond returned to Italy, collected another army, and landed in Albania, but once again failed to defeat Alexius; he died in Apulia in 1111.
33. Smail, op. cit.
34. Cate, op. cit.; see also Fink, op. cit.

Tactical adaptation was only partly responsible for early Frankish victories which gained them a foothold and allowed them to seize and hold Antioch, Jerusalem, and other cities, and to capture and defend existing castles and build new ones. But the Franks probably would not have carved out their various Syrian kingdoms, let alone retain them for nearly a century, had it not been for a supreme enemy weakness. This was political, not military: had the sultan controlled his emirs, or local governors, sufficiently, he could have fielded an army of such strength as to have overwhelmed the relatively slim crusader forces.

Fortunately for the crusaders, the sultan's relations with his Syrian and other emirs were stormy. Moslem rulers such as Kilij Arslan, Zanki, and his son Nūr-ad-Dīn, exercised a hegemony that the sultan resented; conversely, they viewed the sultan's expeditions from Mesopotamia with suspicion. In 1111, for example, when the sultan took the offensive against the Franks, his local emirs offered only lukewarm co-operation to the invading force. The Frankish prince Tancred (Bohemond's nephew) refused battle, and the Turkish forces, finding no worthwhile loot, soon returned home. In 1115, local emirs actually allied *with* the Franks against Moslem invaders. The situation was no better in Egypt, which was wracked by civil war, a fragmentation that lasted until Saladin, the great Egyptian leader, managed to infuse a kind of unity and break Frankish power in Syria.[35]

If enemy political weakness saved the crusaders and allowed them to survive, their own political weakness prevented them from expanding their coastal holdings into a Franco-Syrian empire of any importance. Despite religious trappings, the early crusades represented a colonizing effort—a transplanting of the feudal system to the Middle East. No overall political plan existed. Feudal lords occupied existing castles or built new ones, not in accordance with a single strategy but rather in areas that seemed to offer the best opportunity for exploitation. As Smail has emphasized, the castle did not serve *primarily* a military function, although the security it offered formed a vital ingredient in the feudal holding it dominated. But the Franks did not build a planned defensive complex designed either to repel unwanted invaders or to serve as a springboard for further expansion to important east Syrian cities.

Political weakness on either side in time brought a fundamental change to crusading warfare. Lacking a strong political base, the new feudal kingdoms never grew militarily dominant: knights and foot soldiers were forever in short supply, and local magnates could not afford to risk losing armies. But local feudal lords soon discovered that such was the political fragmentation of the enemy that quite often no need existed to risk battle: natural causes limited depth and duration of enemy incursions. The enemy could burn crops and terrorize peasants,

35. H. A. R. Gibb, "The Rise of Saladin 1169–1189." In Setton, *supra.*

but, lacking equipment to besiege castles and fortified towns, and lacking the strength and staying power necessary to defeat crusading armies, he could not establish a permanent presence and he could not collect loot sufficient to satisfy his soldiers. As one result, his invasion forces, composed of tribal contingents, often melted away, particularly at season's end, when the fighting man was needed at home. In this sense, the art of warfare from the Frankish standpoint became that of *not* fighting battles, or at least restricting them to a minimum.[36]

The crusaders apparently did not realize that good fortune was giving them a breathing space—nearly fifty years—in order to erect a political-military bastion from an indigenous population variously composed of Armenians, Christian Syrians and Moslems. Though apologists later spoke of Frankish assimilation in Syria, the record shows a rule primarily of force with attendant lack of political growth or even change. Local peoples served the Franks because they had to. Frankish behavior offered no particular attraction to local loyalties, particularly when enemy armies frequently challenged Frankish presence. Smail has cited instances of local collaboration with Turks and Egyptians, but perhaps the most telling indication of Frankish failure occurred after the battle of Hattin, in 1187, when ". . . the Franks in the district of Nablus evacuated the area as the Muslim peasants rose *en masse* in favor of the victorious Saladin."[37]

36. Smail, op. cit.
37. Ibid.

Chapter 6

Warfare in the West • Norman conquest of Ireland • The great Mongol invasion of Europe • Vietnam's savior: Marshal Tran Hung Dao • Edward I's pacification of Wales • The English experience in Scotland: William Wallace and Robert Bruce • The guerrilla leader Bertrand du Guesclin • John Zizka and the Hussite wars

STRATEGY AND TACTICS of the Middle Ages, particularly of feudal warfare in Europe, remain obscure. Modern historians tend to argue that combat was not as stylized as we normally think, but rather that it differed from country to country and from commander to commander—in other words, that warfare continued to develop as it had since the birth of time. If the mounted knight enjoyed his place in the sun, his role slowly diminished as mercenaries and citizen soldiers augmented feudal hosts and as armies grew in strength and staying power essential for longer campaigns. If the mounted knight outlasted feudal warfare, he eventually succumbed to weapon development, first the longbow, which shredded French cavalry formations at Crécy and Agincourt, then gunpowder.

Although lacking details, we know that clever commanders continued to employ tactical tricks during these decades and centuries. The feigned flight seems to have been a Norman favorite (possibly the result of Byzantine influence): William of Normandy allegedly used it not once but twice in the same afternoon to break Harold's infantry and win the battle of Hastings in 1066.[1] In the battle of the Standard, in 1138, Prince Henry fought his way through English foot only to find himself and his small cavalry band cut off; ordering his knights to throw away identifying badges, he led them forward to merge with the English and slowly pass through to freedom.

The Normans appear to have used considerable tactical flexibility during the conquest of Ireland (1169–75). In addition to small, seemingly effective armies cored by mounted knights, they relied on three main tactical devices: ". . . the feigned retreat, the flank attack by horsemen, and the sudden surprise."[2] In these campaigns and in defending against Norse incursions from Wales, the Normans, according to Basil Liddell Hart,

. . . showed their skill and calculation by the way in which they repeatedly lured their opponents to battle in open ground where their mounted charges had full effect, by the way they exploited feigned retreats, diversions, rear attacks to break up the opposing formation, and by the strategic surprises, night attacks and use of archery to overcome opposition when they could not lure an enemy from the shelter of his defenses.[3]

Although their military campaigns were facilitated by extreme political dissension in Ireland,[4] their arms and ability were superior to the Irish so long as the latter fought "orthodox" battles. The Normans found more difficult going in bogs and forests, where the Irish set skillful ambushes which often stopped Norman horsemen. One Irish leader delayed a Norman force by cutting trenches across forest paths and throwing up ramparts behind the trenches.[5] Another leader, Dermot MacMurrogh, utilized a similar defense:

. . . In order to keep attackers to the paths and to prevent infiltration into the woods, which might outflank him, Dermot "plashed" the margins of the pathways, in the approaches to his barriers; he made, that is, impenetrable hedgerows of the undergrowth on either side by interweaving cut branches amid the growing shrubs and saplings.[6]

The Normans could not carry war into the bogs with any success, and to the bogs the Irish eventually retired, leaving cities and open country

1. But see Beeler, op. cit., who challenges this traditional version.
2. Oman, op. cit.
3. B. H. Liddell Hart, *The Decisive Wars of History—A Study in Strategy* (London: G. Bell & Sons, 1929).
4. A. J. Otway-Ruthven, *A History of Medieval Ireland* (London: Ernest Benn, 1968).
5. G. A. Hayes-McCoy, *Irish Battles* (London: Longmans, Green, 1969).
6. Ibid.

to the castled supremacy of the English. But the expansion of English supremacy—the successful colonization of Ireland—demanded a continued military effort backed by an influx of settlers. Having neither, the Normans slowly compressed their rule into the greater Dublin area—what became the English Pale. In Oman's words: ". . . Hence came that unhappy division of the island, destined to last for four centuries and more, in which the natives held out in their fastnesses, while the invaders dominated the open land—each levying unending war on the other, yet neither able to get the advantage."[7]

While Western knights continued to depend on weight to give their armies shock power, Eastern armies continued to stress mobility. Like the Franks and Normans, Eastern peoples were also on the move. By the twelfth century, successive migratory waves (which started around 12,000 B.C.) had populated Vietnam, Malaya, the Philippines, Java, Indonesia, and Australia. The dominant power in Southeast Asia was China, which held suzerainty over what are today's Tibet, Korea, and most of Vietnam.

Toward the end of the twelfth century, the Mongols sharply challenged the Chinese position. Genghis Khan (1162–1227) succeeded in consolidating a group of Mongolian tribes, nomads living between Lakes Baikah and Baikal in Asia, and in forming and training an army which in 1214 penetrated the Great Wall of China and captured Peking, capital of the Kin dynasty.

A few years later, while one army remained to fight in China, Genghis led another force west, conquered the Khwarazm Empire (northern India-Turkestan-Persia), and marched north to defeat a Russian army on the Dnieper. This empire did not collapse with the Khan's death, in 1227; his son Ogdai, aided by such civil counselors as the brilliant Yeliu Chutsai and by such outstanding generals as Subutai, defeated the Hin Chinese to win northern China before invading the lands of the Sung dynasty, to the south. Ogdai then led his army across Asia to invade Russia, sack Kiev, conquer most of Poland, and, early in 1241, occupy Hungary.[8] Ogdai's sudden death caused the Mongols to return to Asia, where, after considerable delay, Mangu Khan was elected Great Khan in 1251. Under his rule and that of Kublai, who succeeded him in 1260, the main empire moved east, leaving subordinate empires in Russia and Persia. Although the Mongolian Empire would prove short-lived, the Yuan dynasty, which Kublai established in China, lasted until 1368.

The Mongol conquests represent a tremendous military achievement. Basil Liddell Hart wrote that ". . . in scale and in quality, in surprise and in mobility, in the strategic and in the tactical indirect approach,

7. Oman, op. cit.
8. H. T. Cheshire, "The Great Tartar Invasion of Europe," *The Slavonic Review*, Vol. 5 (London, 1926).

their campaigns rival if they do not surpass any in history."[9] Professor
Bury noted that their success was due to "consummate strategy" and not

. . . to a mere overwhelming superiority of numbers. . . . It was wonderful
how punctually and effectually the arrangements of the commander were
carried out . . . Such a campaign was quite beyond the power of any
European army of the time, and it was beyond the vision of any European
commander. There was no general in Europe, from Frederick II downward,
who was not a tyro in strategy compared to Subutai. It should also be noticed that the Mongols embarked upon the enterprise with full knowledge
of the political situation of Hungary and the condition of Poland—they had
taken care to inform themselves by a well-organized system of spies; on the
other hand, the Hungarians and Christian powers, like childish barbarians,
knew hardly anything about their enemies.[10]

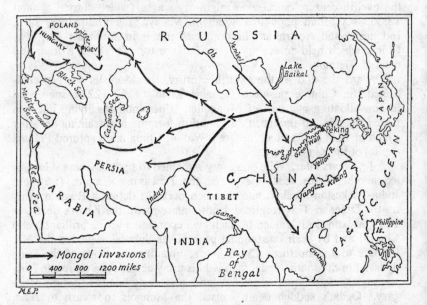

The Mongol armies consisted primarily of horse archers who, in the
Eastern tradition, literally lived on horseback. Armed with bow, lance
and scimitar, the hardy, well-trained warriors used two varieties of bows
and three "calibers" of arrows for various tactical situations. Some authorities believe that, as early as 1218, Genghis Khan used guns and
gunpowder for siege work in the conquest of Turkestan. According to
Marco Polo, who visited Kublai Khan's empire, each warrior marched

9. Liddell Hart, op. cit.
10. Bury, op. cit.; see also P. Kendall, *The Story of Land Warfare* (London:
Hamish Hamilton, 1957).

with eighteen horses and mares in order to supply himself with milk, blood, meat and remounts. Subutai's armies marched in widely separated columns, the flanks ahead of the center; such was the mobility of the cavalry that the columns could converge upon plan, after which they were tactically controlled in the Chinese fashion by a variety of signals.

Tactically, Subutai's armies were not suitable for fighting in hilly, wooded country, nor did they carry siege machines. The most effective defense occurred in Bohemia, where Václav I ". . . saw to it that Prague, Olomouc, Brno, and other towns in Bohemia and Moravia were adequately fortified; he also ordered the monasteries to be turned into strongholds so that the civilian population could take refuge there, while the monks, who were provided with weapons, received instructions to store up food."[11] How effective the Bohemian defense would have proved had the Mongols remained is another matter, but perhaps Václav was aware of their political shortcomings. As it turned out, he was correct: Ogdai's sudden death brought a succession problem and caused the Mongols to return to Asia.

A few years later, the Mongols turned south to Vietnam, an invasion of the Red River Valley with a force, according to ancient annals, doubtlessly exaggerated, of two hundred thousand. ". . . The Vietnamese, as they would so often do later, abandoned their cities and headed for the hills, leaving their capital to be burned by the invaders. But the Mongols, still unused to the tropics and tropical diseases, were defeated by the environment; after a fruitless pursuit of the Vietnamese, they withdrew."[12] About 1268, Kublai Khan led another invasion aimed at conquering the Champa kingdom on the Gulf of Tonkin, an inconclusive campaign described by Marco Polo.[13]

Once fleet of foot, the Mongol armies were growing heavier with the addition of infantry and even war elephants. In 1284, such a host descended for the third time on Vietnam. And now appeared a remarkable man: Marshal Tran Hung Dao, ". . . who withdrew to the mountains, wrote his *Essential Summary of Military Arts,* and began to train his troops for protracted guerrilla warfare! 'The enemy must fight his battles far from his home base for a long time. . . . We must further weaken him by drawing him into protracted campaigns. Once his initial dash is broken, it will be easier to destroy him.' "[14]

Three years passed before Kublai's "initial dash was broken," but he nonetheless had to withdraw. Dao now had his guerrillas plant ". . . thousands of iron-spiked stakes in the Bach-Dang river north of

11. Cheshire, op. cit.

12. Bernard Fall, "Two Thousand Years of War in Viet-Nam," *Horizon,* Spring 1967.

13. Marco Polo, *The Travels of Marco Polo* (New York: New American Library, 1961). Ed. Milton Rugoff.

14. Fall, op. cit.

Haiphong through which the Mongol fleet had to pass. The ships arrived at high tide, when the stakes were submerged. A small Vietnamese naval force cleverly decoyed the enemy into a fight which looked like an easy victory until the Mongol ships found themselves stranded or gored on the stakes by the momentum of the out-flowing tides. That was the moment Marshal Dao's infantry chose to attack and defeat the invaders."[15]

Marshal Dao knew how to use a victory. Bowing to the inevitable, he voluntarily began paying tribute to the Mongols ruling in Peking.

One of the most interesting pacification campaigns of these turbulent years was Edward I's conquest of Wales. In the preceding two hundred years, Anglo-Norman expeditions had only partially subjugated these rude peoples who enjoyed making war against each other almost as much as against the English.

Edward, who came to the throne in 1272 and reigned until 1307, did not return to England until 1274. To his annoyance, the powerful northern Welsh ruler, Llewellyn ap Gruffydd, otherwise the Prince of Wales, refused to do homage. Edward decided to force the issue and invade the country, but wisely took his time in organizing the expedition. In this interim period, he came on a remarkable analysis of earlier campaigns in Wales written by a highly educated and widely traveled cleric who was half Welsh, Giraldus Cambrensis, otherwise called Gerald de Barri. Giraldus had served in Wales and had advised Henry II on his pacification campaigns.[16] He had written a history of the Norman conquest of Ireland; two other works, *Itinerarium Kambriae* and *Descriptio Kambriae,* not only offered generous and generally accurate information on Welsh guerrilla tactics but possibly gave Edward a rough plan of campaign.[17]

Giraldus emphasized the totally hostile environment of this mountainous and wooded target area: dreadful weather, few roads, mostly barren land whose entire settlements disappeared into remote mountain valleys to leave an invading army to fend for itself.

Although Welsh princes preferred to let land and weather defeat an invader, Giraldus left no doubt of their willingness to fight under favorable conditions. A tradition of universal military service existed: ". . . when the trumpet sounds the alarm, the husbandman rushes as eagerly from the plow as the courier from his court." Wearing light armor to retain mobility and armed with bows and spears, the Welsh bands fought in broken country, where they ". . . relied on a single charge accompanied by wild shouts and the noise of trumpets, calculated to de-

15. Ibid.

16. Giraldus Cambrensis, *The Autobiography of Giraldus Cambrensis* (London: Jonathan Cape, 1937). Ed. and tr. H. E. Butler.

17. John Beeler, *Warfare in England 1066–1189* (Ithaca, N.Y.: Cornell University Press, 1966).

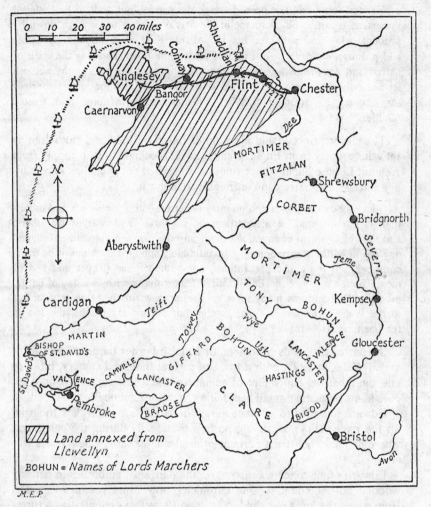

0 10 20 30 40 miles

Conway
Rhuddlan
Anglesey
Bangor
Flint
Chester
Caernarvon
Dee
MORTIMER
FITZALAN
Shrewsbury
CORBET
Bridgnorth
N
Severn
Aberystwith
MORTIMER
Teme
TONY
BOHUN
Kempsey
Cardigan
Teifi
MARTIN
BISHOP
OF ST. DAVID'S
CAMVILLE
Towey
GIFFARD
LANCASTER
BOHUN
Wye
Usk
VALENCE
LANCASTER
Gloucester
VAL ENCE
HASTINGS
St. David's
Pembroke
BRAOSE
C L A R E
BIGOD
Bristol
Avon

▨ Land annexed from
   Llewellyn
BOHUN = Names of Lords Marchers

M.E.P

moralize the enemy." If an attack failed, they disappeared into the woods. But Giraldus warned pursuers to look sharply for ambushes. He also warned that ". . . the Welsh were as easy to defeat in a single battle as they were difficult to overcome in a protracted campaign."[18]

Was it possible to subdue them? It was, if the prince developed a strategy based on enemy weaknesses. Sounding remarkably like Sun Tzu fifteen centuries earlier, Giraldus wrote:

. . . The prince who would wish to subdue this nation, and govern it peaceably, must use this method. He must be determined to apply a diligent and constant attention to this purpose for a year at least; for a people who with

18. Ibid.

a collected force will not openly attack the enemy, nor wait to be besieged in castles, is not to be overcome at the first onset, but to be worn down by prudent delay and patience. Let him divide their strength, and by bribes and promises endeavor to stir up one against the other, knowing the spirit of hatred and envy which generally prevails among them; and in the autumn let not only the marches [the border country], but also the interior part of the country be strongly fortified with castles, provisions, and trusted families.[19]

The clever prince would place an embargo on food and cloth coming into the country from England and a naval blockade to stop supply from Ireland. Let the harsh winter run out, and when the guerrillas were hungry and the land barren and unfriendly to ambush,

. . . let a body of light-armed infantry penetrate into their woods and mountainous retreats, and let these troops be supported and relieved by others; and thus by frequent changes, and replacing the men who are either fatigued or slain in battle, this nation may be ultimately subdued. Nor can it be overcome without the above precautions, nor without great danger and loss of men. Though many of the English hired troops may perish in a day of battle, money will procure as many more on the morrow for the same service; but to the Welsh, who have neither foreign nor stipendiary troops, the loss is for the time irreparable.[20]

Supported by Lords Marchers, or English border barons, Edward invaded Wales in 1277, with a force of several thousand cavalry, infantry and the medieval equivalent of engineers, the whole supported by a secure home base and a small fleet sailing from the Cinque Ports.

Edward intended to advance along the coast ". . . and then to strike up the river valleys, fortifying posts provisionally during the campaign, where he could construct permanent castles afterwards when Wales was annexed."[21]

Edward's first concern centered on the danger of ambushes in densely wooded border country. One chronicler noted that between Chester, from where the army marched, ". . . and Llewellyn's country lay a forest of such denseness and extent that the royal army could by no means penetrate through without danger. A large part of this forest being cut down, the king opened out for himself a very broad road for an advance

19. Ibid.
20. Ibid.
21. J. E. Morris, *The Welsh Wars of Edward I* (London: Oxford University Press, 1901). Edward built ten castles between 1277 and 1295, at a cost of probably £100,000—an immense figure at the time. Several of the castles are extant; see also C. H. Pearson, *History of England During the Early and Middle Ages* (London: Bell & Daldy, 1867); Liddell Hart, op. cit.

into the prince's land, and having occupied it by strong attacks, he entered through it in triumph."[22]

The king built his first forward base at Flint, the timber being brought around by sea. Here he also received considerable troop reinforcements, so that by the end of August he counted over fifteen thousand infantry, a force that included some nine thousand Welsh allies. He used Welsh labor for road and base construction, and, from extant documents, we know that he paid and fed them well.

Pushing on to Rhuddlan by a newly cut road, he again received supply from his fleet. He now marched to Conway and captured the island of Anglesey, described by Giraldus as "the granary of Wales," in time for the harvest.

Edward's carefully conducted campaign had thrown Llewellyn off balance. Deprived of support from tribes which had submitted to the king, short of food with winter approaching, and unable to attract the invaders to the interior, where he wanted to fight, Llewellyn now accepted the inevitable and sued for peace. The treaty of Conway extended English rule and administration deep into Wales. Edward had won a magnificent campaign with a minimum expenditure of life, but to maintain his sovereignty he was forced to build a series of expensive castles and to meet heavy administrative costs.

Peace lasted less than five years. Although King Edward apparently did not intend to absorb Wales into England, he and his lieutenants left no doubts of its subordination to his overlordship:

. . . in one respect Edward was ill-fitted to deal with an uncivilized people. He was over-strict for the times even in England. . . . But his officers were nowhere harsher than in Wales, where the people, unaccustomed to a minute legality, complained that they were worse treated than Saracens or Jews. Old offenses were raked up; wrecking [causing ships to wreck by false signals] was made punishable; the legal taxes were aggravated by customary payments; and distresses [seizure of goods] were levied on the first goods that came to hand, whether Llewellyn's own or his subjects'. . . . David [Llewellyn's brother] was alienated from the English cause by petty quarrels with Reginald Grey, justice of Chester, who insisted on making him answer before the English courts, hanged some of his vassals, and carried a military road through his woods.[23]

Judging the time ripe for rebellion, in early 1282 Llewellyn and David captured and burned a few fortresses ". . . and the Welsh spread over the marches, waging a war of singular ferocity, slaying, and even burning, young and old women and sick people in the villages."[24] But

22. Ibid.
23. Pearson, op. cit.; see also J. D. G. Davies and F. R. Worts, *England in the Middle Ages—Its Problems and Legacies* (London: Alfred A. Knopf, 1928).
24. Ibid.

most strong points held out while Edward, who was unprepared for the rebellion, hastily mobilized an army by summoning troops from all over England and even Gascony. By June, he had collected around seven thousand infantry. Divided into two armies, supported by cavalry and supplied by a small fleet, this expedition marched on Anglesey, which Edward considered "the noblest feather in Llewellyn's wing," and which the navy also attacked.

While the fleet carried out a blockade and soldiers cut down sanctuary forests in the border country, skirmishing continued into early winter, when Llewellyn agreed to negotiate and ". . . presented his list of grievances as justifying the war."[25] Edward refused to discuss them, declaring that Llewellyn's action ". . . was inexcusable, because he had revolted first without appealing to the crown, being himself always ready to hear and investigate."[26]

During a battle in the rugged interior a month after this exchange, Llewellyn, possibly lured by treachery to a meeting of local chieftains, was caught without his armor and run through. Edward sent his head to London, where, garlanded with silver ivy leaves and mounted on a lance, it was carried through the streets and exhibited on the Tower.[27] The campaign continued until David and other chiefs surrendered, in late April.

To judge David, Edward summoned a parliament ". . . of barons, judges, knights and burgesses":

. . . The sentence, which excited no horror at the time, was probably passed without a dissentient voice. David was sentenced, as a traitor, to be drawn slowly to the gallows; as a murderer, to be hanged; as one who had shed blood during Passiontide, to be disembowelled after death; and, for plotting the King's death, his dismembered limbs were to be sent to Winchester, York, Northampton, and Bristol. . . .[28]

This short war cost Edward some ninety-eight thousand pounds, an immense sum even though it included about twenty-three thousand pounds for repair of castles.[29] Supplementing an already large income with taxes on his subjects and with loans from Italian bankers, he had continually to borrow more money to fight further guerrilla wars before he controlled the area.

In pacifying Wales, Edward displayed considerable talent and organizational ability. But geography also helped, for, by occupying certain strategic points, he cut rebel forces from adequate food supply and outside help. Rebel dissidence also aided the royal cause.

25. Morris, op. cit.
26. Ibid.
27. Hoyt, op. cit.; see also Pearson, op. cit.
28. Pearson, op. cit.
29. Morris, op. cit. Amazingly complete records including military and civil payrolls are extant.

Edward encountered a different set of operational factors in his later pacification of Scotland, where rebel forces enjoyed generous space for temporary sanctuary.

The trouble started in 1295. John Balliol, whom Edward had helped to the throne, had incurred baronial ire by paying homage to Edward's

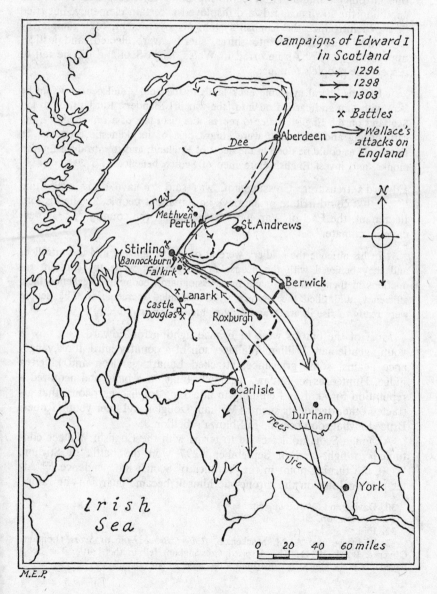

M.E.P.

overlordship. Under baronial pressure, he renounced allegiance to England and formed an alliance with France. The following year, Edward invaded the lowlands and captured Berwick, where his army indulged in a general slaughter of Scots, men and women, an estimated eight thousand to sixty thousand lives, who fell "like the leaves in autumn," as one chronicler put it. After capturing other fortresses and towns and subduing the lowlands, Edward displayed a certain clemency, but tried ". . . to introduce the English system of government, for example the Lowlands were divided into shires, sheriffs were elected, and justices appointed. . . ."[30] As he erred in Wales, so in Scotland did he fail to respect the people's temper:

. . . He was liberal in giving back lands to the nobles and gentry whom he kept with him and carried off into [the war in] Flanders. But he tried to tax Scotland on the English scale; to repress the disorders of a rude country, the cattle-lifting and feuds that were almost part of its domestic economy, as rigorously as could be done in the heart of England; and to introduce English monks, and invest English clergymen of Scotch benefices. . . .[31]

Edward's treasurer, Cressingham, was said to have done everything ". . . that could irritate or aggrieve an impatient people," while his lord lieutenant, the Earl of Warrene, resided out of the country ". . . to escape its climate."

. . . In his absence the soldiery were at once unemployed and uncontrolled, and they behaved with the license of conquerors; while the constant reductions in their number, made by Cressingham's economy, weakened their efficiency, and filled the country with disbanded mercenaries. The people were ready to rise in arms, and only wanted a leader. . . .[32]

Most of the barons were in France fighting for Edward. But now a young gentleman, William Wallace, son of a country laird, took vengeance against some grievance, attacked Lanark garrison and killed a judge. Hunted as an outlaw, he slowly built up a band and acquired a reputation for skill and cunning in attacking English garrisons, that attracted other dissidents such as William Douglas and later young Robert Bruce to what soon became full-blown rebellion.

Although Scots nobles came to terms with the English, Wallace continued to fight and in September 1297 won the battle of Stirling, ". . . the turning-point in the fortunes of Scotch independence."[33] After putting John on the throne—he himself became guardian—he raided

30. Davies and Worts, op. cit.
31. Pearson, op. cit.
32. Ibid.
33. Ibid.; see also A. M. Mackenzie, *Robert Bruce King of Scots* (London: Oliver & Boyd, 1934): The despised Cressingham fell in this battle. The Scots flayed his body and ". . . distributed the hide as souvenirs."

deep into northern English counties and when pursued scorched the earth in order to defeat the king's hungry soldiers.

Little is known of either Wallace or his tactics—A. M. Mackenzie rightly calls him "a cloudy figure." He apparently fought a rigorous guerrilla war; he was later indicted for murders, robberies, and sacrilege in churches. His methods undoubtedly stemmed in part from English severity, and he seems to have won and retained a considerable popular following in these precarious years when he was attempting to move a nation. His over-all strategy backfired in 1298, when Edward cornered and badly beat his army at Falkirk. Relying primarily on the missile (the long bow) as opposed to cavalry charges, the English were said to have taken ten thousand Scots lives.[34] However, as a later historian pointed out: ". . . Edward's victory was decisive, but it was almost profitless. The Scotch left him nothing but the possession of so much desolated land as his army could camp upon."[35]

Wallace escaped to the continent, where he attempted without success to enlist aid from France and from the pope. His best weapon remained the Scots people, especially the lowlanders, who for several years suffered the ravages of the English while still fighting back. The uneven war continued until 1303, when Edward, strengthened at home and at peace with France, led an invasion in such strength as to cause Scots nobles to lose heart and come to terms. William Wallace also petitioned for the king's amnesty—without success. Edward sent him to London, where ". . . he was taken through the streets in a mock procession . . . with a crown of laurel on his head, and tried by a special commission, consisting of three judges." The temper of the day probably explains the severity of sentence:

. . . To Edward and his people—as even to Philip of France, and perhaps to some Scotchmen of the day—Wallace was no better than a brigand, leading an armed rabble against their natural lords, and subverting the foundations of a political order more valuable to every statesman than a mere principle of nationality.[36]

William Wallace was dragged through London streets to the gallows and hanged—but was cut down while still alive and disemboweled.

Robert Bruce, son of a gentleman who had fought on the king's side at Falkirk: as King Robert of Scotland, thirty-two years old, he picked up the standard of revolt and for nearly a quarter of a century waged intermittent warfare against the English. His army was never strong: he never once mustered a thousand cavalry. In the early battle of Methven, he ordered his men to cover themselves with linen smocks to conceal

34. Mackenzie, op. cit., offers an excellent analysis of Edward's tactics.
35. Pearson, op. cit.
36. Ibid.

a lack of defensive armor; Pembroke countered this ruse by agreeing to fight on Monday, then marching on Sunday evening to catch Bruce by surprise and destroy his army.

Bruce escaped with a few followers, and it is doubtful that he would have survived except for space and spirit. Although fear caused many Scots to withhold support of the rebels, the dying Edward's harsh policy turned others to Bruce. Edward's temper toward the end is best expressed by his reply to pleas for the life of a captured Scot baron. "His only privilege," Edward said, "shall be, to be hanged on a higher gallows than the rest, as his treasons have been more flagrant and numerous."[37] He ordered Lady Buchan placed in a cage and exhibited on the ramparts of Berwick castle. He dispatched the Earl of Pembroke to Scotland as governor with

. . . orders that all those taken in arms, and all who sheltered them, were to be hanged or beheaded, while those concerned at all in the death of Comyn [who betrayed Bruce to the king and was murdered], and those who gave them countenance or support, were to suffer his full invention in the way of disembowelling and castration.

Bruce also utilized the space of the highlands:

. . . He was in his own countryside, that he knew well, and he possibly knew that from the people of it he could count on neutrality at any rate. They would not follow him, but they would not betray. What he did was to disappear into the landscape.[38]

He disappeared to survive and then fight back. One of his lieutenants, Douglas, successfully raided Douglas castle, an ingenious and daring effort whispered about the land. Bruce gained recruits. Escaping capture or destruction a dozen times, he fought small engagements and his strength continued to grow. Edward died and John of Brittany replaced Pembroke. By the end of 1308, Bruce controlled most of Scotland north of the Tay. A year later he held his first parliament, at St. Andrews; he also gained rapprochement with Philip of France, a diplomatic move that caused Pope Clement once again to excommunicate him for ". . . damnable perseverance in iniquity."[39]

For five years, Bruce continued retreating before superior English forces while his army sporadically raided northern English counties, which on occasion bought off the invaders for hefty sums. Guerrilla attacks on English-held castles reduced them one by one. In time, Bruce grew strong enough to meet the enemy in pitched battle at Bannockburn, which he won.[40]

37. Ibid.
38. Mackenzie, op. cit.
39. Ibid.
40. Ibid.

Although the Hundred Years' War holds certain orthodox tactical interest,[41] we are mainly concerned with the figure of Bertrand du Guesclin, a guerrilla leader who eventually became High Constable of France.

Du Guesclin was a Breton, a small man with flashing green eyes over a flat nose, ". . . uncouth, querulous, almost illiterate, without fortune. . . ."[42] But with force, with imagination and with a fine disregard for the artificial niceties of knightly warfare.

At eighteen, he headed a small band of fellow Bretons in a war of ambush against the English who occupied Brittany. At thirty, he achieved sudden fame by disguising his small band as woodcutters and capturing the castle of Fougeray.[43]

Appointed to the king's service for this feat, Du Guesclin next opened a guerrilla campaign against an English army besieging the fortress of Rennes. By a series of hit-and-run raids, he slowly drew the bulk of English forces away from the starving fortress, then captured an English food convoy, which he delivered, along with troop reinforcements, to the hard-pressed defenders. Continuing to lead guerrilla campaigns, he became increasingly famous for his rapid movements, night and day, and for the detailed preparation and suddenness of his attacks against enemy flanks and rear.

During a temporary lull in the war, Charles V gave the fiery Breton the task of freeing the French countryside from the barbaric pillaging of the "Grand Companies"—groups of mercenaries formerly in English and French pay and now little better than outlaw groups, whose leaders bore such picturesque names as "Smashing Bars" and "Arm of Iron." These *routiers* had ". . . pillaged and plundered the realm to such an extent," says a chronicler, "that not even a cock was heard to crow in it."[44] Du Guesclin bribed the bulk of these to follow him to Spain. In

41. Fuller, op. cit.; A. H. Burne, *The Crecy War* (London: Eyre & Spottiswoode, 1955); A. H. Burne, *The Agincourt War* (London: Eyre & Spottiswoode, 1956).

42. Éditions G. P., *La merveilleuse histoire de l'armée française.* Paris, 1947; see also Siméon Luce, *Histoire de Bertrand du Guesclin et de son époque* (Paris: Librairie Hachette, 1867).

43. Ibid. From a hidden position, Du Guesclin and his men allegedly had watched most of the English garrison leave the castle. Du Guesclin had observed that no wood had been delivered in some days, so, with bundles of fagots covering their weapons, his party approached the walled château and persuaded the skeleton garrison to lower the drawbridge. Du Guesclin and his men threw their loads on the bridge to prevent its being raised, then rushed to the attack and took the castle, which they held for a year. One of my less imaginative critical readers has pointed out that either the fagots must have been *very* heavy or the defenders *very* weak. I agree.

44. Paul Lacroix, *Military and Religious Life in the Middle Ages and the Renaissance* (New York: Frederick Ungar, 1874).

the battle of Navarrete, against the Black Prince, most of them were killed and Du Guesclin was captured, but later ransomed.

When fighting with England started again, Charles V made Du Guesclin the High Constable, or commander-in-chief, of France. Du Guesclin used Fabian tactics to push the English from the country. With the regular army defending towns and castles in strength too great for English armies to overcome, Du Guesclin used *routiers* to wage almost purely guerrilla warfare: ". . . a war of harassment, surprises, ambushes, sudden assaults, and slow siege."[45] In Basil Liddell Hart's words, ". . . within less than five years he had reduced the vast English possessions in France to a slender strip of territory between Bordeaux and Bayonne. He had done it without fighting a battle."[46]

The diversified combats of the Middle Ages provide but scant defense for the traditional chivalric concept of knightly warfare. Not only was the dragon of rapacious warfare a favorite of the knights, but the dragon of peasant uprisings was a phobia. Nobles ruthlessly suppressed the *Jacquerie,* or peasant uprising, of 1358 in France, that of 1381 in England under Wat Tyler, and the Fleming revolt at Roosebeke in 1382.

But knightly warfare was already in decline, the inevitable result of improved weapons and of the invention of gunpowder, not to mention dynastic feuds such as those in Bohemia, which brought a series of guerrilla campaigns beginning in 1389 and lasting for twenty years. The future Bohemian leader John Zizka served in one of these bands, where ". . . he learned to make the best possible use of the terrain in attack and defense. . . ."[47] Artillery already had played a considerable part in the wars of the Teutonic knights against Lithuanians and Russians—campaigns that featured many guerrilla aspects. Zizka learned the use of fire weapons in Poland, and in fighting the Hussite wars (1419–34)—occasioned by Church-inspired crusades of German and Hungarian knights against the Bohemians—became ". . . the first European commander to make full use of the artillery arm, or to see the value of a mobile barricade of wagons as a factor contributing to the steadiness of a present army."[48]

In defending against the favorite knightly tactic—the cavalry charge—Zizka deployed armored wagons, each sheltering infantry armed with hand guns and crossbows, in a line called a *Wagenburg,* or wagon for-

45. E. Perroy, *The Hundred Years War* (London: Eyre & Spottiswoode, 1951). Tr. W. B. Wells.

46. Liddell Hart, op. cit.

47. Frederick G. Heymann, *John Zizka and the Hussite Revolution* (Princeton, N.J.: Princeton University Press, 1955).

48. H. A. L. Fisher, *Europe—Ancient and Medieval* (London: Eyre & Spottiswoode, 1938); see also Howard Kaminsky, *A History of the Hussite Revolution* (Berkeley, Calif.: University of California Press, 1967).

tress. Between vehicles, he deployed four-wheeled carts holding cannon and protected by infantry armed with pikes. Behind each wing, cavalry waited in readiness to deliver a counterstroke or lead a pursuit. This formation thoroughly baffled invading knights, who unsuccessfully challenged it in more than fifty battles.

A major significance lay in Zizka's utilization of peasants and townsmen in a co-ordinated combat role. As Frederick Heymann concluded: ". . . Thus the Taborite army, in the way Zizka formed it, acquired a degree of rational subdivision, tactical organization, and actual battle co-operation far beyond anything used before in medieval warfare."[49]

49. Heymann, op. cit.

Chapter 7

THE INTRODUCTION and successful application of gunpowder to warfare placed guerrilla operations into general eclipse both in Europe and abroad. A series of peculiar environments unfavorable either to guerrilla or quasi-guerrilla tactics resulted from a technological-tactical competition between emergent European dynastic states. These were sufficiently wealthy to wage almost incessant war in bids for religious-dynastic supremacy at home and imperial supremacy abroad. Although often prolonged and sometimes fought with a ferocity defying even contemporary imagination, these wars were "limited" in the sense of their being fought for specific political objectives usually by professional armies—a state of affairs that in the West was not going to change until the end of the eighteenth century.

In the West, the entire *direction* of war was changing. By the end of the fifteenth century, it was becoming a serious profession, a matter of state interest. One of the first persons to respect this trend was Machiavelli (1469–1527), who, in 1499, witnessed the French invasion of the Italian city-states. In his subsequent, often profound and generally disturbing works, he advised that ". . . the foundation of states is a good military organization"; accordingly, ". . . a Prince should therefore have no other aim or thought, nor take up any other thing for study, but war and its organization and discipline"[1] (which is precisely what Sun Tzu counseled circa 250 B.C.).

His words gained reinforcement by almost constant weapon development. The appearance of the arquebus, whose primitive and unreliable matchlock ignition was eventually replaced first by the wheel lock, then the flintlock, systems, the reluctance of some commanders to employ the new weapons without diluting the ranks of pikemen, the discovery of better casting methods for artillery made more mobile and accurate by the development of the limber and trunnion, the invention of the wheel-lock pistol, the evolution of castles into fortifications capable of withstanding prolonged artillery sieges—each made war more expensive, each moved it increasingly into the hands of the state, which relied more and more on professional armies commanded by great captains who changed tactical values of war without altering its ferocity.

Technology ruled the battlefield. The escalation of violence that it wrought was halted not by choice of rulers and commanders but only because the ghastly wars of religion, the plague, and the excesses of the Thirty Years' War, by ravaging large areas of Europe and sharply limiting the supply of manpower, exercised a moderating influence on the battlefield. With soldiers in short supply, difficult to recruit and expensive to train, commanders became increasingly reluctant to expend them in battle. The French general Turenne (1611–75), who, along with Condé, bridged the interim years between the end of the Thirty Years' War and the reign of Louis XIV (1643–1715), ". . . regarded battle as a last resort, to be accepted with caution and then only when conditions seemed favorable."[2]

This made increasingly good sense in the light of tactical changes. Vauban's socket bayonet fitted to the flintlock musket (the *fusil*—thus, the fusilier) had forever eliminated the pikeman and had caused the old infantry formation in depth (*en profondeur*) to yield to an embryonic line formation. During the last half of the seventeenth century, General Jean Martinet (from whom we take our common noun martinet) trained his French troops to deploy from column into line and advance in three ranks, pausing to fire platoon volleys on command, and finally to attack with the bayonet. The "line" was a geometrical formation—it was a prelude to the famed "square" of lines, which provided

1. Felix Gilbert, "Machiavelli: The Renaissance of the Art of War." In E. E. Earle (ed.), *Makers of Modern Strategy* (Princeton, N.J.: Princeton University Press, 1941).

2. Preston, op. cit.

ideal defense against cavalry charges—and the troops were trained to advance in unison, keeping step at a stately cadence of eighty paces per minute. Naturally enemy artillery fire exacted a tremendous toll from these shoulder-to-shoulder ranks, as did volleys of musket fire delivered at no more than fifty paces (because of technological limitations).

Few commanders could afford the loss wrought by confrontation battles, which were not difficult to avoid. Since the new formations required open and level terrain, a commander not wishing to fight could retire to hilly, wooded country or to a defended strong point or city in order to spend the winter rebuilding forces for a fresh campaign. From this tactical prudence grew the sophisticated tactics of siegecraft and fortification, which further "slowed" battlefield action.

Nature, technology and economics combined to alter this situation, albeit slowly. Man's proclivity to procreation soon repaired former ravages. No less interested an observer than Frederick the Great pointed out that Emperor Ferdinand I had barely supported an army of 30,000, yet, in 1733, Charles VI effortlessly fielded 170,000; Louis XIII supported 60,000 soldiers, but, in the War of Succession, Louis XIV kept between 220,000 and 360,000 men in the field.[3] Technological improvements, for example the ring bayonet and the iron ramrod, started giving an edge to offensive warfare, while riches pouring in from overseas colonies provided rulers with the means to extend the battlefield.

As usual, great captains played a significant role. The efforts of Maurice of Nassau and Gustavus Adolphus to free formations from rigidness and restrictive weight were continued by Marlborough and Frederick the Great. Despite their efforts, war remained very restricted and sharply limited in political purpose, while possessing little tactical subtlety. Charles XII relied primarily on mobile-shock tactics pursued with a reckless charisma to defeat the Russians, Danes, Saxons and Poles in a series of battles, the Great Northern War, fought from 1700 to 1709; his impetuous nature and contempt for Peter the Great and the Russian army brought him defeat in detail at Poltava in 1709 and eliminated Sweden as a major power.

Marlborough's string of victories from 1704 to 1713 hinged on similar tactics, in which surprise played an important role, for example at Blenheim. By discarding care and caution common to the day, he gained complete strategic and tactical surprise, from which the French, fighting well, never recovered; at Oudenarde, he fought and won an "encounter" battle, a decidedly unorthodox practice at the time. Without question Marlborough's victories raised England to great-power status and forced France to sign the Treaty of Utrecht, but all this at a great cost in lives and treasure to gain a peace so fragile as to be chimerical.

3. Frédéric II, *Oeuvres* (*Histoire de mon temps*) (Berlin: Decker, 1846), Vol. 2 of 30 vols. Ed. J. D. E. Preuss.

Frederick the Great also displayed a tactical dualism. He maneuvered a lot, but he also fought a lot. In the *Instructions to His Generals,* he wrote: "In war the skin of a fox is at times as necessary as that of a lion, for cunning may succeed when force fails."[4] But he also advised: "War is decided only by battles and it is not decided except by them."[5]

Another great captain, Marshal de Saxe, echoed this dualism. He wrote in his principal work, *Mes Rêveries,* ". . . I am not in favor of giving battle. . . . I am even convinced that a general can wage war all his life without being compelled to do so." This oft-quoted passage scarcely complements the 1745 battle of Fontenoy, won by De Saxe, who prepared redoubts from which his infantry took the English and Dutch under murderous enfilade fire.

If warfare in this transition period was not particularly subtle, neither did it as a rule involve the general population. Yet, here and there, we find suggestions of what was to come. Tyrone's rebellion in Ireland, at the end of the sixteenth century, was in many ways a guerrilla war, with villagers and farmers frequently involved. When the Earl of Essex failed to stamp out the rebellion, Elizabeth turned to Charles Blount, who utilized tactics that would become all too familiar in the colonial period: he burned crops, razed villages and held hostages. He also introduced light and very mobile cavalry units that operated from fortified towns to scour surrounding areas—altogether a tactical adaptation that in time brought an Irish defeat (though not for long).

In the mid-seventeenth century, the Polish nobility faced a nasty invasion by Ukrainian Cossacks and Mohammedan Tartars whose unorthodox cavalry tactics at first had them on the run. Charles X of Sweden and Frederick William of Brandenburg-Prussia later had their hands full breaking through a ring of Cossack and Polish irregulars who were besieging Warsaw. Charles was finally forced to abandon Poland without having run various rebel bands to ground.

Early in the eighteenth century, prior to the battle of Blenheim, Marlborough defied contemporary custom by ravaging Bavaria, a psychological move intended to cause the Bavarian elector to desert his French alliance, and a practical move in that he denied the area's natural resources to the enemy.[6]

Frederick the Great was nearly captured by irregular mounted bands of Hungarians and Serbs in his first Silesian campaign, in 1741. So effective were these guerrillas that they screened the Austrian advance and almost cost Frederick a defeat. He was so impressed with their tac-

4. Frédéric II, *Oeuvres* (*Militaires*) (Berlin: Decker, 1866), Vol. 28 of 30 vols. Ed. J. D. E. Preuss.

5. Ibid.

6. W. S. Churchill, *Marlborough—His Life and Times* (London: G. C. Harrap, 1933), Vol. 2 of 4 vols. Churchill the historian expressed disapproval of this, Marlborough's "black" month.

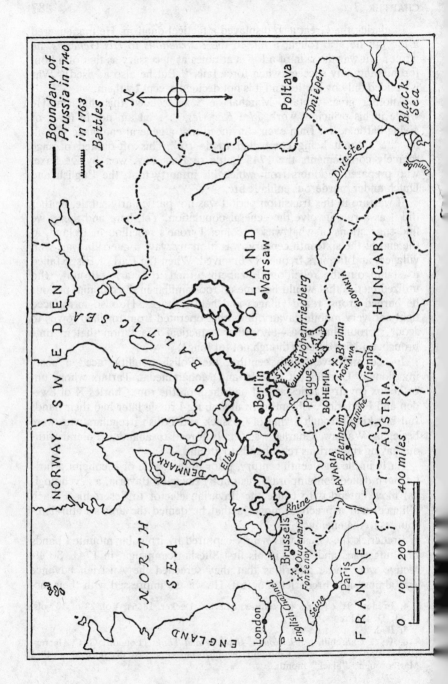

Boundary of Prussia in 1740

in 1763

x Battles

NORWAY

SWEDEN

DENMARK

NORTH SEA

BALTIC SEA

POLAND

Warsaw

Berlin

SILESIA

Hohenfriedberg x

Prague

BOHEMIA

Brünn

MORAVIA

SLOVAKIA

HUNGARY

Vienna

AUSTRIA

Blenheim x

BAVARIA

Danube

Poltava

Dnieper

Dniester

Danube

Black Sea

Elbe

Rhine

Brussels

Oudenarde x

Fontenoy

London

English Channel

Seine

Paris

FRANCE

ENGLAND

0   100   200   400 miles

tics that he organized special light-cavalry units to counter them. In early 1742, he again encountered Moravian irregulars and retaliated by devastating the land and besieging Brünn, neither action very effective. The Hungarians and Moravians provide early examples of guerrilla forces complementing orthodox army operations, in this case those of Austrian and French armies in Silesia, Bohemia and Bavaria.

Frederick encountered another ugly guerrilla situation in the second Silesian war. Leading his army south from Prague in 1744, he found himself in a barren, mountainous land whose peasants had buried their grain and hidden themselves and oxen in the forests. Some ten thousand Hungarian and Croatian hussars buzzed around his line of march, harassing foraging parties, striking columns in short, vicious attacks and cutting lines of communication until couriers failed to get through. Frederick's later, plaintive words describe a kind of warfare that in time would become only too familiar:

. . . It might appear strange that an army as strong as the Prussian army could not hold this area in awe; force it to necessary deliveries [of supply]; to provide food; and to furnish numerous spies to keep it informed of the enemy's least movement. But one should understand that in Bohemia the nobility, priests and bailiffs are very attached to the house of Austria; that the religious difference furnishes an overwhelming obstacle to those people who are as stupid as they are superstitious, and that the [Vienna] court had ordered the peasants, all of whom were serfs, to abandon their hamlets at the Prussian approach, to bury their corn and hide in the neighboring forests—the court further promised to pay for all damage suffered from Prussian arms.

This was a particularly ugly situation for an army that depended largely on local provisions. Frederick continued:

. . . The Prussian army thus found only deserted villages and wilderness: no one approached the camp to sell food; and the peasants, who feared rigorous Austrian retribution, could not be won over despite the sum offered. These difficulties were compounded by a corps of 10,000 hussars which the Austrians had sent from Hungary and which cut army communications in terrain composed only of marshes, woods, boulders, and every possible type of defile. Because of his superiority in light troops, the enemy had the advantage of knowing all that transpired in the king's camp [that is, because of intercepted communications]; nor did the Prussians dare send out scouting parties, at least without sacrificing them, due to the superior enemy parties: thus the king's army, entrenched in the Roman style, was confined to its camp.[7]

7. Frédéric II, op. cit.; see also Vols. 28 and 30 (*Oeuvres militaires*); see also Pierre Gaxotte, *Frederick the Great* (London: G. Bell & Sons, 1941).

The net result forced the king's retreat. So traumatic had been the experience, however, that during this hasty maneuver over seventeen thousand troops deserted. One important official, after describing general discontent, added, "Our mistakes have set more than half the land against us." The experience exercised lasting influence on the soldier-king. A few months later, he won the battle of Hohenfriedberg, but declined to pursue the retreating columns deep into Bohemia.[8] The Austrians continued to use irregulars—the term guerrilla had not yet come into use—with great skill in the Silesian and Seven Years' wars (in which General Laudon emerged as a brilliant guerrilla commander among others). Almost every action in every campaign of these wars had irregular aspects, usually important and in several cases probably decisive. French and Prussian attempts to counter irregular operations greatly varied in result, but, even when successful, involved heavy investments of men and time. *Freikorps,* or voluntary units of irregulars established by the French and Prussians, notably Colonel Mayer's Prussian units, played a considerable role in the Seven Years' War.

While Frederick was so engaged, Corsican guerrillas were contesting Genoese rule of the island. This was scarcely unique. The Corsicans had been resisting someone from the third century B.C.; in those rare periods when they lacked an enemy, they delighted in fighting each other. The most recent trouble started with a revolt against Genoese rule in 1729. When the Genoese introduced German mercenaries, Corsican volunteers began guerrilla warfare. In 1732, the Germans suffered a bad defeat at Calenzana, the guerrillas being aided by villagers who threw beehives into German ranks.[9]

In 1738, the Genoese persuaded France to intervene. The first battalions, under Count de Boissieux, suffered a series of setbacks, but, in 1739, the Marquis de Maillebois took over, broke guerrilla resistance with a series of flying-column operations, and offered the people a reasonably fair peace. The French departed in 1741 and the Corsicans again rebelled.

After several years of intermittent fighting, Corsican guerrillas were up against it. But, in 1755, the twenty-nine-year-old Pasquale Paoli emerged as a national leader. The ubiquitous James Boswell, who later visited General Paoli, wrote of his accession: ". . . There was no subordination, no discipline, no money, hardly any arms and ammunition; and, what was worse than all, little union among the people."[10] Largely by personal persuasion, the tall, young and forceful general eliminated

    8. Ibid.
    9. L. H. Caird, *The History of Corsica* (London: Unwin, 1899).
    10. James Boswell, *The Journal of a Tour to Corsica; and Memoirs of Pascal Paoli* (London: Williams & Norgate, 1951). Ed. with an Introduction by Morchard Bishop.

disruptive vendettas and brought the people to concerted action against the Genoese. Increased autonomy allowed Paoli to introduce reforms ". . . in agriculture, in education, in democratic government, in commerce and in public education."[11]

A legitimate republic might have emerged from Paoli's efforts, but, in 1764, the Genoese persuaded France to occupy the island for four years as payment of a debt, a cynical arrangement causing Rousseau to remark that if the French ". . . heard of a free man at the other end of the world, they would go thither for the pleasure of exterminating him."[12] Paoli's guerrillas forced the small French force into several garrison towns, where they seemed content to wait out their time. But, in 1768, the Genoese sold their interest in the island to France. The following year, in Napoleon's words, ". . . thirty thousand French vomited upon our coasts in drowning the throne of Liberty."[13] Although Paoli's guerrillas fought well, the odds could only have been redressed by foreign intervention. Boswell carried on a vigorous campaign to bring about English intervention and did raise a considerable sum of money to buy arms for Paoli. The English Government was not as impressed as the public with "Corsica Boswell," whose lobbying prompted Lord Holland to the remark, ". . . Foolish as we are, we cannot be so foolish as to go to war because Mr. Boswell has been in Corsica."[14]

The French victory at Ponte-Nuovo forced Paoli to flee and practically ended Corsican resistance. The 1769 campaign cost the French, according to the Annual Register, some four thousand killed, and six thousand dead from either wounds or sickness.[15] Figures are lacking for Corsican deaths, but they must have been high.

Paoli's achievement is the more interesting because he wasn't a very good general. But he did foresee the strength inherent in nationalism. When the French objected that the Corsican nation had no regular troops, he replied: ". . . We would not have them. We should then have the bravery of this and the other regiment. At present every single man is as a regiment himself. Should the Corsicans be formed into regular troops, we should lose that personal bravery which has produced such actions among us, as in another country would have rendered famous even a *Marischal*."[16] On another occasion, he said, ". . . all Corsicans should be soldiers and members of the militia with the heart to defend the motherland." He also persuaded priests to preach ". . . that a martyr's crown awaited a Corsican who died for his coun-

11. Moray McLaren, *Corsica Boswell* (London: Secker & Warburg, 1966).
12. Caird, op. cit.
13. McLaren, op. cit.
14. Boswell, op. cit.
15. Caird, op. cit.
16. Boswell, op. cit.

try."[17] Paoli was not too interested in the philosophy of revolution. He told Boswell, ". . . If a man would preserve the generous glow of patriotism, he must not reason too much. . . . I act from sentiment, not from reasonings."[18]

Nonetheless, he remained realistic. When discussing his war against the French, he told Boswell, ". . . Sir, if the event prove happy, we shall be called great defenders of liberty. If the event shall prove unhappy, we shall be called unfortunate rebels."[19]

A paucity of guerrilla warfare also existed in the early-colonial period, when Western explorers sailing east and west found a wide variety of ancient cultures, such as those encountered by Columbus in the Caribbean. Though most of the island tribes were armed with bows and arrows and palm-tree cudgels, some exhibiting a more bellicose attitude than others, the majority greeted the Spaniards in a friendly if cautious manner. The Europeans, in turn, treated them with a sort of genial contempt, not hesitating to impress them as guides or hostages for their interisland voyages, or even as slaves to take back to Spain.[20]

Some ugly incidents did occur, but whether in the New World or in Africa and later in Asia and the Pacific, the natives, though greater in number and well armed according to their standards, could not stand for long against trained soldiers protected by body armor and armed with muskets and cannon.

Against such disproportionate odds, the native chose from three courses of action: he came to terms with the white man and attempted to profit thereby, as was the case with many coastal and some inland chieftains; or he retreated into jungle depths, moving when danger threatened either from the white man or from native tribes armed with Western weapons and indulging in the profitable slave trade reinstituted into Africa by the Portuguese and extended to the New World by the Spanish, French, English, Dutch and later the Americans; or, as happened mainly in continental areas, he physically contested the occupation of what he deemed his land.

Leaving location and chronology aside, the process of conversion (theft, if you will) remained generally the same: discovery followed by a coastal settlement, protection (ships' guns, a fort, a small garrison), consolidation (winning the tribes), initial exploitation, further discovery by penetration inland, protection (a fort and a garrison), consolidation, further expansion and further exploitation by the Catholic Church and/or the throne, later by private but royally chartered commercial

17. Caird, op. cit.
18. Boswell, op. cit.
19. Ibid.
20. S. E. Morison and Mauricio Obregón, *The Caribbean as Columbus Saw It* (Boston: Little, Brown, 1964).

"companies"—the Virginia Company, the Dutch East India Company, the (British) East India Company—an inexorable process that gained the riches to support innumerable dynastic-religious wars in Europe while laying the groundwork for later, hemispheric wars.

The colonizing process differed in proportion to motives of the home country, strength devoted to the particular effort, and environment, both human and natural, of the target area. The first settlers in America arrived with a minimum of professional military support. In 1607, Jamestown settlers, heeding Captain John Smith's advice, formed ". . . immediately into three groups: one to erect fortifications for defense, one to serve as a guard and to plant a crop, the third to explore."[21]

In Virginia and New England, settlers encountered hostile Indians almost immediately, and for many decades had to rely for survival on ready militia forces. The effectiveness of these varied considerably. In general, the newcomers tried to assimilate the best features of Indian tactics, which stressed many of the features of guerrilla warfare: small-unit operations, loose formations, informal dress, swift movement, fire discipline, terror, ambush, and surprise attack. They were aided by concentration of numbers, and they also became adept at marksmanship, which grew more accurate as weapons improved.

As frontiers expanded to remove the immediate Indian challenge to rear areas, settled colonists began to adopt European methods of warfare. Professor Weigley has noted that by the time of King Philip's War (1675–76) colonial militia tactics had become too formal and European to fight successful Indian-style warfare. Unable to counter "murderous" ambushes, the colonists began relying on Indian mercenaries. Orthodoxy advanced to such an extent that, by the mid-eighteenth century, militia commanders, upon Colonel George Washington's advice, were studying Humphrey Bland's *Treatise on Military Discipline*, ". . . the leading English tactical manual of the day." In 1754, when the French and Indian War started, Washington wrote that ". . . Indians are the only match for Indians; and without these we shall ever fight upon unequal Terms."[22]

The arrival of regular British regiments under General Braddock to fight the French and Indians encouraged the colonial trend toward orthodoxy. These units, splendidly equipped and perfectly drilled in the formal, Continental school made famous by Frederick the Great, were impressive enough and with better leadership and considerable adaptation might have coped satisfactorily with the new tactical environment. Braddock, however, suffered defeat in detail when he encountered an irregular force of French colonials and Indians in the forests of the

21. R. F. Weigley, *History of the United States Army* (New York: Macmillan, 1967).

22. Ibid.: see also J. F. C. Fuller, *British Light Infantry in the Eighteenth Century* (London: Hutchinson, 1925).

Monongahela Valley. His force of fourteen hundred regulars and provincials was shredded by some nine hundred enemy using guerrilla tactics—he lost well over half his men and he himself died from wounds.[23]

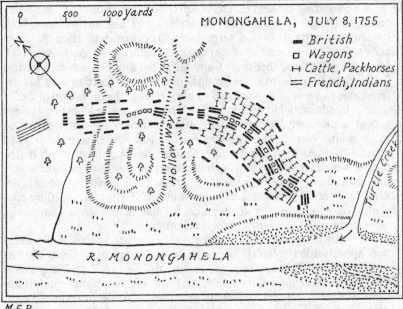

MONONGAHELA, JULY 8, 1755

■ British
□ Wagons
⊢ Cattle, Packhorses
≡ French, Indians

Hollow Way

Turtle Creek

R. MONONGAHELA

M.E.P.

The British reacted by slowing down operations and by making specific tactical changes. In 1755, a Swiss mercenary, Colonel Henri Bouquet, assumed command of a new light-infantry regiment and set about teaching it to fight Indians properly. Bouquet was altogether a remarkable man. A skilled veteran of European fighting, he quickly adapted to the American scene, and we are fortunate to have a lengthy work which, though describing his successful campaigns of 1763, offers an insight into his earlier thinking.[24] A paragraph in the introduction of this work bears quoting:

23. Ibid.: Weigley suggests that had Lieutenant Colonel Thomas Gage, commanding Braddock's vanguard, reacted correctly, ". . . the superior numbers and discipline of the British would probably have effected the rout of the enemy"; but see also Fuller, op. cit., who stresses Braddock's tactical ineptness. After citing British losses as 63 out of 86 officers and 914 of 1,373 men, he concludes: ". . . A French force of nine hundred irregulars, using Indian tactics, had beaten an English column fourteen hundred and fifty strong, using the tactics of Frederick the Great."

24. Anon., *An Historical Account of the Expedition Against the Ohio Indians in the Year MDCCLXIV Under the Command of Henry Bouquet, Esq.*, etc. (London: Reprinted for T. Jefferies, Geographer to His Majesty at Charing Cross, 1766).

. . . Those who have only experienced the severities and dangers of a campaign in Europe, can scarcely form an idea of what is to be done and endured in an American war. To act in a country cultivated and inhabited, where roads are made, magazines are established, and hospitals provided; where there are good towns to retreat to in case of misfortune; or, at the worst, a generous enemy to yield to, from whom no consolation, but the honour of victory, can be wanting; this may be considered as the exercise of a spirited and adventurous mind, rather than a rigid contest where all is at stake, and mutual destruction the object: and as a contention between rivals for glory, rather than a real struggle between sanguinary enemies. But in an American campaign every thing is terrible; the face of the country, the climate, the enemy. There is no refreshment for the healthy, nor relief for the sick. A vast unhospitable desart [sic], unsafe and treacherous, surrounds them, where victories are not decisive, but defeats are ruinous; and simple death is the least misfortune which can happen to them. This forms a service truly critical, in which all the firmness of the body and mind is put to the severest trial; and all the exertions of courage and address are called out. If the actions of these rude campaigns are of less dignity, the adventures in them are more interesting to the heart, and more amusing to the imagination, than the events of a regular war.

To this appreciation he added one of the enemy, for whom he held the greatest respect. In the new tactical environment, the Indian, not the white man, was the real professional:

. . . Let us suppose a person, who is entirely unacquainted with the nature of this service, to be put at the head of an expedition in America. We will further suppose that he has made the dispositions usual in Europe for a march, or to receive an enemy; and that he is then attacked by the savages. He cannot discover them, tho' from every tree, log or bush, he receives an incessant fire, and observes that few of their shot are lost. He will not hesitate to charge those invisible enemies, but he will charge in vain. For they are as cautious to avoid a close engagement, as indefatigable in harrassing [sic] his troops; and notwithstanding all his endeavours, he will still find himself surrounded by a circle of fire, which, like an artificial horizon, follows him every where.

Unable to rid himself of an enemy who never stands his attacks, and flies when pressed, only to return upon him again with equal agility and vigour; he will see the courage of his heavy troops droop, and their strength at last fail them by repeated and ineffectual efforts.

He must therefore think of a retreat, unless he can force his way thro' the enemy. But how is this to be effected? his baggage and provisions are unloaded and scattered, part of his horses and drivers killed, others dispersed by fear, and his wounded to be carried by soldiers already fainting under the fatigue of a long action. The enemy, encouraged by his distress, will not fail to encrease the disorder, by pressing upon him on every side, with redoubled fury and savage howlings.

He will probably form a circle or a square, to keep off so daring an enemy, ready at the least opening to fall upon him with the destructive tomahawk: but these dispositions, tho' a tolerable shift for defence, are neither proper for an attack, nor a march thro' the woods.

Bouquet was an educated man who could remind his readers that ". . . neither is there any thing new or extraordinary in this way of fighting, which seems to have been common to most Barbarians." He offered numerous examples not only from antiquity, but from his own century, pointing to light-infantry formations such as those raised by Marshal de Saxe and Frederick the Great. From his own extensive experience, he knew that as a "general maxim" the Indians ". . . surround their enemy. The second, that they fight scattered, and never in a compact body. The third, that they never stand their ground when attacked, but immediately give way, to return to the charge." It followed, then:

1st. That the troops destined to engage Indians, must be lightly cloathed, armed, and accoutred.
2d. That having no resistance to encounter in the attack or defence, they are not to be drawn up in close order, which would only expose them without necessity to a greater loss.
And, lastly, that all their evolutions must be performed with great rapidity; and the men enabled by exercise to pursue the enemy closely, when put to flight, and not give them time to rally.

He followed these general recommendations with specific advice in considerable detail on such items as clothing, arms, training, construction of camps and settlements, logistics, and various tactical formations —one is reminded of Caesar's work on Gaul. Under his tutelage, the company replaced the battalion as the unit of maneuver; troops learned to fire from kneeling and prone positions, and to march through woods in single file with scouts in front and on the flanks. Such alterations would not work miracles. It was not

. . . to be expected that this method will remove all obstacles, or that those light troops can equal the savages in patience, and activity; but, with discipline and practice, they may in a great measure supply the want of these advantages, and by keeping the enemy at a distance afford great relief and security to the main body.[25]

25. Ibid.; see also Fuller, op. cit.: ". . . First, by means of his advanced posts, he held the enemy at a distance; secondly, he collected his force together; thirdly, by four simultaneous charges, covered by fire, he broke the circle into four segments, that is, forced it to offer eight flanks to his attack; fourthly, he demoralized it by his fire, and, fifthly, pursued and annihilated it by means of his light troops, foot and horse.

"This formation against a savage foe is probably the most ingenious and effective that the history of irregular warfare has to record."

The British also used Indian scouts whenever possible and tried, unsuccessfully, to form an Indian regiment. Lord Howe, who arrived in 1757, retained a famous Indian fighter, Robert Rogers, to instruct him and his men in the fine art of guerrilla warfare. Rogers and other scouts later formed independent companies of frontiersmen who were to carry out scouting missions as well as use Indian tactics to protect lines of communication.[26] The British commander-in-chief in the colonies, Lord Loudoun, attached British officers to these units, and some of them later formed officer cadres for Gage's new regiment formed in 1758—the first light-infantry regiment in the British Army.[27]

Another British general, Brigadier James Wolfe, faced the tactical problems posed by Indians in the Quebec expedition from May to September 1759. His "General Orders" called for constant "care and precaution." But Wolfe introduced a Cromwellian note, not so much from prudery but from sound tactical instinct. He forbade swearing and scalping ". . . except when the enemy are Indians, or Canads [Canadians] dressed like Indians . . . no churches, houses, or buildings of any kind are to be burned or destroy'd without orders . . . the peasants who yet remain in their habitations, their women and children are to be treated with humanity; if any violence is offer'd to a woman, the offender shall be punish'd with death."[28]

Such temporary accommodations to a peculiar tactical environment did not immediately alter an ingrained rigid and inflexible nature of British regiments. Enthusiasm for light infantry did not claim many orthodox commanders, even though, by 1770, each battalion possessed a company of light infantry—but, too often, this unit served more a disciplinary than a tactical purpose, containing the most troublesome soldiers.[29]

American colonists, on the other hand, continued to be influenced militarily by terrain and temperament. Despite the best efforts of Washington and other militia commanders to instill formal British discipline, American formations remained fairly informal.

This was understandable. American settlers possessed a much more individual outlook than their European brethren, and they were better marksmen. The farmers and woodsmen who in 1775 voluntarily took up muskets and rifles to defy British rule were accustomed to hunting small game at a time when laws against poaching and possession of fire-

26. Weigley, op. cit.: Professor Weigley's discussion on deeds claimed versus deeds achieved by Rogers is most interesting.

27. Ibid.; see also Preston, op. cit.; Peter Paret, *Yorck and the Era of Prussian Reform* (Princeton, N.J.: Princeton University Press, 1966). In an introductory chapter, "The Frederician Age," Professor Paret argues convincingly against the generally accepted influence of the American wars on European armies and tactics; see also Fuller, op. cit.

28. Fuller (*The Decisive Battles of the Western World*), *supra*, Vol. 2.

29. Fuller (*British Light Infantry in the Eighteenth Century*), *supra*.

arms prevailed in Europe. The greenest American recruit aimed instinctively at a target, while his European opposite was trained only to point the piece at the enemy and fire volleys on command.

The potential of this type of warfare, particularly when fought by men infected with the emotional virus of revolution, was not wasted on the British commander-in-chief, General Gage. Contrary to most British officials and officers, who deemed the colonial soldier inferior to the British regular, Gage warned at outbreak of hostilities that he would need considerably larger forces and a year or two to subdue the New Englanders. Since other colonies would undoubtedly come to the aid of the North, ". . . he urged that the Ministry estimate the number of men and the sums of money needed, and then double their figures."[30]

Although early colonial militias and the 1st Continental Regiment (authorized by the Continental Congress in 1775) soon gave way to a regular army commanded by General George Washington, light-infantry tactics flourished throughout the revolution, which even in the North displayed guerrilla overtones.

One was the American soldier's use of terrain with which he was only too familiar. General Burgoyne, who himself would surrender to rebel wrath, early warned:

. . . It is not to be expected that the rebel Americans will risk a general combat or a pitched battle, or even stand at all, except behind intrenchments as at Boston. Accustomed to felling of timber and to grubbing up trees, they are very ready at earthworks and palisading, and will cover and intrench themselves wherever they are for a short time left unmolested with surprising alacrity. . . . Composed as the American army is, together with the strength of the country, full of woods, swamps, stone walls, and other inclosures and hiding-places, it may be said of it that every private man will in action be his own general, who will turn every tree and bush into a kind of temporary fortress, from whence, when he hath fired his shot with all the deliberation, coolness, and uncertainty which hidden safety inspires, he will skip as it were to the next, and so on for a long time till dislodged either by cannon or by a resolute attack of light infantry.[31]

Another tactic was the voluntary co-operation sometimes offered by the civil population to the revolutionary army: Burgoyne, in his Saratoga campaign of 1777, faced something akin to a scorched-earth policy as he marched from Montreal to the Hudson. By the time he reached Sara-

30. J. R. Alden, *The South in the Revolution, 1763–1789* (Baton Rouge, La.: Louisiana State University Press, 1957). Hereafter cited as Alden (*South*); see also Christopher Ward, *The War of the Revolution* (New York: Macmillan, 1952), ed. J. R. Alden, Vol. 2 of 2 vols.

31. E. M. Lloyd, *A Review of the History of Infantry* (London: Longmans, Green, 1908).

toga, the Continentals, together with New York and New England militias, had concentrated in strength sufficient to force his surrender.

Another was the individual's role, particularly the marksman armed with the long-barreled Pennsylvania rifle. The Prussian General von Steuben, who arrived at Valley Forge in 1778 to teach Washington's soldiers linear tactics, recognized the difference in individual outlook and marksmanship ability between the farmer-woodsman and the European peasant and dispensed with traditional precision deployment in order to exploit more accurate American firepower.

But, generally speaking, Washington's tactics remained orthodox, nor did he, in Professor Weigley's words, ". . . essay any tactical innovations so unconventional as to approach what later generations would call guerrilla war."[32] Guerrilla warfare, however, did come into its own in the South, where, as we shall see, Lord Cornwallis faced many problems of a modern insurgency.

32. Weigley, op. cit.

Chapter 8

Guerrilla warfare in the southern colonies • The background • Clinton's shift in strategy • Capture of Charleston • "Tarleton's Quarters" • Clinton's occupation policy • Conflict with Cornwallis • Cornwallis takes command • The political situation • Colonial guerrilla resistance • Horatio Gates and the Continentals • Cornwallis' victory at Camden • Guerrilla leaders: Marion, Sumter, Pickens • Cornwallis' punitive policy • His decision to invade North Carolina • British defeat at King's Mountain, and Cornwallis' retreat • Marion's guerrilla tactics • Nathanael Greene and Cornwallis' "country dance" • Battles of Cowpens and Guilford Courthouse • Cornwallis marches for Virginia • Greene's offensive: final guerrilla operations

GUERRILLA ACTIVITY in the South occurred as early as July 1775, in Georgia, where Joseph Habersham organized a local group of "Liberty Boys." In addition to conducting raids such as ". . . seizing six tons of powder from a [British] ship at Tybee Bar," this group ". . . frightened neutrals and friends of Britain into quiet" during that crucial period when the patriots were rallying their forces.[1]

Patriot leaders raised similar groups in other southern colonies—no simple task, since, in many areas, loyalists and neutrals outnumbered patriots. Counterrevolutionary forces had to be fended off while rebels, as in North Carolina, organized a ". . . Provincial Congress and Committee of Safety, raised troops, appointed officers, printed money, levied taxes and otherwise made ready for war."[2]

1. Alden (*South*), *supra*.
2. Ibid.

Some of these hastily organized bands contented themselves with chasing colonial governors and other officials aboard British warships and with burning loyalist homes and plantations and driving off the owners after subjecting them to an unpleasant application of tar and feathers.

Other groups fought semiorthodox actions. Colonel Alexander Lillington, Colonel James Moore and Richard Caswell in North Carolina

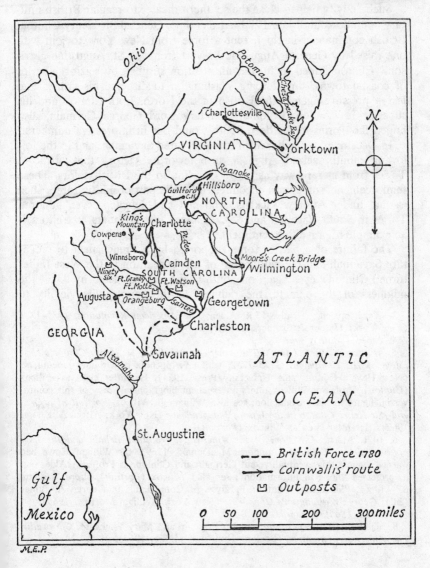

M.E.P.

met a Tory force at Moore's Creek Bridge to win a patriot victory that virtually ended local Tory resistance. Before the action, the patriots had removed bridge flooring and greased the supporting beams, thus completely confounding orthodox Tories.[3] Colonel Richardson, in South Carolina, raised a force of four thousand men which captured loyalist leaders and ". . . not only disarmed hundreds of loyalists but compelled many of them to pledge themselves to pacific behavior in the future."[4]

Such activity helped close the southern theater to regular British military operations until late 1778. At this time, General Sir Henry Clinton, British commander-in-chief, sent a force from New York to join with one raised by General Augustine Prevost from the St. Augustine garrison.[5] Clinton hoped to further an attrition strategy by seizing a series of coastal towns, thus forcing Washington to disperse his armies and lessen pressure against the British in the North. Both Clinton and his superior in London, Colonial Secretary Lord George Germain, also hoped the Tories in the deep South would rise in impressive numbers.[6]

In December, a small British force captured Savannah, and in the following month, seized Augusta, a noteworthy victory that attracted Tories from as far away as North Carolina to the British colors. These reinforcements sometimes encountered hostile patriot militia forces such as that under Andrew Pickens, who met and defeated seven hundred Tories in South Carolina and ". . . hanged five prisoners as traitors,"[7] an example of prevailing sentiment.

The failure of a patriot force supported by a French fleet to recapture Savannah and the withdrawal of this expedition to the West Indies turned Clinton's eyes again on South Carolina.[8] Attracted by ". . . the mildness of the climate, the richness of the country, its vicinity to

---

3. Ward, op. cit.; see also J. R. Alden, *The American Revolution, 1775–1783* (New York: Harper & Brothers, 1954).

4. Alden (*South*), *supra.*

5. William B. Willcox (ed.), *The American Rebellion—Sir Henry Clinton's Narrative of His Campaigns, 1775–1782*, with an Appendix of Original Documents (New Haven, Conn.: Yale University Press, 1954). Hereafter cited as Willcox (*Clinton*). Professor Willcox offers an excellent biographical study of this controversial figure in his Introduction; see also William B. Willcox, *Portrait of a General—Sir Henry Clinton in the War of Independence* (New York: Alfred A. Knopf, 1962). Hereafter cited as Willcox (*Portrait*).

6. J. R. Alden, *A History of the American Revolution—Britain and the Loss of the Thirteen Colonies* (London: MacDonald, 1969). Sir William Howe had warned against this eventuality, but Germain and Clinton, as Professor Alden put it, preferred "hope to information"; see also Willcox (*Portrait*), *supra;* William B. Willcox, "Sir Henry Clinton: Paralysis of Command." In George A. Billias (ed.), *George Washington's Opponents* (New York: William Morrow, 1969).

7. Alden (*South*), *supra.*

8. Willcox (*Clinton*), *supra;* see also Franklin and Mary Wickwire, *Cornwallis: The American Adventure* (Boston: Houghton Mifflin, 1969).

Georgia, and its distance from George Washington,"[9] he sailed south with a large expeditionary force in late 1779.

After considerable delays and difficulties, the British force landed, marched on Charleston and placed it under siege.[10] To isolate the city, in April 1780 Clinton ordered General Lord Charles Cornwallis and a force of nearly two thousand ". . . across Cooper River to intercept all communication between the garrison and the country, a service which he very effectively performed."[11] Clinton may have held an ulterior motive in so dispatching his second in command: the two generals by now were on the worst of terms, the result of Germain and King George having refused to let Clinton resign in favor of Cornwallis.[12] Acrimony aside, the operation was successful, and the commander of the Charleston garrison, Major General Lincoln, surrendered the city in May.

Clinton now sent two corps into the colony's interior, where, as he and Germain had hoped, loyalists came forth ". . . by the hundreds [to] take oaths of allegiance to the crown, and many took up arms in behalf of the King."[13] Cornwallis simultaneously led his corps against ". . . the only body of rebels remaining in arms in South Carolina." This belonged to Colonel Buford, the quarry of a cavalry task force consisting of two under-strength dragoon regiments, the Queen's Dragoons, commanded by a handsome but unscrupulous officer, Lieutenant Colonel Banastre Tarleton. In late May, Tarleton reported to Cornwallis ". . . a march of 105 miles in 54 hours, with the corps of cavalry, the infantry of the legion mounted on horses, and a three-pounder. . . ."[14] Close to the North Carolina border, Tarleton caught up with a detachment of Virginia infantry, who surrendered to him. The British troops conducted a wholesale slaughter, shooting or stabbing 113 of the defenseless men to death and leaving another 150 bleeding to death before marching off with 53 prisoners—a despicable act indignantly described by the great British historian George Trevelyan.[15] To Carolina back-

9. Banastre Tarleton, *A History of the Campaigns of 1780 and 1781, in the Southern Provinces of North America* (London: T. Cadell, 1787).

10. Willcox (*Clinton*), *supra;* the campaign is described in detail; see also Wickwire, op. cit.; Piers Mackesy, *The War for America 1775–1783* (London: Longmans, Green, 1964).

11. Charles, First Marquis Cornwallis, *Correspondence* (London: John Murray, 1859), ed. Charles Ross, Vol. 1 of 3 vols.; see also Wickwire, op. cit.

12. Willcox (*Clinton*), *supra,* the author's Introduction; see also Willcox (*Portrait*), *supra:* Cornwallis had asked for "a separate command away from the main army"; Wickwire, op. cit.: Clinton might have used the opportunity to rid himself of Cornwallis, who, he believed, was undermining his authority in the army.

13. Alden (*South*), *supra.*

14. Charles, op. cit.; see also Willcox (*Clinton*), *supra.*

15. George Trevelyan, *George the Third and Charles Fox* (London: Longmans, Green, 1914); see also Willcox (*Clinton*), *supra:* the general does not mention the incident; see also Fuller (*British Light Infantry in the Eighteenth Century*), *supra,* who registers neither surprise nor indignation.

woodsmen, the senseless act became known as "Tarleton's Quarters"—
a phrase we shall hear again.

Clinton's provost marshals meanwhile were rounding up diehard
rebels and evacuating them along with prisoners of war to coastal islands.
Sir Henry also showered the general population with proclamations and
manifestos ". . . calling upon all well-disposed persons to enrol themselves in the militia for a limited term of service, and announcing severe
punishment against those who should take up arms on the other
side. . . ."[16] Hoping to woo the population further, Clinton announced
a parole system for those persons who promised not to take up arms
against the British. He also promised royal protection to men who took
a special oath of allegiance to the Crown. Cornwallis objected to this
policy of "indiscriminate protection," by which ". . . some of the most
violent rebels and persecutors of the whole province are declared faithful subjects, and are promised to be protected in their persons and properties."[17]

Despite such "gracious offers," a proclamation of May 1780 singled
out ". . . some wicked and desperate men, who, regardless of the ruin
and misery in which the country will be involved, are still endeavoring
to support the flame of rebellion, and, under pretence of authority derived from the late usurped legislatures, are attempting, by enormous
fines, grievous imprisonments, and sanguinary punishments, to compel
His Majesty's faithful and unwilling subjects to take up arms against his
authority and government. . . ." These persons, Clinton promised,
would be severely punished.[18]

By June, organized rebel resistance appeared at an end in Georgia
and South Carolina. The British had established important garrisons
in the interior and along the border, and, with loyalists stirring in North
Carolina, the area seemed under British control. ". . . I am clear
in opinion," Clinton wrote to a friend, "that the Carolinas have been
conquered in Charleston."[19] At Cornwallis' request, Clinton turned
command over to him and sailed for New York.[20]

Clinton's instructions to Cornwallis have long been a subject of controversy. According to the Wickwires, ". . . the burden of . . .
[Clinton's] instructions was clear, if not the means of implementing
them. Cornwallis should pacify South and North Carolina, maintain order in Georgia and the Floridas, and then move north to take Virginia.
Yet Clinton scarcely left his subordinate sufficient troops for such a large
purpose." Under optimum conditions, the Wickwires have pointed out,
Cornwallis needed three thousand men to pacify North Carolina; if

16. Charles, op. cit.; see also Willcox (*Clinton*), *supra*.
17. Charles, op. cit.
18. Tarleton, op. cit.; see also Willcox (*Clinton*), *supra*.
19. Wickwire, op. cit.
20. Ibid.: the authors give details of the command authority.

he ran into no trouble there, he would have to leave two thousand men to garrison the colony, which would give him only a thousand troops to pacify Virginia, ". . . one of the most actively rebellious provinces in North America."[21] Further, Clinton took with him most of the wagons and horses. Cornwallis lacked men, food, horses, wagons, and money. Supplying his interior garrisons alone constituted a major problem.

This does not necessarily make Clinton wrong and Cornwallis right. According to Professor Willcox, Sir Henry instructed Cornwallis ". . . to make the safety of Charleston and the rest of South Carolina his principal objectives, which were not to be endangered by any premature move into North Carolina." Although Clinton favored a lodgment in the Chesapeake Bay area, this perforce lay in the future. Clinton had a lot of shortcomings, but he was no fool. He foresaw Cornwallis working slowly up the Carolina coast in conjunction with the British fleet, developing loyalist bases, then moving inland, building as he went—a methodical but progressive pacification campaign to attract loyalists and consolidate politically and militarily a new theater of war. Once militia forces existed (and the naval situation had clarified), the regular army could continue operations to the north.[22] Lacking sufficient means for the task at hand, Cornwallis would have to generate new means. Clinton and Cornwallis were sufficiently experienced commanders to know that a major command task is to determine operational priorities—that is, equate means to mission. In this case, insufficiency of means dictated Cornwallis' moving carefully. On the other hand, Clinton's orders were often ambiguous, and such were relations between the two as to hinder even normal understanding.

The truth is, I believe, that both commanders erred. Clinton was at fault in opening a new theater of operations with insufficient means and with lines of communication sorely threatened by the French navy. As Professor Willcox has pointed out, in time ". . . division of force . . . led to a division of command." Moreover, the actual situation in the southern theater belied Clinton's expressed optimism, but none of that excuses Cornwallis' subsequent actions. The Charleston base was not politically secure. As Professor Alden has pointed out, ". . . Many patriots, offered a choice between serving under the British flag on the one hand and spoliation, imprisonment, and probably death through hardship and disease on the other, enlisted in the royal forces [and fought for the British in the West Indies, but not against their own people]."[23] Most inhabitants tried to save their lives and property by appeasing the momentary victor—most people answered the dilemma of civil war by

21. Ibid.

22. Willcox (*Portrait*), *supra.*

23. Alden (*South*), *supra;* see also Wickwire, op. cit.: Cornwallis imprisoned over 1,500 American soldiers in ships, where they lived miserably, perhaps 800 of them dying in 13 months.

accommodation in whole or in part. Many of those who swore allegiance to the British or who gave their parole did so under what they rightly regarded as duress, and they were not squeamish in later helping the rebels and even bearing arms against the British.

The political situation, in short, was ticklish, a fact that Clinton perhaps had recognized in wearing a velvet glove. His successor, Cornwallis, continued this policy, at least to a degree. Although confiscating estates of absentee rebels, he returned stolen and confiscated property to royalists and he continued to carry out Clinton's generous parole system. His dashing cavalry commander, Banastre Tarleton, later complained that this ". . . conduct opened a door to some designing and insidious Americans, who secretly undermined, and totally destroyed, the British interest in South Carolina." As for holding the occupying army in check, Tarleton observed that ". . . this moderation produced not the intended effect: It did not reconcile the enemies, but it discouraged the friends. . . ." Tarleton concluded that ". . . the future scene will discover, that lenity and generosity did not experience in America the merited returns of gratitude and affection."[24]

Cornwallis' attitude began to change in June, when submissive Americans in the Charleston area learned that substantial American reinforcements were on their way from the North and began to jump their paroles. One "good citizen," by name Lisle, the second in command of a militia battalion, waited until his men were supplied with arms and ammunition, then hustled them off to join patriot forces in the interior.

Try to imagine his lordship upon receipt of this information. At forty-two years, Cornwallis was chubby and rubicund. Undeniably ambitious —he had left a dying wife to return to this war for a third tour of duty— he was also capable: Professor Weigley regards him as ". . . probably the best British general in America."[25] Cornwallis, at the very least, would have agreed that he was a better general than Clinton. For months, he had been hoping that King George would appoint him commander-in-chief in North America. But the king, to whom Cornwallis reported via Lord George Germain, had held off. Cornwallis deeply resented the rebuff, which he explained in his own mind as the result of Clinton's intrigues against him. He still hoped to replace Clinton. But Clinton was a powerful man, or powerful enough not to be relieved by Cornwallis without sufficient reason. A successful blow by Cornwallis might just provide that reason. One thing certain: he could not afford to fail in his present mission.

And now, sitting at desk, scarlet tunic faint with powder from his wig, bleak eyes flashing over imperious nose, its volutes flared in anger, porcine hand impatiently rubbing long gray sideburns, he dictated a letter

24. Tarleton, op. cit.
25. Weigley, op. cit.; see also Hugh F. Rankin, "Charles Lord Cornwallis: Study in Frustration." In Billias, op. cit.; Mackesy, op. cit.

to Vice-Admiral Arbuthnot explaining his change in attitude: ". . . Nothing can in my opinion be so prejudicial to the affairs of Great Britain as a want of discrimination. You will certainly lose your friends by it, and as certainly not gain over your enemies. There is but one way of inducing the violent rebels to become our friends, and that is by convincing them it is in their best interest to be so."[26]

Off came the velvet glove.

But neither did the naked fist provide an answer. Rebel forces continued to plague the British. In addition to spreading malicious propaganda, the rebels ". . . also employed mild pressure, persecution, terrorization, and killing—not necessarily in that order. Often they terrorized and killed first." A British newcomer to the Carolinas, Brigadier General Charles O'Hara, shortly complained: ". . . The violence and the passions of these people are beyond every curb of religion, and Humanity, they are unbounded and every hour exhibits dreadful wanton mischiefs, murders, and violence of every kind, unheard of before. We find the country in great measure abandoned, and the few who venture to remain at home in hourly expectation of being murdered, or stripped of all their property."[27]

By mid-July, Cornwallis was complaining to Clinton of Sumter's new militia army of fifteen hundred men, as well as of ". . . the want of subordination and confidence of our militia in themselves."[28] General Washington now added to the British burden by sending down a force of Continentals under General Horatio Gates, hero of Saratoga, and, against Washington's wishes, newly appointed by Congress commander-in-chief of the South.

Gates was a good patriot, a poor general. A former British officer turned Virginia squire, he was fifty-two years old, an unhappy-looking man. He commanded a mixed bag: De Kalb's Continentals (Maryland line and Delaware regiment), a handful of horse, some Virginia militia, and Sumter's Carolina militia. De Kalb's troops were already tired, hungry, and sick when Gates caught up to them at Hillsboro in late July.[29]

Gates's appearance in the Carolinas exercised a psychological effect that greatly exceeded his combat potential. Tarleton later wrote that ". . . his name and former good fortune re-animated the exertions of the country: Provisions were more amply supplied by the inhabitants, and the continental troops soon reached the frontier of South Caro-

26. Charles, op. cit.
27. Wickwire, op. cit.
28. Alden (*South*), *supra*.
29. Ward, op. cit.; see also Wickwire, op. cit.: De Kalb had made heavy weather of the march: ". . . lack of food, limited transportation, long stretches of barren and unsettled country, the pestilential voraciousness of insects, violence of thunderstorms, the indifference of the inhabitants to the Revolutionary cause, all these things were strange to De Kalb."

lina."[30] In August, Cornwallis wrote Clinton that ". . . the whole country" between the Pedee and the Santee was ". . . in an absolute state of rebellion, every friend of government has been carried off, and his plantation destroyed."[31]

Gates wisely attempted to exploit the revolutionary air. On the banks of the river Pedee, he issued a proclamation similar in intent to that released by Clinton a few months earlier in Charleston. Gates offered immediate amnesty to all those who had accepted British paroles, on grounds that they had acted under duress. But he excepted those persons who ". . . in the hour of devastation have exercised acts of barbarity and depredation on the persons and property of their fellow citizens," and he warned against further disaffection, now that he was promising them security. Gates's temper is suggested by his remarking on this occasion that the British would long since have been driven from the continent ". . . but for the disaffection of many of the apostate sons of America."[32]

Having so pontificated, Gates continued his march south through barren country, which further wore down his force. At this time, a strange assemblage suddenly appeared in his camp. Its leader was another militia officer, Colonel Francis Marion, soon to become famous as the "Swamp Fox." Marion was a small, wiry, and handsome South Carolinian farmer of no great formal education. In 1759, he had enlisted and fought the Cherokees for two years. At the outbreak of revolution, he was commissioned a cavalry captain in the Second South Carolina Regiment. Trevelyan tells us, obviously with relish, the following: Marion was in Charleston when Clinton's expeditionary force landed. At a dinner party, his host refused to unlock the door until his guests had drunk the Madeira, an announcement that caused teetotaler Marion to exit by way of window. In so doing, he sprained his ankle and was taken to his farm. A few days later, Clinton placed Charleston under siege, but Marion had escaped.[33]

In the back country, Marion organized a ragtag force of locals whom he equipped with sabers ". . . fabricated by rural blacksmiths out of the circular saws of the timber-mills." To feed their pistols, they melted down pewter mugs and spoons. They rode what horses they could find or steal, and their over-all appearance left considerable to be desired. One Colonel Otho Williams was present when Marion and his band reported to Gates. ". . . Their numbers did not exceed twenty men and

30. Charles, op. cit.; see also Mackesy, op. cit.
31. Wickwire, op. cit.
32. Tarleton, op. cit.; he published the entire proclamation.
33. Trevelyan, op. cit.; Bryant later treated his exploits in the poem *Song of Marion's Men*.

boys, some white, some black . . . distinguished by small leather caps, and the wretchedness of their attire."[34]

The Continentals took one look and laughed until fit to bust. Gates was not amused, nor was he impressed with Marion's theories of Indian warfare. Although the guerrillas obviously weren't "apostate sons of America," they obviously weren't soldiers either, and, to get rid of them, Gates sent them on some slight errand.

This was premature, for shortly Gates was going to need all available help. The psychological effect of his army on local inhabitants had both alarmed and infuriated Cornwallis. Having failed to establish a political base, the British commander decided that he must now eliminate the new threat from the North—indeed, as long as the North could support the rebel effort in the South, he could not succeed in pacifying the area. Cornwallis was a man of action—what was needed, he decided, was a battle, a "decisive" battle to prove to the locals which side their bread was buttered on.[35] Determined to fight Gates, Cornwallis had marched north and occupied Camden, while Gates was marching south. In mid-August the two forces stumbled into each other. Gates now attacked the British position near Camden.

Five days after Gates had dismissed Marion, the American army was dead, dying, wounded, prisoner or, like its commander, on the run. ". . . In less than an hour Earl Cornwallis had shattered the only American army in the south . . . the most crushing victory that British arms ever achieved over the Americans in the Revolutionary War."[36] Marion meanwhile seemed to have disappeared. In reality, he was lying low waiting for an opportunity to strike. It came in the form of some hundred and fifty American prisoners being escorted to Charleston. Marion and his guerrillas swooped on the long column, dispatched guards, and freed the captured soldiers, a daring act that made him famous throughout the South.

Other militia-cum-guerrilla leaders began active operations during the dangerous hiatus created by Gates's defeat. Conspicuous besides Marion were Thomas Sumter and Andrew Pickens. Veterans of earlier fighting, they were natural leaders, at home in the tactical environment. Sumter was forty-six, tall, vigorous, and bold, and known as the "Carolina Game Cock." Pickens was five years younger, lean and rugged, an elder of the Presbyterian Church who seldom smiled and never laughed.[37]

These men attracted some followers, but their real popularity stemmed from British pacification methods. In Professor Alden's words,

34. Ibid.; see also Robert D. Bass, *Swamp Fox—The Life and Campaigns of General Francis Marion* (London: Alvin Redman, 1959).
35. Wickwire, op. cit.: the authors offer details of his thinking.
36. Ibid.
37. Ward, op. cit.

". . . the plundering, ravaging, and abuse of civilians by Hessians [mercenaries fighting for the British] and loyalists, and the brutalities of Tarleton, who refused quarter to patriots in the field, drove them to desperation and to bitter resistance."[38] Andrew Pickens, a militia colonel, had accepted British protection and taken the oath of allegiance, but defected, as the Wickwires noted, ". . . taking some men with him, because he considered the destruction of his property by some tories a violation of the protection the British had promised him in return for his oath."[39]

After defeating Gates at Camden, Cornwallis left no doubt of his feelings in a letter to a subordinate commander: ". . . I have given orders that all the inhabitants of this province, who had submitted [that is, accepted British protection in return for a special oath of allegiance], and who have taken part in this revolt, should be punished with the greatest rigor, that they should be imprisoned, and their whole property taken from them or destroyed; I have likewise directed that compensation should be made out of their effects to the persons who have been *plundered* and oppressed by them. I have ordered in the most positive manner, that every militia man who had borne arms with us and had afterwards joined the enemy should be immediately hanged. I have now, Sir, only to desire that you will take the most *vigorous* measures to *extinguish the rebellion* in the district in which you command, and that you will obey in the strictest manner the directions I have given in this letter, relative to the treatment of this country. . . ."[40]

Cornwallis' failure to compute accurately the extent, real or potential, either of royalist sympathy or of rebel support next led him to a fateful decision: the invasion of North Carolina, which he regarded as a sanctuary that supported the insurrection in South Carolina and Georgia. As he informed Clinton, ". . . unless he immediately attacked North Carolina he must give up both South Carolina and Georgia and retire within the walls of Charleston."[41] By his own admission, his southern base was scarcely secure, nor was his military posture particularly prosperous, despite material captured at Camden. But his Camden victory had eliminated threat of imminent invasion by orthodox Con-

38. Alden (*South*), *supra*.

39. Wickwire, op. cit.

40. Charles, op. cit.; see also, Wickwire, op. cit., for a slightly altered version, then another version, much altered by patriots who circulated it, as proof of Cornwallis' brutality. The Wickwires argue that Cornwallis was never as severe as called for by circumstances, but rather that he lost control over ruthless subordinates. Perhaps so. That does not excuse his condoning subordinate behavior such as Tarleton's, which represented ruthlessness without political purpose. Tarleton and other British commanders were practicing quantitative terrorism. Contrarily, Marion and other back-country patriots were practicing selective terrorism with specific political goals.

41. Willcox (*Clinton*), *supra*.

tinental forces, and he also believed that Tories by the thousands would rise to greet and support him. Though displeased with the new plan, Clinton now decided to send an expedition to Chesapeake Bay in order to create a "powerful diversion" and strike at the supply depots which would support Continental units opposing Cornwallis.[42]

In early September, Cornwallis started north to Charlotte, his left screened by a force of loyalist militia under Major Patrick Ferguson.[43] Charlotte turned out to be a dreadful base: ". . . the town and environs abound with inveterate enemies . . . the vigilance and animosity of these surrounding districts checked the exertions of the well affected, and totally destroyed all communication between the King's troops and the loyalists in the other parts of the province. No British commander could obtain any information in that position, which would facilitate his designs, or guide his future conduct . . . accounts of the preparations of the militia could only be vague and uncertain; and all intelligence of the real force and movements of the continentals must be totally unattainable."[44]

The British were still digging in at Charlotte when a patriot militia force fell on Ferguson at King's Mountain. Ferguson was killed, and some three hundred of his force killed or wounded and the rest captured. The Americans hanged nine of the prisoners, partly in revenge for British atrocities—"Tarleton's Quarters" come home—and probably also as a warning to other turncoats. Tarleton later wrote that ". . . the mountaineers, it is reported, used every insult and indignity, after the action, towards the dead body of Major Ferguson, and exercised horrid cruelties on the prisoners that fell into their possession."

Ferguson's defeat increased Cornwallis' isolation, and he wisely decided to retreat, his confusion clear from Tarleton's later report that ". . . owing to the badness of the road, the ignorance of the guides, the darkness of the night, or some other unknown cause, the British rear guard destroyed, or left behind, near twenty waggons, loaded with supplies for the army, a printing press, and other stores belonging to public departments, and the knapsacks of the light infantry and legion."

The expedition moved slowly and ponderously over muddy roads and swollen streams. Cornwallis succumbed to fever. Incorrect information from locals constantly frustrated efforts to locate a suitable area for winter quarters—". . . in all descriptions of country, they are influenced by secret considerations, which direct them to consult their own interest and convenience."[45] The force finally ended in Winnsboro to

42. Ibid.; see also Willcox (*Portrait*), *supra*.
43. Wickwire, op. cit.: the authors offer an excellent biographical sketch of this unfortunate officer; see also Fuller (*British Light Infantry in the Eighteenth Century*), *supra*.
44. Tarleton, op. cit.
45. Ibid.

suffer an uneasy period. Marion had gained immensely by the American victory at King's Mountain. With Gates removed from the picture, the forty-seven-year-old guerrilla leader kept striking at Cornwallis' lines of communication, both to other outposts and to the rear, to keep him off balance until Washington could send reinforcements from the North. Cornwallis had disdained the coast and use of sea power, and henceforth he would pay.

Cornwallis' report to Clinton in early December 1780 suggests the extent of Marion's operations:

. . . Colonel Marion had so wrought on the minds of the people, partly by the terror of his threats and cruelty of his punishments, and partly by the promise of plunder, that there was scarcely an inhabitant between the Santee and Pedee [rivers], that was not in arms against us. Some [guerrilla] parties had even crossed the Santee, and carried terror to the gates of Charlestown. My first object was to reinstate matters in that quarter, without which Camden could receive no supplies. I therefore sent Tarleton, who pursued Marion for several days, obliged his corps to take to the swamps, and by convincing the inhabitants that there was a power superior to Marion, who could likewise reward and punish, so far checked the insurrection, that the greatest part of them have not dared to appear in arms against us since his expedition.[46]

Cornwallis elaborated his feelings on rebel terror tactics when Clinton asked him to explain the deportation of Charleston citizens to St. Augustine, an action objected to by General Washington. After recounting the subversive activities of these persons, Cornwallis wrote: ". . . I have only to say that the insolence of their behavior, the threats with which they in the most daring manner endeavored to intimidate our friends, the infamous falsehoods which they propagated through the town and country, and the correspondence which they constantly kept up with the enemy, rendered it indispensably necessary that they should either be closely confined or be sent out of the province. The milder measure was adopted. . . ." He concluded this long letter:

I will not hurt your Excellency's feelings by attempting to describe the shocking tortures and inhuman murders which are every day committed by the enemy, not only on those who have taken part with us, but on many who refuse to join them. I cannot flatter myself that your representations will have any effect, but I am very sure that unless some steps are taken to check it, the war in this quarter will become truly savage.[47]

Although Cornwallis, as he explained to Clinton, had ". . . always endeavored to soften the horrors of war," he fully condoned Tarleton's

46. Charles, op. cit.
47. Ibid.

punitive operations, and, after Ferguson's defeat at King's Mountain, he also ordered Lieutenant Colonel Thomas Browne to encourage the Indians to attack outlying American settlements.[48] Moreover, the British army had to eat. Lacking a supply service from Camden or Charleston, this meant virtually living off the land. Since food was short, requisitions (usually paid in promissory notes if paid for at all) further alienated the locals to make many active patriot supporters.[49] Not only did patriot forces benefit from increased support, but Cornwallis increasingly found himself deprived of the key ingredient to counterinsurgency warfare: intelligence.

The final phase of the war in the South began in January 1781. Upon hearing of Cornwallis' victory over Gates at Camden, Clinton had sent down a corps, under Major General Leslie, that reached Charleston in December. Strengthened by Leslie's arrival and with his original force rested and reorganized—though still lacking many essentials—Cornwallis decided on a second invasion of North Carolina. But patriot forces also had increased. Congress, following Washington's advice, had placed Nathanael Greene in command of the southern theater.

Greene's major strength consisted of the Continentals of Delaware and Maryland, men of the Virginia line, Sumter's Carolina militia, two small but excellent units: Brigadier General Daniel Morgan's sharpshooting infantry of perhaps eleven hundred men and Lieutenant Colonel "Light Horse Harry" Lee's cavalry of some three hundred; and local guerrilla bands under Marion and other militia officers.

Nonetheless, as Tarleton later wrote, the superiority of the British force, ". . . when compared with General Greene's, gave every reasonable assurance, that with proper care the latter might be destroyed, or driven over the Roanoke; when it was imagined that the loyalists, who were computed to be the greater proportion of the inhabitants, would make indefatigable exertions to render themselves independent of Congress. Such was the opinion of thousands when the King's troops prepared for this expedition. . . ."[50]

The King's troops and their commander, Cornwallis, underestimated Nathanael Greene's abilities. Greene was a common-sense general. Son of a Rhode Island Quaker preacher, he had been an ironmaster until the war, in which he had fought hard and well in rising to his present command. At thirty-eight years, he was fit, a big man, hard as nails. But he also was bright enough to respect a formidable enemy. He once wrote to Anthony Wayne: ". . . Be a little careful and tread softly; for depend upon it, you have a modern Hannibal to deal with in the person

48. Ibid.
49. Wickwire, op. cit.
50. Tarleton, op. cit.

of Cornwallis."[51] Greene now chose to emulate Quintus Fabius Maximus, and even had boats collected so that if necessary his army could retreat across the numerous rivers!

Greene refused to risk his inferior force except on his own terms. He rightly discerned that Cornwallis was operating blind. If guerrillas could cut British communications, either to detachments operating in peripheral areas or to rear garrisons, Cornwallis eventually would have to retire. To confuse and annoy the British general further, Greene sent Morgan to the western frontiers of South Carolina with about 470 light infantry and some 70 light dragoons; he led the rest of his army toward Camden.

Cornwallis responded to Morgan's essay by sending a strong force under Tarleton after him. He himself pursued Greene's main force, but with little success except to tire his troops. In early January, he reported to Clinton: ". . . The difficulties I have had to struggle with have not been occasioned by the opposite army: they always keep at a considerable distance, and retire on our approach. But the constant incursions of refugees, North Carolinians, Back Mountain men, and the perpetual risings in different parts of this province, the invariable successes of all those parties against our militia, keep the whole country in continual alarm, and render the assistance of regular troops everywhere necessary. . . ."[52] He did not report a popular rhyme of the time:

> Cornwallis led a country dance,
> The like was never seen, sir,
> Much retrograde and much advance,
> And all with General Greene, sir.[53]

Cornwallis' hesitant advance—he took ten days to march forty miles —contrasted to Morgan's sure movements. Morgan was an old Indian fighter who had driven a wagon in Braddock's army. An Indian bullet had smashed out the teeth of his lower left jaw; his back carried scars from 499 lashes—the penalty for striking a British officer.[54] Although not as skillful a tactician as Tarleton, he knew the country better, he marched at night, and he persuaded or intimidated locals to refuse information of his movements to Tarleton's patrols. Out of touch with both Morgan and Cornwallis, Tarleton finally brought the former to bay at Cowpens, a disastrous attack that cost Tarleton some nine hundred men.[55]

Cornwallis reacted to this calamity by pursuing Morgan. To increase mobility, he destroyed all heavy baggage, ". . . even his supplies

51. Wickwire, op. cit.
52. Charles, op. cit.
53. Alden (South), supra.
54. Wickwire, op. cit.
55. Ward, op. cit.; Wickwire, op. cit.

of rum," and in the next few months proceeded as far as the northern boundary of North Carolina. Although he chased Greene into Virginia, he did not destroy the American army, a fact that caused local Tories to offer only lukewarm co-operation when he retired to Hillsboro to rest his weary and famished troops.[56]

When Greene returned, in March, with an even larger army, Cornwallis met him at Guilford Courthouse, an inconclusive battle that won the British commander the field but cost him over five hundred casualties he could ill afford. Cornwallis' claim to victory was disputed not only by a torn, bleeding, almost starving army, but by General Phillips in Virginia as ". . . that sort of victory which ruins an army."[57] Nor was Cornwallis' claim respected in London: The Annual Register noted that the battle was ". . . productive of all the consequences of defeat"; Horace Walpole sarcastically wrote, ". . . Lord Cornwallis has conquered his troops out of shoes and provisions, and himself out of troops"[58]; Charles James Fox bluntly remarked ". . . that another such victory would ruin the British army."[59]

With his remaining effectives exhausted, sick and hungry, Cornwallis retired on Wilmington to lick his wounds, his mood clear in a letter to Clinton dated early April: ". . . North Carolina is of all the provinces in America the most difficult to attack (unless material assistance could be got from the inhabitants, the contrary of which I have sufficiently experienced), on account of its great extent, of the numberless rivers and creeks, and the total want of interior navigation."[60]

Clinton made no effort to hide his dissatisfaction, neither at the time nor later, when he noted in his history:

In short, after the most impartial review of Lord Cornwallis' two invasions of North Carolina, the only inference we can draw from them is that without adequate encouragement or the smallest certainty of being joined by any considerable number of the King's friends in that province . . . His Lordship withdrew from South Carolina . . . the chief means of its security and defense, in direct disobedience of the orders left with him by his Commander in Chief; and that, after forcing the passage of several great rivers, fighting a bloody battle, and running eight hundred and twenty miles over almost every part of the invaded province at the expense of above three thousand men, he accomplished no other purpose but the having exposed, by an unnecessary retreat to Wilmington, the two valuable colonies behind him to be overrun and conquered by that very army which he boasts to have completely routed but a week or two before.[61]

56. Wickwire, op. cit.: Colonel Lee's coup, which resulted in sudden death for one hundred loyalists, also dampened Tory enthusiasm.
57. Willcox, op. cit.; see also Rankin, op. cit.; Ward, op. cit.
58. Ibid.
59. Wickwire, op. cit.
60. Charles, op. cit.
61. Willcox (Clinton), supra.

Cornwallis faced a choice of staying in Wilmington, returning to South Carolina, toward which Greene now turned, or going on to Virginia. He chose to march north to the Chesapeake Bay area. The defense of the South now fell to young Lieutenant Colonel Lord Rawdon, at twenty-six years of age a combat veteran of the war. Rawdon commanded about eight thousand troops based on Savannah and Charleston. He maintained a ring of outposts—Ninety Six, Fort Granby, Orangeburg, Fort Motte, Fort Watson, and Georgetown—isolated garrisons manned with 120 to 630 men each, a complex that brings to mind ancient Rome's bastions against the barbarians.[62]

Greene now moved against Rawdon's outer defensive ring. He faced a formidable task, for his main force was neither strong nor well equipped. But Cornwallis' withdrawal left South Carolina loyalists without protection, which frequently meant that they were forced to lend active or passive support to Greene's irregular forces. Greene now ordered these disparate units under Sumter, Pickens, Marion, and Lee to exploit what seemed a God-given opportunity. Lee and Marion's small force struck the first blow by investing and capturing Fort Watson. Like Hannibal, they lacked essential engineering equipment for such a task; unlike Hannibal, they built a siege tower out of logs—"Maham Tower" —and got on with the job.[63] Although Rawdon held Greene's main force off at Hobkirk's Hill, north of Camden, the British commander was soon forced to fall back. Patriot forces now fell on other isolated outposts. Clinton later acidly observed the result:

. . . in the short space of five weeks from the appearance of General Greene's army before Camden [which Rawdon evacuated] we lost or evacuated almost every post we possessed in the Carolinas and Georgia with provisions and stores to an immense amount and upward of 1000 troops killed, wounded or taken—all which heavy misfortunes we might most certainly have escaped had Lord Cornwallis fortunately either marched his army back to Camden after the Battle of Guilford or even retired to Charleston . . . after he had refitted at Wilmington.[64]

Within three months after Cornwallis' departure, Rawdon held only Wilmington, Charleston, and Savannah—royal enclaves that without reinforcement would prove useless until finally evacuated after the fall of Yorktown.[65]

Why did Cornwallis march north?

In his own mind, he could not remain in Wilmington, where he was short of supply. As he wrote Clinton in late April: ". . . Neither my cavalry nor infantry are in readiness to move. The former are in want of

62. Ward, op. cit.
63. Ibid.
64. Willcox (Clinton), supra.
65. Ward, op. cit.

everything; the latter of every necessity but shoes, of which we have received an ample supply. . . ."[66] Tarleton later wrote that Cornwallis was influenced by news of British reinforcements reaching Virginia, and that he also hoped to lure Greene northward. We know that he had a tactical fixation on the North. He told Phillips, Clinton, and Lord George Germain that the conquest of Virginia was necessary to secure South Carolina and win the submission of North Carolina[67]; he could not pacify the South, he believed, so long as its rebels received support from North Carolina and Virginia.[68]

A deeper motive probably inspired his lordship, and this was a total (and impractical) reversal of British strategy. Shortly before departing for Virginia, he wrote Major General Phillips that ". . . if we mean an offensive war in America, we must abandon New York, and bring our whole force into Virginia; we then have a stake to fight for, and a successful battle may give us America. . . ."[69]

He forgot to add that a defeat could cost the same.

66. Charles, op. cit.
67. Ward, op. cit.
68. Wickwire, op. cit.
69. Charles, op. cit.

Chapter 9

England's colonial wars • Indian guerrilla leaders: Sivaji and Tippu • Wellesley's tactical changes • The Vendée rebellion • Hoche's counterguerrilla tactics: "overawing" versus "exasperating" • The Italian lazzaroni *• Napoleon invades Spain • Spanish army disasters • The rise of guerrilla bands • Wellington's early battles and use of guerrillas • French excesses • Guerrilla offensives • French countertactics • Marshal Bessières' testament*

AMERICA was not the only place where England had to fight irregular wars. Early in the seventeenth century, she had established her first trading post in India, whose northern area formed part of the vast Mogul Empire. For a century, the Moguls continued to expand into India, but early in the eighteenth century, the dynasty dissolved, not the least of its problems having been the rise of a new Hindu military power, the Marathas, who fought brilliant guerrilla warfare under the famous leader Sivaji.

In the early-eighteenth century, control of the country rested in the hands of warring viceroys who fell victim one after another to territorial ambitions of England, France, and Holland. In a series of more or less orthodox military campaigns fought before and during the Seven Years' War, Clive largely eliminated French and Dutch threats to British influence: by 1759, England "was the only European race which counted in India."[1]

1. D. H. Cole and E. C. Priestley, *An Outline of British Military History 1660–1936* (London: Sifton Praed, 1936). Hereafter cited as Cole.

England's position was somewhat tenuous. It roughly resembled that of the Romans occupying the coastal fringe of Spain in 206 B.C. In this case, England was reasonably well established in the East, but, in expanding to the South, West, and North, she collided with numerous

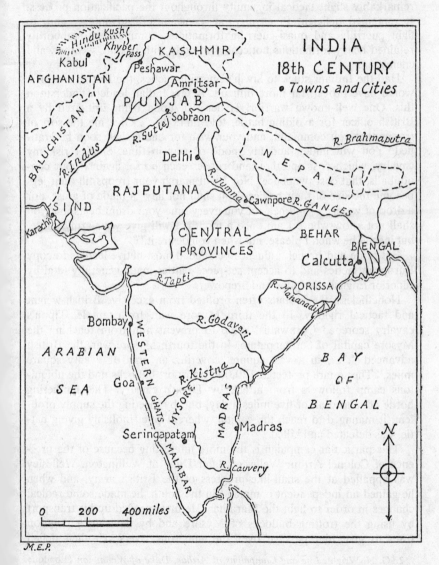

INDIA
18th CENTURY
• Towns and Cities

M.E.P.

tribes, some equipped with European weapons and trained by the French. To neutralize these people would require nearly sixty years of intermittent warfare punctuated by innumerable campaigns against the

Hindus and Muslims in Mysore, the Marathas in the West, and their outlaw offshoot, the Pindaris in central India.

Although the British army displayed admirable perseverance, unquestioned courage and even, on occasion, political acumen, it showed remarkably slight tactical ingenuity throughout the pacification process. It remained deficient in cavalry, an enormous disadvantage, and, to fight guerrilla and quasi-guerrilla formations, commanders stubbornly retained heavy formations noticeably at odds with terrain, weather, and enemy.

Had the Indians stuck to Sivaji's guerrilla tactics, the British conquest would have proved far more difficult. A few Indian leaders understood this. One well-known warrior, Hyder Ali, upon being criticized by a British officer for avoiding battle, told him: ". . . Give me the sort of troops that you command, and your wish for battle shall soon be gratified. You will understand my mode of war in time. Shall I risk my cavalry, which cost one thousand rupees each horse, against your cannonballs, that cost twopence? No: I will march your troops till their legs become the size of their bodies. You shall not have a blade of grass, nor a drop of water: I shall hear of you every time your drum beats, but you shall not know where I am once a month. I will give your army battle, but it shall be when I please, not when you desire it."[2]

But pride and French influence persuaded most native leaders to copy European tactics and to accept set-piece battles made generally fatal by superior English discipline and firepower.

Nonetheless, the Indians often profited from excessive British weight and tactical rigidity. In the third Mysore war, for example, Tippu's cavalry scorched Cornwallis' route to prevent him from reaching the Mysore capital of Seringapatam. In the fourth Mysore war, the British advanced ". . . in a vast square, covering an area of twenty square miles." The square protected 120,000 transport bullocks and the ubiquitous camp followers from attack by Tippu's cavalry. This lumbering horde advanced all of five miles a day, but, by meeting the supply problem, it managed to reach the capital, where Tippu, foolishly giving battle, was defeated and killed.[3]

This particular campaign is the more interesting because of the presence of Colonel Arthur Wellesley, later Duke of Wellington. Wellesley was appalled at the snail-like progress of the British army, and when he gained an independent command in the South, he made some radical changes in order to fight the Marathas. He first speeded up his transport by using the trotting bullocks of Mysore and by devising a pontoon train to give him passage over the numerous rivers. He then defied

2. G. N. Wright, *Life and Campaigns of Arthur, Duke of Wellington* (London: Fisher, Son, n.d.), 4 vols.
3. Cole, op. cit.

standard practice by launching a campaign during the monsoon, when neither Europeans nor Indians were supposed to fight. Finally, he used whatever force he commanded in a prompt, rigorous and decisive manner, both to win battles and to avoid battles.

At one point, in pursuing a rebellious rajah, he found himself in difficult semijungle country with a minimum of information concerning his quarry. ". . . I don't think I ever saw a country naturally so strong as this," he wrote, "and to the strength of which so many additions have been made by the natives themselves. Every village is a strong fortification, of which it would require good troops to take possession; and in some cases ten or a dozen of these villages are connected by made or natural defenses of great strength."[4] His force was small, his time limited. Plainly determined to attack—among other measures, he had his troopers cut underbrush from trails in order to prevent ambush—he told villagers he would kill them unless they tore down defenses and cooperated with him. They chose to do so, and with their help he soon captured the rajah and six other rebels, whom he summarily hanged.

Wellesley's subsequent campaigns in India added a great deal to his knowledge of irregular warfare. This was just as well, for in a few years he would be allied with some of its most able practitioners, Portuguese and Spanish guerrillas.

The French, too, were going to become involved in guerrilla warfare, as a hurtful by-product of the Revolution. In 1793, before Carnot's famous decree called the French nation to arms, republican armies faced a fierce counterrevolution by priest-dominated peasants of Vendée. Finding leaders in local nobles and gentlemen such as Jacques Cathelineau, a linen merchant, these countryfolk picked up scythes, pitchforks, and fowling muskets to win a number of towns from surprised and generally weak republican garrisons. Reinforced with captured arms and fresh volunteers, the inspired irregulars attempted to take Nantes, a defeat in which Cathelineau was killed.

Determined to put down the rebellion, the Convention committed some one hundred thousand troops to the Vendée. Command went to Rossignol, "who was not only a tipsy and dissolute scoundrel, but a stupid and ignorant coward to boot."[5] Generals such as Westermann, l'Échelle, and Kléber carried out a scorched-earth policy until the rebels

4. John Fortescue, *Wellington* (London: Ernest Benn, 1925); see also, Elizabeth Longford, *Wellington—The Years of the Sword* (London: Weidenfeld & Nicolson, 1969); Antony Brett-James, *Wellington at War 1794–1815* (London: Macmillan, 1961).

5. J. R. M. MacDonald, "The Terror." In *The Cambridge Modern History* (London: Cambridge University Press, 1904), Vol. 8 of 13 vols.; see also L. A. Taylor, *The Tragedy of an Army: La Vendée in 1793* (London: Hutchinson, 1913).

looked out only on "heaps of ashes, death and famine."[6] Weakened further by trying to fight set-piece battles and by dissension among leaders, the force splintered, with some peasants returning to their farms. Some fifty thousand with their wives and children retreated across the Loire into Brittany. Their new commander, the twenty-one-year-old Count Henri de La Rochejacquelein, dramatically told them, "If I retreat, kill me; if I advance, follow me; if I fall, avenge me."[7]

The task of pacifying the Vendée base now fell to a young and able general, Lazare Hoche. As Thiers later described his campaign:

6. Ibid.
7. Percy Cross Standing, *Guerrilla Leaders of the World: From Charette to Delvet* (London: Stanley Paul, 1912).

. . . He devised an ingenious mode of reducing the country without laying it waste, by depriving it of its arms and taking part of its produce for the supply of the Republican army. In the first place he persisted in the establishment of entrenched camps. He then formed a circular line which was supported by the Sèvre and Loire and tended to envelop progressively the whole country. This line was composed of very strong detachments, connected by patrols so as to leave no free space by which an enemy who was at all numerous could pass. These posts were directed to occupy every hamlet and village and to disarm them. To accomplish this they were to seize the cattle which usually grazed together, and the corn stowed away in the barns; they were also to secure the principal inhabitants; they were not to restore the cattle or the corn, not to release the persons taken as hostages, till the peasants should have voluntarily delivered up their arms.[8]

By such measures, what Callwell described as "overawing" rather than "exasperating" the enemy, Hoche effectively eliminated the home base of the revolt.[9]

La Rochejacquelein wanted to remain in Brittany until strong enough to return to the Vendée, but older leaders persuaded the force to march north. After failing to capture the seaport town of Granville, the new leaders recommended withdrawal into Normandy. The peasants wished to go home, however, and marched to the Loire. Kléber and Marceau caught them up at Le Mans and Savenay, where probably fifteen thousand of them perished.

This did not end the rebellion. La Rochejacquelein remained in Brittany with a group of followers allied with Breton rebels who called themselves the *Chouans*—literally "long-eared owls." The republican campaign against the main force had exposed the Vendée to further revolt, which defied even the "infernal columns" of General Turreau.

Royalist leaders made a final attempt to save the Chouan survivors in Brittany by landing reinforcements from England. Poor leadership, combined with intraforce rivalries, doomed this to failure, while a vigorous campaign on the part of Hoche destroyed remaining Chouan forces in detail. By the time fighting ended, the once-rich province had become "a desolate and blackened wilderness."

All told, Hoche estimated one hundred thousand insurgent deaths —about one fifth of the Vendean population.[10]

A series of royalist-peasant outbreaks in Switzerland and Italy followed the Vendée revolt. The reader may remember that, in 1796, the young Bonaparte took command of the ragged army of Italy, which he

8. Ibid.

9. C. E. Callwell, *Small Wars—Their Principles and Practice* (London: HMSO, 1899).

10. Standing, op. cit.

reorganized into a splendid fighting force. Having defeated the Austrians and established the Cisalpine Republic, he expelled the Pope and, with connivance of Roman Jacobins, established a Roman republic under Masséna's governorship. In 1798, Masséna's administration bogged down in extreme corruption and led to a mutiny of French troops, followed by local worker uprisings.[11]

King Ferdinand of Naples anxiously watched these developments. Emboldened by Nelson's presence, Bonaparte's absence in Egypt, and the arrival of the overrated General Mack from Vienna, he stupidly raised an army and marched on Rome. Masséna's replacement, the accomplished General Championnet, soon smashed this effort and followed Mack's retreating army to Naples. The French now had to fight outraged Neapolitan *lazzaroni,* or homeless beggars, who proved as anti-republican as the Vendeans. Despite this assistance, King Ferdinand evacuated his court and twenty million ducats to Palermo.[12]

The French meanwhile continued to fight the ill-armed but determined *lazzaroni,* whom they finally defeated, ". . . as much a triumph of tact as of force. Championnet was one of the few French generals of that period who showed skill in dealing with alien peoples. As the fighting waned, he spoke to the *lazzaroni* in their own tongue, promising freedom for their city, every comfort for its population, and the utmost respect for St. Januarius. The words told with magical force; Thiébault marched with a guard of honor to the shrine of the saint, and himself with politic hypocrisy knelt at the altar. . . ."[13]

In January 1799, Championnet established the Parthenopean Republic, but was soon relieved of command for trying to prevent occupation excesses encouraged by the Directory. Not only did the French exact tremendous indemnities—sixty million francs in the case of Naples—but they continued to plunder, while brooking no resistance: at Stanz, Switzerland, in September 1798, French troops massacred 1,000 men, 102 women, and 25 children.[14] Similar harsh policies turned Piedmontese and Neapolitan peasants against the intruders when armies of the Second Coalition invaded Italy early in 1799. By summer, the French republics in Italy had vanished.

The French did not reappear in the South until 1806, when Masséna reoccupied Naples. The Calabrian peasants rebelled, and, in July, a British army under General Stuart landed from Sicily to defeat the French at the battle of Maida. Stuart withdrew his army, but for the next two

11. Felix Markham, *Napoleon* (London: Weidenfeld & Nicolson, 1963).
12. J. H. Rose, "The Second Coalition." In *The Cambridge Modern History* (London: Cambridge University Press, 1904), Vol. 8 of 13 vols.
13. Ibid.
14. Ibid.

years the *lazzaroni* fought a guerrilla war that tied up forty thousand French troops.[15]

None of these guerrilla actions seemed to bother Napoleon in the spring of 1807, when he was casting covetous glances at the Iberian Peninsula.

He wanted this area for two reasons: to exploit "latent Spanish resources, naval and economic," of which he held an exaggerated notion, and more important, to further his "continental system," by which he hoped to force Britain from the war by disrupting her trade with Europe.[16] Nelson's earlier victory at Trafalgar, which ended Napoleon's hope of invading England, had forced this shift in strategy. He would bring England to her knees by economic warfare; as he told his brother, King Louis of Holland, "I mean to conquer the sea by the land."[17]

Napoleon anticipated little difficulty in occupying the Iberian Peninsula. Strong militarily, he was also supremely confident. He held only contempt for his Spanish ally and for the decadent Bourbon court: King Charles IV; Queen María Luisa; her favorite, the young, powerful, and greedy Prince Manuel de Godoy; and finally the stupid heir apparent, Prince Ferdinand. Napoleon had long enjoyed Godoy's connivance— among the rewards, he was promised a piece of Portugal—and he was also being courted by Prince Ferdinand and his cabal.[18]

In July 1807, Napoleon sent Junot's army, some fifty thousand troops, across Spain to seize Lisbon and close it to British merchant shipping. As anticipated, Junot crossed Spain without opposition and even managed to insert French troops in the northern garrisons. Napoleon hastened to consolidate his presence by appointing Murat "Lieutenant of the Emperor in Spain." But as Murat led his columns toward Madrid in March 1808, serious riots broke out in Aranjuez. These were the work of Ferdinand's agents, and they caused the fall of hated Godoy and abdication of panic-stricken Charles. But Ferdinand's ambition was checked when Napoleon summoned the royal family to Bayonne, forced Ferdinand to abdicate, and placed his own brother, Joseph Bonaparte, on the throne.

This proved an egregious political error. The people of Spain did not love their monarch, but they did love their country and certainly had no desire to become a French vassal state. The *Madrileños* already had

15. Markham, op. cit.; see also E. M. Lloyd, "The Third Coalition." In *The Cambridge Modern History* (London: Cambridge University Press, 1904), Vol. 9 of 13 vols.

16. Ibid.

17. Ibid.

18. Raymond Carr, "Spain and Portugal—1793 to c. 1840." In *The New Cambridge Modern History* (London: Cambridge University Press, 1965), Vol. 9 of 12 vols.

contested Murat's presence. In May, when Ferdinand and his entourage left Madrid, the populace revolted. This was an action of ordinary people, not constituted authority. In Madrid, the Spanish garrison ". . . remained inert or gave that assistance to the French authorities for which Murat publicly thanked them. . . ."[19] When the revolt spread to the provinces, in mid-May, ". . . the captains-general and governors, most of them nominees of Godoy, succumbed to a kind of moral paralysis. . . . They appealed for tranquillity and were ignored, but neither would, nor could use the army against the mobs. . . ."[20] The mobs used extreme violence including murder to force ". . . captains-general and local authorities to arm the people and to accept self-constituted local Juntas . . . [which] all over Spain represented the acceptance of the revolution by the local notables."[21] Initially, almost no army officers joined rebel ranks: ". . . it was the men, and groups of junior officers, particularly [artillery] gunners, in liaison with civilian *meneurs* [ringleaders] who made the decisions which brought the army over to the national cause. . . ."[22]

Despite this confusion, the revolt greatly surprised the French. Murat's soldiers were soon driven across the Ebro River. The news caused great rejoicing in London, where the government decided to send an expeditionary force to Portugal.

Although the French recovered and hastily occupied Portugal with sixty-five thousand troops and Spain with eighty thousand, forces sufficiently strong to neutralize local armies, the occupation from the beginning was uneasy, with ". . . murders, assassinations, wholesale butcheries . . . [occurring[in every city."[23] To this opposition, the French reacted promptly and rigorously. Cavalry columns swept down on disordered peasant bands, sabers flashed in the Spanish sun, people died; the troops tortured and executed, burned homes and farms. The troops restored order in some places. But never for long.

The opening phase would have taken a bystander back twenty centuries, to the war between Romans and Celtiberians. Spanish armies attempting to fight pitched battles, for example Cuesta's force, were generally beaten. Those which took to the hills in small guerrilla bands, such as the somatenes in Catalonia, generally prospered. The French soon claimed the important cities and towns, but this was precarious ownership, maintained by shaky communications. Yet, such was the disor-

19. E. Christiansen, *The Origins of Military Power in Spain—1800–1854* (London: Oxford University Press, 1967).

20. Ibid.; see also Charles Oman, *A History of the Peninsular War* (London: Oxford University Press, 1902), 6 vols.

21. Carr, op. cit.

22. Christiansen, op. cit.

23. Wright, op. cit.; see also R. B. Asprey, "The Peninsular War" and "Wellington at Waterloo," *Army Quarterly*, Vols. 77–78, April and July 1959.

ganized state of the defending armies that the war undoubtedly would
have ended in France's favor—but for British intervention.

Wellesley and a small expeditionary force arrived in Portugal in the
spring of 1808, their landing screened by local guerrillas. Needing time
to rebuild the shattered Portuguese army, Wellington had to move cautiously, a crucial period in which his security depended on accurate intelligence from a friendly population.

The French misinterpreted care as weakness. Junot attacked in
August and was beaten at Vimeiro, an important military victory soon
converted to a major political defeat by the outrageous Convention of
Cintra.[24]

Meanwhile Sir John Moore, the British commander, landed a small

24. Fortescue, op. cit.; see also Oman; Wright; Longford. Two British generals,
Burrard and Dalrymple, arrived ahead of the titular commander, Sir John Moore,
to negotiate the treaty, which foolishly authorized the French to return to France
in British vessels, ". . . incidentally taking with them the loot of Lisbon under
the guise of 'private baggage.' " This caused a public outcry in England. A court
of inquiry subsequently exonerated Wellesley, who had signed the document under orders. The damage remained, as did army intrigues: the cabals of the Horse
Guards continued to plague Wellesley throughout the campaign.

army in Northwest Spain. Napoleon reacted by personally leading in
150,000 troops, which soon shattered the remaining Spanish armies. To
give them time to reorganize, Moore struck at a corps of Soult's army,
but, with Napoleon threatening his right, he was forced to retreat
to Corunna, where he was killed, his army escaping by ship. French arms
now reigned supreme—except for the guerrillas.

While the British were fighting in Portugal and Spain and while the
regular Spanish armies were being shredded in orthodox operations,
explosive nationalism had blown a variety of guerrilla bands into existence. These bands were entirely regional. To lead them, ". . . the priest
girded up his black robe, and stuck a pistol in his belt; the student threw
aside his books, and grasped the sword; the shepherd forsook his flock;
the husbandman his home."[25]

One of the first leaders was Juan Martín Díaz. In 1809, he was
thirty-four, a former private of dragoons, illiterate, married, a father,
a farmer in Castile. He gathered together a half dozen trusted neighbors,
a rude lot badly equipped, a deficiency repaired by the ambush of a few
dozen French couriers. In Navarra, a young student, Francisco Javier
Mina, collected a small band and armed it similarly. In La Mancha, a
doctor emerged as leader: Juan Paladea, soon called El Médico; in
Soria, the friar Sapia turned leader; in Catalonia, another doctor,
Rovera; in Salamanca, the famous Julián Sánchez arose.

These and others generally confined early operations to interrupting
French communications. But small successes bred expansion. Bands
multiplied and began attacking convoys and seizing arms and food and
also treasure, for the enemy plundered whenever and wherever possible.

The enemy answered by furnishing larger escorts for couriers, by
sending out innumerable armed patrols, and by showing virtually no
mercy to anyone remotely suspected of aiding the guerrilla effort. Harsh
measures only helped the effort. Cruelty answered cruelty; terror escalated, the French in particular practicing a frenzied rapine such as that
displayed in the capture of Oporto. During Marshal Soult's assault,
swarms of Portuguese civilians were left floundering in a river by a collapsed bridge. The oncoming French battalions cold-bloodedly fired
into this mass until ". . . planks were laid on the pile of dead bodies
that arose from the river; the French passed over, and carried the batteries of Villa Nova."[26] Not content with victory, the French indulged
an orgy of slaughter until some ten thousand Portuguese had been killed.
Meanwhile, Portuguese defenders had reacted predictably against
French prisoners. As French troops ". . . passed through one of the
squares, they beheld a number of their comrades fastened against the
wall in an upright position and still alive, with their eyes forced from

25. Wright, op. cit.
26. Ibid.

the sockets, their tongues cut out, and their bodies and limbs mangled. This spectacle lighted up their fury again and the scene of pillage and assassination was renewed, and continued for some hours longer."[27]

Without such provocation, the French at Ucles tortured the civil populace in order to learn the location of hidden treasures; they burnt the men, then ". . . tore the nun from the altar, the wife from her husband's corpse, the virgin from her mother's arms, and they abused those victims of the foulest brutality in a way to which death was much to be preferred." The Spanish authorities publicized this treatment ". . . as the most certain means of establishing an eternal and fixed aversion in the heart of every Spaniard, for the name of France."[28]

To this ghastly air, Wellesley returned in 1809. As had happened previously, he found the people eminently sympathetic and helpful, and this was important, for, once again, he had to be careful while playing for time. But he also had to push the French from Portugal, which he did by beating Soult on the Douro, then beating Victor at Talavera before retiring on Lisbon.

By this time, Wellesley, who had become Viscount Wellington, knew that he could not rely on Spanish armies, which had nearly cost him a defeat at Talavera. In August 1809, he wrote, ". . . the Spanish troops will not fight; they are undisciplined, they have no officers, no provisions, no magazines, no means of any description."[29]

Wellington knew, however, that Portuguese *ordenanzas* and Spanish guerrillas would give the French little peace, and he cunningly exploited this knowledge in his plans. It is not going too far to say that he envisaged his army as a piece of cheese to attract the rodent enemy into a guerrilla trap.

He now secured his Lisbon base by constructing the elaborate fortifications of Torres Vedras: North of Lisbon, three lines in depth stretched from the sea to the Tagus. A British fleet guarded his flanks; he also swept the country in front ". . . as bare as possible; the sides of hills and streams were 'scarped,' roads destroyed, woods cut down and villages razed so that the French could find no cover for an attack." Simultaneously, General Beresford reorganized and trained the Portuguese army until eventually ". . . about forty per cent of Wellington's fighting force consisted of Portuguese inter-brigaded with British. . . ."[30] At the same time, Wellington anticipated future operations by building a large transport of mules, a sensible decision since the French found supply by wagons an onerous process in a nearly roadless country.

27. Ibid.
28. Ibid.
29. Markham, op. cit.
30. Cole, op. cit.

Considering the pressure from England and from the Regency, Wellington exhibited enormous patience at this time. His preparations lasted nearly a year, *but such was the control of the Spanish and Portuguese countryside by the guerrillas that the French obtained no information as to his activities.* They knew only that guerrilla operations were constantly expanding, a frustrating situation that Napoleon sought to remedy by sending reinforcements and by ordering Masséna's splendid new Army of Portugal to the attack.

Masséna's campaign is a striking example of the arrogance of ignorance. Denied any intercourse with the land, living in a vacuum as it were, he moved to meet an enemy of whom he was totally ignorant. He found Wellington's army in a defensive position outside Bussaco. He learned of Wellington's Portuguese contingent, but, having no notion of Beresford's training program, he dismissed the indigenous troops as so much rabble. He attacked with less than half his force, an effort defeated by about a third of Wellington's army. Wellington was still careful. Why risk his single army attempting to exploit this favorable result, he reasoned, when time could provide a painless victory? Wellington now *retired behind the Torres Vedras defenses.* Masséna, having no idea of their existence, followed him. And while Wellington's army disappeared behind rows and rows of elaborate fortifications to live easily on supplies brought by ship, Masséna's army sat uneasily in a country bereft of provision, with hungry guerrillas constantly nibbling at his communications. The result was inevitable: In March 1810, the starving French army fell back into Spain.

Much of Wellington's tactical success stemmed from this insulating process. Time and again, a French army commander remained in the dark regarding not only Wellington's plans and movements, but also those of other French commanders; time and again, Wellington learned important information from guerrillas. Although he regarded the Spanish army with faintly disguised contempt, he respected the value of sound guerrilla operations; indeed he later promoted Díaz to command of a corps numbering nearly five thousand infantry and cavalry. The Regency, no doubt influenced by Wellington, promoted the elder Mina to full general in command of nearly fourteen thousand infantry and cavalry.

As guerrilla bands gained strength and confidence, their missions increased. So effectively did they interdict French communications that couriers were soon being escorted by "units 300 strong."[31] In some instances, detachment commanders retained replacement drafts with the excuse that the roads were not safe—". . . the number of recruits received at Madrid, Seville, or Salamanca never bore any proper proportion to the total that had crossed the Bidassoa."[32] This naturally

31. C. N. M. Blair, *Guerrilla Warfare* (London: Ministry of Defence, 1957).
32. Oman, op. cit.

exercised a major psychological effect. French commanders soon realized that they owned no more than the ground they occupied, an unsettling thought that the more active guerrilla leaders never let them forget. If the French weakened an outlying garrison, peasants invariably relayed the information to local guerrillas, who then attacked. When, early in the war, French columns were sweeping Navarra in search of the young student Mina and his band, he attacked Tafalla, where he locked the terrified garrison in the castle and departed. In Castile, the wily Díaz, called *El Empecinado* (The Stubborn One), took and held Guadalajara for a day. Militarily these actions were of but slight importance; psychologically they were very important, because they clearly demonstrated that the guerrillas, though greatly outnumbered, held the initiative.

From such actions, the guerrillas progressed to attacking troop formations. In mid-July 1810, a priest, Gerónimo Merino, known as *El Cura,* led an attack against two battalions of French marines en route to reinforce Soult and Masséna. The guerrillas killed thirteen officers and some two hundred men.[33] These attacks increased as bands grew in strength; in autumn of 1810, they were largely responsible for containing three armies of thirty-eight thousand men that Masséna badly needed. Although their total number probably never exceeded twenty thousand, of which only a portion was operational at any one time, they continued to harass and often tie down French forces many times their own size.

By controlling the countryside, guerrillas exercised another important function: they deprived military governors of taxes and food. King Joseph, in Madrid, ". . . could not command a quarter of the sum which he required to pay the ordinary expenses of government. His courtiers and ministers, French and Spanish, failed to receive their salaries, and the Spanish army, which he was busily striving to form, could not be clothed or armed, much less paid."[34] Joseph's natural incompetence already had caused Napoleon to create four autonomous military commands in northern Spain, a decentralization of authority that played into guerrilla hands, besides causing internal army jealousies.

The French fought back in a number of ways, but primarily by outright repression. From start to finish, Masséna's retreat from Portugal repeated the barbarities of Oporto and Ucles. The French impressed peasants as guides and porters, then summarily tortured and shot them; they impaled priests by the throat on sharpened branches of trees and mutilated luckless *ordenanzas,* Portuguese and Spanish recruits, beyond recognition.[35] Sir Thomas Picton, the eccentric British general who, as former governor of Trinidad, was no stranger to torture, witnessed this retreat and wrote a friend, ". . . nothing can exceed the devastation and

33. Ibid.
34. Ibid.
35. Wright, op. cit.

cruelties committed by the enemy during the whole course of his retreat; setting fire to all the villages, and murdering all the peasantry, for leagues on each flank of his columns. Their atrocities have been such and so numerous, that the name of a Frenchman must be execrated here for ages."[36]

Coercion was integral to the second obvious method of attempting to catch the guerrillas. The usual tactic was the "sweep," which invariably returned empty-handed. Repeated failure naturally proved frustrating. The tactic also wore out men and horses, and, since it involved harsh interrogative methods, it simply widened the gulf between conqueror and peasant.

In attempting to catch Sánchez in Castile in 1809, the French general, Marchand, ". . . selected eight of the principal sheepowners in the district, informed them that a guard should be placed in their houses, their persons closely watched, and, if guerrilla depredations did not totally subside in eight days from that notice, the farmer himself should be held responsible. He declared, also, that alcaldes [mayors], lawyers, priests, and surgeons of every village, should answer with their lives, for the violence committed in their districts by these predatory bands, and that he would burn every house which the inhabitants had abandoned at the approach of the French."[37]

His strong edict almost completely backfired: If any Spaniard in the area had somehow missed French intentions, they were now totally informed; further, Sánchez's answer, a widely disseminated refusal to cease operations, justified almost solely by an appeal to patriotism, significantly broadened his base of support.

Even when the French succeeded in capturing a leader and breaking up a band, they accomplished very little. In 1810, the young student Mina was taken prisoner, but his uncle, Francisco Espoz y Mina, soon rallied the remnants of his band. None of these leaders was gentle, and Francisco, though wellborn, was no exception. In expanding his nephew's band, he ran afoul of one Echeverría, ". . . who was the terror of the villages of Navarre, which he oppressed and plundered in a thousand ways, till they complained to me concerning him. I arrested him at Estella on June 13, 1810, caused him to be shot with three of his principal accomplices, and incorporated his own band (600 foot and 200 horse) with my own men."[38]

Once organized, Francisco extended operations as far afield as Álava and Aragon to contribute enormously to Wellington's operations in Portugal. As Oman points out, French army archives list dozens of officers killed or wounded "in a reconnaissance in Navarre" or "in a skirmish with Mina's bands." At one point, Mina was being hunted by

36. Ibid.
37. Ibid.
38. Oman, op. cit.

troops from no less than six major commands, ". . . yet none of the six generals, though they had 18,000 men marching through his special district, succeeded in catching him, or destroying any appreciable fraction of his band."[39]

Mina's survival depended on mercurial operations: ". . . sometimes he was lurking, with seven companions only, in a cave or gorge; at another he would be found with 3,000 men, attacking large convoys, or even surprising one of the blockhouses with which the French tried to cover his whole sphere of activity."[40] Supported by peasants, at times unwillingly, Mina financed his extensive operations by taking stolen treasures from the French, by collecting rents from national and church properties, by fining "bad Spaniards" [those who had co-operated with the French], and by collecting tribute from French customhouses in return for allowing safe passage of imported goods! Mina's operations worked terrible hardships on the land, which the French often scorched in retaliation. But, again, this only strengthened resistance. When the French summarily shot guerrilla prisoners, Mina responded by shooting more French prisoners, an escalation of horror "put to an end by mutual agreement in 1812."[41]

A third method of neutralizing guerrilla operations proved even less effective. This was King Joseph's attempt to raise a counterforce of guerrillas, which he called "Miquelets" after the famed Pyrenean bandits; at the same time, he attempted to form new regiments from Spanish deserters and prisoners, but neither plan worked.[42] The Spanish recruits soon drifted away to rejoin their armies or to fight with the guerrillas.

In desperation Napoleon finally intervened. Sick of squabbling generals and duplicated efforts (for which he was largely responsible), he reorganized his army, eliminating the separate "military governments" in favor of more-centralized command. In 1811, he created the Army of the North, under Marshal Bessières, who enjoyed no better success in counterguerrilla operations than his fellows.

Bessières' later lament paid unwitting homage both to Wellington's strategy and to Spanish guerrillas. Careful study might well have profited commanders of later generations:

. . . If I concentrate twenty thousand men all communications are lost, and the insurgents will make enormous progress. The coast would be lost as far as Bilbao. We are without resources, because it is only with the greatest pains that the troops can be fed from day to day. The spirit of the population is abominably bad: the retreat of the Army of Portugal had turned their heads. The bands of insurgents grow larger, and recruit themselves actively

39. Ibid.
40. Ibid.
41. Ibid.
42. Wright, op. cit.

on every side. . . . The Emperor is deceived about Spain: the pacification of Spain does not depend on a battle with the English, who will accept it or refuse it as they please, and who have Portugal behind them for retreat. Every one knows the vicious system of our operations. Every one allows that we are too widely scattered. We occupy too much territory, we used up our resources without profit and without necessity: we are clinging on to dreams. . . .[43]

43. Oman, op. cit.

Chapter 10

Hofer's Tyrolean guerrillas fight the French • Frederick the Great's warning • The Pugachev rebellion • Napoleon's invasion of Russia • The "conquest" of Vitebsk • Kutuzov's strategy • Peasant guerrillas • Denis Davydov and the partisans • The French retreat • The final disaster • Prussia's levée en masse

T HE SPANISH ULCER," as Napoleon called it, was not his single excursion in guerrilla warfare. In 1809, he had been forced to leave the peninsular campaign in Soult's hands and return to Paris to face a fresh war with Austria. This centered on Tyrol, traditionally a Habsburg possession, but ceded by Napoleon, in 1806, to the Bavarians.

Tyrolean mountaineers loathed their new masters and, in the spring of 1809, rose in mass against them. This was pure guerrilla warfare, under such capable if flamboyant leaders as Andreas Hofer, an innkeeper; Joseph Speckbacher, a peasant; and Joachim "Redbeard" Haspinger, a Capuchin priest. To fight the Bavarian army in the Tyrol, Hofer called several thousand peasants together and, after invoking patriotism, God and presumably motherhood, he directed: "Up then, and at these Bavarians! Tear your foes, aye, with your teeth, so long as they stand up; but when they kneel pardon them!"[1]

1. Standing, op. cit.

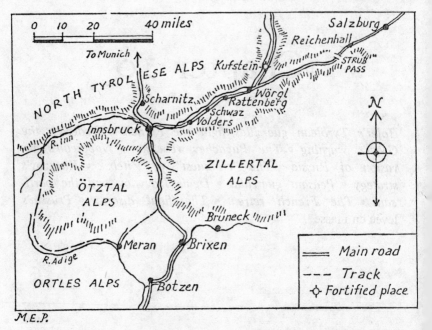

M.E.P.

First blood was drawn against a party of Bavarian engineers attempting to destroy bridges that the Austrian army planned to use. When concealed sharpshooters dispersed this group, the Bavarian commander, General von Wrede, advanced from Innsbruck with a Franco-Bavarian army corps. A young innkeeper, Peter Kemnater, ambushed this force so successfully that it abandoned its guns, which the peasants destroyed. Apparently still not impressed, Von Wrede led a new force toward Brixen, but this was ambushed in a mountain defile where falling rocks and tree trunks merged with accurate fire to decimate the intruders. Simultaneously, Hofer cleared the Passeyr area while Speckbacher won the important town of Innsbruck, a combined effort finally resulting in the capture of the entire Franco-Bavarian force: ". . . all the guns, horses and material of war, the two leading general officers, ten staff-officers, upwards of a hundred lesser officers, 6,000 infantry with seven guns and 800 horses and 1,000 cavalry."[2]

This astounding victory was only temporary. The Austrian army, to which Tyrolean fortunes were tied, was soon beaten by Napoleon. Although the Tyroleans continued to fight magnificently, they met political defeat by the Treaty of Schönbrunn, which re-ceded their country to the Bavarians. Hofer continued to lead a resistance force, but, in December 1809, he was betrayed, captured and, a few months later, shot.

2. Ibid.

Neither "the Spanish ulcer" nor the Tyrolean uprising furnished a warning to Napoleon when it came to invading Russia. This is the more strange because the well-read Napoleon had studied the works of his hero Frederick the Great.

Aware of the Cossack revolt led by Stepan Razin in 1667–71 and mindful of his own painful experiences with guerrillas in Moravia and with Hungarian light horse, Frederick showed a healthy respect for Russian irregular forces in his own writings. Although tending to denigrate the regular Russian army in his earlier writings, Frederick concluded that the Russians nevertheless ". . . are so formidable that no one is able to gain by attacking them, having to cross virtual wastelands to reach them, and there is everything to lose, even in being reduced to a defensive war, if they should come to attack you. What gives them this advantage is the number of Cossacks, Tartars and Kalmuks [irregulars] which they have in their armies; these vagabond hordes of plunderers and incendiaries are capable by their incursions of destroying the most flourishing provinces without the [regular] army even setting foot on them. In order to avoid such devastation, their neighbors treat them with respect."[3]

Frederick was writing of 1740, but subsequent events emphasized the rebellious spirit of the Cossacks. A Cossack leader, Emelyan Pugachev, became the bane of Catherine the Great's existence by leading the major peasant uprising of 1773–74.[4]

Trouble had been brewing for a long time in Russia, the result of increasingly stringent ukases that carried the death sentence to a serf for even questioning his lot. Here and there, serfs did rebel, usually a pathetic effort, an isolated murder of a particularly cruel landlord or greedy tax collector, that met with swift and harsh punishment. Nonetheless, incidents multiplied and finally led to a series of uprisings bloodily put down by the regular army. Nor was unrest settled by Catherine's "liberal" outlook not surprising, since her "major" reform replaced the death sentence to the complaining serf with whipping and transport to Siberia for life.

The Pugachev rebellion began in the heart of the Yaik Cossack country, in the Urals, and at first aimed toward establishing a separate Cossack state. Justified as this might have been, the movement was cloaked in one of the most bizarre forms in history. To win support, the Cossack leader claimed to be Catherine's assassinated husband, Emperor Peter III, who had returned to lead his people from bondage!

That the swarthy Cossack bore no resemblance, physical or otherwise, to Peter, formerly the Duke of Holstein and latterly an idiot, seemingly did not matter. Ignorant and very superstitious peasants traditionally

3. Frédéric II, op. cit.
4. Maurice Hindus, *The Cossacks* (New York: Doubleday, Doran, 1945).

had embraced the reincarnative notion.[5] Pugachev himself seems to have made at least a partial transference of personality in that he surrounded himself with all the trappings of an imperial court, even including "ladies-in-waiting" to his Cossack wife. How much of this served dramatic effect is difficult to judge, but his speeches leave no doubt as to their compelling paternalism: "You, such as you are, I enfranchise you and give eternal freedom to your children and grandchildren. . . . You will no longer work for a lord and you will no longer pay taxes; if we find you toiling on behalf of another, we will massacre you all. . . ." To give the movement identity, Pugachev invoked Cossack traditions: the muzhiks were to have ". . . the privilege of being the most faithful slaves of our own crown; we make them a gift of the cross and of their ancient prayers, of the long hair and the beard, of liberty and independence. . . . When we have destroyed their enemies, the guilty nobles, each man will be able to enjoy a life of peace and tranquility which shall endure for hundreds of years."[6]

Thus inspired, the army of serfs swept across Russia, storming army posts and killing nobles, landlords and officers—a reign of terror not to be outdone in Russia until 1917. In the nineteenth century, the Russian writer Pushkin brought Pugachev to life in his short novel *The Captain's Daughter*,[7] in which the interested reader will find an excellent description of a rebel attack on a small garrison. After soldiers threw down their arms, Pugachev hanged the commandant and his principal aides, then held court on the commandant's porch, ". . . the inhabitants . . . taking the oath of allegiance, coming up one at a time, kissing the crucifix, and bowing to the Pretender. The garrison soldiers were there. The regimental tailor, armed with a pair of blunt scissors, cut off their pigtails. . . ."

Pugachev's ragtag bands grew to the impressive figure of fifteen thousand; in the winter of 1774, they stood only 120 miles from Moscow. From the government's viewpoint, the situation was the more serious because the Russian army was busy fighting the Turks.

But now the Russian victory at Shumla freed the army, the beginning of the end for Peter Pugachev. In desperation, he retreated to the Volga, his scorched-earth policy only bringing more misery to once-devoted followers. Betrayed by his own lieutenants in order to save their lives, he was taken to Moscow, exhibited in a cage, and later beheaded.

Not long after this affair, Catherine wrote the French liberal Voltaire that Pugachev ". . . could neither read nor write, but he was an ex-

5. Bernard Pares, *A History of Russia* (London: Jonathan Cape, 1955).

6. Zoé Oldenbourg, *Catherine the Great* (London: William Heinemann, 1965); see also M. N. Pokrovsky, *Brief History of Russia* (London: Martin Lawrence, 1933), 2 vols. Tr. D. S. Mirsky.

7. A. S. Pushkin, *The Captain's Daughter* (Moscow: Progress Publishers, 1954).

tremely bold and determined man. . . . No one since Tamerlane has done more harm than he has."[8]

To undo the harm, the empress and her ministers invoked a counter-reign of terror in which thousands perished to bring no more than uneasy peace to this troubled land.

Trouble had been brewing between Napoleon and Alexander since 1808, when Alexander expressed his desire to possess Constantinople. The two emperors subsequently clashed over the Polish question and Alexander's trade with England; and the empress dowager of Russia did not help matters by sabotaging Napoleon's marriage to Alexander's sister.[9] Napoleon's temper is evident from a conversation he had with his ambassador to Russia, Armand de Caulaincourt, in the spring of 1811. To Caulaincourt's warning ". . . of the difficulties of the climate, the obstinacy of the Russians and their plan of luring him into the interior by a defensive strategy," Napoleon replied: "Bah! A battle will dispose of the fine resolutions of your friend Alexander and his fortifications of sand. He is false and feeble."[10]

Napoleon nevertheless prepared quite carefully for the pending campaign, which he held to be ". . . the greatest and most difficult enterprise that I have so far attempted." Including allied troops, he collected an army of well over 600,000. Although his strength in Russia never amounted to more than 420,000 to 450,000, his army nevertheless greatly outnumbered the Russian armies.[11]

The Grand Army of 1812, however, was not the polished instrument of earlier campaigns. French soldiers constituted less than half of it; neither allied nor French corps had received enough training, march discipline was poor, the supply system tended to break down, and inadequate facilities existed for sick and wounded. Napoleon also misjudged the attitude of Polish and Russian peasants, who, despite forced requisitions, were supposed to rise in support of the French. Some of these deficiencies might have been corrected, but, by 1812, Napoleon was not in the best physical health and he was totally enslaved by his ego. If all else failed, the Grand Army would march to the beat of his own mystical ambition: ". . . I feel myself driven towards an end that I do not know. As soon as I shall have reached it, as soon as I shall become

8. Oldenbourg, op. cit.
9. E. Stschepkin, "Russia Under Alexander I, and the Invasion of 1812." In *The Cambridge Modern History* (London: Cambridge University Press, 1904), Vol. 9 of 13 vols.
10. Markham, op. cit.
11. Ibid.; see also Stschepkin, op. cit.; Philippe-Paul de Ségur, *Napoleon's Russian Campaign* (London: Michael Joseph, 1958). Tr. J. D. Townsend. The figures vary considerably, from Stschepkin's 680,000 (including 500,000 infantry and 100,-000 cavalry) to Ségur's 617,000, to Markham's 600,000.

unnecessary, an atom will suffice to shatter me. Till then, not all the forces of mankind can do anything against me."[12]

Troubles began to plague the Grand Army almost as soon as its vanguard crossed the Niemen, on June 25, 1812. The unusually fast pace

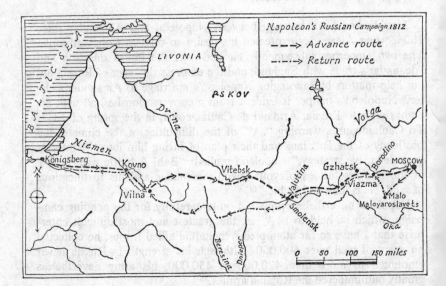

soon told, and the roads filled with sick and stragglers. This was partly the result of a late spring and very bad weather, partly a supply failure and poor march discipline.

Napoleon's ambassador and counselor, Caulaincourt, later wrote that each soldier had been equipped with ". . . ten pounds of flour to last for five days, bread for four days, biscuit for six days."[13] Some of the younger recruits had stupidly thrown away the burdensome flour ration, an action soon regretted. Caulaincourt continued:

. . . This rapid movement [to Vilna], without stores, exhausted and destroyed all the resources and houses which lay on the way. The advance guard lived quite well, but the rest of the army was dying of hunger. Exhaustion, added to want and the piercingly cold rains at night, caused the death of 10,000 horses. Many of the young Guard died on the road of fatigue, cold and hunger.[14]

12. J. F. C. Fuller, *The Conduct of War, 1789–1961* (New Brunswick, N.J.: Rutgers University Press, 1961).
13. Caulaincourt, Duke of Vicenza, *Memoirs* (London: Cassell, 1935), 2 vols. Ed. Jean Hanoteau, tr. Hamish Miles.
14. Ibid.

General Carl von Clausewitz, who fought on the Russian side in this campaign, wrote that a general, returning from Napoleon's headquarters on a political errand, was astonished ". . . at the state of the route of the French Army, which he found strewn with the carcases of horses, and swarming with sick and stragglers. All prisoners were carefully questioned as to the matter of subsistence; and it was ascertained that already, in the neighborhood of Vitebsk, the horses were obtaining only green forage, and the men, instead of bread, only flour, which they were obliged to cook into soup. . . ."[15]

Caulaincourt noted that ". . . the pillage and disorders of all kinds in which the army had indulged had put the whole countryside to flight." Outside of Vitebsk, ". . . we were in the heart of inhabited Russia . . . we were like a vessel without a compass in the midst of a vast ocean."[16] Napoleon's aide, Ségur, later wrote that when the Emperor's immediate entourage rejoiced at the "conquest" of Vitebsk, he turned sharply on them and cried, "Do you think I have come all this way just to conquer these huts?"[17]

A different policy toward the peasants still might have saved French fortunes. Although Russian landowners ". . . grew much milder in 1812, and tried to appease the peasants," the latter probably would have supported the French. But Napoleon, ". . . rather than abetting peasant separatist movements, crushed them ruthlessly on behalf of the nobility."[18] The peasants replied with a scorched-earth policy that cost the French dearly.

A hot and dry summer complicated matters. In mid-July, a German mercenary, Captain Franz Roeder, noted in his journal, ". . . if the Russians want to send half our army to the dogs by the winter, all they have to do is to make us march hither and thither with the individual units kept continually under arms. Then if they give us a few battles we shall be in a tough situation, so long as they have plenty of light troops."[19] Such was the isolation of the Grand Army, such its dislocation, that toward the end of July the astute Captain Roeder wrote a book of wisdom in a single sentence: "Every victory is a loss to us."[20]

Alexander had outlined Russian strategy as early as the spring of 1811, when he wrote the King of Prussia: ". . . The system which has made Wellington victorious in Spain, and exhausted the French armies,

15. Carl von Clausewitz, *The Campaign of 1812 in Russia* (London: John Murray, 1843).

16. Caulaincourt, op. cit.

17. Ségur, op. cit.

18. Eugène Tarlé, *Napoleon's Invasion of Russia, 1812* (London: Allen & Unwin, 1942). Tr. G. M.

19. Franz Roeder, *The Ordeal of Captain Roeder* (London: Methuen, 1960). Tr. and ed. Helen Roeder.

20. Ibid.

is what I intend to follow—avoid pitched battles and organize long lines of communication for retreat, leading to entrenched camps. . . ."[21]

Alexander's own ineptness, a divided high command, and the clamor of nobles for action began to jeopardize this strategy in July. Alexander relinquished supreme command in favor of Barclay de Tolly, who continued to retire until forced to fight a holding action at Smolensk in mid-August. This indecisive battle forced Alexander to replace Tolly with a native son, the sixty-seven-year-old Kutuzov, a veteran campaigner who had fought Napoleon at Austerlitz and greatly respected his abilities.

Kutuzov was old and tired and physically a wreck, but he realized more clearly than the other commanders that time was serving Russia's cause. Unfortunately, he was appointed to the supreme command to give battle. For this purpose, he retired on Borodino, where the two armies met on September 7. In the brief engagement, each side suffered enormous losses; on the following day, Kutuzov began a retreat that would take his armies past Moscow.

Kutuzov was right. Far better to let time and space wear down French regiments, let hunger and sickness do the work of bullets. Fear already was infesting French divisions to compound barbaric behavior of the columns: ". . . the wholesale pillaging by the conquering army, by countless marauders, and sometimes by criminal bands of French deserters, caused the peasants' hatred of the enemy to grow from day to day."[22]

This hatred soon inspired the growth of guerrilla bands. Tarlé has given us the genesis of a partisan detachment. At the end of August, a private in the dragoons, an illiterate named Ermolai Chetvertakov, was taken prisoner but escaped to Basmany, in the South. Here he found one supporter. Killing two French stragglers, they took their uniforms, then killed two French cavalrymen and acquired their horses. These successes helped them recruit forty-seven peasants, an ill-armed band that nonetheless killed twelve French cuirassiers, then a group of fifty-nine French. In time, Chetvertakov's band swelled to over three hundred volunteers operating in the large area around Gzhatsk. Later in the campaign, he led over four thousand peasants against a French battalion supported by artillery and forced it to retreat.[23]

Similar bands sprang up across the land. An infantry private, Stepan Eremenko, taken prisoner at Smolensk, escaped and organized a peasant band of three hundred. A peasant named Ermolai Vasilyev recruited a peasant force of about six hundred armed with rifles taken from the French.

21. Markham, op. cit.
22. Tarlé, op. cit.
23. Ibid.

Although Alexander and his generals, most of whom were landowning noblemen, did not want to arm the peasants, the potential of this new force struck a young lieutenant colonel, Denis Davydov, aide to an army commander, Prince Bagration. A few days before the battle of Borodino, Davydov asked Bagration to help him form small cavalry detachments to work with peasant guerrillas in cutting Napoleon's exposed lines of communication. Bagration persuaded Kutuzov to give Davydov fifty hussars and eighty Cossacks. This was the humble beginning of the Cossack-partisan campaign led by such as Figner, Seslavin, Vadbolsky, and Kudashev, many of whose outstanding exploits were later recorded by Davydov in his pioneer work *The Journal of Partisan Actions*.[24]

Captain Roeder graphically described the reaction of his regiment to a partisan attack in October: ". . . this afternoon the news went round that a few hundred armed peasants and Cossacks, who had their base of operations five leagues [10–15 miles] from here [Viazma] had seized the baggage of the Westphalian regiment and murdered the escort. This threw us into a state of unrest and vigilance." One Major Strecker was sent forth on a punitive expedition, his orders being to scour the countryside by shooting any peasants he encountered and burning all dwellings. Roeder sardonically wrote, ". . . I only hope that he omits at least the final measure for our sakes, in order that we may occasionally find somewhere to spend the night!"[25]

Neither Major Strecker nor other commanders assigned to deal with the harassing problem omitted "the final measure," a shortsighted policy that Napoleon probably approved. Certainly his temper was growing short. He should have reached Moscow with two hundred thousand troops; instead, ninety thousand arrived. According to Caulaincourt, the emperor ". . . attributed all his difficulties simply to the trouble caused by the Cossacks . . . he said he had means of obviating this annoyance by placing detachments of infantry in blockhouses linked in a line of defense, and added that, after giving battle to Kutuzov and driving him further back, he would see to the reorganization of all this."[26]

This countermeasure never appeared. For Napoleon, time was running out. Having gained the nothing of Moscow, he learned too late that the Grand Army, what was left of it, owned exactly what it physically occupied—and this was not enough to even feed it. An unidentified Russian officer described the French presence just prior to the retreat: ". . . Every day the soldiers streamed in thousands from the camps to plunder the city, and many thousand others were scattered throughout the countryside foraging and seeking for bread. Peasants armed with staves lay concealed in the woods and marshes and slew hundreds of

24. Ibid.
25. Roeder, op. cit.
26. Caulaincourt, op. cit.

these marauders every day, and those who escaped the peasants fell into the hands of the Cossacks."[27]

Napoleon's army retreated through land that earlier it had helped scorch. Partisan bands allied with Cossack patrols infested the area to harass columns slowed by hunger and frost and by ponderous baggage trains carrying loot stolen from Moscow. As early as November 6, Ségur wrote: ". . . great numbers of men could be seen wandering over the countryside, either alone or in small groups. These were not cowardly deserters: cold and starvation had detached them from their columns. . . . Now they met only armed civilians or Cossacks who fell upon them with ferocious laughter, wounded them, stripped them of everything they had, and left them to perish naked in the snow. These guerrillas . . . kept abreast of the army on both sides of the road, under cover of the trees. They threw back on the deadly highway the soldiers whom they did not finish off with their spears and axes."[28]

Not far from Moscow, a group of partisans captured one unit of nearly two thousand men. Near Smolensk, Napoleon's vital supply depot, Cossacks and partisans drove off fifteen hundred oxen.[29] Finding no forage in Smolensk, Napoleon had one commissary officer after another put on trial until he learned from Jomini ". . . that a woman Praskovya led a small guerrilla group that attacked and destroyed French foragers."[30]

Kutuzov watched these developments from the south. Pressed to attack by his superiors, he refused. Instead, he shadowed the French army, a "parallel pursuit" that covered 120 miles in fifty days. His own army suffered, but not to the extent of the French—the horses improperly shod for ice-covered roads,[31] soldiers frequently reduced to cannibalism,[32] foragers frustrated by frozen fields, and behind those fields and lurking in woods the whole panoply of impassioned peasants and fierce Cossacks —here was a people's war, as Tolstoy put it, ". . . in all its menacing and majestic power; and troubling itself about no question of anyone's tastes or rules, about no fine distinctions, with stupid simplicity, with perfect consistency, it rose and fell and belabored the French until the whole invading army had been driven out."

No one knows the exact toll. Clausewitz later wrote that of the original force, 552,000 remained in Russia dead or prisoner, along with 167,-000 dead horses and some 1,300 captured cannon.[33]

It was a defeat of such proportion that French veterans could not

27. Roeder, op. cit.
28. Ségur, op. cit.
29. Clausewitz, op. cit.
30. Tarlé, op. cit.
31. Markham, op. cit.
32. Tarlé, op. cit.
33. Clausewitz, op. cit.

encompass it when sitting in the village tavern, eyes filled with tears not from smoke alone. The lesson was not altogether ignored when Prussia declared war against Napoleon the following year and proclaimed a *levée en masse:*

". . . Every man not acting in the regular army or *Landwehr* was to support the army by acting against the enemy's communications and rear. The people were to fight to the death and with every means in their power. The enemy was to be harassed, his supplies cut off and his stragglers massacred. No uniforms were to be worn, and on the enemy's approach, after all food stocks had been destroyed, and mills, bridges, and boats burnt, the villages were to be abandoned and refuge sought in the woods and hills."[34]

34. Fuller (*The Conduct of War, 1789–1961*), *supra.*

Chapter 11

Clausewitz and Jomini on guerrilla war • The French land in Algeria • Abd-el-Kader leads the resistance • Clauzel's strategy and defeat • Valée's Great Wall • Bugeaud's tactics • Shamyl and the Caucasus • Guerrilla warfare in Burma, Africa and New Zealand • The Seminole war in Florida • Effects of industrial revolution on guerrilla warfare • The American Civil War • Forrest, Morgan and Mosby • Sheridan's countertactics • Pope's policy

LESSONS offered by Napoleon's tragic experiences with guerrilla warfare went largely unheeded by later military commanders. After 1815, warfare in Europe went into partial eclipse. Napoleon's "total wars" had taken the starch out of Europe, just as had the earlier Hundred Years' War, Thirty Years' War, and Seven Years' War. Worn by twenty years of battles, European states welcomed a political status quo as determined at the Congress of Vienna and maintained by regular standing armies whose autocratic leadership stultified any attempt to expand the organizational and tactical reforms suggested either by the Napoleonic wars or by the technological progress inherent in the Industrial Revolution. Aside from maintaining internal order and fighting occasional conventional campaigns such as Field Marshal Radetzky's victory over the Piedmontese at Novara, in 1849, the great powers, particularly England, confined themselves to waging colonial wars. From 1815 to 1854, no British army even saw service on the Continent.

In this tactically dormant period, the lessons of Bonaparte's campaigns in Spain and Russia were all but ignored. Neither victorious nor defeated generals wanted to credit rabble action, nor did governments wish to give peasants any notion of exalted status. Napoleon later blamed his difficulties in Russia on the Cossacks, not the partisans. Most guerrilla leaders of the period faded to an illiterate obscurity, unhonored and unsung except in peasant folklore.

Although a paucity of qualified military analysts existed, two principal theorists did emerge in the wake of Napoleonic destruction. Clausewitz, in his famous unfinished treatise *On War* (*Vom Kriege*), only touched lightly on partisan warfare, in a short chapter called "Arming the Nation." A "Prussianized Pole," Clausewitz served extensively in the Napoleonic wars but experienced minimum contact with the battlefield—to the extent that the British war historian Sir James Edmonds later wrote that he ". . . seems to have been a courtier rather than a professional soldier."[1] Although recognizing the "new power" of a "people's war," he saw this in terms of a *levée en masse* that favored the defense. Such a war could only be fought under suitable tactical and psychological conditions; moreover, ". . . we must imagine a people-War in combination with a War carried on by a regular Army, and both carried on according to a plan embracing the operations of the whole."[2]

Partisan operations were to be sharply circumscribed. Neither national levies nor armed peasantry were to attack an enemy army: ". . . They must not attempt to crack the nut, they must only gnaw on the surface and the borders. . . ." Although their potential was definitely limited, ". . . still we must admit that armed peasants are not to be driven before us in the same way as a body of soldiers who keep together like a herd of cattle, and usually follow their noses. Armed peasants, on the contrary, when broken, disperse in all directions, for which no formal plan is required; through this circumstance, the march of every small body of troops in a mountainous, thickly wooded, or even broken country, becomes a service of a very dangerous character, for at any moment a combat may arise on the march; if in point of fact no armed bodies have even been seen for some time, yet the same

1. James E. Edmonds, "Jomini and Clausewitz," *Army Quarterly,* April 1951; see also R. A. Leonard, *A Short Guide to Clausewitz on War* (London: Weidenfeld & Nicholson, 1967); Anatol Rapoport (ed.), *Clausewitz on War* (London: Penguin Books, 1968); Peter Paret and John Shy, *Guerrillas in the 1960s* (London: Pall Mall Press, 1962); Michael Howard, "Jomini and the Classical Tradition in Military Thought." In *Studies in War and Peace* (London: Maurice Temple Smith, 1970).

2. Carl von Clausewitz, *On War* (London: Routledge & Kegan Paul, 1968), Vol. 2 of 3 vols. Tr. J. J. Graham.

peasants already driven off by the head of a column, may at any hour make their appearance in its rear."[3]

Clausewitz pictured partisans as "a kind of nebulous vapory essence." They should ". . . never condense into a solid body; otherwise the enemy sends an adequate force against this core, crushes it, and makes a great many prisoners; their courage sinks; every one thinks the main question is decided, any further effort useless, and the arms fall from the hands of the people . . . on the other hand, it is necessary that this mist should collect at some points into denser masses, and form threatening clouds from which now and again a formidable flash of lightning may burst forth. . . ."

The enemy can only guard against small partisan actions by ". . . detaching numerous parties to furnish escorts for convoys, to occupy military stations, defiles, bridges, etc." His larger garrisons in the rear will remain subject to partisan attack; his force as a whole will suffer "a feeling of uneasiness and dread."[4]

One cannot fault this confirmation of the auxiliary-partisan role, and it is a pity that Clausewitz did not expand his thinking. His own experience in partisan warfare was extremely limited, and apparently so was his historical appreciation of the subject. He found partisan warfare ". . . as yet of rare occurrence generally, and . . . but imperfectly treated of by those who have had actual experience for any length of time. . . ." "A People's War in civilized Europe," he held, "is a phenomenon of the nineteenth century":

. . . It has its advocates and its opponents: the latter either considering it in a political sense as a revolutionary means, a state of anarchy declared lawful, which is as dangerous as a foreign enemy to social order at home; or on military grounds, conceiving that the result is not commensurate with the expenditure of the nation's strength.[5]

Neither Clausewitz's treatment nor his turgid presentation of the subject was apt to arouse much interest in its potential. His incomplete and highly abstruse work was published posthumously in German in 1831. Colonel Graham's English translation did not appear until 1873.[6]

The other leading analyst of the day, General Baron de Jomini, a Swiss officer with considerable battlefield experience in Napoleonic warfare, did not publish his principal study, *A Treatise on the Art of War* (*Précis de l'art de la guerre*), until 1838.[7] As opposed to Clausewitz, who dwelt in Kantian clouds of theory, Jomini realistically (and professionally) analyzed strategy, tactics, and logistics (the word was in cur-

3. Ibid.
4. Ibid.
5. Ibid.
6. Edmonds, op. cit.
7. Baron de Jomini, *The Art of War* (Philadelphia: J. B. Lippincott, 1879).

rent use) from the standpoint of both ancient and contemporary campaigns in an attempt to establish basic principles of war. His work won almost immediate popularity in the West; Edmonds has written that it "was studied everywhere" until placed into eclipse by German victories in 1870–71, which signaled the rise of Clausewitzian influence.

Jomini's opening chapter can still be read with profit. In discussing wars of intervention, for example, he wrote:

. . . When a state intervenes with only a small contingent, in obedience to treaty-stipulations, it is simply an accessory, and has but little voice in the main operations; but when it intervenes as a principal party, and with an imposing force, the case is quite different.

In either instance, ". . . the safety of the army may be endangered by these distant interventions. The counterbalancing advantage is that its own territory cannot then be easily invaded, since the scene of hostilities is so distant; so that what may be a misfortune for the general may be, in a measure, an advantage to the state." Nonetheless, care must be exercised:

. . . In wars of this character the essentials are to secure a general who is both a statesman and a soldier; to have clear stipulations with the allies as to the part to be taken by each in the principal operations; finally, to agree upon an objective point which shall be in harmony with the common interests. By the neglect of these precautions, the greater number of coalitions have failed, or have maintained a difficult struggle with a power more united but weaker than the allies.

In codifying various types of wars, Jomini introduced a separate category, "Wars of opinion."

. . . Wars of opinion between two states belong also to the class of wars of intervention; for they result either from doctrines which one party desires to propagate among its neighbors, or from dogmas which it desires to crush, —in both cases leading to intervention. Although originating in religious or political dogmas, these wars are most deplorable; for, like national wars, they enlist the worst passions, and become vindictive, cruel, and terrible.

After pointing out that religion is often ". . . the pretext to obtain political power, and the war is not really one of dogmas," dogma nonetheless ". . . is a powerful ally; for it excites the ardor of the people, and also creates a party. . . . It may, however, happen, as in the Crusades and the wars of Islamism, that the dogma for which the war is waged, instead of friends, finds only bitter enemies in the country invaded; and then the contest becomes fearful."

. . . The chances of support and resistance in wars of political opinions are about equal. It may be recollected how in 1792 associations of fanatics thought it possible to propagate throughout Europe the famous declaration of the rights of man, and how governments became justly alarmed, and rushed to arms probably with the intention of only forcing the lava of this volcano back into its crater and there extinguishing it. The means were not fortunate; for war and aggression are inappropriate measures for arresting an evil which lies wholly in the human passions, excited in a temporary paroxysm, of less duration as it is the more violent. Time is the true remedy for all bad passions and for all anarchical doctrines. A civilized nation may bear the yoke of a factious and unrestrained multitude for a short interval; but these storms soon pass away, and reason resumes her sway. To attempt to restrain such a mob by a foreign force is to attempt to restrain the explosion of a mine when the powder has already been ignited: it is far better to await the explosion and afterward fill up the crater than to try to prevent it and to perish in the attempt.

Jomini's personal experience in guerrilla warfare, as opposed to Clausewitz, was considerable, but he still treated the subject cautiously, as though he were Pandora well aware of the disruptive force of winds. "National wars," he thought, "are the most formidable of all."

. . . This name can only be applied to such as are waged against a united people, or a great majority of them, filled with a noble ardor and determined to sustain their independence: then every step is disputed, the army holds only its camp-ground, its supplies can only be obtained at the point of the sword, and its convoys are everywhere threatened or captured.

The spectacle of a spontaneous uprising of a nation is rarely seen; and, though there be in it something grand and noble which commands our admiration, the consequences are so terrible that, for the sake of humanity, we ought to hope never to see it. . . .

This uprising may be produced by the most opposite causes. The serfs may rise in a body at the call of the government, and their masters, affected by a noble love of their sovereign and country, may set them the example and take the command of them; and, similarly, a fanatical people may arm under the appeal of its priests; or a people enthusiastic in its political opinions, or animated by a sacred love of its institutions, may rush to meet the enemy in defense of all it holds dear.

After discussing the advantages of forests and mountains to national wars, and offering examples, many already familiar to us, Jomini, with the French disaster in Spain in mind, wrote:

. . . The difficulties are particularly great when the people are supported by a considerable nucleus of disciplined troops. The invader has only an army: his adversaries have an army, and a people wholly or almost wholly in arms, and making means of resistance out of every thing, each individual of whom conspires against the common enemy; even the non-combatants have an interest in his ruin and accelerate it by every means in their power. He holds scarcely any ground but that upon which he encamps; outside the limits of his camp every thing is hostile and multiplies a thousandfold the difficulties he meets at every step.

These obstacles become almost insurmountable when the country is difficult. Each armed inhabitant knows the smallest paths and their connections; he finds everywhere a relative or friend who aids him; the commanders also know the country, and, learning immediately the slightest movement on the part of the invader, can adopt the best measures to defeat his projects; while the latter, without information of their movements, and not in a condition to send out detachments to gain it, having no resource but in his bayonets, and certain safety only in the concentration of his columns, is like a blind man: his combinations are failures; and when, after the most carefully-concerted movements and the most rapid and fatiguing marches, he thinks he is about to accomplish his aim and deal a terrible blow, he finds no sign of the enemy but his campfires: so that while, like Don Quixote, he is attacking windmills, his adversary is on his line of communications, destroys the detachments left to guard it, surprises his convoys, his depots, and carries on a war so disastrous for the invader that he must inevitably yield after a time.[8]

Jomini was closer to the mark of guerrilla warfare than Clausewitz, but neither treatise satisfied the immediate military needs of colonial warfare. Neither spoke of changing objectives or of tactics suitable to defeat thousands of mounted natives with a few hundred regular cavalry, or the proper method of controlling hundreds of square miles with under-strength forces. Nowhere in Clausewitz or Jomini is the tactical adaptation suggested that made the "thin red line," the infantry square, the cavalry squadron, or the gunboat as familiar to professional soldiers as the conventional maneuvers of Napoleonic warfare were to another generation. And yet, a year before Clausewitz died and while Jomini was hard at work on the *Précis,* warfare was already pursuing a tangential course that often mocked mere conventional thought and practice.

Before either Clausewitz or Jomini appeared in print, the French became involved in a major colonial campaign in North Africa.

In the early-nineteenth century, Turkey held Algeria in loose hegemony, ruling through a dey of Algiers, whose army frequently had to fight inland Arab-Berber tribes. The dey's relationship with Europe was none too healthy, since his ports traditionally sheltered pirates who preyed on Western shipping. In 1827, the dey insulted the French consul over a commercial matter, and added injury by allegedly striking him with a peacock-feather fly whisk. Three years later, Charles X, needing a diversion for his unhappy regime (soon to end), dispatched an expeditionary force of thirty-five thousand troops, which easily cap-

8. Ibid.

tured Algiers. Marshal Louis de Bourmont announced: ". . . the whole kingdom of Algeria will probably surrender within fifteen days, without our having to fire another shot."[9] With that, he pushed inland to subdue the tribes.

From the beginning, French military behavior left considerable to be desired. A British admiral and student of the period, C. V. Usborne, later wrote:

. . . To obtain wood for their fires soldiers tore down the doors of houses or cut down fruit trees; they smashed beautiful marble fountains for the pleasure of destruction. They even destroyed aqueducts, which resulted in their own army being short of water. At Blida, taken without resistance on 19 November, 1830, everyone found armed over a large area was shot out of hand. The punitive destruction of crops resulted in scarcity for the army in the following year.[10]

The French expedition caused a famous marabout or holy man, Mahi ed Dine, to proclaim a *jihad,* or holy war, under the military command of his son, Abd-el-Kader.

Sidi-el-Hadji-Abd-el-Kader-Uled-Mahiddin had only a few more years than names. Twenty-four years old, he was a small man ". . . with a long, deadly-pale face, and languishing eyes, an aquiline nose, small, delicate mouth, thin, dark chestnut beard, and slight mustache. He had exquisitely formed hands and feet, which he was continually washing and trimming with a small knife."[11]

Nobly descended from the caliphs of Fatima, the young Mohammedan was generalissimo of several Berber tribes. Upon the outbreak of war, he collected his people in a *smala,* a mobile headquarters of wives, booty, horses, "and a whole army of women and retainers" that at one point numbered sixty thousand, and took to the land.

Abd-el-Kader at first ran rings around ponderous French columns, and might well have driven the French from the land but for one major failing: he could not persuade heterogeneous tribes to join in organized, central government, whose weight he needed to beat the French. The tribes nevertheless fought hard, their motivation being clear in an official report made by the newly appointed Commission on Africa to King Louis Philippe in 1833:

. . . We [France] have seized private properties with no compensation; we have even forced expropriated proprietors to pay for the demolition of their

9. Edward Behr, *The Algerian Problem* (London: Hodder & Stoughton, 1961); see also Tanya Matthews, *Algerian ABC* (London: Geoffrey Chapman, 1961); Joan Gillespie, *Algeria—Rebellion and Revolution* (London: Ernest Benn, 1960).

10. C. V. Usborne, *The Conquest of Morocco* (London: Stanley Paul, 1936).

11. Standing, op. cit.; see also Félix Ponteil, *L'Éveil des Nationalités et le Mouvement Libéral* (Paris: Presses Universitaires de France, 1968).

houses. We have profaned mosques and graves. We have sent to their death, on mere hearsay and without trial, people whose guilt is extremely doubtful. We have murdered people carrying safe-conducts; killed off, on a mere suspicion, whole populations who have since been found innocent; we have put on their trial men regarded as holy in their countryside, because they have had the courage to speak up for their unhappy compatriots. . . . We have surpassed in barbarity the barbarians we came to civilize—and we complain of having no success with them.[12]

When the 1834 peace treaty broke down, the king sent a dashing general, Count Bernard Clauzel, to deal with the stubborn tribesmen. Clauzel had fought in Spain under Marmont, but nothing of the experience with Spanish guerrillas brushed off. Recruiting several regiments of Zouave mercenaries, he undertook a series of expeditions that posed but slight threat to highly mobile Algerian forces. Clauzel exaggerated his reports of success and continued to demand more troops. A major defeat while marching on Constantine cost him his job.[13]

French strategy changed in 1836, when General Bugeaud arrived in western Algeria with some reinforcements. Bugeaud, also a veteran of the Spanish wars, had learned something about guerrilla warfare. After intensively training his troops, he outfitted flying columns and dispensed with ponderous baggage trains in favor of mules and camels. A month later, he beat the emir at Sikkah.[14]

General Valée now assumed supreme command and managed to forge a shaky treaty that let France get on with the colonization effort in the occupied area. But, two years later, Abd-el-Kader reopened hostilities. Valée, who commanded a total force of about fifty thousand, hit on a new strategy. As he wrote the Minister of War in Paris:

. . . in Africa war must be defensive. The Arab will flee constantly before our columns, allowing them to advance as far as the necessity for revictualling them will permit, and he will then return, giving to their withdrawal the appearance of a reverse. Clever tactics in Africa consist of drawing on the Arabs to fight. With this object one must make permanent works. . . . They will certainly attack them. Our success in a battle on a position chosen beforehand will be certain, and the terror which will follow a defeat will bring about the submission of neighboring tribes.[15]

Before anyone in Paris could object, Valée manned a number of posts, ". . . all of which were invested and their communications cut. Strong columns were required to revictual them, and terrible losses resulted. . . . Disaster followed disaster." Valée also started to construct ". . .

12. Matthews, op. cit.
13. Behr, op. cit.
14. Ponteil, op. cit.
15. Usborne, op. cit.

a continuous obstacle round the occupied zone, irreverently called the Great Wall of China." This was to be 120 miles long, an "impassable" ditch supported by 160 blockhouses.[16]

At this point, General Bugeaud replaced Valée. The fiery Bugeaud took instant exception to the Great Wall theory. He reported to his superiors in Paris: ". . . I estimate that in summer four regiments will not be enough to guard the obstacle which will yield seven or eight hundred casualties through sickness in five months. From the moment it is finished war will be impossible outside it. We must withdraw the garrisons of Médéa and Miliana and shut ourselves up in a pestilential area. The army will thus have dug its own grave."[17]

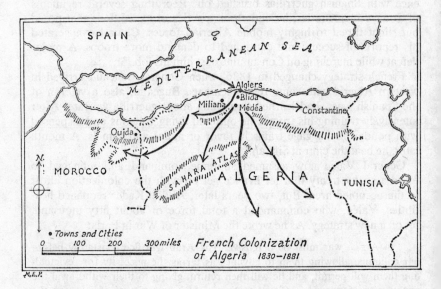

Bugeaud insisted instead on expanding the flying-column tactic. "Père," or "Father," Bugeaud, as his troops called him, had come from the ranks, which was rare enough in that day, but, even more rare, he understood the value of "the ruse, the raid, and the ambush." To accomplish these, he formed and trained small, fast-moving task forces, ". . . a few battalions of infantry, a couple of squadrons of cavalry, two mountain howitzers, a small transport train on mule and camel back."[18] By increased mobility, he gained contact with the emir's troops, then beat them with disciplined firepower. One of his officers, the dashing Saint-

16. Ibid.
17. Ibid.; see also Paul Azan (ed.), *Par l'Épée et par la Charrue—Écrits et Discours de Bugeaud* (Paris: Presses Universitaires de France, 1948).
18. Standing, op. cit.

Arnaud, who later commanded the French army in the Crimea, wrote: ". . . He fights when he wishes, he searches, he pursues the enemy, worries him, and makes him afraid."[19]

Bugeaud's flying columns won a number of important tribal submissions, which the general hastened to exploit with constructive occupation: "The sword only prepared the way for the plough." A mere punitive column advancing into the desert ". . . left no more lasting effect than the wake of a ship in the sea." Bugeaud nonetheless depended more on fear than on persuasion. To bring nomads to heel, he relied chiefly on the *razzia,* or scorched-earth policy, which he ". . . turned into a doctrine of war." Saint-Arnaud wrote: ". . . We have burned everything, destroyed everything. How many women and children have died of cold and fatigue!"[20]

Tribesmen replied in kind, torturing and mutilating captured French soldiers. At times, the French army practiced genocide, as when Colonel Pélissier

. . . lighted fires at the mouth of a cave in which five hundred men, women and children had taken refuge, and all but ten were asphyxiated. *L'affaire des grottes* reached Paris, and became a scandal, denounced in the French Senate as "the calculated, cold-blooded murder of a defenseless enemy. . . ."[21]

The resultant outcry did not prevent the practice from continuing—the government merely imposed stricter censorship.

Realizing that the emir had to be defeated, Bugeaud continued to aim at the *smala,* the emir's floating political-military headquarters. This was eventually smashed by an attack in the best G. A. Henty tradition. King Louis Philippe's son, the Duc d'Aumale, led a cavalry charge of six hundred tired troopers into the teeth of five thousand surprised Berbers. The natives broke and ran, and the young prince captured four thousand prisoners including the emir's mother, his favorite wife, and vast treasure.[22]

As Bugeaud anticipated, this broke organized resistance. The emir now sought sanctuary in Morocco, where Emperor Abd-er-Rahman began helping him rebuild his force. Without gaining permission from Paris, Bugeaud immediately violated this border sanctuary to meet the Moorish army, some 45,000 horsemen, concentrated at the Isly. Bugeaud's force amounted to 6,500 infantry and 1,500 cavalry. Explaining to his troops, that ". . . they are a mob, while we are an army," he at once attacked, and in August 1844, decisively beat them.[23] The sub-

19. Ibid.
20. Behr, op. cit.
21. Ibid.
22. Callwell, op. cit.
23. Usborne, op. cit.

sequent Treaty of Tangier, signed with the Moroccan sultan, provided a wedge for later French expansion into that country.[24]

Bugeaud now claimed most of Algeria and set about administering it through an Arab Bureau, whose officers ". . . had extensive powers, dealt with military and legal matters, collected taxes and engaged in military intelligence activities." Bugeaud's success brought a new horde of European colonists, and, from 1844 onward, the Europeans grew in power while claiming the best farmlands and other concessions at the expense of the tribes.[25]

Abd-el-Kader survived three more years as a fugitive. Finally surrendering, he received a handsome pension from the French, who sent him to Damascus, where he died at the age of seventy-six.[26] His capture did not end resistance, particularly in the Kabylie, where uprisings continued until 1881 and even later.

When Abd-el-Kader began fighting the French, a Mohammedan priest or mullah the Tartar Shamyl, evoked a holy war against the Russians. The czar's army was determined to subdue the rugged Caucasus, some three hundred thousand square miles ". . . of mountains, table-lands, rapid and shallow rivers," the home of Lezghians, Georgians, and Chechens, the land of Daghestan, where ". . . they think no more of taking a life than of taking a cup of tea."[27]

The best modern treatment of this fascinating campaign, in the author's opinion, is found in Lesley Branche's entertaining book *The Sabres of Paradise.*[28] To defy the Russian intruder, Shamyl led his people to the mountains. There he easily repulsed the first forces to come after him. Not least of his advantages was superior firepower, gained from smuggled rifles, the Russian troops being armed only with smoothbore weapons. The enemy also suffered from overconfidence. In 1837, the visiting Czar Nicholas asked some assembled chiefs, "Do you know that I have powder enough to blow up all your mountains?" On another occasion, General Veliamonif told the natives that ". . . if the sky were to fall the soldiers of Russia were numerous enough to prop it up on their bayonets."[29]

This surfeit of manpower and powder was just as well. Expedition after expedition returned from the mountains to report heavy losses against the achievement of a few burned villages. Occasionally, concen-

24. Stéphane Bernard, *The Franco-Moroccan Conflict, 1943–1956* (New Haven, Conn.: Yale University Press, 1968).
25. Gillespie, op. cit.
26. Standing, op. cit.
27. Ibid.; see also S. F. Platonov, *History of Russia* (London: Macmillan, 1925). Tr. E. Aronsberg.
28. Lesley Branche, *The Sabres of Paradise* (London: John Murray, 1960).
29. Standing, op. cit.

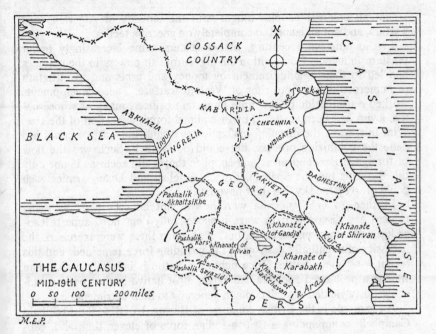

THE CAUCASUS
MID-19th CENTURY
0   50   100   200 miles

M.E.P.

trated forces supported by artillery surprised the guerrillas, and Shamyl was surrounded and twice just barely escaped.

He soon collected another force, however. To insure replacements, he had divided Daghestan into twenty provinces, ". . . placing each under a *naib,* who was bound to provide two hundred horsemen at his bidding. The male population from fifteen to fifty were armed and drilled, and a postal service and foundry for ordnance established. Schamyl's personal command consisted of a thousand superb cavalry. . . ."[30]

Shamyl was also greatly assisted by France and England prior to the outbreak of the Crimean War, in 1854. In one sense, this aid backfired: armaments included artillery pieces which, in untrained hands of the Tartars, proved of little more than nuisance value. Yet Shamyl's insistence on using and protecting his precious guns led him to use more-conventional tactics and resulted in set-piece battles in which he was defeated. This error, combined with an increase in Russian strength at the end of the Crimean War, eventually caused him to surrender. As with Abd-el-Kader, he received a generous pension. He died while on pilgrimage to Mecca.

30. Ibid.

Not all colonial peoples fought with the tenacity of Algerians and Tartars, and not all leaned so completely on guerrilla tactics.

In the nineteenth century, native leaders came increasingly under Western influence. Competition among European powers in the colonies had led to their aggrandizement by money and arms and to initiation of numerous natives into rites of Western warfare. These developments worked on the pride of the more important princes, many of whose native levies had been scattered by disciplined forces a fraction of the size. With this, came the dawning realization that guerrilla warfare could impede the colonizing process, but could not stop it. Such was the flow of foreign troops and arms and supplies that it did seem as if not only the Russians but the Spanish, French, English and Dutch armies each could prop up the sky "on their bayonets."

Further, to fight guerrilla warfare was not an easy task, as many princes had discovered: to wage it successfully demanded superb leadership and enormous patience, but, even when these were exercised, the necessity of eventually destroying the intruding force remained, and this meant a set-piece battle. Since fighting a battle is infinitely easier than waging a prolonged guerrilla campaign, most native leaders perhaps unconsciously yielded to such contact, generally to their detriment.

An example is the British conquest of Burma. In 1824, Sir Archibald Campbell, commanding a British-Indian force of eleven thousand, captured Rangoon and turned north in pursuit of the Burman leader Bundoola, whose headquarters were at Ava, on the Irrawaddy.

Campbell's columns immediately struck a series of fortified stockades, ". . . successive lines of tree-trunks, planted firmly in the ground and laced together with creepers."[31] These defended obstacles forced British columns to deploy and attack. The Burmese would then float away; the British would have to re-form and finally resume their march.

By such methods, Bundoola more than held his own, but in 1825 he foolishly accepted battle and was killed. At this time, Campbell's once-splendid force *numbered thirteen hundred men fit for duty.* With Bundoola out of the way, however, much of the starch disappeared from Burmese resistance. Once reinforcements arrived, Campbell pushed four hundred miles up the Irrawaddy and, in a final set-piece battle, ended the war in his favor.

Native willingness to stand and fight and even to charge invading forces resulted in hundreds of colonial battles in which firepower and disciplined tactics generally proved superior. The colonizing process continued difficult, however. In Burma, Campbell's original regiments had been practically wiped out, with ". . . six out of every seven men engaged becoming casualties, mainly through sickness."[32] In subjugating Madagascar, the French suffered forty-two hundred deaths in only

31. Cole, op. cit.
32. Ibid.

ten months, the result of trying to construct a road through pestilential terrain rather than resistance offered by the Hovas.

Commanders had to remain constantly alert for tactical tricks, invariably some form of ambush that had to be matched by tactical modifications. In Africa, in 1834, Colonel Harry Smith, a Peninsular veteran, formed fast-moving mounted columns to fight the Kaffirs with tactics based on mobility and surprise. In New Zealand, in 1845, the British under Captain George Grey came up against Maori defenses not unlike those Campbell had encountered in Burma. The Maori fortified stockade, called a *pa,* was built sufficiently well to withstand field-artillery fire, and its defenders were quite well sheltered in pits. When a *pa* began to give way, the Maoris retired. Grey beat this system by bringing up heavy artillery and by outflanking the positions, and, when these tactics brought victory, he converted it to peace, if only temporary, by just, and even compassionate, terms.

Until the enemy could be brought to fight, this type of campaign called for extreme patience and tactical imagination. Sometimes the combination of terrain, disease, and enemy cunning proved too formidable even for regular forces, particularly if they were inexperienced and limited in number. In North America, in 1835, a Seminole Indian ambush of Captain Dade's army column in Florida opened a six-year guerrilla campaign that heavily taxed slim army-navy-marine resources. As Professor Weigley has pointed out, the Army at the time

. . . was not much better prepared for guerrilla warfare against the Seminoles in Florida than Napoleon's soldiers had been for the guerrillas of Spain. This was true despite experience in fighting forest Indians and the irregular campaigns that Americans themselves had sometimes waged during the Revolution. A historical pattern was beginning to work itself out: occasionally the American Army has had to wage a guerrilla war, but guerrilla warfare is so incongruous to the natural methods and habits of a stable and well-to-do society that the American Army has tended to regard it as abnormal and to forget about it whenever possible.

At first, various generals tried unsuccessfully to bring the Seminoles to battle. Quartermaster General Thomas Jesup grew so frustrated that he resorted to an ugly expedient used two thousand years earlier by the Romans in Spain: He brought Seminole chieftain Osceola to council under a flag of truce and then imprisoned him, an act which ". . . outraged public opinion and Congress, and the effect on the Seminoles seems to have been mainly to infuriate them and stimulate their resistance." Colonel Zachary Taylor fared better. After beating the Indians in a pitched battle, he began a pacification program:

. . . he divided the entire disaffected region into districts twenty miles square, proposed to establish a stockade and a garrison in each district, and commissioned each district commandant to comb his district on alternate days.

Before this had a chance to work, a disagreement caused Taylor to ask for relief. His successor, Colonel William J. Worth, indulged a punitive campaign, burning crops and dwellings, which he sustained straight through 1841:

. . . The cost to Worth's own men in fever and dysentery was high, but the method succeeded. The Indians were broken into small bands that barely subsisted, and concerted resistance to United States authority came to an end.[33]

Even where force of arms told and treaties were signed, the pacification process continued. Throughout the century, dissident tribes and nations continued to revolt in Africa, India, and Burma, just as Indian tribes continued to rise in the western part of North America.

But these isolated efforts were increasingly doomed, for, where the native found it difficult if not impossible to repair losses in men and material while maintaining tribal cohesion sufficient to wage war, the Industrial Revolution was constantly increasing the capability of colonizing powers to fight prolonged campaigns. Not only did growing populations furnish manpower necessary to sustain colonial wars, particularly when nations refrained from fighting each other at home, but such technological improvements as the percussion cap and more accurate artillery greatly enhanced the striking power of expeditionary forces against native irregulars.

These new weapons scarcely eliminated the guerrilla. By adding weight to war already heavy, they eventually were going to ease his task. If the percussion cap reduced rifle misfires from 40 per cent to 4 per cent, and if the breech-loading rifled artillery piece increased rate and accuracy of fire, they also demanded far more ammunition, which meant increasingly large and vulnerable logistic "tails." If improved agricultural and industrial production could support larger armies fighting in diverse theaters of war, these still had to be moved, controlled and supplied by the railroad and telegraph, which were particularly vulnerable to enemy action.

The American Civil War displayed to the world the awesome influence of technology on war, particularly the killing power of rifle and cannon in defense, but it also produced some lively examples of army vulnerability to partisan warfare.

From the beginning, the war featured definite guerrilla overtones—not unnaturally, since the South was numerically inferior and since the war quickly spread to diverse areas, some highly favorable to guerrilla tactics. Moreover, by environment and temperament, the Southerner naturally inclined to irregular war.

This showed even on the battlefield, where the Confederate soldier's highly individualistic comportment contrasted strongly to formal Union

33. Weigley, op. cit.

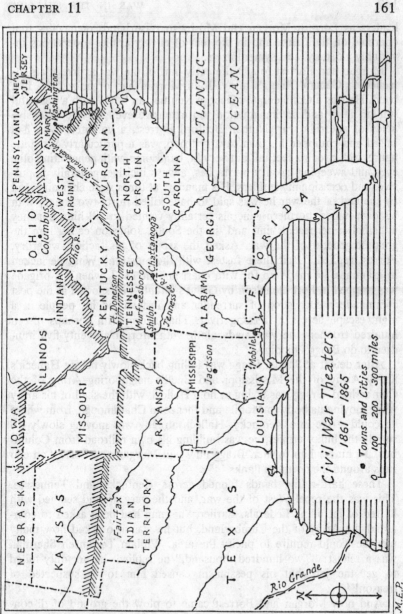

Civil War Theaters
1861 – 1865

● Towns and Cities

0   100   200   300 miles

ranks. The Confederate, undisciplined but intensely enthusiastic, fought more as an independent skirmisher. As Fuller noted ". . . the Federal soldier was semi-regular and the Confederate semi-guerrilla." The South wisely exploited this capability by allowing such capable if flamboyant leaders as Forrest, Morgan and Mosby to raise bands of cavalry that operated on the flanks and in the rear of enemy armies—operations invariably aided by local sympathizers.

Morgan and Forrest fought the early part of the war as irregulars attached to General Bragg's army. John Morgan had organized the first band. He was a Confederate officer, a Kentuckian ". . . with a beautiful suit of hair" and an imagination too extensive even for the extensive fields of guerrilla war. Nathan Bedford Forrest, a volunteer who had raised and equipped his own cavalry troop, was a particularly romantic figure, well over six feet tall but very fit, handsome, with penetrating blue eyes and sweeping cavalry mustaches, always incisive, generally impulsive, and occasionally ruthless. His manners at times were charming, but by the end of the war he was said to have killed thirty-two enemy with his own hands; northern generals certainly wanted to kill him, but they nonetheless respected him, and, in the South, Johnston called him the greatest general of the war. Asked the secret of his tactical wizardry, Forrest replied, "I git there fustest with the mostest." What he lacked in grammar, he made up for with charisma. In 1862, when his brigade was trapped in Fort Donelson by Grant's infantry, he snorted at the post commander's suggestion of surrender and instead led his people in a night escape across a freezing river. That spring with perhaps fifteen hundred troopers, he was ready along with Morgan's twenty-five hundred to do Bragg's bidding.

After defeat at Shiloh, Bragg was falling back slowly before Halleck's heavy Army of the Mississippi and Buell's neighboring Army of the Cumberland. Bragg was trying to hold Halleck with the shell of his army while moving its body to Mobile and thence to Chattanooga, from where he could strike into Kentucky. Halleck already was moving slowly—to supply the bulky armies, he was building his own railroad from Columbus. To hinder him further, Bragg now sent Morgan and Forrest on end runs around the northern flanks.

These hard-riding bands fanned across Kentucky and Tennessee. This was the rebel West of the war, and the very ground seethed with hatred of intruding Federals. Earlier, Sherman had been asked to command the Army of the Cumberland, but he was also asked how many men he would require to pacify the area. William Tecumseh Sherman was a realist: "Two hundred thousand," he replied—he not only failed to get the job, but his pessimism caused him to be suspected of treason![34]

And now Morgan and Forrest came to plow the ground of discontent. They found local partisans galore—partisans ready to join their bands, partisans to scout and report enemy dispositions, partisans to

34. Fletcher Pratt, *A Short History of the Civil War* (New York: Pocket Books, 1948).

help them fall on isolated garrisons, burn ammunition and stores, capture prisoners, cut railroad and telegraph lines—in general, make life a festering hell for the confused Northerners.

Forrest's raid culminated in a splendid *coup de guerre,* the capture of Crittenden's reinforced brigade at Murfreesboro, a gigantic bluff in view of Forrest's meager force, but one that worked and allowed him to destroy half a million dollars' worth of Federal supplies as well.

Morgan also prospered. In turning Union defenses upside down, he suffered a hundred casualties but took over a thousand prisoners and, by brisk recruiting among partisans, enlarged his band from nine hundred to two thousand. Grant, who had replaced Halleck, had to pull infantry from his line to serve as railroad guards. Such was the manpower drain that he asked to abandon the railroad, but Halleck, now in Washington, disapproved this. His progress became snaillike; Bragg beat him and Buell to Chattanooga, and the war went on.

Forrest continued screening Bragg's flanks and striking at opportune targets. In December, he bailed Bragg out again by hitting Grant's lines of communication between Jackson and Columbus. After knocking out seven hundred Union cavalry, ". . . he started along the railroad, eating up the line and the small posts that protected it as a robin eats a worm. His flank-guards roamed fearlessly through the countryside, the telegraph wires went down everywhere and Union regiments wandered helplessly in a land of no information, searching for him while he made his way back to the Tennessee [River], the flatboat and eventually to the flanks of Bragg's command. Grant's supply line was ruined, it would take months to rebuild it and for more than a week he had not even telegraphic communication with the north."[35]

In the spring of 1863, Bragg sent Morgan on another raid to throw the Army of the Cumberland off balance. Morgan performed brilliantly, burning, destroying, capturing prisoners, tapping telegraph wires to send false orders to Union commanders, tearing down wires, eluding regiments and divisions sent to get him. So successful were his operations that he disobeyed orders and crossed the Ohio River to fight in Indiana and Ohio. His was a fantastic effort, altogether covering over a thousand miles in twenty-four days. But, as Federal forces and local militias turned out, his casualties grew heavy, his men and mounts tired, and finally he surrendered with the remnants of his band.[36]

A third Confederate officer, a small and wiry man named John Mosby, was more fortunate. Serving under Jeb Stuart as a captain, Mosby took twenty-nine volunteer troopers through enemy lines to General Stoughton's headquarters, north of Fairfax. With incredible audac-

---

35. Ibid.
36. He later escaped from a prison camp but was killed leading a cavalry charge at Knoxville.

ity, he personally penetrated the general's headquarters, reached his bedroom, awakened him, and told him he was prisoner. To eliminate argument, he added, "Stuart's cavalry are in possession of the place [which in a sense was true] and Stonewall Jackson holds Centreville [not true]." The ensuing dialogue remains an all-time classic in the department of captured West Pointers:

STOUGHTON: "Is [General] Fitzhugh Lee here?"
MOSBY: "Yes."
STOUGHTON: "Then take me to him. We were classmates."

(This order may explain President Lincoln's remark upon being told of the capture of Stoughton and a number of horses: "Well, there won't be any difficulty in making another general, but how am I to replace those horses?"[37])

Based in the Shenandoah Valley and supported by partisans, Mosby continued his whirlwind raids to increasing Federal fury. As opposed to Forrest and Morgan, he kept his band small, but still inflicted enormous damage. In 1864, when Early burned Chambersburg, Pennsylvania, Grant found his excuse to scorch Mosby from the valley; after gaining Lincoln's approval, he ordered two corps to the task, and he told Sheridan: ". . . If you can possibly spare a division of cavalry, send them through Loudoun County to destroy and carry off the crops, animals, negroes, and all men under fifty years of age capable of bearing arms. In this way you will get rid of many of Mosby's men. . . . Give the enemy no rest. Do all the damage to railroads and crops you can. Carry off stock of all descriptions, and negroes, so as to prevent further planting. If the war is to last another year, we want the Shenandoah Valley to remain a barren waste."[38] Although Sheridan promised to ". . . leave them nothing but their eyes to weep with," he still did not capture Mosby, now a colonel with a considerable price on his head.

Passions ran high in this war, the inevitable result of total war encompassing a considerable portion of a great nation. But guerrilla warfare evoked a special and deadly kind of anger. Henderson wrote in his splendid work *Stonewall Jackson* that as early as 1862 Pope ordered that in Virginia ". . . the troops should subsist upon the country, and that the people should be held responsible for all damage done to roads, railways, and telegraphs by guerrillas."[39] When later pillaging and rape brought increased resistance, Pope ordered that every Virginian in Union-held areas must take an oath of allegiance. One of his generals, the German Von Steinwehr, arrested five prominent citizens as hostages ". . . to suffer death in the event of any soldiers being shot by bushwhackers." The Confederate Government replied ". . . by declaring

37. Standing, op. cit.
38. Ibid.
39. G. F. R. Henderson, *Stonewall Jackson and the American Civil War* (London: Longmans, Green, 1961).

that Pope and his officers were not entitled to be considered as soldiers. If captured they were to be imprisoned so long as their orders remained unrepealed; and in the event of any unarmed Confederate citizens being tried and shot, an equal number of Federal prisoners were to be hanged. . . ."[40]

Sherman later wrote in a report to Washington, ". . . Forrest is the devil. There will never be peace in Tennessee until Forrest is dead."[41] Morgan and his band, when captured, in the spring of 1863 were treated harshly, ". . . like felons rather than prisoners of war."[42] At war's end, northern officials talked of arresting Forrest as a war criminal. Sherman's march through Georgia was as much an act of passion as one of necessity: a giant "search-and-destroy" operation that insured the hatred of those searched and destroyed.

Union treatment of guerrillas seems to have been based on Old Testament thinking. Guerrilla prisoners were summarily executed in Grant's command, and probably no Union commander was entirely guiltless in this respect. One of them, General Paine, at wits' end in western Kentucky, actually published this proclamation: "I shall shoot every guerrilla taken in my district, and if your southern brethren retaliate by shooting a Federal soldier, I will walk out five of your rich bankers, and cotton men, and make you kneel down and shoot them. I will do it, so help me God."[43]

40. Ibid.
41. Standing, op. cit.
42. Ibid.
43. Richard Bennett, *The Black and Tans* (London: Hulton, 1959).

Chapter 12

The American army's preference for orthodox warfare • Brussels conference of 1874 • Indian wars in America • General Custer's disaster • Upton's mission to Europe • Influence of Prussian militarism on the American army • Alfred Mahan and American expansionism • Guerrilla wars in Cuba • General Weyler's tactics • McKinley and American intervention

GUERRILLA OPERATIONS in the American Civil War, though striking, were also limited. Raids by irregular bands of horsemen tearing up railroad tracks and cutting telegraph wires did not decide the war. The decision derived from elaborate strategies, from naval blockades and mass movement of large armies, from conventional if changing battlefield tactics, from big battles and enormous casualties.

A professional officer, John Bigelow, may have treated Sherman's Civil War tactics in his textbook *Principles of Strategy*,[1] but military students continued to concentrate on the battles of Shiloh and Gettysburg and Spotsylvania and Fredericksburg in preference to the spectacular raids of Morgan and Forrest and Mosby, which the orthodox officer held as freakish manifestations in a side show of war.

Had the North lost the war, its conventional outlook might have al-

1. John Bigelow, *Principles of Strategy* (Philadelphia: J. B. Lippincott, 1894).

tered; but, since it won, its principals regarded the irregular aspects as unseemly if not obscene. Other powers understood and agreed. In 1874, an international conference in Brussels, solemn in its stupidity and sounding awesomely like Alice's friend the Queen, announced to the wonderland world that guerrillas in order to be recognized as lawful belligerents must answer to a specific commander, wear a distinctive badge, carry arms openly and conform in operations to the laws and customs of war.[2]

While dark-suited diplomats, paunches suitably adorned with heavy gold watch chains, so pondered and decreed, a portion of the American army was fighting rudely clothed Indians who neither could, nor had any wish to, understand diplomatic proceedings in Brussels. These tribes, diverse in location, numbers and combat capability, knew only that their way of life was yielding with each army stockade raised, with each spike pounded into the Union Pacific railroad track, with each white homestead built and ground broken. They protested by force of arms whenever and wherever possible. From 1865 to 1898, the army fought the amazing number of 943 actions against Indians. This military record should have produced a splendid breed of professionals adept in irregular warfare.

And it did.

But on a very small scale and in a sharply circumscribed tactical specialty.

The Civil War army, of over a million men, soon fell to some forty thousand, rose briefly to fifty-seven thousand during Reconstruction, then sank to around twenty-seven thousand, where it remained until the Spanish-American war.[3] Three major territorial areas administering 255 military posts claimed this small force. One of them, the Department of the Missouri, consisted of an expanding line of rude stockades supporting a cavalry troop or two in addition to small infantry garrisons. The Midwest and West still resound with their names: Fort Dodge, Fort Kearney, Fort Carson, Fort Reno—these and others a cumulative glove covering the fist of continental expansion.

But an awkward glove for a very big fist. The tactical problems for these troops in some ways paralleled those faced by other colonizing powers. Protesting Indian tribes rarely acted in concert, and tended to avoid set-piece battles except on their own terms. They preferred guerrilla tactics, an ambush or a hit-and-run raid, usually hideous affairs in which bow and arrow vied with repeating rifle (supplied along with whiskey by traders and renegades) to produce carnage cruelly topped by tomahawk and scalping knife giving vent to primitive frustrations.

Small in numbers, these war bands moved fast, struck hard, and dis-

2. R. B. Asprey, "Guerrilla Warfare." In Encyclopaedia Britannica, 1969, Vol. 10.

3. Weigley, op. cit.

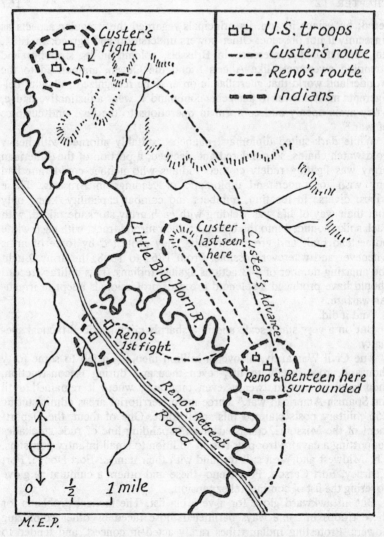

U.S. troops
—·—· Custer's route
— — — Reno's route
■■■■ Indians

Custer's Fight

Custer last seen here

Custer's Advance

Little Big Horn R.

Reno's 1st fight

Reno & Benteen here surrounded

Reno's Retreat Road

N

0   ½   1 mile

M.E.P.

appeared. Little pattern existed in either their strategy or their tactics. Successful countertactics hinged on intelligence and mobility. To supply the former, the army used friendly Indians; to provide mobility, it depended on horses. Troopers enjoyed the advantage of disciplined fire and movement. They suffered from lack of numbers; from the rugged terrain and vast spaces, which usually precluded an artillery train; and from communication difficulties with other posts, which prevented coordinated action.

As Marshal Bugeaud had discovered in Algeria, the lighter the column the better—but this could be abused, particularly where the commander lacked intelligence. The classic example of how not to fight the Indians occurred in the spring of 1876 during Sheridan's campaign against the Sioux and Northern Cheyennes. Sitting Bull's force was thought to be in the Little Missouri area, and Crazy Horse was somewhere in the Powder River area in Wyoming. General Terry was sent to smoke them out and defeat them. His cavalry consisted of two columns, one commanded by General Crook, one by General Custer. These commanders were to operate in extremely rugged terrain familiar neither to themselves nor to their troopers.

The first warning came in March, when Crazy Horse jumped and badly hurt Crook's force. In June, scouts reported Sitting Bull in the Yellowstone country, somewhere in the valley of the Little Big Horn. Terry now sent Custer's 7th United States Cavalry, a regiment of some seven hundred troopers, into this virtually unknown country against an enemy of unknown strength. Upon approaching Sitting Bull's home grounds, Custer compounded Terry's error by splitting his regiment into a strong advance guard under Major Reno, who was to "charge the village" while Custer's force worked through the hills. Reno ran into an ambush and was badly hurt but managed to survive until Terry's main force arrived. Custer's command, 265 men, was surrounded and slaughtered. The relief force saw their scalped comrades, charged forth in fury —and found space.[4]

Such defeats were rare. The press of civilization, of people and the railroad, increasingly pushed the Indian into barren country, which he would finally forsake for the reservation. Technology might not have given the army superior firepower, but it did offer the means to campaign the year around. As Weigley notes, ". . . thus supported, the Army again and again won its most decisive victories in the winter. Then George Custer won the battle of the Washita; then George Crook and Nelson Miles crushed Sitting Bull and Crazy Horse; then Chief Joseph [of the Nez Percé] vowed to Howard and Miles to fight no more forever."[5] Unlike the European process, which involved military superiority, commercial exploitation and ultimately political failure, the American process depended on military superiority and tribal genocide. In short, the Europeans milched the conquered, the Americans tried to eliminate them.

The Indian wars form a fascinating chapter in American history. They

4. Ibid.; see also Callwell, op. cit., who cited this campaign in his chapter on division of force. Although he held that such division was often necessary in small wars, and practically essential in guerrilla wars, he nonetheless cautioned the commander to be careful when operating independently with limited force and with inadequate knowledge of enemy and terrain.

5. Weigley, op. cit.

also provide splendid examples of minor tactics. If these primarily were *cavalry* tactics, they nonetheless could have been codified and expanded into a significant doctrine that might have altered the growing American preference for European-style warfare.

This may have been in Sherman's mind. The top army commander, at that time called the Commanding General, William Tecumseh Sherman, reigned from 1869 to 1883. Formerly in command of the Division of Missouri, Sherman retained interest in western fighting and, in the mid-seventies, sent a three-man commission to study British colonial campaigns. The prime mover of this body, which traveled first to Asia and India, then to Europe, was a Sherman protégé, a much decorated Civil War veteran named Emory Upton.

A humorless pedant, General Upton already had wrestled with the challenge to orthodoxy posed by technology, specifically the repeating rifle and breech-loading artillery: ". . . a systematic search for means to escape tactical impasse."[6] His new tactics, adopted by the army in 1867, called for a build-up of the skirmish line by fire and movement. This tactical trend had begun a century earlier with the development of Jäger battalions in Europe and light-infantry regiments in the American revolution. It had advanced in the Napoleonic wars—Clausewitz and Jomini both concentrated on the problem—and in the American Civil War. Today's tactics are still based on this notion, which has never totally answered the ascendancy of the defense.

Colonial warfare in Asia did not much impress the orthodox, infantry-oriented Upton, who infinitely preferred European warfare. This was the day of emergent Prussian militarism. Prussia's dramatic victories of 1864, 1866 and 1870–71 signaled a battlefield of breech-loading rifles and artillery, large and carefully organized conscript armies, meticulously planned railway nets and mobilization schedules—all arranged by an omnipotent general staff.

The German system cast a profound influence on Upton. His report, "The Armies of Asia and Europe," recommended ". . . that the United States adopt a modified form of the German cadre army."[7]

Some of Upton's contemporaries already were influenced by Clausewitz, whose massive *On War* was published in English in 1873. Prussian militarism seemed a logical and even enviable extension to Clausewitzian doctrine, a thought pursued by Upton in another work, *The Military Policy of the United States*. This posthumously published work called for war by superior numbers and armament, or weight rather than mobility and its natural corollary, deception. To Upton and his followers, and they were many and impressive, the military road ahead was plain to behold.

6. Ibid.
7. Ibid.

It was not so plain to either the American people or their Congressional representatives, who held the purse strings. Army budgets remained as penurious after Upton's death as before. When purse strings finally loosened, it was for a reason remote from Upton's thinking, and one he probably would not have welcomed.

The conquest of the American continent was still continuing when a navy captain fatefully influenced a small but powerful group of Americans already inclined toward expansionist thinking. This was Alfred T. Mahan, who in 1890 published a work called *The Influence of Sea Power upon History, 1660–1783*.[8]

In this and subsequent works, Mahan argued that Britain's world-power status rested on naval supremacy, by which she controlled the balance of power on the land mass of Eurasia. To complement this strategy, America must continue her present construction of a powerful and modern battle fleet capable of controlling North American waters. Such a fleet would need forward bases, coaling stations, and a supply fleet, all of which called for the co-operation and possible acquisition of certain foreign territories. The effort, besides assuring America her due place among the world's great powers, would pay moral, religious, and economic dividends.[9]

By a spate of magazine articles published during the next seven years, Mahan attempted to convince the reading public that it could not sleep easily until the country had forged Cuba, the Isthmus of Panama (soon to be pierced by a canal), and Hawaii ". . . in a single system vital to American security."[10]

These strategic arguments for limited imperialism impressed a number of important officers, such as George Dewey, and civil officials and politicians, such as Benjamin Tracy, Henry Cabot Lodge and Theodore Roosevelt, who each accepted Mahan's theories and influenced, in turn, other important government voices.

But Mahan's arguments impressed other influential circles: American businessmen did not object to the idea of new foreign markets and of competing in Asia and Africa with European powers, though most of them wanted nothing to do with American colonies as such. Men of good works, ministers and missionaries, spoke of the moral and religious responsibility of the strong toward the weak—the old "white man's

8. A. T. Mahan, *The Influence of Sea Power upon History, 1660–1783* (London: Sampson, Low, Marston, 1900); see also *The Influence of Sea Power upon the French Revolution and Empire 1783–1812* (London: Sampson, Low, Marston, 1892), 2 vols.; *Sea Power in Its Relations to the War of 1812* (London: Sampson, Low, Marston, 1905), 2 vols.

9. R. W. Leopold, *The Growth of American Foreign Policy* (New York: Alfred A. Knopf, 1965); see also W. W. Rostow, *The United States in the World Arena* (New York: Harper & Brothers, 1960).

10. Leopold, op. cit.

burden" argument. A favorable emotional climate also existed. The glory of nation building had worn thin. Men were bored, frustrated by the economic depression of 1893; they wanted activity, and a foreign excursion did not seem repugnant.

None of these factors alone would have pushed America into an imperialist phase, anyway, beyond the acquisition of Caribbean and Hawaiian bases. But, in 1895, the Cuban insurrection began to form a powerful catalyst.

When the insurrection broke out, the Cleveland administration was having difficulties with England in Venezuela, and Cleveland favored a hands-off policy. But as fighting continued and was dramatically reported by a sensationalist press, public opinion began to swing in favor of the rebels.

The newly elected McKinley at first ignored increasing pressure for intervention. In his inaugural address, he said: ". . . We want no wars of conquest; we must avoid the temptation of territorial aggression."[11]

Unfortunately, McKinley's words rarely impressed the nation's policy makers. The historian S. E. Morison later described McKinley as "a kindly soul in a spineless body."[12] His attempts to cool the situation made little progress. The insurgents, if not winning, were at least holding their own; convinced of eventual American intervention, they were demanding total independence, which the Spanish refused to consider.

The Spanish had only themselves to blame for the contretemps. From time to time, powerful American voices had stressed Cuba's proximity to the United States and called for annexation. Simultaneously, dissident groups backed by wealthy exiles in New York had formed in Cuba to protest against continued Spanish rule. Finally, Madrid should have been warned by the war of 1868, a ten-year insurrection put down only with difficulty and with attendant frowns of disapproval from the Grant and Hayes administrations.

The fighting began when eastern planters rose under Carlos Manuel de Céspedes. Himself a plantation owner, Céspedes freed his slaves and raised the standard of revolt. His force counted less than one hundred fifty irregulars, but within a month had grown to some twelve thousand, who controlled large areas of Oriente province. The Spanish continued to govern principal towns, and, early in 1869, a Spanish force inflicted a severe defeat on guerrillas outside Bayamo, causing perhaps two thousand casualties.[13]

11. Ibid.

12. S. E. Morison, *The Oxford History of the United States 1783–1917* (London: Oxford University Press, 1928), Vol. 2 of 3 vols.

13. Hugh Thomas, *Cuba or The Pursuit of Freedom* (New York: Harper & Row, 1971). I have relied largely on this comprehensive work in the following brief accounts of the 1865 and 1895 insurrections.

Spanish tactics combined old with new. Although the captain-general, Domingo Dulce, called for moderation, his commanders relied heavily on punitive measures. In the spring of 1869, General Valmaseda ordered

. . . that in the eastern province all males over fifteen found away from home without cause would be shot. All women and children not living in their houses were to be concentrated in fortified towns. All houses were either to carry a white flag or be burned down (unless occupied by Spanish troops).[14]

Subsequent commanders relied on similar edicts, the guerrillas replied in kind, violence and savagery ruled. To contain the Cubans in the East, the Spanish built a thirty-mile fortified ditch across the narrow neck in Oriente province. Although a guerrilla force breached this on one occasion, it allowed the Spanish a certain control by concentration of force and helped in maintaining communications with town garrisons in Oriente.

Rebel forces raised considerable havoc so long as they used guerrilla tactics, a lesson driven home by Céspedes' nearly disastrous defeat at Bayamo. Their chief disadvantage stemmed from divided counsels: the slave question caused considerable dissension, and leaders also disagreed on whether to attack rich plantations in the West. Arms were in short supply, and although encouraging voices sounded from the United States, the administration made no move to intervene. In time, Spanish weight told. A good many rebel leaders fell or were captured; others grew discouraged. Spanish columns isolated remaining units, which submitted one by one.

The Spanish could scarcely claim victory. The prolonged campaign fought by an army that grew to about seventy thousand men drained countless troop reinforcements from the mother country at a politically awkward time. Spanish deaths amounted to an estimated two hundred and eight thousand, Cuban deaths perhaps fifty thousand. The war cost $300 million, an immense sum, which the Spanish added to the Cuban debt, thus deepening resentment.[15]

The war won Spain only postponement. Perhaps her rule could have survived had she put through reforms leading toward autonomy. But political anarchy at home prevented viable policy abroad. And the war had helped form forces of nationalism that were to explode within a few years. If it claimed the lives of many leaders, it also trained other leaders and gave the people heroes: Carlos Manuel de Céspedes, Antonio and José Maceo, Calixto García, José Gómez, Eduardo Machado, Tomás Estrada Palma—names perhaps unfamiliar to North American readers, but names no less glorious for that, and glorious not only to

14. Ibid.
15. Ibid.

Cubans but to many other Latin Americans, names that thenceforth tripped frequently from persuasive nationalist tongues.

One of the most persuasive belonged to José Martí, founder, in 1892, of the Cuban Revolutionary Party.[16] Scholar and romanticist, lawyer and poet, Martí worked hard to bring on the 1895 insurrection. Killed a few weeks after its outbreak—he was forty-two years old—he in turn became a legendary hero to the next two generations, who marked well his sobering admonition: ". . . Anyone is a criminal who promotes an avoidable war; and so is he who does not promote an inevitable civil war."

The war of 1895 began in spring of that year with rebel landings from Costa Rica and Santo Domingo. The Spanish doubled their forces to thirty-two thousand, commanded by the hero of Morocco, General Martínez Campos. By June, the Spanish build-up had reached over fifty thousand, a force opposed by six to eight thousand rebels operating mainly in Oriente province, where ". . . all classes openly or secretly backed the rebellion—even sometimes members of the Civil Guard."[17]

Martínez Campos accurately defined the problem to his prime minister in the same month: Spain was faced with a rebellion of major proportions. Ruthless measures were called for; he himself did not feel able to implement them and recommended General Weyler for the job. He warned, however:

. . . Even if we win in the field and suppress the rebels, since the country wishes to have neither an amnesty for our enemies nor an extermination of them, my loyal and sincere opinion is that, with reforms or without reforms, before twelve years we shall have another war.[18]

Martínez Campos retained command until early in 1896. The rebels meanwhile consolidated control of much of Oriente province. As in the earlier rebellion, the Spanish continued to govern important towns; unlike in the earlier rebellion, forceful guerrilla leaders, Máximo Gómez and José Maceo, carried war to the western provinces:

. . . Gómez and Maceo . . . with 500 infantry and over 1,000 cavalrymen, broke out of the old line of *trochas* from Júcaro to Morón, outmanoeuvring the Spaniards by sheer speed, working in many, often ill-coordinated bands, concentrating on the destruction of property, usually ordering the inhabitants out of their houses before they were burned and their possessions looted. The rebels rode onwards to a good tune, the *Himno Invasor* . . . the banners of liberty flying, living off the land, creating an inextinguishable legend.[19]

16. Manuel Urrutia Lleó, *Fidel Castro and Company, Inc.: Communist Tyranny in Cuba* (New York: Frederick A. Praeger, 1964).
17. Thomas, op. cit.
18. Ibid.
19. Ibid.

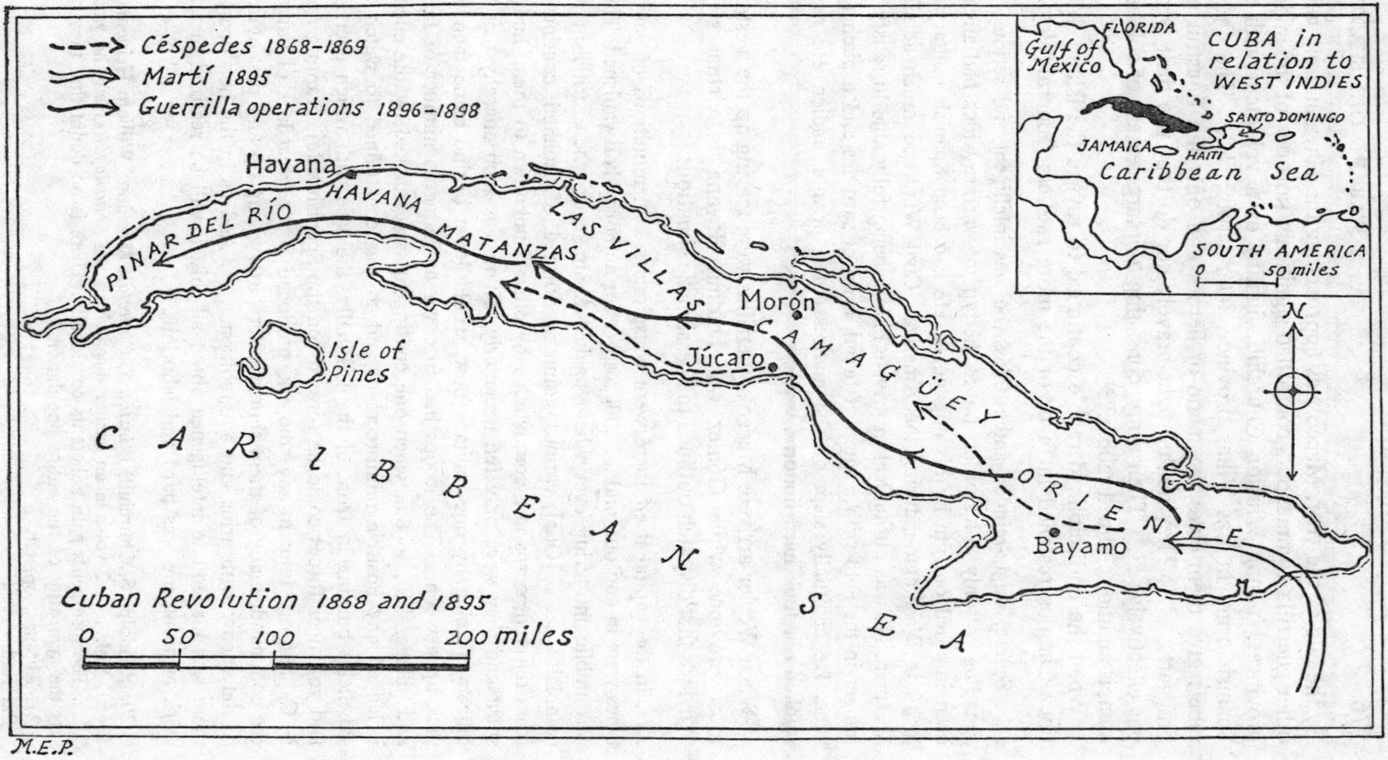

CUBA in
relation to
WEST INDIES

FLORIDA

Gulf of
México

SANTO DOMINGO

HAITI

JAMAICA

Caribbean Sea

SOUTH AMERICA

50 miles

ORIENTE

Bayamo

CAMAGÜEY

Morón

Júcaro

LAS VILLAS

MATANZAS

HAVANA

Havana

PINAR DEL RÍO

Isle of
Pines

CARIBBEAN SEA

Céspedes 1868-1869
Martí 1895
Guerrilla operations 1896-1898

Cuban Revolution 1868 and 1895

0   50   100   200 miles

M.E.P.

By the end of the year, Maceo was approaching the Havana area, while other guerrilla commanders controlled significant portions of the middle provinces. Young Winston Churchill, fighting as a volunteer with the Spanish army in Las Villas province, later wrote: ". . . The Cuban rebels give themselves the name of heroes and only are boastful and braggarts. . . . They neither fight bravely nor do they use their weapons effectively. . . . Their army, consisting to a large extent of coloured men, is an undisciplined rabble."[20]

When the undisciplined rabble continued to ravage the island, Martínez Campos resigned in favor of the more ruthless General Weyler:

. . . Severe, single-minded and ruthless, he was intelligent and serious, responding not only to his orders but to the type of warfare which had already been imposed on him by his opponents. He had been Spanish military attaché in Washington during the American Civil War, and much admired Sherman. He was puritanical in private habits, being fully able to satisfy his hunger in the field with a lump of bread, a tin of sardines and a pitcher of wine. He habitually slept on the mattress of a private soldier. He never smoked nor took hard liquor. . . .[21]

When Weyler arrived, Maceo's guerrillas were tearing up the westernmost province while Gómez was holding Havana in virtual siege. Weyler's first dispatch outlined the pessimistic situation:

. . . in the capital itself there were conspiracies . . . munitions of various types were in and out, and . . . all respect for authority had vanished. There was public muttering everywhere against Spain, everywhere criticism and complaint. . . . [Our] various columns, formed of isolated contingents from different corps and commanded by officers unknown to them, had no spirit and they were only fed irregularly. There was such anarchy that the officers, passing by one military post, would leave behind some men and pick up new ones. The troops had to cover an immense number of farms and villages . . . so that when one contingent was attacked by the enemy, it lacked any positive reinforcement and so was constrained to watch the canefields burning in front of them. Finally, the ease with which guerrillas and volunteer forces could be formed [on the Spanish side], granting ranks as Captain or Major to any who ask, produced . . . a great lack of unity in the command, many of them shortly afterwards giving up and passing over to the enemy with arms and ammunition. . . . And as in the headquarters there was inadequate intelligence about all this, it will be realized that the work awaiting me was hard and laborious.[22]

20. Randolph S. Churchill, *Winston S. Churchill* (London: William Heinemann, 1966), Vol. 1 of 2 vols. In an earlier dispatch to the *Saturday Review,* he wrote: ". . . The insurgents gain adherents continually. There is no doubt that they possess the sympathy of the entire population."
21. Thomas, op. cit.
22. Ibid.

An able general, Weyler quickly adapted to the tactical challenge. He began to divide the island into operational spheres—the first of a series of measures that would become only too familiar in future counterinsurgency campaigns. Like Scipio Africanus in Spain in 137 B.C., like Bugeaud in Algeria in 1836, Weyler attempted to regain tactical mobility by reorganizing cavalry and infantry and by eliminating remote outposts. He also recruited militias for town defense and organized units of Cuban counterguerrillas, ". . . these being often much more feared than the Spaniards by the rebels."[23] To deny rebels support and allow his columns unfettered maneuver, he herded thousands of Cubans into "fortified towns" and "military areas," which often proved little more than concentration camps. He ordered all the people of the eastern provinces to register, and he gave his area commanders emergency powers including that of summary execution.

These measures, invoked during 1896 and 1897, worked variously, but definitely helped to check guerrilla operations, particularly in the West. That they did not give Weyler "victory" is explained by several factors. Weyler's army, though well armed and fairly well organized, was not the best: its officers, in part, were venal and corrupt, its men illiterate and often uncaring. A British observer in Cuba at the time, Lieutenant Barnes of the 4th Hussars, later made a comprehensive and penetrating analysis of the Spanish failure. The main problem, Barnes noted, was

. . . the intense hostility of the inhabitants. They could get no good information of the rebel movements, while the rebels were never in doubt about theirs. An insurgent was distinguished from the peaceful cultivator only by his badge which could be speedily removed, and by his rifle which was easily hidden. Hence the Government forces, whether in garrison or operating in the country, were closely surrounded by an impalpable circle of fierce enemies who murdered stragglers, intercepted messages, burned stores, and maintained a continual observation.[24]

In addition, poor roads hindered Spanish mobility, while smallpox, malaria and yellow fever ". . . filled the hospitals and drained the fighting units." But, as Barnes pointed out to his superiors,

. . . all these are obstacles to success rather than causes of failure—these latter must be looked for in the tactics and conduct of the Spanish forces. There was a complete absence of any general plan. Columns moved about haphazard in the woods, fighting the enemy where they found them and returning with their wounded to the towns when they were weary of wandering. Their method of warfare was essentially defensive. They held great numbers of towns and villages with strong garrisons. They defended, or tried to defend, long lines of communication with a multitude of small block-

23. Ibid.
24. Callwell, op. cit.

houses. They tried to treat the rebels as though they were merely agrarian rioters and to subdue the revolt by quartering troops all over the country. The movement was on a scale far exceeding the scope of such remedies; it was a war, and this the Spanish Government would never recognize. Over all the petty incidents of guerrilla skirmishing, the frequent executions and the stern reprisals threw a darker shade.[25]

In time, Weyler corrected some of the tactical deficiencies, and his various measures succeeded in "compartmenting" operations with attendant gains such as the death of José Maceo in Pinar del Río. Nonetheless his dissatisfaction was evident in his orders of December 1896:

. . . I observe that the columns operating in Havana and Matanzas provinces, instead of camping in places or mountains frequented by the enemy, go nightly to the towns or mills in their zone to sleep. This has grave consequences for the operations, since it makes it easier for the enemy to know the route which the columns will take the next day, and also their number and morale. At the same time, the soldiers are more tired: . . . for these reasons, please arrange that all columns of both provinces, when setting out for operations, take with them three days' worth of rations and four of biscuits; with these, and with the cattle that abound in these provinces, it is easy to sustain the forces for six days in operations, camping on the mountains and at crossroads being able from the encampments to send picked troops swiftly for reconnaissance for four kilometres around, while the encampment is being prepared. In this way the enemy will be kept in a constant state of uneasiness. . . . My aim is that during my stay in Pinar del Río there should not remain a place or a mountain which will not have been crossed by the responsible column, while all really suspicious places will have been camped in.[26]

Spanish excesses disturbed the American public as much as rebel successes thrilled it. Such was the exaggerated and bellicose tone of the day's yellow press—mainly the Hearst, Dana, and Pulitzer papers fed in part by Estrada Palma's group in New York—that McKinley increasingly found it difficult to steer a neutral course.

Hope of a Spanish-Cuban solution meanwhile was growing increasingly dim. By early 1897, Weyler was reporting the western provinces pacified and rebels on the run in Las Villas. Although his *trochas* had impeded and in some cases broken rebel communications and although considerable quarrels were rending the rebel camp, the guerrillas were far from defeated, particularly in Oriente province. Spain had sent an estimated two hundred thousand soldiers to Cuba (of whom tens of thousands died, most from disease), the Philippines were draining more troops and money, and the climate of America was turning increas-

25. Ibid.
26. Thomas, op. cit.

ingly in favor of intervention. In the spring of 1897, a new government in Madrid tried to mollify Cuba's powerful neighbor by promising the Cubans autonomy (but not independence) and by recalling Weyler, now notorious as "the Butcher" because of the high mortality rate among the four hundred thousand hapless natives penned in concentration camps.[27]

These steps proved too little and too late. In fairness to more lurid press accounts, Spanish promises of reform were halfhearted, nor did the Madrid government respond favorably to McKinley's offer to purchase Cuba for $300 million. A case also existed for intervention on humanitarian grounds, and, by 1898, the humanitarian appeal had broadened in America. By 1898, the strategic, economic, moral, religious and emotional influences of a young and in some respects greedy nation had fused to form a powerful interventionist voice whose cry caused President McKinley to send a battleship, USS *Maine,* to Havana.

The dispatch of the *Maine* was not a bellicose act. When its sinking under circumstances still obscure led to war with Spain, General Upton's professional military Utopia was not even around the corner. The American army numbered around twenty-five thousand, its infantry and cavalry were reasonably well trained in minor tactics, it had adopted the excellent Krag-Jörgensen rifle; but its organization was appallingly bad, its artillery deficient, many of its senior officers were Civil War veterans. Professor Arthur Schlesinger (the elder) later wrote: ". . . Politics entered into the appointment of officers; and mismanagement, lack of plans, and general confusion interfered seriously with the mobilization, provisioning, and transport of troops."[28]

In April 1898, Congress authorized an increase in regular-army strength to nearly sixty-five thousand and also authorized calling up volunteer and state-militia units. By the end of the war, in August, army strength topped 270,000, twice the number desired by harassed army planners, who lacked camps, uniforms, weapons, and machinery to provide them.[29] Confusion prevailed at all levels, severe epidemics broke out, and the press did not help matters by pointing out raucously and consistently manifold errors that in some instances reached scandalous proportions. Despite such hindrances, General Shafter's expeditionary force finally landed in Cuba, Teddy Roosevelt scampered up San Juan Hill, the enormous but demoralized Spanish garrison surrendered, and the army settled down to a relatively quiet occupation.

Meanwhile, however, acting on secret and prearranged instructions earlier transmitted by Assistant Secretary of the Navy Theodore Roose-

27. Leopold, op. cit.
28. A. M. Schlesinger, *Political and Social History of the United States* (New York: Macmillan, 1926).
29. Morison, op. cit.

velt, Commodore Dewey had sailed his squadron of six warships secretly from Hong Kong. Early on May 1, he slipped into Manila Bay, sank the Spanish fleet, and besieged the city. To exploit his gains, he requested a landing force of five thousand men. Responding favorably, President McKinley ordered the War Department to furnish an expeditionary force that would complete ". . . the reduction of Spanish power in that quarter" and give ". . . order and security to the islands while in the possession of the United States. . . ."[30]

These orders were to open a new chapter in American arms—one undreamed of by General Emory Upton and his army disciples of the orthodox battlefield.

30. G. F. Kennan, *American Diplomacy, 1900–1950* (London: Secker & Warburg, 1952).

Chapter 13

Spanish rule of the Philippines • Rizal and the 1896 insurrection • Aguinaldo's rise • Dewey's victory at Manila Bay • The American problem • General Merritt's expeditionary force • The American attitude • The Treaty of Paris • Outbreak of insurrection

THE PHILIPPINE ISLANDS offered a slightly more complicated situation than Cuba. Toward the end of the century, this enormous archipelago supported a population of nearly 7 million. Spanish rule, particularly the "paternal authority" of friars, had enslaved natives for nearly four hundred years. The warlike Moros had challenged this dismal state of affairs since the beginning of the eighteenth century—sporadic revolts put down with almost unbelievable harshness.[1] Resistance spread in the nineteenth century, and, in 1896, a major revolt broke out, largely the work of Dr. José Rizal backed by a terrorist society, the Katipunan, or Patriots' League.

Rizal was almost unique in the islands: at thirty-five, he was traveled and educated, ". . . a poet, philosopher, surgeon, and an artist," and was the author of a popular protest novel, *Noli Me Tangere* (Touch

1. Rafael Altamura, *A History of Spain* (New York: D. Van Nostrand, 1949).

Me Not).[2] Rizal's revolt triggered a reign of terror under a new governor, General Polavieja, described by an English observer as ". . . an amazing personage, who has never won a battle and never failed to lose one."[3]

Polavieja's troops summarily executed Rizal and hundreds of his followers, but the Katipunan remained intact and revolt spread throughout Luzon. It was not pretty, but hatred never is. The Catholic Church, responsible for much of the misery, proved a particular target. In the village of Imus, ". . . thirteen friars fell into their [native] hands. One was killed by being gradually cut to pieces. Another was set afire, after being saturated with petroleum; still another was pierced through the length of his body by a bamboo split then doused in oil while alive and turned over a moderate fire."[4]

Isolated bestiality does not make a successful revolution. Polavieja's successor, General Primo de Rivera, soon exploited the rebels' willingness to fight pitched battles. Badly armed and with little formal military training, they invariably lost. The revolution could well have been doomed had not a natural leader come to the fore.

Don Emilio Aguinaldo was a Filipino Trotsky. The son of landowning parents in Cavite province, the twenty-nine-year-old rebel was a mixture of Chinese and Tagalog blood. He had studied law in Manila without gaining a degree; in a predominantly Catholic country, he was a Mason; he was said to have been mild and soft-spoken, yet, for years, he had exercised a charisma that placed him among the young leaders of the revolution.

In August 1896, he personally led a successful assault against the garrison in his home town. By October, ". . . he had become the accepted military commander of the revolution." Showing exceptional administrative ability, he organized a Central Revolutionary Committee and a Filipino Congress, which established a shadow government. In 1897, Aguinaldo was elected president and generalissimo. When a disgruntled associate began a splinter movement, Aguinaldo had him arrested, court-martialed, and shot.[5]

During the next year, the movement survived a series of vicissitudes that demonstrated the perfidy of the new Spanish governor, General Primo de Rivera, to Aguinaldo and the revolutionary junta. Rolling with the punches, Aguinaldo and his principal lieutenants fled to Hong Kong, where they received limited aid from the U. S. Navy (through Com-

2. Leon Wolff, *Little Brown Brother* (New York: Doubleday, 1961). I have relied heavily on this lively, detailed and very well written book in this and the following chapter.

3. H. B. Clarke, *Modern Spain 1815–1898* (London: Cambridge University Press, 1906).

4. Wolff, op. cit.

5. Ibid.

modore Dewey) and also from the U. S. State Department (through Consul Wildman).

After Dewey's victory at Manila Bay, in early May, the revolutionary junta returned to Luzon. By late spring of 1898, Aguinaldo and his military commander, General Luna, boasted an army of nearly thirty thousand. With the bulk of Spanish forces contained in Manila, and with Dewey's fleet in control of harbors and sea, the rebels proclaimed the Visayan Republic and published a declaration of independence.

Aguinaldo's words no doubt flowed from the heart, but his mind also was at work. He was already disturbed by what appeared to be America's contradictory attitude. Only the previous December, in a warmup speech for war with Spain, President McKinley had said of Cuba: ". . . I speak not of forcible annexation, for that cannot be thought of. That, by our code of morality, would be criminal aggression." In Aguinaldo's mind, this principle would apply to the Philippines. But neither Dewey nor Wildman had seemed wildly enthusiastic about supporting the rebel movement, and they all but ignored the Filipino declaration of independence.

Aguinaldo was a realist, however. He needed American help: Dewey's fleet, troops for the assault of Manila, loans to get his government organized. Knowing that he was going to receive American help, whether or not solicited, he told his people by proclamation:

. . . Compatriots! Divine Providence is about to place independence within our reach. . . . The Americans, not from mercenary motives, but for the sake of humanity and the lamentations of so many persecuted people, have considered it opportune to extend their protecting mantle to our beloved country. . . . At the present moment an American squadron is preparing to sail for the Philippines. . . . There where you see the American flag flying, assemble in numbers; they are our redeemers![6]

Redeemers or conquerors?

A large portion of the American populace no doubt regarded themselves as redeemers who would establish organized government, as in Cuba—and get out.

These were not the sentiments, however, of a strong and influential expansionist group who expanded Mahan's doctrines to fit the new situation—with Mahan's full concurrence, may it be said. With the annexation of Hawaii assured, they raised their sights to the Philippines, arguing that Filipinos could not govern themselves. If America were not to assume the task, then the inevitable anarchic vacuum would be filled either by Japan, particularly dangerous in view of recent victory over China, or by England, Germany, Russia, or France. America, too, needed overseas trade, and here was a splendid opportunity to anchor

6. Ibid.

in new territory—a base from which to nibble at the crumbling Chinese pie.

To some Americans, it seemed as if God were extending America's lease on manifest destiny; to others, a mystic element entered. Shortly before the outbreak of war, the Washington *Post* told its readers:

. . . A new consciousness seems to have come upon us—the consciousness of strength—and with it a new appetite, the yearning to show our strength . . . ambition, interest, land hunger, pride, the mere joy of fighting, whatever it may be, we are animated by a new sensation. We are face to face with a strange destiny. The taste of Empire is in the mouth of the people even as the taste of blood in the jungle. It means an Imperial policy, the Republic, renascent, taking her place with the armed nations.[7]

The executive instrument essential to planting the American flag in the Philippines, the American army's expeditionary force, was not the sharpest ever forged. Command went to Major General Wesley Merritt, a sixty-two-year-old seasoned campaigner: he had served as a young general with enormous distinction in the Civil War, a reputation enhanced by service in the Indian wars. Now heavy, with white, wavy hair and hard gray eyes, he was also something of a realist. Looking at his two regiments of regulars, the 14th and the 23rd Infantry, supported by a few artillery batteries, he complained in mid-May to President McKinley that such a force would prove insufficient ". . . when the work to be done consists of conquering a territory 7,000 miles from our base, defended by a regularly trained and acclimated army of from 10,000 to 25,000 men [the Spanish] and inhabited by 14 millions [sic] of people, the majority of whom will regard us with the intense hatred both of race and religion."[8]

Although Merritt's force eventually was fleshed out to eighty-five hundred with National Guard and volunteer units, these reinforcements had to be armed with the old Springfield .45 caliber rifle, a single-shot monster whose black powder puffed like a locomotive over the firer's head. Other essentials remained in short supply, nor were matters remedied upon arrival in the Philippines at Camp Dewey, a former peanut farm:

. . . The heat was oppressive and rain kept falling. At times the trenches were filled with two feet of water, and soon the men's shoes were ruined. Their heavy khaki uniforms were a nuisance; they perspired constantly, the loss of body salts induced chronic fatigue. Prickly heat broke out, inflamed by scratching and rubbing. Within a week the first cases of dysentery, malaria, cholera and dengue fever showed up at sick call.[9]

7. S. E. Morison and H. S. Commager, *The Growth of the American Republic* (New York: Oxford University Press, 1962), Vol. 2 of 2 vols.
8. Wolff, op. cit.
9. Ibid.

Merritt and his generals slowly overcame these initial difficulties. In August, Major General Elwell Otis arrived with reinforcements that nearly doubled American strength. Merritt meanwhile was moving his army alongside Filipino units for the cardboard assault of Manila, which fell in August.

This victory failed to repair deteriorating American-Filipino relations. Considering the state of the 1898 world, and particularly the Great Power concept, perhaps an amicable relationship was impossible. Strategic and economic arguments for outright annexation were strong, and Spanish efforts to send a relief force and the rude behavior of a German task force in Manila Bay reinforced them.

But overriding these arguments was a paternalism that must have brought bile to Aguinaldo's throat. Nowhere is this better expressed than in an early report of the Philippine Commission, a presidentially-appointed body headed by Jacob Schurman, which concluded:

. . . lack of [Filipino] education and political experience, combined with their racial and linguistic diversities, disqualify them, in spite of their mental gifts and domestic virtues, to undertake the task of governing the archipelago at the present time. The most that can be expected of them is to cooperate with the Americans in the administration of general affairs . . . and to undertake, subject to American control or guidance (as may be found necessary), the administration of provincial and municipal affairs. . . .

Should our power by any fatality be withdrawn, the commission believe that the government of the Philippines would speedily lapse into anarchy, which would excuse, if it did not necessitate, the intervention of other powers and the eventual division of the islands among them. Only through American occupation, therefore, is the idea of a free, self-governing, and united Philippines Commonwealth at all conceivable. And the indispensable need from the Filipino point of view of maintaining American sovereignty over the archipelago is recognized by all intelligent Filipinos and even by those insurgents who desire an American protectorate. The latter, it is true, would take the revenues and leave us the responsibilities. . . .[10]

The Commission's arguments had certain merits. Spanish rule had deprived most people of formal education. The Commission reported that Spanish regulations provided one male and one female teacher for each five thousand inhabitants—". . . this wretchedly inadequate provision was never carried out."

But the Commission, peering from Olympian heights of Western political behavior, failed to recognize either the volatility or the pride of these "backward" peoples, a volatility and pride dangerously compressed by four centuries of misrule. Spanish excesses had filled Filipino hearts

10. *Report of the Philippines Commission to the President* (Washington: U.S. Government Printing Office, 1900).

with hatred. An officer of Dewey's squadron had earlier written home: ". . . But the more we knew the Filipino the more we got to know what hatred is. . . . Their hatred of the Spaniard was the accumulation of the hatred of their forefathers for generations, added to their own."[11]

Hatred is a nebulous emotion but is inextricably related to pride. In the eyes of most Westerners, pride and poverty are poles apart; and, all too often, we assume that a poor man *ipso facto* lacks pride, particularly if his skin is not white. The American soldier of 1898 proved true to this philosophy. An army major in an official report noted, ". . . almost without exception, soldiers and also many officers refer to the natives in their presence as 'niggers' and natives are beginning to understand what the word 'nigger' means."[12]

Top American officials, Dewey and Merritt and Otis, added to mounting antagonism by cavalier treatment of Aguinaldo and his officials, whose protests over the continuing arrival of American reinforcements were insolently brushed aside. As American presence mounted and American intentions became clear, tentacles of native ill feeling began to leave the Spanish corpse to quiver about the newcomers. Aguinaldo meanwhile emphasized Filipino intentions by convening a congress that, in September 1898, wrote a constitution for the new republic.

American officials remained unimpressed and successfully communicated their negative attitude to Washington and to influential portions of the American public. Imperialist feeling was now running high despite fulminations of the Anti-Imperialist League, whose members included some of the most respected men in the nation. To suggested alternatives, for example a protectorate role similar to that proclaimed for Cuba, or limited acquisition, say the island of Luzon alone, the expansionists turned a deaf ear.

In October, the American Government opened negotiations with Spain in Paris. Needless to say, neither Aguinaldo nor his representatives were invited to participate. In November, they learned that the Treaty of Paris granted the United States control of the Philippines, the Sulus, and Guam in return for a payment of $20 million to Spain.

Considerable soul-searching accompanied the ratification process, but the necessary Senate majority was won.[13] President McKinley, who before Dewey's victory confessed he ". . . could not have told where those

11. Wolff, op. cit.
12. Ibid.
13. Morison and Commager, op. cit. Senator Lodge called it ". . . the hardest fight I have ever known." The victory raised a storm of protest from liberal elements. Mark Twain's letter "To the Person Sitting in Darkness" charged ". . . McKinley with 'playing the European game' of imperialism, and suggested that Old Glory should now have 'the white stripes painted black and the stars replaced by the skull and cross bones.' "

darned islands were within two thousand miles," bowed to the inevitable. As he later told a group of visiting clergymen:

. . . The truth is I didn't want the Philippines, and when they came to us, as a gift from the gods, I did not know what to do with them. . . . I thought first we would take only Manila; then Luzon; then other islands, perhaps, also. I walked the floor of the White House night after night until midnight; and I am not ashamed to tell you, gentlemen, that I went down on my knees and prayed Almighty God for light and guidance more than one night. And one night it came to me this way—I don't know how it was, but it came: (1) That we could not give them back to Spain—that would be cowardly and dishonorable; (2) That we could not turn them over to France [!] or Germany—our commercial rivals in the Orient—that would be bad business and discreditable; (3) That we could not leave them to themselves—they were unfit for self-government—and they would soon have anarchy and misrule over there worse than Spain's was; and (4) That there was nothing left for us to do but to take them all, and to educate the Filipinos, and uplift and civilize and Christianize [!] them, and by God's grace to do the best we could by them . . . and then I went to bed, and went to sleep, and slept soundly. . . .[14]

McKinley awakened to a nightmare. The treaty, which struck Aguinaldo like a thunderbolt, only intensified Filipino aspirations to independence. To the leaders, it was now clear that war was imminent, war of a kind suggested by preliminary native operations: by rifles smuggled from Manila in coffins supposedly carrying the dead; by orders for secret attacks against American installations in Manila.

That winter, the cloud of ill feeling continued to swell. Soon it enveloped Manila and hung over the two armies, the one now facing the other. On February 4, 1899, an American sentry fired on and killed a Filipino soldier. Firing opened along the line. The Philippine Insurrection was on.

14. C. S. Olcott, *William McKinley* (New York: Houghton Mifflin, 1916), Vol. 2 of 2 vols.

Chapter 14

American victories in the Philippines • Otis' optimism • MacArthur's expedition • American reverses • Mr. Bass tells the truth • Enemy tactics • American countertactics • MacArthur's pacification program • Frederick Funston and the capture of Aguinaldo • Taft establishes civil rule • The Samar massacre • General "Roaring Jake" Smith: "I want no prisoners . . ." • General Bell's "solution" • Taft's countersolution • End of insurrection • The tally sheet

THE INSURRECTION should have ended quickly. But so should the rebellion of 1896, once the Spanish killed José Rizal and sent the native army to the hills. In 1899, the Americans incontestably won the first battle, a two-day orthodox infantry attack supported by naval gunfire. This action cost 59 American lives and 278 wounded; the insurgents lost from two to five thousand dead, their army fleeing to the north. Aguinaldo's guerrilla plans for Manila came to nought thanks to American army precautions. The New York *Times* informed its readers, ". . . It is not likely that Aguinaldo himself will exhibit much staying power. . . . It seems probable that after one or two collisions the insurgent army will break up."[1]

General Otis agreed. When a peace emissary arrived from Aguinaldo's headquarters, Judge Florentine Torres, to suggest a cease-fire, Otis

1. Wolff, op. cit.

". . . sternly replied that the fighting having once begun must go on
to the grim end." Three days later, Otis cabled Washington, ". . . His
[Aguinaldo's] influence throughout this section destroyed. Now applies
for cessation of hostilities and conference. Have declined to answer."[2]

Or, rather, he answered by conventional military tactics, which he
felt certain would result in the capture of Luna's army and the end of
the insurrection. These involved sending out task forces to find, fix and
destroy. On an island the size of Ohio, they found little, fixed virtually
nothing, but destroyed numerous villages. That spring, MacArthur's
brigade captured the rebel capital of Malolos at a cost of nearly 550
casualties, but one capital was as good as another to the rebels. Luna's
army dispersed, drifted north, and re-formed.

By spring, the war was going badly for the Americans. Otis increasingly resembled Job facing one disaster after another. His restless soldiers liked nothing about the Philippines—not the weather, the people,
the tinned-salmon rations—nothing. He had already lost a large number
of volunteers whose terms had expired, sick bays and hospitals over-
flowed with patients, impatient generals were carping at his halting
tactics and, even worse, American correspondents were beginning to
fathom insurgency warfare.

In June, the American journal *Harper's Weekly* published a dispatch
that its respected correspondent, Mr. Bass, had smuggled to Hong Kong.
Influential American readers learned that

. . . since the fourth of February various expeditions have taken place,
principally in the island of Luzon. These expeditions resulted in our taking
from the insurgent government certain territory. Some of this territory we
have occupied; the rest we have returned to the insurgents in a more or less
mutilated condition, depending on whether the policy of the hour was to
carry on a bitter war against a barbarous enemy, or to bring enlightenment
to an ignorant people, deceived as to our motives.[3]

After stating that the American outlook ". . . is blacker now than
it has been since the beginning of the war," Mr. Bass offered some reasons: ". . . First, the whole population of the islands sympathizes with
the insurgents; only those natives whose immediate self-interest requires
it are friendly to us. . . ." The in-again-out-again policy was ridiculous:

. . . The insurgents came back to Pasig, and their first act was to hang the
presidente for treason in surrendering to the Americans. Presidents do not
surrender towns to us any more. When we returned to Pasig we found
the place well fortified, and we suffered some loss in retaking it. This process
might go on indefinitely. . . . These expeditions, lacking the purpose of hold-

2. Ibid.
3. Ibid.

ing the land conquered, alienate the population already hostile, encourage insurgents, teach them true methods of fighting, and exhaust our men.

As for Otis' tactics:

. . . To chase barefooted insurgents with water-buffalo carts as a wagon-train may be simply ridiculous; but to load volunteers down with two hundred rounds of ammunition and one day's rations, and to put on their heads felt hats used by no other army in the world in the tropics, in order to trot these same soldiers in the broiling sun over a country without roads, is positively criminal. Out of as strong and robust an army as ever wore shoe leather, there are five thousand men in the general hospital. . . .

The press soon suffered a surfeit of copy. In June, a rebel force ambushed four thousand Americans and cut them to ribbons. That summer, the rebels began discarding uniforms, the better to pursue guerrilla tactics. Ambushes became common, and so did the question: Who is the enemy? Lieutenant Colonel J. T. Wickman, commanding the 26th Infantry of U. S. Volunteers, later explained some of the tactical problems to enthralled senators:

. . . In November, 1899, at Jaro, a large flag of truce was used to entice officers into ambush. By order of the commander all persons displayed white flags in the country where our troops operated. This was not for protection, but to give warning to insurgents to hide their guns and disguise themselves. Privates Dugan, Hayes and Tracy, of Company F, were murdered by the town authorities at Calinoz. Private Nolan, at Dingle, was tied up by the ladies while in a stupor; the insurgents were sent for and cut his throat with a sangut. The body of Corporal Donehy, of Company D, was dug up, burned, and mutilated at Dumangas. Private O'Hearn, captured by apparently friendly people near Leon, was tied to a tree, burned for four hours with a slow fire, and finally slashed up. Lieutenant Max Wagner was assassinated on the road to Pototan, October 1, by insurgents disguised in American uniform. . . .[4]

To these and other atrocities, the Americans retaliated by using the "water cure" on natives reluctant to talk: four or five gallons of water were forced down a man's throat, then squeezed out by kneeling on his stomach.[5] If he lived, he usually talked. The guerrillas retaliated by more torturing and mutilating. Americans responded by burning villages and killing indiscriminately. The sick figure rose; morale declined. Otis initiated heavy censorship of news dispatches and was heard to say

4. *Hearings Before the Commission on the Philippines of the United States Senate in Relation to Affairs in the Philippine Islands* (Washington: U. S. Government Printing Office, 1902), Vol. 2 of 2 vols.

5. Ibid. (Vols. 1 and 2).

it was ". . . as though the AP were in the pay of the Filipino junta in Hong Kong." Eleven correspondents mailed a dispatch from that crown colony:

. . . We believe that, owing to official dispatches from Manila made public in Washington, the people of the United States have not received a correct impression of the situation in the Philippines, but that these dispatches have presented an ultra-optimistic view that is not shared by the general officers in the field.[6]

Otis now resolved to end the war. He had over forty-five thousand troops, with more en route, and, in September, he ordered a three-division operation designed to clear northern Luzon and capture Aguinaldo. Of the three columns, Lawton's fared the worst. Such was the terrain and the rain that the cavalry often averaged only a mile a day! Supply wagons became hopelessly mired. After five weeks, the troops

. . . had been on half-rations for two weeks. Wallowing through the hip-deep muck, lugging a ten-pound rifle and a belt filled with ammunition, drenched to the skin and with their feet becoming heavier with mud at each step, the infantry became discouraged. Some men simply cried, others slipped down in the mud and refused to rise. Threats and appeals by the officers were of no avail. Only a promise of food in the next town and the fear that if they remained behind they would be butchered by marauding bands of insurgents forced some to their feet to struggle on.[7]

Lawton's cavalry finally broke loose by abandoning wagons and living off the land. This column, under Colonel Young, fell on Aguinaldo's rear guard near San Pedro and captured his mother and son. Aguinaldo and his guerrillas escaped—not surprising, since in six weeks Lawton's task force had covered only 120 miles.

With the rebels underground, the war lost any semblance of orthodoxy—excepting Otis' tactics. These consisted in fanning a series of outposts out from Manila, a serious drain on his forces, which now numbered around sixty thousand. Incredibly he seemed to think that he was winning. In a popular magazine of the day, *Leslie's Weekly,* he stated, ". . . You asked me to say when the war in the Philippines will be over. . . . The war in the Philippines is already over . . . all we have to do now is protect Filipinos against themselves. . . . There will be no more real fighting . . . little skirmishes which amount to nothing." In December 1899, he cabled Washington no less than four times that the war was over![8]

6. Wolff, op. cit.
7. Ibid.
8. Ibid.

His commanders, or some of them, were growing more realistic. General Lawton described the insurgents as ". . . the bravest men I have ever seen." General Arthur MacArthur noted, ". . . wherever throughout the archipelago there is a group of the insurgent army, it is a fact beyond dispute that all the contiguous towns contribute to the maintenance thereof. . . . Intimidation has undoubtedly accomplished much to this end; but fear as the only motive is hardly sufficient to account for the united and apparently spontaneous action of several millions of people."[9]

As Otis pushed outposts farther and farther from the capital, and as punitive expeditions began seeking out neighboring islands, resistance increased. Supply lines became favorite targets. Sometimes guerrillas simply blocked paths and trails by interwoven vines, sometimes they "mined" them by burying sharp bamboo sticks. Rebels constantly cut telegraph lines; villagers stole rifles and ammunition; small bands fell on garrisons or ambushed supply parties. In the first thirteen months, the army reported 1,026 engagements, with 245 Americans killed, 490 wounded and 118 captured, versus 3,854 rebels killed, 1,193 wounded, 6,572 captured.[10]

In an election year, pacification was moving much too slowly for McKinley's pleasure. In May 1900, he replaced Otis with MacArthur, whose force now numbered seventy thousand. MacArthur continued the old and tried something of the new. At first, nothing worked. An amnesty program brought in only some five thousand people to swear allegiance to the flag—the American flag; a rifle-recovery program, thirty pesos per weapon, produced an insulting 140 pieces. He continued sending punitive expeditions to other islands, which he blockaded with gunboats; he bribed island chiefs, who took the money but could not stop the fighting.

MacArthur wanted to impose much stricter measures, but his hands were tied by the bitter autumn elections in America. Imperialism was a major theme. Aguinaldo, seeing a Democratic victory as his only hope, called for general escalation of resistance in order to keep the issue in American headlines.

The Republican victory came as a terrible blow to the insurgent cause: MacArthur received another seventy-five thousand soldiers and, at the end of the year, placed the islands under martial law. Mass arrests and imprisonment followed. For the first time, the insurgent cause faltered. A native Federal Party, pledged to accept American sovereignty, began to grow in popularity. A few dissident tribes already had come over to the American side, and, for some time, troop commanders had been using native irregulars. In February 1901, Congress authorized

9. Ibid.
10. Ibid.

MacArthur to recruit ". . . a body of native troops, not exceeding 12,-
000, called 'Scouts'"—these to consist initially of thirty to fifty companies of one hundred men each, commanded by American officers.[11]

The scouts played an integral role in the first real break in the war.
Among dispatches taken from a captured courier was one from Aguinaldo ordering a distant guerrilla chief to send him four hundred troops
at once. According to the courier, Aguinaldo was operating in northeastern Luzon, in the mountains of Isabela province. The man who learned
this information was Frederick Funston, a thirty-six-year-old brigadier
of volunteers, a rugged, brave and intelligent redhead. Funston at once
decided to exploit this valuable intelligence by an imaginative, courageous and deceptive plan that hopefully would allow him to attack
enemy political-military leadership.

With some difficulty, he persuaded seniors to allow him to disguise
eighty-one Maccabebe scouts as *insurrecto* replacements responding to
Aguinaldo's orders. Funston and four volunteer officers disguised as
prisoners accompanied the draft. After a hazardous march of over a
hundred miles, this extraordinary party penetrated Aguinaldo's inner
sanctum, took him prisoner, and returned to American territory—one
of the most successful *ruses de guerre* of all times. Aguinaldo subsequently swore allegiance to the American flag and issued a proclamation
of surrender.

The second break in the war came soon after Aguinaldo's capture.
In early July 1901, President McKinley appointed William Howard Taft
to be chairman of the second Philippines Commission and also civilian
governor of the islands. By this time, the President was thoroughly disillusioned with God's advice. When the portly judge told McKinley that
he did not approve of American policy and did not want the Philippines,
the President is said to have replied, "Neither do I, but that isn't the
question. We've got them."[12]

McKinley furnished his new governor some powerful arms and armor.
MacArthur's replacement, General Adna Chaffee, became subordinate
to Taft's civil control. To insure Taft's authority, he was given control
of every penny of American money spent in the Philippines, including
that paid to officers and men of the army, navy, and marines!

So armed, Taft set about the immense task of establishing viable
civil government.

Neither Aguinaldo's capture nor Taft's appointment ended the fighting, but rebel operations now began to resemble writhing ganglia of a
headless body. Increasingly desperate, the southern rebels turned to outright bestiality such as the massacre of an army infantry company, Company C of the 9th Infantry, at Balangiga, on the island of Samar.

---

11. *Fifth Annual Report of the Philippines Commission—1904* (Washington:
U. S. Government Printing Office, 1905), Vol. 1 of 2 vols.
12. Olcott, op. cit.

Although this massacre succeeded primarily because of the company's lax security precautions, the army commander exacted swift retribution, choosing as his instrument a combat-experienced and very tough marine, Major L. W. T. Waller, of Boxer Rebellion fame. Waller reported with his punitive force to an army officer, Brigadier General "Roaring Jake" Smith, who told him, ". . . I want no prisoners, I want you to burn and kill; the more you burn and kill, the better it will please me."[13] Waller sensibly confined operations to seeking out the guerrilla camp and destroying it along with some insurgents.

An army general, Brigadier General Bell, employed extremely harsh tactics in cleaning out Malvar's guerrilla band on a neighboring island:

. . . there were to be no more neutrals; inhabitants were to be classified as active (not passive) friends or enemies. The latter, regardless of age or sex, were to be killed or captured. Everyone had to live within designated military zones and nowhere else. The municipal police were disarmed. Outside the concentration zones all food supplies were to be confiscated or destroyed. An eight p.m. curfew went into effect. Any Filipino found on the streets after that hour was to be shot on sight. Whenever an American soldier was killed, a native prisoner would be chosen by lot and executed. Native houses in the vicinity of telegraph lines cut by the insurrectos would be burned.[14]

This program certainly would have been approved by "Butcher" Weyler, the Spanish general in Cuba whose excesses were a major reason for America going to war. Early in 1902, Bell personally led a campaign that resulted in Malvar's capture. Bell later codified the experience into a universal that undoubtedly influenced his fellows: ". . . To combat such a population," Bell wrote, "it is necessary to make the state of war as insupportable as possible . . . by keeping the minds of the people in such a state of anxiety and apprehension that living under such conditions will soon become unbearable. Little should be said. The less said the better. Let acts, not words, convey the intention."[15]

Bell's conclusions by no means stood at odds with the opinion of a good many Western colonizers. He forgot to state, however, that inept relocation methods resulted in mass epidemics, which claimed over fifty thousand native lives. How many innocent natives were shot is not known. A witness of Bell's methods, a young lieutenant and later judge, James Blount, wrote, ". . . The American soldier in officially sanctioned wrath is a thing so ugly and dangerous that it would take a Kipling to describe him."[16]

Fortunately for the American cause, Taft already was insisting on

13. R. B. Asprey, "Waller of Samar," *Marine Corps Gazette,* May and June 1961.
14. Wolff, op. cit.
15. Ibid.
16. Ibid.

M.E.P.

a humane approach; indeed, he forced Chaffee to court-martial Waller for executing some native guides whom Waller had found treacherous, and when the court-martial revealed General Smith's punitive instructions to the marine major, he forced the court-martial of Smith.[17]

17. Asprey, op. cit.

Taft had at once recognized the need to win native support. Using forceful diplomacy, he persuaded the Vatican to sell America 410,000 acres of prime farmland for over $7 million, then sold land parcels to the natives on easy terms. He also laid the groundwork for a vast civil-affairs program, which was to continue for many years. To start the necessary educational program, he caused one thousand American teachers to be recruited and brought over to the islands.

Taft also de-emphasized, as rapidly as possible, the military role in suppressing the insurrection. He relied instead on civil government but-tressed by a constabulary police force and the growing Philippine Scouts. In 1903, Taft reported:

. . . this arrangement presents some anomalies which seem greater to the military commander than to the civil government; but however unsymmetri-cal the union of the two forces under a constabulary officer may seem to be, it has had the immense advantage of enabling the civil government, with na-tive troops, to suppress disorder. It is of the utmost political importance that the regular soldiery, under a command more or less independent of the civil government, should not be called in to suppress disorders and to maintain the authority of the civil government until all the forces of natives, whether constabulary or scouts, should be used for this purpose. . . . In this country it is politically most important that Filipinos should suppress Filipino dis-turbances and arrest Filipino outlaws.[18]

After Aguinaldo's renunciation of revolt, Taft treated remaining re-sistance groups as *ladrones,* or outlaws, which some of them were. Although they were offered full amnesty if they surrendered, the "bandolerismo statute," of late 1902, promised either death or imprison-ment for not less than twenty years ". . . for any person proved to be a member of a *ladrone* band (of three or more) . . . and any person aiding a member of such a band. . . ."[19]

To counter the natural advantage of the country to either guerrilla or outlaw, Taft authorized ". . . the provincial governors to withdraw the outlying barrios of towns to their respective centers of population and, in a sense, to reconcentrate the residents of the outlying bar-rios. . . ." Taft went on:

So effective is this system against *ladrones,* if carried on properly, and so comparatively easy is it for the people in this country, without great suffer-ing or inconvenience, to move from one part of the country to another, erecting temporary houses of light material, that in Tayabas, which at one time was much afflicted with ladrones under a man named Rios . . . who has now expiated his crimes on the gallows, the so-called reconcentration

18. *Report of the Philippines Commission* (*1900–1903*) (Washington: U. S. Government Printing Office, 1904).
19. Ibid.

was used voluntarily by the towns that were invaded by Rios and carried to a successful conclusion before the central authorities were advised of the methods pursued.[20]

By 1903, Taft had given at least some native populations an incentive to protect either what they had or what they believed the future was to offer them. By such methods, Taft slowly won over the bulk of the population. Although sporadic revolts would continue until 1916, by mid-1902 the major insurrection was over.

The final figures were grim: more than four thousand Americans dead (thousands would later die from tropical diseases), thousands wounded; the insurrectos lost about twenty thousand killed; civilian deaths were estimated at two hundred thousand.

The end of the affair came as a great relief to the American people, but it left numerous citizens disturbed. Senator Hoar, an outspoken opponent of imperialism, addressed his colleagues:

. . . What has been the practical statesmanship which comes from your ideals and sentimentalities? You have wasted six hundred millions of treasure. You have sacrificed nearly ten thousand American lives, the flower of our youth. You have devastated provinces. You have slain uncounted thousands of the people you desire to benefit. You have established re-concentration camps. Your generals are coming home from their harvest, bringing their sheaves with them, in the shape of other thousands of sick and wounded and insane. . . . Your practical statesmanship has succeeded in converting a [grateful] people . . . into sullen and irreconcilable enemies, possessed of a hatred which centuries cannot eradicate.[21]

20. Ibid.
21. Wolff, op. cit.

Chapter 15

Small-war characteristics • Importance of leadership • Technology and increased weight • British, Russian and French failures • General Gordon and military blackmail • Charles Callwell's classic work: Small Wars

THE LESSONS derived from American experience in the Philippines made no great impact on military thinking of the day. In consolidating and expanding overseas empires, European powers had fought scores of campaigns, literally hundreds of battles, that in part or whole foreshadowed the American campaign. The army of each of these countries had faced similar situations, had made the same errors, had suffered but finally survived. Not only had this process happened to these armies, but it continued to happen—each military generation seemed determined to repeat past errors.

Nor was this altogether obtuseness.

For one thing, one small war rarely resembled another: each generally produced specific challenges that had to be met with specific and sometimes highly unorthodox tactical modifications. The colonizing giants of the time, Britain, France, Spain, and the Netherlands, supported armies that were too diversified in make-up and interest, too independent in operational responsibility, and too widely separated geographically in an age of limited communications for a healthy exchange of information.

Most colonial forces had begun as "company" armies, and only slowly reverted to crown control, but even they tended to remain closed shops, with their own standards and traditions, and showing very little interest in operations elsewhere—an insularity displayed simultaneously by American frontier forces and still displayed by remote garrisons today. In India, two armies existed side by side: the Indian army and the British army, the latter looking down on the former as decidedly inferior and able to teach it nothing. The combined experience of the two forces offered rich lessons in irregular warfare, but these were comfortably ignored by British forces elsewhere.

For another thing, colonial powers were spoiled: Military successes had far outweighed disasters, and it is a seeming axiom in war that only losers want to know why.

Major reasons for this military prosperity have been mentioned earlier: In brief, science and wisdom ruled over superstition and ignorance. The tendency of native forces to indulge charges and set-piece battles against smaller but well-armed and disciplined forces grew as the century waned. Time after time, small colonial armies smashed native hordes ten and twenty times their size.

Good leadership continued to play a vital role in the process. Despite certain civil failures, British military reverses must be laid in essence to poor generals. Conversely, successes stemmed in part from leaders such as "Fagin" Napier and Hugh Rose and Horatio Kitchener, each of whom fought and beat vast native armies; in the case of the French, Gallieni and Lyautey each conducted extremely successful pacification campaigns, which we shall examine shortly.

At the same time, a lack of native leadership often aided the Europeans. After the battle of the Sobraon, in 1846, for example, an Indian officer commented on the narrow margin of the British victory: ". . . The Khalsa fought as no man ever did in India before, but it was evident that their leaders knew not how to manage an army; when they had decided advantages in their hands they failed to make any use of them; their cavalry never came near the battlefield that I ever heard of. . . ."[1] The three major leaders of the Indian Mutiny, Nana Sahib, Tantia Topi and the Rani of Jhansi, were repeatedly beaten in set-piece battles.

Technology also continued important, with the edge going to European powers but scarcely to the exclusion of natives, whose weapons increasingly improved and frequently included artillery. Tactical employment of weapons was something else again, and here technology favored the disciplined force, particularly in the defense. With each progression

1. Cole, op. cit.

in the rifle—the Minié to the Enfield to the Snider to the Martini-Henry to the magazine rifle adopted in 1889, the Lee-Metford—speed, range, accuracy, and impact improved, just as it did with embryonic automatic weapons, the Gardner and the Gatling, and with artillery, first the breechloader in 1886, then the quick-firing gun in 1891.

These improvements, as was earlier the case, proved a mixed blessing because again they added weight to columns already heavy. Sir William Lockhart's 1897 expedition south of the Khyber numbered ". . . 35,000 troops with 20,000 more on their lines of communication."[2] But now natives were armed, at least in part, with breech-loading rifles, and the wormlike columns provided first-rate targets. European tactics of halting, dismounting, off-loading mountain guns, and deploying, usually to find nothing, was tiring, time-consuming, and frustrating.[3] The 1897 expedition showed beyond doubt ". . . that much more flexible tactics and more powerful artillery must be utilized, since as regards weapons the tribesmen were fighting on level terms and with the country very much in their favor."[4]

Long before 1897, some native forces had displayed disturbing ability to survive for a surprising length of time after strong points were overrun and armies dispersed. The British had the devil's own time in running down leaders of the Indian Mutiny, and one wonders what would have happened had Tantia Topi chosen to wage guerrilla warfare from the outset, or even midway through the campaign.

But other factors joined with tribesmen and terrain to complicate the problem, to tarnish, as it were, the sterling series of tactical successes. Some very serious reverses—for example, the opening phase of the first Afghan war, of 1839–42, the Indian Mutiny of 1857, the opening disasters of the Zulu war at Isandlhwana and Rorke's Drift, the Russian setbacks against the Turkomans, the costly and inconclusive first Boer war, of 1881, the early French disasters on Madagascar, Gordon's demise at Khartoum—dotted these decades of colonial campaigns.

The British were badly mauled in the first Afghan war not only because of civil failure to appreciate military problems—the entire expedition was strategically ludicrous—but also because of a failure in arms. As two modern British officer-historians, Cole and Priestley, concluded:

. . . The tragedy of Kabul [where General Elphinstone and his garrison were treacherously slaughtered] must be regarded as the penalty of overconfidence resulting from previous success. British arms had been so con-

2. Ibid.
3. Nor were more suitable tactics ever devised. The latter-day Indian campaigns so well described in Robert Henriques' splendid novel *No Arms, No Armour* and in John Masters' exciting novels must have closely resembled the Victorian campaigns.
4. Cole, op. cit.

sistently triumphant against overwhelming odds that it had come to be thought that imbecile plans, senile generals, too few British troops, a preposterous baggage-train and indifferent arms hardly mattered.[5]

The tragedy of the Indian Mutiny stemmed also from overconfidence, since a number of measures could have been taken against this contingency. A series of minor mutinies already had suggested trouble, and considering the ratio of armed native to armed European, 300,000:40,-000, the East India Company should have been on guard. Moreover, its conquest of Upper Burma in 1852 raised the ratio in favor of the native, and if, in the event, the culprits were Bengalese, still the Bengalese constituted about two thirds of the company's army. Finally, the Crimean war (1854–55) further weakened Britain's military posture in India, both in numbers and reputation, which added to the mutinous climate. Britain should now have learned, just as France should have learned from the Seven Years' War, the danger of conventional European wars to the colonial presence.

Gordon's stand at Khartoum taught a corollary lesson. His presence in the Sudan was a direct result of Britain's annexation of Egypt, in 1882, an act that had been forced on Gladstone. Although he did not want Egypt, once he had it he could not give it back. As if it did not constitute a sufficient problem, he inherited the chaos of the Sudan. Wanting to withdraw entirely from this vast territory, he assigned General Gordon the operational task without realizing the extent of Gordon's emotional involvement in the country. Gordon, like Napoleon, had a private arrangement with Destiny and was in no mind to be put off by the best interests of the British Government. By refusing to evacuate Khartoum, he indulged in a military blackmail for which he paid with his life, but only after greatly embarrassing his country.

Colonial forces of other countries similarly erred. In Algeria, the French for years failed to understand the tactical problem and wasted innumerable lives and treasure in attempting to apply false solutions. Initial French failures at Madagascar stemmed from poor intelligence, which caused Duchesne to waste thousands of lives trying to build an unnecessary road into the interior.

In general, the lessons of these and other setbacks (as well as those of most victories) seemed to make but fleeting impression on senior military minds. Details of each campaign were recorded (some inaccurately), and a few commentators appeared in print from time to time. General Skobeleff wrote at length of his 1880 campaign; the French officers later wrote of their campaigns.[6] We also find mention in con-

5. Ibid.
6. General Skobeleff, *Siege and Assault of Denghil-Tépé* (London: HMSO, 1881). Tr. J. J. Leverson; General Gallieni, *La Pacification de Madagascar* (*Opérations d'Octobre 1896 à Mars 1899*) (Paris: Librairie Militaire R. Chapelot,

temporary military literature of the occasional work such as Captain Peach's *Handbook of Tactics—Savage Warfare.*[7]

Until 1896, however, little codification of either strategy or tactics existed for this complicated period of irregular warfare. If the young officer studied anything more than various drill manuals, it was likely to be a standard work such as Brigadier General Clery's *Minor Tactics,* which slavishly preached the 1866 and 1870 orthodox battle doctrine.[8]

In 1896, in London, a work of a much different nature was published by a young major: Charles Callwell's *Small Wars—Their Principles and Practice.*[9]

Callwell wrote from considerable experience. A regular British officer of the Royal Field Artillery, he was also a scholar and linguist. He had fought in the second Afghan war, in India, and in 1881 had participated in the final operations against the Transvaal Boers, in Africa. Transferred to the Staff College in 1885, the twenty-six-year-old captain submitted an essay, "Small Wars," which won a gold medal from the Royal United Service Institution. During subsequent tours of duty in Intelligence and as an observer of the Greek-Turkish war, he published works on the armies of Romania, Turkey, and the minor Balkan states as well as one with the intriguing title *Hints on Reconnaissances in Little Known Countries.*[10] Meanwhile his essay on small wars had caused so much comment that he expanded it into what became the official textbook on the subject.[11]

1900); H. Lyautey, "Du rôle social de l'officier" and "Der rôle colonial de l'Armée," *Revue des Deux Mondes* (1891 and 1900). The extensive correspondence of the French officers, much of it concerning professional matters, has been largely preserved and published. See, for example, H. Deschamps and P. Chauvet, *Gallieni Pacificateur* (Paris: Presses Universitaires de France, 1949); P. B. Gheusi, *Gallieni et Madagascar* (Paris: Éditions du Petit Parisien, n.d.); H. Lyautey, *Lettres du Tonkin* (Paris: Éditions Nationales, 1928), 2 vols.; H. Lyautey, *Lettres du Tonkin et de Madagascar (1894–1899)* (Paris: Librairie Armand Colin, 1933, 3rd Edition); H. Lyautey, *Lettres du Sud de Madagascar (1900–1902)* (Paris: Librairie Armand Colin, 1935); Pierre Lyautey, *Lyautey L'Africain—Textes et Lettres du Maréchal Lyautey présentés par Pierre Lyautey* (Paris: Librairie Plon, 1953), 4 vols.; etc.

7. Callwell, op. cit.

8. C. F. Clery, *Minor Tactics* (London: Kegan Paul, Trench, 1887). Clery's experience as chief of staff of the Egypt Army does not seem to have altered his orthodox tactical views in the slightest.

9. Callwell, *supra* (1896). He followed this with revised editions in 1899 and 1903.

10. These are official publications, short and dull: 1888, *The Armed Strength of Roumania;* 1890, *Hints on Reconnaissances in Little Known Countries;* 1891, *Handbook of the Armies of the Minor Balkan States;* 1892, *Handbook of the Turkish Army;* all published in London by HMSO.

11. *Dictionary of National Biography 1922–30* (London: Oxford University Press, 1937). After distinguished service in the Boer war, Callwell continued to publish military work, sometimes of a critical, sometimes of a frivolous, nature,

In the opening pages of *Small Wars,* Callwell took pains to pacify the orthodox military reader. He did not wish to quarrel with ". . . the system of regular warfare of today. Certain rules of conduct exist which are universally accepted. Strategy and tactics alike are in great campaigns governed, in most respects, by a code from which it is perilous to depart."

So far, so good.

But contiguous to orthodox wars are small wars. A small war ". . . may be said to include all campaigns other than those where both the opposing sides consist of regular troops. It comprises the expeditions against savages and semi-civilized races by disciplined soldiers, campaigns undertaken to suppress rebellions and guerrilla warfare in all parts of the world where organized armies are struggling against opponents who will not meet them in the open field. . . ."

. . . Why are the European nations involved in small wars? Small wars are a heritage of extended empire, a certain epilogue to encroachments into lands beyond the confines of existing civilization, and this has been so from early ages to the present time. Conquerors of old, penetrating into the unknown, encountered races with strange and unconventional military methods and trod them down, seizing their territory; revolts and insurrections followed, disputes and quarrels with tribes on the borders of the districts overcome supervened, out of the original campaign of conquest sprang further wars, and all were vexatious, desultory, and harassing. And the history of these operations repeats itself in the small wars of today.

The great nation which seeks expansion in remote quarters of the globe must accept the consequences. Small wars dog the footsteps of the pioneer of civilization in regions afar off. The trader heralds almost as a matter of course the coming of the soldier, and commercial enterprise in the end generally leads to conquest. Foreign possessions bring military responsibilities in their train which lead to petty warfare. Spain and Portugal in the age of maritime discovery found that it was so, and Great Britain, France and Russia experience it now.

Callwell sounded like a latter-day combination of Sun Tzu, the emperors Maurice and Leo, and Marshal de Saxe. In establishing what a small war is and why it came about, he continued:

. . . The conditions of small wars are so diversified, the enemy's mode of fighting is often so peculiar, the theaters of operations present such singular features, that irregular warfare must generally be carried out on a method totally different from the stereotyped system. The art of war, as generally

---

which earned him service enemies. Passed over for promotion to general, he retired in 1909. Recalled to duty in 1914, he served with distinction, winning promotion to major general and a knighthood. He retired after the war and died in 1928, shortly after editing Field Marshal Sir Henry Wilson's diaries.

understood, must be modified to suit the circumstances of each particular case. The conduct of small wars is in fact in certain respects an art by itself, diverging widely from what is adapted to the conditions of regular warfare, but not so widely that there are not in all its branches points which permit comparisons to be established.

The young officer offered three broad classes of small wars: campaigns of conquest or annexation; campaigns for the suppression of insurrections or lawlessness, or for the settlement of conquered or annexed territory; campaigns undertaken to wipe out an insult, to avenge a wrong, or to overthrow a dangerous enemy.

Not only did small wars differ from regular warfare, but often from each other. In several hundred somewhat prolix pages, Callwell examined major differences from strategic and tactical viewpoints, expounding at length on problems of staff and command, intelligence, communications, supply, and general operations in a host of small-war environments. He followed this with detailed chapters on offensive and defensive tactics in a variety of terrain, pursuits and retreats, feints, surprises-raids-ambushes, night attacks, fighting in hill and bush country, guerrilla warfare. He illustrated critical analyses with campaign episodes, some of which I have cited previously in this book. Throughout this pioneering work, he often demanded extreme tactical modifications, citing verse, chapter, and text of British and European military failures as proof of his conclusions.

Callwell differentiated between small wars and guerrilla wars, but pointed out that they share many common characteristics. In introducing his section on tactics, he presciently wrote:

. . . The military forces of today are complicated organisms which the stress of combat tends to disturb, the more elaborate the machinery the more liable it is to be thrown out of gear by rough handling or by sudden shock; it is owing to this indeed that the art of war has assumed so definite a shape. But irregular warriors have not so highly sensitive a tactical system, they are prepared to disperse should the fates prove unpropitious, and each fighting man enjoys individual independence. In these small wars, in fact, the enemy does not offer an intricate organization as an object for the commander of the regular troops to direct his energies against.

Rather than despising the savage, Callwell continued, his words echoing Bouquet's sage advice of a previous century (see Chapter 7), the orthodox must remember that

. . . irregular warriors are generally warriors not by training but by nature. The fighting instincts of the regular soldier are, in spite of his training and his military calling, dormant till he goes on active service. He lives in a land with a settled social system, where life is secure and where the rights of prop-

erty are protected by laws which are obeyed . . . [the savage] acquires a
military sagacity and skill in the use of such weapons as he has at his command which the trained soldier never can aspire to. The one trusts to his
own wits in the hour of danger, the other looks to his superior for guidance.
And so it comes about that, leaving actual courage and also of course arms
out of account, the regular troops are individually inferior to their opponents
in these wars. They do not possess the same fertility of military resource, they
have not the same instinctive capacity for contriving ambushes and for carrying out surprises, they are amateurs while their adversaries are professional fighting men.

The individual assumes an even greater role in guerrilla warfare,
which depends so much on small-unit action and on over-all charismatic
leadership:

. . . No one today remembers who led the Khalsa armies at Sobraon or the
Beluchis in Scinde, but Abd-el-Kader and the Circassian Schamyl figure
among the great soldiers of the age. Charette and Andreas Hofer still live in
history, not as patriots only but also as masters of one form of the art of war.
And Tantia Topi owes his reputation not to Kalpi and Cawnpore but to the
months when, with a dwindling following and bound to a declining cause,
he kept the field while the British hunted him in vain.

Of the entire *genre* of small wars, from the orthodox commander's
viewpoint guerrilla war is the worst *species:*

. . . Guerrilla warfare is what the regular armies always have to dread, and
when this is directed by a leader with a genius for war, an effective campaign
becomes well-nigh impossible. . . .

After proving this disturbing point with historical examples, Callwell
offered some hope for the resolute and energetic orthodox commander,
but he warned that

. . . The guerrilla mode of war must in fact be met by an abnormal system
of strategy and tactics. The great principle which forms the basis of the art
of war remains—the combination of initiative with energy; but this is applied
in a special form. The utmost vigor and decision must be displayed in harassing the enemy and in giving him no rest; the hostile bands may elude
the regular detachments, but their villages and flocks remain. The theater of
war must be sub-divided into sections, each to be dealt with by a given
force or by a given aggregate of separate detachments. Defensive posts must
be established where supplies can be collected, whither raided cattle can be
brought, and which form independent bases. To each such base must be
attached one or more mobile, self-contained columns, organized to be ready
to move out at a moment's notice, and equipped so as to penetrate to any
part of the district told off to it and to return, certain of supplies for the task.

Callwell emphasized the necessity for good intelligence exploited by mobility. He favored the "flying column" of either horse or foot, or both, a tactical formation introduced by Hoche in the Vendée and used with such success by Bugeaud in Algeria, the British in Afghanistan and Burma, and the Americans against the Red Indians. He warned, however, that

. . . in no class of warfare is the need of self-reliant subordinate officers so urgent as in operations of this nature, and the lack of such may spoil the best matured combinations of the chief.

Despite the gold medal and official recognition, Callwell's work did not cause a *volte-face* in British military thinking. The time was not ripe for a young man to hold school on his elders—has it ever been?—and indeed Callwell's professional career suffered because of his disturbing and generally accurate conclusions. Although his work failed by omission in that he insufficiently stressed the political task of pacification campaigns, it nonetheless should have been studied and respected by military commanders throughout the empire.

Instead, his teachings apparently failed to reach home, at least in such quarters as British garrisons in Burma and South Africa. The pacification of Upper Burma (1885–90) demonstrated the validity of many of Callwell's teachings. So did the second Boer war, which started in 1899, a turbulent three years in which various British generals managed to commit just about every past error pointed out by Callwell. Ironically, the young author himself served with distinction in this unhappy war—in 1903 he published a revised edition of his work that incorporated the newest lessons.

Chapter 16

THE FIRST BURMA WAR (1820) established the British presence in three important provinces; the second war (1852) extended British control and placed a co-operative ruler, Mindon Min, on the throne of Upper Burma. Mindon's death, in 1878, ended a relatively quiescent period that witnessed extensive commercial exploitation of the country by British companies.

Mindon's son, Thibaw, was not a strong ruler. Controlled by a reactionary palace group working through Queen Supayalat, Thibaw terminated most of Mindon's reforms and also began quarreling with British commercial interests. When the king opened negotiations with France in 1883, the British Government grew thoroughly alarmed; the quarrel continuing, in 1885 a British military expedition occupied Mandalay and deported Thibaw and his queen. A few months later, Britain annexed Upper Burma and its tributary states and made the entire country a province of the Indian Empire.

The British expedition under General Prendergast had overcome organized resistance with little difficulty. But the British did not capture Thibaw's army, which dispersed with many of the soldiers forming guerrilla bands to carry on the war. The ease with which the larger of these groups gave way to a further British military effort at first caused the interlopers to underestimate the pacification task. They did not realize the extent of the rebellion or its deep-seated nature. Preferring to blame brigands, or dacoits, they failed to understand that spontaneous risings were not alone ". . . led by officers of various grades of the disbanded royal armies" but also by ". . . village headmen, former officials in the service of the king, princes of the blood, and even Buddhist monks. . . ."[1]

To pacify and administer its newest acquisition, the British divided the vast area of some 160,000 square miles into fourteen (later seventeen) districts, each headed by a deputy commissioner ". . . with a British police officer to assist him and such armed force of police, as could be assigned to him. . . ." In the early months, the onus of pacification, however, fell on a Burma Field Force of about fourteen thousand troops commanded by Major General George White.[2] Only six months after formal annexation, White outlined the military problem in a report to superiors in India:

. . . These bands are freebooters, pillaging wherever they go, but usually reserving the refinement of their cruelty for those who have taken office under us or part with us. Flying columns arrive too late to save the village. The villagers, having cause to recognize that we were too far off to protect them, lose confidence in our power and throw in their lot with the insurgents. They make terms with the leaders and baffle pursuit of those leaders by roundabout guidance or systematic silence. In a country itself one vast military obstacle, the seizure of the leaders of the rebellion, though of paramount importance, thus becomes a source of greatest difficulty.[3]

White attempted to solve the problem by establishing a network of 141 military posts, the weakest consisting of forty riflemen. Patrols of not less than ten men theoretically maintained the peace; if a post could not suppress a local rising, strategically placed garrisons supplied reinforcements. Difficult terrain necessarily limited reaction time as well as operational radius of patrols; where possible, troops traveled by a new type of river boat, ". . . a very light-draught paddle-wheeler, with

1. Maung Htin Aung, *A History of Burma* (New York: Columbia University Press, 1967); see also Maung Htin Aung, *The Stricken Peacock—Anglo-Burmese Relations 1752–1948* (The Hague: Martinus Nijhoff, 1965).
2. Charles Crosthwaite, *The Pacification of Burma* (London: Edward Arnold, 1912).
3. Ibid.

simple machinery and fair speed, with accommodation for half a company of rifles and a couple of officers. . . ."[4]

Although the post system hurt guerrilla operations, it did not stop them. The chief commissioner of Burma from 1887 to 1890, Sir Charles Crosthwaite, later wrote that ". . . when the soldiers passed on, the power of the British Government went with them, and the villagers fell back under the rule of the guerrilla leaders and their gangs." Moreover, troops often remained ignorant of conditions in their immediate areas; districts reported to be "quite peaceful" or "comparatively settled," Crosthwaite wrote, ". . . were often altogether in the hands of hostile bands. They were reported quiet because we could hear no noise. We were outsiders. . . ." The posts also bred an unhealthy reliance on fixed force:

. . . It was found necessary from the first to restrain firmly the tendency of the local officials to fritter away the strength of the force in small posts. The moment anything occurred they wanted to clap down a post on the disturbed spot; and if this had been allowed to go on unchecked there would not have been a man left to form a movable column or even to send out a patrol of sufficient strength.[5]

Although the military phase proved necessary, Crosthwaite concluded:

. . . The people might be held down in this way, but not governed. Something more was necessary. The difficulties were to be overcome rather by the vigorous administration of civil government than by the employment of military detachments scattered over the country. A sufficient force of armed police at the disposal of the civil officers was therefore a necessity.[6]

Crosthwaite's answer was to recruit what eventually amounted to fifteen thousand military police from India. Replacing military posts as rapidly as possible with police protection, he relied on troops for special operations against particularly troublesome areas and also to carry out an extensive village resettlement program—a shifting in some cases of entire villages in order to deprive guerrillas of support. Although he reported a greatly improved situation by mid-1888, he had come under some fire for harsh methods of pacification. He himself later complained of

. . . the demands from the Secretary of State for information, which came through the Government of India, [and] wasted a great deal of time. Members of Parliament who cannot force themselves into notice in other ways, take up a subject like Burma, of which no one knows anything, and asks

4. Ibid.
5. Ibid.
6. Ibid.

[sic] questions which the Secretary of State has to answer. . . . Correspondents of newspapers, not so much perhaps out of malice—although that is not quite unknown—as from the necessities of their profession are greedy for sensational news. They know that the English public prefer to think that their servants abroad are either fools or scoundrels. If everything is reported to be going well and the officers to be doing their duty, few will credit it, and none will be interested in it. But hint vaguely at dark intrigues or horrible atrocities, ears are cocked at once, and the newspaper boys sweep in the pence.[7]

A modern Burmese historian, Professor Maung Htin Aung, would soundly have defended the British press in its attempts to uncover sordid facts of pacification. Professor Htin Aung has written that Crosthwaite was a ruthless administrator responsible for thousands of civil deaths. By singling out for persecution families ". . . who had supplied the headmen of villages for several generations," Crosthwaite hoped to destroy any threat from natural leaders.

Alas, he accomplished this in part but some survived. If Sir Charles hoped to break the Burmese spirit, he must have been a disappointed man. Sporadic resistance continued for years and so did Burmese desire for independence. People suffered and died, but the survivors, as Htin Aung wrote, ". . . quietly built little pagodas on the sites of the executions and kept alive the spirit of nationalism. . . ."[8]

The second Boer war had been brewing for nearly twenty years. The failure of the 1899 Bloemfontein conference, followed by Jameson's ill-prompted raid, merely heightened existing tensions to bring war in October.

That the Boers could fight and fight well was already proved by the first Boer war, of 1881, when mounted settlers had run rings around Sir George Colley's small British army. The colonizing process, and particularly the Kaffir wars, had produced a nation in arms with a commando system that enabled the country to ". . . put every male of fighting age into the field."[9] Few would dispute the Boer's mastery of rifle or horse. His fighting spirit was obvious. President Kruger, in his truculent exchanges with Rhodes and his South Africa Company and with the Cape government, had left no doubt of his determination to fight, and he had emphasized his attitude by importing modern arms including large cannon from Germany.

In October 1899, Kruger mustered a total force of about fifty thou-

7. Ibid.
8. Htin Aung, op. cit.
9. Cole, op. cit.; see also L. S. Amery (ed.), *The Times History of the War in South Africa* (London: Sampson, Low, Marston, 1902), Vol. 2 (1902) of 5 vols.

sand, mostly mounted men thoroughly at home in the vast land. Against this impressive force, Sir Redvers Buller commanded a dispersed British army of about twenty thousand supported by some ten thousand ancillaries—colonials, volunteers, and police.[10]

Although Buller would soon gain substantial reinforcements, Kruger held the initiative. Instead of invading Cape Colony, which was perfectly possible, and which might have resulted in a speedy Boer victory, Kruger attacked British forces immediately at hand. In short order, his commandos invested British garrisons at Ladysmith, in the Northeast, and Mafeking and Kimberley, in the Northwest. These moves, Kruger reasoned, would bring the British north, where he could fight them on his own terms.

Buller reacted predictably: One column, under Sir William Gatacre, moved up the center railway toward Bloemfontein; another column, under Lord Methuen, marched along the western railway toward Kimberley; a final column, under his own command, headed for the Tugela River toward Ladysmith. In addition, Sir John French's first-rate cavalry force was operating in the Northwest, but, by now, both troopers and mounts were tiring.

Buller's greatest enemy was space. His base ports, Cape Town and Durban, lay hundreds of miles apart; Pretoria, capital of the Transvaal, was eight hundred miles from Cape Town. Buller's columns had to cross an area the size of France and Germany. Lack of animal transport and almost no roads tied infantry to single-line railroads. Lack of communications and distance between railways caused Buller to forfeit tactical control. Lack of training and dubious command procedures caused columns to proceed without flank or frontal security. Lack of maps caused commanders to use guides, who generally proved unreliable.

By mid-December, each of the columns was badly mauled and had stopped short of its goal. The press lumped these initial reverses together in the eye-catching term "Black Week" it was, but it stemmed from the neglect of years.[11]

Early in 1900, however, a remarkable command team arrived to repair matters: Field Marshal Lord Roberts, veteran of forty-one years of Indian fighting, a man who respected his enemy before beating him; his chief of staff, Major General Lord Kitchener, hero of Omdurman, until recently Sirdar of the Egypt Army, not yet fifty years old, a cold, blue-eyed taskmaster who trampled on tradition when necessary to get things done, a hard man who slaughtered the Dervishes in the Sudan, then contemplated having the Mahdi's skull made into a drinking cup.

Roberts, at sixty-eight years of age, was a small, one-eyed, peppery,

10. Ibid. See also E. S. May, *A Retrospect on the South African War* (London: Sampson, Low, Marston, 1901). The author is particularly interesting on the artillery's role.

11. Amery, op. cit. (Vol. 3, 1905).

and able soldier who, just as important, was familiar with war in large theaters and with the particular military problem on hand. Upon disembarking in Africa, he learned that his son had just been killed in the Tugela fighting. With his one good eye, he wept briefly, then turned to the military problem: he would bring the war to Kruger, no doubting that, but scarcely on Kruger's terms. Roberts would use the supply umbilical of the western railway as far as the Modder River, but here he would wean his army in favor of animal transport and turn to advance on Bloemfontein, his interim base for a final advance to Pretoria.

To organize enough transport and to mount colonials into a semblance of a cavalry division required a month of hard and frustrating work, as Kitchener wrote to a friend:

. . . We are getting along a little bit, but we have not a single saddle for love or money; all our water-bottles are so small as to be useless. It was exactly the same in the Sudan, when I had to fit out the whole of the British troops with water-bottles which they had to pay for. Not a single emergency ration, so the men have to fight all day on empty stomachs. I could go on, but what is the use? I am afraid I rather disgust the old red-tape heads of departments. They are very polite, but after a bit present me with a volume of their printed regulations generally dated about 1870 and intended for Aldershot maneuvers, and are quite hurt when I do not agree to their printed rot.[12]

Roberts pushed north in early February, an approach march undetected by Cronjé at Magersfontein. Cronjé paid dearly for ignorance. With Roberts temporarily indisposed, Kitchener took over and lightning struck. Cronjé, surprised and outflanked by French's cavalry, ran due east, his retreat impeded by a train of heavy supply wagons that he stubbornly refused to abandon. Once French had entered Kimberley and cleared the British flank, Kitchener sent him after Cronjé, who was struggling to cross the Modder River at Paardeberg. Still refusing to sacrifice his train—De Wet's commando was supposed to be rushing to his aid—he was caught and forced to surrender.

Despite this happy turn of events, Kitchener and Roberts still had problems: enteric fever, caused by bad water, was sweeping through the ranks; French had lost hundreds of horses; supply was short; and De Wet's considerable commando was somewhere in the area. Roberts nonetheless pushed east toward Bloemfontein. De Wet delayed him but was not strong enough to stop him, and in mid-March the British force reached the important capital.

Roberts was extremely short of supply by now; he ". . . had no cavalry, no mounted infantry and no artillery with horses in effective condition." Enteric fever continued its violent course and he had to clear Boer

12. George Arthur, *Life of Lord Kitchener* (London: Macmillan, 1920), Vol. 1 of 3 vols.

partisans from his right flank. He took seven weeks to put matters to his satisfaction before advancing north along the railway toward Pretoria.

His campaign now began to resemble Halleck's and Grant's march through Tennessee with Forrest and Morgan tearing at their lines of communication. As fast as Roberts' soldiers repaired the tracks, Boer guerrillas tore them up. Out of seventy-five thousand troops, Roberts was forced to use nearly half guarding his single line of communications! And these were none too many. Upon reaching Johannesburg, he cabled the War Office that his troops ". . . were living from hand to mouth," the result of short supply. But now his strategic goal, Pretoria, was in sight. After a brief halt, he continued his push on this capital and, after a final battle, entered it in early June.

In Roberts' mind, his march, by ending organized Boer government, should have ended the war. President Kruger was on the run—indeed he soon sailed for Europe in a futile attempt to find helpful allies.

What Roberts failed to realize was a slow but certain change in Boer leadership that had been going on since Cronjé's disaster at Paardeberg.

Younger commanders such as Christiaan de Wet and Louis Botha

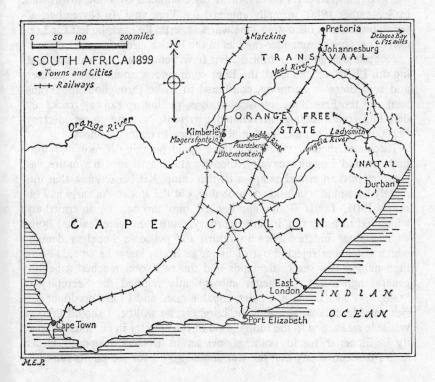

had long since realized the futility of trying to fight European-style war against heavy British columns. Turning increasingly to guerrilla warfare, they had been joined by such natural leaders as De La Rey and Jan Smuts.

These and other leaders were now based, albeit tenuously, east of Pretoria, in the Delagoa Bay area. To them, Kruger's departure mattered but little—his command already was fragmented, the commandos having fought more or less separately for months. Their commandos were not only intact, but could still tap human and material resources to keep on fighting until the British tired and offered a fair peace. Some of the more fanatic held to a never-surrender policy, but it is probably fair to say that the majority were pragmatists in this sense. In any event, theirs was the decision to keep fighting, and to it De Wet added a powerful spice by very nearly capturing Lord Kitchener.

Considering the situation, the Boers acted boldly. Once in Pretoria, Roberts quickly made good his losses. Reinforcements, both human and material, began to pour in. While Kitchener and French flailed flying columns about the countryside in mostly useless attempts against the guerrillas, Roberts consolidated his command over the towns and, in September 1900, formally annexed the Transvaal. In November, after stating that in his opinion the war was virtually over, he left for London to become commander-in-chief of the British army.

Roberts was unduly optimistic. Far from being over, the war was heating up. Living off the land, the Boer commandos, sometimes separately and sometimes in harmony, continued to strike throughout the Transvaal and the Free State, blowing bridges, pulling up railway tracks and derailing trains, falling on isolated garrisons, burning stores, destroying convoys—all in mocking denial of the British claim to victory.

Kitchener reacted vigorously, first by jury-rigging a mounted force built around French's cavalry, then by starting to turn the entire vast territory into an armed camp—a British camp. Kitchener knew that ultimately he would win, and so, probably, did the Boers. As early as February 1901, Louis Botha approached him through an intermediary, which led to a meeting in late February. Both men were realists. Botha wanted Boer independence in return for peace, a hopeless demand which Kitchener rejected out of hand, as Botha knew he would. Botha then named less severe demands and the two soon reached a healthy general agreement. Kitchener subsequently notified the Secretary of State: ". . . L. Botha is a quiet, capable man, and I have no doubt carries considerable weight with the burghers; he will be, I should think, a valuable assistance to the future good of the country in an official capacity." Kitchener found nothing onerous in Botha's proposed terms: ". . . It seems a pity that the war should go on for the points raised by

Botha, which appear to me all capable of adjustment."[13] Arrogant in its ignorance and in its power, the British Government in the form of Sir Arther Milner caviled over giving amnesty to the Cape Colony rebels, a debatable refusal to one of Botha's major demands. Stalemate ensued, and, toward the end of March, Botha dropped further negotiations.

Kitchener's hopes for an early peace thus dashed, he turned again to the military problem. Lacking necessary intelligence and essential mobility, his approach tended toward the defensive, his lines of communication now becoming his paramount concern. To guard these, he divided the territory into specific military areas. To each he assigned large numbers of his ever-increasing army to build a series of blockhouses, at first along the railway and on vital bridges. These structures consisted of ". . . two skins of corrugated iron nailed on to wooden frames, the space between being filled up with gravel and earth." Each housed one non-commissioned officer and seven men; it was supported by its neighbor, generally a thousand yards removed, to which in time it became linked by barbed wire.[14]

During 1901, the area of operations grew into a labyrinth of such blockhouses. At the end of 1901, Kitchener's new chief of staff, Ian Hamilton, wrote to Lord Roberts:

. . . Although I had read much of blockhouses, I never could have imagined such a gigantic system of fortifications, barriers, traps and garrisons as actually exists. This forms the principal characteristic of the present operations, supplying them with a solid backbone and involving permanent loss of territory to the enemy, which former operations did not.[15]

Kitchener supported this system with a force of about 240,000, an illusory figure greatly reduced by sickness: in June 1901, the net fighting strength stood ". . . at under 164,000 men."[16] Passive defense—blockhouse garrisons, base garrisons, railway guards, depot cadre and the like—required 100,000 men. Active defense in the form of mounted "flying columns" used the rest. Kitchener sent these columns on "drives" of the increasingly segregated areas. Such drives sometimes involved

13. H. de Watteville, *Lord Kitchener* (London: Blackie & Son, 1939). Although Botha could not guarantee acceptance of any agreement by his fellows, the opportunity to end the war should have been more fully explored; had it proved successful, it would have prevented enormous suffering and expense.

14. Amery, op. cit. (Vol. 5, 1907). Eventually these were replaced by octagonal, umbrella-roofed structures more cheaply constructed from prefabricated corrugated iron sheets, the invention of a Major Rice; ". . . ordinary barbed wire was used at first, but the Boers became such adepts at cutting it that a quarter-inch unannealed steel wire, specially manufactured in England, had to be substituted."

15. Arthur, op. cit. (Vol. 2).

16. Ibid.

a single column or less, sometimes five or six columns, ". . . with as many as five thousand mounted men abreast."[17]

Kitchener did not expect great bags of prisoners. He had had enormous experience in this type of warfare both in Egypt and Africa: in July 1901, he wrote the Secretary of State, ". . . these flying columns, on extended operations in this vast country, only in great measure beat the air, as the mobile Boers clear off the moment they hear of the columns being sometimes twenty miles away."

Kitchener wanted to keep the commandos off balance and out of touch with each other. To deprive them of hearing of the columns, he began to clear key areas of people, moving women and children into concentration camps, where he kept them despite a fearful outcry from home. To deprive commandos of livelihood, food, and mounts, Kitchener burned farms in the best Sherman tradition. He also deported Boer prisoners—some twenty-four thousand—to overseas camps.[18]

Kitchener suffered any number of setbacks. He was not at all pleased with his army. He thought its discipline was dreadful, and he could not understand the insouciance of younger officers who showed a near camaraderie to the enemy instead of treating them like dervishes. The difficulty stemmed in large part from an essentially defensive army composed largely of non-professionals with little patience for the frustrations inherent in attrition warfare. Kitchener did his best to impose disciplined behavior, but as late as March 1902, command laxity resulted in Methuen's column being ambushed. Kitchener wrote: ". . . I am having one officer tried for the loss of the convoy, and six officers tried for Methuen's disaster. These trials probably will result in other trials, as we get at the truth."[19]

At this stage, Kitchener was becoming increasingly pessimistic and even unsure of himself. On one occasion, he wrote Lord Roberts, ". . . I wish those who say that the war should be over would come out and show us how to do it."[20] And in March 1902, only weeks before the Boer capitulation, he wrote apropos of the Methuen disaster, ". . . The dark days are on us again."

The dark days were about to lighten. The Boers, reduced to some twenty thousand men, lacked food, mounts, medicine. Continual hardship, desertions, pursuit had flagged once-ebullient spirits. Peace seemed inevitable and, considering various amnesty statements of the enemy, even enviable. They quit in the spring of 1902.

From 1899 to 1902, the Boers had put 90,000 men in the field. Of these, they lost an estimated 4,000 killed, thousands more wounded and taken prisoner; poor sanitary conditions in the concentration camps

17. De Watteville, op. cit.; see also Amery, op. cit.
18. Cole, op. cit.
19. Arthur, op. cit.
20. Ibid.

accounted for perhaps 20,000 civilian deaths. The British army, which altogether mustered 450,000 men, lost 6,000 killed in action, over 20,000 wounded, and about 16,000 dead from wounds and disease. The war cost England over £200 million, not to mention the investment necessary to rebuild the ravaged country.[21]

21. Cole, op. cit.; see also Amery, op. cit. (Vol. 7, 1909), for a breakdown of the figures.

Chapter 17

Hubert Lyautey • His background • Gallieni's tactics against Indochinese "pirates" • Origin of the tache d'huile *concept • Gallieni's influence on Lyautey • Pacification of Madagascar • Tache* d'huile *tactics in Algeria • Pacification of Morocco • Lyautey: success or failure?*

MAJOR CALLWELL laid far more stress on military problems of colonization than on political problems, a priority natural for a professional soldier. He did not seem to realize that a solution of the political problem, either in whole or in part, could have diminished or eliminated the military problem—an interesting fact uncovered by the more successful commanders of the colonial era.

The French general Hubert Lyautey ranks as one of these. Born and bred a royalist, Lyautey was a devout Roman Catholic who became interested in social reform while a student at St. Cyr. Intensely bright, he pursued this interest during early, prosaic postings. As a squadron commander at St. Germain in 1887, he startled fellow officers by showing concern for the mental welfare of his troops: ". . . he arranged a large room supplied with tables, a library, lamps, where the men found books, games, a billiard-table, writing-paper. . . ."[1] His continued interest in

1. André Maurois, *Marshal Lyautey* (London: John Lane, Bodley Head, 1931). Tr. H. Miles. I have relied extensively on this work, but see also an authorized

social welfare brought him into contact with some of the leading French intellectuals, and he soon began to publish controversial articles in the better journals.

Writing in 1889–91, Lyautey thought he saw in the French officer corps of some twenty thousand a potential social force that could bring about necessary reforms. Internal changes in the corps were first necessary: He argued, for example, that an officer must know his men better than his horses, which was not usually the case. Provided the officer acquired a social conscience, however, he could indoctrinate conscripts with essential principles of patriotism and nationalism necessary for a renascence that ultimately would repair the humiliating 1870 defeat by the Prussians.[2] Although the thirty-seven-year-old major conceived this activity within the traditional monarchist-church framework, his ideas created a mild sensation and marked him in some quarters as a socialist and revolutionary. To save his career, sympathetic seniors posted him to Indochina.[3] (See map, Chapter 45.)

Lyautey arrived in Saigon in 1894. The French already had staked claim to most of Indochina: Cochin China had been a colony since 1862, and Annam a protectorate since 1885. The governor-general, De Lanessan, ruled these areas with a philosophy that he explained to Lyautey on a train trip to Hanoi:

. . . In every country there are existing frameworks. The great mistake for European people coming there as conquerors is to destroy these frameworks. Bereft of its armature, the country falls into anarchy. One must govern *with* the mandarin and not *against* the mandarin. The European cannot substitute himself numerically; but he can control. Therefore, don't disturb any tradition, don't change any custom. In every society there exists a ruling class, born to rule, without which nothing can be done. Enlist that class in our interests.[4]

Although the French had managed to pacify the southern areas and most of the Tonkin Delta by this time (see Chapter 42), De Lanessan's rule did not cover the northern provinces of Tonkin, ceded by China to France by the treaty of Tientsin and ". . . declared Military Territories, administered by superior French officers, who had to deal with the pirates infesting these regions."[5]

biography: Sonia E. Howe, *Lyautey of Morocco* (London: Hodder & Stoughton, 1931); and previously cited correspondence.

    2. Peter W. Paret, *French Revolutionary Warfare from Indochina to Algeria— The Analysis of a Political and Military Doctrine* (New York: Frederick A. Praeger, 1964).

    3. Maurois, op. cit.
    4. Ibid.
    5. Howe, op. cit.

As Joseph Buttinger has pointed out in his comprehensive two-volume work *Vietnam: A Dragon Embattled,* the pirates were often nationalists fighting for independence, a fact overlooked, perhaps intentionally, by most French officials:

. . . the French, totally mistaken about the nature of their enemy and the difficulties of pacifying a nation as old as the Vietnamese, relied exclusively on brute force. "We had at this time no idea," wrote a witness of conquest and pacification, "of the importance and quality of these Vietnamese bands; our first columns merely traversed the country without occupying it; they were putting, a little too indifferently, steel and fire into every village where they met the slightest trace of resistance." The commanders of these columns, who equated spreading terror with creating order, turned more peasants into partisans than the mandarins who agitated for armed resistance. . . .

. . . [The French] subscribed to the principle of "collective responsibility," which meant summary executions of noncombatants, "the last expedient in all wars against partisans by regular troops that cannot touch their opponents." De Lanessan and others described what this principle meant in practice: "Every village that has given refuge to a band of guerrillas or not reported their passage is declared responsible and guilty. Consequently, the chief of the village and two or three principal inhabitants are beheaded, and the village itself is set on fire and razed to the ground." Prisoners, of course, as Captain Gosselin reports in his revealing book, were always shot, "on orders from above." Severe repression worked the inevitable result:
. . . even the meek among the people, and certainly the terror-stricken, hated the French, and no man of honor among the leaders cooperated with them as long as the partisans continued their fight. "Those who collaborated with us," says a historian of this and later periods of trouble, "succumb to the lure of money, or even worse to unrestrained and unscrupulous ambition. Nobility of soul, disinterestedness, and courage are to be found in the opposition. Against this coalition of moral forces nothing can be done."

The tactical result was equally inevitable:

. . . The official military history of Indochina again and again tells how the troops engaged in hunting down the guerrillas, although numerically strong, well equipped, and often well led, missed their objective wherever the French had no friends. . . . "A column is helpless against these brigands, who, at the approach of our troops, disperse in the villages, where, thanks to the complicity of the population and probably the indigenous officials, they cannot be found. . . . Moreover, our troops are paralyzed by an absolute lack of information. The commanders of our posts do not have the money to buy informants." The enemy, on the other hand, got all the information he needed without having to pay. "As soon as a patrol starts out, the pirates are warned, while we," wrote one official historian, "walk in a hostile country as though blind."

A few outstanding and experienced French officers had questioned first, and then begun changing, this policy. Colonels such as Servière, Vallière, Pennequin, and Gallieni had recognized the political element of the problem:

. . . These men combined military with psychological action, apart from being the first to take advantage of the country's peculiar geographical circumstances. This they did by the application of measures valid to this day as a condition of success against guerrilla warfare: They counteracted the support, or even merely the sympathy, of the people toward the guerrillas through social, economic, and political measures designed to elicit equal if not greater support.[6]

As temporary chief of staff in Hanoi, Commandant Lyautey was soon conferring with the commander of the effort, the forty-four-year-old Colonel Gallieni, who had made his colonizing reputation in the Senegal and Sudan. Gallieni at once impressed the new arrival, both with the scope of the pacification problem and his solution. As Gallieni later wrote:

. . . The tactics of the pirates were to retire into the most hidden places of the great thickets of the forest, there to organize their defenses in such a way as to compel their assailants to approach very close over open ground, and then to take them unawares between crossfires, at the very moment when the numerous obstacles arranged all around and outside the principal defenses had to be overcome.

Gallieni relied on surprise and mobility—a system of converging mobile columns—to attack these various strongholds, but this was only part of the answer. As he explained to Lyautey: ". . . Piracy is not a necessary historical fact. It is the result of an economic condition. It can be fought by prosperity." Although superior discipline, firepower and mobile tactics could in time subdue the pirates, military success meant ". . . *nothing* unless combined with a simultaneous work of organization—roads, telegraphs, markets, crops—so that with the pacification there flowed forward, like a pool of oil, a great belt of civilization."[7]

Gallieni did not realize it, but he had fashioned a strategic device used by the ancient Greeks, the *epiteichismos,*

. . . which meant the fortification of some place or region to put pressure upon an enemy. . . . In the first stage of the Peloponnesian war the enterprising Athenian general, Demosthenes, occupied a position on the west coast of the Peloponnesus, which led indirectly to the capture of a force of

6. Joseph Buttinger, *Vietnam: A Dragon Embattled* (New York: Frederick A. Praeger, 1967), Vol. 1 of 2 vols.
7. Maurois, op. cit.

Spartans, and directly, and more permanently, to producing a place of secure refuge for Spartan helots who wished to escape from being Spartan serfs . . .[8]

Gallieni's radical approach appealed enormously to the socially aware Lyautey. The two hit it off so well that Gallieni arranged for the young major to become his chief of staff. In subsequently submitting a plan of campaign to the governor-general, Lyautey showed the extent of Gallieni's influence on his thinking:

. . . It should not be overlooked that the pirate is a plant which will grow only in certain soils, and that the surest method is to make the soil uncongenial to him. . . . Similarly with regard to territory given over to brigandage: armed occupation, with or without fighting, is as the ploughshare; the establishment of a military cordon fences it and isolates it definitely, if an internal frontier is in question; and finally the organization and reconstitution of the population, its arming, the setting-up of markets and various cultivations, the driving of roads, are all as the sowing of the good grain, and render the conquered region impervious to brigandage.[9]

A year later, Lyautey continued this policy in Madagascar, where he was summoned by Gallieni, the new resident-general. Having decided to govern *against* the mandarin, Gallieni had stirred up the Hovas and now had a revolt on his hands. He assigned Lyautey to the command of an area ruled by a Hova rebel, a former royal governor, Rabezavana. Lyautey reverted to the methods of Tonkin: he used mobile converging columns to deprive the rebel force of herds and food supply; simultaneously he pinched off bits of territory while showing the people the advantages of coming over to his side, where they would be protected and allowed to earn a good living. Deprived of support, Rabezavana surrendered within a month. Lyautey not only treated him with utmost courtesy, but to the astonishment of all, placed him in charge of the region which he had formerly ruled—where he served loyally and well.[10]

This experience confirmed much of Lyautey's earlier thinking. In an article published during this period, "The Colonial Rule of the Army," he described the pacifying process as ". . . an organization on the march." He continued:

. . . Military command and territorial command ought to be joined in the same hands. When the high military officer is also the territorial administrator, his thoughts, when he captures a brigand's den, are of the trading-post he will set up after his success—and his capture will be on different lines.[11]

8. Adcock, op. cit.
9. Maurois, op. cit.
10. Ibid.
11. Ibid.

In other words, he will not search and destroy—he will conquer, preserve, and build.

After playing a major role in pacifying Madagascar, Lyautey returned to France to command a hussar regiment prior to retiring from the army. At this point, he happened to meet the new Governor-General of Algeria, Jonnart, who complained about the army's failure to stop guerrilla raids of rebels based in eastern Morocco. Impressed with Lyautey's comments, Jonnart persuaded the minister of war to send the colonel to take command of the turbulent southern Oran area. (See map, Chapter 28.)

The job carried promotion to brigadier general, but Lyautey found a cool reception by his superior at Oran, who did not relish an "outsider" challenging his theretofore supreme control. The fifty-nine-year-old Lyautey, in turn, found little to admire. At Aïn-Sefra, he discovered that artillery and transport remained under the Oran commander's control, which meant slow reaction to raids.

But the tactical villain remained bulk and weight, just as it had in the British army in Africa and the American army in the Philippines. At Lyautey's request, a light column paraded before him. Noting the men's high laced boots, haversacks laden as if for a campaign of six months, vast convoys for men who could feed on a handful of dates, the tall general turned to the local commander and asked: "What do you call a *heavy* column in this country?"[12]

Lyautey reported back to Jonnart in Algiers and told him he would take the job only under certain conditions:

. . . I want to have my territory as a whole. I want to have under my orders not only all the military services, but also all the political services, the intelligence officers, everything. . . . And then, in case of urgency, I want to be able to have direct telegraphic communication with the Minister of War, without having to do so by way of the Oran division . . . If you desire the pacification of southern Oran, this is essential.[13]

Jonnart agreed, undoubtedly to his Oran commander's fury. He made a wise decision, however, for Lyautey was one of the few senior officers in the French army who was temperamentally and professionally suited for the task.

Lyautey's immediate problem centered on the old Algerian rebel Bou-Amama, who was allied with a young Moroccan, Bou-Hamara, a conjurer turned pretender to the sultan and called the Rogui. They operated from a Moroccan sanctuary, the Tafilelt, which they kept under submission while their bands swept across the border to raid French outposts and Algerian tribal settlements. Success had greatly emboldened

12. Ibid.; see also C. V. Usborne, op. cit.
13. Maurois, op. cit.

them: they had attacked a convoy in which Jonnart himself was traveling, and in the previous year a *harka* of some four thousand warriors had invested the French military post at Taghit. Although the French army was authorized to pursue the guerrillas inside Morocco, their slow columns rarely ran down the fast-moving bands, and they were forbidden to build permanent outposts on the other side of the border.

Lyautey was not as anxious as his predecessors to mount punitive expeditions, and he also scornfully rejected the string of small border outposts that failed to prevent rebel incursions. Instead he began to apply his *tache d'huile* technique: winning separate tribes by offering them protection under the French flag, then providing social services ranging from medical clinics to markets—a ". . . military-political pacification and occupation . . . the gradual advance on a wide front instead of a single deep (column) penetration."[14] He used light columns to break up enemy concentrations and to meet subsequent threats, ". . . but the emphasis lay on the *tache d'huile* or oil-spot technique—a methodical, necessarily slow expansion of French control."[15]

This reads rather tamely today, but, at the time, many of its aspects were quite revolutionary. Not far to the south, in German East Africa for example, the white man ruled with the *kiboko*—". . . a whip made of hippopotamus hide, and most white men, women and even children, as well as every *akida* [Arab or Muslim-educated overseer], carried one and used it. It was not as much an instrument of punishment or discipline but of terrorism, and it was used everywhere to turn the native into cringing animals ready to do everything their masters demanded of them. . . ."[16] Such treatment caused the unsuccessful Maji-Maji rebellion of 1905, which in turn led to brutal reprisals: ". . . according to an official German estimate, 120,000 natives out of about 2,000,000 were killed and thousands more died from starvation caused by troops laying waste the country. Only now did German policy begin to change with the introduction of schools and mission stations."[17]

In Algeria, Lyautey was trying to avoid such difficulties and still ac-

14. Paret, op. cit.
15. Ibid.
16. Leonard Mosley, *Duel for Kilimanjaro* (London: Weidenfeld & Nicolson, 1963).
17. Ibid.; see also Charles Hordern, *Military Operations East Africa 1914–1916* (London: HMSO, 1941), Vol. 1: ". . . the Maji-Maji rebellion was so named from the Swahili word *maji*, meaning water. The tribes were incited by medicine men to believe that possession of a certain medicine rendered a warrior invulnerable to bullets, which would turn to water. The revolt was in several respects an astonishing example of fanatical native mass-psychology, successfully worked up against Europeans on the basis of this belief. . . . The revolt was finally quelled by extensive and merciless destruction of crops and villages, with consequent famine and disease, the number who died in the rising and as a result of it being estimated at over 100,000."

complish his mission, by using the army not as an instrument of repression but as a positive social force, "the organization on the march." This was an extremely clever concept, a sort of imperialist infiltration in that his showplaces of civilization, by attracting other tribes to the fold, undermined the solidarity and authority of rebel chieftains.

To accomplish this, Lyautey relied strongly on intelligence, on propaganda, on the correct behavior of his troops and, above all, on his own charisma. He took a great deal of trouble cementing relationships with tribal authorities. The extent of his involvement can be seen from an incident soon after he assumed command. Ordered by Paris to evacuate Berguent, a water point his troops had seized inside the Moroccan border, he cabled a protest to the minister of war and concluded:

. . . Moreover, having personally pledged myself to populations in the name of France that we should not abandon them and would protect them, and having thus brought them to rally to us and recover security and trades unknown for seven years past, I could not honorably proceed myself to this step; and if it is maintained, I respectfully request to be immediately relieved from my command in such a way that I may appear solely responsible with regard to the inhabitants, and so that they may realize that it is I alone who have improperly pledged the word of the French Government, and, seeing me disowned, can suspect only myself and not the honor of the Government of the Republic.[18]

As it turned out, Jonnart's successful diplomacy solved the crisis by allowing Lyautey's troops to retain the post.* By year's end, he had consolidated the area, which he protected by several large forts that supported strong but mobile patrols.

Lyautey's success came at a good time for his career. France was about to expand into Morocco, the result of a deal with England that gave the latter a free hand in Egypt.

Morocco in 1904 was a heterogeneous collection of Arabic tribes tied into a loose federation linguistically by Arabic language, spiritually by Islamic religion. This vast area fell under titular rule of a sultan whose practical control extended as far as his troops, or about 20 per cent of the country. Scores of fierce Berber tribes held the rugged mountainous country in semianarchy manifested by frequent intertribal blood feuds and massive revolts against the sultan's government.

Lyautey already had neutralized some of these dissident tribes when he was promoted to the Oran command, in 1906, and charged with the protection of the entire Algerian-Moroccan border. In 1907, he extended

18. Maurois, op. cit.

* This example of military blackmail is reminiscent of Gordon at Khartoum. In this case it was quite unnecessary, since, a few months later, the 1904 treaty with England gave France carte blanche in the area.

operations into eastern Morocco by occupying Oujda. Three years later, he had created

. . . a real buffer state [which] now covered our Algerian frontier, and thrust back the zone of insecurity by several hundreds of kilometres. The populations were already acquiring a taste for ordered life, less costly than anarchy, the kaids for regular administration, more fruitful than the petti-fogging of former times, the Maghzen for the well-gathered revenues of a country which had never recognized its authority. . . . The policing of the wide territories had cost France but little: 4,000 men had been enough in the Oujda area, 1,600 on the Haut-Guir. Further, the Shereefian troops [of Morocco] and budget were gradually to replace the soldiers and money of France. Rarely had a soldier conquered with so little expense. . . .[19]

In 1910, General Lyautey, married now to a colonel's widow, returned to France to command an army corps at Rennes. But the treaty of Fez caused serious revolts in French Morocco, and in 1911 Lyautey was sent to Rabat as resident-general.

Lyautey was now nearly seventy, but advancing years seemed only to give him added energy. After putting down the revolts, he turned to administering French Morocco. As was his wont, he upheld the au-thority of tribal leaders,

. . . and all local customs and local religious practices were preserved intact. Wherever French troops went . . . they immediately taught the local people better methods of agriculture, showed them how to grow more and better crops, dug better water holes, built hospitals, and set up market-places where prices were low and where the items offered for sale were diversified as never before. . . . Lyautey built railroads, highways, and schools. He improved the land, put people to work, and opened mines. Both the modern metrop-olis of Casablanca, one of Africa's largest and finest cities, and the busy town of Kenitra [renamed Port Lyautey] were Lyautey's creations.[20]

Although Lyautey did not hesitate to employ military force when necessary—in 1912, he sent Colonel Mangin to crush a revolt in Mar-rakesh—he believed in applying it in limited amounts. When Mangin exceeded himself in the 1913 fighting in the Middle Atlas massif, Lyautey relieved him of command. And when expansionists in Paris urged him to invade "independent" Morocco, he wrote:

. . . This country ought not to be handled with force alone. The rational method—the only one, the proper one, and also the one for which I myself was chosen rather than anyone else—is the constant interplay of force with politics. I should be very careful about attacking regions which are "asleep,"

19. Maurois, op. cit., quoting Britsch.
20. David Woolman, *Rebels in the Rif* (Stanford, Calif.: Stanford University Press, 1969).

which are lying still, which are waiting and questioning, which would burst
into flames if I entered them, at the cost of many men and much trouble,
whereas, once all the neighboring regions are dealt with, these others will
find themselves isolated and will fall into our hands by themselves. . . .[21]

At the outbreak of World War I, the Ministry of War ordered Lyautey
to evacuate the interior of Morocco and occupy a few coastal enclaves
while sending the bulk of his troops to France. Arguing that evacuation would bring rebellion, Lyautey persuaded the government to hold
the interior with *minimum* forces. By judicious use of territorials, Lyautey prevented serious revolt and even managed to increase the territory under his control during the war.

Lyautey's pacification formula produced short-term gains for long-term losses. Among its numerous built-in booby traps, it represented
one man's idea rather than a national ideal. Essentially a totalitarian
concept, it could be and subsequently was subverted by the dictates of
other colonial administrators materially far more greedy and politically
far more myopic than Lyautey.

Lyautey himself was a one-man show, a prima donna in the Gordon
tradition. Dramatic and flamboyant, something of a mystic, he was
married to ideals that the majority of his countrymen had long since
divorced. Like kings before him, he was convinced that he knew better
than his government, and in some instances he probably did. At times,
the Third Republic seemed like no government, and Lyautey was not
alone among prominent officials in refusing obeisance to its oft-changing
and oft-contradictory ministerial decrees.

This attitude can be defended if not carried too far. The fractious
nature of French politics, particularly in the first decade of this century,
increased the responsibility of French officials. To carry on sometimes
required intelligent disobedience of orders. Most successful leaders in
history at some point have risked their careers by intelligent disobedience. When disobedience, intelligent or otherwise, becomes habit, however, it turns to mutiny, and then anarchy is the result.

Lyautey was by no means alone in exploiting the turbulent political
scene to gain immense operational freedom. From Gallieni and Jonnart he learned not to respect the state but to outwit it. By the time
he rose to prominence, a lack of control already had spelled a loss of discipline sufficient to allow the growth of unhealthy autonomy in the French
colonial empire. Lloyd George recognized this when he referred to
Lyautey as "that prince of pro-consuls."[22] He could have referred
similarly to other French governors-general and he would have been

21. Maurois, op. cit.
22. Usborne, op. cit.

correct—in the early part of the century, France already was becoming a prisoner of her empire.

Lyautey aided this pernicious trend. Although he preached a careful admixture of civil and military effort in administering colonial areas, in practice the military officer absorbed civil responsibility, thus giving rise to the unhappy system of the *officier-administrateur,* which called for ". . . 'special' officers trained and interested in political, social and economic affairs." As Professor Peter Paret has pointed out, this concept was fundamental to a philosophy that we shall come to later, that of the *guerre révolutionnaire,* familiar to Indochina, Algeria, Morocco, and Tunisia, and one that contained the seeds of its own destruction.[23]

This perhaps was the inevitable result of refusing the notion of political growth. Lyautey did not believe that colonies would ultimately emerge as independent, self-governing nations. In Morocco he allowed numerous *colons* to purchase large and choice land tracts at low prices and to work them with minimum-wage labor. His administration made little attempt to train Moroccan administrators or even to develop a stabilizing middle class. By allowing tribal chiefs to retain authority, he insured continued misery of millions, and by supporting a weak and inefficient sultan, he laid the groundwork for the catastrophic Rif rebellion in neighboring Spanish Morocco.

In the main, these were also his country's errors, and they were not confined to France. Lyautey's success in keeping the peace merely compounded rather than solved them. Although he paid lip service to political necessities, he never forgot that the rifle, the French rifle, ruled. Along with most of his fellow humans, he was a slave to the policy of the now. Lyautey refused the past, he blessed the present, he denied the future.

He wrote his own epitaph unknowingly many years before he died. This was in Algeria, after he had ridden around his neat bivouacs wishing his splendid legionaries, his spahis, Zouaves, his Chasseurs d'Afrique, and his *tirailleurs* a happy year. Flushed from his tour of power, he returned to his desk to write a friend. After an almost orgiastic description of troop esprit in the neatly formed camps, he added: ". . . I don't give a damn for the morrow—the present is enough for me."[24]

23. Paret, op. cit.
24. Maurois, op. cit.

Chapter 18

Background to the Mexican revolution • The rebellions of Miguel Hidalgo and José Morelos • Santa Anna's dictatorship • Guerrillas and the War of the Reforms • Marshal Bazaine and Mexican guerrillas • The Porfiriate and the 1910 revolution • Early guerrilla actions • The guerrilla armies of Pancho Villa and Emiliano Zapata • The political, social and economic revolutions • Civil war • American intervention • Zapata's and Villa's deaths

GUERRILLA WARFARE played a spotty but important role in the Mexican revolution, which was fought from 1910 to 1920. This complex upheaval started as a political revolution, but so intense was a need for sweeping social and economic changes that the fighting developed into a series of bloody civil wars. The conflict should prove of particular interest to the North American since it helps to explain a Mexican xenophobia only slowly disappearing and one founded in part on North American territorial acquisition and commercial exploitation, in part on diplomatic and military intervention during the fighting. Washington intervened forcibly on several occasions. Lacking accurate information and not understanding the dynamic forces at work in the impoverished country, the Wilson administration greatly embarrassed itself and extricated its military forces only with difficulty.

Wilson's confusion is not difficult to understand. The Mexican revolution seemed to pale in comparison with the dramatic events in Europe.

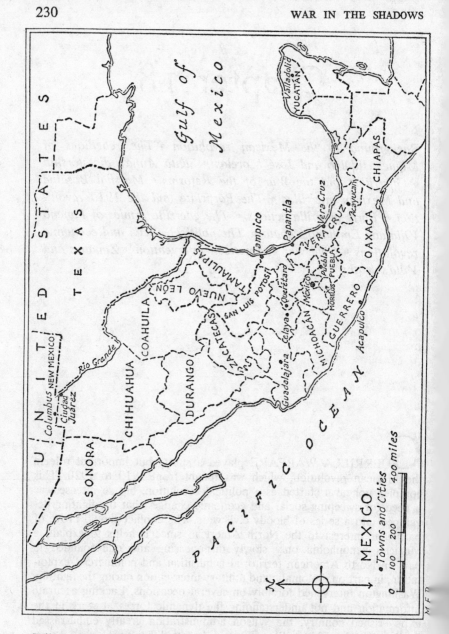

Wilson and his advisers did not and perhaps could not understand that
World War I would end a phase of history, while the Mexican revolution would foreshadow a new and as yet incomplete phase.

Although the outbreak of the Mexican revolution surprised everyone, including the revolutionaries, it did not suddenly explode. Rather, it seethed from a centuries-old fermentation familiar to many other areas of the world, a powerful concoction that created and nurtured the host of elements that exploded in 1910. In Victor Alba's words:

. . . Everything the future was to bring was already foreshadowed: a frustrated middle class, indignant at the arrogance of foreign capital; an urban youth longing for freedom of thought and expression; a proletariat in constant protest; a stultified and downtrodden peasantry, which sent off occasional sparks of rebellion; a certain number of theorists of change, which all the other groups confusedly hungered for; and a few organized and militant groups with programs for action.[1]

Aztec chieftains, who depended on military might for survival, did not use guerrilla tactics to any significant degree either in fighting internecine wars or in defending against Spanish incursions, and this is the main reason that they steadily gave ground to the intruder. Early Mayan victories against small Spanish expeditions possibly helped to mask innate superiority of Spanish arms, horses, armor and cannon to pave the way for Hernán Cortés' successful conquest, but pride also played an important role.

Cortés ruled harshly, but he nonetheless recruited large native armies to fight for him. Professor Kirkpatrick has described a punitive expedition into one rebellious region, Pánuco, where the Spanish commander, Sandoval, burned four hundred chiefs ". . . in the presence of their people: he then nominated or acknowledged the successors of these victims as native chiefs of the people and left the country beaten down into uneasy submission."[2] In later periods, as many as two hundred thousand natives served Spanish arms.

Spanish colonizing efforts continued to breed local uprisings. Later in the sixteenth century, the Mayas fought the intruder for over twenty years, ". . . a cruel and devastating war that ended in mutual exhaustion"; they finally submitted to become virtual slaves, as had their brethren to the north. These early centuries of Spanish colonialism are not, in general, marked by violent rebellions, however. Sir Nicolas Cheetham, whose recent book *A History of Mexico* is recommended, has argued that this ". . . was due to the fundamental good sense and humanity of the viceregal regime."[3] It was also due to the Indians'

1. Victor Alba, *The Mexicans—The Making of a Nation* (London: Pall Mall Press, 1967).

2. F. A. Kirkpatrick, *The Spanish Conquistadores* (London: Adam & Charles Black, 1934).

3. Sir Nicolas Cheetham, *A History of Mexico* (London: Rupert Hart-Davis, 1970); see also William H. Prescott, *The History of the Conquest of Mexico* (Chicago: University of Chicago Press, 1966); Salvador de Madariaga, *The Fall of the Spanish American Empire* (London: Hollis & Carter, 1947); Hubert Herring, *A History of Latin America* (London: Jonathan Cape, 1955).

generally docile nature, to frequent and fierce epidemics, to economic necessity, and, in large part, to lack of political organization and communications, not to mention arms and armies.

The viceregal system of rule may have held advantages and in general kept the peace, but Mexico is a large land area and communications were rude. The prevailing system of settlement, the *encomienda,* begun by Cortés, created powerful colonial barons who in many ways resembled feudal lords presiding over serfs. At the colonist's death, the holding reverted to the crown, but, in time, the barons retained their holdings, or *haciendas,* which frequently increased until relatively few persons owned most of the valuable land. The government could not function everywhere and did not always function well, and, in a relatively short time, local creoles frequently exploited the native to a sickening degree.

The Spanish hold on Mexico began to slip when the Napoleonic wars brought civil war to Spain. In 1808, an interregnum occurred, with a *gachupín* government ruling on orders from the regency in Spain, a confused period soon exploited by Mexican liberals.

North of Mexico City, in the mining area of Querétaro, an active group of dissidents had sprung up under the aegis of a young army officer, Ignacio Allende, and a parish priest, Miguel Hidalgo, a tall, self-styled prophet of fifty-seven years. In mid-September, Hidalgo summoned parishioners by tolling church bells, then treated them to a harangue that ended with the cry, "Death to the Gachupines."

The peons reacted swiftly and impressively: Within two weeks, Hidalgo had raised an army of tens of thousands. Calling himself Captain-General of America, he led this ill-trained host against a series of town garrisons. At first he was successful, but when he and Allende fell out over command of the army, a government force badly mauled the rebels. More dissension followed as Hidalgo struggled to hold his capital of Guadalajara and fend off General Calleja's government troops, a series of actions marked by extreme cruelty on both sides. Hidalgo finally met defeat in conventional battle, which dispersed his army. He was captured, cast out of the Church, and executed in the summer of 1811. Despite his failure, he is still regarded as the father of the Mexican nation. In Cheetham's words:

. . . In his concern for the welfare of the people he was well ahead of his times, and he may rightly be considered the precursor of the whole social movement of the 1911 revolution, on which the political philosophy of modern Mexico rests.[4]

General Calleja's problems did not end with Hidalgo's demise. Although the rebel army had been destroyed, numerous officers and men

4. Cheetham, op. cit.

escaped to the mountains, there to organize guerrilla bands. This period produced a particularly able guerrilla leader, José María Morelos, a short, stocky village priest who had been a pupil and later lieutenant of Hidalgo. Sent to the country southwest of Mexico City (today's Guerrero), Morelos recruited a strong guerrilla force that was capable either of fighting Calleja's army or retiring to the hills if necessary.

Morelos fought Calleja's army for four years. He not only held his own in early encounters, but, in 1812 and 1813, gained the initiative until he controlled a sizable area running nearly across the country between Acapulco and Vera Cruz. Such was his strength in late 1813 that he arranged a conference of rebel delegates to whom he proposed an independent Mexico: ". . . a republic, universal suffrage for all citizens without distinction of race, the abolition of privilege and the breaking up of the great estates belonging to private landowners and the Church."[5] Creole conservatives rejected such radical notions, and a split developed, which gave Calleja a needed breathing space. As the new viceroy, he now reorganized his army and again went after Morelos. The two forces met outside Valladolid, where the rebel leader fought and lost two battles. In 1814, government forces recaptured the main towns and retained the initiative against the rebels, now split into two camps. Morelos was captured in 1815, cast out of the Church, and executed.

Morelos' death severely damaged the movement, as did conciliatory efforts by Calleja's successor, Apodaca. One by one, guerrilla bands made peace with the government, until only two important leaders were holding out: Guerrero, in the mountains east of Acapulco, and Félix Fernández, in the difficult terrain behind Vera Cruz.

The political confusion that embraced Spain at this time extended to Mexico and cost its people dearly. A young officer, Agustín de Iturbide, who had distinguished himself in Calleja's campaigns, sought to appease Guerrero with a plan that would make Mexico an independent kingdom. In the middle of these negotiations, Iturbide pulled off a military coup and proclaimed himself emperor of Mexico. A good many generals, including Antonio López de Santa Anna, refused such arbitrary promotion. Breaking away from Iturbide's government, they declared for a republic and forced Iturbide to abdicate, in 1823.[6]

This action unfortunately set the pattern for a century of Mexican politics: a military coup—what was called a *pronunciamiento*—followed by corrupt government and eventually a countercoup, with very little good accruing to the long-suffering Mexican peon. Although guerrilla warfare did not play a dominant role in these years, it was never far removed from the scene. The Mexican army failed to use it in its war

5. Ibid.
6. Ibid.; Iturbide exiled himself to London but soon returned to Mexico and was shot.

with the United States (possibly from pride) and was severely beaten, a defeat that cost almost a third of its territory. The man who finally toppled the disastrous Santa Anna dictatorship, Juan Álvarez, depended only in part on guerrilla tactics—the Santa Anna regime was so rotten and the army so demoralized that the rebels won a relatively easy victory. In the civil war that followed—the War of the Reforms—guerrillas operated behind the opposing armies, but, too often, these were little more than bandit groups exploiting an already confused and ravaged countryside.

Guerrilla warfare came into its own, however, during the abortive effort of Emperor Napoleon III to restore a Mexican monarchy and put the Habsburg Archduke Ferdinand Maximilian on the throne. The Monroe Doctrine had theretofore prevented direct foreign intervention, but in 1862 the United States had its hands full with its own civil war. An allied army, mostly French but with Spanish and British contingents, landed at Vera Cruz and began to fight inland. By spring, the French were fighting alone; after a setback at the battle of Puebla, Napoleon sent reinforcements, and the army ably commanded by Marshal Bazaine entered Mexico City. The liberal government of Benito Juárez now moved north to Paso del Norte (Ciudad Juárez), which it defended while waiting for American intervention. By the spring of 1864, organized resistance to French arms had virtually ended, but, throughout the occupied areas, guerrilla actions flared.

None of these actions was particularly important by itself, but together they constituted a challenge to authority. And the challenge gained strength because that authority itself was divided: Napoleon was not pleased with what had become an expensive campaign—he had fielded some thirty thousand troops; and Maximilian's supporters, the clergy and landowners, were not pleased at his refusal to reinstate various privileges; and Bazaine was not pleased, because his army knew no rest and he was spending a great deal of money in fruitless pursuit of these wretched guerrilla bands.

For some time, Bazaine had been arguing for solution by force: he wanted to treat the guerrillas as outlaws, with summary execution of those captured. Maximilian eventually agreed. An overzealous Mexican officer fighting for the French now summarily executed two captured generals. The guerrillas retaliated. With each French reprisal, the guerrillas gained new recuits—and the war continued.

But Napoleon was in trouble: at home, a strong and arrogant Prussia was threatening him, and abroad, the United States Government was demanding his army's recall. Early in 1867, he bowed to these pressures and withdrew his army. Unable to stand alone, Maximilian surrendered and was court-martialed and shot.[7]

7. Ibid.

Maximilian's death put Juárez and the liberals back in power. Unfortunately, Juárez soon died and the party split into three factions, each devoted to self-aggrandizement. For forty years, leaders such as Manuel González and particularly Porfirio Díaz sold Mexico to anyone who would buy it. Their peculations included selling huge tracts of public land, including mineral rights, to a chosen few—either Mexican or foreign speculators—along with railways and mining and later oil concessions. A political elite, the *científicos,* preached laissez-faire economics that virtually ignored social problems, particularly those of the Indians, who still constituted 30–40 per cent of the population. Porfirio's ruling political philosophy was short but scarcely sweet: "bread and the stick."

Under the Porfiriate, of several decades, grand larceny became a way of life: Porfirio and his henchmen disposed of 50 million hectares (one hectare equals nearly two and one half acres) of land, much of it going to foreign ownership and management—about $3.5 billion poured into the dictator's coffers from 1880 to 1910. The Catholic Church once again became a large landowner, as did Porfirio's regional bosses, the hated *jefes políticos.* One Mexican rancher owned 2.5 million hectares in Chihuahua; the Cedros *hacienda* in Zacatecas comprised 750,000 hectares; thirty-two persons owned the sugar-growing state of Morelos; three thousand families owned *half of Mexico.* Landowners frequently forced peasants from common land (the *ejidos*) and dispossessed tribes that had occupied territory for generations. Of 10 million peasants working the land, 9.5 million owned nothing.[8]

This perhaps would have been tolerated had it resulted in a decent way of life. Instead, the *haciendas* offered conditions familiar to the feudal ages:

. . . Wages were sometimes as low as twenty-five centavos a day; corporal punishment was a normal practice and most peasants fell hopelessly into debt with the *hacienda* store. The diet was insufficient and their housing primitive in the extreme; disease was rife and a school was rarely available for their children. . . . Lands lay fallow, the Indians struggled on the brink of starvation and Mexico was obliged to import foodstuffs for its townspeople.[9]

As one historian wrote, Díaz did ". . . much to develop his country. But he did nothing to develop his people."[10]

8. Alba, op. cit.; see also Ronald Atkin, *Revolution! Mexico 1910–1920* (New York: John Day, 1969); Charles C. Cumberland, *Mexico—The Struggle for Modernity* (New York: Oxford University Press, 1968).

9. Cheetham, op. cit.

10. Atkin, op. cit.; see also Patrick O'Hea, *Reminiscences of the Mexican Revolution* (Mexico City: Editorial Fournier, 1966). O'Hea was a plantation manager before and during the revolution.

His people sometimes protested. A disciple of the French socialist Charles Fourier, one Rhodakanaty, had started a small labor movement in 1866. One of his disciples, Julio Chávez, led a short-lived peasant rebellion in 1869—he was captured and shot. The movement continued during the 1870s and was fed by the writings of Marx and Bakunin. Significantly, these doctrines held little appeal to the peons, who were far more attracted by the promise of immediate reforms.[11] That did not mean they were opposed to armed uprising. In 1885, the Yaqui tribes of Sonora rose against the government and, for fifteen years, under such capable leaders as Cajeme and Tetabiate, fought a guerrilla war. When government weight finally told, the army rounded up some eight thousand tribesmen and deported them to Yucatán to work on the plantations virtually as slaves. Other revolts occurred, but either the army or a gendarme force, the despised *rurales,* put them down rapidly and cruelly.[12]

Down but not out.

The countryside was never completely safe during the Porfiriate, and even if the *rurales* suppressed active opposition, peasant hatred continued to grow. Serious uprisings occurred in Tenochic in 1892, in Papantla in 1895, in Acayucan in 1906, and in Viesca in 1908.[13]

A revolutionary movement also existed. In 1906, two anarchists, the Flores Magón brothers, well known for their revolutionary newspaper *Regeneración,* formed a Liberal Party whose slogan was "Land and Liberty." These and other labor leaders also incited a series of provincial strikes in mines and factories. A frightened government overreacted—troops put down one strike by killing some two hundred workers.[14]

But a more dangerous situation was developing in Porfiriate ranks. Porfirio and his ancient henchmen had grown increasingly isolated and intransigent. Had they been intelligent, they would have read the increasing demonstrations and uprisings as proper warning of vast social unrest—like Horatio seeing the king's ghost, they would have said, "This bodes some strange eruption to our state." A few of the younger Porfiristas recognized the danger and began to demand reforms. When the dictator, soon to turn eighty, refused to name a successor, a party member named Francisco Madero broke away and organized a group called the Anti-Re-electionists. Madero was in his thirties, a small, restless man, rich and well educated, a teetotaler and vegetarian. Arrested during the 1910 presidential elections, Madero upon release fled to Texas, denounced Díaz's re-election as fraudulent, named himself provisional

11. Alba, op. cit.
12. Atkin, op. cit.; see also Frank Tannenbaum, *Peace by Revolution: An Interpretation of Mexico* (New York: Columbia University Press, 1933).
13. Alba, op. cit.
14. Cheetham, op. cit.

president, and issued a reform program called the Plan of San Luis Potosí.[15]

No mass uprisings followed, but Madero's lieutenants in Chihuahua, Abraham González and Pascual Orozco, raised a number of mounted bands which, using guerrilla tactics, effectively harassed immobile army garrisons. One subordinate leader, typical in some ways, was named Doroteo Arango. A mestizo with a touch of negro blood, at sixteen years of age he had killed the *hacendado's* son, who had raped his sister, and fled to the hills to become a cattle thief. The thirty-year-old Arango knew little of Mexican politics, but, hating government and landowners, he came down from the hills, rounded up fifteen horsemen, and joined Madero. Soon feared by the federals for fantastic mobility and surprise attacks, he became famous as Francisco "Pancho" Villa and shortly commanded a force of some five hundred horse.[16]

Although the army was disorganized and riddled with corruption, it withstood rebel attacks in a war that was cruel from the beginning. Porfirio's generals, deeming the rebels to be bandits, ordered all prisoners shot. The rebels retaliated by executing government officials and all officers (but allowing soldiers to join rebel ranks). Subordinate guerrilla leaders also paid off old scores: on one occasion, Pancho Villa ordered two hundred Chinese killed in one town simply because he hated Chinese.[17]

In relatively short order, rebel forces controlled enough of Chihuahua for Madero to transfer his revolutionary government from Texas. Meanwhile, revolts continued to break out in the North, and also in the South, in the sugar provinces.

Those readers who remember Wallace Beery's superb portrayal of Pancho Villa will inevitably connect the Mexican revolution with Villa, but a guerrilla leader named Emiliano Zapata played an even more significant role. John Womack has recently written an excellent biography of this rebel leader: *Zapata and the Mexican Revolution*.[18] Zapata was a tenant farmer in the southern province of Morelos. Incensed at feudal conditions, he became outspokenly critical and was banished to the army. Discharged in 1910, he returned to Morelos, already restive with a few small guerrilla bands operating from the hills. Recognizing the futility of this meager effort, Zapata set out to organize a peasant uprising.

Zapata was neither a Marxist nor a Communist. The historian Frank

15. Ibid.; see also Alba, op. cit.; Stanley K. Ross, *Francisco I. Madero—Apostle of Mexican Democracy* (New York: Columbia University Press, 1955).

16. Atkin, op. cit.; see also O'Hea, op. cit., who writes from a basis of personal acquaintance with Villa.

17. Atkin, op. cit.

18. John Womack, *Zapata and the Mexican Revolution* (London: Thames & Hudson, 1968).

Tannenbaum described him as ". . . a man of no learning, of no broad social contacts, a simple, vigorous human being . . . who knew that his people had been robbed of their lands, and that it was his call to return these lands to them." His program reflected Madero's stated agrarian and social reforms, and neither program was dissimilar to that of the Taiping rebels in 1850 (see Chapter 24).

Ronald Atkin, who has also written an excellent new study of the period, *Revolution Mexico 1910–1920,* describes Zapata as ". . . a small, slender man with a sensuous Asiatic face, mandarin mustache and eyes as black and hard as obsidian. Unlike the rough, rude Villa, Zapata was a dandy. He always wore symbolic, theatrical black—a fitted jacket and tight trousers with silver trimming down the seams. He wore enormous, silver-laden sombreros and his taste extended to fine horses and beautiful women."[19] Deadly earnest in social-economic protest, he rallied peasants by the thousands with the cry: "Men of the South, it is better to die on your feet than live on your knees!" Give us land and liberty, he thundered—and his cry reverberated throughout the province.

Within nine months, Zapata had raised an army of three thousand peasants, a spontaneous and self-supporting uprising: ". . . We have begged from the outside not one bullet," Zapata boasted, "not one rifle, not one peso; we have taken it all from the enemy."[20] The uprising spread quickly, and, in general, regional leaders such as José Trinidad Ruíz, Salazar, Neri, and a man with the unlikely name of De la O proved highly effective guerrilla fighters.[21]

Zapata's initial success was all the more wondrous in view of government forces in Morelos—about a thousand troops under General Casso López and perhaps five thousand *rurales.* John Womack explained their general impotence:

. . . the only places they effectively held were the towns they were stationed in, the district and major municipal seats. In some cases, especially among the *rurales,* the commanders were excellent; and on paper they had crafty tactics for their mounted police—constant pursuit, night marches, mobile provisioning. But almost all officers and troopers came from other states . . . and they were so ignorant of the twisting trails and ravines they now had to maneuver through as they were unfamiliar with the local villagers, whom they inevitably harassed and who then informed on them to the rebels. The planters too resented the expense and disruption the soldiers and policemen caused. The result was that the federal forces rarely budged from their quarters.[22]

19. Atkin, op. cit.
20. Ibid.
21. Alba, op. cit.
22. Womack, op. cit.

The Díaz government could not withstand the combined onslaught against its authority. When negotiations with the rebels broke down in early 1911, fighting resumed. In the North, Orozco's guerrillas captured Ciudad Juárez; in the South, Zapata's bands took Cuautla.

These victories toppled the government.[23] After a short and confused interim government, Madero won election to the presidency. But he was already in trouble with his own party. More like a boy on a pony than a man on horseback, Madero proved far too weak for the enormous task he faced, one he did not even understand. Madero insisted that the people wanted a political revolution, whereas they were vigorously demanding fundamental social and economic changes. But Madero failed to offer even a political revolution. A poor administrator, he quickly lost control to conservative ministers, and, instead of pushing through vital and promised reforms, he followed a vacillating policy that merely bred new discontent.

De la Barra's interim government had already sent an army under General Victoriano Huerta against Zapata, who had withdrawn his guerrillas to the mountains. Madero halted this punitive pursuit, but Zapata, rightly suspicious of the new president, refused to disarm his guerrillas. When Madero failed to push through promised land reforms, Zapata announced his own reform program. In November 1911, ". . . standing on a table in a mountain hut . . . while the Mexican flag was raised and a band played the National Anthem," Zapata read out the Plan of Ayala. Like that of the Taipings in 1850, the program markedly resembled Marxist teachings:

. . . immediate seizure of all foreign-owned lands and of all properties which had been taken away from villages, the confiscation of one-third of the land held by hacendados friendly to the Revolution and full confiscation against owners who "directly or indirectly" opposed the Plan. . . . All land held by the Zapatistas was immediately turned over to the people, and crude huts went up in the productive fields of fifty-three of the richest haciendas in the country, which were declared forfeit "to the sovereign cause of liberty and equality."[24]

Once again, peasants by the thousands flocked to fight under Zapata's banner, a grim death's-head.

After announcing his new program, Zapata resumed fighting in the South. In January 1912, Madero sent a new governor to Morelos, Francisco Naranjo, Jr., a fairly liberal man who carefully studied the situation. ". . . I found that Morelos lacked three things," he said later,

23. Cheetham, op. cit.; Porfirio Díaz fled to Paris and died four years later.
24. Atkin, op. cit.

"first plows, second books, and third equity. And it had more than enough latifundios, taverns and bosses."[25] Naranjo had put his finger on the problem, but was unable to effect necessary reforms. Meanwhile, federal troops under Brigadier General Juvencio Robles were marching through the state, burning towns, relocating peasants, shooting guerrillas. When these punitive measures failed and the guerrilla force continued to grow, Madero relieved Robles with General Felipe Ángeles. Ángeles took an altogether new tack and attempted to bring peace to the torn country by general amnesty and good sense. His measures soon began to deprive the guerrillas of recruits and of support from the towns, and, had the provincial administration acted forcefully and intelligently, it could probably have stopped the fighting altogether.

As it was, it refused to enact the proposed reforms. Zapata, in turn, had changed tactics by ordering his guerrillas to burn cane fields in order to deprive peons of work and thus create recruits. His forces shortly swelled until subordinate leaders were fielding units with as many as eight to twelve hundred guerrillas.[26]

In the North, Pascual Orozco felt himself slighted by the new government and, early in 1912, also resumed fighting, though scarcely for a revolutionary cause. His new patron was a millionaire cattle baron who wanted to embarrass Madero's government and cause it to fall. In the event, Orozco was soon challenged by Pancho Villa and then defeated by a federal army under command of General Huerta, an able if drunken and dishonest soldier incongruously known to his admirers as "the Mexican Cromwell." As if Madero did not have enough problems, he now ran afoul of the United States Government.

Public opinion in America originally had favored the revolutionary cause, at least sufficiently to cause President Taft to recognize and even assist the Madero government while officially holding to a neutral policy.[27] But American commercial interests in the country were strong: American companies owned three quarters of the mines, half the oil fields (England owned the other half), and vast cattle ranches in the North—all together, by 1910, an investment of some $2 billion.[28] The tragic exploitation of people and property was in keeping with North America's curious little imperialistic fling that had begun with the Spanish-American War. An American fleet patrolled the Gulf Coast, its purpose according to Philander Knox, Taft's Secretary of State, to keep Mexicans ". . . in a salutary equilibrium, between a dangerous

25. Womack, op. cit.
26. Ibid.
27. Atkin, op. cit.; among hundreds of American volunteers to the rebel forces was a future film star, Tom Mix.
28. Alba, op. cit.

and exaggerated apprehension and a proper degree of wholesome fear."[29]

The American ambassador to Mexico, Henry Lane Wilson, a fifty-five-year-old archconservative, was firmly wedded to American commercial interests. This group, which formed a powerful colonial lobby called The Committee of the American Colony, deplored the notion of a reform government and, through Wilson, did what they could to defeat Madero. Whether through intention or ignorance, Wilson, who admired Porfirio Díaz, badly misreported the actual situation from the beginning of the revolution. The Mexican Government had interpreted the lull that followed the original outbreaks as a sign of weakness, whereas it was a period of rebel reorganization and recruitment. This was a fundamental error—we shall encounter it again and again—and Wilson went along with it: ". . . The conspiracy lacks coherence and the government will easily suppress it," he reported, also commenting on ". . . the lack of intelligent leadership" among the rebels.[30] Even when the situation clarified, Wilson persisted in denouncing

. . . the President's [Madero's] ineptitude, his hostility to the United States and his fatal leanings toward radicalism. By manipulating or disregarding his [Wilson's] own instructions he contrived to give the Mexicans a misleadingly harsh impression of his government's attitude towards the Madero regime. Although the revolution had not taken place without some loss of American lives and property, it was grossly dishonest of Wilson to exaggerate these incidents and to pretend that disorder was increasing, whereas the truth was that by mid-1912 peace had been restored in the whole of Mexico outside the area overrun by Zapata.[31]

Ambassador Wilson misrepresented the situation so badly that Washington adopted an anti-Madero policy and moved troops to the border. The ambassador's machinations helped anti-Madero forces to overthrow, indeed to murder, the president and the vice-president in early 1913 and install General Huerta in power. Huerta was a dreadful man —an alcoholic, dope addict, thief, and despot—and neither Taft nor his successor, Woodrow Wilson, recognized his government, nor did three northern Mexican states, where revolution again broke out.

The governor of Coahuila, Venustiano Carranza, challenged the Huerta government by announcing still another reform program, the

29. Atkin, op. cit.; see also Peter Calvert, *The Mexican Revolution, 1910–1914— The Diplomacy of Anglo-American Conflict* (London: Cambridge University Press, 1968): a detailed and excellent political-diplomatic analysis.
30. Atkin, op. cit.
31. Cheetham, op. cit.

Plan of Guadalupe. Huerta's army at first forced the rebels north but did not destroy Carranza's army. Based at Nogales, on the Sonora-Arizona border, the rebel force was commanded by Álvaro Obregón, thirty-three years old, a former schoolteacher and factory worker who, along with his associates, Adolfo de la Huerta and Plutarco Elías Calles, would soon become important revolutionary characters (and eventually presidents).

Another rebel leader was about to come into his own in neighboring Chihuahua. This was Pancho Villa, who had returned from Texas to organize a new force of mounted irregulars. Such was his charisma that he had little trouble in attracting men to his banner. When federal troops captured and executed his titular commander, General Abraham González, Pancho Villa became military commander of the state.

Villa was not as good a guerrilla fighter as Zapata, but he was as picturesque. A teetotaler and non-smoker, he was a crack pistol shot; as Ronald Atkin wrote, he loved women, ice cream, and war. As long as he commanded a small band, he prospered, but as his force increased, he began to encounter problems that he failed to solve and that eventually brought him to heel.

The opposing forces spent most of the summer of 1913 in strengthening themselves. Huerta's strategy was to defend the towns along the railway, leaving the countryside to the rebels. This was a holding action while he maneuvered to gain American recognition of his government.

Woodrow Wilson despised Huerta and what he stood for and steadily refused to recognize him. But, in the spring of 1913, the British Government offered to recognize Huerta in return for a promise of "free elections" as soon as possible. Germany, France, Spain, and Japan played along, but Wilson relieved his ambassador and refused to name a new one. Leaving the embassy under control of a chargé d'affaires, Wilson sent a personal emissary to the war-torn country. John Lind, former governor of Minnesota, proposed a cease-fire with "free elections" to follow, with Huerta abstaining from candidacy. Carranza refused the plan and announced that the Constitutionalists would execute anyone recognizing a president elected under it! In the event, the elections proved a farce and Huerta continued as dictator.

But an uneasy dictator.

Carranza's armies had been steadily growing. Pancho Villa now commanded some eight thousand men, a force armed and equipped in part by captured government weapons, in part by arms smuggled from the United States and paid for by "contributions" and "loans" exacted from towns in the best medieval tradition. Villa's army even included a modern hospital train staffed with sixty American and Mexican doctors.[32]

32. Atkin, op. cit.

In bold contrast, his disparate force included lieutenants as unorthodox as they were cruel: Tomás Urbina, the Lion of the Sierras, an illiterate whose signature was a heart; Fausto Borunda, called the Matador because he always killed prisoners; Rodolfo Fierro, another brute, who on one occasion killed three hundred federal prisoners on the spot.[33] Such men were called "finger generals"—". . . their nickname coming from the practice of appointing officers by pointing a finger . . . and saying, 'You, be colonel; you, general; you, governor.'"[34] Along with other leaders, they turned up in small bands that included wives, children, and animals; the resultant army strongly resembled the Algerian *smala,* an awkward mob that perforce traveled by rail. Villa exercised unquestioned authority over most of these bands. His personal following was high at this time. Although not understanding the goals of the revolution (nor did the other leaders, with the exception of Obregón and Calles), Villa did understand the peon's desire for land, and, like Zapata, distributed it liberally. He used his guerrilla army in civic works—repairing streets and building schools. Villa also had gained two important aides: General Felipe Ángeles, a professional and capable soldier, and Martín Luis Guzmán, his secretary (who later wrote novels based on his experience).

Villa's army fought well in the early battles. In September, he and Obregón began to push southward. The tactical problem consisted of attacking towns defended by government troops. In the early attacks, Villa developed what became a favorite tactic, *un golpe terrífico* (a terrible blow) delivered by a flank attack of cavalry (a tactic repeatedly used by Frederick the Great). Villa was so impressed with its success that he organized an elite and independent unit, the *Dorados,* three squadrons of one hundred horse each.

Both Obregón and Villa scored impressive victories in the autumn fighting. The rebel cause prospered further when President Wilson, early in 1914, changed his policy of "watchful waiting" and allowed the rebels to buy arms in America.

But nothing was pleasant about the war. The rebel attacks were costly, and interspersed with this confused campaign were small bands looting, raping and killing—a terrible period reminiscent of the Thirty Years' War. Neither side gave or expected quarter. Horrified by the brutality, President Wilson sent an army officer, General Hugh Scott, to Villa's camp. Scott explained how the habit of executing prisoners repelled American citizens and gave him a British army manual on the treatment of prisoners and conquered areas: ". . . Villa was fascinated. He had

33. Ibid.; see also O'Hea, op. cit., who personally knew many of these subordinates.
34. Alba, op. cit.

it translated into Spanish and distributed among his officers." Scott claimed that he reprieved the next four thousand prisoners. But, in Atkin's words,

. . . Villa still executed the *Colorados* whenever he captured them, explaining that they were peons, just like the revolutionaries, and that no peon could volunteer to fight against the cause of liberty unless he were a wicked man.[35]

The ghastly war continued through the winter. But intense rivalries had been developing between Carranza, the "First Chief" of the Constitutionalists, and his military commanders, and also between Obregón and Pancho Villa. The rebel armies nonetheless continued to advance toward Mexico City. Huerta's cause was virtually lost. He received a temporary boost in popularity in April 1914, when Washington intervened by seizing a ship loaded with munitions, an action that led to the famous Tampico incident and an American force landing at Vera Cruz, killing two hundred defenders and occupying the port. But even this incredibly inept move could not save him—in July he abdicated, and, a month later, the federal army left Mexico City.

But matters were scarcely pacific in the rebel camp. Frightened of Villa's growing power and truculent attitude, Carranza now steered him away from the capital. When Villa protested, Carranza stopped coal deliveries to his camp. Villa, who depended on trains to move his *smala,* was stymied—and Obregón's army beat him to Mexico City.

Villa did not long remain stymied. At the end of September, when he was again marching south, he issued a manifesto that defied Carranza's authority. Carranza's rule also faced a threat from the South: Emiliano Zapata, who controlled a large area south of Mexico City, was pushing toward the capital as well. Like Villa, Zapata had held to a rigorous social-economic interpretation of the revolution. In taking over the countryside of Morelos, Puebla, and Guerrero, he ruthlessly eliminated landowning opposition, killing plantation managers, burning haciendas. To retain control of the land, he summarily distributed it to peons, who farmed it while carrying rifles. Zapata thus strengthened his power base, and in some ways proved a more formidable enemy than the northern forces. But the states under his control paid a terrible price: whole villages destroyed; thousands of men conscripted and deported north as laborers by government forces; plantations razed and burned; crops destroyed.

Zapata remained strong, however, and, combined with Villa, proved too powerful for Carranza, who moved his government to Vera Cruz,

35. Atkin, op. cit.; see also O'Hea, op. cit.: Scott's success may have been exaggerated—he did not speak Spanish.

leaving Mexico City to Villa and Zapata. This proved only a temporary setback. Neither rebel leader knew what to do with his power, and soon evacuated the capital. Obregón had used the breathing space to reorganize his army and again take to the field. Fighting seesawed until April 1915, when Obregón tempted Villa to attack his army entrenched at Celaya, west of Mexico City. Villa's military adviser, General Felipe Ángeles, was away, and Villa had failed to learn the lessons of the Russo-Japanese war: horses were useless against trenches defended by barbed wire and soldiers firing rifles and machine guns. A series of abortive attacks cost him perhaps ten thousand killed and broke his army.[36] Retreating north, he halted now and again to fight losing battles. His close friend Tomás Urbina deserted with the treasury; other leaders and their guerrilla followers faded away.

Villa reached his northern sanctuary of Chihuahua with a greatly decimated army. A few months later, another blow fell when Washington, which had recognized Carranza's government, stopped arms from reaching Villa. Partly in retaliation, in January 1916, Villa's troopers held up a train in Sonora and cold-bloodedly murdered sixteen American engineers; in March, his band raided Columbus, New Mexico, and killed eight American soldiers and ten civilians. In response to the public outcry, President Wilson gained Carranza's permission to send a punitive expedition under General John Pershing into the northern provinces.

Pershing's expedition failed for two reasons: his troops were neither trained nor equipped for guerrilla warfare, and his operations were constantly hampered by Carranza, who was only too aware of the prevailing Mexican hatred for Yankee intervention. On the one occasion that Pershing's cavalry found Villa, it could not pursue, because its horses were worn out. The Americans were operating in hostile country, and soon learned that even federal troops resented their presence. They scored a few successes: on one occasion, a cavalry column surprised a group of rebels and killed forty-four of them; on another occasion, a young lieutenant, George Patton, surprised and killed the commander of Villa's famed *Dorados*. But these were slight when compared to the investment in and embarrassment brought by the expedition. The New York *Herald* bluntly stated that

. . . through no fault of his own, Pershing's Punitive Expedition has become as much a farce from the American standpoint as it is an eyesore to the Mexican people. . . . Each day adds to the burden of its cost . . . and to the ignominy of its position. General Pershing and his command should be recalled without further delay.[37]

36. Alba, op. cit.
37. Atkin, op. cit.

Although Pershing's operations were increasingly restricted—as of July, his patrols could operate only 150 miles into Mexico—the campaign lasted into early 1917.

Pancho Villa continued to operate in the North, though with only sporadic success. In the summer of 1919, another American force, under Brigadier General James Erwin, brought his small army to bay and defeated it. Small bands of Villistas survived; Villa himself outlasted his enemy, Carranza, whose rule had brought continued disaster to Mexico. In 1920, the First Chief fell out with Obregón and was murdered while trying to escape the country. Obregón made peace with Villa and kept him quiet by giving him a large hacienda, which he ruled in the best overlord tradition until he was ambushed and killed in 1923.

Emiliano Zapata also suffered a violent end. Unlike Pancho Villa, Zapata continued to fight guerrilla warfare against the Carranza government. General Pablo González commanded the campaign in Morelos against what he called "the Zapata rabble." González answered Zapata's guerrilla tactics with wholesale spoliation: ". . . Whole villages were burned; crops were destroyed; women and children were herded into detention camps and every man González could lay his hands on was hanged."[38] Zapata replied with wholesale terrorism against landowners and army officers:

. . . Some victims were crucified on telegraph poles or on giant cactus trees; others were staked out over ants' nests and smeared with honey, or sewn up inside wet hides and left to suffocate as the hides dried in the sun. One of Zapata's favorite execution methods was to stake out a man on a rough framework of branches over the top of a fast-growing maguey cactus. During the night the thorn-tipped blossom stalk of the plant would grow a foot or more, driving itself inch by inch through the staked-out victim.[39]

Although the Carranza government introduced a new constitution in 1917, Zapata refused to submit to what he believed was reactionary government. Fighting continued into 1919, when Zapata fell victim to an elaborate ruse: an army colonel sent word that he wished to desert along with his regiment. To prove his good intention, he attacked a government force and killed fifty-nine soldiers! Duly impressed, Zapata met him at a rendezvous and was instantly shot dead. The colonel received fifty thousand pesos and a promotion.[40] Following Zapata's death, resistance in Morelos diminished and finally settled into uneasy peace.

The Mexican revolution was expensive. In addition to millions of dollars spent by each side on arms, armies, and ammunition, it cost an estimated three million lives.[41] It left the country virtually bankrupt, with

38. Ibid.
39. Ibid.
40. Alba, op. cit.
41. Atkin, op. cit.

industries and mines at a standstill and virulent hatreds among the populace that would persist for decades. Nor did it accomplish all basic revolutionary aims. But it did clear the way for a system of government that, despite many faults, has without question improved the lives of its peoples—a task of reconstruction not yet completed.

Chapter 19

Guerrilla fighting in World War I • Lettow-Vorbeck in German
East Africa • The background • A guerrilla army forms •
Lettow-Vorbeck's problems • The Boer campaign against him •
His incredible retreat • The cost • Lettow-Vorbeck's secret
• British weaknesses • Meinertzhagen's prediction

THE STATIC NATURE of World War I prevented guerrilla operations on the western front but not in subsidiary theaters. Brilliant campaigns were fought in East Africa and Jerusalem—campaigns that bore
primarily a military hallmark in that each contributed to the fortune of
its parent army, although in totally different fashion.

The war produced two other peripheral actions, however, of a primarily political hallmark: one was the revolt in Ireland, where rebels
used guerrilla methods, mainly terrorist activities, to gain a political aim.
The rebellion only indirectly affected the war, in that by hurting and embarrassing England it helped the Central Powers; in other words, the
rebels used the war as an ally.

The other action was the Russian Revolution, which had been brewing for decades. Achieved by quasi-guerrilla methods, it directly affected
the war in favor of Germany, who did all within her power to bring it
about. But here, too, the war proved the true catalyst. And it was the

chaos and confusion brought by war that allowed a reasonable expression of the will of the majority to be subverted by a Bolshevik minority —albeit a minority inspired by charismatic leadership that cannot be denigrated merely because of unfortunate results.

These four actions hold diverse and interesting lessons, each for different reasons. Taken together, however, and related to the lessons of former centuries, they complete the legacy seized on by Lenin and converted by him and his followers into a new political-military approach to warfare.

At the outbreak of World War I, a forty-five-year-old German army officer, Lieutenant Colonel Paul von Lettow-Vorbeck, commanded German East Africa's (later Tanganyika, today's Tanzania) garrison force, a *Schutztruppe* that, together with the police force, numbered about 260 white officers and 4,600 *askaris,* or natives. Though virtually surrounded and cut off from overseas supply by British blockade, Lettow-Vorbeck refused to consider his civilian superior's plea for neutrality. Instead, he insisted on military action in order to pin down "as many troops as possible" and thereby cause England to provide reinforcements otherwise destined for France.

Lettow-Vorbeck told his own story after the war, but it has recently been presented in Leonard Mosley's splendid book *Duel for Kilimanjaro,* on which I have in part based the following brief account.[1]

Shortly after outbreak of war, the British decided to occupy the coastal towns of German East Africa. In early November, two reinforced brigades from India landed near Tanga, in the North, an effort that was supposed to have been supported by another brigade coming overland. This help never arrived, and so inept was the amphibious operation that Lettow-Vorbeck's guerrillas, aided by swarms of local and furious bees, soon caused the enemy to re-embark.

This disaster cost the British eight hundred dead, five hundred wounded, and several hundred taken prisoner; it cost Lettow-Vorbeck fifteen European and fifty-four *askari* lives, it brought him recruits by the hundreds, and it also supplied ". . . twelve machine guns, hundreds of rifles, 600,000 rounds of ammunition, coats and blankets enough to last for the rest of the war."[2]

But Lettow-Vorbeck was after much bigger game. He wanted to entice a large British expeditionary force into German East Africa—an immense country, whose 650,000 square miles of jungle, forests,

1. Mosley, op. cit.; for another recent account, see Brian Gardner, *German East* (London: Cassell, 1963).

2. Ibid.; see also General von Lettow-Vorbeck, *My Reminiscences of East Africa* (London: Hurst & Blackett, 1920). Lettow-Vorbeck claimed that the British suffered closer to 2,000 deaths rather than 800; he also claimed the capture of 16 machine guns.

bushlands, heat, rain, and disease would not gladly suffer large armies. He reasoned that if guerrillas continued to cut the all-important Uganda railway, the British would be stung into the desired reaction—and each soldier lured south would be one less available to be sent to Europe.

Throughout 1915, his small guerrilla bands, usually two Europeans and eight *askaris,* operated from Mount Kilimanjaro's wooded slopes, destroying bridges, blowing up trains, ambushing convoys, and capturing arms, ammunition, horses, and mules. At the same time, Lettow-Vorbeck was recruiting and training a guerrilla-type army, which, by late 1915, reached a peak strength of three thousand whites and eleven thousand *askaris.*

Lettow-Vorbeck was supremely suited to carry out this ambitious program. A large, physically tough man, he was a professional soldier who had fought in China in the Boxer Rebellion. In 1904, he had campaigned against the Hottentots in Southwest Africa, had been wounded, but had learned a great deal about guerrilla warfare from these superb bush fighters, who, as the British had earlier experienced with the Zulus, moved faster on foot than the European on horse! Lettow-Vorbeck ". . . took away with him from south-west Africa a lesson he never forgot—that in savage lands it is not necessarily the big army that will win the campaign, even if it eventually wins the war."[3]

In trying to mobilize German East Africa's resources, Lettow-Vorbeck often fought an uphill battle. His nemesis was the governor, Heinrich Schnee, a vapid little man who wished to keep the area neutral. A more complex and less determined man than Lettow-Vorbeck might have bowed to his nominal superior's desire. Lettow-Vorbeck was not particularly complex, but he was determined, and, above all, he was a realist. Reasoning that neutrality would preserve nothing if Germany suffered defeat, he argued that, in time of war, military authority must rule. As a German army officer, he felt it incumbent to fight in the best way he could, a decision soon condoned by the German emperor himself. Schnee never did agree—a stormy and prolonged relationship that forever hindered Lettow-Vorbeck's operations.

A perpetual shortage of arms, ammunition, and supply also plagued the colonel. The British disaster at Tanga and guerrilla forays in the North provided him with needed arms. The British also helped by bombarding coastal towns and turning the apathetic European population into active participants willing to donate goods and services to the army. In the spring of 1915, a German freighter evaded the British blockade and crash-landed on the coast to disgorge eighteen hundred rifles, 4.5 million rounds of ammunition, two six-centimeter guns, four machine guns, shells, explosives, tents, and communication materials.[4]

3. Ibid.; see also General von Lettow-Vorbeck, *Mein Leben* (Munich: Koehlers, 1957).
4. Lettow-Vorbeck (*Reminiscences*), *supra;* see also Hordern, op. cit.

But the Royal Navy prevented another such windfall, and Lettow-Vorbeck's diversely located units were never entirely free from ammunition shortages. They soon became dependent on home-made or ersatz items such as candles, soap, quinine, medicines, cigars, cigarettes, beer, whiskey, boots made from antelope skin (the soles cut from captured British saddles). Later in the war, as the British occupied the towns and pushed inland, most of these items disappeared, with resultant hardship to the guerrillas.

Hardship, however, meant that Lettow-Vorbeck was accomplishing his basic mission. Early British failures and concomitant guerrilla successes had deeply offended British *amour-propre* and decided London on a campaign designed to eliminate the troublesome Lettow-Vorbeck. In early 1916, a mounted brigade of Boers arrived in Nairobi, the vanguard of an impressive force commanded by Major General Jan Smuts, once a hunted guerrilla himself. Smuts commanded a two-year offensive that ended in stalemate, with Lettow-Vorbeck's force, though weakened, still very operational.

General van Deventer next took over the chase, and in late 1917 forced Lettow-Vorbeck to begin a long retreat south into Portuguese East Africa, *a three-thousand-mile trek* that ended back in the German colony in the autumn of 1918. Here he rebuilt his shattered force and by November was again wondering where to strike. At this point, the European armistice ended his war.

At a cost of some 2,000 killed, 9,000 wounded, and 7,000 prisoners or missing, besides six or seven thousand native carriers dead (mostly from disease), he had contained 160,000 British troops besides various Portuguese and Belgian expeditions from south and west. In hunting him, the British lost an estimated 10,000 killed, 7,800 wounded, and about a thousand missing or captured in addition to nearly 50,000 native carriers dead. Belgian and Portuguese casualties amounted to 4,700.[5]

How to explain this fantastic record?

Lettow-Vorbeck and his *Schutztruppe* must take most of the credit. He adopted and retained a simple and clear-cut mission, one which his subordinates fully understood and one for which they were trained. He knew his natives, allowed them their customs, offered them understanding, compassion, and success. He knew his country, and consistently paced operations to terrain and weather. He constantly improvised, never ceased experimenting with field expedients. Above all, he remained an indomitable commander who recognized but was not deterred by his own weaknesses, who gained strength when the enemy demanded surrender. Once, when he was fever-ridden and nearly blind, he led his exhausted horse into camp. His adjutant noted, ". . . I am not sure

5. Ibid.; see also Mosley, op. cit.; Gardner, op. cit.

which one more resembled a skeleton. One thing is certain. The horse will not last the next twenty-four hours, but the colonel will."[6]

He did not go into this war lightly. He knew that he was but a small cog, a very small cog on the wheel of total war. He did not know that the British did not intend to use black soldiers on the western front; he could not have dreamed of the tactical stupidity of a battle such as the Somme, which in one day cost the British fifty thousand dead—so he did not realize that the few thousand white soldiers he and his people were retaining by their own agony would not greatly have influenced the European war.

These facts do not shrink the dimensions of his unique accomplishment. Britain had to supply and pay an enormous army, a total bill of £72 million, and she also had to withstand the severe buffeting of German psychological warfare, which constantly harped on the British failure to run down Lettow-Vorbeck.

Nor do facts lessen the import of his decision. He knew that he was inviting wrath to his country, that people would suffer and die, that he himself would have to surmount an endless stream of personal and organizational problems in order to survive. Anyone doubting the ghastly seriousness of his approach need read only his own words concerning organization and training of the first guerrilla groups which operated from Kilimanjaro slopes against the British railway:

. . . I had to teach the Europeans that it was possible, in these waterless wastes, to drink their own urine to quench their thirst. It was a bad business when anyone fell ill or was wounded, with the best will in the world it was impossible to bring him along. To carry a severely wounded man from the Uganda Railway to the German camps, as was occasionally done, was a tremendous performance.[7]

So tremendous, Mosley adds, that ". . . he gave orders that it was to stop. A wounded man was relieved of his gun and ammunition, shot through the head, and left to the lions, hyenas or the vultures."[8]

Lettow-Vorbeck was as ruthless with his own body. By early 1917, he was enduring his fourth bout of malaria; sand flies and jiggers lived in his skin, at times he could scarcely walk on a scabbed and festered left foot, his teeth were infected, and he had scratched his one good eye on long elephant grass. By autumn of that year, enemy columns were closing from all directions while enemy aircraft droned relentlessly overhead. His once splendid force numbered only about two thousand

6. Mosley, op. cit.
7. Ibid.
8. Ibid.

rifles, including two hundred Europeans, and some three thousand bearers, who were now frequently deserting. But Lettow-Vorbeck was not ready to quit, at least without trying to wring some profit from disaster:

> . . . All I knew was that henceforth we would at least have this over the enemy—we could withdraw quickly anywhere we wished, for we had no more dumps to protect, no more hospitals to worry about. The enemy would have to involve increasing numbers of men in his search for us and would progressively exhaust his strength.[9]

Does a greater example of command optimism exist in the literature of war?

In addition to Lettow-Vorbeck's natural and acquired attributes, he derived considerable strength from his enemy's weaknesses. In 1914, the British high command both in Africa and India epitomized the arrogance of ignorance. Major General Aitken, who commanded the task force of eight thousand that sailed from India to Tanga, ". . . openly expressed his contempt for the Germans. He maintained that they made poor officers and that their native troops were ill-trained and badly directed . . . and he went on record as saying that he was confident his troops would have thrashed the enemy by Christmas."[10] The record does not offer his comments after the disastrous landing, defeat, and reembarkation of survivors, which cost him his job and relegated him to the status of colonel on half pay.

The British East African command erred in the opposite direction. The governor, Sir Charles Belfield, did not want a war and ". . . refused to co-operate with his military commanders."[11] The senior military commander, Major General Wapshare, was later described by his intelligence officer, Captain Meinertzhagen, as ". . . a kindly old gentleman, nervous, physically unfit and devoid of military knowledge."[12] The aggressive young captain found Brigadier General Tighe pleasant but useless, drink having given him gout and a bad liver.[13]

Neither of these commanders was qualified to divine the military problem, which called for a strategic defensive with strong, mobile patrols to neutralize guerrilla depredations along the Uganda railway. Instead, aided by the wisdom of the supreme command in London, they thought in terms of "expeditions"—vast "sweeps" to envelop and destroy the enemy.

9. Ibid.
10. R. Meinertzhagen, *Army Diary 1899–1926* (London: Oliver & Boyd, 1960).
11. Ibid.
12. Ibid.
13. Ibid.

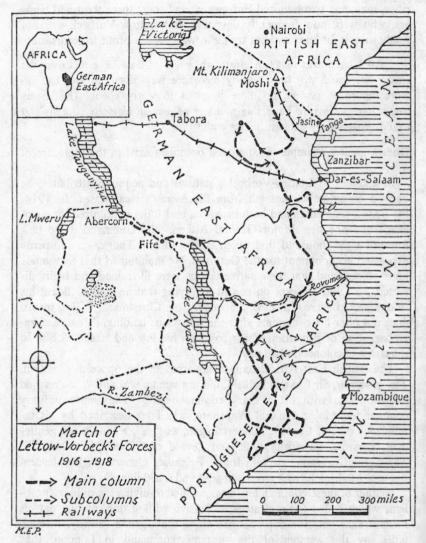

March of
Lettow-Vorbeck's Forces
1916-1918

- -➤ Main column
- - -➤ Subcolumns
+ + + Railways

M.E.P.

The conventional approach merely helped Lettow-Vorbeck. Had the British not landed at Tanga, had they not bombarded coastal towns, he would have had the devil's own time raising any sort of an effective force. He could never have raised an army large enough to invade neighboring countries, and if he had tried, the British and Portuguese disposed of ample forces to stop him. He should have been allowed to wither on the vine. He knew this, and this is why he set about making himself an excresence, an insulting, disgusting presence that the British, in their own minds, had to eliminate.

As he hoped, they chose to wipe him out not by a qualitative approach that would have neutralized his operations, but rather by a quantitative approach that represented the summit of Lettow-Vorbeck's dreams.

Wapshare's first effort, an overland expedition of eighteen hundred troops and fifty-five hundred bearers ended in the little coastal town of Jasin just south of the border, where, after four companies were lost to an enemy attack, it withered "away from sickness and heat."

The highly vaunted Boers did not fare much better. Meinertzhagen found Van Deventer contemptuous in his ignorance of this war ". . . between coolies and kaffirs":

. . . I tried to explain to them that they had not the slightest idea of climate and health conditions, neither had any of them any experience of fighting in thick bush. I told them I thought that perhaps two years might finish the campaign. They smiled and told me I did not understand the Boer.[14]

Meinertzhagen was correct. In the spring of 1916, Smuts sent Van Deventer south in command of 1,200 mounted troops and 8,600 infantry and artillery. Lettow-Vorbeck wisely stayed out of sight, letting rain and the tsetse fly fight for him. On April 6, Van Deventer counted 1,150 mounted strength, on April 12, 800, and on April 16, 650. By the end of the month, he had a fighting strength of 3,000 left out of 10,000.[15]

Other expeditions fared equally ill. By autumn of 1916, ". . . out of 54,000 horses, mules, donkeys and oxen which had been fed into the supply lines south of the Central Railway . . . all but 600 had died."[16] This appalling expenditure of men, animals and effort would have been difficult to defend even if "victory" had resulted. But "victory" was nowhere in sight. And yet, continued adversity only increased Smuts's tenacity—precisely as Lettow-Vorbeck hoped. The capture of Lettow-Vorbeck became an obsession to Smuts. Van Deventer, in turn, never saw the forest for the trees, never totally modified his conventional thinking to fit the task at hand. Only late in the campaign did the British approach the obvious target of the natives—and then with excellent success, but by then it was too late to matter.

Anyone can be wise after the event, but in the case of this campaign the facts were on hand by summer of 1916. Only one officer in the Brit-

14. Ibid.
15. Mosley, op. cit.
16. Ibid.

ish camp looked at them objectively. This was Captain Meinertzhagen, and during that summer he wrote:

> . . . Von Lettow . . . is not going to be caught by maneuver. He knows the country better than we do, his troops understand the last word in bush warfare and can live on the country. I think we are in for an expensive hide-and-seek, and von Lettow will still be cuckooing somewhere in Africa when the cease-fire goes.[17]

17. Meinertzhagen, op. cit.

Chapter 20

Thomas Edward Lawrence • His background • The original Arab revolt • Lawrence's first impressions and estimate of the situation • He joins the rebellion • Arab reverses • Lawrence recovers the initiative • His illness • Moment of truth: a new tactical doctrine • His tactics analyzed • The Arab contribution

WHILE LETTOW-VORBECK was training black guerrillas in remote Kilimanjaro hills, a young British intelligence officer in Cairo was tinkering with a different type of war. This was Thomas Edward Lawrence, who was to become famous to the world as "Lawrence of Arabia."

T. E. Lawrence was an illegitimate Welshman, a twenty-six-year-old reserve lieutenant, a short man, slightly built, his boyishly fair countenance belying either an Oxford honors degree or an extensive knowledge of the Near East gained from several years of archaeological digging in northern Syria, a vocation actively encouraged by British Intelligence.

Scholar, linguist, historian, writer, artist, and poet, Lawrence had not proved a quiescent staff officer in GHQ, Cairo. ". . . A subaltern on the staff, without a Sam Browne belt, and always wearing slacks, scorching about between Cairo and Bulaq on a Triumph motor-cycle, he was an offense to the eyes of his senior officers."[1] His ready criticism of the way the Near East war was being fought against the Turks infuriated most of his seniors. The British surrender of Kut-el-Amara, in Mesopotamia, where he served as negotiator, only heightened his disgust.

Lawrence fortunately did not believe in empty criticism. He not only told his superiors what was wrong, but he insisted that an Arab revolt was the best way to beat the Turks. In talking this up, he appeared at times brilliant, at times frivolous, generally impudent, often rude. He probably would not have endured in any but the British army, which tolerated eccentrics on the grounds that the genius of a few amply repaid the sacrifice.

Not too many officers listened to Lawrence, fewer still agreed. But one who did agree was Kitchener Pasha, now Lord Kitchener, Secretary of State for War, who offered encouragement to the Arabs. The chief of British Intelligence in Cairo, Major General Clayton, also recognized the possibilities of a revolt and encouraged Lawrence to investigate further. A handful of other high-ranking diplomats and officers agreed, and they helped pave the way for Lawrence to exercise what most held to be perverted military thought, others a whimsical imagination, a few genius.

Lawrence's hoped-for revolt broke out in the Hejaz—the skinny Arabian province flanking the Red Sea—in the summer of 1916. Husein, the sherif of Mecca, succeeded in capturing that holy town from the Turks. But his force as well as those commanded by his sons, Feisal, Ali and Abdullah, were badly organized and lacked arms and equipment. By September, Feisal's and Ali's armies were marking time southwest of Medina; Abdullah, having won Taif (and the surrender of the Turkish governor-general), hovered northeast of Medina with his warriors. In the minds of many ranking British staff officers in Cairo, the Arab revolt had failed.

Lawrence disagreed, believing instead that lack of leadership explained the present dormant state. Arab nationalism, he thought, could become an ideal sufficient to unite all tribes in a war against the Turks —but a leader was needed to translate this into action. At this crucial point, GHQ dispatched a ranking and eminently qualified British diplomat, Ronald Storrs, to Jidda to help Abdullah and his father, Husein, through still another crisis. Lawrence meanwhile had been using influential friends to wangle his transfer to the Arab Bureau; he now *took leave* to accompany his good friend Storrs. On the trip down the Red

---

1. David Garnett, (ed.), *The Letters of T. E. Lawrence* (London: Jonathan Cape, 1938); a number of good general biographies are available: Robert Graves, *Lawrence and the Arabs* (London: Jonathan Cape, 1927); Basil Liddell Hart, *T. E. Lawrence* (London: Jonathan Cape, 1934); Anthony Nutting, *Lawrence of Arabia* (London: Hollis & Carter, 1961); Robert Payne, *Lawrence of Arabia— A Triumph* (New York: Pyramid Books, 1963).

Sea, Lawrence became close friends with Husein's chief of staff, an Arab-Circassian ex-colonel in the Turkish army, Aziz el Masri, whose advice, albeit cynical at times, greatly helped Lawrence in the difficult months ahead.

The three men landed at Jidda on October 16, a scene Lawrence later used to open his first major work, *Revolt in the Desert*,[2] a short version of his subsequent classic *Seven Pillars of Wisdom*.[3] Emir Abdullah did not overly impress the young intelligence officer. Lawrence found him too clever, his sincerity discouraged by personal ambition; he was ". . . too balanced, too cool, too humorous" to be *the* leader of the revolt, too discouraged to be the armed prophet who ". . . would set the desert on fire."[4]

Storrs now persuaded Husein to allow Lawrence to visit Ali and Feisal. Lawrence met Ali and his nineteen-year-old half brother Zeid at Rabigh. Ali, too, proved disappointing. Though possessing a ". . . dignified and admirable manner," the thirty-seven-year-old sherif, weakened by tuberculosis, lacked any ". . . great force of character," was ". . . nervous and rather tired," and was not possibly up to the task ahead. Zeid possessed a certain fire, but was too young for the task.[5]

From Rabigh, Lawrence traveled cross-country, a long and dangerous trip by camel, to Feisal's camp at Hamra. This tall, slender, black-bearded prince at once impressed Lawrence as a natural leader. Ensuing talks in which he found the thirty-one-year-old ruler to be ". . . hot-tempered, proud and impatient" confirmed his first impression. Although Feisal was tired and discouraged, he was willing to fight.

As he explained to Lawrence, the Arabs, after initial successes, had lost the initiative to the Turks. In his opinion, the enemy would now try to advance on Rabigh and recapture Mecca. To void this plan, Feisal proposed to fall back and then move against the Hejaz railway while his brothers, Abdullah and Ali, struck the Turkish base at Medina. But Feisal needed arms, ammunition and other aid if he was to keep going.

Lawrence welcomed Feisal's aggressiveness as well as the fighting spirit he discerned in numerous tribes. As he visited various tribal levies and talked to individual fighters, he began to form his own idea of the best tactical contribution the Arabs could make. He concluded that Feisal's tribesmen, if supplied with light guns, ". . . might be capable of holding their hills and serving as an efficient screen behind which we could build up, perhaps at Rabigh, an Arab regular mobile column,

2. T. E. Lawrence, *Revolt in the Desert* (London: Jonathan Cape, 1927).

3. T. E. Lawrence, *Seven Pillars of Wisdom* (London: Jonathan Cape, 1973); for an excellent background study of the revolt, see Ronald Wingate, *Wingate of the Sudan* (London: John Murray, 1935).

4. Lawrence (*Seven Pillars of Wisdom*), *supra*.

5. Ibid.

capable of meeting a Turkish force (distracted by guerrilla warfare) on terms, and of defeating it piecemeal. . . ."[6]

At this stage of his thinking, Lawrence envisioned a Hejaz war ". . . of dervishes against regular troops. It was the fight of a rocky, mountainous, barren country (reinforced by a wild horde of mountaineers) against an enemy so enriched in equipment by the Germans as almost to have lost virtue for rough-and-tumble war. The hill-belt was a paradise for snipers; and Arabs were artists in sniping. Two or three hundred determined men knowing the ranges should hold any section of them; because the slopes were too steep for escalade. . . ." Similarly, the valleys lent themselves to easy ambush that should frustrate and probably prevent Turkish transit. ". . . Without treachery on the part of the mountain tribes," Lawrence decided, it seemed impossible that ". . . the Turks could dare to break their way through." But,

. . . even with treachery as an ally, to pass the hills would be dangerous. The enemy would never be sure that the fickle population might not turn again; and to have such a labyrinth of defiles in the rear, across the communications, would be worse than having it in front. Without the friendship of the tribes, the Turks would own only the ground on which their soldiers stood; and lines so long and complex would soak up thousands of men in a fortnight, and leave none in the battlefront.[7]

After promising Feisal as much help as possible, Lawrence returned to the coast convinced of the possibilities of an effective rebellion. On the return voyage, he found unexpected allies in two important Englishmen. One was Admiral Sir Rosslyn Wemyss, commanding the Royal Navy in the Red Sea, a close friend of the sherif of Mecca; the other was Sir Reginald Wingate, soon to become High Commissioner of Egypt. These officers read Lawrence's reports, which prompted Wingate to wire Cairo:

. . . Following observations of Lieutenant Lawrence a man of great experience and knowledge. . . . Assistance in material and especially quick-firer guns and machine-guns is vital if they [the Arabs] are to be kept in the field. If given this there is no reason why they should not continue to operate successfully for an indefinite time. Their morale is excellent and their tactics and leadership well-suited to present objective.[8]

Thanks to Wemyss and Wingate, Lawrence wafted into Cairo on a lofty cloud of importance. Pleasantly surprised at being closeted with top commanders, he even momentarily forgave their myopic incompe-

---

6. Ibid.
7. Ibid.
8. Payne, op. cit.; see also G. MacMunn and C. Falls, *Military Operations, Egypt and Palestine* (London: HMSO, 1928, Vol. 1, and 1930, Vol. 2).

tence in order to plead his case—the Arab need for immediate arms and supply as well as for British-officer instructor-advisers. Again to his surprise, his recommendations turned quickly into formal orders. Then, to his consternation, he himself was ordered to report to Feisal as adviser and liaison officer.

Lawrence's protests at his new assignment were genuine. He had never fancied himself a troop leader and certainly not a leader of Arab irregulars. So ill-prepared was he in practical military matters that at Yenbo, on the way to Feisal's headquarters, he took a crash course in demolitions from a British expert. His friend Aziz was still there, desperately trying to whip the native army into some semblance of military organization. Although four British planes had arrived, Cairo had not sent much other aid and no officer-instructors. News from the various rebel forces was favorable, however. At Yenbo, ". . . the feeling was busy and confident."

This changed in short order. The hill tribes that formed Feisal's barrier forces gave way to the first major Turkish assault. A Turk cavalry column had pushed on, nearly captured young Prince Zeid's force and now was looking hungrily at the Yenbo base. This unexpected success brought Feisal with his five-thousand-strong camel corps to screen Yenbo, but he in turn was attacked and driven back into the town, where he was protected by the guns of hastily concentrated British warships. These proved too much for the Turks, who backed off to sit like a hungry dog, one eye on Yenbo, one eye on Rabigh.

Lawrence now pulled a master coup by persuading Feisal to march two hundred miles up the coast to the small port of Wejh, from where he could more easily interdict the Hejaz railway. This was a shrewd psychological move that more than neutralized recent Turk successes. Feisal's army on the march, some ten thousand mounted and foot warriors, emphasized the extent of the rebellion and brought dozens of tribes into the fold. From Wejh, taken easily thanks to British warships and slight Turkish resistance, Feisal's agents continued north and east to plead the cause of Arab nationalism and pave the way for further moves by the rebel army.

An equally important result showed in the Turkish camp The Turks could not pursue Feisal. Sickness already was tearing at their columns, and hostile tribes were slicing their thin lines of communication. They lacked both transport and will to pursue Feisal north They could probably have captured Yenbo, but Lawrence made that effort unattractive by sea evacuation of stores. They could have marched on Rabigh, but the Arabs there could retreat on Mecca; meanwhile, so the Turks reasoned, Feisal could wheel about and strike Medina. So, instead of pursuit, the Turks chose to fall back on Medina, where half the force guarded the city, half the railway that supplied the city.

Lawrence did not yet know it, but he had hit upon a successful formula for war in the desert. At the moment, other thoughts occupied his mind. Returning to Cairo, he learned of a French plan to land a British-French force at Akaba, and hurriedly returned to Wejh to persuade Feisal against it. Instead, Lawrence sold him on a plan for a land assault of Akaba by *Arab* forces once Feisal had won necessary tribal submissions.

But now Lawrence learned from Cairo that the Turks were planning to evacuate Medina. Although this move would have suited the Arabs, the transfer of some twenty-five thousand Turkish soldiers would threaten British operations in the Beersheba area. Accordingly Cairo wanted to disrupt the move at all costs. This would involve cutting the all-important Hejaz railway—the umbilical cord to Turkish supply from Syria to Medina—and attempting to disrupt any march made by the Turks, preferably by an Arab attack against Medina. Feisal agreed to help. To win Abdullah's co-operation, Lawrence left on another long and dangerous trip, some two hundred miles across the sands to Ais, northwest of Medina.

Readers of Lawrence's books will remember this journey as the one that forced him to kill one of his guides in order to prevent a blood-rift in the ranks—a soul-searing episode that added to personal ravage caused by back boils, dysentery, and enteric fever. Arriving at Ais more dead than alive, he briefed Abdullah and collapsed.[9]

Lawrence nearly died in Abdullah's camp. High fever brought delirium and visions, and these slowly changed to intense pain from a renewed plague of boils as he returned to reality. Lying in a sun-baked tent, a latter-day Job in a military wilderness, he asked himself the why of war against the Turks.

Nothing about it fitted conventional theories of warfare:

. . . the textbooks gave the aim in war as "the destruction of the organized forces of the enemy" by "the one process battle." Victory could only be purchased by blood. This was a hard saying, as the Arabs had no organized forces, and so a Turkish Foch would have no aim: and the Arabs would not endure casualties, so that an Arab Clausewitz could not buy his victory.[10]

Were the textbooks correct?

Only if one accepted the theory of "absolute" war. The Arab war, however, could not be called absolute: The destruction of the Turkish army by armed confrontation lay hopelessly beyond Arab means.

Was it possible that war did not have to be absolute? Clausewitz, whom Lawrence greatly admired, admitted a number of reasons for fighting a war; two eighteenth-century commentators, De Saxe and

9. Lawrence (*Seven Pillars of Wisdom*), *supra*.

10. T. E. Lawrence, "Guerrilla Warfare." In Encyclopaedia Britannica, 1957, Vol. 10.

Guibert, had preached the virtues of "limited" wars, which should be fought (and won) with as few battles as possible.

If one looked on the Arab war as a rebellion, the picture changed. The Arab aim ". . . was geographical, to extrude the Turk from all Arabic-speaking lands in Asia."[11] In gaining the domination of territory,

. . . Turks might be killed, yet "killing Turks" would never be an excuse or aim. If they would go quietly, the war would end. If not, they must be driven out: but at the cheapest possible price, since the Arabs were fighting for freedom, a pleasure only to be tasted by a man alive.[12]

Lawrence's strategic and tactical analysis hinged on three elements, ". . . one algebraical, one biological, a third psychological."

The algebraical element meant "measuring" invariables of the war to arrive at specific conclusions. The Arabs wanted about 140,000 square miles of territory. If they built a regular army and attempted to occupy this area, the Turks would entrench, and, at best, a stalemate would develop. Suppose, however, that Arabs instead formed

. . . an influence, a thing invulnerable, intangible, without front or back, drifting about like a gas? Armies were like plants, immobile as a whole, firm-rooted, nourished through long stems to the head. The Arabs might be a vapor, blowing where they listed.[13]

To meet a vapor attack, an attack in depth with ". . . sedition putting up her head in every unoccupied one of these 100,000 square miles," the Turks would need a fortified post every four square miles:

. . . 600,000 men to meet the combined ill wills of all the local Arab people. They had 100,000 men available. It seemed that the assets in this sphere were with the Arabs, and climate, railways, deserts, technical weapons could also be attached to their interests. The Turk was stupid and would believe that rebellion was absolute, like war, and deal with it on the analogy of absolute warfare.

The biological factor, what Lawrence called bionomics, respected relations between the organism and its environment. In war, this is the relation of man to battle, the giving and taking of blood until a decision is reached. This could not help the present situation: The Arabs were irregulars, limited in number, ". . . not units, but individuals, and an individual casualty is like a pebble dropped in water: each may make only a brief hole, but rings of sorrow widen out from them. The Arab army could not afford casualties." The Turkish army could afford casu-

11. Lawrence, *Seven Pillars, supra.*
12. Ibid.
13. Ibid.; cf. Clausewitz, op. cit.

alties, but only in men. Materials in the Turkish army were at a premium; therefore ". . . the death of a Turkish bridge or rail, machine or gun, or high explosive" would be more profitable than the death of a Turk.[14]

Lawrence's final factor was the psychological, "the ethical in war"— what Xenophon had called the diathetic. The *will* of the Arab had to repair numerical and material weaknesses. His mind had to be influenced, and not alone his mind, but those of his enemy and his enemy's allies. The French theory of war combined moral and physical factors. Years before, Foch had written that the moral is to the physical as three to one, and on this comforting axiom the French built the disastrous opening strategy of World War I: the *offensive à outrance,* or all-out offensive, that sent hundreds of thousands of French soldiers to unnecessary death. Lawrence separated the factors: ". . . the contest was not physical, but moral, and so battles were a mistake." He was not interested in regimental traditions and elite corps, but rather in men's minds: ". . . the printing press is the greatest weapon in the armory of the modern commander."[15]

The sum of these three factors dictated an indirect approach to war:

. . . the Turkish army was an accident, not a target. Our true strategic aim was to seek its weakest link, and bear only on that till time made the mass of it fall. The Arab army must impose the longest possible passive defense on the Turks (this being the most materially expensive form of war) by extending its own front to the maximum.[16]

To accomplish this, the Arabs needed ". . . a highly mobile, highly equipped type of force, of the smallest size," which would variously strike at Turkish line of communications. Size was not important, since ". . . the ratio between number and area determined the character of the war, and by having five times the mobility of the Turks the Arabs could be on terms with them with one-fifth their number."[17]

This was a latter-day approach to De Saxe's eighteenth-century philosophy. To the incredulity of professional British and French officers raised in Napoleonic tradition, Lawrence argued that battles are unnecessary, that they ". . . are impositions on the side which believes itself weaker, made unavoidable either by lack of land-room, or by the need to defend a material property dearer than the lives of the soldiers." The Arabs had plenty of land-room and nothing of material value to lose,

. . . so they were to defend nothing and to shoot nothing. Their cards were speed and time, not hitting power, and these gave strategical rather than

14. Lawrence, "Guerrilla Warfare," *supra.*
15. Ibid.
16. Ibid.
17. Ibid.

tactical strength. Range is more to strategy than force. The invention of bully-beef had modified land-war more profoundly than the invention of gun-powder.[18]

Conversely, the Arabs had no need to take Medina either by expensive assault or tiresome siege. Let the enemy stay there, or anywhere else, in the largest possible numbers, then destroy him by "killing" his line of communications.

Toward this end, the Arabs added to the sea bases of Yenbo and Wejh by taking Akaba. From these bases, they developed "ladders of tribes" to their advanced bases, from where they seized ". . . Tafileh and the Dead Sea; then Azrak and Deraa, and finally Damascus."[19] With this, the Turks in Arabia were virtually at the mercy of their enemies. In Lawrence's opinion, the Arabs were on the verge of proving Marshal de Saxe's dictum ". . . that a war might be won without fighting battles." In gaining incontestable control of some one hundred thousand square miles, the Arabs had killed, wounded, or captured about thirty-five thousand Turks at little loss to themselves. The Turkish garrisons were totally on edge, morale stood at rock bottom, and undoubtedly the whole army would have collapsed had not General Allenby's immense victory in Palestine summarily driven Turkey from the war.[20]

The enormity of war on the western front, the precipitate fall of the Turks, and the Arab failure to obtain their political aim in the Near East have tended not so much to dim as to confuse the extent of Lawrence's accomplishment. Postwar commentators concentrated on war in the West at the expense of such secondary theaters as Palestine. Most writers treated the Arab war as a guerrilla side show, interesting enough, probably some help to old Allenby, who won the affair in Palestine, but not having much to do with "real" war.

This judgment ignores two essential points. One is that Lawrence and his Arabs were fighting a separate war, a carefully defined war of insurrection that, although dependent on British arms and finances, helped Allenby enormously. Lawrence was not afraid of more Turks; indeed, he wanted more Turks, since enemy quantity enhanced friendly quality. As he pointed out, the Turks would have needed six hundred thousand soldiers to establish ". . . a fortified post every four square miles," nor would this effort necessarily have given them control of the territory, since each Turkish soldier would merely ". . . own the ground he sat on, and what he could poke his rifle at."[21]

18. Ibid.
19. Lawrence, *Seven Pillars, supra.*
20 Lawrence, "Guerrilla Warfare," *supra.*
21. Lawrence, *Seven Pillars, supra.*

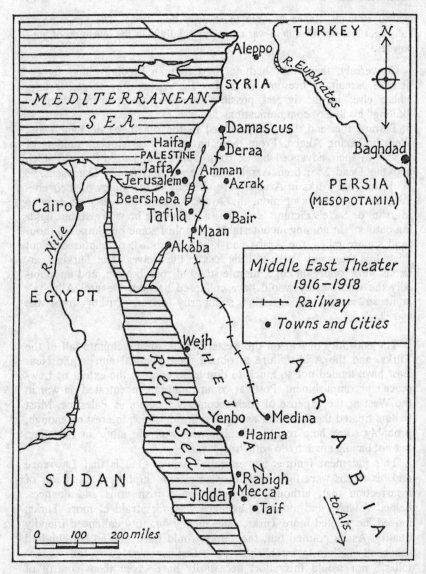

The second point is the "personalized" nature of Lawrence's war. He did not insist on grafting his own and his country's military standards on a body incapable of reception. Instead, and thanks to linguistic ability, imagination, perception, intellectual and moral honesty, and, not least, immense energy, he went to the tribes, found a leader, determined a viable goal, weighed capabilities, and hit on a type of war compatible to leadership, capabilities, and the political goal. The estimate of the situation that Lawrence brought forth from the sand dunes in 1917 is a military equivalent of the British constitution—one of the most interesting unwritten documents of all time.

His political preparation of the area greatly simplified Allenby's subsequent operations, which stood in strong contrast to those in neighboring Mesopotamia, where the British

. . . remained substantially an alien force invading enemy territory, with the local people passively neutral or sullenly against them, and in consequence had not the freedom of movement and elasticity of Allenby in Syria, who entered the country as a friend, with the local people actively on his side. The factors of numbers, climate and communications favored us in Mesopotamia more than in Syria; and our higher command was, after the beginning, no less efficient and experienced. But their casualty lists compared with Allenby's, their wood-chopping tactics compared with this rapier-play, showed how formidably an adverse political situation was able to cramp a purely military operation.[22]

In fighting his own war, Lawrence displayed a versatile strategy and tactics at odds with orthodox military thinking. Under his aegis, the Arab army ". . . used the smallest force in the quickest time at the farthest place."[23] Although he was highly experimental, he always respected his cardinal dictum that ". . . range is more to strategy than force." Raiding parties struck and ran, and this was fundamental, since it denied the enemy a target. In turn, Arab casualties remained minimum: ". . . many Turks on the Arab front had no chance all the war to fire a shot, and correspondingly the Arabs were never on the defense, except by rare accident."[24]

Essential to such operations was ". . . perfect intelligence, so that plans could be made in complete certainty. . . . The headquarters of the Arab army probably took more pains in this service than any other staff." Simple armament was equally essential. Lawrence preferred light machine guns, which the Arabs used as automatic rifles, ". . . snipers' tools, by men kept deliberately in ignorance of their mechanism, so that the speed of action would not be hampered by attempts at repair." Demolitions were important, with each irregular receiving at least rudimentary training in their use. Camels provided standard transport. On occasion, Lawrence used armored cars manned by Englishmen with gasoline either carried by camels or brought in by air. Although they performed well under certain conditions, ". . . the tactical employments

22. Ibid.
23. Ibid.
24. Lawrence, "Guerrilla Warfare," *supra*.

of cars and camel-corps are so different that their use in joint operations is difficult. It was found demoralizing to both to use armored and unarmored cavalry together."[25]

Lawrence's tactics might have been countered, at least in part, by intelligent Turkish adaptation. In 1923, Lawrence wrote Colonel A. P. Wavell:

. . . If the Turks had put machine guns on three or four of their touring cars, and driven them on weekly patrol over the admirable going of the desert E. [east] of Amman and Maan they would have put an absolute stop to our camel-parties, and so to our rebellion. It wouldn't have cost them 20 men or £20,000 . . . *rightly applied.* They scraped up cavalry and armored trains and camel corps and block-houses against us: because they didn't think hard enough.

Lawrence dismissed several other possible Turkish countertactics: well-destruction would not have helped, nor did airplanes, which they used:

. . . Bombing tribes is ineffective. I fancy that air-power may be effective against elaborate armies: but against irregulars it has no more than moral value. The Turks had plenty machines, and used them freely against us—and never hurt us till the last phase, when we had brought 1,000 of our regulars on the raid against Deraa. Guerrilla tactics are a complete muffing of air-force. . . .

The Turks did miss

. . . one other thing of which every rebellion is mortally afraid—treachery. If instead of counter-propaganda (never effective on the conservative side) the money had been put into buying the few venal men always to be found in a big movement, then they would have crippled us. We could only dare these intricate raids because we felt sure and safe. One well-informed traitor will spoil a national rising.[26]

Lawrence's most amazing feat was assimilating himself to his environment, or, put another way, the ability to respect the Arabs as individuals leading their own way of life. Many of Lawrence's achievements stemmed from this relatively simple outlook. He refused to impose Western standards on people he regarded as civilized. A good example is his failure to respect the military principle of concentration of force. He could not achieve this, because tribes would not mix and one tribe could not operate in another's territory. As a result, he fought the war with ". . . the widest distribution of force," but this increased fluidity of operations, while the tribal concept insured a flow of replacements and, more important, avoided intertribal wars.

25. Ibid.
26. Garnett, op. cit.

Lawrence's insistence on individual importance remained paramount. Since lines of communication and supply troops did not exist, every soldier was a front-line soldier. But he could not be committed in strength; rather, by relay, by individual action, which levied severe strain and exacted from the soldier ". . . special initiative, endurance and enthusiasm." To maintain this, demanded charismatic leadership. English officer-advisers were purposely few in number, not more than one per thousand troops, and ". . . those who were present controlled by influence and advice, by their superior knowledge, not by an extraneous authority."[27]

The sum of the experience was enormous, suggesting to Lawrence that:

. . . irregular warfare or rebellion could be proved to be an exact science, and an inevitable success, granted certain factors and if pursued along certain lines. Here is the thesis: Rebellion must have an unassailable base, something guarded not merely from attack, but from the fear of it: such a base as the Arab revolt had in the Red Sea ports, the desert, or in the minds of men converted to its creed. It must have a sophisticated alien enemy, in the form of a disciplined army of occupation too small to fulfil the doctrine of acreage: too few to adjust number to space, in order to dominate the whole area effectively from fortified posts. It must have a friendly population, not actively friendly, but sympathetic to the point of not betraying rebel movements to the enemy. Rebellions can be made by two percent active in a striking force, and ninety-eight percent passively sympathetic. The few active rebels must have the qualities of speed and endurance, ubiquity and independence of arteries to supply. They must have the technical equipment to destroy or paralyze the enemy's organized communication, for irregular war is fairly Willisen's definition of strategy, "the study of communication," in its extreme degree, of attack where the enemy is not. In fifty words: Granted mobility, security (in the form of denying targets to the enemy), time, and doctrine (the idea to convert every subject to friendliness), victory will rest with the insurgents, for the algebraical factors are in the end decisive, and against them perfections of means and spirit struggle quite in vain.[28]

This was not an accidental theory, neither was it applied hit and miss. In 1933, Lawrence wrote a most revealing letter to Basil Liddell Hart, who was about to publish a major work:

. . . You talk of a summing up to come. Will you (if you agree with my feeling) in it strike a blow for hard work and thinking? I was not an instinc-

27. Lawrence, "Guerrilla Warfare," *supra;* see also Liddell Hart, op. cit., who cites Lawrence's "Twenty-Seven Articles"—"a theory of the art of handling Arabs . . . [written] as a confidential guide to newcomers from the British Army." These could be studied with profit by today's Western advisers to foreign armies.
28. Ibid.

tive soldier, automatic with intuitions and happy ideas. When I took a decision, or adopted an alternative, it was after studying every relevant—and many an irrelevant—factor. Geography, tribal structure, religion, social customs, language, appetites, standards—all were at my finger-ends. The enemy I knew almost like my own side. I risked myself among them a hundred times, to *learn*.

The same with tactics. If I used a weapon well, it was because I could handle it. . . . To use aircraft, I learned to fly. To use armored cars, I learned to drive and fight them. I became a gunner at need, and could doctor and judge a camel.

The same with strategy. I have written only a few pages on the art of war—but in these I levy contribution from my predecessors of five languages. You are one of the few living Englishmen who can see the allusions and quotations, the conscious analogies, in all I say and do, militarily.

Do make it clear that generalship, at least in my case, came of understanding, of hard study and brain-work and concentration. Had it come easy to me I should not have done it so well. If your book could persuade some of our new soldiers to read and mark and learn things outside drill manuals and tactical diagrams, it would do a good work. I feel a fundamental crippling incuriousness about our officers. Too much body and too little head. The perfect general would know everything in heaven and earth.

So please, if you see me that way and agree with me, do use me as a text to preach for more study of books and history, a greater seriousness in military art. With 2,000 years of examples behind us we have no excuse, when fighting, for not fighting well. . . .[29]

Lawrence also heavily emphasized the factor of faith—the why of the irregular war or rebellion. And here he was skating on dangerous ice. Later critics condemned him for pursuing an unrealistic political goal.[30] He himself defined this goal as winning a vast territory so that Arab tribes could live in a loose confederation of freedom. Knowing the power politics of that imperialist day, for Lawrence was a realist as well as a romanticist, did he imagine that this could be the case at war's end?

The answer is difficult. Ignoring the creation of the *Seven Pillars of Wisdom,* the tragedy of his subsequent life is explained in part by massive disillusionment. How much this stemmed from the Paris conference is difficult to say. Lawrence accompanied Feisal to that august gathering and strongly pleaded the Arab cause, but this could have been prompted by a sense of loyalty or, more likely, a conscience stricken by having led the Arabs up the garden path, as he admitted in *Seven*

29. Garnett, op. cit.

30. R. Aldington, *Lawrence of Arabia—A Biographical Enquiry* (London: Collins, 1955); see also P. Knightly and C. Simpson, *The Secret Lives of Lawrence of Arabia* (London: Nelson, 1969).

Pillars. In August 1923, he wrote of this work to his close friend Mrs. Thomas Hardy:

... It is meant to be the true history of a political movement whose essence was a fraud—in the sense that its leaders did not believe the arguments with which they moved its rank and file: and also the true history of a campaign, to show how unlovely the back of a commander's mind must be. . . .[31]

But other factors undoubtedly played a role in the tragedy—his illegitimacy, early mental and moral confusions, the terrible rigors of prolonged desert campaigns, and finally physical and mental torture suffered at Deraa.

Probably all these combine to form the explanation, but the emotional factor must reign supreme. No one can doubt the idealistic motivation of the Arab revolt. Lawrence found this during his first reconnaissance, in 1916, and he correctly realized that, if properly exploited, it could move mountains. He revealed its strength, but also its devouring nature, in the opening page of the *Seven Pillars of Wisdom:*

... We were a self-centered army without parade or gesture, devoted to freedom, the second of man's creeds, a purpose so ravenous that it devoured all our strength, a hope so transcendent that our earlier ambitions faded in its glare. As time went by our need to fight for the ideal increased to an unquestioning possession, riding with spur and rein over our doubts. Willy-nilly it became a faith. We had sold ourselves into its slavery, manacled ourselves together in its chain-gang, bowed ourselves to serve its holiness with all our good and ill content. The mentality of ordinary human slaves is terrible—and we had surrendered, not body alone, but soul to the over-mastering greed of victory. By our own act we were drained of morality, of volition, of responsibility, like dead leaves in the wind.[32]

Victory is an illusory word.

31. Garnett, op. cit.
32. Lawrence, *Seven Pillars, supra.*

Chapter 21

The Irish revolution • Asquith reacts • Rise of Sinn Fein • Michael Collins and the Irish Republican Army • The IRA and terrorist tactics • The Royal Irish Constabulary • The Black and Tans • The Auxies • Sir Nevil Macready's iron fist • Sinn Fein replies • The war escalates • Partition and British departure • The cost • Question of terrorist tactics • Definition of terror • Rule by terror • Paradox of terror: the double standard • Terror in the East

THE IRISH REVOLUTION began in Dublin on Easter Monday 1916. Padhraic H. Pearse, at thirty-seven years of age a veteran member of the Irish Republican Brotherhood, voiced the insurrectionary words from the wide steps of the general post office. His brogue heavy in lazy, warm air, Pearse proclaimed the end of English rule in favor of a free republic; as his oratory washed by a few startled citizens, fellow conspirators set up a series of fortified strong points in and around the city. By the time authorities awakened, rebels held city center, seemed hopeful of general uprising.

No general uprising.

Although many Irishmen resented English rule, they found nothing attractive about the militant IRB, with its organizational appendages the Sinn Fein (Ourselves Alone) and the Irish Volunteers. For sixty years, power had resided in the Irish Nationalist Party, whose eighty members vigorously and often cacophonously represented their country in the House of Commons. At the outbreak of World War I, John Redmond, speaking for country and party, had pledged Ireland to the war effort. In spring of 1916, some sixty thousand of her sons were serving in France. Heavy casualties, harsh taxation and other wartime measures, many of a niggling nature so dear to bureaucratic hearts, had somewhat soured the glorious opening notes, but martial displeasure was a long way from open rebellion.

And, on that Easter Sunday, most citizens watched apathetically and perhaps even apprehensively, and not a few secretly rejoiced when government recovered to proclaim martial law, arrest ringleaders and several hundred followers, and end the revolt. A popular nationalist paper, *The Freemen's Journal,* judged the abortive effort to have been ". . . an armed assault against the will and decision of the Irish nation itself constitutionally ascertained through its proper representatives."[1]

The attempted *putsch* may have affronted public opinion by challenging legal authority, but it was not entirely sinister. Irish leaders had been demanding home rule for a long time; indeed, such a bill was languishing in the Statute Book in London, deferred until the end of the war.[2] The IRB action should have been construed as an exaggerated demand for political autonomy, the indiscretion of ringleaders punished by mild prison sentences and fines, other "troublemakers" released— life presumably then continuing in its pleasant if turbulent fashion.

But now the English Government erred egregiously. Preoccupied with reverses on the western front, Asquith foolishly let the Dublin military command court-martial and execute the ringleaders (including Pearse). In the first two weeks of May, fifteen Irishmen were shot, a process that George Bernard Shaw warned was ". . . canonizing the prisoners." Asquith belatedly stopped the executions and hurried to Dublin. He was too late. As Beckett has pointed out, ". . . Ireland was quickly passing under the most dangerous of all tyrannies—the tyranny of the dead."[3]

The IRB efficiently exploited widespread resentment, which continued to spread despite the government's conciliatory efforts. Prompted by England's new ally, America, whose Irish population commanded a large vote, Lloyd George in spring of 1917 declared a general amnesty of political detainees and prisoners; in July, he convened an Irish Convention, which unfortunately settled nothing. Former prisoners scurried back to subversive tasks, prison (as usual) having only sharpened rev-

1. J. C. Beckett, *The Making of Modern Ireland 1603–1923* (London: Faber & Faber, 1966).

2. W. S. Churchill, *The World Crisis* (London: Thornton Butterworth, 1929), Vol. 5.

3. Beckett, op. cit.

olutionary zeal. A real cause existed now—". . . the grass soon grows over a battlefield but never over a scaffold."[4]

That scaffold had taken more than rebel lives. It had choked the legitimate party virtually out of existence. In its place rose Sinn Fein, under such able if diverse leaders as De Valera, Arthur Griffith, and Michael Collins.

The militants would scarcely lack ammunition. In 1918, the government announced its intention to introduce conscription. The Irish people rose in protest, the English Government backed down, thousands of young volunteers flocked to the now not-so-covert IRB colors. To combat growing subversion, Lloyd George's government seized Sinn Fein leaders, another mistake, in that the arrest of De Valera and Griffith left the future of the movement to fire-eating Michael Collins, who wanted outright insurrection.

In 1919, Collins reorganized the Irish Volunteers into the Irish Republican Army (IRA) and commenced limited war. The government answered by declaring Sinn Fein and its elected assembly, the Dail, illegal. Incidents mounted, and, by 1920, a virtual state of war existed.

Collins had no intention of repeating the mistakes of 1916. His was a ragtag army of high-spirited volunteers with little military training, no uniforms and a wild assortment of weapons—Hotchkiss machine guns, Lewis guns, German Mausers, Mannlichers, Winchester repeaters, British army Lee-Enfields, sporting rifles and shotguns, hand grenades and mines—mostly stolen from legal authority.[5] The IRA probably never exceeded fifteen thousand members; according to Collins, its effective strength was ". . . not more than three thousand fighting men." He divided these into brigades, battalions, and companies, but, despite this military veneer, his real strength consisted of small "flying columns" of fifteen to thirty men who trained in guerrilla warfare, particularly the hit-and-run raid and the ambush—terrorist tactics that included assassination.[6] By creating a reign of terror, Collins hoped to make ". . . regular government impossible, and the cost of holding the country so great that the British would be compelled to withdraw."[7] His primary targets were the police and the military, but he soon included prominent government officials and progovernment Unionists. In 1920, his terrorists killed 176 policemen and wounded 251; they also killed 54 soldiers and wounded 118, besides killing and intimidating numerous civilians. They blew up police and military barracks, burned courthouses and tax

4. Churchill, op. cit.
5. Bennett, op. cit.
6. Ibid.; see also Giovanni Costigan, "The Anglo-Irish Conflict, 1919–1922," *University Review*, Dublin: Spring 1968; on occasion, flying columns were larger—in 1921, Tom Barry commanded 104 men in an ambush of British forces at Crossbarry.
7. Beckett, op. cit.

collectors' offices, destroyed coast-guard stations, robbed the mails, and even sheared girls' heads ". . . because they had been seen talking to soldiers or constables."[8] On the evening before Easter, they destroyed 315 barracks of the Royal Irish Constabulary (R.I.C.) in a single night. Such was the extent of their activities that the English viceroy, Lord French, reported the Sinn Fein as ". . . an army numbering 100,000 . . . properly organized in regiments and brigades, led by disciplined officers. . . . They are a formidable army."[9]

The Royal Irish Constabulary numbered about ten thousand men neither organized nor trained to combat insurgency. Unlike England's unarmed police, the Constabulary was ". . . a para-military force, armed with carbines, bayonets, revolvers and grenades." When counter-subversion became a principal activity, their plain clothesmen were loathed by the IRA, who regarded them as spies. In addition to armed attacks, the IRA conducted effective psychological warfare against the Constabulary:

. . . De Valera stigmatized the R.I.C. as "England's janissaries," and called upon his compatriots to ostracize them. "These men must not be tolerated socially," he ordered, "as if they were clean, healthy members of our social life. They must be shown and made to feel how base are the functions they perform, and how vile is the position they occupy." Policemen, he emphasized, must be made "to understand how utterly the people of Ireland loathe both themselves and their calling," so as to "prevent" young Irishmen from dishonouring both themselves and their country by entering that calling."[10]

Dublin walls sometimes carried the chalked words: "Join the R.A.F. and See the World. Join the R.I.C. and See the Next."[11]

By now, a significant minority of the population actively sympathized with the movement—one authority estimates over one hundred thousand offering *active* support; a large percentage remained apathetic, frightened by Collins' terror. Police morale fell, resignations increased, recruitment fell off. Worse yet, the police had begun to abrogate constituted authority: ". . . Barracks and court houses were abandoned in the remoter parts of the south and west of the country . . . [where] *Sinn Fein* police, young men with green armlets, kept what order there was, and the *Sinn Fein* courts administered their own rough justice with variable, and sometimes impressive success."[12]

8. Edgar Holt, *Protest in Arms—The Irish Troubles 1916–1923* (London: Putnam, 1960).
9. Costigan, op. cit.
10. Ibid.
11. Ibid.
12. Bennett, op. cit.

"The Irish Question" was progressively dividing the home government. A substantial group of parliamentarians and other officials wanted to deal gently with the rebels; a more substantial group opposed them:

. . . The Prime Minister [Lloyd George] refused to believe that Sinn Fein had any real popular support in the guerrilla struggle that was raging. In October 1920 he denounced "the small body of assassins, a real murder gang, dominating the country and terrorizing it."[13]

The Chief Secretary for Ireland, Sir Hamar Greenwood, and the military commander at Dublin House, General Sir Nevil Macready, believed that only harsh methods would "win" the war—or, rather, the fight against "treason and murder."[14]

The punitive attitude prevailed and resulted in two police forces being recruited in England. One was a large unit of British ex-soldiers who served as constables. Wearing khaki tunics, breeches, and puttees, large tam-o'-shanter bonnets, and belts, bandoliers, and holsters of black leather, the members of this unit, eventually numbering twelve thousand, earned the colloquial name of Black and Tans, derisory in that this was a well-known pack of fox hounds in County Limerick.

The other unit was the "Auxiliary Division" of the Royal Irish Constabulary. Known as "Auxies," this unit eventually numbered about fifteen hundred, mostly British ex-officers who wore their old uniforms (minus rank) and Glengarry caps; they later wore dark green and khaki uniforms and fought in one-hundred-man "shock companies" under their own officers.

The government further strengthened Macready's hand by emergency legislation enacted in July 1920, a bill that ". . . gave wide powers to the military command, including authority to arrest and imprison without charge or trial anyone suspected of *Sinn Fein* associations, to try prisoners by court-martial, to hold witnesses in custody and imprison or fine them for failing to produce evidence, and to substitute military courts of inquiry for coroners' inquests."[15] Macready pleaded for authority to declare martial law throughout the country, and in January 1921, had declared it in eight southern counties.[16]

The results of this repressive policy were disastrous. Police-state methods turned Ireland into a hostile land, with British forces occupying tiny enclaves and those not entirely secure.

Neither the Auxiliaries nor the Black and Tans were trained in counterinsurgency warfare. From the beginning, they presented easy targets to Irish terrorists. In attempting to ferret out miscreants, their heavy hands

13. Costigan, op. cit.
14. Ibid.
15. Holt, op. cit.
16. Costigan, op. cit.

often fell on innocent civilians, thus further alienating an already hostile population. Each repressive measure worsened matters. No one citizen trusted the other. The old man in the worn trenchcoat standing quietly in a crowd might whip out a pistol and shoot a policeman; the young blade with the pretty girl might throw a hand grenade at a military post. Then the Crossley tenders—awkward lorries holding eight to ten police— would race to the scene, the Black and Tans arresting without caution, interrogating without discretion, on occasion employing torture.[17]

Puffs of hatred rose from the green land, a cloud floated over the island. In return for executing one insurgent, Kevin Barry, Tralee rebels ambushed a lorry load of Black and Tans, killed five, and captured two. Police and soldiers descended on the town, demanded the return of the two prisoners, and, to emphasize the demand, ". . . wrecked shops and houses with hatchets and crowbars and set fire to the County Hall." And in vain: the ". . . *Sinn Feiners* had thrown the two men alive in the furnace of the local gas-works."[18] At Kilmichael, an IRA flying column ambushed and killed an Auxie patrol. In turn, police squads fell on private houses, summarily executed citizens suspected of being Sinn Feiners. Toward the end of 1920, when the IRA began burning warehouses in Liverpool, the government authorized "official punishments" including the destruction of homes believed to harbor sympathizers, not to mention more-active suspects. This quickly backfired: for every cottage destroyed, the IRA burned down an official's much more valuable house. In his recent book *Out of the Lion's Paw,* Constantine Fitzgibbon has dramatically spelled out the give and take of hatred:

. . . Like all guerrilla wars it was a dirty fight, atrocities breeding atrocities, vengeance following upon revenge. Murder was a weapon of war acceptable to both sides, though on the whole the Irish murdered selectively, the British with less discrimination. Some British units tortured their prisoners; some Irish tortured captured informers. There was much treachery, and little gallantry. The sudden ambush on the mountain lane; the raid in the night and the English officer or Irish leader shot in front of wife and children; the knife between the shoulder-blades in the dark, slum alley-way; the moment of awareness in the public house when the victim suddenly realizes that these men are not his friends, that he is alone with them, and that his lower lip is beginning to tremble; the lorry careering down a long village street, its machine-guns blazing blindly into unidentified little homes; drunken soldiers burning half Cork as a reprisal; Michael Collins's squad of professional assassins stalking their victims through the quiet and leafy suburbs; big, beautiful Georgian country houses blazing in the night, because their owners probably had Unionist sympathies; infuriated soldiers shoot-

17. Ibid.
18. Holt, op. cit.

ing into the massed spectators at a football match; and always the glance over the shoulder, the backward glance of fear. That is guerrilla warfare.[19]

In early 1921, the vicious exchange was heartily condemned by no less than the Archbishop of Canterbury, who, speaking in the House of Lords, condemned IRA violence, but also British reprisals. ". . . You cannot justifiably punish wrong-doing by lawlessly doing the like. Not by calling in the Devil will you cast out devilry." A few months later, Lloyd George voiced the dilemma: ". . . I recognize that force is itself no remedy, and that reason and goodwill alone can lead us to the final goal. But to abandon the use of force today would be to surrender alike to violence, crime and separatism, and that I am not prepared to do."[20] Privately he told colleagues that he refused ". . . to shake hands with murder."[21] So saying, he authorized another troop increase: by May 1921, British forces numbered about 50,000—some 35,000 regular troops, 12,500 Royal Irish Constabulary (including Black and Tans), and about 1,500 Auxiliaries.[22]

Strength settled nothing. By spring of 1921, the Cabinet had concluded ". . . that the only way to make sure of winning the Irish war was to raise an additional 100,000 troops and special police, together with thousands of armored cars, and then to cover the whole of southern Ireland with blockhouses and barbed wire, so that great drives on the Boer War model could be made to round up the whole I.R.A." Wiser heads pointed out that British public opinion would topple any government suggesting such a move.[23]

The matter might have ended there but for a good reason: the other side was also getting desperate. Collins' two-fold strategy had failed: Murderous raids and ambushes had, without question, disrupted normal government, but had not driven the English from the country, nor did the English seem on the point of leaving. The general public, always mercurial, was tiring of semianarchy—as Yeats had it: ". . . now days are dragon-ridden, the nightmare / rides upon sleep." Compromise now seemed the only way to end agony.

In July 1921, the British Government proposed what could have become law in 1914: a partition, with an Irish Free State in the South— a self-governing dominion similiar in status to Canada. A treaty to this effect was signed in December, and British forces were quickly withdrawn. Peace lasted only a short time. In spring of 1922, civil war erupted between pro- and anti-treaty factions. But this was Irish fighting

19. Constantine Fitzgibbon, *Out of the Lion's Paw* (London: MacDonald, 1970).
20. Holt, op. cit.
21. Costigan, op. cit.
22. Churchill (op. cit.) put the figure at 60,000.
23. Churchill, op. cit.

Irish, so only Irish could win (or lose). This time, the rebel-rebels lost. A year later, the country settled into disturbed peace appropriate to its historical tradition of lilting turmoil.

The Irish revolution raised moral questions scarcely justified by number of casualties. A ranking British official, the Chief Secretary for Ireland, estimated British army losses at 566 killed. General Macready counted 750 rebel-army losses. A contemporary authority believes that fewer than 2,000 civilians lost their lives.[24] Compared to the blood bath of World War I, these figures represent a mild shower.

Yet the use of terror as a major rebel weapon genuinely shocked many English people. In discussing its use by insurgents, even Winston Churchill's normally silky pen jerked a convulsive protest that relied more on contradiction of terms than on rational consideration of traditional and moral aspects.[25]

This naïve reaction was perhaps inevitable in a land still hypnotized by its own majesty and power, a land that was outgrowing the use of force at home but still relied on it to rule an empire, thus a land that had become accustomed to a double standard of application while refusing to admit the paradox of definition.

These good people would probably have agreed with a contemporary definition of terror as "extreme fear" and "an object of dread."[26] Not only can terror be employed as a weapon, but any weapon can become a weapon of terror: terror is a weapon, a weapon is terror, and no one agency monopolizes it. The point is made with artistic brilliance by Goya, whose *Los Desastres de la Guerra* depict the "excesses" of the Spanish guerrilla war against France; the paradox is emphasized by the corpse-strewn battlefields of World War I caught in the camera's cold eye. Terror is the kissing cousin of force and, real or implied, is never far removed from the pages of history. To define (and condemn) terror from a peculiar social, economic, political, and emotional plane is to display a self-righteous attitude that, totally unrealistic, is doomed to be disappointed by harsh facts.

The paradox of terror, so conveniently ignored by English public opinion, particularly middle- and upper-middle-class opinion during the Irish rebellion, is ages old. Celtiberian slaves working New Carthage silver mines must have regarded Roman legionaries as objects "of dread" inducing "extreme fear." To enslaved minds, the legionaries were weapons of terror designed to keep the slaves in the mines—and apparently they worked very efficiently toward this end. From time to time, these and other slaves secretly rose to attack the Romans, who, upon

24. Costigan, op. cit.
25. Churchill, op. cit.
26. Chambers Twentieth Century Dictionary. London: 1968.

seeing a sentry assassinated or a detachment ambushed and annihilated, no doubt spoke feelingly about the use of terrorist tactics.

But who had introduced this particular terror to this particular environment? The Romans. Had they other options? Certainly: they could have kept their hands off the Iberian Peninsula, or they could have governed it justly and wisely (as a few officials tried to do). Instead, they came as conquerors ruled by greed, and, in turn, they ruled by oppression maintained by terror. What options did the natives hold either to rid themselves of the Roman presence or to convert it to a more salutary form? Only one: force. What kind of force? That which was limited to what their minds could evoke. Lacking arms, training, and organization, they had to rely on wits, on surprise raids, ambushes, massacres. Was this *terror* or was it *counterterror?*

The paradox survived the Roman Empire. The king's soldiers frequently became weapons of terror, just as did the rack and the gibbet. Feudal government of the Middle Ages rested on force (as opposed to the people's consent), often on terror exercised through the man-made will of God reinforced by hangman's noose or executioner's ax. No student of the period can seriously condemn the protesting peasant as a terrorist, for here, as in the case of Romans in Spain and indeed of most governments, European monarchs and ruling nobility held options of rule ranging from the most benevolent to the most despotic. Their subjects, however, held limited options: submit or rebel. If they chose rebellion, the options were again limited, the main reliance being placed on native wit. But since native wit was often sharply circumscribed, most rebellions were doomed to expensive failure. Whatever the effort, whether a single peasant who in the fury of frustration picked up a scythe and severed the tax-collecting bailiff's head from his body, or the group of peasants who grabbed pitchforks to stand against the king's soldiers—the effort, more often than not, was not *terror* but, rather, *counterterror.*

The paradox survived the Middle Ages and is implicit in many instances cited in preceding pages. But as bourgeois rule began to replace feudalism in Western nations, the paradox of terror began to wear a camouflage convenient to Christian conscience. As the people's will slowly asserted itself, as dynasties fell or became sharply altered in character, the pattern of rule slowly began to change. As nations came into being, as rule by law began to replace rule by whim, as the concept of democratic government began to claim men's minds, parliamentary processes visibly diminished the role of force and thus of a particular type of terror in civilized government.

The process greatly varied. In England, the bourgeois revolution of 1689, finally consolidated in 1832, established a climate in which rule by law and stable government grew to proud tradition. In France, the bourgeois revolution gave way to reaction unsuccessfully challenged by the proletariat in 1848, an enduring conflict, a climate that barely tolerated rule by law, with the inevitable result of semianarchic government. Each European nation treated the transition from feudalism to bourgeois rule in a different way and at a different time, and each in turn has faced the challenge of the proletariat in a variety of ways and with greatly differing results in which terror has never been far removed.

The paradox of terror remained very much alive in the imperialist philosophy of even the most advanced Western nations. By devious mental exercises conducted in the spiritual gymnasium of Christianity, colonizing powers defended the double standard: force used by themselves became benevolence; counterforce used by natives became terror. The conceit is clearly expressed in Cornwallis' denunciation of Marion and his guerrillas during the American Revolution.

It appeared in both subtle and blunt ways. Most of us do not think of a well-meaning missionary as a terror weapon. But he was just that to political functionaries of some tribes, in that he represented a distinct threat to the existing social-political-economic-religious structure, besides serving as harbinger of white armies that would take tribal lands and place the tribe in perpetual bondage. The missionary was a threat. The missionary was as much a threat to the savage's way of life as, to choose a military analogy, the musket was to the knight's way of life. Some readers will remember the touching scene in *Orlando Furioso* when the knight rowed out to sea and tossed the captured firearm overboard while cursing its invention and hoping it was the only one of its kind, because it would mean the end of knightly warfare. The thought process of the savage was similar when he tossed the first missionary into the cooking pot.

A more blatant example of Western hypocrisy occurred at the end of the nineteenth century, at the Hague conference on the rules of land warfare. One resolution proposed to abolish dumdum bullets. This was a splendid idea: a dumdum bullet is an ordinary cartridge with an X cut on the end, the improvised surgery insuring that the ball, when striking an object, preferably human, will expand and, upon leaving the object, tear away a great portion of flesh. If ever a weapon is terrible, it is a dumdum bullet, and it is not difficult to imagine the effect on an ignorant native's mind, for here terror was heightened by a seemingly magic quality of the white man's military art.

Yet, at this conference, the British refused to abandon the use of the dumdum, because of its proven efficiency in breaking up native charges![27]

The hypocrisy of Western governments also displayed itself in home

27. (Hague Conference on land warfare.) Lest the American reader nod smugly, he should remember that American soldiers used dumdum bullets in the settling of the West and during the Philippine Insurrection; the Japanese, incidentally, used them on Iwo Jima (and probably elsewhere) in World War II. Rumors of usage by both sides have been reported from Vietnam. They are also used during the annual Canadian-Norwegian slaughter of baby seals.

rule, but in a more subtle form than either a missionary or a dumdum bullet. Neither the rise of democratic government nor technical innovations wrought by the Industrial Revolution resulted in Utopia. Industrialization benefited many people, but it also brought grave social inequities to threaten seriously and frequently the fabric of social government in the most enlightened nations.

The overt terror of the king's soldiers, the lord's bailiffs, the rack, and the gibbet was replaced with the covert terror of industrial slavery: in England, the Lancashire cotton mills, the industrial centers of the Midlands, the Ebbw Vale coal pits, the doss houses; in America, the New England railways, the Chicago meat plants, the Allegheny coal mines, the Colorado copper mines—these and other by-products of *laissez faire* economics spelled miserable wages, torturous hours, dangerous and unhealthful working environments, accidents with no compensation, minimum if any retirement benefits, massive layoffs, widespread unemployment, slums, child labor, inadequate schools: altogether a portrait of hopelessness, the dignity of human beings cast like some sort of industrial refuse into gigantic slag heaps to form a social state in which death often became preferable to survival, a state mocking the cultural pretensions of Western civilization.

The deadening process of this social disease was accompanied by a hatred difficult for our affluent society to understand or even to comprehend. But it did exist, and it did assert itself. For then, as now, where man is deprived of dignity and hope, hatred sets in, and a corollary of hatred is a desire for vengeance. And if death is made to appear as good or even preferable to life, then an act of terror against an object of hatred is a simple and even rewarding matter, for the bite of the rifle's bark is momentary, and, as Socrates put it, the sleep is long and can be no less comfortable than life and may be more so.

And yet, to rational man, terror and counterterror are abhorrent and, except for isolated cases, they did not become favored weapons of the discontent in western Eurasia or in America. Men used terror on occasion, and at times the history of labor and, in some instances, agrarian movements in the respective countries is bloody and ugly, and the history of all countries is spotted with political assassinations. But this falls far short of a terror-ridden environment, of systematic repression on the one hand and systematic assassination on the other, far short of outright insurrection. In general, the working classes in western Eurasia and America avoided using terrorist methods primarily because of the lurking knowledge reaching to the depths of the labor movement that legislative processes inspired by the principle of one man-one vote were trying to eradicate social horrors evoked by industrialization and unmitigated greed of some landlords and factory owners. In short, the labor movement chose the ballot, not the bullet, evolution by selective trade unionism, not revolution by the mass proletariat. Particularly in

England, a peculiar and in some ways unhealthy calm accompanied the process. In despair, Karl Marx wrote to a friend in 1870: ". . . England possesses all the necessary conditions of social revolution; what she lacks is a universal outlook and revolutionary passion."

If social malaise of such intensity gripped enlightened nations, we can imagine its extent in the autocracies and colonies, where the major labor force remained strapped to the feudal concept of land ownership. In fulminating against social abuses in nineteenth-century France or England or twentieth-century America, neither Zola nor Dickens, neither Dreiser, Sinclair nor London, equaled Tolstoy's or Turgenev's narrative power, simply because of the much more orderly canvas of the West, where man was not yet divorced from his government, where hope for improvement still survived.

British and American workers may have been ill-paid and ill-treated and themselves and families host to a wide variety of social indignities, for any one of which society, industry, and government should have been ashamed, but they were not quelled by the knout under the least possible pretext, their demonstrations were not usually fired upon by troops, they were not subject to mass arrest and detention, they were not executed in wholesale lots when their whispered protests brushed authoritarian ears. Violence was not their chosen way of life, and this is the main reason that English public opinion was so shocked by the "Irish outrages."

That English public opinion was shocked does not alter the fact of terror that reigned in numerous countries throughout the nineteenth and into the twentieth centuries. In 1914, an act of terror began the events that led to the first world war in history. In 1917, a reign of terror culminated in a revolution that changed the political face of the world.

Chapter 22

THE FALLOUT of radical thought produced by the explosion of the French Revolution filtered only slowly into the reactionary air of czarist Russia. Falling gently and slowly, it penetrated not the minds of peasants and serfs, those unfortunates whose isolated protests marked the decades with the patterned emphasis of tombstones, but, rather, it infected the palace hierarchy, made particularly receptive by the oppres-sive air of Nicholas I's reign. ". . . By virtually proscribing all forms of political, social and philosophical speculation," E. H. Carr noted, Nicholas "threw the whole intellectual movement of three generations into a revolutionary mould."[1]

The Decembrist uprising of 1825 was the result: ". . . a palace revo-lution," in Bernard Pares's words, "that did not succeed," but ". . . al-most the first that had anything like a political program." Pares, along

1. E. H. Carr, *Studies in Revolution* (London: Macmillan, 1950).

with most modern historians, marks this revolt ". . . as the first act in the Russian Revolution."[2]

As might be expected, the Decembrist uprising elicited harsh penalties from young and autocratic Czar Nicholas I. Although Nicholas continued to work for peasant reforms, oppression of the intelligentsia continued throughout his long reign (1825–55). But thought has always survived oppression, and if Pushkin and Lermontov were forced to premature deaths because of liberal views, others survived. The provocative thinking of the German philosophers Kant, Fichte, Schelling, Hegel, and Feuerbach, the radical writings of the socialist theorists Saint-Simon, Fourier, and Louis Blanc—all reached Russia and were embraced by the Belinsky-Stankevitch school, which produced such important political theorists as Michael Bakunin and Alexander Herzen.

The intellectual movement gained impetus during the opening years of Alexander II's more liberal reign. In discussions preceding the freeing of the serfs, specific liberal and revolutionary schools of thought appeared. The 1861 emancipation act directed liberal thinking almost exclusively to the peasant question and brought demands for further reforms. As early as 1861,

. . . a students' meeting developed into a riot and was charged by the Cossacks. In June, students' clubs with their uniforms were forbidden; the numerous bursaries [scholarships] for poor students were withdrawn, and meetings were to be held only by special permission. In the autumn there were serious riots followed by mass expulsions, strict processions of the students and attacks of the troops; three hundred students were imprisoned. . . .[3]

Two important revolutionary movements appeared in these years. The young Pisarev opted for ". . . an insurrectionary freedom from all authority and convention," a movement described by Ivan Turgenev in his novel *Fathers and Children* and one that he termed the Nihilists. Another appeared under the aegis of Chernyshevsky, who, influenced by the utilitarian philosophy of Bentham and Mill, broke with the liberal Herzen to demand radical reforms in his *Unaddressed Letters:*

. . . Fly-sheets began to appear, calling for terrorist acts against the government—such as that addressed *To Young Russia* in 1862, in which even the murder of the Emperor was advocated. About this time fires broke out in St. Petersburg and were attributed either to Revolutionaries or to Poles. . . . Chernyshevsky was tried and, on loose evidence, sent for twenty-four years to Siberia; Pisarev was sentenced to two years' imprisonment. Both their magazines were suspended.[4]

2. Pares, op. cit.; see also Alan Moorehead, *The Russian Revolution* (New York: Harper & Brothers, 1958).
3. Pares, op. cit.
4. Ibid.

The attempt on Alexander's life in 1866 virtually ended the liberal aspects of his reign. But repression could not stem various liberal movements that for a short time had been allowed to develop and were now nurtured from the West. In 1869–70,

. . . the political influence of western Europe became yet more marked. The example of the Paris commune, the growth of socialism and anarchism, and the widespread agitation carried on with the aid of clandestinely imported literature, exercised a stimulating and encouraging effect. . . .[5]

Where some new movements preached non-violent methods, notably Lavrov's, who picked up the shreds of Pisarev's nihilist movement, others, such as Michael Bakunin's, called for all-out violence to achieve revolution. Writing from Geneva in 1868, Bakunin, in his book *Cause of the People,*

. . . called on all to free themselves first and foremost from religion, but also from all traditions of hereditary property and the family; the State, he said, had to be destroyed. Bakunin's creed was anarchism; the future society was to be based on a number of free local communities; the means of production were to be controlled. Bakunin called for an armed rising. "It is not difficult," so he lightly wrote, "to raise any village"; and his appeal was to many more attractive than the milder methods advocated by Lavrov.[6]

Bakunin's theories collided squarely with those expressed by Karl Marx, who urged that revolution should be achieved within the framework of the state. They came closer on the subject of violence. Though no particular advocate of violence, Karl Marx wrote in his world-shaking economic study *Das Kapital,* first translated into Russian in 1872, that ". . . force is the midwife of every old society pregnant with a new one."[7]

But Russia was not ready for Marxian theories. Instead, in 1872 a group of propagandists attempted to spread the revolutionary word to the peasants. Several thousand men and women—the forerunners of the Narodniks—discovered to their dismay that peasant ignorance, drunkenness, apathy, and misplaced faith in the czar, not to mention the size of Russia, poor communications, and powerful secret police and army made revolution by persuasion a difficult task.

Disappointed members of this group soon began returning to the cities, where ". . . they lived without passports and waged a systematic war on the police." Here they frequently joined revolutionary movements of the intelligentsia, who had continued to spread thoughts by

5. T. G. Masaryk, *The Spirit of Russia* (London: Allen & Unwin, 1919), Vol. 1 of 2 vols.

6. Pares, op. cit.

7. E. H. Carr, *Karl Marx—A Study in Fanaticism* (London: J. M. Dent & Sons, 1934).

the printing press and by word of mouth, the punctuation marks acts of terror. The first revolutionary society, *Land and Liberty,* formed in St. Petersburg, was dedicated

. . . to bring about an economic revolution from below by militant methods. It had a closely systematized staff, which was to produce strikes and riots wherever possible and was also to conduct propaganda. Its "heavenly chancellery" manufactured false passports, and its "disorganization department" planned acts of terrorism. A demonstration of December, 1876, in front of the Kazan Cathedral, where the chief speaker was the propagandist Plekhanov, led to further arrests and sentences. Among the revolutionaries the tide flowed ever stronger in the direction of terrorism.[8]

Professor Mazour has pointed out that although the new party recognized terroristic acts, it ". . . accepted these not as a policy of political opposition, but only as an expedient weapon of revolutionary defense. Terror could be directed only against individuals who served as instruments of oppression; it had no place in a society where political institutions allow the citizen freedom and justice."

. . . Terroristic activity [stated the 1876 program of the executive committee of the party] consists in the destruction of the most harmful persons in the Government, the protection of the party from spies, and the punishment of official lawlessness and violence in all the more prominent and important cases in which such lawlessness and violence are manifested. The aim of such activity is to break down the prestige of Governmental power, to furnish continuous proof of the possibility of carrying on a contest with the Government, to raise in that way the revolutionary spirit of the people and inspire belief in the practicability of revolution, and, finally, to form a body suited and accustomed to warfare.[9]

The government's answer to such tactics, repression rather than reform, was exactly what revolutionists needed to keep themselves in business and to propagate such "hard-core" bodies as *The Will of the People,* which went so far as to publish the death sentence of Czar Nicholas.

. . . These conspirators were not more than a few hundred in number. Their weapon was the bomb. While they fought the Russian police the public remained passive, but the sympathies of many were certainly, if anything, rather with the revolutionaries, who thus were often able to obtain indirect help or shelter. They were organized in sections and worked efficiently; and they had good information as to the Emperor's movement. . . .[10]

8. Pares, op. cit.
9. A. G. Mazour, *Russia—Tsarist and Communist* (New York: D. Van Nostrand, 1962).
10. Pares, op. cit.

Not all revolutionaries embraced a philosophy of terror. Notably G. V. Plekhanov, the father of Russian Marxism, pleaded with his fellows to forgo terrorist methods, which he regarded as a waste of time. His stand split the party into Populists and Terrorists. Other liberal groups abhorred the idea of terror. The government could quite easily have isolated and neutralized the minority extremists, but, in 1878, when the czar appealed for public support,

. . . in Kiev and Harkov the Zemstvo Liberals met in conference, and pointed out that while all guarantees of individual liberty were violated by the police, and while the demands of the public were persistently ignored, it was thereby precluded from giving any effective support to the throne. . . .[11]

Extremists recognized the all-too-fragile base of their organization. Their continued existence in part depended on publicity derived and sympathy aroused from mass arrests and large trials, which emphasized the rape of justice as well as keeping vital issues before the public eye. Proposed liberal reforms of General Melikov, the important first step toward constitutional government, had they been put into effect, would have terminated the reason for terrorist activities. The czar already had signed the first of these when two nihilists, Rysakov and Grinevetsky, assassinated him, in 1881.

A reform government or even a government interested in reform might still have succeeded in providing a suitable constitution, but Alexander III, ". . . big, strong and stupid," gave way to the most reactionary of his advisers. Although the revolutionary movement was virtually paralyzed by governmental repression, individual acts continued to plague authorities throughout Alexander's reign (1881–94): in the country, isolated peasant protests; in the cities, student strikes and riots; and, from 1880 onward, increasing industrial unrest and open strikes.

The government replied in kind with "the *okhrana* procedure":

. . . This law, under which all Russia was at least partially governed . . . gave to local and imperial officials the right of search; the right to imprison any suspect for two weeks—the two weeks might be indefinitely extended by order of the Minister of the Interior; the right to exile a subject for five years without a trial or without bringing charges; the right to forbid residence in a given area for an indefinite period; the right to suppress meetings, even those for which official permission had been given; the right to dismiss employees of the Zemstva and town councils; and the right to hand civilians over to military courts-martial. Even this list is not exhaustive. . . .[12]

11. Ibid.
12. W. B. Walsh, *Russia and the Soviet Union* (Ann Arbor, Mich.: University of Michigan Press, 1958).

In 1894, the weak Nicholas II insured continuation of this dreadful state of affairs by promising his advisers ". . . an unswerving adherence to the principle of autocracy,"[13] an injudicious statement that elicited a sinister warning by pamphlets distributed in St. Petersburg: "You have begun the struggle, and the battle will not be long delayed."[14]

Autocracy would have been acceptable had it produced necessary reforms in country and city. Despite the 1861 emancipation act, the plight of the Russian peasant under the vicious "commune system" beggared description. Prince Peter Kropotkin may have been an anarchist, but his words condemning Czar Nicholas' call for "order" in Russia were damning in their truthfulness. What is order? Kropotkin asked:

. . . It is misery and famine become the normal state of society . . . it is the peasant of one-third of Russia dying of diphtheria, typhus, of hunger from hardship, amidst piles of grain making their way abroad. . . . It is land taken from the peasant in order to raise cattle to feed the wealthy; it is land left fallow rather than restored to him who asks for nothing more than land for cultivation.[15]

Russian industrialization, delayed until the last decades of the nineteenth century and brought to surging life by the financial genius Sergius Witte, drew numerous half-starved peasants to the cities and mines, where their lot was as bad as in the country.

Revolutionary parties were beginning to look to the worker for support. Plekhanov, who had broken with the anarchists and finally fled to Switzerland, published a Russian translation of the *Communist Manifesto* in 1882. A year later, along with Vera Zasulich, Paul Axelrod, and Leo Deutsch, he founded ". . . the first Russian Marxist group and planted the roots of Marxism in the new industrial proletariat of Russia."[16] This movement spawned "reading circles" in the larger Russian cities, and it was in one of these in St. Petersburg that, in 1893, the twenty-three-year-old Lenin became convinced that the newly created working proletariat ". . . would provide the driving force and the ideological justification of the Russian revolution."[17]

The rise of industrial strife contributed greatly to the revolutionary cause. The pioneer Bolshevik historian M. N. Pokrovsky wrote that ". . . in the space of six years (1881–86) the historians of the Russian labor movement have to record 48 large strikes affecting altogether more than 80,000 workers . . ."[18] Lionel Kochan has pointed out in

13. Pares, op. cit.
14. Masaryk, op. cit.
15. Lionel Kochan, *Russia in Revolution 1890–1918* (London: Weidenfeld & Nicolson, 1966).
16. Carr, *Studies in Revolution, supra.*
17. Ibid.
18. M. N. Pokrovsky, op. cit., Vol. 1.

his recent, excellent book *Russia in Revolution 1890–1918* that ". . . the strikes of the 1890s had political overtones and were organized"[19]; the germ of the later soviets, or workers' councils and trade unions, appeared in St. Petersburg textile strikes of 1896–97. In 1896, 118 strikes occurred, 145 in 1897, and 215 in 1898.[20] These and other demonstrations were ruthlessly suppressed, at first by police, both official and company-hired, but increasingly by troops. Where the army intervened in industrial disputes 19 times in 1893, it intervened 271 times in 1901 and 522 times in 1902.[21] Here was a dangerous condition, for where the worker originally began demonstrating and striking for economic betterment, slowly he was moving toward divorce from the harridan monarchy to marry the floozily attractive blonde of radical political change.

A few, a very few government officials recognized what was happening. In 1898, General Trepov, head of the police, presciently wrote:

. . . If the minor needs and demands of the workers are exploited by the revolutionaries for such profound anti-governmental aims, then is it not up to the government as soon as possible to seize this weapon, that is so rewarding for the revolutionaries, from their hands and itself to assure the fulfilment of the task . . . the police are obliged to be interested in the same thing as the revolutionary.[22]

Colonel Zubatov, head of the Moscow security police and himself a considerable man of mystery, enlarged this idea by attempting to separate ". . . the workers' economic action from the revolutionary political struggle," encouraging unions to air and study workers' problems by appropriate courses and discussion groups. Zubatov succeeded so well that he quickly lost control of the movement, whose solidarity alarmed industry, government, and foreign investors. With his summary dismissal, in 1903, the movement lost momentum, but was revived by a peasant-priest-double agent, Georgi Gapon, who organized St. Petersburg workers into ". . . a cross between a trade union, a mutual aid society and even an underground revolutionary organization."[23]

But if authorities wished to separate trade unionism and revolution, Lenin saw the one leading to the other. The shooting of workers at the Obukhov works, in May 1901, had caused him to write on the subject of armed insurrection. In 1904, Lenin wrote in *Iskra* (*The Spark*):

. . . It is up to the working-class to extend and strengthen its organizations, to intensify tenfold its agitation among the masses, taking advantage of

19. Kochan, op. cit.; see also Mazour, op. cit.
20. Walsh, op. cit.
21. Kochan, op. cit.
22. Ibid.
23. Ibid.

every vacillation on the part of the government, *making propaganda for the idea of insurrection,* demonstrating its necessity on the example of all those half-hearted steps, foredoomed to failure, that are being made such a fuss of at present [the Zemstvo conference]. . . .[24]

Prompt and radical industrial and agrarian reforms undoubtedly could still have channeled the organizational trend into an evolutionary direction heartily desired by upper- and middle-class liberals and moderates including professional classes and an increasing number of university students. The new revolutionary parties lacked organization, they represented a minority, and they disagreed as to how revolution should be achieved.

The Social Revolutionary Party, which inherited the Populist movement, believed that revolution must come from the peasants. Certainly the land was stirring under protest. New railroads were slowly breaking down the barrier between city and country, which meant a far larger audience for inflammatory propaganda pouring from the cities. The drunken, apathetic peasant of Turgenev's novels was becoming militant. An official police report of 1898 has him indulging in the most basic form of guerrilla warfare:

. . . From reports reaching the Ministry of the Interior it is seen that in certain provinces, predominantly southern and south-eastern, there has recently emerged a series of peasant disorders in the form of systematic damage to the landowners' fields and meadows, together with the driving away of cattle under the protection of men armed with sticks, staves and pitchforks, and attacks on the landowners' watchmen and guards or considerable illegal timber-cutting in the landowners' woods, and brawls with the foresters. When the guards seize the peasants' cattle, the peasants, hoping to free it, *often moving by whole villages,* carry out armed attack on the buildings and farmhouses of the landowners and divide up the working and even the living quarters, attacking and wounding servants and guards.[25]

In sharp contrast to the agrarian movement, the Social Democrats held, as did Marx, that revolution must come from the working proletariat of the cities. But here, in 1903, another split and a serious one developed: the Mensheviks, dominated by Plekhanov, believing that the movement must be as broad-based as possible, essentially a trade-union concept; the Bolsheviks holding for the thirty-three-year-old Lenin's ". . . conception of a small dedicated body of professional revolutionaries" to steer the masses—in Max Weber's words, the "principle of the small number," with the Marxian result of the dictatorship of the proletariat—and this is what prevailed in 1917.

Each movement relied on propaganda, masses of it, and also on ter-

24. Pokrovsky, op. cit.
25. Kochan, op. cit.

ror—terror to disorganize the government, terror to draw reprisals and thus involve the whole population and widen the gulf between people and government, terror to protect the movement from spies, *agents provocateurs,* and traitors. Revolutionary parties already had suffered a high casualty rate—Lenin's brother, for example, was hanged in 1891 —that necessitated cellular internal structure with emphasis on secrecy to cloak the cunning, tough, brave, and fanatical survivors.

The Socialist Revolutionaries carried out terror missions by a small, secret, and entirely voluntary group whose members were unknown even to the party's central committee. This committee ". . . designated the targets but only the combat organization determined and put into practice the mode of execution."[26]

The bravery and skill of party agents may be gathered by Lionel Kochan's description of Von Plehve's [the Minister of Interior] assassination in 1904:

. . . It was no mean achievement to frustrate the extraordinary security precautions surrounding the minister. His office could only be reached by way of circuitous corridors. He dared not travel without an escort of police-cyclists and police droshkys, in a carriage protected by closed blinds of nickel-plated steel, proof against revolver bullets and shrapnel. To no avail. The two terrorists, Sazonov and Sikorsky, made use of a vehicle disguised to simulate the type of van used to collect letters from the pillar-boxes of the capital. With this they intercepted Plehve's entourage as it passed by the Warsaw railway station in St. Petersburg. Sazonov threw the bomb. A correspondent of the English newspaper, the *Daily Telegraph,* witnessed the explosion and noted that ". . . Plehve's end was received with semi-public rejoicings. I met nobody who regretted his assassination or condemned the authors."[27]

So fanatic were these agents that most of them willingly accepted death, confident that their places would soon be filled by other, equally ardent visionaries. The young Kaliayev, who killed Grand Duke Sergei in 1905, told the court:

. . . I am not a defendant here, I am your prisoner. We are two warring camps. You—the representatives of the imperial government, the hired servants of capital and oppression. I—one of the avengers of the people, a socialist and revolutionist. Mountains of corpses divide us, hundreds of thousands of broken human lives and a whole sea of blood and tears covering the country in torrents of horror and resentment. You have declared war upon the people. We have accepted your challenge. Having taken me prisoner, it is now within your power to subject me to the torture of slow extinction or to kill me outright, but you cannot hold trial over me. No matter how much

26. Ibid.; see also Masaryk, op. cit.; Walsh, op. cit.
27. Kochan, op. cit.

you may seek to exercise your sway, there can be no justification for you as there can be no condemnation of me. Between you and me there can be no reconciliation, as it cannot be between absolutism and the people. We are still the same enemies, and if, having deprived me of liberty and the opportunity to speak directly to the people, you have seen fit to institute this solemn judgement upon me, I am in no way obliged to recognize you as my judges. . . . Let us be tried by this great martyr of history—the Russia of the people.[28]

These chilling words did not yet represent "the Russia of the people," either in the cities or on the land. The true tragedy of the Russian revolution is the unheeded cry of the majority of the people for evolution toward a better life—for basic subsistence, basic liberties defended by representation in a constituent assembly as the first step toward constitutional monarchy, moves favored by a surprising number of landowners and industrialists and by nearly all professional classes.

But Czar Nicholas II refused to budge from autocratic absolutism; his ministers of state remained nearly as hidebound in frightened intensity. To worsen matters, the war with Japan in 1904–5 led to an unmitigated series of military disasters, each lending itself to the thunder of anti-government propaganda that kept Russian air charged with revolutionary fervor.

Czar and government not only refused the relatively modest demands of the people, but fear caused them to deny these demands, by police and army repression. In January 1905, peasant-priest-double agent Gapon caused near crisis by leading a general strike in St. Petersburg. On Sunday, January 9, the tall, bearded Orthodox priest, purple robes flapping in the Neva breeze, gold cross glittering on his chest in the cold winter's sun, led perhaps two hundred thousand workers and their wives and children to the Winter Palace in St. Petersburg, there to present a people's petition of grievances to the czar. The unarmed, hymn-singing multitude reached the Narva Gate, where it halted before infantry bayonets. And then, without warning, hidden Cossack cavalry units charged the columns of demonstrators while infantrymen fired point-blank into the massed throngs.

Thus Bloody Sunday, a thousand or more people killed, thousands wounded. Bloody indeed, and not only from a humanitarian standpoint. Bloody Sunday caused the Russian worker and the peasant to question the omniscience theretofore enjoyed by the paternalistic figure of the czar. Bloody Sunday cut the first chunk from the broad-base support enjoyed by Nicholas. In many people's minds, the need not for political reforms but for *radical* political reforms became dominant for the first time. In Lenin's words: ". . . The revolutionary education of the proletariat made more progress in one day than it could have made in

28. Ibid.

months and years of drab, humdrum, wretched existence." Moreover, the precipitate display of force solved nothing. The fully charged air of the cities now exploded into a continuous series of protest acts including isolated mutinies in army and navy.

The crisis resulted in the famous October Manifesto, of 1905, seemingly an official surrender. This document guaranteed fundamental civil liberties including freedom of the press, extended the sorely limited franchise, and reformed the Duma, or parliament, into a legislative body. A general amnesty followed, the peasants were tossed some overdue land reforms, and trouble began to decrease.[29]

People reacted variously to this document. The Octobrists, a new, conservative party, embraced it; so did the right-wing Kadets, in the hope that a legislative Duma could evolve into a constituent assembly. As perhaps foreseen by the government, the manifesto caused violent disagreements among the Social Democrats and other revolutionary parties. The Mensheviks and some of the Socialist Revolutionaries wanted to believe in it. Genuinely inspired, the manifesto could have made history with minimum bloodshed. But it was not genuine. Its intention was as thin as its paper, and Trotsky was right to denounce it as ". . . a cossack's whip wrapped in the parchment of a constitution."

The manifesto was a brake. The fast-moving events of 1905 had caught government off guard, its repressive forces severely weakened by war in the Far East. The manifesto was to gain time for government to regroup its forces. In this it succeeded admirably, first by quieting the peasant with mild land reforms, second by breaking the united political front of the cities into two general pieces, then by causing internal dissension in the radical portion. When renewed violence broke out in December with a workers' uprising in Moscow, the government put it down swiftly and continued to repress a new wave of demonstrations, student riots, strikes, and peasant uprisings that lasted well into 1906.[30]

Despite the return of troops from the Far East in early 1906, the government held little reason to feel secure. Between November 1905 and June 1906, 288 police officials were killed and 383 were wounded. ". . . Altogether, up to the end of October, 1906, 3,611 government officials of all ranks, from governor-generals to village gendarmes, had been killed or wounded."[31] The new repression could not stop agitation or propaganda, and each function expanded as the impotency of the Duma became increasingly obvious.

The 1905 revolution introduced a new and most important organizational factor, the soviet of workers' deputies. A soviet was a group of

---

29. George Vernadsky, *A History of Russia* (New Haven, Conn.: Yale University Press, 1945); see also Hugh Seton-Watson, *The Decline of Imperial Russia, 1855–1914* (London: Methuen, 1952).

30. Pares, op. cit.

31. Kochan, op. cit.

elected representatives—one representative per thousand workers—who became a sort of mature strike committee to further workers' demands. The factory soviet, however, soon broadened its base of support by representing more than one factory and by transcending any one political party. The St. Petersburg soviet, which came to life in autumn of 1905, soon grew to 226 members representing 96 factories, and also representatives of five trade unions.[32] This organizational concept quickly spread to other cities and even resulted in soviets of peasants and soldiers: ". . . There were peasants' soviets and military soviets and student soviets and village soviets and city soviets 'from St. Petersburg to Tiflis, and from Warsaw to Vladivostok.'"[33] The St. Petersburg soviet led the October 1905 uprising, the Moscow soviet led the December uprising. The idea was to attain a unity of action far superior to that rendered possible by the emasculated trade unions now permitted.

Lenin did not recognize the true potential of the supposedly apolitical soviets, but Leon Trotsky did. In his visionary mind, they fitted nicely into revolution by the "principle of the small number." They would remain outside party jurisdiction but would be regarded as ". . . the embryo of a provisional revolutionary government," the gun of the political party. Having direct and virtually instant contact with the masses, they became prime targets, along with the trade unions, for Bolshevik propaganda.

The forces that exploded into the 1917 revolution were now in play, except for World War I. From 1906 on, a repressive and unyielding government pitted itself against a declamatory if divided people. In discussing the White Terror following the 1905 revolt, Professor Masaryk wrote,

. . . My pen is reluctant to describe the infamies of this reign of terror. In actual fact, every one in Russia is still [1913] an outlaw. It may be said without exaggeration that during the white terror the fear of death ceased to exist. It had been driven away by pogroms; by the death sentences of courts martial and field courts martial; by arrest and martyrisations in the prisons and on the road to Siberia; by the extremities of cruelty and torture; by the frequency of suicide in the prisons; by illness, epidemic, disease and famine. . . .[34]

The pathetic aspirations of moderate liberals, primarily the Kadets, to legislative reforms through the Duma came to naught; the militancy continued, but outlawed parties operated underground in sporadic and often unco-ordinated jabs and thrusts, the casualty rate remained high

---

32. Ibid.
33. Walsh, op. cit., quoting Khrustaleyev-Nosar.
34. Masaryk, op. cit.

with exiles and executions the order of the day. In September 1907, during the vacation of the Duma, the premier, Stolypin,

. . . set up field courts-martial which dealt drastically with revolutionary crime, the whole of the proceedings being ordinarily completed in four days. The usual sentence of these courts was death, and 600 persons were executed. . . .[35]

Stolypin's police and soldiers continued to move ruthlessly across the face of Russia. From 1905 to 1910, the government handed down 7,101 death sentences and carried out 4,449 executions.[36] Nor did repression end with Stolypin's assassination, in 1911. In 1912, troops put down a strike in the Lena gold fields in Siberia by firing on unarmed men, killing 170 and wounding nearly four hundred. Important strikes followed, to culminate in the massive St. Petersburg general strike of July 1914, which fizzled only in the wash of war's outbreak.

But when cannons sounded and cause called, land-hungry peasants and underprivileged workers swallowed grievances to fight for country and czar. Country proved a better cause than czar, who failed with his army as with his people. Russia's disastrous war with Japan might never have been fought, so little were its lessons respected. With a few exceptions, uniformed fools, mostly aristocrats, commanded the army. The army lacked artillery, airplanes, communications, transport, medical services. Its weapons were obsolete and in short supply: millions of mobilized men lacked rifles and even boots.

The emergency of war changed nothing of this hapless picture. Mismanagement, incompetence, corruption, cupidity, nepotism—each bloomed following mobilization. Food supplies quickly grew short, both in the army and at home. Industrial production slowed. Well-meaning officials submitted corrective plans only to see them shelved by Czarina Alexandra, now totally under the demoniac influence of the "Mad Monk," Grigori Rasputin; and when Nicholas II was persuaded to become commander-in-chief of the army, with headquarters at Tsarskoe Selo, Alexandra became virtually the ruler of Russia.

A palace revolution might have salvaged something from the growing ruin of government. No palace revolution occurred. Instead, the czar and his generals ordered new and voracious offensives that devoured hundreds of thousands of men. At the end of June 1915, Russian losses numbered an estimated 3.8 million and had to be replaced with men taken from factories, mines, and fields. In all, 15 million were mobilized; about half were listed as killed, wounded, or missing. Survivors faced ever-growing shortages in arms, food, and equipment; at home, people faced near starvation. Production slowed, almost ceased. Riots and

35. Pares, op. cit.
36. Masaryk, op. cit.

strikes in cities proclaimed the growing temper and were ruthlessly suppressed.

But abysmal conduct of the war had gnawed away final and frail supports of government. Finally, even the troops rebelled: in February 1917, the St. Petersburg garrison, ordered to break up a massive hunger demonstration, refused its orders. Demonstrations and riots increased in intensity in early March, and still the garrison, some 160,000 troops, refused to act. A general strike brought three hundred thousand workers into the streets, and now mobs began running amok, attacking police stations, storming law courts, breaking open jails.[37] Police either were killed or fled—or joined the revolution. While ministers paled and the Duma fretted, the troops, with a few exceptions, still refused to act. On March 12, regiments began to mutiny, and that was the end of monarchy. The czar abdicated; the vacillating Duma finally established a provisional government in the form of an Emergency Committee. Frantic revolutionaries meanwhile had been trying to assess events, then harness the revolutionary force. The result was a Soviet of Workers' and Soldiers' Deputies, an organization not unlike that which had emerged in 1905; its Executive Committee soon challenged the Duma's Emergency Committee, and eventually, using armed Red Guards, seized power from it.

The St. Petersburg soviet consisted of about twenty-five hundred deputies including most Socialist Revolutionary and Social Democratic leaders. These formed a Central Executive Committee to carry out policy determined by a small and elite Praesidium. Bolsheviks were not strongly represented in this early body, but nonetheless the differences between it and the provisional government were fundamental.

Russia's attitude toward the war provided the major issue. The Lvov-Kerensky government, strongly influenced by the allied powers France, England, and America, pledged Russia to continue fighting. Unaware of the real situation, the American ambassador urged recognition of the new government, which was given on March 22, 1917; Britain, France, and Italy quickly followed suit and even sent labor delegations ". . . to reconcile the differences between the Provisional Government and the Socialists."[38] They were going to take some reconciling: on March 27, the Petrograd soviet issued a proclamation to the people of the world calling for ". . . concerted and decisive action in favor of peace." The Soviet "defeatists" had accepted what the bourgeois right-wing and moderate liberals had failed to realize: that the Russian people had no intention of continuing the war. The allied powers, by demanding continued Russian participation—as Elihu Root succinctly put it, "no fight,

37. Moorehead, op. cit.; see also N. N. Sukhanov, *The Russian Revolution, 1917* (London: Oxford University Press, 1955). Ed. and tr. Joel Carmichael.

38. Vernadsky, op. cit.; see also G. F. Kennan, *Russia Leaves the War* (London: Faber & Faber, 1956).

no loans"—helped to widen the already dangerous gulf between the
Kerensky government and the Russian people.

To this turbulent, divisive climate, the little, bald-headed, sharp-eyed
Lenin returned in 1917 (under German auspices from Geneva by
means of the famous sealed railroad car across Germany). He was
shortly joined by the tall, imperious Trotsky, an intellectual revolutionary in the Menshevik mold, who had sailed from America. The revolution had surprised both of them, but, unlike the Mensheviks, they
realized that, if properly controlled, it could result in a smashing socialist victory.

In Lenin's mind, the Petersburg soviet formed ". . . the germ cell
of a workers' government." With its quasi-military Red Guards, its af-
finity to workers (the mainstay of the revolution), its contacts in other
cities and in the armed forces, the soviet should be able to usurp the
function of the badly disorganized and divided provisional government.
Once this happened, the small but well-organized Bolsheviks, in turn,
should be able to wrest control of the soviet from the majority but divided Mensheviks and Socialist Revolutionaries.

Lenin carefully tailored his appeals to these general objectives. In
contrast to the muddled program offered by the Lvov-Kerensky government, Lenin offered a simple three-point program: immediate peace;
immediate distribution of land to peasants and seizure of factories by
workers; all power to the soviets.[39] In contrast to Mensheviks and most
Socialist Revolutionaries, who did not believe the time propitious, Lenin
demanded an immediate socialist revolution; in addition, the Bolsheviks,
by every means possible, urged extension of soviets into cities and villages to undertake ". . . the task of organizing insurrection and of serving as organs of revolutionary state power."[40]

Lenin was fighting an uphill battle. In June 1917, the Bolsheviks held
only 105 seats in the All-Russian Soviet Congress, the Socialist Revolutionaries holding 285, the Mensheviks 248. This called for a great deal
of razzle-dazzle to keep the Bolsheviks alive, and in this respect Lenin
was a past master. "Loot the looters," he screamed to hysterical masses.
"Peace to the village huts," he cried, "war against the palaces." Rubbish
slogans, certainly—but flaring as effective matches in that highly tindered
air.

Other parties performed a great deal of Lenin's work for him. The
Bolshevik presence should have caused the provisional government to
forget its differences, at least temporarily, and govern, but right-wing
and moderate liberals and numerous Social Democrats and Socialist Revolutionaries refused to take either Lenin or his group seriously, a
pathetic display of the arrogance of ignorance.

39. Vernadsky, op. cit.
40. Kochan, op. cit.

Lenin and his lieutenants realized what the provisional government and the allied powers failed to realize: the Russian people, particularly workers and peasants, were demanding an end of war and immediate and fundamental changes in their ghastly existence. Kerensky undoubtedly sensed the feeling, but failed to control it. He respected it with the "Declaration of Soldiers' Rights," in May 1917, and he appointed political commissars in the army ". . . and charged them with the responsibility of political leadership."[41]

The declaration proved fatal to army discipline, and Lenin quickly exploited the new political commissars through army soviets. Kerensky's provincial civil commissars, taken from the old zemstvo committees, ". . . had almost as little contact with the people as the authorities whom they displaced," and this greatly simplified the work of the village soviets.[42] Finally, Kerensky erred fatally by ordering an offensive against the Austrians, in July 1917.

This effort collapsed within a few days, with entire regiments marching to the rear. The extent of the catastrophe caused Lenin to call on soldiers and sailors in St. Petersburg to seize the government. Lenin was premature; the Party paid the price: Trotsky arrested, Lenin fleeing to Finland, the Bolsheviks momentarily shattered.

But instead of exploiting this development, Kerensky refused to break with the St. Petersburg soviet, thus further alienating upper, middle, and officer classes. Moreover, by turning the disorganized and demoralized army over to General Kornilov, a strong man to whom he gave virtually dictatorial powers, he created a dangerous rival.

In September, Kornilov attempted his own putsch. This failed not because of Kerensky's leadership, but, rather, because workers and soldiers refused to countenance it. As Professor Vernadsky pointed out, it left Kerensky ". . . a prisoner of political and economic anarchy," unable to prevent radical socialists from taking the initiative. In September, an increasingly demoralized Kerensky was forced to release Trotsky from prison and overlook Lenin's secret visits from Finland.

In October, Trotsky became president of the St. Petersburg soviet, and Bolsheviks won control of the all-important Military Committee of this body. On November 7, the Bolsheviks arrested Kerensky's cabinet members and stampeded the Second All-Russian Congress of Soviets into adopting the Bolshevik program, to be carried out by the new government of Russia: the Council of People's Commissars; president: Lenin; Commissar for Foreign Affairs: Trotsky; other key billets: Rykov, Stalin, Lunacharsky. Kerensky fled, the Bolsheviks put down a liberal-student uprising in Moscow, and, on November 20, opened secret negotiations with Germany to end the war. Moving swiftly to con-

41. Vernadsky, op. cit.
42. Ibid.

solidate his coup, Lenin directed Dzerjinsky to organize a powerful secret police, the Cheka, which immediately invoked a reign of terror designed to eliminate all bourgeois (non-socialist) opposition and to cow lesser adversaries into obedience.

A major stumbling block remained: the Constituent Assembly, whose 703 deputies, elected in late November, included only 168 Bolsheviks. Prior to its first meeting, in January 1918, Lenin's police arrested all non-socialist deputies, murdering two in the process. When socialist deputies, mainly Socialist Revolutionaries and Mensheviks, refused to accept Lenin's self-proclaimed government, the Bolsheviks withdrew from the assembly. On January 20, the Central Executive Committee of the Soviets disbanded the assembly by decree, forcibly removing the deputies.

In less than three months, the work of over thirty years had brought a new government to Russia. Whether it could effectively rule remained to be seen.

Chapter 23

Lenin's problems • The Red Terror • Treaty of Brest-Litovsk • Trotsky builds the Red army • Lenin on guerrilla warfare • Allied intervention • President Wilson's ambiguity • Whites versus Reds • The guerrilla aspects of civil war • Lenin's tactics • Reason for allied failures • Kolchak's and Denikin's shortcomings • Cost of allied intervention • Lenin's victory • The Communist International: short-term losses, long-term plans

LENIN faced massive internal and external problems in consolidating his theft of the Russian revolution: a rapidly demobilizing imperial army, the German enemy pressing against the southern provinces, the Ukraine in revolt, grave shortages of food and materials, minimum agricultural and industrial production, lack of foreign credits and supply, rampant inflation.

Politically, the upper, middle, and professional classes and a large portion of bureaucracy and peasantry loathed the Bolsheviks and refused to co-operate with the new government. Deposed military commanders such as Kolchak in Siberia and Alexeiev, Kornilov, and Denikin in the South were organizing former imperial officers into nucleus "White" armies that were attracting regional guerrilla dissidents such as Cossacks, Georgians, and Ukrainians, a growing movement supported by the allied powers, who were muttering thinly veiled threats of open intervention should Russia sign a separate peace with Germany.

The challenge of survival brought forth an intensified display of leadership, discipline, organization, fanaticism, guile, and ruthlessness that already had served Lenin so well. In speaking of political-social change, Bismarck once remarked, ". . . you can't make an omelet without breaking eggs." Lenin put it rather more forcefully: ". . . No dictatorship of the proletariat is to be thought of without terror and violence." Dzerjinsky's Cheka abridged these words to the "Red Terror," a hideous period characterized by torture and summary execution in wholesale lots, summary imprisonment and deportation to Siberia, and, finally, slow starvation of "unproductive elements" by refusal of food-ration cards.

Nor did the peasants escape. To "deepen the revolution," the government sent teams of agitators and Red Guards to organize village soviets and start the all-important flow of food to the cities. When peasants refused to yield hoarded grain supplies, special "food battalions" of Red Guards and secret police relentlessly seized them.[1] To break up united peasant opposition and discredit the Socialist Revolutionaries, Lenin used divide-and-conquer tactics, in this case turning the poorest peasants into "Committees of the Poor," which he pitted against rich and middle-class peasants with the slogan "Loot the Looters"—words used rather differently but a few months earlier.

To rid himself of the German incubus, Lenin signed the treaty of Brest-Litovsk in early March 1918. By this, he ceded vast amounts of Russia: eastern Poland, Lithuania, Estonia, and Latvia to Germany; the Ukraine to be independent; part of Transcaucasia to Turkey—altogether a whopping 26 per cent of the Russian population, 27 per cent of her arable land, 75 per cent of her coal industries.[2] The treaty also brought down the wrath of the allied powers and virtually insured allied intervention. Lenin accepted these consequences as the cost for precious time which he urgently needed to reorganize his forces to face imminent civil war.

Bolshevik military fortunes in early 1918 rested on a heterogeneous collection of Red Guards plus various imperial units such as those under Muraviev, a former czarist colonel, which had defected to the revolutionaries. The Red Guards consisted of armed bands of former workers and soldiers. They varied greatly in size, allegiance, and effectiveness. The St. Petersburg contingent, ten to fifteen thousand strong, was commanded by a former mechanic, Clement Voroshilov. In February, Voroshilov marched his force of irregulars to the southeast to fight and beat the counterrevolutionary Volunteer Army, a successful cam-

1. Vernadsky, op. cit.
2. Ibid.; see also Pares, op. cit.

paign which gained him the support of a number of independent guerrilla bands and swelled his force to some thirty thousand. Other Red Guard units served the party in Moscow and the lesser cities and towns, but Lenin was well aware that this force could not long shelter Communist existence from the dark and rapidly forming clouds of counterrevolution.

In February 1918, Lenin appointed Trotsky chief of the Military Revolutionary Committee, with orders to build a "Workers' and Peasants' Army." Acting swiftly and imperiously, Trotsky started to fashion a Red army suspiciously at odds with revolutionary ideals. Abolishing the Soldiers' Committees created by Kerensky, he replaced them with Communist political commissars, who organized secret Communist cells in each unit. He caused the government to reintroduce conscription, which brought him four hundred thousand men by spring—conscripts armed and equipped from imperial army stocks. Bowing to the inevitable, Trotsky now turned over army organization and training to former czarist officers, most of whom were starving and welcomed any work, but some of whom were coerced into service by the Cheka:

. . . the former tsarist officers were given curt notice to serve the new master in the country—the proletariat. They were to teach toiling men "how to fight the bourgeoisie. . . ." Should they desert their posts, their "fathers, mothers, sisters, brothers, wives, and children" would pay for the betrayal.[3]

Trotsky also set up a special Central Operations Department, to control the numerous guerrilla bands scouring the countryside.[4]

That these steps were not popular, and that the Bolshevik hierarchy did not like independent guerrilla bands, was made abundantly clear by a letter from Lenin to party organizations:

. . . Hundreds and hundreds of military experts are betraying us and will betray us; we will catch them and shoot them, but thousands and tens of thousands of military experts have been working for us systematically and for a long time, and without them we could not have formed the Red Army, which has grown out of the guerrilla force of evil memory, and has been able to score brilliant victories in the East. Experienced people who head our war department rightly point out that where the Party policy in regard to the military experts and the extirpation of guerrilla spirit has been adhered to most strictly, where discipline is firmest, where political work among the troops and the work of the commissars is conducted most thoroughly, there, generally speaking, the number of militia experts inclined to betray us is the lowest, there the opportunities for those who are so inclined to carry out their designs are the slightest, there we have no laxity in the army, there its organization and morale are best, and there we have the most victories. The guer-

3. Mazour, op. cit.
4. Edgar O'Ballance, *The Red Army* (London: Faber & Faber, 1964).

rilla spirit, its vestiges, remnants and survivals have been the cause of immeasurably greater misfortune, disintegration, defeats, disasters and losses in men and military equipment in our army and in the Ukrainian army than all the betrayals of the military experts.

Our Party Program, both on the general subject of bourgeois experts, and on the particular program of one of their varieties, the military experts, has defined the policy of the Communist Party with absolute precision. Our Party is combating and will "ruthlessly combat the supposedly radical, but actually ignorant and self-conceited belief that the working people are capable of overcoming capitalism and the bourgeois order without learning from the bourgeois experts, without utilizing them, and without going through a *long schooling* of work side by side with them."[5]

While Trotsky and Lenin so labored, counterrevolutionary fortunes also waxed. In April, the British landed troops at Murmansk, Archangel, and Vladivostok; American, French, and Italian landings followed, and the Japanese moved into eastern Siberia in considerable strength.[6]

The allied pretext was protection, from the Germans in Finland, of ammunition stores already delivered to imperial Russia. The real motive was to help Kolchak's counterrevolutionary army of Whites forming in the East. Pressed by his allies, and also thinking to neutralize Japanese aspirations on the Asia mainland, President Wilson only grudgingly authorized American forces to land. He instructed the force commander, Major General W. S. Graves, to remain neutral but to support neighboring Czech forces.[7] Since the Czechs were counterrevolutionary, this, in effect, showed the American hand; in short order, American forces were fighting with the British against the Reds. Nothing so well illustrates the confusion and downright ignorance that influenced the president at this critical juncture—the perhaps inevitable result of inept diplomatic reporting, primarily the failure of sixty-seven-year-old Ambassador David Francis, combined with the inaccurate and often con-

5. V. I. Lenin, *Selected Works* (Moscow: Foreign Languages Publishing House, c. 1961), Vol. 3 of 3 vols.

6. Vernadsky, op. cit.; by September 1919, troop strengths numbered: Japanese (eastern Siberia), 60,000; U.S.A., 8,500; British, 1,500; Italian, 1,400; French, 1,096.

7. About 40,000 Czech prisoners had formed brigades to fight on the Russian side against the Central Powers. After the treaty of Brest-Litovsk, they asked for transfer to the western front, which could only be accomplished, due to enemy battle lines, by their sailing from Siberian ports. When, in marching to these ports, their columns were strung from the Volga to Vladivostok, Trotsky, apparently acting under German orders, attempted to disarm and intern them. They successfully rebelled against the Bolsheviks and became an integral if dubious quantity in the counterrevolution.

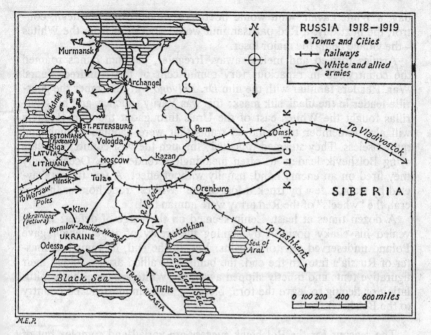

RUSSIA 1918—1919
- Towns and Cities
-+-+- Railways
→ White and allied armies

Murmansk

Archangel

Helsinki

ST. PETERSBURG

ESTONIANS (Iudenich)
Riga
LATVIA
LITHUANIA

Vologda

Perm

Omsk

To Vladivostok

K O L C H A K

SIBERIA

MOSCOW

Kazan

Minsk

To Warsaw
Poles

Tula

R. Volga

Orenburg

To Tashkent

Ukrainians (Petlura)

Kiev

Kornilov-Denikin-Wrangel

UKRAINE

Astrakhan

Sea of Aral

Odessa

Black Sea

TRANSCAUCASIA

Caspian Sea

Tiflis

0 100 200 400   600 miles

M.E.P.

flicting reports submitted by a host of the president's personal and quasi-personal representatives.[8]

The two-year war that ensued was as unlike war on the western front as Lawrence's campaign in Arabia. None of the armies was well organized, armed or equipped, or even well commanded, yet each won impressive local successes that, properly exploited, probably could have proved decisive. Battle plans were either non-existent or meaningless. The White armies spent months in "winning" hundreds of square miles and in reality controlled no more than the ground occupied by the feet of their horses. When their always insufficient numbers stretched thinly enough across the vast Russian steppes, a Red army would strike a weak point of the line to send the entire army hurtling back on its supply. One

8. G. F. Kennan, *The Decision to Intervene* (London: Faber & Faber, 1958). This work and its accompanying volume, *Russia Leaves the War, supra,* are vital for an understanding of this period, particularly the American participation. As Ambassador Kennan pointed out, Vice Consul Felix Cole had sent a lengthy appreciation from Archangel on June 1. This report, in Kennan's words ". . . what has subsequently proved to be the most penetrating and prophetic of all statements by western observers on the prospects for allied intervention in Russia," concluded by recommending delay. Ambassador Francis did not approve and did not cable any of it; it traveled by courier mail and reached Washington on July 19, too late to influence the president's decision.

day, a White cavalry unit would liberate a village from Bolshevik control; the next day, a Red partisan unit would liberate it from the Whites —the village being the major loser.

Armies formed and melted away. Irregular, partisan bands roamed the countryside in rapacious fury reminiscent of the Hundred Years' War. Readers familiar with the film *Dr. Zhivago* will remember the guerrilla leader in the black silk mask: this was Vasily Blücher, and his guerrillas fought the Whites east of the Urals throughout the war. Readers will also remember the armored trains that were genuine enough and quite useless. They steamed raucously through the vast countryside carrying Bolshevik leaders to often meaningless rendezvous. Occasionally they fired on an enemy band, usually without effect. A few troops traveled by train, a few by truck. Most of the "Whites" rode horses. In general, the "wheels" of the Red army were human feet.

A dozen times at least, Lenin seemed on the verge of defeat: he revealed his shaky position by signing the treaty of Riga, which gave Poland undeserved territorial gains. Yet, in the end, he remained master of Russia's fate. In the end, the bumptious allied armies folded their figurative tents and quietly slipped away, the White armies either capitulating or fleeing to leave the torn, bleeding, and famine-stricken country to the Bolsheviks.

The reasons for the Bolshevik success are varied and complex but of immense importance to any study of revolutionary warfare.

On the Bolshevik side, the single overriding key to victory was Lenin's superb leadership, which in time gave the Bolshevik effort the inestimable advantage of unity and fixity of purpose. The hallmark of this leadership was flexibility both of conception and execution.

Before 1917, Lenin's idea of world revolution bore scant similarity to what happened, but this did not deter him from exploiting what he instantly recognized as a unique historical opportunity. In late 1917, no one recognized the precariousness of the Bolshevik position better than Lenin. Great may have been his revolutionary ambitions and broad his objectives, but when the failure of western Eurasian socialists to launch proletariat revolutions became clear, Lenin shelved his grand domestic ambitions and objectives and subordinated himself and his lieutenants to the grim task of survival.

In accomplishing this task, he continued to display a cunning political and military flexibility that often overrode basic tenets held not only in the Communist party but also in Western political and military circles. If it suited his purpose, he never hesitated to yield, either politically or militarily. At times, the government aided the army; at times, the army aided the government: each remained subordinate to the Communist party.

To free his hand to start with, he surrendered immense territories to Germany. And yet, what did he gave away? He yielded territory already controlled by Germany (territory that a strong Russia could one day recover), and he antagonized allied powers who were already antagonized and already aiding White armies as best they could.

To feed his hard-core strength, the workers and soldiers and their families, he endangered peasant support by forcing distribution of crops without adequate compensation. To build an army, he reintroduced the dreaded conscription, enlisted former Czarist officers and shamelessly used their talents, retaining some and discarding others at the end of the emergency.

He relied on a similar policy to fight the civil war. Retreat was not an ugly word so long as it spelled tactical sense. Space existed solely to trade for time: time for the allied powers to quarrel, time for socialist pressures in England and France to exert themselves, time to exploit enemy political and military errors, time for Russian guerrillas to cut Kolchak's and Denikin's lines of communication; time for loyal Russian peasants to scorch the earth; time for Red armies to form and march from north to south and from east to west to stem off still another enemy incursion.

A number of factors influenced the play. The Red army could not have existed without the supply and ammunition depots taken over from imperial forces. The essentially defensive military task (including the final successful counterattacks against the White armies) was immensely aided by operations on interior lines.[9] Lenin's lieutenants and most of the Bolshevik hierarchy, recognizing the literal "do or die" situation, shared his fixity of purpose.

Patriotic motivation also helped. The Bolsheviks may have stolen the revolution, but that scarcely made the idea of revolution less popular. The Red army may have been a dubious proposition from the standpoint of capability, as a generation of Western critics have tenaciously and often tediously pointed out, but it was in every sense a people's army and as such it formed a growing organism in which self-sacrifice often vied with refusal to accept defeat. Tables of organization and equipment (TO&E), vital to Western military structures, may have been nonexistent, but Voroshilov nonetheless transformed his ragtag collection of Red Guards and guerrillas into the Red Fifth Army, and his soldiers, in being beaten by Denikin and in finally beating Denikin, died just as splendidly as those of more properly organized units on the western front.

The Red army may have been battered and close to defeat, it may have lacked proper organization, modern weapons, artillery, communi-

9. This military term may become clearer by analogy to a beehive: the more territory the Bolsheviks lost, the more compressed became their lines of communication, until they could strike with concentrated forces at any intruder from any direction.

cations, airplanes, medical services—but it did not disintegrate under stress, as did the imperial armies, and, by the end of 1920, it numbered over five million, admittedly an inefficient force that supported only sixteen field armies of varying effectiveness, but nonetheless a force that insured Bolshevik control of what was left of Russia.[10]

The French philosopher Jean Paul Sartre once wrote: "The alternative to transcending one's limitations is death." Throughout the civil war, Lenin respected his and Bolshevik limitations. A classic example occurred toward the end, when the Red army had pushed Polish forces from the Ukraine and was driving on Warsaw. A desperate Marshal Pilsudski had sued for an armistice; Bolshevik terms included provisions essential to eventual Russian domination of Poland: for example, citizens' militia of workmen, land grants for all families of Polish men killed or wounded in the war—in other words, the Bolsheviks held the master hand. But now the French intervened with fresh aid and, most importantly, with the services of Maxim Weygand, one of the few capable generals of World War I. Within days, the Red army was routed with a loss of some seventy thousand prisoners.[11] Lenin could have pursued this war further, for many of the factors that so far had aided him remained at work. Undoubtedly, some of his associates urged him to this course. Instead, he signed the disadvantageous treaty of Riga. But he had accomplished his major objective, expelling the Polish army from Russian territory; and he now freed his hand to deliver the *coup de grâce* to Wrangel's final White effort in the South.

A great deal of Lenin's success hinged on his capability of exploiting enemy errors. He did this so constantly and so swiftly and efficiently as to cause the student of the period to suggest that neither the Russian revolution nor the Russian civil war was won so much by the Bolsheviks as the one was lost by the provisional government, the other by the egregious errors of the counterrevolutionary Whites in loose concert with the Western powers.

Intervention in another country's affairs is a delicate matter at best. Whatever happens, the intervening agent is apt to reap the lion's share of the blame if things go wrong and none of the resultant credit if they go right. Primarily for this reason, the objective of the intervening party must be sufficiently important to warrant the risk to prestige. Its importance can be defined only by a careful spelling out of one or more specific aims, as opposed to a conglomerate ambition made the more meaningless by the frippery of legalistic and moralistic window dressing. As an operating rule of thumb: the more vague the stated objective, the less the validity and, in natural corollary, the less the chance of attainment.

10. O'Ballance, op. cit.
11. Churchill, op. cit.

But that is only the beginning. Assuming the specific objective is judged sufficiently important, it must be realistically attainable; that is, if disaster is to be avoided. First-rate minds using first-rate intelligence must weigh the effect of the intervening agent on the balance of the struggle, a process that involves consideration of national forces available for the act of intervention. If the amount of available force is clearly insufficient for the task, either at the inception or as it develops, then the importance of the objective must be reassessed in view of the obvious disadvantages including potential catastrophe.[12]

The allied intervention in the spring of 1918 failed on each count. No single interallied objective existed, but, rather, a nebulous ambition to re-create an eastern front against the Germans, either by persuading the Bolshevik government to this action or by replacing this government with another that would embrace allied interests. A lack of specific objectives prevented allied powers from determining a combined course of action, a deficiency the more glaring in view of the pinchpenny forces committed.

Several reasons explain this failure. The German offensive in France in the spring of 1918 automatically precluded a major allied diversionary effort, at least in northern Russia. Added to this were Anglo-French suspicions of each other's foreign policy, and Wilson's reluctance to intervene openly in Russian affairs, a natural reluctance reinforced by not wanting to give Japan a pretext to secure a permanent foothold in Siberia. Finally, allied representatives in St. Petersburg failed to determine either the depth of the revolution or Bolshevik ability to retain control of it.[13]

This was a catastrophic failure, but an understandable one. The diplomats and generals on hand were engrossed with the world war. They had switched support almost instantly from the imperial government to the provisional government, and they had been prepared to support the Bolshevik government had it agreed to keep Russia in the war. The chief of the American military mission in St. Petersburg had believed that he could persuade Trotsky to this course; the French and the British had even furnished officer adviser-instructors to the embryo Red army, an extraordinary move sharply terminated when Lenin opened peace negotiations with the Germans.[14] Britain and France already were aiding the White movement when Lenin abrogated Bolshevik responsibility for imperial Russian war debts and other obligations, in February 1918.

The erroneous estimate of allied observers hinged in large part on ignorance of conditions inside Russia. The majority of allied representa-

12. In rare instances, the action will still be approved, a handy example being the British sacrificial commitment to Greece in 1940.

13. Kennan, op. cit.

14. O'Ballance, op. cit.; see also Kennan, op. cit.: the U.S. assistant military attaché briefly participated in this effort.

tives did not speak the language, nor did this seem necessary, since the czar and czarina always corresponded in English, and since the court and diplomatic language was French. In those years an enormous gulf existed in all countries between the educated and the working and peasant classes, and the diplomatic corps saw no reason to bridge it, an attitude explicit in the vapid and saccharine writings of the British ambassador's daughter, Meriel Buchanan.

This attitude, natural perhaps, but nonetheless disastrous, meant that in 1918 allied representatives, with few exceptions, were linguistic prisoners of upper, middle, and professional classes who, desperately longing for active intervention, painted a canvas of falsely bright colors. It meant that they had no idea of the turmoil existing deep inside the country; knew nothing of working-class and peasant attitudes; could not talk or listen to Socialist Revolutionaries or Social Democrats or many other persons except through interpreters; lacked accurate information concerning strength, plans, or even progress of White armies, except what they were told by generally dubious sources.[15]

Taken together, this led to an illusory belief, in allied circles, that Bolshevik control was transitory, and this arrogance of ignorance was expanded into a completely unwarranted assumption that a display of allied flags would cause counterrevolutionary Whites to rally into a cohesive force capable of defeating the upstart Reds. When this did not happen, the allied forces found themselves increasingly paralyzed, their influence sharply curtailed. The November 1918 armistice greatly complicated matters. Although the French and British governments wanted to take more positive action in Russia, their leaders were wary of political repercussions—understandably so, in view of their immense losses in the war, not to mention their teetering on the edge of bankruptcy. Instead of reinforcing northern sectors, the British had to satisfy themselves by occupying the Transcaucasian oil fields, from where they fed increasing amounts of arms and supplies to General Denikin. The French did send troops into the Odessa area, a halfhearted effort neutralized by the Reds, whose propaganda caused some French soldiers to defect!

The allies acted more decisively in the spring of 1919, when the Supreme Council, in Paris, offered the Kolchak Whites "munitions, supplies and food to establish themselves as the government of all Russia" in return for specific political guarantees.[16] In June 1919, the British

15. Kennan, op. cit.; after citing a linguistic failure, Kennan posed ". . . the uncomfortable question: on how many other occasions were those American representatives—ignorant as most of them were of the language in which the political life around them was transpiring—betrayed in this manner by their interpreter, and how much was added, in this way, to the confusion and misunderstandings of the time?"
16. Vernadsky, op. cit.

stepped up deliveries to Denikin, sending him ". . . a quarter of a million rifles, two hundred guns, thirty tanks and large masses of munitions and equipment" as well as two hundred military adviser-instructors.[17] Had Paris promises materialized, they might have reversed the failing situation. But Paris promises vanished in the smoke of the conference table. In August 1919, Lord Curzon noted:

. . . The situation is so complex, and the difficulties of arriving at a decision which is acceptable to all are so great that, in some instances, it would be no exaggeration to admit that there is no policy at all.

In these circumstances, the Great Powers when they meet—and too often it must be confessed that refuge is taken in inaction—adopt an uncertain line of conduct; the financial burden tends to fall almost exclusively on the shoulders of those who either have the greatest capacity or the least unwillingness to pay. . . .[18]

Churchill later wrote of allied statesmen: ". . . Some were in favor of peace and some were in favor of war. In the result they made neither peace nor war."[19] In the end, they evacuated, a perhaps inevitable decision but one that, first discussed publicly, proved catastrophic. To save their lives, thousands of Russians now left allied and White army ranks to go to the Red camp, which, never averse to making capital propaganda, was distributing verses such as the following:

> The uniform is British,
> The epaulettes, from France.
> Japan sends tobacco.
> Kolchak leads the dance.

> The uniforms are tattered.
> The epaulettes are gone.
> So is the tobacco, and
> Kolchak's day is done.[20]

The numerous and serious allied shortcomings paled in comparison with those of the White armies. Here dissension ruled, both internally and externally. Although a joint plan of attack and eventually a jointure of forces might have defeated the Red army, neither was achieved, even regionally.

Not only did southern armies pursue separate campaigns, but General Denikin, who had replaced General Kornilov after his suicide in early 1918, constantly alienated the peoples vital to his operational success. Unlike Lenin, he did not understand compromise: He broke with

17. Churchill, op. cit.
18. Ibid.
19. Ibid.
20. Walsh, op. cit.

the powerful Don Cossacks, whose chief, or *ataman,* Krasnov, was will-ing to use German arms and equipment; he held but slight sympathy for land reforms, none for autonomous provincial government.

In his numerous and sometimes extensive incursions, Denikin alien-ated the peasants, not alone by letting his armies live off the land and by commandeering grain and forage as ruthlessly as the Bolsheviks, but also by attempting to give the estates back to their private owners!

He treated provincial groups such as the Cossacks, the Georgians, and the Ukrainians not as allies but as subject peoples of the govern-ment he was going to re-establish. As a result, he forfeited an immense amount of potential strength. Instead of exploiting the loyalty of peas-ants already disillusioned by Bolshevik rule, he often caused them to fight as a third force, the Greens; in the Ukraine, for example, ". . . the peasant anarchist Nestor Makhno led partisans against, successively, Denikin's Whites, Trotsky's Reds, Wrangel's Whites, and finally every-body, until he fled to Rumania in 1921."[21] The brilliant French author André Malraux later depicted the senseless turbulence through a ficti-tious character, Katow, in *Man's Estate (La Condition Humaine)*:

. . . On the Lithuanian front, his battalion had been captured by the Whites. Their arms gone, the men stood lined up on the vast snowy plain that was scarcely visible in the greenish light of the dawn. "Communists stand out!" They knew that it meant death. Two-thirds of the battalion had stepped for-ward. "Take off your tunics. Dig the trench." They had dug. Slowly, for the ground was frozen. To right and left of them the White guards stood waiting, impatient and ill at ease, with a revolver in each hand, for spades might be used as weapons. The center was left empty for the machine-guns trained upon the prisoners. The silence was immeasurable; it had the immen-sity of the snow which stretched as far as the eye could see. There was only the noise the frozen clods made as they hit the ground. Crisp thuds that came quicker and quicker. Even with death before them, the men were hurrying—to get warm. Several had begun to sneeze. "That'll do. Stop!" They turned round. Behind them, beyond their comrades, were massed old men, women, and children from the village; but scantily clothed, wrapped in blankets. Gathered there to profit by the lesson. Many shook their heads, as if they were making every effort to look away, but were spellbound in their anguish. "Take off your trousers!" For uniforms were rare. Many hesitated, on account of the women. "Take off your trousers!" Wounds had appeared, one by one, bound up with rags; the machine-guns had shot very low and almost all of them were hit in the legs. Many folded their trousers, though their great-coats had been thrown aside anyhow. They were lined up once more, at the edge of the trench this time, facing the machine-guns, white against the snow; flesh and shirts. As the cold pierced them they sneezed incessantly, one after another, and those sneezes were so intensely

21. F. L. Schuman, *Russia Since 1917* (New York: Alfred A. Knopf, 1957).

human beside the grimness of that dawn, that instead of firing the machine-gunners had waited—waited till Life be more discreet. They had made up their minds in the end. On the following evening, the Reds recaptured the village; seventeen whom the shots had failed to finish were saved; Katow among them. Silhouetted against the snow, almost transparently bright in the eerie light of the dawn; convulsed with sneezes; so many shapes, they faced the machine-guns. . . .[22]

(Not for nothing did Pushkin cause Lieutenant Grinev, riding through the land torn by Pugachev's revolt, in 1773, to cry: "God defend you from the sight of a Russian rebellion in all its ruthless stupidity!")

A similar failure in leadership infected the Siberian command, where, after the 1918 armistice, Admiral Kolchak established a dictatorship. Almost at once, he alienated Socialist Revolutionary forces in the area and thus lost peasant support; halfhearted and contradictory measures began losing him support of potentially powerful Czech forces.

When counterrevolutionary fortunes looked up, in spring of 1919, Kolchak foolishly attempted a jointure with the allied-Russian force at Murmansk instead of a straight drive to join Denikin in the South. This abortive lateral movement presented a long exposed flank, which the Reds struck to send the White army spinning back in confusion.

In summer of 1919, the British military representative, General Knox, reported that in Kolchak's armies ". . . the men are listless and slack, and there is no sign of their officers taking them in hand. The men do not want rest, but hard work and discipline. . . . The enemy boasts he is going to Omsk, and at the moment I see nothing to stop him. As it retires the army melts, the men desert to their villages or to convey their families to safety. . . ."[23]

While this deterioration was in progress, General Denikin was enjoying unprecedented success in the South. Between April and October 1919, his forces took ". . . 250,000 prisoners, 700 guns, 1,700 machine guns and 35 armored trains; and at the beginning of October he reached Tula, within 220 [sic] miles of Moscow, with forces approximately equal to those of his opponents, namely, about 230,000 men." On September 22, 1919, Winston Churchill told the British Cabinet: ". . . General Denikin has under the control of his troops regions which cannot contain less than thirty millions of European Russians, and which include the third, fourth and fifth great cities of Russia. . . ." But Denikin lacked ". . . the resources—moral, political or material—needed to restore prosperity and contentment. . . ."[24] Worse than that, however, he refused to come to political terms either with General

22. André Malraux, *Man's Estate* (*La Condition Humaine*) (London: Penguin Books, 1972). Tr. Alistair MacDonald.
23. Churchill, op. cit.
24. Ibid.

Yudenich, advancing from Estonia on Petersburg, or with the Poles or with the Baltic States, or with Petlura, the Ukrainian leader. At the apogee of his autumnal advance, Denikin stopped to fight Petlura, a fatal error that opened his twelve-hundred-mile front to successful Red counterattacks. Thus the end of Denikin. The heir to his bankruptcy, General Wrangel, did attempt to introduce social and political reforms, at least verbally, but the movement never recovered its former momentum.

The collapse of the White armies did not surprise everyone in allied councils. During one of the Paris conferences, Marshal Foch is said to have remarked, "These armies of Kolchak and Denikin cannot last long because they have no civil government behind them."[25] An astute participant could have taken this a step further and asked what a military "victory" would have accomplished? Considering the prevalent political anarchy, the demonstrated inability of conservative-moderate-liberal-socialist elements to come to terms, an inability made the greater by their best leaders' now having been eliminated by the Red Terror, the peasant demands for land reform, and the nebulous but nonetheless autocratic designs of Denikin and Kolchak, the answer would have been political disaster: a divided Russia with the great powers occupying spheres of influence, which would inevitably have led to German-Japanese dominance.

Had these possibilities been respected, then intervention might not have been taken so casually and so aimlessly. Churchill, in *The World Crisis,* plaintively asks, ". . . Could they [the statesmen at Paris] not have said to Kolchak and Denikin: 'Not another cartridge unless you make terms with the Border States, recognizing their independence or autonomy as may be decided.'" Yes, they could have—and *before,* not after, the landings. And if the replies had not been eminently suitable, the landings need never have occurred and the allied powers would have profited immensely thereby.

For the allied intervention solved nothing and cost a great deal, a cost extending far beyond the cruelty of false hopes raised in the breasts of people far too small to escape the web of events, or beyond the thousands of Russians who did flock to allied colors only to be sacrificed ultimately to Red vengeance.

In spring of 1918, millions of Russians remained ideologically uncommitted to either the White or the Red cause. For decades, revolutionary parties in Russia had been preaching the evils levied on the masses by foreign capitalists, and now, as Bolshevik propaganda pointed out, here on Russian soil were foreign armies to protect the investments of these capitalists.

Judging from the effect of the later Polish incursion into Russia—

25. Ibid.

denounced, for example, by no less a figure than Brusilov, former commander-in-chief of the imperial army—the psychological effect of allied intervention could not but have been adverse. Very probably, the intervention better served Reds than Whites, and one cannot help wondering if Lenin otherwise could have achieved his "backs to the wall" fusion.

Allied intervention, more than any one factor, insured Communist hatred of the Western world. Taken with subsequent Western moves, it formed a convenient international bogeyman on whom to blame the disastrous effects of the postcivil-war famine, Lenin's further and ruthless consolidation of Communist power, the inefficiencies and errors of the regime during the post-Lenin power struggles, and the repressive cruelties of the Stalin and post-Stalin regimes.

Withdrawal of allied forces from Russian soil, defeat of the White armies, and lifting of the naval blockade in January 1920 yielded Lenin a somewhat Pyrrhic victory. Russia was plainly exhausted, her industry at a halt, finances ravaged by hopeless inflation, agricultural production at an all-time low. Serious peasant revolts in 1920–21 further clouded the picture, as did droughts that brought widespread famine in 1921–22. In less than two years, Russia lost perhaps five million people from starvation, a figure that probably would have doubled but for the humanitarian and now scarcely remembered efforts of the American Relief Administration.

Lenin answered this internal crisis by launching his famous New Economic Policy. The NEP, by recognizing the value of incentives to agricultural and industrial production, clearly abrogated basic Marxist principles and was welcomed in the West as an admission of Communist failure. This judgment was premature. The NEP represented a step backward, a temporary mollification of social-economic forces, in military terms the reduction of an awkward salient—but not a reversal of strategy. For, while Lenin was juggling with economic factors, his mind remained intent on achieving world revolution.

Lenin had never regarded the Russian revolution as an isolated phenomenon. As a Marxist, he had to adjust chronologically, in that revolution was supposed to have occurred first in Germany, then spread throughout Europe and the world. This slight anachronism in no way invalidated his belief in world revolution or in the Communist party as its major organizational force. In spring of 1919, at the height of his country's internal doubt and confusion, he presided over the First Congress of the Communist International—what would become dreaded throughout the world as the Comintern.

Little doubt or confusion reigned at this congress, where Lenin and Trotsky ran the elections and wrote the governing manifesto, a tedious document hopefully calling on the workers of the world to unite and revolt. The Second Congress of the Comintern, called in July 1920, decided on a more indirect approach, of preparing the "world revolution" through "a systematic program of propaganda."

Winston Churchill properly identified the new tactics in *The World Crisis:*

. . . The Bolsheviks do not work only by military operations, but, simultaneously or alternatively with these, they employ every device of propaganda in their neighbors' territories to make the soldiers mutiny against their officers, to raise the poor against the bourgeois, to raise the workmen against the employers, to raise the peasants against the landowners, to paralyze the country by general strikes, and generally to destroy every existing form of social order and of democratic government. Thus a state of so-called peace, i.e., a suspension of actual fighting with firearms, may simply mean that the war proceeds in a still more difficult and dangerous form, viz., instead of being attacked by soldiers on the frontier, the country is poisoned internally and every good and democratic institution which it possesses is undermined.[26]

Despite this gloomy analysis, had the Comintern been a cash-and-carry business, it soon would have gone broke. But it was not a short-term arrangement. To shift metaphors, it resembled an angry octopus whose head remained in Moscow while innumerable ganglia slithered into every corner of the globe.

The ganglia suffered a high casualty rate: Béla Kun's Communist government in Hungary lasted less than six months. The proletariat of western Eurasia and England responded flaccidly: these states were confused and exhausted, and, despite spurts of Communist enthusiasm in England and the new Czechoslovakia, by 1920 the less militant socialist parties controlled the workers. In America, the national temper and postwar prosperity made the task of selling rebellion tantamount to peddling whiskey to a prohibitionist. Bolshevik agitators received nearly as cool a reception in the Near and Middle East, where only a small proletariat existed and where the reasoned atheism of communism repelled rather than attracted: religion indeed was the opium of the masses, nor did they desire to quit smoking. The Far East offered more fertile grounds, and, in 1920, Lenin called the first "congress of the Peoples of the East" for ". . . the purpose of stirring up and using Asiatic nationalism."[27] Two years later, Comintern agents were active in China, where again the situation permitted no dramatic inroads.

Several factors softened these various rebuffs. By working through the Comintern, Lenin minimized damage to his foreign policy, including the business of the market place: ". . . an Anglo-Soviet Trade Pact

26. Ibid.
27. Walsh, op. cit.

was concluded in 1921, and during the years 1921–22 nineteen treaties of peace or of friendship were concluded between the new Soviet state and its neighbors."[28]

Nor did the professional revolutionary, long inured to failure, expect to accomplish miracles overnight. If an encircling ganglion were crushed or cut off, the party relied on the biological principle of *l'autotomie*— the virtually automatic regeneration of the hapless limb. For if the party's long arms failed to crush postwar political structures of Germany, Italy, France, Spain, and England, they nonetheless began to weaken foundations by establishing local Communist parties and serving as the line of communication necessary to feed these units with money and propaganda while honeycombing the area with secret party cells.

Widespread unrest greatly aided the process of fomenting revolution from within. The cumulative effects of the Industrial Revolution, the preliminary backlash of colonialism, the social-economic disruption of World War I—each played a contributory role in the social ferment of the day. From this ferment arose a variety of political genies, of democratic states whose weak and uncertain leadership bred reluctance to accept social challenges imposed by international communism, of fascist states dedicated to eliminating challenge imposed by fear with the blunt instrument of force, of nationalist states spurred by challenge but remaining aloof from the ideology—a political potpourri, a confused, frightened, and often brutal world in which revolution and its kissing cousin, guerrilla warfare, were to play significant roles.

28. Ibid.

PART TWO

Mao and Revolutionary Warfare

A revolution is not a dinner party, or writing an essay, or painting a picture, or doing embroidery; it cannot be so refined, so leisurely and gentle, so temperate, kind, courteous, restrained and magnanimous. A revolution is an insurrection, an act of violence by which one class overthrows another. . . .

MAO TSE-TUNG

Chapter 24

The "sleeping giant" of China • Early revolts • Rise of the Manchus • Foreign intervention • The Opium War • Foreign exploitation • The Taiping rebellion • Peking faces increasing resistance • Rise of regional armies • China's second war with England • End of the Long-Hair revolt

UNLIKE RIP VAN WINKLE, the "sleeping giant" of China did not suddenly awaken to a new world. Instead, she emerged in a series of internal fits and external starts familiar to a somniloquist reluctant to face a day of gloom and drizzle. In her instance, the awakening began in the eighteenth century—a labored and sometimes perverted renascence that continues today.

Nor is Napoleon's term essentially correct. Although China shut herself from the West about the time Shih Huang Ti ("the First Emperor") built the Great Wall (200 B.C.), rather than a "sleeping giant" she resembled a fragmented colossus sheltering behind a spiritual-physical screen. In the minds of her rulers, China occupied ". . . the center of the universe, and the outer galaxies, except when they bothered China, were of no concern to her."[1] To keep them at safe distance, Chinese

1. Franz Schurmann and Orville Schell (eds.), *China Readings 1 (Imperial China—The Eighteenth and Nineteenth Centuries)* (New York: Penguin Books, 1967). Hereafter cited as Schurmann. The reader will find this 3-volume work essential to further study of ancient and modern China.

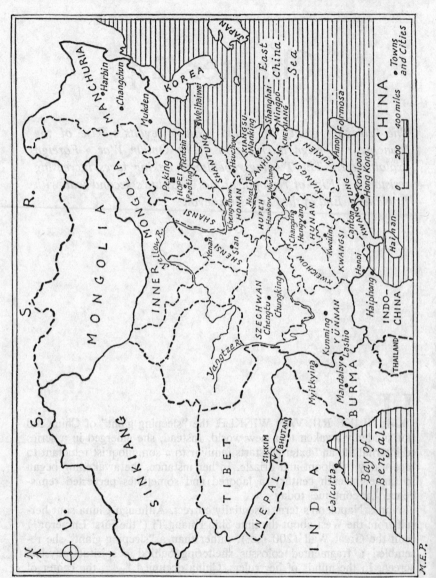

rulers relied on a protective ring of tribute-paying states. Japan, Korea, Manchuria, Turkestan, Tibet, Burma, and Annam

Internal rule derived from a Confucianist-Taoist-Buddhist religious philosophy in which Confucianist teachings remained dominant. Chinese scholars taught the Tao (the Way) as the key to human behavior: as long as everyone subscribed to the Tao, peaceful harmony would result. The Tao divided society into "gentlemen" and "small men." ". . . It was the gentleman's duty to exercise benevolent rule over the small men: emperor over his subjects, magistrate over the people, husband over wife and children." This would yield a "flat," or peaceful, existence: ". . . No disturbances in the realm, the village, or the home, no passion in the life of man, serenity in old age where death calmly supplanted life."[2]

The "flat" concept of existence was not exactly exciting. Like Plato's *Republic*, it formed a philosophic rationale for an involved type of benevolent despotism (the two words are incompatible). Although in earlier centuries China produced some remarkable discoveries in the sciences and some original and exquisite work in humanities and arts, her political structure stood still. Enforced isolation from the rest of the world and the gulf between the ruler-scholars and her vast millions led at first to tarnishing and then erosion of her political-economic-social structure. Scholars telling scholars what scholars already know is not conducive to original thinking, and, by the eighteenth century, China's learned outpourings, increasingly formal and restricted, were becoming devoid of reason, holding little or no practical connection with the people's problems.

These were immense, increasing almost daily. As is invariably the case, benevolent despotism, despite its Platonic sheen of logic, trampled promiscuously on basic human rights, in this case yielding the Chinese peasant an existence that in the nineteenth century would become subhuman. Harsh provincial rulers and rapacious landlords played evil roles in plenty, but to their work must be added frequent and catastrophic floods, droughts, and epidemics. Pearl Buck's novels in no way exaggerate the human degradation and despair suffered by hundreds of millions of human beings.

This perpetual semistarvation status of millions instantly condemns the efficacy of the "flat" theory of government demanded by Confucianist ruler-scholars. In any event, the concept proved largely illusory, for under its ostensibly placid surface, human emotions spilled over into countless protests and riots that failed to spread only because of lack of communications.

The basic Chinese conflict between ruler and peasant was traditional. Suggested in the ancient *Book of Songs*,[3] it is manifest in later regional peasant societies. The most famous of these secret organizations, the White Lotus, stemmed from the late fourth century. Originally a religious society, it slowly evolved into a revolutionary order that helped

2. Ibid.
3. Arthur Waley, *The Book of Songs* (London: Allen & Unwin, 1937).

overthrow first the Sung dynasty (960–1279), then the Mongols (1280–1368).[4]

A peasant-monk, Chu Yüan-chang, led the revolt against Mongol rule. Chu had begun leading guerrilla raids on villages when he was twenty-five. Winning an immense following by his policy of forbidding guerrillas to exploit or steal from common people, Chu captured Nanking in 1356 and extended his control south of the Yangtze River. Later, his army toppled the ruling Mongols, and he became the first Ming emperor, Hung Wu.[5] The Ming dynasty lasted until 1644, when the Manchus replaced it. Provincial uprisings continued to plague Manchu authority, but lack of cohesion and communications generally isolated these attempts sufficiently for the emperor's soldiers to "flatten" them. In 1795, however, the White Lotus society attempted unsuccessfully to overthrow the dynasty. Failure only encouraged other, more successful rebellions.

Economics formed the nub of the difficulty. According to the *Veritable Records* of the Ch'ing dynasty, China's population from 1750 to 1850 increased from 143 million to 430 million.[6] Simultaneously, land under cultivation decreased, a process already familiar to western Eurasia but partially offset there by the Industrial Revolution. No such revolution occurred in China to ameliorate the misery and starvation that increased from year to year.

Nor did the Peking government help matters. Caught in a political web, it struggled only fitfully to escape. Its fatigue increasingly told in the provincial bureaucracy, which found itself hamstrung by overcontrol from Peking, whose authoritative government was growing increasingly corrupt. The ruling air was not merely tainted with corruption, it exuded it. Professor Harrison has listed a few examples: ". . . forced crop payments, the pocketing of bribes, fraudulent land registrations (productive land registered as waste land), illegal imposts, the unjust allocation of assessments, the juggling of rates of exchange, and the increasing immunities of the landlords."[7]

Here was a dislocative air, a complicated admixture of obsolescent and corrupt government ruling harshly but ineffectually over starving millions. The ingredients for trouble were plain enough to see, but now a new one was added. This was the great catalyst of modern-day revolution: the foreign state.

More precisely, foreign states. Portuguese and Spanish traders started

4. Dun-jen Li, *The Ageless Chinese* (New York: Charles Scribner's Sons, 1965).

5. Robert Payne, *Mao Tse-tung* (London: Abelard-Shuman, 1967).

6. John A. Harrison, *China Since 1800* (New York: Harcourt, Brace & World, 1967). I have relied on this splendid and immensely readable work throughout these chapters on China.

7. Ibid.; see also L. C. Goodrich, *A Short History of the Chinese People* (London: Allen & Unwin, 1969).

nudging the southern periphery in the early sixteenth century. By 1715, the Dutch and the English were trading out of Canton, but only with increasing difficulties. The remote Peking government—the throne that ruled through an omnipotent Grand Council—regarded Westerners as tributary guests forced to pay for the privilege of trading with China. A host of intermediary officials, provincial viceroys and governors, extended the emperor's hand, as did port and customs officials and Chinese merchants, who added their own "squeeze."

Why, then, did foreigners stay in Canton?

First, immensely profitable trade. The British East India Company, operating out of India, brought in raw cotton, metals, and woolens, and carried away cotton cloth, tea, and silk.[8] Added to this legitimate effort was contraband smuggling of opium, which increased throughout the eighteenth century. The British East India Company must bear onus for this pernicious trade from which a number of aristocratic fortunes derived. The company administered Bengal, where most of the opium was grown and prepared, and in time came to depend on the exorbitant profits to pay for its operations in India. But the profits were shared by a great many persons, including Chinese merchants and officials, who generally received the death penalty if caught. In Canton in 1828, ". . . it was estimated that about 90 percent of the total foreign import trade was in opium."[9] A few years later, the company lost its trade monopoly with China: other English merchants moved in and so did Americans, many of them unscrupulous traders.

Peking's attempts to halt the illicit trade were suspicious by their ineffectiveness, but such was the nature of China's monolithic government, so tenuous the chain of command, that orders issued at the top rarely led to compatible action at the bottom.

In 1839, the throne sent an Imperial Commissioner, Lin Tsê-hsü, to Canton to end the trade once and for all. Lin seized all opium stores and, in reply to English intransigence, closed Canton to British ships. The Governor-General of India declared war on China, the famous "Opium War" of 1841-42, which clearly exposed Chinese military weakness to British arms. British occupation of Canton and the coastal cities of Amoy and Ningpo led to lopsided treaties which gave England the almost uninhabited island of Hong Kong, opened Shanghai and major southern ports to Western trade under foreign-imposed "fair and regular" tariffs, established the extraterritorial principle governing land

8. Harrison, op. cit.; see also Tsiang Ting-fu, "The English and the Opium Trade." In Schurmann, *supra*. Some Western apologists, for example Cole and Priestley (op. cit.), have argued ingeniously (if speciously) that the relatively low profits from legitimate trade ". . . forced the west, primarily England, into the opium trade."

9. Harrison, op. cit.; also Schurmann, op. cit.

for foreign homes and businesses, and made England a "most favored nation."

As Professor Harrison has pointed out, the last clause established a disastrous precedent, for all subsequent treaties with other nations, such as that signed with America in 1844, contained a similar clause: ". . . internationally, China became a legal pauper, living on the good will of the treaty nations. The war of 1841–42 contained the seeds of a kind of cultural, economic, and political destruction unknown in any previous war in Chinese history."[10]

The treaties provided only surface solutions to profound problems. Opium smuggling continued, the ghastly "pig trade" in Chinese emigrants sprung up, Chinese pirates and Portuguese mercenary incursions in the South China Sea led to an increased presence of Western navies, and as Western merchants exploited extraterritorial privileges in the ports, unpleasant incidents repeatedly occurred with local Chinese.

A competent government would have had its hands full coping with this awkward transitional period. The rigid Peking government could not possibly have met the challenge. Living in splendid isolation in Peking, it continued to practice government by remote control. Its lesser officials merely exacerbated existing problems, either by sharing the throne's aversion to the foreign presence and thus creating rather than dissipating difficulties, or by profiting from the foreign presence and falsely reporting essential facts to Peking.

Simultaneously, Peking was faced with a worsening internal situation. Sporadic revolts, which had marked early decades of the century, were steadily increasing. In 1850, by far the most serious of these occurred: the Taiping peasant-based rebellion, which quickly spread to threaten the very existence of the Manchus.

The Taiping rebellion began in the remote southern province of Kwangsi, the work of a peasant-student named Hung Hsiu-ch'üan. Hung was born into a poor peasant family of Hakkas in Kwangtung in 1814.[11] His parents sacrificed greatly to send him to school. At four-

10. Harrison, op. cit.; see also Schurmann, op. cit. Professors Schurmann and Schell noted that ". . . the Nanking Treaty (1842) signed at the conclusion of the war represented China's point of no return. Hereafter, the tide of foreign penetration could not be reversed." In London, Lord Palmerston was aware of this: ". . . There is no doubt that this event, which will form an epoch in the progress of the civilization of the human races, must be attended with important advantages to the commercial interests of England."

11. The Hakkas, or "guest settlers," emigrated from northern China in the fourth century to settle in Kwangtung and Southeast Asia, where they eventually numbered some twenty millions. They assimilated slowly: after fourteen centuries, the Hakkas still spoke a different dialect and practiced different customs and habits, which kept them at odds with the local inhabitants, a condition undoubtedly existing today.

teen, he became a village teacher and, in subsequent years, studied in Canton to pass state examinations, an essential step to becoming a minor bureaucrat. Failing exams four times running, he suffered a nervous breakdown manifested by a vivid religious vision. He had been exposed briefly to missionary Christianity, and he ". . . now saw himself as the son of God and the younger brother of Jesus Christ, chosen at God's command for a special mission: to destroy the demons on earth and establish the Kingdom of God."[12]

Hung's desire was not altogether farfetched, at least regarding demons. In principle, these were the Manchus at Peking; in practice, they were provincial tax collectors, who, supported by despised soldiers, covered the southern provinces like locusts. Virtually any call for action against their rapacious demands would have proved popular, and the peasants of eastern Kwangsi, where Hung launched his revolt, in 1847, quickly flocked to his banner.

Here again was guerrilla warfare in its purest form: a few thousand peasants armed with pitchforks and calling themselves the "God-Worshipers." Based in the Thistle Mountains, a remote area safe from imperial infantry and cavalry incursions, these dissidents began striking out at the demon tax collectors, at first by raids on villages to gain support and recruits.

Hung's early successes attracted such a variety of anti-Manchu secret societies that the "God-Worshipers" became a blending of religious, nationalist, and social elements, which, as Professor Franke has written, ". . . constituted the Taiping Rebellion's point of departure."[13] The movement grew rapidly; in 1850, Hung's followers, now many thousands, proclaimed him the T'ien-wang, or Heavenly King, of the T'ai P'ing T'ien-kuo, or Heavenly Kingdom of the Great Peace.

What sounds to us like religious mumbo jumbo formed a most effective appeal to Chinese peasants. The Christian aspect magnetized people thoroughly disillusioned with Confucianist-Taoist rule; it also attracted sympathy of Western missionaries and, in consequence, that of some Western governments (themselves variously at odds with the Peking government). Despite outlandish titles, the political structure of the Taipings suited the problem of absorbing diverse power elements: Hung, the Heavenly King, ordained a number of plain Kings, whose followers continued to spread the word to draw in additional strength. Hung used a number of devices to tie these heterodox groups of peasants, coolies, country intellectuals, pirates, miners, and even businessmen into a common band. The Manchus had introduced the queue, or pigtail—the Taipings cut it off; the Manchus shaved the forehead—the Taipings let their hair grow, thus earning the official name "the Long-Hair Rebels."

12. Wolfgang Franke, "The Taiping Rebellion" (tr. by Franz Schurmann). In Schurmann, *supra*.
13. Ibid.

Most of all, however, Hung relied on the appeal of a social-political-economic manifesto that bore a remarkable resemblance to Karl Marx's work of 1848, but was conceived independently of it and was based ideologically on elements of Christianity and structurally on the pre-Christian Chou dynasty.[14]

Hung's manifesto is often termed primitive communism, just as Christ has been called the first Communist. Hung attempted to use religion as an instrument to effect sweeping land and social reforms. In the Kingdom of Heaven, the state owned everything. It assigned land on an equitable basis with surplus grain production going into a state granary. A state bank paid for tools and seed and for weddings, births, and funerals. Women were fully equal to men, but had to marry, though theoretically someone of their own choice. The state abolished prostitution and foot-binding and forbade opium, tobacco, and alcohol. The God-Worshipers could only practice their own brand of Christianity. The new state would deal with Western nations, but only on an equal basis, which meant, among other things, the end of extraterritorial privileges. Hung's manifesto, which also called for immediate calendrical and linguistic reforms, is altogether a remarkable document, and in 1851 it represented the most sweeping demand for change in China's long history.

Equally remarkable was Hung's army. Oriented religiously from inception, soldiers were taught to respect peasant rights. They could neither requisition food without payment nor enter dwellings without permission. They received intense religious instruction, could neither drink, gamble, nor smoke, and stood subject to execution for either rape or desertion. This surely must have been one of the purest armies in history, and since the phrase is contradictory, we must conclude that modern scholarship errs on the romantic side.

Still, in mid-nineteenth century, an army with such pretensions, at least in part consummated, differed radically from the badly organized, ill-disciplined, and utterly dissolute government forces, which plundered and raped at will. Undoubtedly, *esprit de corps* played a significant role in Hung's early and impressive victories. At first, Hung employed guerrilla tactics, striking the enemy at his weakest points and bypassing major garrisons, which eventually became "islands" in a hostile sea. His army continued to grow, and, in 1852, when it numbered some fifty thousand, he left his Kwangsi base and marched into Hunan. After converting the guerrilla formations at least in part to orthodox units armed with captured weapons, he further expanded, falling on Hankow, Wuchang, and Hanyang, then sailed his army down the Yangtze to Nanking, a rich prize that fell in March 1853. In October, one of his armies

14. Ibid.

reached Tientsin and marched on Peking, but was turned back by a strong force of imperial cavalry.

Having established headquarters in Nanking, Hung now turned south to consolidate his gains, an effort quickly traded for the more prosaic task of retaining them. For now "moral decay" set in. In Professor Franke's words,

. . . shortly after the capture of Nanking the Heavenly King and other leaders, against all commandments of the revolutionary movement, began a life of excesses—high living, luxury, many concubines. Decay at the top naturally was contagious to those in the lower echelons.[15]

Internecine quarrels certainly played a role: a power struggle in Nanking in 1856 allegedly took some twenty thousand lives, including those of a great many of the early Taiping leaders. Professor Harrison marked 1856 as the apogee of the rebellion. From then on, ". . . corruption, nepotism, the attrition of leadership, the failure to carry out promised reforms, the loss of zeal by the masses, and simple war weariness all took their toll."[16]

Hung's early successes stemmed in part from Peking's failure to recognize the true nature of events. In early 1852, Emperor Hsien Fêng read an estimate of the situation prepared by one of his wisest and most trusted advisers. This stated in part:

. . . Secondly, the thieves and bandits are too numerous and it is difficult for good people to live peacefully. . . . Recently it is heard that the bandits' power has become more severe. They plunder and rape people in the daylight and kidnap the people for ransom. People cannot help but appeal to the officials. When the officials go in to arrest, an announcement is proclaimed in advance, and till the government [force] reaches the spot the local gentry usually tell a lie that the bandits have fled. Sometimes it is trickily said that the bandit is killed by putting another prisoner to death in order to substitute the case and yet actually the bandit does not die. When the case of plunder is not cleared up, the lost articles are not returned and the family of the suffering host is already bankrupt, he has to swallow his voice, sip his own tears and has no more strength to reappeal. Even if he does, and fortunately soldiers are dispatched to meet together and to arrest the bandits, nevertheless the soldiers in ordinary times all have connections with the bandits and at the very time they will set the latter free after getting a bribe and leave no footstep to trace. Sometimes, on the contrary, they take the pretext of calling them bandits to frighten the foolish villagers and forcing them to pay a heavy bribery. Otherwise, they will be burned and they will

15. Ibid.
16. Harrison, op. cit.

be tied up with fetters. . . . Today the bad soldiers and harmful government employees who foster bandits and set bandits free appear everywhere. This is another one of what your minister calls distress among the people.[17]

It is interesting to substitute "guerrillas" for "bandits" in his report.

The emperor and his advisers probably interpreted Hung's early raids as the work of bandits, and they may have misread other uprisings, such as the Nien Fei rebellion in Anhui and neighboring provinces, an extensive guerrilla movement led by the White Lotus society, and the Triad movement, which came to control much of Shanghai from 1853–56.

Even had the Peking government earlier recognized the threat, military weakness would have prevented effective action. As late as 1853, the viceroy of Hunan province complained:

. . . Our whole country swarms with rebels. Our funds are nearly at an end, and our troops are few. The commander of the imperial forces thinks he can put out a bonfire with a thimbleful of water. I fear that we shall hereafter have some serious affairs, and the great body of the people will rise up against us and our own followers will leave us.[18]

So grim was the situation from Peking's point of view, that, in 1854, the emperor authorized regional armies of defense, a move previously avoided because of the potential threat to central authority. Viceroys and governors either organized militias or built up existing illegal ones. Some of these in time performed excellent work, the outstanding example being Tsêng Kuo-fan's army in Hunan province. Backed by landed gentry, Tsêng recruited from villages and based training on Confucianist principles as strong as, if not stronger than, Hung's Christian principles. Stressing leadership and discipline, he fed and paid the troops regularly, forbidding them to live off the land. Although a scholar and bureaucrat, Tsêng seems to have had excellent strategic sense and, in a relatively short time, began claiming the initiative from the insurgents.

Peking also benefited both from Hung's failure to co-ordinate his own rebellion more fully with those of various other secret societies, and from Hung's alienating the Western powers.

England, France, and the United States played a complex, confusing, and sinister role in the internal affairs of China at this time. Continuing quarrels with Chinese port officials and merchants led to England's second war with China, an on-again-off-again affair involving France, Russia, and the United States, and finally terminated by Lord Elgin's Anglo-French force burning the complex of buildings known as the Sum-

17. Ibid.
18. Payne, op. cit.

mer Palace, an invaluable architectural masterpiece north of Peking—
an "unnecessary act never forgotten or forgiven by the Chinese."[19]

The resultant treaties, again very unequal documents that favored
the Western powers, increased foreign jurisdiction over Chinese waters,
inland and seaboard ports, and trade; extended the foreign presence to
the North, including Peking, and in the South inland to the larger cities
of the Yangtze Valley; and legalized the opium trade.

Hung's announced reforms did not now look nearly so attractive to
the Western nations, which began supplying arms to the Manchus and
helping the emperor build the Ever Victorious army composed of Chinese, European, and American mercenaries. Commanded by Li Hung-
chang, the new army, working in conjunction with regional armies,
slowly pushed the Long-Hairs back to Nanking. Hung's heavenly kingdom fell in the summer of 1864. With his suicide and execution of his
principal lieutenants, the movement quickly disintegrated.

The regional armies next put down neighboring rebellions. By 1866,
the Manchu government could claim the end of the rebellion.

19. Harrison, op. cit.

Chapter 25

Cost of the Taiping rebellion • Failure of the Reformers • Continued foreign exploitation • Chinese resistance • The Boxer rebellion • Enter Sun Yat-sen • The 1911 revolution • End of the Manchus • Birth of the Kuomintang • The war lords rule • Sun Yat-sen's revolt • The Communists join the Kuomintang • Enter Chiang Kai-shek • His march north • He breaks with the Communists • His dictatorship

SUPPRESSION of the Taiping rebellion offered Peking rulers scant cause for rejoicing. Central China was bled white—some authorities believe that *the rebellion claimed forty million lives!* Internal chaos had helped Western powers to increase their grip on China's economy, and they now began shamelessly dividing the country into spheres of interest for further commercial exploitation. Virtually bankrupt, Peking was forced to borrow large sums from Western bankers in order to fight a costly campaign against Moslem rebels in northwestern provinces. Simultaneously, foreign states began chipping away at China's traditional "buffer" states: England in Burma, France in Vietnam, Russia in Manchuria, and Japan in Korea.

The rebellion also left the throne in precarious hands. Emperor Hsien Fêng's death, in 1861, transferred power to his six-year-old son, who ruled through a clumsy regency composed of his uncle, Prince Kung, and *two* dowager empresses: one the widow, the other a former concubine and the heir's mother, who became Dowager Empress Tz'ŭ Hsi. Of the three, she proved by far the most powerful and certainly the most durable, her reign lasting until 1908. Vain and ambitious, she was also dangerous, almost constantly playing off one power faction against another to maintain herself in power.

But imperial power had greatly weakened. Regional armies, necessary to suppress the rebellion, now answered to their own leaders—to embryonic war lords such as Tsêng Kuo-fan, who thenceforth had to be persuaded rather than ordered to a course of action. Most of these new leaders were conservatives, however, and many of them supported Prince Kung in his attempt to effect the T'ung Chih Restoration.

The Reformers, as this group came to be called, recognized that China was powerless to contest foreign dominance so long as she remained industrially underdeveloped. The Reformers introduced a "self-strengthening" movement, an internal renascence founded on Confucianist principles, that produced some very real reforms in foreign affairs, education, and industrialization. This effort was enhanced by a group of young scholars who, educated at Yale, returned to China to preach the need for political, economic and social reforms along Western lines.[1]

Such enthusiasm was scarcely widespread, and the work of the Reformers resembled the Herculean task of cleansing the Augean stables. One after the other, their laudable goals fell victim to numerous and powerful counterforces.

Neither the dynasty nor ultraconservative Confucianist elements could accept widespread reforms. The dowager empress paid lip service only. As if the urgently needed measures were a bowl of cherries, she selected one or two to please her political palate, but soon brushed the course aside in favor of the meat of power.

But even this creature, with her distorted set of values, was not the supreme villain. That title goes to the foreign powers. What once was petty larceny turned now to grand larceny: from 1865 on, the ". . . mercantile, missionary, and ministerial" classes, in Sir Robert Hart's words, vied with each other in the humbling of the Chinese people.[2] A moral superiority difficult to believe (except that we still see it today) clothed the entire foreign presence. Diplomats and businessmen paid little heed to the work of the Reformers, whose reforms they considered of value only so long as they helped keep the Manchus in power and thus maintain the flow of golden eggs from the goose of state. Nor were missionaries any more sympathetic to the effort. Their self-imposed task was not limited to replacing what they considered mumbo-jumbo cultism of Buddhists, Taoists, and Confucianists with Christian gospel, but em-

1. Harrison, op. cit.
2. Ibid.

braced that of infusing all of China with Western culture. The prevailing conceit is only too plain in the words of one of them, Arthur Smith, who wrote in 1894:

. . . What China needs is righteousness, and in order to attain it, it is absolutely necessary that she have a knowledge of God [!] and a new conception of man, as well as of the relation of man with God. . . . The manifold needs of China we find, then, to be a single imperative need. It will be met permanently, completely, only by Christian civilization.[3]

The representatives of Christian civilization at that time resembled a pack of blooded wolves in the final pursuit of quarry. England already had claimed the southwestern ramparts of the Chinese empire, namely Burma; France had claimed the south, namely Vietnam, from where she was pushing into Cambodia and Laos. In 1894, China collided with Japan in the north, a brief war, a Chinese defeat that emphasized Peking's archaic military system and administrative impotence. The treaty of Shimonoseki placed Japan on the Asian continent and further burdened Peking with enormous reparations.[4] Germany meanwhile forced China to award her virtual hegemony in Shantung province. The French acquired a lease on Kwangchowan, on the southwestern coast of Kwangtung, and began pressing into southern China. Russia forced China to grant permission for a railroad across Manchuria. Britain demanded and secured long leases on Weihaiwei and Kowloon. In 1899, Sir Robert Hart noted: ". . . The fact is everybody's for exploiting China. . . ."[5]

China's continuing decline naturally increased the already wretched plight of the Chinese people. If, somehow, a particular benefit seeped down to a community through the maze of official-foreign filters, then either flood, drought, locust plague, or corrupt soldiery quickly undid the good work, leaving the usual residue of misery and poverty.

The Chinese people reacted variously. In a land where life expectancy probably did not exceed twenty-five years, where infant daughters were disposed of at birth like unwanted kittens, in such a land survival was the main problem. Millions of Chinese sought survival from the worn and precious earth, and in so doing remained unwilling slaves to the "flat," Confucianist concept of government.

A lesser group, known contemptuously to their fellows as "rice-bowl Christians," came to accept the foreign presence: to adopt the new religion, to serve humbly in mines, factories, railroads, warehouses, and

3. Ibid.
4. It also brought Japan into conflict with Germany, Russia, and France. The three powers forced her to yield the strategic Liaotung area to China for a further enormous sum.
5. Harrison, op. cit.; see also Sir Robert Hart, *These from the Land of Sinim— Essays on the Chinese Question* (London: Chapman & Hall, 1903).

private homes of foreign masters. And because foreigners lived in insulated enclaves remote from real China, most of them accepted the comfortable premise of a placid people while failing to recognize the existence of underlying currents. These were caused by still another minority, a revolutionary minority, which in the best Chinese tradition was widening old channels and creating new.

Dissident groups of militant rebels, although scattered and disorganized, had continued to exist in post-Taiping decades. Their activities took two forms: uprisings against the dynasty, which, although invariably quelled, continued to occur, for example the preliminary Boxer risings in 1898–1900; and uprisings against foreigners, usually terrorist displays such as the dreadful Tientsin massacre of 1870, which spelled hatred with missionary blood.

Bandit depredations also existed and at times proved convenient to foreign powers—the murder of two German missionaries in Shantung province, for example, led to direct German military intervention and control of the area in 1897.

The throne answered all such incidents officially with virtual diplomatic prostration before foreign representatives, whose *amour-propre* was further soothed with enormous reparation payments which China could ill afford. Unofficially, the dowager empress probably encouraged some of the anti-foreign efforts. Certain secret societies such as the White Lotus were involved in their activities; the Boxers were a conglomerate led by the I Ho Ch'üan (Righteous Harmonious Fists), who directed the major rebellion of 1900, a movement seconded by the throne, which went so far as to declare war on the foreign powers, although the dowager empress may have done this to save the throne from the Boxers.

The Boxer movement, in addition to the I Ho Ch'üan societies, included small regional bodies, the outgrowth of provincial militias established to fight the Taiping Long-Hairs. Some authorities say that the name stemmed from the ancient sport of Chinese boxing; others hold that the prebattle ritual dance caused Westerners to think of boxing. The rebellion seems to have been internally inspired, free from outside influence. For the most part, the Boxers were ignorant peasants who practiced sorcery and superstition, actually believing that they were immune to bullets. In early 1900, they broke loose in northern China, attacking missionary settlements and slaughtering missionaries and thousands of Chinese Christians. Although some provincial leaders put down the risings, others turned a blind eye, as did the throne, which in June sent government units to join rebels in besieging foreign legations in Peking. An international expedition, when finally formed, made short work of the besiegers, the war ending abruptly in August. Harsh peace terms exacted an indemnity of six to seven hundred million dollars, including a principal payment of nearly $331 million in gold.[6]

The Boxer calamity did not spell the end of rebellion. Throughout the 1890s, leading members of the Chinese intelligentsia had been calling for necessary reforms. The outlook of these men varied greatly, and their failure to present a united front to the throne was the major reason for the continuing series of disasters. Chang Chih-tung, one of the most able, saw the major need as military reform, a thought abhorrent to the throne as a public confession of ". . . the corruption, incompetence and nepotism of the officer corps of the various armed forces, as well as the failures of the arsenals."[7]

Two outstanding scholars, K'ang Yu-wei and Liang Ch'i-ch'ao, pressed for political, economic, and social reforms on what they called progressive Confucianist lines under dynastic supervision. In 1898, they persuaded the emperor, Kuang Hsu, to defy the dowager empress and the ultraconservative elements around him and issue the necessary proclamations. This, a sort of palace revolution in reverse, failed, because the emperor lacked a proper army to back him. The dowager empress, in league with Yüan Shih-k'ai, the viceroy of Chihli, who controlled the Northern Army, forced the emperor to abdicate and took over once again as regent. She executed six of the Reformers, and the others fled abroad. Here they found other dissidents, true revolutionaries such as Dr. Sun Yat-sen, who for years had been arguing for a fundamental change in favor of Western democracy.

In 1898, Sun Yat-sen was thirty-two years old. The son of a poor farmer in Kwangtung province, he spent his childhood in China. At the age of eleven, he went to Hawaii, where a brother sent him to an Anglican church school. At seventeen, he returned to China, but soon left in favor of medical school in Hong Kong, where he practiced for two years as a doctor before becoming a full-time revolutionist. Returning to Hawaii, he established the Hsing Chung Hui (Revive China Society), a movement of ". . . twenty small Chinese shopkeepers" pledged ". . . to expel the Manchus, recover China, and establish a republic."[8] After several futile attempts at revolution and some narrow escapes, Sun joined another revolutionary, Huang Hsing. In Japan they established the T'ung Meng Hui (United League), a small but militant group that called for a social and economic revolution.

This brought them in conflict with expatriate Confucianist reformers who wanted a carefully conducted political revolution with economic and social reforms to follow eventually. The United League wanted action: ". . . between 1907 and 1911 the *T'ung Meng Hui,* despite its

6. Harrison, op. cit.
7. Ibid.
8. Ibid.

lack of a real organization in China, attempted eight armed revolts in Southeast China in an effort to capture the provinces of Kwangtung, Kwangsi, or Yunnan for a base of operations."[9]

Their efforts failed for want of a true revolutionary force. Like the Confucianist reformers, they looked across a wide gulf to the ordinary people of China, the hodgepodge millions of peasants and coolies who in part constituted the provincial secret societies and armies that threatened the throne, itself a weakened and divided regency since the dowager empress' death in 1908.

Neither the T'ung Meng Hui nor the Confucianists prompted the 1911 revolt. The throne's arbitrary and unfair attitude in the matter of a provincial railroad question brought the people of Szechwan province to arms in autumn of 1911. The revolt quickly spread through the Yangtze Valley, where even army regiments mutinied. A thoroughly alarmed dynasty now called the former viceroy-strong man of Chihli province, Yüan Shih-k'ai, from retirement and gave him command of the Northern Army, with orders to put down the revolt.

This proved impossible: by mid-November, all but four provinces had seceded in favor of a provisional republic with headquarters at Nanking. Republican leadership consisted of provincial officials and army commanders with revolutionaries present as poor relations. Sun Yatsen, who was in America when the trouble began, did not appear until the end of December. These disparate groups eventually hammered out a republican form of government that promised a constitution, a cabinet answering to a bicameral parliament, and a president, Yüan Shih-k'ai. The Manchus abdicated in February 1912, a virtually bloodless end to three centuries of bloody rule.

Unfortunately the new government answered none of China's problems. Despite republican trappings, Yüan headed a reactionary government supported by the foreign powers, the Northern Army, and a political bloc of conservatives called the Progressive Party. He was opposed principally by the T'ung Meng Hui, which, in 1912, became the Kuomintang, the dominant political party in the new parliament.

But the Kuomintang lacked popular appeal. Its leaders preached a muddled blend of social-economic reforms and the party comprised divisive elements, none holding the real support of the people or even much power. Yüan, with his Northern Army, shared real power with provincial military governors, each with his own army, and none held the people's interests at heart.

The people, in short, were left with reactionary and corrupt government at both national and provincial levels, yet general ignorance, lack of organization, and apathy prevented them from seeking another

9. Ibid.

change—they failed, for instance, to support Sun Yat-sen's two attempts at revolt in spring of 1913.

Sun and his followers already had recognized their early mistake in thinking that a constitution and parliament would hold Yüan in hand. Thoroughly alarmed at his steadily increasing reactionary rule, they now tried to check him by parliamentary authority.

The showdown came in autumn of 1913. As was the case with the Manchus, the growth of provincial powers reduced the central government's income to a trickle, and Yüan could get money only by loans—ruinous in the extreme—from foreign powers. That spring, Yüan had negotiated such a loan in the immense sum of £25 million. The governing conditions were so restrictive and humiliating that President Woodrow Wilson forbade American participation. When Yüan sought approval of this measure, the Kuomintang caused parliament to disapprove. In reply, Yüan dissolved the Kuomintang, whose key members fled to Japan.

This cleared the way for Yüan's dictatorship. But even a dictatorship —the simplest, if most repulsive, form of government—could scarcely thrive when subject either to threat of regional competitors, each backed by arms, or to continuing encroachments of foreign powers, particularly Japan, who used World War I to replace the German presence in Shantung province, a sinister prelude to the famous "Twenty-one Demands"—compliance with which would have reduced China to a vassal state. In 1915, probably with Japan's backing, Yüan stupidly tried to establish a new monarchy (with himself as emperor), an idea quickly abandoned because of widespread protest which split China, the southern half becoming a hotbed of revolution.

Yüan died in 1916, to leave China in the hands of provincial military governors, powerful war lords who ruled with scant heed of Peking. Between 1916 and 1926, the impotent central government was run by ". . . six Presidents . . . [who] had a total of nineteen Prime Ministers, none with a tenure of more than a year."[10] Whoever the president, he ruled only through the grace of local war lords, and a more squabbling bunch of dissembling chieftains probably never existed.

Anarchy spawned two other national forces. In 1917, Sun Yat-sen and his Kuomintang followers took advantage of the South's open break with Peking and returned to Canton to establish "the Military Government of the Republic of China."[11] Unable to gain a popular base of government, Sun depended in large part on the local military governor's support. His fortunes and those of his followers fluctuated accordingly, Sun at times taking refuge in Shanghai. During this period, Sun wrote the *San Min Chu I* (Three Principles of the People), a wooly but none-

10. Ibid.
11. Ibid.

theless influential dissertation calling for nationalism, democracy, and the people's welfare as goals for his party, now renamed the Chinese Revolutionary Party. As Professor Harold Isaacs has pointed out, up to mid-1919 ". . . his hope was to bring about the peaceful and benevolent transformation of Chinese society after first securing power for himself and his followers by purely military means. This was the aim of his long series of invariably fruitless military adventures and alliances."[12]

Meanwhile, considerable revolutionary activity had been building in the North. The immediate motivation was the disastrous Versailles decision that approved Japan's dominating presence in Shantung province, the outcome of one of those wretched secret agreements that England and France were forever signing. Despite China's presence at the peace table, the powers voted in Japan's favor. On May 4, 1919, students at Peking University rioted against the Peking government, burning the houses of pro-Japanese ministers. Governmental suppression of this and other strikes and demonstrations gave birth to a revolutionary May Fourth Movement, ". . . a catalyst that united large-scale organizations —students, labor, merchants, and guilds . . ." in an almost total rejection of the West and a reappraisal of traditional values.[13]

Having rejected the West and seeing the inability of political leaders to come to terms with reality, segments of this movement eyed the triumph of the Russian revolution and began moving toward communism. In 1920, the Socialist Youth Party emerged from the ferment in the Shanghai area. This, the first instance of organized communism in China, is the more interesting because of its non-ideological motivation: One of its two founders, an internationally trained scholar named Ch'ên Tu-hsiu, ". . . turned to Communism as the most efficient method for modernizing China"; his cofounder, Li Ta-chao, ". . . a fanatic nationalist, saw in Communism the weapon for destroying imperialism."[14] Whatever their reasons, the decision was welcome to Moscow, and in 1921 a Comintern agent, Voitinsky, helped them establish the Chinese Communist Party.

But another Comintern agent, Maring, already had recognized a more viable revolutionary force in Sun Yat-sen's Chinese Revolutionary Party. The May Fourth Movement had caused Sun to broaden his party's base by flirting with student and trade-union movements, in which he played increasingly influential roles. Maring's reports induced Lenin's government to send a top diplomat, Adolf Joffe, for lengthy talks with Sun. Joffe offered to help reorganize and arm the Kuomintang so that it could lead a revolution; although China would achieve ". . . national

12. Harold Isaacs, *The Tragedy of the Chinese Revolution* (Stanford, Calif.: Stanford University Press, 1962).
13. Harrison, op. cit.
14. Ibid.

union and national independence,"[15] this was not to be a Communist revolution, since communism was ". . . unsuitable to Chinese conditions."[16]

Surrounded by mostly hostile war lords, looking at a hostile Peking government and hostile foreign powers, recognizing the Kuomintang as still disorganized and virtually bankrupt, Sun accepted Joffe's offer. Joffe planned to use the Kuomintang only as a stepping stone to an eventual Communist takeover, and almost immediately began arguing for a marriage of convenience between the Kuomintang and the Chinese Communist Party.

Enter Chiang Kai-shek: thirty-four years old, a small, thin soldier whose varied and, in part, seamy career stood at odds with the Confucianist asceticism he so ostentatiously professed. Born in Chekiang province, Chiang had grown up in great poverty, his father, a small farmer, having died when he was nine. At the age of eighteen, he entered China's first military academy, at Pao-ting. An honor student, he was sent to Japan for further training. Here he fell under the revolutionary influence of Sun Yat-sen's teachings, and in 1911 participated in the overthrow of the Manchus; in the dismal aftermath of that effort, he ". . . disappeared somewhere into Shanghai's murky underworld."[17] For nearly a decade, he lived a quasi-covert life, apparently under protection of the notorious Green Gang, a highly organized group of cutthroats that would make the Mafia look like a boy-scout troop. After a brief stint of service with a "Fukienese warlord," Chiang came to the attention of Sun Yat-sen, with whom he quickly rose in favor.[18]

In 1922, Chiang headed a military mission to Moscow while two Russian Communists, Mikhail Borodin and Vasily Blücher (alias General Ga-lin), worked with Sun to reform the Kuomintang along Leninist, or pyramidal-command, lines.[19] In 1923, still another shift of regional power allowed Sun's return to Canton, where, strongly supported by the Comintern, he reorganized the Kuomintang into an independent political force with its own police and army elements.

A year later, Chiang Kai-shek, somewhat disillusioned with Soviet rule, returned from Moscow to set up the famous Whampoa military academy. Provided with arms, money, and advisers from the Comintern, he began training cadre officers for the new Kuomintang army. Also in 1924 Sun decided, against the wishes of many of his Chinese advisers, to admit Chinese Communists into the Kuomintang, thus beginning a twenty-five-year power struggle.

15. Isaacs, op. cit.
16. Schurmann, op. cit. (Vol. 2).
17. T. H. White and A. Jacoby, *Thunder Out of China* (New York: William Sloane, 1946).
18. Ibid.
19. This organizational concept is retained on Taiwan today.

Man's ego plays an enormous role in the affairs of man. Like many statesmen before and since, Sun refused to accept the possibility of his own death. He believed that he could control the Communists—". . . if Ch'en disobeys our Party, he will be ousted."[20] He probably planned to squash the Communists, once revolution became a fact, in exactly the same way the Communists planned to squash him—his death, early in 1925, precludes a positive answer.

Sun's error was Faustian; in fostering revolution, he contracted with the devil. He had asked the Kuomintang to be too much to too many people. Its membership ranged from ultraconservative elements—landlords and merchants, even war lords—to moderates, to left-wing liberals, to Communists, but with no single faction claiming a broad base of support from the people. Revolution filled the air, but Sun and his lieutenants failed to harness the human energy. This did not diminish revolutionary potential: if nothing else, rapacious landlords and greedy foreign powers kept that alive. The Soviet Government, now in the hands of Joseph Stalin, continued to deal overtly and covertly with the Peking government, with the Kuomintang, with the Communist element of the Kuomintang, and with the very powerful northern war lords. Other Western powers continued to exercise extraterritorial privileges while exploiting China's internal economy.

The major codicil in Sun's will was a promotion of party factionalism, not only among conservatives, moderates, leftists, and Communists, but in each of the splinter groups. Chiang Kai-shek's retention of power depended as much on rejection of extreme conservatism as on retention of communism, and from 1925 until his break with the Communists, in 1927, he constantly juggled the power factors, his success stemming far more from control of the army than from his ability to reconcile dissident groups. The only cohesive element at work during this period was negative: the inability of any group to carry out the revolution alone.

The revolution moved north in spring of 1926, but a more disparate revolutionary force never marched. The vanguard consisted of the People's National Revolutionary Army—three corps that totaled less than one hundred thousand soldiers, under the over-all command of Chiang Kai-shek.

Two of these corps marched north to the Wuchang-Hankow area on the Yangtze; the third, under Chiang's personal command, moved north up the coast toward Shanghai. Nationalist-Communist agents, such as the young Mao Tse-tung, had spent years preparing the Yangtze Valley by organizing sympathetic trade unions in the cities and peasant associations in the countryside. The Nationalists had also come to terms with the major war lord in the area, the famous "Christian General," Fêng Yü-hsiang, who baptized his troops en masse with a fire hose.[21]

20. Schurmann, op. cit.
21. A. A. Vandegrift and R. B. Asprey, *Once a Marine* (New York: W. W. Norton, 1964).

The two corps on the left advanced with little difficulty and, in October, occupied Wuchang and began consolidation of the entire target area. On the right, Chiang ran into trouble with some local war lords and did not reach Shanghai until March 1927. Although the city was his for the taking—the work of local Communist agents—Chiang now paused.

For some time, Chiang had been receiving disquieting reports from the West. In January, the Kuomintang government had moved from Canton to Hankow, where, under the aegis of its forceful Russian adviser, Mikhail Borodin, it began consolidating power in the Yangtze Valley area, but scarcely in the manner desired by Chiang and his most powerful backers. The new government allowed its Communist elements full sway: prodded by professional agitators, labor unions and peasant associations seized and distributed private property—a violent period accompanied by a flow of both Chinese and foreign blood. In short, the revolution was assuming Bolshevik dimensions totally anathematic both to Chiang and to the middle-conservative elements of the Kuomintang.

For several weeks, Chiang hesitated. But when it became clear to him that the moment of truth was at hand, he acted quickly, decisively, and brutally. Leagued with conservative business elements of Shanghai, including foreigners and the notorious bandit gangs, on April 12, 1927, he launched a surprise attack against the area's Communists. This, the beginning of the infamous White Terror, quickly spread to other power centers; he followed it by setting up a Nationalist government at Nanking. Chiang's army undoubtedly would have fought the Hankow forces but for the war lord Fêng Yü-hsiang, whose army stood between them.[22]

Before either side could bribe Fêng, the Communists overplayed their hand. Joseph Stalin, fresh from his triumph over Trotsky, ordered the Chinese Communist Party (which was subordinate to the Comintern) to take over the revolution. This extraordinary order, naïve in the extreme, caused an immediate and terrible resentment throughout the Kuomintang. It virtually shattered the Communist movement. Borodin and other Soviet agents escaped to Russia; their Chinese opposites, those who survived the White Terror, went into hiding.

Chiang Kai-shek exploited this development by hammering the remaining elements of the Kuomintang into an embryonic Nationalist government, which by 1928 claimed control of China.

A brave claim. Internally, the Kuomintang remained greatly divided: war lords showing fangs too sharp to be ignored yapped in defense of sectional interests and foreign powers representing vast financial empires. Chiang was too strong to abdicate, too weak to protest. So

22. Malraux (*Man's Estate*), *supra*, has presented a striking picture of this turbulent scene.

he compromised: the highly vaunted revolution had stirred up the forces of power without removing the evils of their burden from the people. Chiang merely replaced Manchuism and warlordism with a dictatorship. His suppression of the Autumn Uprising of 1927—a peasant movement —was as thorough and heartless as any of the numerous Taiping suppressions.

And yet, ironically, Chiang was too weak to forge even an effective dictatorship. The slave of Confucianist thinking and the pawn of commercial interests, domestic and foreign, Chiang found himself blocked from reform on almost every side. The bulk of Chinese people remained miserable. Here and there, they continued to protest their misery. Here and there, small groups, led by Communists, waged guerrilla war. Here and there, the idea of social revolution lived on. Here and there, a few forceful leaders had survived to fight.

One of them was Mao Tse-tung.

Chapter 26

Mao Tse-tung • Childhood and education • Conversion to communism • Mao turns to the peasants • ". . . A revolution is not a dinner party. . . ." • The Autumn Harvest Uprising • Mao's defeat • Guerrilla warfare • Mao's formula • A winter of discontent • The Changsa defeat • Mao's shift in strategy • Chiang Kai-shek's "bandit-suppression campaign" fails • Mao's growth in strength • Falkenhausen's counterguerrilla tactics • The Long March to Shensi • Its accomplishments • Mao resumes the offensive • The United Front against the Japanese invaders

MAO TSE-TUNG was born in 1893, the son of hard-working peasants in Hunan province, in central China. As a "middle peasant," Mao's father, a harsh taskmaster and disciplinarian whom Mao loathed, was able to give his son the almost unheard-of luxury of a provincial education through high school level. Mao responded by reading whatever he laid his hands on, an eclectic assortment ranging from traditional Confucianist classics to the great Chinese historical novels and to translations of Western works in economics, political theory, and history.[1]

In these formative years, Mao learned more away from the classroom, where life was a constant fight for survival. In addition to normal

1. Stuart R. Schram, *Mao Tse-tung* (New York: Simon & Schuster, 1967); see also Harrison, op. cit.; Schurmann, op. cit. (Vol. 3); Mao Tse-tung, *On Guerrilla Warfare* (New York: Frederick A. Praeger, 1962). Tr. and with an Introduction by S. B. Griffith. (Hereafter cited as Mao Tse-tung (Griffith).) Dr. Griffith's excellent introduction includes a biographical sketch of Mao; see also Payne, op. cit.

stresses, the recurring plagues, famines, and floods, the tax collectors, landlords, and bandits, Mao witnessed something of the revolutionary turmoil surrounding the fall of the Manchus. As a keen student, he also realized the new government's inadequacy to solve old problems, particularly those affecting hundreds of millions of Chinese peasants. Mao soon became a socially aware and resentful young man; service as a private soldier, as servant to officers in an army ridden with nepotism, corruption, and inefficiency, only increased his resentment. When he went to work in the Peking University library, in 1917, he was, at twenty-four years, the Chinese version of an angry young man.

Angry young men are prone to swallow morphia-ridden political panaceas in much the same way that country people take to cure-all elixirs. Mao found his nostrum at Peking. Under tutelage of hard-line Marxists such as Li Ta-chao, his library boss, and Ch'ên Tu-hsiu, Mao soon became a convinced Communist, ". . . a man who had discovered his mission: to create a new China according to the doctrine of Marx and Lenin."[2] In 1921, he helped organize the Chinese Communist Party in Shanghai. Thenceforth he served as an activist in the revolutionary movement, which was still a joint Kuomintang-Communist affair.

In keeping with fundamental principles of Marxism-Leninism, the new Communist Party concentrated on organizing the Chinese proletariat into trade unions. It found a fertile field. The war had swollen the labor population to some two million persons, a miserably paid and ill-treated force particularly receptive to Communist propaganda. Party newspapers, youth movements, schools, clandestine meetings—each prospered in the factories and along the wharves and in the mines. An old party hack, Ho Kan-chih, later wrote that between 1922 and 1923 the party arranged ". . . over a hundred big and small strikes, with more than three hundred thousand workers taking part. Most of these strikes were crowned with complete success."[3] As a political agent, Mao Tse-tung found himself in the middle of this activity, eventually becoming chairman of the Hunan branch of the Trade Union Secretariat, a front organization. As such, he led ". . . the strikes of Changsha, the Anyuan Colliery, and the Shuikoushan Lead Mine."[4]

Despite this emphasis on the proletariat, the result of Comintern influence, some Chinese Communists had turned to organizing peasants of the central provinces. In 1921, P'eng P'ai started the first peasant association, in Kwangtung province; in five years, membership rose from a few thousand to 665,000, with other significant increases in Honan and Hunan provinces. Probably because of Mao's rural background, he was early assigned to agitation-propaganda activities in his home prov-

2. Mao Tse-tung (Griffith), *supra.*
3. Ho Kan-chih, "Rise of the Working Class Movement." In Schurmann, op. cit., Vol. 2.
4. Ibid.

ince, Hunan. He excelled in this work and, in 1926, was elected chairman of the All-China Association of Peasant Associations.[5] But even Mao was surprised at the outbreak of peasant violence in support of the Kuomintang army's northern march. Early in 1927, he spent a month touring Hunan province. In a prescient report to the Central Committee, he emphasized the need for party reorientation, with concentration on peasant forces:

. . . For the present upsurge of the peasant movement is a colossal event. In a very short time, in China's central, southern and northern provinces, several hundred million peasants will rise like a mighty storm, like a hurricane, a force so swift and violent that no power, however great, will be able to hold it back.[6]

In but months, Mao reported, membership of Hunan peasant associations had jumped from a few hundred thousand ". . . to two million and the masses directly under their leadership increased to ten million." Showing no sympathy for the victims of revolution to date, ". . . the local tyrants, the evil gentry and the lawless landlords," he mocked protests of conservative Kuomintang elements. If peasants on occasion were going too far, their excesses still did not match those of earlier governments. Besides,

. . . a revolution is not a dinner party, or writing an essay, or painting a picture, or doing embroidery; it cannot be so refined, so leisurely and gentle, so temperate, kind, courteous, restrained and magnanimous. A revolution is an insurrection, an act of violence by which one class overthrows another. A rural revolution is a revolution by which the peasantry overthrows the power of the feudal landlord class.[7]

The break between Chiang Kai-shek and the Hankow government, followed by Chiang's general purge of all Communists, may have removed luster from Mao's enthusiasm, but it in no way dimmed his basic convictions. At great danger to his own life, he willingly participated in the Autumn Harvest Uprising, of September 1927. This abortive effort, which centered in Hunan province, caused him to question one of the Chinese Communist Party's basic tenets: that unarmed and untrained peasants could bring about revolution. In the event, he commanded four "auxiliary" regiments, but these were scarcely strong enough to stand against the Nationalist army. Disobeying party orders,

5. Schurmann, op. cit. (Vol. 2).

6. Mao Tse-tung, *Selected Works* (Peking: Foreign Languages Press, 1965), Vol. 1.

7. Ibid. Payne has pointed out that his words gain an added bite when the adjectives are identified with the Confucianist *Analects*.

he broke off the action to seek sanctuary with remnant followers in the Chingkang Mountains of southern Hunan-Kiangsi-Fukien provinces.[8]

Late in 1927, Chiang announced the end of the Communist threat. He was wrong: The Communists were down, but not yet out. Early in 1928, the capable Chu Teh joined Mao, as did other fugitive survivors. In a manner reminiscent of Hung Hsiu-ch'üan, who started the Taiping rebellion from the mountains of Kwangsi province in 1847, the two Communists organized fellow fugitives, local bandit groups and peasant volunteers into a small, rudely equipped guerrilla army to keep alive the almost defunct revolution.

Unlike Hung, Mao and Chu respected the need for a political base. They turned local peasant associations into *su-wei-ai*, or soviets, of ". . . soldiers, peasants, and workers which assumed administrative control over the Red areas."[9] They also established local militia forces which Mao called ". . . the Red guards and the workers' and peasants' insurrection corps." Mao later explained that the militia's job was ". . . to suppress counter-revolution, to protect the township government, and, when the enemy comes, to assist the Red army and the Red guards in war."[10] The first insurrection corps started as an underground force in Yungsin but became overt once the army won command of the area. At best, the work moved slowly: in the winter of 1928, according to Mao, the Red Guards possessed a mere 683 rifles of assorted calibers. Moreover, Communist methods of land sequestration and redistribution had antagonized a good many "rich" and "middle" peasants in the area.

Despite Communist weakness, the movement survived and grew stronger. Using the plow of propaganda to till fertile "poor" peasant soil into acquiescence if not wholesale support, Mao and his fellows relied on coercion, including terrorist methods, to gain financial support from local merchants and landlords. Intelligence provided by peasants enabled guerrillas to fight local provincial forces on their own terms, utilizing mobility and surprise—short, sharp actions that avoided pitched battles.

In these early, crucial months, Mao's guerrillas profited from Chiang's concentration on more immediate problems besetting the Kuomintang as well as from his patronizing attitude, which led him consistently to underrate his enemy, whom he contemptuously dismissed as "communist-bandits."

Mao and Chu, on the other hand, paid closest attention to Kuomintang power struggles, which so obviously influenced the amount of Na-

8. Mao Tse-tung (Griffith), *supra*.
9. Schurmann, op. cit. (Vol. 2).
10. Mao Tse-tung, *Selected Works* (Vol. 1), *supra*.

tionalist army strength that would be used against them. As Mao wrote in 1928:

. . . When splits take place within the ruling classes . . . we may adopt a strategy of comparatively venturesome advance and expand the independent regime over a comparatively large area by fighting. Yet all the same we must take care to lay on a solid foundation in the central districts so that we shall have something to rely upon and nothing to fear when the White Terror comes. When the political power of the ruling classes is relatively stable, as in the southern provinces after April this year, our strategy must be one of gradual advance. We must then take the utmost care neither to divide up our forces for venturesome advance in the military field, nor to scatter our personnel and neglect to lay a solid foundation in the central districts in the field of local work (including the distribution of land, the establishment of political power, the expansion of the Party, and the organization of local armed forces).

Mao regarded the instability of national rule as a prerequisite for setting up ". . . an armed independent regime," but success, in his opinion, also depended on:

. . . 1) a sound mass basis [i.e., a willing peasant population]; 2) a first-rate Party organization [i.e., completely disciplined to pursue basic objectives]; 3) a Red army of adequate strength [as Mao later wrote, "Political power comes out of the barrel of a gun."]; 4) a terrain favorable to military operations [including a sanctuary area]; and 5) economic strength sufficient for self-support [i.e., to come from local sources such as landlords or merchants, from the people themselves, and from outside agencies such as the Comintern].[11]

While Mao was so theorizing, Communist success remained very limited. The ragged force euphemistically called the Red army suffered severe shortages of arms and equipment. Recruits reported literally with pitchforks, spears, and fowling pieces, weapons later replaced with captured rifles. Officers and soldiers alike received a ration of rice and five cents a day for ". . . cooking oil, salt, firewood, and vegetables"—a monthly payroll of more than ". . . ten thousand dollars, which are obtained exclusively through expropriating the local bullies [landlords and merchants]," and was not always met.[12]

In the freezing mountain sanctuary, soldiers shivered in light cotton clothing; over eight hundred lay ill from cold, malnutrition, and wounds but the army lacked doctors and medicine. To hold the ranks together, leaders relied on discipline engendered and maintained through ideology. A party political representative supervised each soldiers' council

11. Ibid.
12. Ibid.

at each command level down to and including the company; political indoctrination surpassed practical training in frequency and intensity, as is evident from Mao's 1928 report. This proved the more important because, in the relatively barren border areas, the White Terror had frequently cooled revolutionary fervor: "Wherever the Red Army goes," Mao wrote in 1928, "it finds the masses cold and reserved; only after propaganda and agitation do they slowly rouse themselves"[13]—and Mao held no intention of letting such apathy infect his army. His was scarcely an easy task, and his words reflect a winter of discontent: "We have an acute sense of loneliness and are every moment longing for the end of such a lonely life. . . ."[14]

Still, the Red flag flew and the ragtag army continued to elude government forces. In mid-1929, Mao and Chu moved from the remote Chingkang Mountains to a new base in southwestern Kiangsi province. A more realistic land policy gained them considerably wider support here, and, with an influx of recruits, they reshaped their army to win a number of significant local victories.

But Li Li-san, Chou En-lai, and other members of the Central Committee of the Chinese Communist Party, long since operating underground in Shanghai, misread the limited success of their agrarian counterparts. Still under Russian influence and convinced that revolution must come from the proletariat, Li and his associates, in 1930, ordered Mao and Chu to begin a series of attacks against southern cities, which would be "prepared" internally by labor strikes and uprisings. This called for a complete reversal of Communist tactics to carry out a campaign for which the Red army was neither trained, organized, nor equipped.

Mao and Chu acquiesced for a number of reasons: they and their followers were still subordinate to the Central Committee, they needed arms and ammunition which victories would bring, and they still partially believed in mass revolution led by the proletariat. The first attacks succeeded, although at a cost in lives that they could ill afford. But at Changsha, in September, they suffered a nearly disastrous defeat. They ended the ill-fated campaign by retreating into the hills of Kiangsi; despite orders of the Central Committee, they refused any further attempt to bring about a proletarian revolution.

The campaign against the cities convinced Mao and Chu that victory must come from peasant and countryside, not worker and city. As Dr. Griffith has written, this was ". . . the single most vital decision in the history of the Chinese Communist Party."[15] Mao and Chu decided this in September 1930. A refutation of Marxism-Leninism, it was also a demonstration of where real Communist leadership lay in China, and

13. Ibid.
14. Ibid.
15. Mao Tse-tung (Griffith), *supra.*

it helps to explain a great deal of the subsequent Chinese relationship with the Soviet Union.

Taking heart from the Nationalist victory at Changsha in the autumn of 1930, Chiang Kai-shek announced a "bandit-suppression campaign." Commencing in November, this looked better on paper than it proved in fact. Mao and Chu refused the Nationalist invitation to battle (except on their own terms), preferring a Fabian strategy designed, in Mao's later words, to lure the enemy deep and, with the aid of intelligence provided by peasants, destroy him piecemeal. This was particularly appropriate in view of Chiang's forces, which already were displaying deficiencies that he never could repair: riddled with inefficient and corrupt leadership, his divisions flailed over the land like locusts, further alienating peasants, the ill-treated, illiterate soldiers frequently deserting to the Communists. Attempts at reform were badly hampered by ". . . the political and ideological disunion within the Nationalist Party. . . . Between 1929 and 1932 three separate Nationalist governments were in some sort of operation."[16] Chiang's political concepts also hurt him: ". . . Since the Kuomintang was publicly against any rural reforms save such as could be comprehended within its vision of Confucianism, their return meant the return of the landlords."[17]

For these reasons, Chiang's first campaign fell apart at the seams. A second, equally unsuccessful effort failed in the spring of 1931. Chiang himself commanded an army of some three hundred thousand in the third campaign, but made little progress before having to march north to meet Japanese military incursions in Manchuria.

As Kuomintang fortunes plunged, Communist fortunes soared. Shortly after Chiang's precipitate departure in summer of 1931, the Comintern persuaded the Central Committee of the Chinese Communist Party to proclaim existence of the Chinese Soviet Republic. On November 7, the Chinese Red army raised this flag at Juichin, in southwest Kiangsi, and Mao Tse-tung became the new republic's president. At this time, his area of operations covered a large part of Kiangsi and extended into Fukien, Hunan, and Hupeh—an area containing around 25 million Chinese. Mao's army had grown to an impressive sixty thousand, with recruits continuing to come in.

In 1932, Chiang returned to the attack in the South. His fourth "encirclement and annihilation" campaign succeeded only in capturing some small Communist bases in Hupeh province. Impressed by Communist resistance and somewhat humbled by the poor performance of the Nationalist armies, he prepared carefully for the fifth campaign, which he opened in October 1933. Advised by a German group of officers headed by able General von Falkenhausen, Chiang now committed his most

16. Ibid.
17. Harrison, op. cit.

loyal divisions as core of an expeditionary force of over half a million men supported by artillery and some two hundred airplanes. Drawing on the lessons of the Boer war, Falkenhausen advanced this force slowly and methodically, evacuating peasants from villages and consolidating gains by building a massive series of mutually supporting blockhouses.

Although Mao's army numbered perhaps 250,000, continuing pressure soon began wearing the ranks thin. Deprived of peasant support, and thus of information and food, Mao's people slowly withdrew into the hills. One by one, Communist bases fell. By June 1934, Mao held only three small areas, each encircled by Chiang's divisions.

To Mao and Chu, and indeed to the Central Committee, the exact form of the revolution now became academic. Unless leaders of the new Soviet Republic acted quickly, they and their army would be exterminated. They finally decided to seek sanctuary in the remote northern province of Shensi, whose hills already sheltered a small Communist group. Their actual destination, the loess caves of Pao An, lay twelve hundred miles away "as the crow flies." Since Nationalist divisions and war lords friendly to Chiang interdicted virtually the whole route, the Communists would have to escape around Robin Hood's barn: southwest deep into Yünnan, then north through the tortuous mountains of Szechwan, all together some six thousand miles of difficult terrain, much of it contested by war lords, Chiang's armies, and by hostile tribes.

In October 1934, like Xenophon's Greeks twenty-three centuries earlier, the Communists burned granaries, backpacked meager possessions, fought through Chiang's encircling army, and began one of the most extraordinary marches in man's history.

A fighting withdrawal, the Long March, as it has come to be known, lasted over a year. Professor Tibor Mende later wrote that the march

. . . led across eleven provinces, over remote regions inhabited by suspicious peoples, through murderous marshy lands overgrown by grass, and in face of continuous danger from local and governmental forces. It is claimed that the three Communist armies who participated in the march crossed eighteen mountain chains and twenty-four large rivers, broke through the armies of ten war lords, defeated dozens of Kuomintang regiments, and took temporarily sixty-two cities.[18]

Of an estimated 130,000 persons who left Kiangsi, no more than thirty thousand arrived in Shensi—Mao Tse-tung's wife numbered among the dead.

The Communist ledger of hardship and sacrifice nonetheless held a profit column. The first and by far most important entry: the Long March established the Chinese Soviet Republic in a new, temporarily

18. Tibor Mende, *The Chinese Revolution* (London: Thames & Hudson, 1961).

safe sanctuary. In remote loess caves of Pao An (Protracted Peace), Mao reorganized battered ranks of party and army. Neither proved an easy task: Losses had been heavy, but survivors breathed the zeal of ideologically devoted men. This was the hard core. Some of the leaders are alive today, men whose unquestioned and varied talents were partly fired in the crucible of the Long March.

The Long March produced other advantages. As Mende and others have pointed out, stories of the epic retreat soon circulated throughout China to belie Kuomintang claims of total victory over the Reds. The Long March also brought Mao into contact with other Communist groups, whose civil and military leaders accepted his authority. The Communists perforce had to deal with a variety of peasant and nationalist groups, and lessons learned from such contacts played an invaluable role in later propaganda missions.[19]

Despite the chaotic, nightmarish quality of the march, Mao never lost sight of the future. The political factor remained paramount in his mind. For as his armies struggled over mountains and through rivers, he assigned small agitation-propaganda cadres to remain in likely areas to talk up the revolution. In time, he would send trained teams to reinforce these cadres, and he left secret caches of arms and ammunition for their later use.[20]

Considering the problems at hand, the Communists resumed operations in surprisingly short time. As his initial target, Mao chose neighboring Shansi province. In February 1936, three Red army columns, numbering some thirty-four thousand men, crossed the Yellow River, brushed aside provincial forces of the governor, Yen Hsi-shan, and occupied large areas, where they ". . . collected grain and money, shot rich landlords and tax collectors, recruited thousands of peasants for their armies, and began organizing the rural masses."[21] By their own account, they returned to Shensi with some eight thousand volunteer recruits, not only peasants, but students, bureaucrats, shopkeepers, workers, and soldiers.[22]

Mao was not yet out of trouble. His incursions into Shansi decided Chiang Kai-shek to complete the extermination campaign begun in Kiangsi. To carry this out, he deployed the Northeastern and Northwestern Defense Armies, a heterogeneous collection of some 150,000 troops, along the Yellow River under command of "Young Marshal" Chang Hsueh-liang, who established "Bandit-Suppression Headquarters" at Sian.[23]

19. Ibid.
20. Ibid.
21. Mao Tse-tung (Griffith), *supra.*
22. S. B. Griffith, *The Chinese People's Liberation Army* (New York: McGraw-Hill, 1967). (Hereafter cited as Griffith (CPLA).)
23. Ibid.

Chiang's fear of the Communists as the real threat to China was not shared by all members of the Kuomintang. A considerable faction disagreed outright, and for good reason: not only did the Japanese virtually control Hopei province, in the North, but they were slowly pushing into Kiangsu and Honan provinces, farther south. Worse yet, Chiang's failure to stem these incursions became Mao's gain. By taking up the cause of resistance to the Japanese invader, and in the process villainizing Chiang Kai-shek and the Kuomintang, Mao gained a fantastic psychological advantage. As Professor Harrison has pointed out, the Communists ". . . appropriated nationalism from the Nationalists and made it a powerful Communist weapon."[24]

The denouement of this internal drama had already begun, the *deus ex machina* being the external force of the Soviet Union. Aware of Japanese aspirations on the Asian continent, Stalin had never broken with the Kuomintang, whose power he regarded as essential to checking Japan's invasion of China. Now, threatened by the rising prominence of Hitler in the West, he ordered Mao Tse-tung to make common cause with Chiang Kai-shek through a United Front.

Although such an alliance upset Mao's revolutionary timetable, this was in any event flexible and Mao stood to profit in other ways. Since 1932, he had been calling for war against Japan, and much of the Communists' popular appeal derived from this position. He had even found an ally of sorts in Marshal Chang Hsueh-liang, on whom Chiang Kai-shek was depending to hold Mao in check and eventually destroy him. The security derived from Mao's improved relationship with Chang in Sian probably explains why Mao was able to move his headquarters to the town of Yenan, which, in December 1936, became the capital of the Chinese Soviet Republic.

Chiang Kai-shek refused the notion of a United Front, despite considerable pressures from within the Kuomintang. In mid-1936, he ordered Marshal Chang to attack the Communist bases in Shensi, an order refused not only by Chang but by subordinate war lords. In December 1936, a furious Chiang Kai-shek traveled to Sian, where he ordered Chang ". . . to mount a full attack against the Communist bases in Shansi."[25]

Chang not only refused, but literally kidnaped the president of China and issued a manifesto calling for an end to civil war in favor of united action against Japan. Mao undoubtedly was involved in this move, although to what extent is not known. Professor Harrison believes that Chiang probably would have been executed but for Stalin's intercession on his behalf. Although details are lacking, Chou En-lai apparently pre-

24. Harrison, op. cit.
25. Ibid.

sented the Comintern position to Chang in Sian. As it turned out, Chang released Chiang Kai-shek toward the end of December.

Although Mao hated to let Chiang go—Edgar Snow wrote that Mao ". . . flew into a rage when the order came from Moscow to release Chiang"[26]—he hastened to make political capital from Chiang's release. In a much publicized letter to the Generalissimo, Mao reminded him that he owed his freedom to the Communists, who had intervened solely in order for China to get on with the war against the Japanese invader; if Chiang would cease fighting the Communists, Mao offered to call off revolutionary activities in return for a joint war effort against the Japanese.

Formal agreement between Nationalists and Communists emerged in September 1937, shortly after the Japanese captured Peking and Shanghai and began to fight toward Chiang's new capital at Nanking. But only for the moment was the very real threat of the foreign invader to overshadow severe internal antagonisms.

26. Edgar Snow, *Random Notes on China 1936–1945* (Cambridge, Mass.: Harvard University Press, 1957).

Chapter 27

Mao's theory of "people's war" • *His writings analyzed* • *Communist organization, equipment and training of guerrilla units* • *Their missions* • *Mao's debt to Sun Tzu* • *Secret of Communist tactics* • *Mao's "identification strategy"* • *His war against the Japanese invader*

THE YEARS IN THE SOUTH that culminated in the Long March made Mao Tse-tung undisputed leader of the Chinese Communist Party. And now, in the loess caves of Pao An, the forty-three-year-old Communist leader began to frame the theory and doctrine of "people's war" —a thesis that would influence his world to an immeasurable degree.

As Professor Stuart Schram has pointed out, Mao did not arrive easily at this doctrine. Prior to the Long March, however, he had concluded that revolution in China depended ultimately on ". . . three essential principles . . . the central role of the army, the importance of rural base areas, and the protracted character of the struggle," and he also had tested and improved many of its strategic and tactical aspects.[1]

1. Mao Tse-tung, *Basic Tactics* (New York: Frederick A. Praeger, 1966). Tr. and with an Introduction by Stuart R. Schram. (Hereafter cited as Mao Tse-tung (Schram).)

Fundamental to the process was guerrilla warfare, and, in 1937, he defined its revolutionary role in a definitive work called *Yu Chi Chan,* or *Guerrilla Warfare.*[2] Mao followed this with a book titled *All the Problems of the Anti-Japanese Guerrilla War.* In the same year, he delivered a series of complementary lectures on guerrilla tactics to a group of young officer cadets. Subsequently published under the title of *Basic Tactics,* they have only recently been translated into English.[3]

Although Mao paid lip service to the united front by naming the Japanese as the enemy in these works, his thoughts centered more on the Kuomintang armies. Too weak to fight the Japanese on his own, he would rely on the Kuomintang until the invader had been defeated; he would use one war as a means of growth to fight another, or, as he later put it, ". . . to drive out Japanese imperialism and build an independent, free and happy new China."[4]

Whichever the enemy, Mao looked on a country

. . . half colonial and half feudal; it is a country that is politically, militarily, and economically backward . . . a vast country with great resources and tremendous population, a country in which the terrain is complicated and the facilities for communication are poor. All these factors favor a protracted war; they all favor the application of mobile [that is, orthodox] warfare and guerrilla operations.[5]

Mao carefully elaborated on this statement:

. . . The concept that guerrilla warfare is an end in itself and that guerrilla activities can be divorced from those of the regular forces is incorrect . . . in sum, while we must promote guerrilla warfare as a necessary strategical auxiliary to orthodox operations, we must neither assign it the primary position in our war strategy nor substitute it for mobile and positional warfare as conducted by orthodox forces.

With regard to the whole war, ". . . mobile warfare is primary and guerrilla warfare supplementary; with regard to each part, guerrilla warfare is primary and mobile warfare supplementary."[6] Since Mao's force, known as the Eighth Route Army, was fighting "a part," he called for a basic strategy of "guerrilla warfare." But, he warned, ". . . lose no

2. Mao Tse-tung (Griffith), *supra.* This work was translated into English in 1939 by S. B. Griffith, at the time a young marine officer and Chinese-language student in Peking, and was published in the *Marine Corps Gazette* in 1940 (and largely ignored by America's professional military body).

3. Mao Tse-tung (Schram), *supra.*

4. Mao Tse-tung, *Selected Works, supra.*

5. Mao Tse-tung (Griffith), *supra.*

6. Ibid.

chance for mobile warfare [operations of regular armies] under favorable conditions."[7]

Whether fighting the Japanese or later the Kuomintang armies, Mao demanded a three-phase war. Phase One, as Dr. Griffith has described it,

. . . is devoted to organization, consolidation, and preservation of regional base areas situated in isolated and difficult terrain. Here volunteers are trained and indoctrinated, and from here, agitators and propagandists set forth, individually or in groups of two or three, to "persuade" and "convince" the inhabitants of the surrounding countryside and to enlist their support. In effect, there is thus woven about each base a protective belt of sympathizers willing to supply food, recruits, and information. The pattern of the process is conspiratorial, clandestine, methodical, and progressive.[8]

Phase Two steps up the action:

. . . Acts of sabotage and terrorism multiply; collaborationists and "reactionary elements" are liquidated. Attacks are made on vulnerable military and police outposts; weak columns are ambushed. The primary purpose of these operations is to procure arms, ammunition, and other essential material, particularly medical supplies and radios. As the growing guerrilla force becomes better equipped and its capabilities improve, political agents proceed with indoctrination of the inhabitants of peripheral districts soon to be absorbed into the expanding "liberated" area.[9]

Phase Three is decisive: the enemy's destruction by orthodox military operations which do not necessarily deny guerrilla operations but place them in a subsidiary role.[10]

The hallmark of this blueprint is flexibility. The phases are coactive: Phase Two and even Phase Three may concern one theater of operations, Phase One another. While the process normally proceeds upward, Phase Three may retrogress into Phase Two and even Phase One. Timelessness, or protraction, also plays an important part—a single phase may last two, ten, or twenty years.

Echoing Clausewitz, whom he had studied, Mao insisted on subordinating combat to an over-all political strategy:

. . . Because ours is the resistance of a semicolonial country against an imperialism, our hostilities must have a clearly defined political goal and firmly established political responsibilities. Our basic policy is the creation of a national united anti-Japanese front. This policy we pursue in order to gain our political goal, which is the complete emancipation of the Chinese people.[11]

7. Mao Tse-tung, *Selected Works, supra.*
8. Mao Tse-tung (Griffith), *supra.*
9. Ibid.
10. Ibid.
11. Ibid.

Guerrilla warfare cannot be separated from national policy:

. . . What is the relationship of guerrilla warfare to the people? Without a
political goal, guerrilla warfare must fail, as it must if its political objectives
do not coincide with the aspirations of the people and their sympathy, co-
operation, and assistance cannot be gained. The essence of guerrilla warfare
is thus revolutionary in character. . . . Because guerrilla warfare basically
derives from the masses and is supported by them, it can neither exist nor
flourish if it separates itself from their sympathies and co-operation.[12]

Mao returned to the political priority in a later chapter of *Yu Chi
Chan,* a chapter that most of today's Western military commanders seem
unable to understand. Some of Mao's generals seemed equally obtuse:

. . . There are some militarists who say: "We are not interested in politics
but only in the profession of arms." It is vital that these simple-minded militarists be made to realize the relationship that exists between politics and
military affairs. Military action is a method used to attain a political goal.
While military affairs and political affairs are not identical, it is impossible
to isolate one from the other.[13]

Mao's insistence on the overriding importance of the political factor
resulted in his concept of the "three unities":

. . . These are political activities, first, as applied to the troops; second, as
applied to the people; and, third, as applied to the enemy. The fundamental
problems are: first, spiritual unification of officers and men within the
army; second, spiritual unification of the army and the people; and, last,
destruction of the unity of the enemy.[14]

The first of the unities represented a radical departure from oriental
military tradition. Although admitting need for obedience in any army,
Mao held that ". . . the basis for guerrilla discipline must be the individual conscience." Mao wanted only "pure and clean" volunteers
"willing to fight." As opposed to discipline achieved through physical
beatings or tongue-lashings, revolutionary discipline

. . . must be self-imposed, because only when it is, is the soldier able to
understand completely why he fights and why he must obey. This type of
discipline becomes a tower of strength within the army, and it is the only
type that can truly harmonize the relationship that exists between officers and
soldiers.

In Mao's army, ordinary soldiers, as well as guerrillas, must ". . . enjoy political liberty"—by which he meant that such questions as

12. Ibid.
13. Ibid.
14. Ibid.

". . . the emancipation of people must not only be tolerated but discussed, and propaganda must be encouraged." Further, ". . . officers should live under the same conditions as their men, for that is the only way in which they can gain from their men the admiration and confidence so vital in war. It is incorrect to hold to a theory of equality in all things, but there must be equality of existence in accepting the hardships and dangers of war." Through all this, ". . . we may attain to the unification of the officer and soldier groups, a unity both horizontal within the group itself, and vertical, that is, from lower to higher echelons."[15]

As quaint as all this sounds to the Westerner, it is really no more than the Napoleonic-Fochian concept that the moral is to the physical as three to one. But the reader should keep in mind that few commanders in history have been able to attain this ratio in practice, and that it formed a radical departure from the *Lumpensoldat* concept of China's feudal and Nationalist armies. In view of the Communist performance in Kiangsi, the survival of the inner core during the Long March, and some of the exploits of the Eighth Route Army against the Japanese and the Nationalists, no Westerner should summarily scorn it as just another of "Mao's thoughts." No less qualified an observer than Lieutenant Colonel Evans Carlson, U. S. Marine Corps, who ". . . traveled on foot for more than 2,000 miles [as an official observer] with Eighth Route Army guerrillas in 1937 and 1938," was deeply impressed ". . . by the uncomplaining endurance of the soldiers during long and dangerous marches behind Japanese lines. On one occasion, he recorded a march of 58 miles in thirty-two hours—a feat the more remarkable because it was performed in mountainous country by a battalion of 600 men. Most of the distance was covered in moonlight." Carlson later wrote: ". . . The explanation lay in the ethical indoctrination of the individual. Each man possessed the *desire* to do what was right; it was right to perform his duty."[16]

The army's "internal unity of spirit" must extend to the local people. Mao covered troop behavior among the population with three general rules:

1. All actions are subject to command.
2. Do not steal from the people.

15. Ibid.
16. Griffith (CPLA), *supra*. Carlson, a mystical sort of man with decidedly liberal views, was so impressed with Communist military performance that he later incorporated many of its tactical tenets into the Raider concept which he imposed on the U. S. Marine Corps, his chief ally being Lieutenant Colonel James Roosevelt. Two Raider regiments eventually emerged. Although these highly trained units performed well, particularly in the opening battles of Tulagi and Guadalcanal, most senior marine commanders objected to them as wasting resources, both men and material, in making elite units from units already elite. Cf. A. A. Vandegrift and R. B. Asprey, *Once a Marine, supra*.

   3. Be neither selfish nor unjust.
He amplified these "rules" with eight "remarks":
   1. Replace the door when you leave the house.
      [Visitors in the Chinese countryside frequently removed the doors
      to use as beds.]
   2. Roll up the bedding on which you have slept.
   3. Be courteous.
   4. Be honest in your transactions.
   5. Return what you borrow.
   6. Replace what you break.
   7. Do not bathe in the presence of women.
   8. Do not without authority search the pocketbooks of those you
      arrest.[17]

Again, such behavior constituted a radical departure from that of both
Nationalist and Japanese soldiers, justly detested throughout China for
rapine and brutality. But, in Mao's mind, such behavior was essential
to the spiritual unification of the army and the people:

. . . Many people think it impossible for guerrillas to exist for long in the
enemy's rear. Such a belief reveals lack of comprehension of the relationship that should exist between the people and the troops. The former may be
likened to water and the latter to the fish who inhabit it. How may it be said
that these two cannot exist together? It is only undisciplined troops who
make the people their enemies and who, like the fish out of its native element,
cannot live.[18]

Finally, Mao charged the Eighth Route Army to destroy ". . . the
enemy by propagandizing his troops, by treating his captured soldiers
with consideration, and by caring for those of his wounded who fall
into our hands. If we fail in these respects, we strengthen the solidarity
of our enemy."[19]

The interdependence of the three unities is clear, and indeed essential to the concept of the peasant-guerrilla as the basis of the army:

. . . Without question, the fountainhead of guerrilla warfare is in the masses
of the people, who organize guerrilla units directly from themselves.[20]

Mao lists seven ways in which guerrilla units are originally formed.
The "fundamental type" is formed from people automatically springing
to arms to oppose the invader. This is the "pure" type of guerrilla warfare, earlier illustrated in this book:

. . . Upon the arrival of the enemy army to oppress and slaughter the people, their leaders call upon them to resist. They assemble the most valorous

   17. Mao Tse-tung (Griffith), *supra*.
   18. Ibid.
   19. Ibid.
   20. Ibid.

elements, arm them with old rifles or bird guns, and thus a guerrilla unit begins.

Background and experience are unimportant. Only courage is essential:

. . . That you are farmers is of no difference, and if you have education, that is so much the better. When you take your arms in hand, you become soldiers; when you are organized, you become military units.

Mao held for on-the-job training:

. . . Guerrilla hostilities are the university of war, and after you have fought several times valiantly and aggressively, you may become a leader of troops, and there will be many well-known regular soldiers who will not be your peers.[21]

In addition to spontaneous resistance, guerrilla warfare may be fought by units assigned from the regular army, by a combination of regular army soldiers and peasant-guerrillas, by units of local militia, by enemy deserters, and by former bandits and bandit groups. Each category poses special problems in recruiting and organizing, but the catalytic agent is political and the effort worthwhile, since ". . . it is possible to unite them to form a vast sea of guerrillas. The ancients said, 'Tai Shan is a great mountain because it does not scorn the merest handful of dirt; the rivers and seas are deep because they absorb the waters of small streams.' "[22]

Mao's basic guerrilla unit, the squad, comprised nine to eleven men. Two to four squads formed a platoon, two to four platoons a company, and so on through battalion and regimental levels. These units operated within a "military area" commanded by military and political officers and divided into districts and counties. This dual command, military-political, extended to companies and even to platoons when operating independently. Auxiliary, or "self-defense," units, of rudely organized militia, performed local sentry duties, provided intelligence, arrested traitors, and prevented ". . . the dissemination of enemy propaganda." On occasion, they functioned as combatants and, in addition, were to

. . . furnish stretcher-bearers to transport the wounded, carriers to take food to the troops, and comfort missions to provide the troops with tea and rice. If a locality can organize such a self-defense unit as we have described, the traitors cannot hide nor can bandits and robbers disturb the peace of the people. Thus the people will continue to assist the guerrillas and supply manpower to our regular armies.[23]

The small guerrilla unit did not require sophisticated arms. Two to

21. Ibid.
22. Ibid.
23. Ibid.

five Western-style rifles were sufficient for a squad, ". . . with the remaining men armed with rifles of local manufacture, bird guns, spears, or big swords." Members of militia and self-defense units ". . . must have a weapon even if . . . only a knife, a pistol, a lance, or a spear." Each guerrilla district commander should establish an armory to make and repair rifles and produce cartridges, hand grenades, and bayonets. However, ". . . guerrillas must not depend too much on an armory. The enemy is the principal source of their supply."[24]

Each guerrilla carried a minimum of clothing and equipment. Clothing must be procured by higher echelons, since it is an error to take clothes from prisoners. In general, equipment becomes more sophisticated as unit size increases. Larger units will carry telephone and radio equipment as well as propaganda materials, which ". . . are very important. Every large guerrilla unit should have a printing press and a mimeograph stone. They must also have paper on which to print propaganda leaflets and notices. They must be supplied with chalk and large brushes."[25] Medical services are also most important, and if Western medicines cannot be procured from "contributions," then local medicines must be used. The logistics requirement at all times is held to a minimum:

. . . The equipment of guerrillas cannot be based on what the guerrillas want, or even what they need, but must be based on what is available for their use.[26]

Mao assigned a number of over-all missions, or "responsibilities," to guerrillas:

. . . to exterminate small forces of the enemy; to harass and weaken large forces; to attack enemy lines of communication; to establish bases capable of supporting independent operations in the enemy's rear; to force the enemy to disperse his strength; and to coordinate all these activities with those of the regular armies on distant battle fronts.[27]

In discussing strategy and tactics essential to accomplishing such missions, Mao borrowed freely from Sun Tzu's thesis of the indirect approach (see pages 34-36):

. . . Guerrilla strategy must be based primarily on alertness, mobility, and attack. It must be adjusted to the enemy situation, the terrain, the existing lines of communication, the relative strengths, the weather, and the situation of the people.

24. Ibid.
25. Ibid. Cf. Lawrence, *The Seven Pillars of Wisdom, supra:* ". . . The printing press is the greatest weapon in the armory of the modern commander."
26. Mao Tse-tung (Griffith), *supra.*
27. Ibid.

In guerrilla warfare, select the tactic of seeming to come from the east and attacking from the west; avoid the solid, attack the hollow; attack; withdraw; deliver a lightning blow, seek a lightning decision. When guerrillas engage a stronger enemy, they withdraw when he advances; harass him when he stops; strike him when he is weary; pursue him when he withdraws. In guerrilla strategy, the enemy's rear, flanks, and other vulnerable spots are his vital points, and there he must be harassed, attacked, dispersed, exhausted and annihilated.[28]

Surprise and deception are the hallmark of guerrilla tactics: ". . . Cause an uproar in the east, strike in the west." As Mao explained to smooth-faced cadets training to fight the Japanese in 1938: ". . . When the army wants to attack a certain place, it does not advance there directly but makes a detour by some other place and then changes its course in the midst of its march, in order to attack and disperse the enemy. 'The thunderclap leaves no time to cover one's ears.' "[29] Surprise offsets numerical weakness: ". . . Fierce wind and heavy rain offer a favorable occasion for a guerrilla attack, as do thick fog, the darkness of night, or circumstances in which it is possible to strike at an exhausted enemy." Above all offensive tactics, Mao favored ambush, ". . . the sole habitual tactic of a guerrilla unit."[30]

As opposed to orthodox warfare, which is frequently static, Mao wanted

. . . constant activity and movement. There is in guerrilla warfare no such thing as a decisive battle; there is nothing comparable to the fixed, passive defense that characterizes orthodox war. In guerrilla warfare, the transformation of a moving situation into a positional defensive situation never arises. The general features of reconnaissance, partial deployment, general deployment, and development of the attack that are usual in mobile warfare are not common in guerrilla war.

Instead of fixed defense, Mao calls for

. . . alert shifting . . . when the enemy feels the danger of guerrillas, he will generally send troops out to attack them. The guerrillas must consider the situation and decide at what time and at what place they wish to fight. If they find that they cannot fight, they must immediately shift.

Although the guerrilla will defend his own operational bases, these must be abandoned when necessary. ". . . We must observe the principle, 'To gain territory is no cause for joy, and to lose territory is no cause for sorrow.' "[31]

28. Ibid.; see also Sun Tzu, op. cit.: Dr. Griffith has made an excellent comparative study in his Introduction.
29. Mao Tse-tung (Schram), *supra.*
30. Ibid.
31. Mao Tse-tung (Griffith), *supra.*

Nevertheless, ". . . the operations of a guerrilla unit should consist in offensive warfare." Offensive tactics, he was careful to stress, demand ". . . careful planning . . . those who fight without method do not understand the nature of guerrilla action. A plan is necessary regardless of the size of the unit involved; a prudent plan is as necessary in the case of the squad as in the case of the regiment." Good planning depends on superior intelligence, and this can be gained only from the people, who, in turn, must withhold such from the enemy. In the end, it is peasants who give the guerrilla liberty of action essential to maintaining the initiative: ". . . When an army loses the initiative, it loses its liberty; its role becomes passive; it faces the danger of defeat and destruction."[32]

The validity of functional theory lies in practice. We have seen already that much of the Red army's success in occupying, consolidating and enlarging base areas lay in almost magical appeals of basic Communist social and economic reforms. In working with peasants of northern China, Communist agents undoubtedly exaggerated the quality of their wares—in another work, the author has described them as offering Barnum-style promises to people who had never seen a circus. But this scarcely lessened the impact of immediate reforms, which resembled an elixir that may not have cured the disease but at least alleviated considerable pain.

Communist magic rested on refutation: refutation of everything evil in traditional rule. Although the United Front temporarily tied Mao's hands in so far as seizure and redistribution of land were concerned, the Communists continued to abolish usury, reduce rents, and lighten taxes; the Red army no longer seized and executed landlords (at least not en masse), but it did grade them carefully as to productivity under the credo originally and ironically voiced by Dr. Sun Yat-sen: "Land to those who till it."[33] By refuting if not necessarily replacing evil, the Communists restored to the common peasant two emotional ingredients that make the difference between existing and living: dignity and hope. To the long-suffering peasant, the price tag of discipline, of unquestioned loyalty and obedience to the Party, seemed reasonable.

Discipline formed the foundation of the meticulous organization imposed on peasant communities and based on the village soviet, proceeding upward to district, county, provincial, and central levels. As Edgar Snow wrote in his classic work *Red Star over China:*

. . . Under the district soviet, and appointed by it, were committees for education, cooperatives, military training, political training, land, public health, partisan training, revolutionary defense, enlargement of the Red

32. Ibid.
33. Edgar Snow, *Red Star over China* (New York: Random House, 1938).

Army, agrarian mutual aid, Red Army land tilling, and others. Such committees were found in every branch organ of the soviets, right up to the Central Government, where policies were coordinated and state decisions made.[34]

This activity swelled the rolls of the Communist Party, which also organized and propagandized village youth and even children. By so involving the peasant population, the Communists forged virtually indestructible base areas impervious to the adverse influence of both Nationalists and Japanese invaders. Professor Harrison offered a striking example of the success of what I call "identification strategy": In 1935, the "best" provincial governor in China, Yen Hsi-shan, of Shansi province, ". . . literally eradicated the Communists in his province," yet admitted ". . . that, given their head, 70 per cent of his people would go over to the Communists." The successful Communist invasion of Shansi the following year bore out his pessimism. Although he drove out the intruders with the help of Nationalist troops, in 1937 ". . . he invited them back to help fight the Japanese thrust at Shansi."[35]

The Japanese war also favored identification strategy. Professor Harrison goes so far as to call this invasion ". . . the real revolutionary force in China," and there is no doubt that Japanese occupation and fighting played a horribly destructive and divisive role that in the end favored Mao Tse-tung more than Chiang Kai-shek.

Nationalist armies, in retreating from Peking, Shanghai and Nanking in 1937, suffered enormous losses. Alone and increasingly isolated from foreign military aid (the Russians alone providing pilots, planes and money), Chiang Kai-shek was desperately trying to rebuild his army and could risk no part of it in a new campaign against the Japanese. In the north and north-central provinces, this left the field open to the Communists.

Under the terms of the United Front, the Red army became the Eighth Route Army, of three divisions comprising about forty-five thousand troops, under command of Mao's old Kiangsi comrade, the able Chu Teh. This army, by partially filling the military hiatus, served as an organized rallying point for national resistance. Mao also controlled perhaps another forty-five thousand troops, whose standards, though not blatantly unfurled, attracted numerous followers.

Adding to Mao's military largess, the Japanese army behaved in a manner to insure the popularity of Communist armies. Older readers will remember the infamous "Rape of Nanking," which shocked the civilized world in 1937. Such bestiality hallmarked the earlier Japanese invasion and occupation of Hopei province. The Japanese behaved in China precisely like Hitler's people in the Ukraine a few years later—

34. Ibid.
35. Harrison, op. cit.

as supermen dealing with inferiors. Naturally, any organized force wanting to fight against such treatment found immediate and widespread popularity among the people, particularly among those peasants already impressed with Communist land and tax reforms.

The Japanese also erred tactically. In the 1932 invasion of Manchuria and subsequently, their armies showed well—strong, splendidly equipped, tactically well disciplined, flexible, capable of long marches and devastating night attacks. With continuing prosperity, their military commanders, never self-deprecating, grew increasingly arrogant.

In September 1937, one of them, Lieutenant General Itagaki Seishiro, marched his division into an ambush cunningly laid by Lin Piao, commanding the 115th Division of the Eighth Route Army. In a brief but furious action, Itagaki suffered perhaps five thousand casualties besides losing most of his arms and supply trains, including the paymaster's money chests—the first major Japanese defeat and one trumpeted to the world by jubilant Chinese Communists.[36]

Mao was much too smart to try for a repeat victory of this nature. Instead, he concentrated on occupying and consolidating three major "base areas" in Shansi province. From here, his units fanned out to establish "guerrilla areas," which supported what Mao called "mobile-striking war"—guerrilla tactics which ". . . harassed and irritated the Japanese and tied thousands of troops, who might otherwise have been employed to better advantage, to static guard duties."[37]

The war continued in this fashion until 1940: Chiang and the Nationalists on the defensive outside of Chungking; Mao and the Communists, securely based in Shansi, on the limited tactical offensive with successes in the countryside but unable to contest Japanese control of the cities.

While Chiang's military fortunes waned, Mao's fortunes waxed—to the extent that, in 1940, he organized the New Fourth Army to fight south of the Yangtze, in Chekiang province. Already seriously alarmed at the growth of Communist power, Chiang reacted vigorously to this move. Ordering the New Fourth Army north, out of "Nationalist territory," Chiang ambushed it as it was crossing the Yangtze. Chiang then placed an economic embargo on Communist-held areas and followed this with troop operations against the Communists.

Mao, meanwhile, was facing another threat—from the Japanese general Tada Hayao, who took command of the North China Area Army in late 1939. As Kitchener had done in South Africa and Chiang in Kiangsi, Tada began systematic construction of forts, in this case by

36. Griffith (CPLA), supra.
37. Ibid.

thousands of impressed coolies. This, his "cage policy," was described in an American military intelligence report:

. . . Deep and wide ditches or moats were dug and high walls built along the sides of the railways and highways in Central and Southern Hopeh in order to protect them from attacks and, more important, to blockade and to break up the Communist base areas. At the same time, hundreds of miles of new roads with protecting ditches were built with the object of cutting up the guerrilla bases into small pieces which would then be destroyed one by one. The number of blockhouses along the railways and roads, manned by Japanese soldiers, was greatly increased. . . .[38]

Mao answered this threat in part by a massive guerrilla offensive, the "Hundred Regiments Offensive," launched in August 1940: this co-ordinated operation continued

. . . with several interludes, for three months. In its overt aspects, the campaign was a success. Guerrillas made hundreds of cuts in rail lines; derailed trains, blew up small bridges and viaducts, attacked and burned stations; destroyed switches, water towers, and signal-control equipment, and otherwise seriously damaged and temporarily disarranged the railway system in North China. As a substantial dividend, Japanese garrison forces, necessarily concentrating on counterguerrilla operations and major restoration projects, were unable to get into the countryside to confiscate the autumn harvest. The Communists . . . reported more than 20,000 Japanese killed; 5,000 puppet troops killed and wounded; 281 Japanese officers captured, and 18,000 puppet prisoners. They claimed that almost 3,000 forts and blockhouses had been destroyed and large quantities of arms and ammunition taken.

As Dr. Griffith pointed out, these figures were undoubtedly exaggerated.[39]

The Communist offensive nonetheless hurt the Japanese. Tada's successor, General Okamura Yasuji, attempted to repair the damage, in the summer of 1941, with what he called a "three-all policy"—"Kill all, burn all, destroy all." As the year closed, Okamura's powerful mobile columns began pushing back Communist guerrillas in numerous areas. Simultaneously, Mao's relations with Chiang Kai-shek were worsening. By the end of 1941, China's chances for survival seemed remote, even if a rapprochement should occur between Nationalists and Communists.

Then, suddenly, the entire situation changed. On December 7, 1941, the Japanese bombed Pearl Harbor, which brought America into the war. China no longer stood alone against the Japanese enemy. This radi-

38. Ibid.
39. Ibid.

cal shift in the power position was going to bring significant and indeed fatal consequences to the torn and bleeding country.

But this introduces another phase in the Eastern struggle. We must now return to the West and to revolutions of another sort, in which guerrilla warfare, unaided by Marxist motivation, also played a decisive role.

Chapter 28

The Rif rebellion • Spain and Morocco • Condition of the Spanish army • The Regulares and the Tercio • Spanish pacification policy • Early operations • Guerrilla resistance • Abd-el-Krim • Spanish defeat • The war continues • Africanistas versus Abandonistas • Primo de Rivera's "line"

THE 1904 TREATY that turned England and France loose in Egypt and Africa also opened northern Morocco to Spanish influence. In 1912, France formally placed this area under a Spanish protectorate.

It was not a great prize. Consisting of some eighteen thousand square miles, it supported no less than sixty-six tribes (subdivided into numerous clans and subclans), many of them tucked away into formidable mountain areas where they lived a way of life established long before the birth of Christ and where they spoke dialects often unintelligible to other tribes. Illiterate and poor, these peoples were nonetheless proud. Many tribes were also bellicose (bloody intertribal feuds were common), and they were also resentful of any foreign incursion into what they regarded as their country. Particularly was this true in two of the five major tribal areas, the Jibala, in the West, and the Rif, in the East.

Spanish proponents of an aggressive colonial policy in Morocco, particularly members of army and Church, argued that a successful conquest would help repair Spain's status as a world power after its disastrous defeat by America, and would also provide new markets and enormous mining profits and would secure the southern approach to the Spanish mainland.

Not everyone agreed: From 1904 on, Spain itself was divided: the Africanistas holding for conquest; ". . . the Spanish masses . . . either apathetic or apprehensive about engaging in further military action."[1] The latter were particularly wise. In trying to develop mining areas in the Rif, the Spanish stirred up local tribes and had to fight a brief but bloody war in the Melilla area in 1909, a Spanish "victory" of Pyrrhic proportions: Besides costing the Spanish some four thousand casualties, it aroused severe internal protest in Spain and also displayed to friend and foe alike the army's general ineptitude. Two years later, the army clashed with western tribes.

Spain thus acquired a restive protectorate in 1912. An ill-disciplined army coupled with a feckless colonization policy scarcely improved the situation, and World War I, which introduced German influence, created more friction points.

In the main, these existed in the West, or Jibala area, ruled by the powerful chieftain Ahmed er Raisuli, and in the East, or Rif area, ruled by Abd-el-Krim. Theoretically subordinate to the sultan's deputy at Tetuan, the khalifa, these rulers in practice all but ignored him, nor did they prove willing onlookers to Spanish invasion. Not that they ruled supreme: internecine tribal wars in the respective enclaves as well as traditional enmity between Jibilans and Rifians sharply circumscribed their powers. Nonetheless, they remained important forces, to be reckoned with by the wise, ignored by the foolish.

To bring peaceful unity to northern Morocco would have taxed the talents of ten Lyauteys. Spain lacked even one such. In 1919, Major General Dámaso Berenguer assumed the post of high commissioner, with headquarters in Ceuta. Berenguer came from an army family. A heavy man—some said fat—with a pleasant if brooding face, a sensitive mouth hidden by pointed mustachios, Berenguer, at forty-six years, was a man of considerable experience in Morocco, where he had campaigned for years and in the process had organized and trained a native constabulary: a paramilitary organization called the Regulares. He knew and admired Lyautey and tried to emulate his colonial policy:

. . . he was convinced that the most prudent course lay in presenting a peaceful show of force. He neither expected nor wished to use this power against the Moroccans in the fashion of a conqueror. He did expect to establish an indigenous administration in Spanish Morocco and to achieve

1. Woolman, op. cit.; see also L. Bertrand and C. Petrie, *The History of Spain* (London: Eyre & Spottiswoode, 1934).

Spain's ends through it. Berenguer viewed the pacific occupation of the Spanish Protectorate as a political rather than a military problem.[2]

In attempting to carry out a sane policy, Berenguer faced innumerable disadvantages. The state of his army was dreadful. Most officers were venal martinets, the obese generals often unable to read a map.[3] Factionalism riddled junior-officer and non-commissioned-officer ranks; many units supported *juntas de defensa,* or military defense councils, which very nearly approached seditious intent. The troops were ill-trained, generally illiterate, peasants. Most of their pay was siphoned off by superiors. Badly disciplined, they lacked equipment, proper arms, essential services, even good food. Replacements and supply arrived in irregular driblets from the mainland. The war ministry, in Madrid, sent vacillating, often contradictory, orders, and both civil and military appointments frequently went to King Alfonso's favorites.

One of these, a contemporary of Berenguer, became his military commander, at Melilla, in the Northeast. Manuel Silvestre was a fire-eating colonel, a dashing cavalry officer whose body was said to hold the marks and scars of sixty wounds.[4] Silvestre's adjutant, on one occasion, stated command policy: ". . . The only way to succeed in Morocco is to cut the heads off of all the Moors."[5] Despite Silvestre's brutal and bellicose attitude, his troops were no better trained than Berenguer's, in the West.

To repair some of these military deficiencies, Madrid authorities organized an entirely new command, the Tercio, or Spanish version of the French Foreign Legion. Command went to Major José Millán Astray, a forty-year-old combat tiger whose claws dipped to necrophilia: ". . . Death in combat is the greatest honor," he wrote. "One dies only once. Death arrives without pain, and is not so terrible as it seems. The most horrible thing is to live as a coward." Known in Spanish history as the "glorious mutilated one," Millán Astray left an eye, an arm, and a leg in Morocco.[6]

One of Astray's commanders left a different sort of personal imprint. This was a young major, also holding a formidable combat record in Morocco: Francisco Franco-Bahamonde, twenty-eight years old in 1920, when the Tercio appeared, a little man, five feet three inches tall, un-

2. Woolman, op. cit.

3. A. Barea, *The Track* (London: Faber & Faber, 1943). Tr. Ilsa Barea; see also Rupert Furneaux, *Abdel Krim—Emir of the Rif* (London: Secker & Warburg, 1967). Barea, who served as an engineer corporal, was undoubtedly prejudiced against the regular army, but his criticism in general is variously confirmed in other contemporary accounts and by later, serious commentators. Furneaux noted, for example, ". . . in 1920 the [Spanish] army's strength stood at 100,000 men and 12,000 officers, a disproportionate number whose ranks were headed by 690 generals and 2,000 colonels."

4. Furneaux, op. cit.

5. Woolman, op. cit.

6. Ibid.

interested in women or drink—". . . a first-class organizer, a harsh disciplinarian, and a fearless fighter." He once declared vigorously in his high-pitched voice: "I don't want medals. I want promotion."[7]

The Tercio was still forming in 1920, when Berenguer commenced military operations designed to extend Spanish hegemony into the hinterland of Morocco. His plan was simple: a western force, in all some forty-five thousand troops based on Ceuta, to march some fifty miles south to occupy the town of Chaouen in order to splinter Jibilan power; Silvestre's eastern force, of perhaps twenty-five thousand, based on Melilla, to march west to Alhucemas Bay in order to split the Rifian movement.

Berenguer's column moved out in September 1920. Before the expedition reached Chaouen, one General Girona, disguised as a charcoal burner, entered the citadel and persuaded the chiefs by threat and bribery to surrender. Two circumstances marred this neat piece of work: a surprise attack by local tribesmen, countered only with considerable casualties; and the execrable behavior of Spanish troops, the officers (by bringing in their own whores) vying with the men (who defiled mosques and otherwise insulted locals). Still, Berenguer had achieved his primary mission—a new base to support operations that in time would lead to Raisuli's capture. Neither he nor his staff seemed unduly concerned about a line of communications stretching some fifty miles over difficult terrain occupied by generally hostile tribes.

Silvestre's march west from Melilla also proceeded quite smoothly. Ignoring Berenguer's injunction of caution, the fiery Silvestre moved rapidly through country made more barren by a series of poor harvests. Spanish columns dealt quickly and ruthlessly with any opposition, burning houses and crops, collecting whatever cattle they could find—altogether a punitive display that quickly alienated the local populace.

By spring of 1921, Silvestre's vanguard stood on Sidi Driss, not far from its objective of Alhucemas Bay, to the west. His army already had advanced about eighty miles west of Melilla, its front extending south some thirty-five miles to Zoco el Telata, smack in the Rif hinterland. To consolidate this impressive advance, Silvestre depended on ". . . 144 outposts, blockhouses, and small forts,"[8] many of them isolated and weakly defended.

To garrison nearly a hundred fifty outposts including larger forts that required eight hundred or more soldiers, Silvestre spread his army of about twenty thousand Spanish and five thousand Moroccan Regulares rather thinly across the face of conquest, a minor blemish but one compounded by poor morale, lack of combat readiness, and by tenuous supply lines between relatively isolated posts. The relative ease of the advance had powdered over these imperfections, which Silvestre, in his

7. Ibid.
8. Ibid.; see also Usborne, op. cit.

ardent desire to kiss victory, chose to ignore. Not only did he plan to push onto Alhucemas Bay but, according to an intimate, he relished the thought of battle: ". . . We need a victory so overwhelming that it will convince the Moors that they cannot afford the price of resistance to Spanish domination."[9]

Unknown to Silvestre, a coterie of spies were keenly observing the progress of his columns and the state of his local defenses, their reports (often delivered verbally, since illiteracy ruled) going to a twain of remarkable nationalists, the brothers Abd-el-Krim.

Mohamed and Mhamed Abd-el-Krim were the sons of a Rifian nobleman, a judge (some say schoolteacher) both anti-Spanish and anti-French, a not unnatural attitude for an educated Moroccan, and one undoubtedly accentuated by German propaganda during World War I. The elder Abd-el-Krim gave each of his sons a university education that resulted in a successful career in journalism for Mohamed and graduate study in engineering for Mhamed, ten years younger.

As a journalist in Melilla, Mohamed grew increasingly disillusioned with Spanish colonial policy, particularly its blatant intent to exploit Morocco's mineral wealth. Imprisoned by the Spanish in 1917, he escaped and returned to journalism, but in 1919 threw over his job, joined his father in the mountains ringing Ajdir, and summoned Mhamed from Madrid. In 1920, his father was poisoned to death in a tribal feud. But, by this time, the three had decided to raise a rebellion designed to oust the Spanish and create a Moroccan or at least a Rifian state, and now the surviving brothers turned to this task.

Neither brother was particularly imposing. Mohamed, traditionally known as Abd-el-Krim, at thirty-nine years of age was what London tailors describe as S&P—short and portly. Mhamed was taller and slimmer. Both were dark and both wore the standard Rifian dress, a dark-brown homespun wool *jellaba* with loose-fitting sleeves and a cowl, bagged trousers, grass sandals, and white cotton turban.

Abd-el-Krim affected a black beard and sweeping mustache. Small dark eyes flicked from an otherwise benign face to suggest a contradictory character: Abd-el-Krim would lovingly pat children on the head; but he would also stand by approvingly while Rifian guerrillas slit a Spanish officer's throat. Denied a hereditary charisma such as that bestowed, for example, on Attila, Shamyl, or Feisal, Abd-el-Krim seems to have relied on superior education and knowledge of Spanish ways to impress various tribal chiefs. In no way ostentatious, he used remoteness to impress the ordinary native, who in time willingly proffered him demigod

9. Ibid.

status.[10] Mhamed cheerfully played a subordinate (but key) role and remained not only loyal but of enormous help to his older brother.

The brothers needed all such strength to accomplish their self-appointed task. The territory called the Rif, an area about the size of Massachusetts, contained eighteen major tribes, divided and subdivided into several dozen, a bewildering complex whose jealous chieftains, some of whom covertly dealt with the Spanish, had to be alternately threatened and cosseted for support. In the formative days, money and arms constituted perennial problems. Building a regular army was out of the question. Instead, the tribes slowly accumulated rifles and bullets, either by barter from Spanish soldiers (such was the demoralized state of the Spanish army) or smuggled in from Algeria or French Morocco. This painstaking effort finally resulted in several thousand armed men, but these were greatly dispersed. According to one authority, Abd-el-Krim's original cadre, or *harka,* numbered only 125 men, but this number quickly increased.[11]

Until the spring of 1921, Silvestre heard only rumors of this guerrilla force. His attitude is best judged by his response at that time to Abd-el-Krim's warning for him to remain east of the Amerkan River. Silvestre told a friend: ". . . This man Abd el Krim is crazy. I'm not going to take seriously the threats of a little Berber *Caid* whom I had at my mercy a short while ago. His insolence merits a new punishment."[12] To Berenguer's word of caution, Silvestre replied, "I shall drink tea in Abd el Krim's house at Ajdir whether he wills it or not."[13]

In May 1921, Silvestre pushed a detachment across the Amerkan with orders to establish an outpost on the hill of Abarran. But now native auxiliaries, the Regulares, mutinied, and, together with local tribesmen, fell on the Spanish force, killing 179 out of 250. Other Rifian guerrillas attacked the Spanish base at Sidi Driss, inflicted about a hundred casualties, and disappeared.

These opening strikes caused fierce argument between Silvestre and the high commissioner, Berenguer, who wanted his military commander to backtrack. Silvestre instead continued to expand by building a new

10. Vincent Sheean, *Personal History* (New York: Doubleday, Doran, 1936). At great personal risk, Sheean, an American newspaper correspondent, twice visited Rif country. On the first occasion, he was impressed by a group of tribal chiefs who ". . . spoke of the glory of Abd el-Krim, the splendor of his victories over the Spaniards, the certainty with which those who fought for Abd el-Krim would go to heaven and all others to hell. . . ." On the second occasion, when the Rifian bloom of victory was wearing off, Sheean wrote in his notebook of Abd-el-Krim: ". . . his courage is magnificent. His ideas have not changed, have even been reinforced by the present danger. From what I saw of him today I knew that I had no idea of him before. He has a grandeur, added to by the circumstances of horror and great danger. But in spite of this he is humorous, funny. . . ."

11. Furneaux, op. cit.
12. Woolman, op. cit.
13. Furneaux, op. cit.

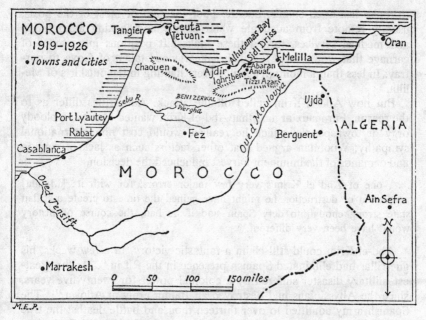

MOROCCO
1919-1926
• Towns and Cities

Tangier Ceuta Tetuan Alhucemas Bay Sidi Driss Oran

Chaouen Ajdir Ighriben Abaran Anual Melilla Tizzi Azan

Port Lyautey sebu R. BENI ZERWAL Wergha Ujda

Rabat Fez Berguent ALGERIA

Casablanca Oued Tensift M O R O C C O

Oued Moulouya

Ain Sefra

• Marrakesh

0   50   100   150 miles

N

M.E.P.

outpost three miles south of a small fort at Anual. When the enemy failed to contest this work, Berenguer's immediate panic subsided; a leading Madrid paper quoted him ". . . as saying that the Spanish people could be sure that the work of pacification in Morocco was proceeding successfully, with only isolated losses, and that therefore no new troops would be needed."[14]

Shortly after this comforting statement appeared, Abd-el-Krim's guerrillas struck again, this time an attack in force against the new outpost at Ighriben followed by attacks two days later against Anual. Ighriben quickly fell, as much from a water shortage as enemy fire. An alarmed Silvestre meanwhile hurried to the Anual base. Several factors, including an ammunition shortage, caused him to order a retreat on the following day. With this, all discipline vanished, the retreat becoming a rout with few survivors. Hatred of the past caused shame of the present: guerrillas fell on small groups of Spanish soldiers, jabbed and slashed bodies with knives and bayonets, gouged out eyes, cut off genitals and jammed them in the victim's mouth, ran stakes through helpless bodies. Silvestre disappeared, presumably tortured and killed.

The initial victories brought whole tribes to the Rifian banner. Guerrillas continued to strike luckless garrisons, sending survivors panic-stricken to Melilla. Here and there, senior officers corralled these hordes

14. Woolman, op. cit.

to make last-ditch stands, but the poor location of most of the posts, usually remote from adequate water supply and lacking ammunition and medical services, turned these makeshift positions into scenes of carnage that would have taxed the experienced talent of Goya to portray. In less than a month, guerrillas were fighting in the outskirts of Melilla.

But now Abd-el-Krim called off the attack. Authorities differ as to the reason. Furneaux argued that Abd-el-Krim wanted to avoid a bloody orgy of townspeople, which he realized would cost him international sympathy; Woolman argued that other factors such as lack of cannon and demands of the imminent harvest influenced the decision,

. . . one of Abd el Krim's very few major errors, for with its [Melilla] possession or destruction he might have gained the time to create a Rifian state strong enough to defy Spain—and if he had, the course of history would have been very different.[15]

Abd-el-Krim could still claim a fantastic victory. In a few weeks, his guerrillas had eliminated Spanish presence in the Rif in ". . . the greatest military disaster suffered by a colonial power for twenty-five years, since the Abyssinians had destroyed an Italian army at Adowa."[16] The Spanish army admitted to over thirteen thousand battle deaths; the true figure probably approached nineteen thousand. The Spanish lost nineteen thousand rifles, several hundred machine guns and cannon, and over one thousand prisoners who were later ransomed for fat prices.[17]

Berenguer reacted by recalling his own expeditionary force and sending massive reinforcements to Melilla, an effort spearheaded by the recently formed Tercio. Though badly shaken, the Spanish Government sent Berenguer new troop levies, reinforced with armored cars and airplanes. By 1922, the high commissioner disposed of some 150,000 troops, but as Woolman has pointed out, Spanish policy perforce had changed ". . . from one of outright conquest to the far less ambitious one of limited occupation and political control through bribery of certain caids and chiefs."[18]

Increased numbers allowed Berenguer to occupy major towns and, in the West, to encircle once again the wily Raisuli. Berenguer's successor, General Ricardo Burguete, who took over in mid-1922, chose to make a deal with this powerful leader, in effect buying his "retirement" (at a monthly subsidy of twelve thousand dollars) in order to free troops from the Jibala area.

In the East, the Army reoccupied much of the territory evacuated

15. Ibid.
16. Furneaux, op. cit.
17. Ibid.: Abd-el-Krim used the ransom money to buy more arms.
18. Woolman, op. cit.

after the Anual disaster, but as they moved into mountain country, progress slowed and then stopped. Spanish troop reinforcements proved virtually useless in fighting guerrillas, which left the lion's share to the Tercio and Regulares, both outfits suffering a high proportion of casualties. Moreover, the Rifians were growing sophisticated. In March 1922, one group used a captured cannon to sink a Spanish warship in Alhucemas Bay; another band attacked and destroyed a force of armored cars. When, later in the year, Burguete pushed forward to Tizzi Azar as a preliminary move to an all-out-offensive, Abd-el-Krim's guerrillas fell on the outpost, a bloody action costing the Spanish about two thousand casualties and decisively ending their offensive plans.

Instead, Burguete decided on a blockade punctuated by naval bombardment. This punitive action failed, because villagers moved inland, nor did the blockade prevent money and arms reaching guerrillas from Tangier—Vincent Sheean has described the relative ease of traveling back and forth either by sea or land.[19]

This series of military failures widened the internal political rift that had long been developing in Spain between Africanistas, who demanded Spanish conquest of Morocco, and Abandonistas, an increasingly powerful group which wanted total withdrawal from the colony. The Abandonistas now won an important round by forcing Burguete's recall in favor of a civilian high commissioner. Unfortunately, neither this man nor another civilian successor could solve the "Moroccan question."

Spanish ineptitude and dissension contributed to the growth of Abd-el-Krim's ambitions. Early in 1923, he took the title of emir, or prince, of the Rif, and in June attacked the key position of Tizzi Azar—again held by the enemy—a failure that cost him heavy casualties and, incidentally, led to Franco's taking command of the Tercio.

The ensuing stalemate brought the Rifian Government to the conference table, in the bowels of a Spanish ship off the coast of Morocco. Since Abd-el-Krim wanted total Spanish withdrawal, and since the Spanish offered ". . . a kind of independence—economic and administrative —to the Rifian tribes," the talks came to nought.[20] Instead, the Spanish began to fortify the "Silvestre Line" in depth. Abd-el-Krim responded, in late August, by attacking a Spanish convoy, another costly tactical failure.

This seesaw state of affairs was working in Abd-el-Krim's favor. The war, which was costing Spain some £20 million a year, was causing virtual anarchy on the mainland, where, at Barcelona, a regiment des-

19. Sheean, op. cit.

20. Woolman (op. cit.) has offered an interesting sidelight on the Spanish attitude. The Spanish called Abd-el-Krim's delegate, Mohamed Azerkan, "Punto," because "as a boy he had cadged 'puntos'—cigarette butts—from the Spanish officers."

tined for Morocco mutinied in protest. And now, in late summer of 1923, Primo de Rivera, an army general and politician of extensive experience at home and abroad, brought off a bloodless coup and established himself as dictator of Spain.

A large man of keen wit and robust physical appetites—he was to die in Paris, ". . . his last hours divided between brothel and confessional,"[21]—Primo de Rivera at fifty-three years held a charismatic appeal that made him many things to many people. Reputedly an Abandonista regarding Morocco, he had been brought to power by a group of royalist generals. Soon after taking over, he announced withdrawal plans, which caused Marshal Lyautey, nervously looking on from French Morocco, to exclaim: "My God! An army retreats when it must but it does not announce the fact to the enemy in advance."[22]

Once installed, however, Rivera fell under army influence:

. . . his military policy changed from one of outright disengagement in Morocco to one of aggression. . . . The new dictator promised "a quick, dignified, and sensible" solution to the Moroccan problem.[23]

Hollow words, these: Raisuli, in the Jibala, was becoming increasingly demanding in his "retirement," while, in the East, Abd-el-Krim continued to ride a wave of local and international popularity. As underdog biting the heel of Spanish colonialism, he attracted worldwide sympathy, particularly from nationalist leaders in other colonial countries, but also from French Communists; he probably received financial aid from British and German mining interests as well.

His power easily allowed him to retain initiative in the Rif and to extend operations into Jibala territory, his brother Mhamed being increasingly active in this area. But the Spanish also helped him win new tribes by an inane policy of bombing villages populated mostly by women and children.[24] To the Spanish claim that airmen dropped preliminary warning leaflets in Arabic and Thamazighth, Woolman has evidenced the telling point that most tribesmen were illiterate!

So successful was the guerrilla action, that Abd-el-Krim continued attacking throughout the summer, his total impact such that several Spanish outposts owned no more than the ground enclosed by wire. The entire picture so distressed Rivera, that after an inspection tour in 1924 he declared, ". . . Spain cannot continue to maintain her soldiers on

21. Hugh Thomas, *The Spanish Civil War* (London: Eyre & Spottiswoode, 1961).

22. Furneaux, op. cit.

23. Woolman, op. cit.

24. Furneaux, op. cit.

isolated crags."[25] Coming full circle in thought, he announced withdrawal to a fortified line, telling an American correspondent:

. . . Abd el Krim has defeated us. He has the immense advantages of the terrain and a fanatical following. Our troops are sick of war, and they have been for years. They don't see why they should fight and die for a strip of worthless territory. I am withdrawing to this line, and will hold only the tip of this territory. I personally am in favor of withdrawing entirely from Africa and letting Abd el Krim have it. We have spent untold millions of pesetas in this enterprise, and never made a *céntimo* from it. We have had tens of thousands of men killed for territory which is not worth having. But we cannot entirely withdraw, because England will not let us. . . . England fears that if we withdraw, the territory will be taken by France. . . . They don't want a strong power like France here![26]

Contrary to the Spanish dictator's belief, England presented less of an obstacle to withdrawal than his own army, particularly fanatic Africanistas spearheaded by the Tercio. Only when Franco threatened to resign command of the foreign legion did Rivera modify his plans: a compromise that in the West placed the one-hundred-thousand-man army behind a fortified "Primo Line," the idea being to strengthen and reorganize units into a new striking force. Grudgingly accepted by the army, various withdrawals of outer posts began in September and were carried out under almost constant harassment by guerrillas. This effort culminated in evacuation of the important base of Chaouen, a forty-mile anabasis beginning in November and ending a month later at Tetuan, *the Rifians having pursued the rear guard, Franco's Tercio, to the city gates.* Rifian casualties were never published. Spanish dead numbered an estimated eight hundred officers and seventeen thousand men—some authorities say more.[27] The words of a Spanish officer survivor form a fitting epitaph: ". . . We made war against shadows, and we lost thirty men to their one!"[28]

For the time being, the Spanish army in the West was safe behind the "Primo Line": ". . . a series of typical blockhouses about a quarter of a mile apart, each built on dominating ground wherever possible and equipped with strong searchlights. The spaces between the blockhouses, particularly around Tangier, were usually mined."[29] All this did not much impress the American correspondent Vincent Sheean: After a lengthy stay with rebel hosts, he was ushered quite easily through the line at night.

25. Ibid.
26. Woolman, op. cit.
27. Furneaux, op. cit.
28. Woolman, op. cit.
29. Ibid.

Chapter 29

*Abd-el-Krim and the great powers • French intervention •
Rebel strength • The Rif offensive • Escalation • Abd-el-Krim's
fall • Spain's "victory" • The spread of colonial uprisings • The
Royal Air Force and pacification • Air Control versus Ground
Control • Air Control analyzed*

ABD-EL-KRIM'S PRIMARY PROBLEM was not the Spanish
army but, rather, European powers that did not want an independent
Moroccan state. His several overtures to the British to help him remove
the Spanish presence were brushed aside; the British, after all, governed an enormous colonial empire and frowned on any trend toward
self-government. Spain would not acquiesce, not only because Primo
de Rivera was staking his political reputation on favorable settlement
of the Moroccan question, but also because the government thought
that Spain's international prestige rested on a favorable settlement.

Far more important, however, was the attitude of France, to whom
the thought of an independent Moroccan state was particularly abhorrent. France had been having her own troubles with rebellious tribes in
French Morocco: ". . . It was Lyautey's belief that tribes which had
once enjoyed French rule desired no other, but events in the north had

already shaken this theory. . . ."[1] Even in 1924, France did not wish to test her strength in the rest of Morocco and in Tunis and Algeria. An independent Moroccan state would automatically void the sultan's overall authority—and that, in colonial administrative minds, would begin the end. Or, as Marshal Lyautey put it: ". . . A maggot-breeding spot in the Rif would be a grave threat to civilization and the peace of the West."[2]

Thus a political paradox emerged: Although Abd-el-Krim remained respectful of French military power and did not wish to antagonize France, his success in the North automatically brought him into conflict with his powerful colonial neighbor. When his expansion sloshed over into French Morocco, the French began to build a *casus belli*.

Already in 1924, Lyautey had crossed the Wergha River and created a northern front under the able General Chambrun, a line of intersupporting posts, backed by aircraft, that constituted a direct challenge to Rifian control of the disputed area. If Lyautey displayed some concern over the strength of the "Wergha Line," higher echelons refused to accept his pessimism, even denying his request for additional troops.[3] The French Minister of Foreign Affairs, Aristide Briand, expressed comfortable arrogance to an American correspondent:

. . . You have seen the great Abd el Krim. These native chiefs . . . we know them well. They are really simple fellows. Properly handled, they respond to kindness. There is, of course, not the slightest chance that this one will ever attack us.[4]

Lack of military strength formed Abd-el-Krim's second major problem. His army was strong enough to contain the Spanish in two coastal enclaves, but not to drive them out of Spanish Morocco and certainly not to fight the French at the same time. He would never command a stronger army than that of 1925, but, out of a total force estimated variously at 80–120,000, he commanded perhaps a maximum 10,000 riflemen augmented by a pathetically small artillery unit of some 350 gunners. Although his combat areas featured strategically located supply dumps and were connected by a primitive telephone system, the work of a German renegade, his army remained primitive in the extreme.[5]

Neither did his political organization represent any great achievement. Despite a political "cabinet" of mostly young and keen revolutionaries, Abd-el-Krim remained a dictator whose respect for republican institu-

---

1. Usborne, op. cit.
2. Woolman, op. cit.
3. Usborne, op. cit.
4. Woolman, op. cit.
5. Ibid.; see also Usborne, op. cit. The German was Joseph Klems, one of the few European mercenaries employed by Abd-el-Krim. Klems supposedly inspired Sigmund Romberg's operetta "The Desert Song."

tions he claimed to admire diminished as his responsibilities increased. His command of the diverse northern tribes was never too secure, and it is problematical that he ever could have forged the cohesive state he talked about—any more than Feisal could have melded Syrian tribes into a viable political entity in 1918. Abd-el-Krim's widespread but relatively fragile political base probably explained his aversion to settlement with Spain on a partial-protectorate basis as opposed to his demand for total Spanish withdrawal.

His conflict with France centered on control of a border tribe, the Beni Zerwal. When this tribe opted for war against France, the Rifians were forced to a decision. Woolman marks this in the early months of 1925:

. . . Provoked by French depredations, worried about his food supply, goaded by questions of honor and prestige, and lured on by his own over-confident advisers, Abd el Krim was drawn into the fatal decision to attack the French. . . . Fear and desperation must have been the deciding factors.[6]

The rebels attacked in April, their goal the major French base at Fez. Its capture, they believed, would force France to a reasonable settlement in the North. Abd-el-Krim's brother, Mhamed, commanded the operation, which involved an estimated four thousand tribesmen, with another four thousand in reserve. The dispersed attacks caught the French by surprise. Rebel units tore through Chambrun's careful defenses and, in a few days, advanced to a line some twenty miles north of Fez.

Supported by border tribes the French had expected to remain loyal, the rebels within a month wiped out northern French garrisons. Many fought literally to the last man:

. . . By the end of June, the Rifians had taken forty-three of sixty-six French posts. They had captured an estimated 51 cannon, 200 machine guns, 5,000 rifles, millions of cartridges, 16,000 shells for cannon, 60,000 grenades, and 35 mortars with 10,000 shells. They had carried off at least seventy Frenchmen and 2,000 mercenaries as prisoners, and no one cared to report publicly how many French troops had been killed and wounded.[7]

On the surface, this represented a fantastic victory. In reality, it amounted to a painful sting, though of sufficient dimensions to bring a

6. Woolman, op. cit.; see also Furneaux, op. cit., who has pointed out that Abd-el-Krim attained unity ". . . by the employment of the powerful shame compulsion, the *aar*," which caused tribes to forgo feuds in favor of a common cause. The protective alliance, or *liff*, spread throughout the Rif and finally to the southern tribes, whose call for help against the French could not be ignored—thus, Furneaux has implied, Abd-el-Krim was hoist with his own political petard.

7. Woolman, op. cit.; see also Usborne, op. cit. Each source provides excellent details of the fighting.

combined Franco-Spanish peace offer. In July, these powers offered a guarantee of Rifian autonomy, but refused to create a Rifian state. Abd-el-Krim turned them down.

He probably erred. Lack of army organization and supply difficulties, not to mention tenacious resistance of the enemy, already were robbing him of momentum. He suffered a political setback from refusal of important tribes north of Fez to come over to him. And now French strength began to tell. In July, the government relieved Lyautey as military commander in favor of the able General Naulin. Marshal Pétain, the hero of World War I, inspected the entire front, his report causing Paris to dispatch one hundred thousand more troops. Meanwhile, French military commanders conferred with Spanish opposites to come up with a combined quasi-pincer operation: the French to drive north into the Rif, the Spanish to pull off a large-scale amphibious landing at Alhucemas Bay and drive in to Abd-el-Krim's headquarters at Ajdir.

The Spanish landing began on September 7. The following day, the first assault waves, men of the Tercio under Franco, set up a beachhead rapidly expanded to eight thousand troops including artillery, a force soon raised to twelve thousand. Despite Spanish air bombing and strafing, artillery fire and use of poison gas, the Rifians continued to resist the Spanish advance practically yard by yard. Rifian determination, coupled with rugged terrain, held the Spanish to small gains—an average four hundred yards per day at heavy cost in lives, but nonetheless the invaders pushed through to Ajdir, the Rifians retiring south. Farther east, another Spanish force pushed inland and, in October, joined a French column coming from the south.

Although the campaigns cost the Spanish and French heavily, by November French numbers had risen to over 300,000, Spanish numbers to 140,000 with reinforcements constantly arriving. The Rifians also had suffered heavy casualties—losses compounded by poor harvests and large areas of scorched earth. Typhus now scourged the sad, hungry tribes. Desultory winter operations further weakened Abd-el-Krim's army, for if guerrilla bands struck successfully here and there, he could not prevent the Franco-Spanish build-up from continuing, nor could he alleviate constantly increasing tribulations of the diverse tribes. Wanting also to take advantage of favorable public opinion in France and Spain (and other Western nations) to his cause, he bowed to the inevitable and asked for peace talks. Grudgingly the Spanish and French governments agreed to a conference at Ujda in April.

Abd-el-Krim's hopes for a reasonable peace were almost immediately dashed by increased European arrogance, not unnaturally, since the powers were negotiating from a military strength of about forty to one. While talks dragged on, French and Spanish army commanders shuffled troops for a final offensive. When the talks dragged to a halt in early May, the temporary allies struck, their armies within the month overrunning most organized resistance in the central Rif. In late May 1926, Abd-el-Krim surrendered to the French. To the fury of the Spanish, they exiled him to the island of Réunion, in the Indian Ocean, giving him a comfortable estate and a generous annual subsidy—altogether a fortunate end, since capture by the Spanish undoubtedly would have meant execution.

Abd-el-Krim's exile did not end the campaign, which continued into 1927, with sporadic resistance up to 1934. But these were relatively minor actions, and Spain, by the end of 1926, could claim "victory."

The Spanish army's failure to subdue Abd-el-Krim's rudely armed and loosely organized tribesmen without French help emphasized the impotent state of Spanish arms, just as Primo de Rivera's dictatorship emphasized the puerile state of Spanish politics.

The military struggle in Morocco left Spain exhausted, sick in mind and spirit, a giant, disjointed body increasingly prone to disastrous factionalism and internal strife.

Rivera's attempts to repair political and economic deficiencies proved fruitless. With dissolution of his dictatorship, in January 1930, a power vacuum developed. King Alfonso's failure to fill it led to his self-imposed exile in 1931 and to the ill-fated Second Republic, with its equally ill-fated liberal constitution.

This was part of the price of "victory" in Morocco. It would result in catastrophic civil war in less than five years.

Spain and France were not the only great powers that had to fight guerrilla actions in the years following World War I. Uprisings and rebellions broke out in most colonial areas—even the United States became embroiled with guerrillas in the New World.

In occupying and policing mandated portions of the old Ottoman Empire, the British began to rely on air power. World War I had brought birth of the Royal Air Force (RAF), whose leader, Hugh "Boom" Trenchard, was a man of imagination, force and political shrewdness. Part of Trenchard's postwar task, a large part, was to justify RAF existence, not an easy job in view of innate hostility forcibly expressed (and often demonstrated) by army and navy, and in view of still unproven virtues of the relatively new weapon.[8]

Trenchard used any occasion to demonstrate air power's versatility. Of twenty-five operational squadrons, he based nineteen overseas, where they performed a wide variety of both peace-keeping and house-keeping tasks. In early 1920, he scored a significant success when RAF planes intimidated the Mad Mullah and helped end his rebellion in Somaliland. The RAF's main chance came a few months later, when

8. Andrew Boyle, *Trenchard* (London: Collins, 1962).

a small uprising in Mesopotamia (today's Iraq) caught fire and spread despite suppression efforts by some sixty thousand British troops. (See map, Chapter 20.) Worried by political implications of the widening conflict, Britain's new Secretary of State for Colonies, Winston Churchill, sought Trenchard's help. The Chief of the Air Staff turned to with a will: Once again, the bomber worked magical effect against recalcitrant tribes and helped bring peace, though only after British forces had suffered some two thousand casualties and Whitehall had spent about £100 million.[9]

The total experience led Trenchard to argue for a new RAF mission, that of substituting air for ground power in keeping the king's peace in vast Middle Eastern reaches. Trenchard and his fellows contended that, in suitable operational areas, what they called Air Control would prove more effective than Ground Control. One of air power's most effective voices, Marshal of the RAF Sir John Slessor (who was very active as a young flier in those early days and whose arguments gain great strength from an innate charm and intelligence evident to all fortunate enough to know him), later wrote in his excellent book *The Central Blue:*

. . . The Ground Method is that traditionally employed by the Army for many years, and was indeed the only one in the days before the aeroplane. It involves invasion by a column on the ground, sometimes permanent but more often temporary, of his territory. There was an increasing tendency as time went on for the Air Force to be the spearhead or striking force, followed up by the Army as the occupying force; but the method was unaffected and remained that of invasion, the crushing of resistance by the enemy's fighting men, followed by occupation. The trouble was that the areas of undeveloped tribal territory within the Empire or on the fringes of British-administered territory were in those days so vast that occupation could not be complete. So the Ground Method really boiled down to one of temporary and partial occupation, with the establishment of garrisons at suitable places whence more or less mobile columns could be despatched into the tribal areas when necessity arose.

The job of these columns was to occupy temporarily the country of the offending tribe; if possible to inflict a sharp lesson in the form of casualties to their fighting men; to exact the necessary retribution in the form of fines or rifles surrendered or by destroying property or crops, and then withdraw. It was fatal to leave small detachments of troops unsupported in potentially hostile territory—for instance the overrunning of the little garrison of Rumaitha in the Iraq rebellion of 1919 increased the number of insurgents against us from 85,000 to over 130,000 in one night. That meant that even when we had garrisons right in the heart of tribal territory they had to live in one central strongly fortified cantonment—as at Razmak. When there was some tribal affair which had to be dealt with then, having dealt with it, the column

9. Sir John Slessor, *The Central Blue* (London: Cassell, 1956).

still had to withdraw behind the wire into cantonments. It was always the Air Staff contention that this method, known unkindly by its critics as "Burn and Scuttle" or "Butcher and Bolt" was very expensive and did not in fact achieve the object of maintaining order in these remote and inhospitable lands.[10]

Trenchard and his staff argued that air power by its mobility and fire potential could not only reach remote tribal areas immediately but that it could coerce far more humanely and at much less cost than ground power, though control of more developed areas such as Palestine would require ground operations.

Their general idea was to conduct gunboat diplomacy from the air. Trenchard believed that ". . . the mere presence of an apparently all-seeing, all-powerful mobile force, however small, would encourage the lawless to settle down and learn civilized ways."[11] Where tribes refused, they would be warned and, if failing to come to heel, they would be punished—their villages bombed and herds dispersed—until they changed their minds. By reacting selectively to tribal disturbances, Air Control would reduce the expense and unfavorable publicity attendant upon raising a punitive ground expedition. Slessor saw it as a sort of "inverted blockade" that kept the enemy from his country in order to win his submission without inflicting human casualties and with minimum material damage. In the words of the old RAF manual, it was to interrupt ". . . the normal life of the enemy people to such an extent that a continuance of hostilities becomes intolerable."[12]

These arguments greatly impressed Winston Churchill. Mesopotamia's fragile peace depended in part on Emir Feisal, who became king in late 1921. Wanting to prop up a weak throne at minimum expense, Churchill embraced the concept of Air Control (as, curiously considering his later writings, did Lawrence of Arabia, who was serving briefly as his adviser). Trenchard's plan, vigorously and successfully advocated by Churchill at the Cairo Conference in 1921, called for ". . . eight R.A.F. squadrons, a supply of armored cars, auxiliary services, several armored trains, an air ambulance unit and a few gunboats. . . . The main policing duties would devolve on Arab levies trained and led by British officers."[13] Essential to the plan was a resident commissioner and a group of civil political officers stationed in outlying areas.

Air Control did not immediately leave the ground. The army did its best to sabotage the operation—when Sir Henry Wilson refused to furnish troops, Trenchard organized his own ground forces, including

10. Ibid.
11. Boyle, op. cit.
12. Slessor, op. cit.
13. Boyle, op. cit.

armored-car units. The effort encountered other delays and some operational difficulties, not to mention an early misunderstanding as to punishment.

Shortly after operations had commenced, Trenchard instructed his Middle East commander, Geoffrey Salmond:

. . . The air force is a preventative against risings more than a means of putting them down. Concentration is the first essential. Continuous demonstration is the second essential. And when punishment is intended, the punishment must be severe, continuous and even prolonged.

Trenchard insisted on numerous humane precautions, including leaflet warnings at least twenty-four hours before a raid. His biographer concluded that often a "demonstration" flight was enough to quell an uprising.[14]

One of Trenchard's and Churchill's principal arguments centered on RAF ability to mete out selective punishment. Trenchard's attitude was clear in an early letter written to a squadron commander in India who complained ". . . about the hazards of operational flying against turbulent tribesmen in the Himalayan foothills":

. . . You state that it is impossible to see snipers. Nobody ever expected to see them and I should have thought this idea of looking for them ought to have been long since dead in India. . . . I admit all the hardships the pilots undergo . . . but I do feel so much . . . that the load must be borne without speaking about it. . . . Indiscriminate bombing should never be allowed. Surely this was dead five years ago.[15]

What the commander wants and what he gets are often different. Early in the Air Control experiment, some young political officers, wanting to make ". . . a special example . . . of an exceptionally unruly tribe," brought down winged wrath to the extent that the RAF report read:

. . . The eight machines . . . broke formation and attacked at different points of the encampment simultaneously, causing a stampede among the animals. The tribesmen and their families were put to confusion, many of whom ran into the lake, making good targets for the machine-guns.[16]

Air Commodore A. E. Borton, commanding in Baghdad, noted that this gave ". . . a vivid if rather ferocious glimpse of the type of warfare we have to wage."[17]

It was the last type of warfare envisaged by either Trenchard or

14. Ibid.
15. Ibid.
16. Ibid.
17. Ibid.

Churchill, and the report brought a sizzling rocket from the latter to Trenchard:

. . . I am extremely shocked. . . . If it were to be published it would be regarded as most dishonoring to the air force and prejudicial to our work and use of them. To fire wilfully on women and children is a disgraceful act, and I am surprised you do not order the officers responsible for it to be tried by court-martial. . . . By doing such things we put ourselves on the lowest level. Combatants are fair game and sometimes non-combatants get injured through their proximity to fighting troops, but this seems to be quite a different matter.[18]

This early aberration aside, subsequent results more than pleased most concerned persons. As Lawrence of Arabia had argued at the Cairo Conference, the new arms' deterrent effect generally sufficed to keep the peace. General Haldane, commanding the army in Iraq, was favorably impressed, as was the high commissioner, Sir Percy Cox, ". . . a humane man of pronounced liberal views," Boyle tells us, "zealous in his hatred of undue coercion." The British Government was also pleased: Where eighty battalions initially kept the peace in Mesopotamia and Palestine, three battalions eventually remained in Mesopotamia, a tremendous financial saving.

Other benefits resulted. We must remember that air power was in its infancy—Charles Lindbergh did not fly the Atlantic until 1927. Flying over trackless deserts and daily contact with frontier defense forces and political officers proved invaluable experience to future commanders. More than this, however, the need to patrol desert areas meant charting air routes, a time-consuming and frequently hazardous prelude that was nonetheless essential to British interests in the air age. The day's primitive machines, courageously flown in the most appalling extremes of weather with minimum navigational aids, foretold many future possibilities. The RAF carried mail, passengers, and supply; the planes helped centralize administration and they delivered civil officers to remote areas when necessary; they evacuated sick and wounded; in 1928, they flew over the Hindu Kush (familiar to Alexander the Great twenty-three centuries earlier) to evacuate the beleaguered British colony at Kabul. (See map 1, Chapter 9.)

A cost-conscious British Government judged Air Control operations so successful that it extended the plan to cover the Northwest Frontier of India, Trans-Jordan, the Aden protectorate, and, in a modified form, Palestine.

The concept of Air Control suffered from two major difficulties: it inherited the onus of enforcing a colonial policy that was becoming in-

18. Ibid.

creasingly less acceptable to world (including British) opinion; and it proved of limited application.

More-liberal minds of the period held that the sole justification for British control of Mesopotamia and ancillary territories—indeed, for British and great-power control of *any* area—was to bring more benefit than harm to the peoples concerned. Here as elsewhere in the British Empire, the overlords unquestionably improved the lot of some of these peoples. Introducing law and order of sorts in place of constant raids and small tribal wars was a major contribution, as was introduction in some areas of schools, hospitals and reasonably efficient administration.

This was fine—as far as it went. It could even have been noble, had Britain been prepared to invest time, effort, and money essential to preparing these peoples for eventual self-government. No such intention existed. Rather, it was colonialism on the cheap. All great powers practiced it, America included, as we shall see. It was exploitive in the worst sense—it was maintaining a primitive status quo in order to ease commercial exploitation of natural commodities, in this case primarily oil.

Within this framework, neither Air Control nor Ground Control could serve other than a holding, or deterrent, function. British rule was by force and coercion rather than consent, and when that force found physical expression, either by punitive columns or air-delivered bullets and bombs, it was rule by terror—more-selective terror than employed by ground columns, as Sir John Slessor argues, but nonetheless terror, as anyone knows who has had his house or town or city bombed. The British were ruling, in short, without the consent of the governed, and so long as this was the case, the instrument of rule did not much matter in the end: coercive rule builds and expands antagonisms into forces of rebellion which eventually explode. Like Ground Control before it, Air Control inhibited but did not stop native political ambitions. It helped produce short-term gains for long-term losses.

The second point is the limited application of Air Control. The psychological effect of air power—remember that the natives had never seen an airplane—played a major role in the new concept. When demonstration failed to keep the peace, we have noted that the RAF stepped up pressure by political or diplomatic warning, and if that failed, by overt punishment ". . . severe, continuous and even prolonged." We are told that in practice this meant bombing a village (after due warning) and dispersing a flock—economic pressure, in other words, which usually did the job.

Two observations follow: such pressure could be applied only in compatible environment, preferably desert, and such pressure proved effective only against fragmented tribal society, either nomadic or primitive agrarian. Air Control could not work in more-developed countries, such as Palestine, a limitation readily admitted by Sir John Slessor.

But what Sir John and other proponents failed to consider is the rationale behind the concept of Air Control. Deterrence all too often is a euphemism for blackmail by force. But what if a person or tribe or country refuses to be blackmailed? In the case of the Middle East, what would have happened had deterrence, warning, and physical punishment failed to bring around a tribe? Logically, the RAF would have had to continue punishment until the tribe no longer was capable of resistance. But this contradicts the principle of selective, or "humane," application of punishment, forwarded by air-power proponents, for if bombing one village and dispersing one herd do not work, then presumably punishment must embrace two villages and two herds and so on. This is the genesis of escalation, a subject we shall come to much later in this book. The point is that far from being selective in face of genuine resistance, Air Control would have had to resort to destroying villages and herds and starving people into submission. Carried to its logical conclusion, this is genocide.

Chapter 30

The British army and colonial uprisings • Sir Charles Gwynn's Imperial Policing • The Moplah rebellion • Guerrilla warfare in Santo Domingo • American marine tactics • Guerrilla warfare in Nicaragua • Augusto César Sandino • American marine tactics: ground and air • The American effort analyzed • The Spanish Civil War • Guerrilla aspects • Hemingway and the ideological element • Stalin's attitude • International brigades

BRITISH ARMY LEADERS never accepted the validity of the Air Control concept, in part because it threatened army pre-eminence, in part because application was so limited. Throughout the 1920s and early 1930s, empire forces faced a number of rebellions and small wars, several of which were analyzed in a book published in 1934: *Imperial Policing*, by Major General Sir Charles Gwynn.[1]

An army's police duties, Sir Charles argued, fell into three categories. The first was to fight small wars in order to establish or re-establish civil control (a subject brilliantly treated a half century earlier by another British officer, Charles Callwell—see Chapter 15). The second was to maintain or restore order when normal civil control either does not exist or has temporarily broken down. The third was to assist civil control

1. Sir Charles Gwynn, *Imperial Policing* (New York: St. Martin's Press, 1934). See also Sir Andrew Skeen, *Passing It On—Short Talks on Tribal Fighting on the North-West Frontier of India* (London: Gale & Polden, 1932).

without assuming governmental responsibility. Such was the advanced state of empire that the second task had now replaced the first in importance:

. . . The principal police task of the Army is no longer to prepare the way for civil control, but to restore it when it collapses or shows signs of collapse. Subversive movements take many forms and are of varying intensity; but even when armed rebellion occurs, it presents a very different military problem from that of a deliberate small-war campaign. There is an absence of a definite objective, and conditions are those of guerrilla warfare, in which elusive rebel bands must be hunted down, and protective measures are needed to deprive them of opportunities. The admixture of rebels with a neutral or loyal element of the population adds to the difficulties of the task. Excessive severity may antagonize this element, add to the number of rebels, and leave a lasting feeling of resentment and bitterness. On the other hand, the power and resolution of the Government forces must be displayed. Anything which can be interpreted as weakness encourages those who are sitting on the fence to keep on good terms with the rebels.

The British army was facing three main classes of disorder. One was the revolutionary movement ". . . organized and designed to upset established government." Another was rioting or other lawbreaking ". . . arising from local or widespread grievances." A third was communal disturbances ". . . of a racial, religious or political character not directed against Government, but which Government must suppress."

The first category particularly interested Sir Charles, who presciently observed:

. . . Revolutionary movements, again, may be divided into violent and, professedly, non-violent movements. The former may be on a scale which amounts to fully organized rebellion, necessitating operations in which the Government forces employ all the ordinary methods of warfare. More commonly, however, they imply guerrilla warfare, carried on by armed bands acting possibly under the instructions of a centralized organization, but with little cohesion. Such bands depend for effectiveness on the capacity of individual leaders; they avoid collisions of a decisive character with Government troops. Their aim is to show defiance of Government, to make its machinery unworkable and to prove its impotence; hoping by a process of attrition to wear down its determination. Their actions take the form of sabotage, of ambushes in which they can inflict loss with a minimum of risk, and attacks on small isolated detachments. By terrorizing the loyal or neutral elements of the population, they seek to prove the powerlessness of the Government to give protection, and thus provide for their own security, depriving the Government of sources of information and securing information themselves.

The suppression of such movements, unless nipped in the bud, is a slow business, generally necessitating the employment of numbers out of all proportion to the actual fighting value of the rebels, owing to the unavoidable dispersion of troops and the absence of a definite objective. It becomes a battle of wits in which the development of a well-organized intelligence service, great mobility, rapid means of inter-communication and close cooperation between all sections of the Government forces are essential.

Normal military operations did not suffice to meet these challenges. The military police task differed fundamentally from normal, or orthodox, operations in that it had to achieve its object with *minimum* exercise of force. In carrying out the task, officers

. . . must be guided in most cases by certain general principles rather than by definite orders, and, as a rule, they have to decide what is the minimum force they must employ rather than how they can develop the maximum power at their disposal.

Training for such operations is therefore a difficult task: ". . . To a very large extent the Army must depend on traditional doctrines, on discipline, and on its own common-sense."

Just how difficult the task was, the author made clear in a series of chapter analyses beginning with the Amritsar riots of 1919 (see map 1, Chapter 9), which resulted from Mahatma Gandhi's arrest and which were ineptly controlled due to overreaction on the part of security forces, which killed a great number of people. A more intelligent application of force, however, resulted in satisfactory suppression of an ugly riot situation in Egypt in the same year.

The Moplah rebellion, of 1921, in the Madras District of India, was one of the most instructive from the guerrilla-warfare standpoint. This was a religion-biased uprising; almost immediately, a British army force using orthodox tactics ". . . broke the center of the rebellion" and arrested a principal leader, Ali Musaliar.

This prompt action ". . . eliminated the chief military objective" without ending the rebellion. But now the Madras government and its security forces seemed at a loss. Both civil and military officials interpreted an ensuing lull as rebel weakness. Instead of firm, positive action including rapid trial and sentencing of rebel leaders, authorities adopted a vacillating attitude, the Indian Government forbidding courts-martial of rebels (one result of the Amritsar debacle).

Moplah rebels meanwhile were organizing for further action. They were not well armed, and although they enjoyed protective terrain they lacked outside reinforcement (no Communist element was involved). Their object was to wage guerrilla warfare: not to fight the army, but ". . . rather to prove the impotence of Government" by sabotage and selective terror against Hindus. Incidents soon developed. By October, the situation had deteriorated to the degree that the government was reporting to London,

. . . active war against the British Government is openly being waged by a number of armed bodies . . . [estimated] from 8000 to 10,000 men whose policy is to avoid open encounter and to lie in ambush and snipe at the troops. The Madras Government also state that the Moplahs have spies everywhere, that their information is very much better concerning the movements of our troops than any information obtainable by our troops, and that they attack and plunder the houses of Hindus and maltreat the inmates as they will and are to a great extent masters of the country. . . .

The general commanding Madras District summarized the situation as it developed in October:

. . . The rebel change of tactics from open to guerrilla warfare has developed steadily and increasing signs of more efficient and intelligent handling are apparent. More people become implicated as rebellion continues. New recruits are brought in by terrorization and attraction of loot. . . . Active rebellion is not adopted by every Moplah, but behind the bands ambushing, dacoity and looting is [sic] participated in by remainder as opportunity offers. In the intervals they revert to peaceful life. In the military sense the situation is not out of hand, but tendency will be for bulk of population to become part-time, as opposed to whole-time rebels, for active bands to become smaller, more elusive and numerous and for dacoity to increase. . . .

London responded by sending more troops. At this point, security forces had been operating by patrols based on various village centers, but now more extensive operations began, including at least one massive "drive" that failed. The author noted:

. . . These [new] measures did not, however, by any means bring quick and decisive results; the rebellion was now too well organized and the temper of the rebels at white heat. Some surrenders took place, but on the other hand there were cases in which those that surrendered again took the field. The lot of those who rendered assistance to, or were in sympathy with, the Government became increasingly hard. Still the continuous pressure was bound to have effect in the long run. . . .

By early December, security forces had broken up the larger bands. To run smaller groups to ground now became the task of separate battalions assigned to specific areas. Simultaneously, security forces gradually transferred control to police and civil authorities and phased out altogether at the end of February. The tally was impressive: 2,300 rebels killed, 1,650 wounded, and 5,700 captured. Security forces claimed 39,000 "voluntary surrenders." The number of civil deaths caused by rebel terrorist acts was unknown but high. Troop casualties numbered 137!

In analyzing the action, Sir Charles noted that the original rebellion had evolved into a small war,

. . . that is to say, that the troops were called on to act with the maximum force they could develop under the conditions imposed by the terrain and the methods adopted by the enemy.

There was, however, no strategic objective the capture of which would decisively affect the enemy's operations, and the will of the Government could be imposed on the enemy only by a process of attrition and exhaustion, the result of a continuous unrelenting pressure.

Although in the nature of a small war, it may be noted that it opened with a purely police operation in aid of which a small detachment only of troops was called in. Similarly, it was left to the police to sweep up the last fragments of resistance when the troops had sufficiently restored order to permit the civil power to resume control. The military intervention, although it involved war-like operations, was in essence, therefore, police work on a large scale.

Sir Charles believed that the government's major error lay in limiting military powers under martial law, which hindered security forces in preventing neutrals from helping the rebels. He also pointed to a lan-

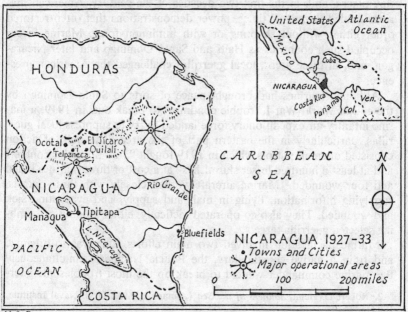

M.E.P.

guage difficulty which made troops dependent on police intelligence. Operations depended primarily on infantry, although on occasion trucks gave extra mobility and armored cars effectively patrolled roads. Artillery played almost no role and air power none. One tactical observation must be quoted, if only because of its similarity to Byzantine writings and to Bohemond's experience in 1098 (see Chapter 5):

. . . It has been noted that punitive columns, more especially in the earlier phases of the rebellion, were always liable to be rushed or sniped on the march, and protective measures had to be adapted to the circumstances and nature of the country. The governing principle was that the column with its protective detachments should cover sufficient ground to prevent the whole column being rushed simultaneously, but each of its components required to be a compact body, in immediate readiness to stand a rush till it received assistance from portions not attacked. Distances between protective detachments and the main body were reduced in the interests of mutual support to the extent consistent with covering a sufficient area, and often did not exceed 100 yards. Compactness and instant readiness were points that admitted no relaxation in the protective bodies.

America meanwhile was involved with guerrilla warfare in attempting to pacify certain Caribbean and Central American countries. Almost perpetual revolution and troublesome banditry plagued most of these tiny places, and, in the first two decades of the century, American marines landed dozens of times, power demonstrations that often restored order either without shooting or with minimum force. Marine forces occupied such countries as Haiti and Santo Domingo and later Nicaragua, and, in these areas, local guerrillas challenged the American presence.

Although marines had brought peace of sorts to Santo Domingo by the end of World War I, trouble continued to break out. In 1919, a marine infantry-air expeditionary force landed to try to suppress local guerrillas, particularly in the eastern part of the area. The bulk of action consisted of small patrols which in 1919 fought ". . . 50 major contacts and at least a hundred lesser skirmishes" at a cost of three marines killed and four wounded.[2] Marine aircraft worked closely with these patrols, supplying information, flying in mail and supply, and evacuating sick and wounded. They also co-operated tactically, either strafing or bombing selected guerrilla targets.

Marine pacification involved two main efforts. One was to organize and train a native constabulary, the Policía Nacional. Simultaneously the marine commander wanted to break up the most troublesome guer-

2. Robert D. Heinl, *Soldiers of the Sea* (Annapolis, Md.: U. S. Naval Institute, 1962).

rilla bands. In the eastern district, the marines employed a device we shall encounter again:

. . . After blocking off bandit-infested areas, troops and *Guardias* rounded up virtually every male for a series of mass line-ups in which carefully hidden informers picked out known bandits. These line-ups were often conducted in the open at night under flood-lights while the informers were stationed in darkened tents. After five months of the "cordon system," nine successful roundups had been carried out, and more than 600 courtroom convictions for banditry resulted. Following this crackdown, the cordons were discontinued because of the resentment aroused by such methods among those who were innocent.[3]

The Americans also declared an amnesty period in which guerrillas could surrender without prejudice. They also formed and trained ". . . five special anti-bandit groups . . . from among Dominicans who had suffered at bandit hands." By spring of 1922, the country was reasonably quiet, and, in 1924, the American Government withdrew the last of its forces.

A few years later, another marine infantry-air task force landed in Nicaragua to prevent a revolution. President Calvin Coolidge sent a personal representative, Henry L. Stimson, to mediate between rival political parties. Stimson found a military deadlock and a country tired of civil war. He recommended the ". . . gradual political education of Nicaraguans in self-government through free elections" supervised by United States Marines. Marines would disarm both armies and maintain internal order while training a Nicaraguan constabulary to take over the policing task. Leaders of both parties accepted this solution, which unfortunately involved two unfounded assumptions, both basic: that all Nicaraguans would embrace the principle of free elections as a satisfactory method of choosing leaders; that the presence of American marines would insure peace.[4]

Within two weeks of the Peace of Tipitapa, renegade bands began raiding towns to plague marine detachments posted about the country. The most serious challenge came from a former officer, Augusto César Sandino, who, instead of turning in his arms, vanished with some 150 followers into the remote mountains of his home province, Nueva Segovia.

Brigadier General Logan Feland, commanding the marines, started after Sandino almost at once. He garrisoned such northern towns as Ocotal, Telpaneca, Quilalí, and El Jícaro, which served as bases for ag-

3. Ibid.
4. Bryce Wood, *The Making of the Good Neighbor Policy* (New York: Columbia University Press, 1961); see also A. A. Vandegrift and Robert B. Asprey, *Once a Marine,* op. cit.

gressive patrolling intended first to disrupt rebel operations, next to defeat them entirely.

Sandino was riding quite high at this point. In July 1927, he attacked the Ocotal garrison, of some thirty-seven marines and forty-seven *guardias*. Fortunately, an air patrol spotted the fight and summoned help: that afternoon, five De Havillands peeled off smartly to plaster rebel positions with twenty-five-pound bombs and strafe them with machine-gun fire. Surprised by this unheard-of tactic, Sandino lost fifty-six known killed, with an estimated one hundred wounded. The garrison lost one dead and five wounded. Two months later, Sandino attacked another garrison but was beaten off, again with heavy casualties.[5]

Despite Sandino's ability and willingness to attack fortified positions in strength, American officials refused to accept him as anything more than another bandit leader. The marines constantly underestimated his military strength and extent of civil following. Instead of reinforcing the marine effort, Washington recalled a regiment; simultaneously, the Nicaraguan Government assigned new Guardia Nacional units to more heavily populated areas.[6]

This was a mistake, because Sandino was much more than a bandit. A native Nicaraguan, he had fought with Pancho Villa in Mexico, where he subsequently worked, and caught the raging revolutionary fever. Along with tens of thousands of Nicaraguans, he deeply resented American overlordship reflected in Nicaragua's political system, which primarily served local politicians and such North American commercial interests as United Fruit Company. He returned to Nicaragua determined to fight for independence despite American intervention. He had revolutionary connections in Mexico and Honduras (and later the United States), he had virtually an automatic following of disgruntled Nicaraguan peasants, and he held a good grasp of guerrilla tactics. He built a fortified mountain base, Chipote, not far from Honduras.

In locating and trying to eliminate this headquarters, marine patrols found themselves in considerable difficulty. Sandino's guerrillas had grown up in the country. They knew the jungle and the peasants, whom they used in a variety of ways, not hesitating to gain co-operation by selective terrorism when necessary. More than once, marine patrols walked into well-laid ambushes, which they survived, though not without casualties, only through disciplined fighting ability and timely support in some cases from aircraft.

Early reserves brought a fresh build-up in marine strength, and in January 1928, an infantry-air attack captured Sandino's base but netted only a few prisoners. Marine and guardia units now garrisoned more towns and stepped up patrolling, including night work. Pressure con-

5. Robert B. Asprey, "Small Wars—1925–1962," *Leatherneck,* 1962.
6. Heinl, op. cit.

tinued on Sandino's guerrillas. By mid-1928, he had lost sixteen hundred men, who had turned themselves in under government amnesty (and who received ten dollars for each rifle).[7] But Sandino was patient, determined, wily, and intelligent. Despite shortage of arms, lack of money, generally poor lieutenants, and bad communications, he led marines a merry chase for more than five years. Though generally neutralized and often hard-pressed, he was still at large when the marines left the country.

The marines faced two major difficulties. One was the tactical environment, particularly the eastern area, where Sandino operated in ". . . swamp, jungle, banana plantations, mahogany forests, and occasional gold mines."[8] Getting Sandino meant sending patrols and expeditions, one after the other, through seemingly impenetrable terrain devoid of communications and any roads but an occasional trail where an ambush could await each turn. ". . . In one [cavalry] march which kept us afield 31 days," wrote a veteran captain, "we actually marched 23 days with four night marches besides, and in my last long spell afield, we actually marched 39 out of 45 days from home."[9]

Local commanders lacked sufficient men, horses, mules, rations, and equipment. Intense heat, broken only by torrential downpours, filled jungle country with anopheles mosquitoes and myriad ticks, which soon covered human flesh with festering, very painful sores. After marching for weeks under such conditions and usually falling into at least one ambush, an expedition such as Captain Edson's celebrated four-hundred-mile effort into the interior time and again would reach a reported enemy camp only to find it vacated. Marine operations served a major purpose, however. They kept Sandino disorganized while a viable Guardia Nacional was being trained, and, in so doing, they prevented him from disrupting national elections held in 1928, 1930 and 1932 (a brief spurt of democracy that soon yielded to military dictatorship).

Organizing and training an effective Guardia Nacional proved extremely difficult. Corruption ruled the country and its officials to the extent that when marines first took over the guardia, they could not persuade recruits that they would be paid—former guardia officers had expropriated payrolls as a matter of course.

Patient and determined work finally resulted in an organization of sorts. In 1929, guardia units commanded by marine officers and noncommissioned officers began replacing marine units, and in the following year took over most offensive duties, albeit with marine air support. After a brief time in Honduras, Sandino returned, now backed by left-wing groups in Mexico and the United States. The guardia, though not without faults, countered his new efforts. In early 1934, a year after ma-

7. Ibid.
8. Ibid.
9. Asprey, op. cit.

rines had left Nicaragua, the guardia lured Sandino to Managua (some said the bait was a woman), where he was shot and killed.

Unfortunately, subsequent political events largely vitiated the American effort, in part because, both politically and militarily, intervention left so much to be desired. In discussing American operations in the Philippines, Nicaragua, Santo Domingo, and Haiti, the outstanding guerrilla expert of the Marine Corps, Colonel Samuel B. Griffith, wrote in 1950:

. . . Each of these areas was almost totally undeveloped; each was isolated with relative ease; in none were guerrillas properly equipped, organized, or led. And yet the campaigns in each of them assumed considerable proportions, and absorbed a great deal more military energy than would have been necessary had there been a sound operational concept. No such concept was evident in Nicaragua, for example, where a few hundred poorly equipped "Sandinistas" made monkeys out of thousands of Marines and native troops for six years. There were isolated instances of success, which occurred when local commanders applied political, economic, and psychological weapons to the problem, or when they made themselves more mobile than the guerrillas. However, no district in Northern Nicaragua was "pacified" by military means alone.[10]

Guerrillas played a peripheral but still interesting role in the Spanish Civil War. As if in remembrance of things past, the war began with an army revolt in Morocco, at Melilla, where soldiers and members of the Civil Guard arrested all Republicans and Republican sympathizers and summarily executed the leaders. With the Nationalist flag hoisted, the rebellion spread the following day to the mainland. (See maps, Chapters 9 [Map 3] and 28.)

Lines were quite clearly drawn. The bulk of the army, about forty thousand men, sided with rebel officers, but these soldiers for the most part were two-year conscripts of more use for garrison than for combat purposes.[11] About two thirds of the Civil Guard, or some twenty-two thousand men, opted with the rebels, as did about one thousand Assault Guards, fourteen thousand Carlist Requetés, fifty thousand Falangist irregulars, and thousands of volunteers. But the rebel mainstay consisted of the Army of Africa, of which about sixteen thousand soldiers of the Tercio and Moroccan Regulares stood ready to come to the mainland under Franco's command.

About a third of the army, some twenty thousand conscript troops, scattered and ineffectual, remained loyal to the Republic. About two hundred officers remained loyal, including thirteen generals. Major military strength consisted of trade-union militias, including the paramilitary

10. Samuel B. Griffith, "Guerrilla," *Marine Corps Gazette,* August 1950.
11. Thomas, op. cit.

Asaltos, reinforced by bands of untrained and generally unarmed workers and peasants. Most of the navy remained loyal.

The first phase bore a certain resemblance to 1808 uprisings against the French. In trying to defend legitimate government against regular army, Civil Guard, and paramilitary Falangist units, badly armed and organized Republican forces relied primarily on guerrilla warfare—almost as if the Nationalists were a foreign invader like Napoleon's armies in 1808. Anarchist, socialist, and Communist leaders begged the government to arm the workers; other voices called for a genuine people's war. In invoking the memory of 1808, the Communist leader Dolores Ibarruri, famous as La Pasionaria, broadcast a demand for ". . . resistance throughout the country, urging the women of Spain to fight with knives and burning oil, and ending with the slogan, 'It is better to die on your feet than to live on your knees! *No pasarán!**"[12]

In these confused days, Spain became a mélange of battles. In the cities, regular-army garrisons attempted to overcome Republican forces and in places succeeded. In other cities, the Republicans held, their ragged units reinforced by angry workers or by peasants streaming in from the countryside, their weapons hoes and flails. In smaller cities and villages, hastily organized guerrilla bands of workers and peasants sometimes fell on surprised local garrisons, usually shooting the lot.

This early fighting fitted the 1808 pattern and could have inspired a latter-day Goya to another *Dos de Mayo,* which depicts the revolt against Murat's soldiers, or to that other great canvas in the Prado which shows postrebellion executions, or to any of the famous *Los Desastres* etchings. Extreme cruelty crowned these many battles. The British authority Hugh Thomas later estimated that a month of fighting cost perhaps a hundred thousand Spanish lives and hundreds of thousands wounded.[13]

But the war quickly veered from the 1808 situation. Readers of Ernest Hemingway's classic novel *For Whom the Bell Tolls* will remember the old crone Pilar describing an initial uprising in her village.[14] After eliminating the army garrison, local guerrillas rounded up middle-class "fascist" citizenry, forced them to run a gantlet of flails and finally flung them over a cliff to their deaths. Hemingway based this brutally dramatic scene on an uprising in the Andalusian town of Ronda, ". . . where 512 people were murdered in the first month of war."[15]

* "They shall not pass"—the famous rallying cry of the French at Verdun in 1916.

12. Ibid.; see also Dolores Ibarruri, *They Shall Not Pass* (London: Lawrence & Wishart, 1966).

13. Thomas, op. cit.

14. Ernest Hemingway, *For Whom the Bell Tolls* (London: Penguin Books, 1955).

15. Thomas, op. cit.; see also Carlos Baker, *Hemingway: The Writer as Artist* (Princeton, N.J.: Princeton University Press, 1967).

Brutality aside, the significance lies in the temper of the Republicans, for they were simultaneously defending Republican government against Fascist rebels and rebelling against middle-class liberal participation in that Republican government. In a more quiet way, Elliott Paul described the same ideological play in his account of the Nationalist conquest in Ibiza, *Life and Death of a Spanish Town,* but probably the best fictional account of the political turbulence, at least on the Republican side, is offered in André Malraux's *L'Espoir (Days of Hope—*an artistic *tour de force).*[16]

Any resemblance to the strategic situation of 1808 soon ceased. The war quickly escalated. Germany and Italy vied in supplying rebels with arms and men; Republicans received weapons from Mexico and France, planes, tanks, and artillery from the Soviet Union and Comintern-recruited voluntary battalions.

In short order, civil war assumed many conventional aspects. Communiqués began to speak of lines, offensives and counteroffensives planned by professional staffs and executed by divisions and brigades supported by aircraft, tanks, and artillery.

Armies of both sides expanded: the Nationalists to perhaps six hundred thousand, the Republicans slightly less. German pilots tested Douhet's theories of strategic bombing, eliminating the town of Guernica to determine psychological and economic effects of mass bombing of civilians. Up in the Basque country, fliers worked out "carpet bombing" techniques. German advisers working with Nationalist armies realized the futility of committing armor in pinchpenny packets. In these and other ways, the Spanish war presaged World War II.

Despite such conventional trappings, two factors make the war of interest for our purposes: one is the overtone of guerrilla warfare, the other the role played by Russian communism.

Republican armies never did attain full growth, the result of a deficiency in arms and training but also the result of earlier guerrilla orientation. At outbreak of war, union militias lacked formal military training. Volunteers often trained on the way to the front; a fortunate few received an eight-day course in Madrid. The Fifth Regiment, which became famous in the Sierra fighting, started with two hundred survivors from earlier Madrid battles; by the end of August 1936, this regiment had fielded sixteen thousand volunteers.

Individual charisma played an important role in Republican forces, but this bore a definite political tint. One character prominent in the early fighting was a former Anarchist terrorist and professional killer, Buenaventura Durruti, who led an Anarchist column from Barcelona

16. Elliott Paul, *Life and Death of a Spanish Town* (London: Peter Davies, 1939); André Malraux, *Days of Hope (L'Espoir)* (London: Penguin Books, 1970). Tr. S. Gilbert and A. MacDonald.

to "liberate" Saragossa. Prevented from reaching this city, he went on the defensive in the area of Pina. There his violence ". . . had made him actually loathed by the peasants . . . and his column had been forced to leave by their silent hate."[17] A few months later, he was shot and killed, presumably by one of his own gang.

El Campesino fared much better. This was Valentín González, a large, physically strong peasant whose heavy, black-bearded face became a symbol of resistance throughout Republican ranks. When Nationalists first marched on Madrid, El Campesino rounded up ". . . 29 men, two lorries, rifles and one machine gun." A consummate showman, he named his command Group Chapaev, after a popular guerrilla leader of the Russian revolution. Reinforced by volunteers, he deployed his men in the Somosierra passes against Franco's oncoming columns. In time, Group Chapaev grew to become the 46th Division, but its commander, who remained intensely individualistic and obstructive to the over-all effort, retained two companies of guerrillas for special operations.[18]

The paucity of arms, particularly of artillery, tanks, and aircraft, stamped many Republican units with semiguerrilla characteristics. A Republican veteran of the Basque fighting offered a splendid picture of his army:

. . . We were a strange army composed of students, mechanics and peasants, led by a handful of regular officers. We wore navy blue coveralls, and we used whatever weapons were handy—French rifles, which were last used during the Franco-German War of 1870, and the most up-to-date rifles from Czechoslovakia. . . . We also had homemade dynamite bombs—three sticks of dynamite in a tomato can with a sixteen-second fuse. We lit the fuse with a cigarette.[19]

Such armies fought for months in the Basque hills:

. . . We fought best at night. We would dig into the hills, and send out scouting parties to find the weak points of the enemy, and push them back. By night we advanced, but during the day, without supporting artillery, airplanes and tanks, we were often forced back. Yet we could not afford to retreat, because there was so little ground to retreat to. . . .[20]

No army could stand forever against such odds, but the Nationalist task was never easy. After the Republicans fell in the Asturias, ". . .

17. Thomas, op. cit.
18. Robert Payne, *The Civil War in Spain* (London: Secker & Warburg, 1962).
19. Ibid.
20. Ibid.

18,000 maintained themselves as guerrilla forces in the Leonese mountains, so delaying new offensives by the Nationalist armies."[21]

Franco's armies in the South did not face the extensive guerrilla action familiar to Napoleon's armies, and for several reasons. Much of the south-central Spanish countryside was barren and sparsely populated, devoid of roads. Nationalists advanced in columns, and effective resistance could only have come from contiguous terrain, particularly mountain passes.

The people living in and around cities, towns, and villages did not form a homogeneous body defying an invader. To a great many persons on Nationalist lines of march, Franco and his generals appeared as liberators, and these persons, Monarchists, Carlists, and Fascists, did not hesitate to identify Republicans. Similar groups existed in larger cities, where the famous Fifth Columns performed limited acts of sabotage, provided information to Nationalists, and emerged from hiding when their armies moved in. Advancing Nationalists showed virtually no compassion to consolidating gains. Potential cadres of resistance fell to swift, brutal action—Republicans, including prisoners of war, were marched to the nearest bull ring, lined up, and shot.

Some escaped. Hemingway based his guerrilla band, immortalized in *For Whom the Bell Tolls,* on a realistic situation. His assortment of Republican fugitives chose a cave high in the ". . . forested slopes of the Sierra de Guadarramas 60 miles north-west of besieged Madrid and behind the Fascist lines."[22] Similar small bands existed in the same area, but a number of difficulties prevented these guerrillas from realizing their full potential.

One was lack of training and supply: Robert Jordan, the idealistically motivated American who joined them, backpacking in his own dynamite in order to blow a vital bridge, was a forerunner of allied teams who brought skills and arms to World War II guerrilla bands.

Another problem was Nationalist use of airplanes to find and attack guerrillas forced into the open—readers may remember the gripping scene of El Sordo's band trapped on a hilltop.

A third problem was lack of communication and control: the Republican general, Golz, ordered Jordan to blow the bridge on a certain hour of a certain day; in the event, the main attack aborted, but no method existed to cancel Jordan's orders, which meant a needless waste of lives, including his own.[23]

21. Thomas, op. cit.: Sporadic guerrilla resistance lasted in the Cantabrian Mountains until 1939. Remnants of Republican bands made a serious effort at a comeback in the Pyrenees in 1945-47.

22. Baker, op. cit.

23. Ibid.; see also Thomas, op. cit. Hemingway based the character of General Golz on one General "Walter," who was the Polish Communist general Karol Swierczewski. He based the tactical situation on an actual Republican offensive

Jordan's own failure and Golz's failure and the Republic's failure were foreshadowed when Karkov, the *Pravda* correspondent, told Jordan in Madrid that although things were better and that reliable units were emerging in the army, the basic problem remained:

. . . "But an army," Karkov went on, "that is made up of good and bad elements cannot win a war. All must be brought to a certain level of political development; all must know why they are fighting, and its importance. All must believe in the fight they are to make and all must accept discipline. We are making a huge conscript army without the time to implant the discipline that a conscript army must have, to behave properly under fire. We call it a people's army but it will not have the assets of a true people's army and it will not have the iron discipline that a conscript army needs. You will see. It is a very dangerous procedure."[24]

It was a very dangerous procedure in another sense. The Communist attempt to capture the Republican cause and subvert it to the Soviet Union's political convenience presaged the future as much as dive-bombing or armor warfare, though in a far more subtle, in a political, way. Nowhere was the dualism of communism better illustrated than in Spain, nowhere the intricacy of Soviet thought better displayed.

Far from appealing to Stalin, the Spanish Civil War came at a most inconvenient time. Since 1934, he had been moving toward an alliance with Britain and France against the threat of Hitler and Mussolini: The Soviet Union had joined the League of Nations, had signed a defense pact with France, and had ordered the Comintern to push a policy of the Popular Front, whereby local Communists allied with left-wing and liberal-middle-class parties against Fascism. A Nationalist or Fascist victory in Spain naturally held little appeal to the Kremlin. But a Socialist-Communist victory, as Thomas has pointed out, would have antagonized the U.S.S.R.'s important potential allies Britain and France, and might even have led to war. Still consolidating his internal rule (the massive purges were to resume in 1937), Stalin was not ready for war.

All this explains why Stalin did not exactly leap into the Spanish fray. Although he sent food, raw materials, and money, he at first refused to send arms. Under extreme pressure, he dispatched professional Comintern agents into Spain besides authorizing an international Comintern movement to provide "humanitarian" aid to Republicans. Only when Italo-German military aid to Nationalists became widely reported, did Stalin change his mind and dare to circumvent Franco-British non-

planned along the Segovia front. Although Colonel Dumont's XIV International Brigade broke through Nationalist lines at San Ildefonso, the attack ran out of steam at La Granja, due in part to jealousy between Walter and Dumont, and possibly also to betrayal, as Hemingway suggested.

24. Hemingway, op. cit.

intervention policy, and then only under further pressure from non-Russian Communists.

Military supplies did not begin trickling into Spain until late September 1936. Soviet aid eventually reached respectable proportions, including several hundred aircraft with pilots and ground crews, tanks, artillery, trucks, and military advisers and instructors, but it was given grudgingly and paid for, in advance, with Spanish gold.

Stalin's opportunistic attitude contrasted with that of non-Russian Communist members of the Comintern. This amazing organization exerted an influence both inside and outside Spain far beyond anything suggested by its limited numbers. Through a maze of "front" organizations, which fooled a great many non-Communist liberals, the Comintern recruited, trained, armed, and equipped perhaps forty thousand foreigners who served at one time or another in one of seven international brigades.

No matter the slapdash character of these units, particularly in early days, their formation bespoke a determined and disciplined effort, which, allied with the small but disciplined Communist Party in Spain, very nearly captured the Republican cause. This was a classic example of exploiting liberal idealism, and it was not lost on Hemingway, whose American protagonist, Robert Jordan,

. . . fought now in this war because it had started in a country that he loved and he believed in the Republic and that if it were destroyed life would be unbearable for all those people who believed in it.[25]

Jordan was not a Communist, but he willingly had placed himself

. . . under Communist discipline for the duration of the war. He accepted their discipline for the duration of the war because, in the conduct of the war, they were the only party whose program and whose discipline he could respect.[26]

No matter that the effort failed, that Jordan and many others of his kind died, that the Republicans suffered ultimate defeat. As German and Italian air and ground officers returned to their respective countries rich in battle experience, Communist survivors also returned rich in another kind of battle experience. They were still too weak to launch revolutions in their own countries. They would need another war for that. But they were prepared to wait, and as it turned out, they hadn't to wait for long. Less than six months after the close of the Spanish Civil War, World War II began.

25. Ibid.
26. Ibid.

Chapter 31

World War II • German and Japanese victories • Guerrilla warfare begins • Allied support of resistance movements • Special Operations Executive (SOE) • Office of Strategic Services (OSS) • The British-American policy analyzed • The Communist element • Reasons for a quantitative approach • Churchill and Roosevelt

ON SEPTEMBER 1, 1939, Hitler loosed the full force of Germany's infantry-armor-air power against Poland, whose army was so obsolete that Polish cavalrymen *armed with lances* charged German tanks. In less than a month, the *Wehrmacht* overran this tragic country in violent demonstration of a new type of warfare, the *Blitzkrieg,* or lightning war, which Western military leaders failed to comprehend.

After a winter of uneasy quiet, Hitler moved again, this time occupying Norway in order to gain naval and air bases. On May 10, 1940, he struck. Denmark quickly capitulated, Holland fell to aerial bombing and paratroopers, German armored columns pushed through the supposedly impassable Ardennes in a giant sweep into France.

In fourteen days, German armored columns encircled allied armies in northwestern France, forcing the British to evacuate nearly a third of a million men from Dunkerque. Meeting only scattered resistance, the Germans continued south across the Aisne and the Seine. On June 16, Marshal Pétain surrendered the French army.

Hitler followed this victory with an air offensive against England. By breaking the back of the Royal Air Force, he hoped to soften the island's defenses for an across-the-channel invasion. His plan buckled before a determined aerial defense—the famous Battle of Britain—from which the Spitfire fighter emerged superior to the Messerschmitt; in early October 1940, the *Luftwaffe* conceded its first defeat, a crucial one in that heavy German losses of aircraft and pilots could not readily be replaced.

Hitler's ally Mussolini next launched two offensives: one against Greece, the other against the British in North Africa. By early 1941, the Italian dictator was in severe trouble in each theater. To rescue him, Hitler sent an armored force under General-leutnant Erwin Rommel to Africa; in early April 1941, a German army invaded Yugoslavia, pushed through in five days and, with forces based in Hungary, Bulgaria, and Romania, went on to conquer Greece and seize Crete by a daring, if costly, airborne assault.

With this flank protected, Hitler turned east: in late June 1941, three powerful German armies invaded the Soviet Union. By early November, vanguard divisions had pushed seven hundred miles, to within fifteen miles of Moscow. But now cold weather and a Russian counteroffensive forced them on the defensive along the entire front.

On December 7, 1941, Japanese bombers flying from a secretly concentrated task force of aircraft carriers attacked Pearl Harbor, America's major Pacific naval base. Within hours, the bulk of the American battleship fleet had been sunk. In ensuing weeks and months, Japanese ground, air, and sea forces seized allied bases throughout the Pacific and Southeast Asia. French Indochina, Siam, and Malaya at once capitulated; Singapore fell, then Burma, the Dutch East Indies, the Philippines, Guam, Wake. By spring of 1942, the enemy was threatening Australia from nearby New Guinea and from bases in the neighboring Solomon Islands.

By spring of 1942, then, battle lines east and west were drawn. For the next three years and more, mighty armies, giant naval fleets, and vast air armadas clashed again and again in a global war without precedent.

And a global war that spawned an immense variety of irregular-warfare operations. For, whatever the conquest, whoever the conqueror, the clash of fundamental ideologies combined with brutal occupation policies resulted in resistance that varied from the lone saboteur to guerrilla armies. Wherever possible, hard-pressed allied powers eagerly embraced such movements, their general policy being to help anyone willing to fight the enemy. Technological advances, particularly the airplane, the portable radio transmitter, the parachute, and the submarine, enabled them in time to support almost any group anywhere.

No real precedent existed for the over-all situation—massive global war: massive global resistance. To exploit the potential, England established "an independent British secret service" known as Special Operations Executive (SOE). America followed suit with the Office of Strategic Services (OSS). Russian support of guerrillas either inside or outside the country became the Red army's responsibility, but with numerous political ramifications. In China, Chiang Kai-shek similarly controlled his guerrillas, though much less effectively; Mao Tse-tung continued to use guerrilla forces as the keystone of political-military operations earlier described.

As might be expected, guerrilla operations world-wide varied considerably in size, composition, motivation, mission, and effectiveness. Such were differences in enemy strength and counteractions, in political environments, in guerrilla leadership, and in allied assistance and supervision, that one resistance action often bore only generic resemblance to another.

This lack of cohesive operation lessens neither the single nor the collective value of the experience and its contribution to guerrilla warfare. Neither does it eliminate some "constant" factors that can be retrieved from various operational theaters, which we shall get to in a moment.

But since we are still living with some results of allied support of various resistance groups, we should examine first not only its genesis and extent but the reasons for it.

The immense task of supporting resistance movements and of trying to form them into a cohesive weapon that would fire at allied will fell to an organization not heretofore seen in warfare. This was a British group, Special Operations Executive (SOE), which functioned under the Ministry of Economic Warfare, itself activated only in 1939 and later directed by a prominent laborite and socialist, Dr. Hugh Dalton. The interested reader will find detailed information on this mysterious and complex organization in two serious works: M. R. D. Foot's *SOE in France,* an official but nonetheless lively and at times controversial work; and E. H. Cookridge's *Inside SOE,* which offers a more dramatic and wider survey of SOE operations. Literally dozens of works complement these two, and many are listed in the respective bibliographies.[1]

SOE traced from a small research section of the British General Staff, the GS-R, which in 1938–39 prepared two anticipatory pamphlets, *The Art of Guerrilla Warfare* and *Partisan Leader's Handbook.* At this time, only a few British officers realized the potential of guerrilla warfare—a

---

1. M. R. D. Foot, *SOE in France* (London: HMSO, 1966); E. H. Cookridge, *Inside SOE—The Story of Special Operations in Western Europe 1940–45* (London: Arthur Barker, 1966).

surprising fact in view of British military history, particularly the small wars of the nineteenth century, the Boer war, Lawrence's campaigns, the Irish rebellion, and the Palestine fighting of the 1930s. One who did was a forty-five-year-old lieutenant colonel, Colin McVean Gubbins, a regular soldier decorated for bravery in World War I who subsequently served in the Irish rebellion and in India during the riots. In the 1930s, he made personal reconnaissances in Poland and the Baltic States, where he envisaged the possibility of guerrilla actions, and in 1939 he headed the intelligence section of a British mission to Warsaw and narrowly missed capture by the Germans. He next organized, trained, and commanded the first Striking Companies, which fought in Norway and later became the Commandos. Gubbins and a few men with similar backgrounds were called to SOE, where most of them subsequently served with great distinction—as did many civilians with nonmilitary backgrounds.

But, for every Gubbins, a thousand regular officers existed who, wedded to orthodox military tradition, disdained irregular warfare. Cookridge later described early confrontations of regulars with "the others":

. . . The horrified generals, brigadiers, admirals and air marshals were confronted by men some of whom had never heard a shot fired in anger, and who talked about politics, ideologies, psychology and subversion. Employing saboteurs and guerrilla leaders was alien to the traditions of Sandhurst men. Many of them were still fighting the last war but one, and dreamed of the Charge of the Light Brigade. . . .[2]

And not alone Sandhurst men! At a time when German bombers were battering Britain, Air Marshal Portal objected to an SOE operation designed to ambush and kill German pathfinder bomber pilots. Portal wrote to a responsible official:

. . . I think that the dropping of men dressed in civilian clothes for the purpose of attempting to kill members of the opposing forces is not an operation with which the Royal Air Force should be associated. I think you will agree that there is a vast difference, in ethics, between the time honored operation of the dropping of a spy from the air and this entirely new scheme for dropping what one can only call assassins.[3]

Such service delicacy in part prompted Winston Churchill to place SOE under the Ministry of Economic Warfare rather than either the War Office or the Foreign Office. In July 1940, the new minister, Hugh Dalton, called for a "democratic international":

. . . We must organize movements in enemy occupied territory comparable to the Sinn Fein movement in Ireland, to the Chinese guerrillas now oper-

2. Cookridge, op. cit.
3. Foot, op. cit.

ating against Japan, to the Spanish Irregulars . . . in Wellington's campaign or—one might as well admit it—to the organizations which the Nazis themselves have developed so remarkably in almost every country in the world. We must use many different methods, including industrial and military sabotage, labor agitation and strikes, continuous propaganda, terrorist acts against traitors and German leaders, boycotts and riots. . . .[4]

In approving the formation of SOE, Winston Churchill exhorted Dalton: ". . . And now set Europe ablaze."

In more prosaic language, SOE was ". . . to create and foster the spirit of resistance in Nazi-occupied countries" and, once a suitable climate of opinion existed, ". . . to establish a nucleus of trained men who would be able to assist 'as a fifth column' in the liberation of the country concerned whenever the British were able to invade it."[5] In time, the first task fell to a sister organization, the Political Warfare Executive (PWE).

From the very beginning, SOE proved politically promiscuous. As Foot wrote,

. . . the body's task was to help break Nazi power, and its politics were simply anti-Nazi; they did not favor or disfavor any other political creed at all. . . . SOE was ready to work with any man or institution, Roman Catholic or masonic, trotskyist or liberal, syndicalist or capitalist, nationalist or chauvinist, radical or conservative, Stalinist or anarchist, gentile or Jew, that would help it beat the Nazis down.[6]

The American equivalent to SOE, the Office of Strategic Services, or OSS, was the brainchild of a World War I hero and civilian attorney, William J. "Wild Bill" Donovan.[7] OSS began life as the Office of Coordinator of Information. Personnel experienced in irregular warfare were virtually non-existent. For nearly forty years, America's armed forces had fought almost no irregular-warfare campaigns. Few persons, if any, remembered lessons learned in the Philippine insurrection at the turn of the century. Pershing's Mexican-border expedition was more a matter of a cavalry force marching hither and yon than one fighting guerrilla warfare. Although marines saw considerable action in Nicaragua and Haiti in the 1920s, this was limited to a handful of officers and men (see Chapter 30). As one result, the organization was slow in getting organized; as another, it recruited numerous officers who later proved unsatisfactory.

4. H. Dalton, *The Fateful Years* (London: Muller, 1957).
5. Foot, op. cit.
6. Ibid.
7. S. Alsop and T. Braden, *Sub Rosa—The OSS and American Espionage* (New York: Harcourt, Brace, 1963); see also R. Harris Smith, *OSS—The Secret History of America's First Central Intelligence Agency* (London: University of California Press, 1972).

Transformed into the OSS by a presidential order of June 1942, it became a federal agency responsible for covert operations in enemy-occupied areas. As such, it naturally came together with SOE in London, where it embraced SOE's politically promiscuous policy, not alone in Europe but in the Balkans and Middle and Far East.[8]

In the turbulent years of their existence, SOE and OSS enjoyed numerous successes and suffered numerous failures, and we shall look at some of these shortly. A good many persons, including most professional military officers, have held subsequently that failures overshadowed successes. The greatest error, according to later critics, lay in indiscriminately arming various resistance groups, some of which were politically antagonistic to the West.

While reserving judgment for the moment, we must point out that although SOE and OSS played the executive role in arming and supporting these groups, the ultimate responsibility belonged to Churchill and Roosevelt, as well as to certain of their strategic advisers, civil and military, who placed short-term military goals ahead of long-term political goals.

Winston Churchill set the Anglo-American pace in this respect by demanding British support of anyone willing to kill Germans. As he once said, ". . . If Hitler invaded Hell, I would make at least a favorable reference to the Devil in the House of Commons." By the time OSS emerged as an entity, America had accepted this policy and quite naturally enlarged it to include the Japanese.

In retrospect, in view of complicated and greatly varying local political situations, it seems far too simple a policy, altogether unworthy of the British, who were scarcely naïve in international politics.

Its chief disadvantage centered on the dissidents themselves. Although many of these were patriots willing to die for love of country, most of them wanted fundamental political changes in that country once the war ended. In many countries—not all—the most determined opponents of Fascist conquerors were Communists, who wanted postwar control.

Two decades of attempted suppression had inured local Communist parties to an underground existence ideal for the present situation. Where advantageous terrain existed, such as in Yugoslavia, the raised standard, hastily painted over in nationalist colors, attracted thousands of well-meaning citizens, of whom many, in the end, became converts.

In countries less suitable for guerrilla warfare, Communists operated more covertly. Their infiltration and organizational ability, in almost all cases, paid immense dividends by insinuating party members into responsible resistance roles while superb propaganda techniques won new adherents to the cause: in virtually all cases, they ended the war in a

8. Foot, op. cit.

far stronger position than they began it—as witness Communist attempts to take over France and Italy in immediate postwar years.

Similarly in the Far East, SOE armed dissident groups, in some cases nationalist, in some cases Communist, in Burma and Malaya. OSS furnished arms and equipment to Mao Tse-tung in China and even to Ho Chi Minh in Vietnam, and in supplying guerrillas in the Philippines, they inadvertently supported the Communist movement there.

Why were Churchill and Roosevelt willing to play games with the devil?

Britain's initial position, established and maintained by Winston Churchill and graced by Cabinet and government, is not difficult to understand. After the fall of France, the island kingdom literally stood alone, resources of empire as yet unharnessed, the Soviet Union allied with Germany, the United States just beginning to awaken. A desperate Churchill stared at a doomed England. Unlike Dr. Faustus, who wanted mere knowledge, Churchill demanded survival.

But after light entered these dark days, after the U.S.S.R. was fighting Germany and after the U.S.A. had come into the war, why did the game continue?

Although mystery still shrouds the issue, the key reason—and one all too often overlooked—centered on the possibility of developing an atomic bomb. Background development of this weapon is complex— the reader can study it in such works as Leslie Groves's *Now It Can Be Told* and Lewis Strauss's *Men and Decisions*.[9] According to Strauss, the term "atomic bomb" first occurred in a letter to him from the brilliant Hungarian immigrant Leo Szilard. Commenting on a nuclear breakthrough by two German physicists, Drs. Hahn and Strassmann, Szilard wrote on January 25, 1939:

. . . I see, however, in connection with this new discovery potential possibilities in another direction. These might lead to a large-scale production of energy and radioactive elements, unfortunately also perhaps to atomic bombs. . . .[10]

A month or two later, Szilard, working with such colleagues as Drs. Teller, Zinn, Wigner, and Fermi, suggested to Strauss the possibility of a nuclear "chain reaction," a suggestion that by March 1939 changed to a distinct possibility with chances "above fifty percent." Similar investigations meanwhile were occupying other scientists, such as Dr. Blackett in England and Dr. Joliot-Curie in France, not to mention those in Germany, Italy, and the Scandinavian countries.

9. Leslie Groves, *Now It Can Be Told* (London: André Deutsch, 1963); Lewis Strauss, *Men and Decisions* (New York: Macmillan, 1963).
10. Strauss, op. cit.

By spring of 1939,

. . . Szilard was gravely worried by the possibility of an early German success in producing a new weapon based on nuclear fission. The liberation of vast energy from a quite small amount of material had suggested to him the feasibility of making a weapon which would utterly dwarf any chemical bomb and with which, should Hitler be the first to achieve it, the conquest of Europe would be quickly accomplished. . . .[11]

This led to the famous "Einstein letter" to President Roosevelt, in autumn of 1939. After reviewing atomic research to date, Einstein stated the probability of achieving ". . . a nuclear chain reaction in a large mass of uranium," a new scientific phenomenon which ". . . would also lead to the construction of bombs, and it is conceivable—though much less certain—that extremely powerful bombs of a new type may thus be constructed. . . ." Einstein left little doubt of German interest:

. . . I understand that Germany has actually stopped the sale of uranium from the Czechoslovakian mines which she has taken over. . . .[12]

The incubus of the Germans developing an atomic weapon grew after the invasion of Norway, in spring of 1940. By midsummer,

. . . the eagerness shown by the Germans to capture a Norwegian plant producing heavy water gave color to the apprehension that *the German military establishment was vigorously engaged in some kind of atomic weapon project*. We knew that several kilograms of heavy water were produced daily at Trondheim. . . .[13]

Just when Roosevelt communicated these fears to Churchill is not clear in published records. In any event, Churchill was well served scientifically. In early 1940, a group of civil and military experts—they would be known as the Maud Committee—convened at Oxford to begin trying to determine if an atomic bomb could be made and if the venture would be worth the trouble![14]

Enough progress in atomic physics had been made on the continent and in England for everyone to know the value of heavy water, deuterium oxide, for experiments in atomic energy. When Germany invaded France, French scientists managed to spirit away their supply of the precious stuff to England. But British intelligence soon learned that German scientists in the Norsk Hydro Elektrisk plant near Vemork, just west of Rjukan, had ordered Norwegian engineers to increase heavy-

11. Ibid.
12. Ibid.
13. Ibid.; my italics.
14. R. W. Clark, *The Birth of a Bomb* (London: Phoenix House, 1961); see also Cookridge, op. cit.

water output to three thousand pounds a year.[15] In late 1941, SOE learned that this figure had risen to ten thousand pounds for the next year. Continuing intelligence estimates heightened allied apprehensions regarding German manufacture of a bomb. According to Admiral Strauss,

. . . the fears in 1941 and later that the Germans would be first with an atomic bomb were reinforced by Hitler's frequent and cryptic references to devastating "secret weapons. . . ."[16]

The Norwegian effort led to a British Combined Operations plan to blow up the hydroelectric plant. In late November 1942, two gliders attempted to land special teams in the area, a disastrous failure in which most participants were either killed in crash landings or executed by the Germans. A later effort by a very brave Norwegian team partially closed down operations, and later RAF raids continued to damage the plant. In early 1944, a Norwegian agent, Knut Haukelid, who had participated in the earlier raid, learned that the Germans were shipping a half year's production of heavy water to Germany. Haukelid and two companions managed to plant explosives that blew up the ferry and destroyed fifteen thousand liters of heavy water.[17]

The allies did not know that in 1943 Albert Speer, Hitler's armaments chief, already had drastically limited nuclear research. A shortage of heavy water further hindered German scientists, whose researchers in any case were lagging far behind their Western counterparts. Strauss does not state when the veil began to part, but does remark that,

. . . as the war with Germany drew to a close, it became more and more clear that the apprehensions as to what the Germans were doing in atomic energy had been exaggerated.[18]

By this time, however, England and the United States long since had embarked on quantitative support of dissident peoples.

Juxtaposed to this overriding and eminently justified fear of Germany producing an atomic weapon were the dominant personalities of Roosevelt and Churchill. Each was convinced of his ability to control the world's destiny: a splendid egotism reinforced by a host of erroneous information furnished by outstanding specialists of both countries; by cunning Communist strategy which downplayed Communist preeminence in certain areas; and, in Roosevelt's case, by an anti-colonial attitude distinctly at odds with Churchill's imperial desires. Above all, an

15. Ibid.
16. Strauss, op. cit.
17. Clark, op. cit.; Cookridge, op. cit.; see also Knut Haukelid, *Skis Against the Atom* (London: William Kimber, 1954).
18. Strauss, op. cit.

egotism that completely ignored the possibility of death—either natural or political—of either leader.

In view of these quixotic personalities and the momentous issues at stake, the initial decision to support whoever would kill Germans (or Japanese) is perhaps defensible if only on grounds of survival. It was on just such grounds that Stalin ordered Communist parties everywhere to form united fronts with bourgeois groups against the Fascist enemy— and such is the universal desire for survival that one must wonder if Stalin would have insisted on making political hay of the resistance in Eastern Europe had he been apprised of the possibility of German production of an atomic bomb.

But, once the danger passed, and, in the case of the atomic threat, Strauss marks this in 1944 at the latest, a re-evaluation by Western powers was in order. In view of the momentous forces of war then swirling over the world, it was perhaps expecting too much for concerned governments to have stopped for a moment to cast critical eyes on resistance movements and to ask themselves: where are we going and why? Such were the day's operational confusions, such the political ignorance of the allied powers, that intelligent examination might not have changed allied resistance policies for the better. This we shall never know, because these policies were not re-examined. Like Topsy, the resistance effort continued to grow.

Chapter 32

*European resistance analyzed • The complex political element
• German occupation policy • German errors • Growth of
underground movements • Resistance in Czechoslovakia, Poland, Italy, and Norway*

DURING MOST of World War II, resistance forces in Poland,
Czechoslovakia, Norway, Denmark, Holland, Belgium, France, and Italy
concerned themselves with a more subtle type of guerrilla warfare than
practiced, for example, in the Soviet Union and Yugoslavia.

In the former countries, a variety of factors hindered attempts to
build operational guerrilla armies. Lack of suitable terrain for sanctuary
purposes, inadequate internal communications, conflicting national
temperaments and political attitudes—each sharply influenced resistance
efforts. While attempting to build secret guerrilla "armies" that would
emerge at the appropriate time to fight in conjunction with allied land
armies, these partisans operated either as individuals or in small groups
to carry out tasks of terror, subversion and sabotage. Equally important missions included securing and transmitting intelligence on enemy
strength, activity, and movements, and in helping allied soldiers, princi-

pally downed airmen, to evade capture while escaping to neutral countries.

In performing these manifold missions, resistance members in all countries constantly risked imprisonment, torture, deportation, and death. Although many participants died and, in many instances, records were lost or destroyed (or not kept), sufficient sources survived to give us a good insight into operational aspects of this type of warfare and the numerous factors that created and sustained it.

The indigenous populations of occupied countries formed the most important factor. A pleasant fiction persists in Western thinking that the political situation in occupied countries was of a black-and-white composition: a few traitors, but the bulk of the population violently anti-Nazi.

Unfortunately, it was not this simple.

Each of the above-named countries did contain citizens who either overtly or covertly embraced the Fascist cause—the quisling, or outright traitor, element who argued primarily that fascism was necessary to defeat communism or socialism, the collaborator who came to terms with the enemy for other reasons.[1]

These groups often differed radically within themselves. Some quislings and collaborators, motivated by a pathological fear of communism, desired German control; others wanted more local autonomy under some sort of protectorate arrangement. Other motivations played a part. As C. M. Woodhouse later wrote of the Greek resistance:

. . . The worst that can be said against the Greek collaborators, which is bad enough, is that they acquiesced in the occupation either for personal gain, or because they believed that the Germans had won the war, or because they saw no hope of survival for themselves and millions of others except by collaboration.[2]

For every citizen so inclined, thousands regarded fascism as the antithesis of civilization. But this group, too, differed within: some anti-Fascists—the *attentistes,* or fence-sitters—refused to take a stand; some preferred mild accommodation to the enemy to avoid reprisals; others, under no circumstances, would permit the conqueror an easy occupation. Of the latter group, some fought solely for unselfish motives; a good many, including most Communists, used the effort to strengthen the party's position in postwar years.

The extremists did not represent majority feeling. Hundreds of thousands, indeed millions, of people found themselves in the middle, perhaps loathing the conqueror but rationalizing that the conquest was an

---

1. Hugh Seton-Watson, *The East European Revolution* (London: Methuen, 1956). Professor Seton-Watson has differentiated among no less than five major types of quislings and collaborators (pp. 106–7).
2. C. M. Woodhouse, *Apple of Discord* (London: Hutchinson, 1948).

accomplished fact and that one had a duty to support one's dependents. This middle group, people generally bewildered by war's overwhelming forces, comprised a wide range of attitudes: citizens who accommodated the enemy for profit, or from fear, or because, in their minds, no reasonable alternative existed, or for an ulterior motive of serving him with one hand and stabbing him with the other, or for gaining time in order to plan escape to an allied country or to a guerrilla refuge.

These internal groups varied considerably from country to country. Norway, for example, whose citizen Vidkun Quisling inspired a new word in the English language, presented a relatively conservative example, with only a small Communist party to complicate matters. An interesting play of forces still occurred, the wartime equivalent of Henrik Ibsen's *An Enemy of the People,* a sad and tragic situation well portrayed in John Steinbeck's novel, *The Moon Is Down.*

France furnished a much more desperate example, the inevitable reaction of a country tired, sick, and divided even prior to the German invasion. As Michael Foot asked:

. . . What was there in fact in France in the way of political resistance? At first, as serious French historians admit, there was very little indeed, but plenty came with time. Time brought many controversies. Was it best to accept the fact of German domination and collaborate, or to follow the aged marshal [Pétain] in an attempt at an independent policy, or to resist? If to resist, with what object—to restore the Third Republic, or one of the monarchies; or to build a new kind of France, and if so with marxist or Christian or agnostic inspiration? And under American or British or Russian or purely French sponsorship? And under which French military leader? Differences about which side to take in these numerous disputes split French society asunder, from top to bottom; not since the Dreyfus affair at the turn of the century had such cleavages opened between teachers and students, priests and congregations, parents and children, brothers and sisters, husbands and wives.[3]

The conflict between acceptance and resistance has recently (1971) been examined in a brilliant television production, *Le Chagrin et la Pitié,* which treats the German occupation of a small town, Clermont-Ferrand.

Despite a confused and divided citizenry in occupied countries, the German conqueror everywhere faced a certain amount of *natural* resistance—fanatical patriots of every political party who would prostrate themselves to the enemy only in death, the incredibly brave civilian counterpart to Polish cavalrymen who charged German tanks with lances.

In overcoming such resistance and in consolidating occupation, German conquerors naturally tapped pro-Fascist sections of the population.

3. Foot, op. cit.

These generally included important industrialists and prominent businessmen who either inclined toward or embraced a Fascist form of government, but it also included a less desirable element—quasi-Nazi groups containing the scum of society just as did the original storm-trooper units in Germany. In utilizing the bullying tactics of this element, the Germans at once offended a considerable portion of citizenry otherwise prepared to remain acquiescent.

The Germans also offended by their almost unbelievable display of the arrogance of power. The true Nazi, and in 1940 a good many more of these existed than in 1945 and subsequently, doubted not that Germany shortly would rule the world. Military and civil governors quickly began turning their newest acquisitions into German satrapies.

Regarding all foreigners as inferior, they practiced patronizing attitudes that endeared them to no one, nor did they hesitate to invoke severe occupation policies: inconvenient curfews and travel restrictions; confiscation of houses and buildings; strict rationing; hurtful taxes; impossible production norms; plundering of private and public property; arrest and deportation or outright elimination of Aryans and non-Aryans, with emphasis on Jews and Communists.

While these actions did not necessarily create resistance movements, they did aid incipient movements to survive by enlisting sympathies of otherwise apathetic citizens.

As resistance survived and developed, the conquerors replied with most-brutal reprisals: mass arrests, imprisonment, torture, deportation to forced-labor and concentration camps, and summary executions, including those of hostages and innocent persons. The striking scene of German reprisals against guerrillas in Warsaw offered in Anatole Litvak's contemporary film *The Night of the Generals* became relatively commonplace in other occupied countries.

The Germans complemented this effort by introducing wholesale conscription for service either in armed forces or for labor in factories at home and abroad. Besides further alienating the general population, this drove thousands of young men to mountain and forest sanctuaries, where some of them in time formed effective guerrilla bands such as the French *maquis*.

In total, then, German policy not only helped resistance movements to survive but enabled them to grow at a time when England and the Soviet Union were able to offer little or nothing in the way of material help.

Perhaps the outstanding lesson of this period of European resistance is the innate booby trap contained in reprisal philosophy. Reduced to its simplest terms, reprisal illustrates the fallacy of answering lawless behavior with lawless behavior—and this seems to be a universal *bête noir* of the military mind.

One story of Czechoslovakian resistance, possibly apocryphal but offered as truth by a former British intelligence officer who recently related it to the writer, illustrates this point. Contrary to general belief, the Germans were not badly received when they took over most of Czechoslovakia. Perhaps for this reason, occupation authorities did not rule as harshly as elsewhere, and thus did not face as much of a resistance problem. Although members of the intelligentsia and a large number of the middle class suffered under occupation, workers and peasants, in general, fared reasonably well—or well enough so that they did not indulge in spontaneous resistance.

Lack of resistance is said to have greatly annoyed the exiled president, Eduard Beneš. Beneš allegedly was responsible for a plan to assassinate the German governor, Reinhard Heydrich, the theory being that this act would cause widespread reprisals, which would turn the citizenry against the occupying enemy. With Winston Churchill's alleged cognizance and co-operation, Beneš arranged for SOE to drop a team of specially trained Czech volunteers into the occupied country. Whatever the details, Heydrich *was* assassinated, in the spring of 1942, by an SOE-supported operation, and this did cause widespread reprisals, such as the destruction of Lidice, a mining village, all of whose inhabitants were either executed or deported. The German storm eventually passed but it embittered a large part of the population, which in part supported a resistance movement lasting until the war's end, though not to the intensity desired by Beneš![4] Czech resistance remained segmented:

. . . Those who resisted most, and suffered most, were the intellectuals and the civil servants and army officers of the old republic. . . . The 38,000 executions of Czechs during the six years of Nazi rule came mostly from the middle class.[5]

Czechoslovakian resistance also suffered from internal political differences, lack of suitable terrain, poor communications with allied countries, and energetic German security measures.

Although guerrilla bands appeared in Moravia in late 1944, they seem to have accomplished but little. The main resistance centered in Slovakia, where, in mountain reaches of the center and north, a secret Slovak army as well as a guerrilla movement slowly formed. (See maps, Chapters 7 [Map 1] and 34.)

4. Private information; see also Seton-Watson, op. cit., who noted that German repression became more severe in the autumn of 1941. After sabotage of a munitions plant and power station, Himmler appointed Heydrich as Protector, or governor: ". . . For eight months Heydrich conducted a regime of terror, with firing squads, concentration camps and deportations to forced labor"; see also Charles Wighton, *Heydrich—Hitler's Most Evil Henchman* (London: Odhams Press, 1962); Miroslav Iranov, *The Assassination of Heydrich* (London: Hart-Davis, MacGibbon, 1974). Tr. Patrick O'Brian.
5. Seton-Watson, op. cit.

A Russian partisan, Sidor Kovpak, had sent in Slovakian partisans in 1943 to work up partisan warfare in Slovakia. In June 1944, mixed partisan detachments of Czechs and Russians began parachuting in:

. . . by the end of August, thirty such detachments, averaging a score of men each, had arrived. They served as a stiffening and organizing element for the local partisan forces which the underground Communists in Slovakia were organizing.[6]

By August, a partisan force totaling perhaps eight thousand was in full operation. With Soviet armies pushing over the Carpathians, the German high command sent troops into the previously unoccupied area. Two divisions of the secret army almost at once defected to the Germans. The remainder, including guerrillas, attempted to hold an area known as Free Slovakia. Unfortunately, Western allies could not effectively supply this force. Although the Russians sent in another three thousand partisans and some ammunition,[7] they refused a large-scale supply effort, nor did the Red army advance as planned—a situation which, as we shall see, was similar in some ways to the Warsaw rising of the same period. German attacks subsequently overran Free Slovakia and forced the guerrillas to the mountains, where most of them perished.[8]

The political factor even more strongly influenced the Polish resistance movement. A substantial portion of the population, particularly peasants and urban socialists, while remaining opposed to communism, nonetheless wanted a new postwar political order. This forced reactionary leaders, mainly army officers at home and abroad, into an uneasy alliance that, coupled with Communist diversions, frequently dissipated the total resistance effort.

As in other occupied countries, Germany did her best to generate maximum resistance. In that part of western Poland annexed to the German Reich,

. . . all available industrial and agricultural resources were to be fully exploited and expanded for the benefit of the Reich. At the same time the population was to be germanised. Jews and the most intractable Poles, especially members of the intelligentsia, were deported to the General Government [the rest of Poland]. Large numbers of able-bodied male Poles were deported to other parts of the Reich to work in factories or fields. . . . The Polish language was not permitted in administration or schools within the annexed territories. . . .[9]

6. J. A. Armstrong (ed.), *Soviet Partisans in World War II* (Madison, Wis.: University of Wisconsin Press, 1964).
7. Ibid.
8. Seton-Watson, op. cit.; see also Blair, op. cit.
9. Seton-Watson, op. cit.

What was left of Poland, the area called General Government, was to be stripped. Governor-General Hans Frank at the Nuremberg trials voiced German policy: ". . . Poland shall be treated as a colony; the Poles shall be the slaves of the Greater German World Empire."[10]

Jews could not be tolerated. By spring of 1943, over three hundred thousand had been deported from Warsaw alone; in April, the German army attacked the remaining one hundred thousand unarmed Jews living in the Warsaw ghetto and eliminated them. The Germans established special concentration camps where Jews from Poland, central Europe, and western Russia were murdered—one estimate places the figure at four million.[11]

The ruthless German policy almost immediately generated widespread Polish resistance. Sikorski's government in exile in London remained in reasonably close contact with indigenous resistance forces, which it directed ". . . to build up a secret government, administration, army, press and even law courts and schools."[12] Resistance in general became the responsibility of the Home Army and of special groups, including guerrilla detachments, formed by various political parties.

Although the Home Army and other units performed some effective guerrilla actions, the long distance from England hindered supply by air. Nor was terrain particularly suited to guerrilla operations: the forests, where some guerrilla groups existed, were generally remote from major German installations and lines of communication. Poor internal communications also tended to prevent co-ordinated actions. But these deficiencies could in part have been overcome had Soviet Russia played a true allied role.

Unfortunately, she did nothing of the sort. Her attitude became clear as early as 1940, when she siphoned off a portion of General Anders' army-in-exile, placed it under command of a Polish Communist, Lieutenant Colonel Berling, and affixed it to a puppet exile group called the Union of Polish Patriots. Russia also made common cause with the indigenous Communist movement, which supported a People's Army and which, joined with the Union of Polish Patriots, formed the Lublin Committee, in July 1944. Meanwhile Russia had been dropping Polish and Russian saboteurs inside Poland, an effort that frequently brought German reprisals. In turn, local peasants, on occasion, fought these saboteurs—to German advantage.

Mainly for these reasons, Polish resistance consisted of sporadic, small-scale actions while local patriots built an underground army supplied with weapons either flown in from England or manufactured in un-

10. Ibid.
11. Ibid.; this figure was taken from Wilhelm Höttl's later testimony. Although Höttl is notoriously unreliable, no doubt exists as to the huge number of victims; see also H. Krausnick, *Anatomy of the SS State* (London: Collins, 1968).
12. Seton-Watson, op. cit.

derground factories or captured or stolen from the Germans. General Anders later estimated the size of this force at 380,000, of whom 40,000 were in Warsaw.[13]

When Russian armies approached the Vistula, in early August 1944, the Home Army rose in Warsaw, unfortunately a premature action, the result either of poor communications or a Communist trap designed to eliminate organized resistance to a postwar Communist take-over.[14] Whatever the reason, the Home Army, supported by most Warsaw civilians, fought off joint attacks of five German divisions for sixty-three days before surrendering. Although Polish resistance continued in the western provinces, the Warsaw disaster took the heart from it.

In addition to internal political differences, terrain also played an important role in shaping European resistance, as we have seen already in the cases of Czechoslovakia and Poland. Lack of natural sanctuary greatly inhibited initial resistance groups, which were little more than cells, lacking head, tail or body. Holland, Denmark, Belgium, and France offered few suitable areas for guerrilla operations, the exceptions being mountainous regions in Belgium and France. But these, and other sanctuaries in Poland and Czechoslovakia, did not lend themselves to raids essential to procure weapons and supplies.

The mountains of northern Italy proved more hospitable, and here large guerrilla groups eventually did form. But here also an ugly political factor existed. In 1944, when allies began supporting the Italian resistance in the North, it rested in a Committee of National Liberation of Northern Italy, with operations run by a Corps of Volunteers of Liberty, both organizations containing strong Communist elements. Such was the day's feeling, such the overwhelming priority awarded to purely military considerations, that the allies never hesitated in supplying quantitative aid even though one of the two resistance chiefs of staff was Luigi Longo, the Communist who had served with distinction in Spain.[15]

This resistance movement grew to perhaps ninety thousand members, who could not have survived without allied support delivered through SOE and OSS missions, which operated in separate areas. Whether the return on this considerable investment was adequate is debatable. Although the resistance hindered Kesselring's operations and final with-

13. W. Anders, *An Army in Exile* (London: Macmillan, 1949).
14. Ibid.; according to Anders, he and his military colleagues in London advised against the rising, but the civil government, generally at odds with the military (and themselves), disagreed and authorized it; see also Foot, op. cit.: For a long period, SOE was the "sole liaison" between the Polish ministries of interior and national defense, "an impossible but typical Polish situation"; see also Seton-Watson, op. cit., who has suggested a Russian dilemma that could explain the Soviet failure to advance, and even to refuse the use of Soviet airfields to allied supply planes.
15. Blair, op. cit.

drawal, Communist guerrilla groups used a large portion of arms and money in consolidating their own positions. As one result, the Italian Communist Party became the most powerful in postwar Europe and still represents a major force in Italian politics.

Norwegian sanctuaries offered a different problem, in that mountain retreats actually proved hostile to guerrillas. As C. N. M. Blair has pointed out, food to feed guerrillas had to come either from thinly populated valleys easily controlled by small German garrisons or from air drops made difficult by distance and adverse weather conditions.[16] Until the end of the war, guerrilla operations in Norway consisted of small groups sometimes buttressed by teams parachuted in for special operations. Meanwhile, SOE was arming a secret army, the Milorg, which, by early 1944, was administered in eleven districts ". . . with an effective strength of 33,000 well-disciplined and armed men."[17] At war's end, this organization threw off its wraps, accepted German surrender, and maintained order until the government-in-exile returned.

Without arms, equipment, or food, and without organization, communications, or training, early resistance groups created little more than nuisance value—but a value greatly enhanced by German overreaction, as explained above. But it was up to SOE, and later OSS, to exploit the potential of these groups, an effort that encountered numerous difficulties, frustrations, and failures, but one that also paid handsome dividends.

16. Ibid.
17. Cookridge, op. cit.; an interesting "non-violent" resistance also developed and played an important role in over-all resistance—see Magne Skodvin, "Norwegian Non-Violent Resistance During the German Occupation." Adam Roberts (ed.), *The Strategy of Civilian Defense* (London: Faber & Faber, 1967).

Chapter 33

*French resistance in World War II • The political caldron •
De Gaulle and the BCRA • Conflict with SOE • SOE's early
difficulties • The German occupation policy • Growth of resistance • German errors • Rise of the* maquis *• Guerrilla
warfare increases • SOE/OSS special units • Guerrilla support
of allied landings • The cost*

FRANCE was SOE's most important target in Europe, and SOE almost at once found difficulty in trying to work effectively in that country.

The reader will recall that, after the fall of France in 1940, a considerable body of French soldiers managed to escape either to England
or to Algeria. In London, this group formed the nucleus of the Free
French under a dynamic officer, Charles de Gaulle, who was not then
known outside the French Army. In Algeria, a similar group formed
somewhat later under General Giraud, De Gaulle's rival. In France itself, Nazis or no Nazis, the political caldron never stopped bubbling,
and this was even more the case when Germany split the country into
Occupied and Unoccupied France, with Marshal Pétain heading the
État français, or what the allies called Vichy France.

Just how responsible SOE officials overlooked this political turbulence is difficult to imagine, particularly in view of unsettled French
politics of the 1930s. But overlooked it was. As Professor Foot wrote,

. . . at first SOE's staff was ingenuous enough to imagine that all anti-German Frenchmen would work happily together; this was at once discovered to be wrong. Strong anti-Nazi elements in Vichy France refused to have any dealings with General de Gaulle, who in turn rejected anything and anybody that savored of co-operation with Pétain's regime.[1]

General de Gaulle had his own ideas for developing French resistance, a subject on which he was particularly touchy. As he later wrote,

. . . The most urgent thing was to install an embryo organization within the national territory. The British, for their part, would have liked to see us simply send over agents with instructions to gather, in isolation, information about the enemy with reference to defined objectives. Such was the method used for espionage. But we meant to do better. Since the action in France would be carried on in the midst of a population which would, we thought, be teeming with well-wishers, we meant to set up networks. By binding together hand-picked elements and communicating with us through centralized means these would give the best return.[2]

De Gaulle assigned the function to an amateur, the brilliant Major André Dewavrin, who, under the alias of Colonel Passy, headed the *Bureau Central de Renseignements et d'Action,* or BCRA.

BCRA conflicted with SOE almost immediately. SOE had established Section F to build resistance groups inside France. It now established another section, Section RF, to work with BCRA.[3] But the British soon discovered highly restrictive aspects of French policy:

. . . to the Gaullists, the question of who was to be in power in France after the Germans had been driven out was always *the* question; and they necessarily mistrusted bodies of armed men at large in France of whose allegiance they were uncertain.[4]

The British Government and SOE did not view the situation through the same politically colored glasses. Section DF, for example, which was trying to establish escape routes in France for downed airmen, did not give a hoot about the politics of those Frenchmen willing to risk their lives for this vital effort. And, while SOE attempted to appease De Gaulle with Section RF, it nonetheless retained Section F, whose agents

1. Foot, op. cit.
2. Charles de Gaulle, *War Memoirs* (London: Collins, 1955), Vol. 1 of 6 vols. Vol. 1 (Text and Documents) tr. J. Griffin; Vols. 2 and 3 (Text and Documents) tr. R. Howar.
3. Foot, op. cit.; see also Cookridge, op. cit.; Bickham Sweet-Escott, *Baker Street Irregular* (London: Methuen, 1965); Eric Piquet-Wicks, *Four in the Shadows* (London: Jarrolds, 1957).
4. Foot, op. cit.

worked secretly with other politically aligned resistance groups. The bulk
of these agents were non-French and, according to Foot,

. . . knew little of French politics and cared less; and when they had a political aim at all, beyond helping in the overthrow of Hitler and Pétain, it was
simply that of the British War Cabinet: to give the French every chance of
a quite unfettered choice of their own system of government once the war
was won.[5]

Free French discovery of Section F's separate existence created a
furor. In De Gaulle's words,

. . . A regular competition therefore started immediately, with us appealing
to the moral and legal obligation of Frenchmen not to join a foreign service,
and the British using the means at their disposal to try and gain for themselves agents, and then networks, of their own.[6]

Hard feeling continued—but so did Section F. At this time, SOE held
the most important cards: It got first crack at arriving French refugees,
who, if suitable for resistance work, were often recruited without BCRA
knowledge. It also owned the few arms and delivery systems available,
all training centers, and, not least, the money. Later, when the United
States entered the picture, Roosevelt's antipathy to De Gaulle further
strengthened SOE's hand.

In time, Section F ". . . built up almost a hundred independent cir-
cuits—networks of subversive agents on French soil; it armed several
scores of thousands of resisters, who fought well."[7] Communists numbered among those armed, but, seeing which way political winds blew,
quickly came to terms and remained in uneasy alliance with the Free
French. Similarly, BCRA and SOE eventually worked quite well together. The one needed the other, they both needed Communists, and
Communists needed them.

SOE faced other difficult problems. A year after the organization's
inauguration, one of its members, veteran diplomat Bruce Lockhart,
commented in a letter to Anthony Eden on "inter-departmental strife
and jealousies." Professor J. R. M. Butler, Britain's official military historian, later wrote: ". . . In its early months SOE suffered from the
suspicions of an upstart felt by older organizations, and was embittered
by personal animosities."[8]

The disruptive tendency was probably inevitable, considering the nature of the organization, the prima-donna temperament of many of its

5. Ibid.
6. De Gaulle, op. cit. (Vol. 1); Vol. 1 (Documents) contains an acrimonious
exchange of letters between De Gaulle and Anthony Eden on the subject.
7. Foot, op. cit.
8. J. R. M. Butler, *History of the Second World War, Grand Strategy* (London:
HMSO, 1957), Vol. 2.

members and the complexity and secrecy of its functions. A sometimes ludicrous hush-hush atmosphere developed: that expressed in American intelligence circles by the satirical security classification TOP SECRET BBO—burn before opening. Duplication also existed, mainly the result of the private battle of Giraud and De Gaulle in Algiers for control of the Free French. This caused SOE to establish Section AMF to work with the Free French in Algeria, and this meant more forces at work in the French interior.

SOE personnel usually encountered a frosty reception from the Foreign Office, whose junior diplomats ". . . as a rule regarded the organization with disdain. . . ."[9] The Foreign Office only grudgingly consented to one of SOE's most spectacular early successes, the capture of an enemy liner off the west coast of Africa in the spring of 1941. In the case of SOE operations inside Vichy France, diplomatic disdain frequently turned to alarm.[10]

Nor was the covert organization always popular with the armed forces, which ran their own intelligence-collection operations and even their own escape routes, a conflict well brought out in Airey Neave's recent book *Saturday at MI-9*.[11] The armed forces also organized special operational forces such as Commandos, which sometimes operated independently, sometimes in conjunction with SOE. Operational conflicts on occasion resulted:

. . . On one notorious occasion an SOE-controlled group reconnoitring the dockside at Bordeaux for an attack that night saw its targets sink under the impact of limpet mines—provided, ironically enough, by SOE—planted by canoe-borne marines [Commandos]. . . .[12]

A final complication occurred in the form of America's equivalent to SOE, the Office of Strategic Services, or OSS. The new organization consisted of three sections: research and analysis, intelligence collection, and special operations. As was the case with SOE, OSS grew too rapidly and recruited too many persons, some of whose qualifications were more suited to drawing-room soirées. Its fundamental and continuing enmities with other American organizations—the armed forces, the Federal Bureau of Investigation, and the Department of State—often resulted in wasteful duplication of facilities and operations, the classic example being in the China theater, as will be seen in a subsequent chapter.

OSS at first did not collide with SOE, at least not in western Europe. In autumn of 1942, an agreement between American and British chiefs of staff fused special operations of each organization in northwestern

9. Foot, op. cit.
10. Ibid.
11. Airey Neave, *Saturday at MI-9* (London: Hodder & Stoughton, 1969).
12. Foot, op. cit.; see also R. H. Smith, op. cit.

Europe into a section called SOE/SO, an arrangement reflected in Algiers by a combined Special Forces Headquarters (SFHQ). In time, OSS won its operational spurs to indulge in operations sharply at variance with SOE, though not so much in France as in Italy and the Far East. A ranking SOE official later wrote:

. . . By the end of the war their [OSS] bitterest detractors would be forced to admit that they had become quite as good as the British at getting secret intelligence and at carrying out special operations, and I personally thought they were doing better.[13]

SOE would have suffered major problems even under ideal circumstances if only because of the state of the art at the time: political naïveté, operational inexperience, communications difficulties, limited delivery means, top-heavy organization. But the quantitative approach it insisted on resulted in a duplication of covert operations, which sometimes severely complicated basic SOE missions, generally resulting in reduced efficiency and sometimes in operational catastrophes both in France and elsewhere.

Some catastrophe was perhaps unavoidable in the political confusion of the day. One example is the premature uprising of the Warsaw Poles, another the Slovak rising of 1944—previously discussed.

But other failures resulted from operational inefficiency including downright carelessness. A major SOE operation in the Netherlands furnished a striking example. For two years, a German *Abwehr,* or army intelligence, agent used a captured code to lure allied agents to destruction by means of false radio messages, a sorrowful but dramatic tale told by the officer responsible, Colonel H. J. Giskes, in *London Calling North Pole.*[14] Another Abwehr agent, a German sergeant named Hugo Bleicher, trapped numerous allied agents in France by posing as Monsieur Jean or Colonel Henri, again a sad but immensely dramatic tale told in Bleicher's book *Colonel Henri's Story.*[15]

Considering the extent of the German effort, the thousands of agents and secret police and scores of military units involved, such successes were remarkably few and almost always hinged on concentrating on agent communications. One of the most valuable lessons offered by French resistance is the relative ease with which resistance members operated in occupied areas, where by no means all of the civil population was friendly to the allied cause. A large number of postwar memoirs underlined this lesson, my own favorites being George Millar's *Horned*

13. Sweet-Escott, op. cit.; R. H. Smith, op. cit.
14. H. J. Giskes, *London Calling North Pole* (London: Arthur Barker, 1966).
15. Hugo Bleicher, *Colonel Henri's Story* (London: William Kimber, 1954). Ed. Ian Colvin.

Pigeon and *Maquis,* Peter Churchill's *Of Their Own Choice,* and Bruce Marshall's *The White Rabbit.*[16]

Although concerned allied organizations and incredibly brave agents can take some credit, much of it must go to the enemy, whose inept occupation procedures for the most part not only failed to exploit the divisive environment but caused many Frenchmen to take a stand, if only of inert sympathy, in favor of the resistance.

The Germans at first behaved themselves. As Blake Ehrlich wrote in *The French Resistance:*

. . . After the armistice of June 25, 1940, the Germans made every effort to show themselves to be "correct." . . . The serenity, the charity, the unity of the Germans, even the radiant health, elegant uniforms and superb machines of the soldiery, left the French with little resource. . . .[17]

Eric Piquet-Wicks, who served in Section RF and was close to Passy, later wrote of "a certain lethargy" in the unoccupied zone in the early years. General de Gaulle noted that, in 1940, although some indications of resistance feeling appeared,

. . . no sign led one to suppose that French people in appreciable numbers were resolved on action. The enemy, wherever he was, ran no risk in our country. As for Vichy, few were those who contested its authority. The Marshal [Pétain] himself remained very popular. . . . At bottom, the great majority wanted to believe that Pétain was playing a deep game and that, when the day came, he would take up arms again. The general opinion was that he and I were secretly in agreement. In the last resort, propaganda had, as always, only slight value in itself. Everything depended on events. . . .[18]

A small natural resistance, those who would never quit, did exist. Ehrlich cited one Berthe Marquaille, who hid soldiers left behind at Dunkerque and later helped them to escape; denounced by a neighbor in her village of Lézennes, she was executed by the Germans. A small group in Nancy helped evacuate nearly seven thousand escaped prisoners of war in a year and a half; the group later became an important resistance *réseau,* or network.

As early as August 1940, the Germans responded to acts of sabotage by ordering a curfew and seizure of hostages. This solved very little, and continuing repressive measures served to expand isolated and unco-ordinated resistance nuclei. Anti-German posters appeared, un-

16. George Millar, *Horned Pigeon* (London: William Heinemann, 1946); George Millar, *Maquis* (London: William Heinemann, 1945); Peter Churchill, *Of Their Own Choice* (London: Hodder & Stoughton, 1952); Bruce Marshall, *The White Rabbit* (London: Evans Brothers, 1964).

17. Blake Ehrlich, *The French Resistance* (London: Chapman & Hall, 1966).

18. De Gaulle, op. cit. (Vol. 1).

derground newspapers multiplied, sabotage continued.[19] The German invasion of Russia brought French Communists to life. Peculiarly prepared for resistance work, as De Gaulle later wrote, ". . . by their organization in cells, the anonymity of their hierarchy and the devotion of their cadres," they believed in striking whenever and wherever possible, violence that brought savage reprisals and enlarged the resistance.

In August 1941, Pétain admitted the growing problem in a radio address:

. . . From several regions of France I can feel an evil wind blowing. Unrest is taking hold of people's minds. Doubt is seizing their souls. The authority of the Government is being called in question. Orders are being carried out badly. A real uneasiness is striking at the French people.[20]

In September 1941, resistance fighters killed the colonel commanding Nantes garrison, an officer in Bordeaux, and two German soldiers in Paris. The Germans shot forty-eight French citizens in Nantes and fifty in Bordeaux in retaliation. A month later, De Gaulle broadcast from London:

. . . It is absolutely natural and absolutely right that Germans should be killed by Frenchmen. If the Germans did not wish to receive death at our hands, they had only to stay at home. . . . But there are tactics in war. War must be conducted by those entrusted with the task. . . . For the moment, my orders to those in occupied territory are not to kill Germans there openly. This for one reason only: that it is, at present, too easy for the enemy to retaliate by massacring our fighters, now, for the time being, disarmed. On the other hand, as soon as we are in a position to move to the attack, the orders for which you are waiting will be given.[21]

Resistance elements controlled by Gaullist officers generally conformed to these orders. Other units, including most Communist maquis, did not. Continued reprisals and German behavior in general helped resistance to grow, as did inept enemy propaganda and German refusal to release over a million French prisoners of war being used as a labor force in Germany. The creation of and reliance on special French police forces such as Joseph Darnand's Service d'Ordre de la Légion—which in 1943 would become the brutal and hated *Milice*—also did much to antagonize an increasingly restless population.[22]

19. The importance of the clandestine press during the German occupation has generally been overlooked and deserves more study. See, for example, George Tanham, *Contribution à l'Histoire de la Résistance Belge* (Brussels: University of Brussels Press, 1971), Chapter 5.

20. De Gaulle, op. cit.

21. Ibid.

22. Ehrlich, op. cit.; Foot, op. cit.: Darnand's original organization was a fascist group supposedly composed of loyal gentlemen but in reality, in George Millar's words, claiming ". . . the scum of the jails, brutalized of the most brutal, cream

In mid-1942, the Germans erred seriously by introducing a forced-labor scheme, the dreaded STO, or *Service du Travail Obligatoire*, under which men of military age were taken to Germany. Although the Germans shipped twenty thousand men a week from Paris, thousands more fled to the hills and mountains, there to form the famed maquis.[23] A recruiting leaflet of the time suggests their over-all frame of mind:

. . . Men who come to the maquis to fight live badly, in precarious fashion, with food hard to find; they will be absolutely cut off from their families for the duration; the enemy does not apply the rules of war to them; they can not be assured any pay; every effort will be made to help their families, but it is impossible to give any guarantee in this matter; all correspondence is forbidden.

Bring two shirts, two underpants, two pair wool socks, a light sweater, a scarf, a heavy sweater, a wool blanket, an extra pair of shoes, shoe laces, needles, thread, buttons, safety pins, soap, canteen, knife and fork, flashlight, compass, a weapon if possible, and also if possible a sleeping bag. Wear a warm suit, a beret, a raincoat, a good pair of hobnailed shoes.

You will need a complete set of papers, even false, but in order, with a work card to pass you through road-blocks. It is essential to have food ration tickets.[24]

German occupation of Vichy France in response to allied landings in North Africa further extended the meaning of the war to the French nation—in other words, it stirred up what Lyautey would have termed an "asleep" area and forced people to take a position for or against resistance.

German security services, the Abwehr and Gestapo, were not up to the increased task. German countermeasures suffered from competing counterespionage organizations and police forces whose ". . . senior staffs were obsessed by service intrigues, and their junior staffs were often as incompetent as they were cruel. . . ."

. . . The nature of the Nazi state machine ensured that many German counter-espionage agents were more interested in promoting the status of

of the offal." According to Ehrlich, each member swore ". . . to fight against democracy, against Gaullist dissidence and against the Jewish leprosy." Darnand became head of Vichy police, ". . . with power over all law enforcement agencies under French control." In 1943 his "legion" became the Milice, described by Ehrlich as ". . . a fully equipped little army of young Frenchmen, with special spy services to uncover resistance and to infiltrate resistance movements. They were noted for their joyous viciousness. . . ." Foot notes that they ". . . lived and worked in their home towns and villages, and used their local knowledge expertly. . . . They might be found at work in any part of France. . . ."

23. Ibid. *Maquis* ". . . is a Corsican word for the dense brush of the hill country, to which Corsicans historically repair when they are in trouble."

24. Ehrlich, op. cit.

their own organization as compared with its rivals at home than in actually coping with the activities of allied agents in the field.[25]

As early as October 1942, the German high command was becoming apprehensive, Hitler himself ordering:

. . . In future, all terror and sabotage troops of the British and their accomplices, who do not act like soldiers but rather like bandits, will be treated as such by the German troops and will be ruthlessly eliminated in battle, wherever they appear.[26]

Hollow words, these. By the end of 1942, Marshal von Rundstedt noted:

. . . It was already impossible to dispatch single members of the Wehrmacht, ambulances, couriers, or supply columns without armed protection to the First or Nineteenth Army in the south of France.[27]

SOE did not actively promote guerrilla warfare at this time, but instead was trying to build a secret army by furnishing necessary arms and equipment to the newly formed maquis. Among the problems, logistics loomed large. SOE's original plan for building secret armies in France, Poland, and Czechoslovakia had called for organizing, training and arming 130,000 underground fighters. In spring of 1941, the British Chiefs of Staff rejected the plan, which would have required 8,000 sorties by the RAF, as "utterly unrealistic."[28] SOE countered with a proposal to arm 45,000 men in France and the Low Countries, but that would have required 2,000 RAF bomber sorties at a time when the RAF was averaging only that number per month.[29] With aircraft at a premium, French resistance received only meager arms and supply during 1942.

Progress nonetheless resulted. In February 1943, when Commander Yeo-Thomas (the White Rabbit), Colonel Passy, and Pierre Brossolette slipped into France, they found five distinct resistance groups. Of the Gaullist formations, the Organisation Civile et Militaire was the most highly organized and had the best security. The Front National, a Communist organization that supported the Franc-Tireurs et Partisans, or FTP, without question ". . . formed the strongest and most effective Resistance group. . . . They claimed to carry out roughly 250 attacks and to kill between 500 and 600 Germans every month."[30] In time, the FTP furnished nearly a third of the maquis. Although they refused

25. Foot, op. cit.
26. Ibid.: In North Africa, Rommel refused to pass on this order to his subordinates.
27. Ibid.
28. Cookridge, op. cit.
29. Sweet-Escott, op. cit.
30. Marshall, op. cit.

to relinquish control of their units, they agreed to join the other organizations in establishing a secret army commanded by General Delestraint —a co-operation prompted more by need for recognition, arms, and money than by patriotism.

In June, the Gestapo, which had penetrated the National Committee of Resistance, suddenly struck. General Delestraint (known as General Vidal), was shot: ". . . The national organization was shattered and Resistance groups throughout the country suffered heavy losses."

Despite this major setback,

. . . the second line of the leadership and the hard core of local and regional groups had survived. Surprisingly, only a small percentage of supplies were lost. Elated by the capture of many prominent Resistance leaders, the Germans had failed to find the hideouts and dumps of arms, ammunition and explosives which SOE had been delivering on an increasing scale. In many areas, reception committees, reorganized and led by local leaders, continued to welcome new supplies and new SOE instructors, liaison officers and radio operators from Britain.[31]

In October 1943, the German commander-in-chief in France, General von Rundstedt wrote to Hitler, noting ". . . with alarm the rapid increase in rail sabotage." In September, he reported, ". . . there were 534 very serious rail sabotage actions, as compared to a monthly average of only 120 during the first half of the year." Vichy police reported ". . . more than 3,000 separate attempts by Resistance saboteurs to wreck the railway system, of which 427 resulted in very heavy damage while 132 caused derailment with serious loss of German troops." Continuing destruction forced the Germans to import 20,000 German railway workers, and ". . . SS units had to be diverted from the front to guard stations, locomotive sheds, workshops and thousands of miles of track by day and night."[32]

London still did not want a general uprising. In August 1943, SOE planners had stated the secret army's mission during allied landings:

. . . a preliminary increase in the tempo of sabotage, with particular attention to fighter aircraft and enemy morale; attacks on local headquarters, simple road and telephone wrecking, removal of German explosive from mined bridges likely to be useful to the allies, and more and more sabotage as the air battle reached its climax; and then, simultaneously with the seaborne assault, an all-out attack on roads, railways and telephones, and the harassing of occupation troops wherever they could be found by any available means. This last injunction was bound to lead in places to guerrilla; but guerrilla was not called for in the original plan. . . .[33]

31. Cookridge, op. cit.
32. Ibid.
33. Foot, op. cit.

Some resistance units, particularly those dominated by Communists, refused to lie low and insisted on striking the enemy wherever possible. One source reported that, between June 1943 and May 1944, 1,822 locomotives were destroyed or badly damaged, 200 passenger carriages destroyed and 1,500 damaged, 2,500 freight wagons destroyed and 8,000 damaged.[34]

In January 1944, some maquis chiefs refused to obey De Gaulle's instructions to lie low until D-Day, and guerrilla activity notably increased. In words reminiscent of a French marshal in Spain in 1810, Von Rundstedt later wrote:

. . . From January, 1944, the state of affairs in Southern France became so dangerous that all [German] commanders reported a general revolt. . . . Cases became numerous where whole formations of troops, and escorting troops of the military commanders were surrounded by bands for many days and, in isolated locations, simply killed off. . . . The life of the German troops in southern France was seriously menaced and became a doubtful proposition.[35]

In the first three months of 1944, guerrillas destroyed 808 locomotives (as opposed to 387 destroyed by allied air action).[36]

French and British planners in London meanwhile incorporated guerrilla warfare into plans for the Normandy landing: Plan Green to sabotage all railway lines; Plan Violet all telephone lines; Plan Tortoise all main roads. In mountainous districts, ". . . the Resistance must create redoubts and mobilization centers from which the personnel could be reinforced when the moment came."[37]

Special command teams, the Jedburghs, would help the secret army. Each team consisted of two officers—French, British, or American— and a sergeant radio operator, with each man trained in guerrilla tactics:

. . . Their objects were to provide a general staff for the local resistance wherever they landed, to co-ordinate the local efforts in the best interests of allied strategy, and where possible to arrange further supplies of arms.[38]

Special Air Service, or SAS, units, consisting of thirty to sixty ". . . heavily armed, Commando-trained men," complemented this effort. So did Operational Groups, or OGs,

. . . airborne commandos of thirty-two men, who could be split up into two or four independent groups. They are trained for special missions, the de-

34. Cookridge, op. cit.
35. Foot, op. cit.
36. Cookridge, op. cit.
37. Robert Aron, *De Gaulle Before Paris—The Liberation of France June–August 1944* (London: Putnam, 1962). Tr. H. Hare.
38. Foot, op. cit.; see also Alsop and Braden, op. cit.

struction, or indeed the protection, of some precise objective and came directly under headquarters in London. Once their particular mission had been carried out, the O.G. had orders to join the nearest F.F.I. and assist them in their ordinary activities.[39]

The Aloès Mission completed the list; this was a complete headquarters that would go into action after the landings. Jedburgh, SAS, and OG units were to parachute into rendezvous areas prearranged with resistance groups.

In March 1944, De Gaulle formally created the French Forces of the Interior, or FFI, to which SOE/OSS became subordinated; in the subsequent battle for France, FFI, however, remained subordinated to Supreme Headquarters Allied Expeditionary Forces (SHAEF).

A lack of aircraft had continued to hinder the supply effort. As late as November 1943, Yeo-Thomas inspected a maquis camp in the Department of the Lot:

. . . The thirty men in the camp were disciplined, well fed and happy. Divided into groups of five each commanded by an NCO ("*Sixaines*"), all the armament they possessed between them consisted of one Sten gun with a hundred rounds, three French rifles with five rounds each and ten revolvers with ten rounds each: there were no grenades at all. The available arms were used by all in turn for instructional purposes, drill, weapon-stripping and field craft exercises by night. Lack of ammunition prevented target practise.[40]

In a second guerrilla camp, of thirty men, he found only one rifle and ten rounds of ammunition.

Yeo-Thomas was largely responsible for persuading Winston Churchill to divert more planes to the effort. Increased American air force participation also helped. In the first six months of 1944, in addition to large shipments of explosives and ammunition, SOE dropped into France 45,354 Sten guns, 17,576 pistols, 10,251 rifles, 1,832 Bren guns, 300 bazookas, and 143 mortars.[41] On D-Day, June 6, 1944, about twenty thousand resistance fighters were fully armed; another fifty thousand were armed ". . . in some degree."[42]

French and SOE views of commitment differed. In spring of 1944, De Gaulle's headquarters sent an agent into France with instructions to various resistance leaders:

. . . he explained to them that it would be folly to mount a general action. The liberation of territory by the Allies, even on the most favorable suppo-

39. Aron, op. cit.
40. Marshall, op. cit.
41. Cookridge, op. cit.; see also Foot, op. cit.: SOE logisticians eventually hit on four categories of transport aircraft "loads." The smallest, Load A, consisted of 12 containers that held 6 Bren guns, 36 rifles, 27 Sten guns, 5 pistols, 52 grenades, field dressings, and several thousand rounds of ammunition.
42. Cookridge, op. cit.

sition, could only be progressive. The Resistance operations in France must therefore be launched in succession, district by district, and on orders from London. In no circumstances were they to assume the nature of a general insurrection, but to be limited to local sabotage operations and such guerrilla warfare as the Allied authorities might require. . . .[43]

In the event, prearranged signals from the SOE, broadcast by BBC, called for a general insurrection.

Commencing in June, in one week guerrillas cut or blew up over one thousand railroad lines to prevent eight enemy divisions from immediately entering the battle of the beaches. On June 6, the German high command, for example, ordered the Second SS Panzer Division to march from Montauban to the Normandy beachhead, normally a three-day effort. Confined to roads because of railway sabotage and constantly attacked by maquis, the division did not arrive at Alençon until June 18. The Eleventh Panzer Division, hastily summoned from Russia, reached the French border in eight days but required another twenty-four days ". . . to cross France from Strasbourg to Caen."[44]

Not all maquis units prospered. A maquis of about five hundred Frenchmen and sixty Spanish stationed on the Plateau des Glières fought a thirteen-day withdrawal against several battalions of German troops in February 1944.[45] As the French had feared, premature action on D-Day sometimes cost dearly. Some small groups, such as a fifteen-man unit in Caen, were captured and executed to a man the day after D-Day. On D-Day, a Corcieux maquis, of thirty-four men, attacked a German garrison of several hundred soldiers at Taintrux, in the Vosges area, a failure costing most of them their lives and bringing severe reprisals on the civilian population.[46] In other areas, notably near Saint Marcel, in Brittany, pitched battles developed between large maquis forces reinforced by SAS and OG units. On June 18, a powerful German force attacked and drove the maquis from its redoubt area, but at a cost of over five hundred German dead. On June 24, maquis on Vercors Plateau fought off a large-scale German attack but suffered severe casualties before withdrawing.

In general, the maquis served brilliantly, not only on and immediately after D-Day but throughout crucial summer months. On July 18, 1944, a pro-Nazi French official complained by letter to Ambassador Otto Abetz:

. . . It is no longer possible today for private persons or for Wehrmacht vehicles to travel along the roads of France. It is impossible to go freely from

---

43. Aron, op. cit.; Professor Foot has informed me that ". . . those BBC messages calling out resistance all over France were sent on Eisenhower's direct order, against the advice of his technical advisers of several levels and nationalities.
44. De Gaulle, op. cit. (Vol. 2).
45. M. J. Bird, *The Secret Battalion* (London: Muller, 1965).
46. Aron, op. cit.

Paris to Lyons, from Lyons to Bordeaux, from Paris to Châteauroux, from Châteauroux to Angoulême. . . . The roads of Brittany are impractical. Behind the Normandy front, the Chief of Staff of the Army, whose head-quarters are at Le Mans, has told me that German convoys are far from safe owing to particularly active maquisards. The roads from Paris to Nancy and Verdun, and from Paris to Mézières, have been cut by the Maquis, that is to say that within a short distance from the German frontier the men of the Maquis attack officers of the Wehrmacht. . . . The Maquis forces are so numerous that one is forced to the conclusion that, since the month of May, a veritable mobilization has taken place in the towns and villages of central France, as well as in the south and southeast.[47]

According to the historian Robert Aron, between July 10 and August 4 in the department of Côtes-du-Nord, the maquis put 2,500 Germans out of action, cut 300 telephone and high-tension lines, effectively sabotaged railways, derailed 40 trains, ambushed 50 convoys and captured 200 vehicles, burned 10,000 gallons of German gasoline, and captured a prison and liberated 32 Frenchmen condemned to death.[48]

Similar actions took place throughout France. One resistance veteran later wrote a classic account of a maquis ambush:

. . . in a few minutes an unending stream of armored cars, motorcars, motorcyclists, lorries and occasional tanks appeared . . . the speed of advance was extremely slow—about five miles an hour—and there were frequent halts to remove a tree trunk, investigate a supposed trap, or reconnoitre the roadside. All this was a sure proof—if we needed one—that the maquis guerrillas were feared, and were succeeding in their main intention of delaying the enemy. The troops we saw were both German infantry and *miliciens*. . . .

As guerrillas watched, noise of a distant ambush caused the convoy to halt, and then from the left a small maquis section opened fire:

. . . My two companions and myself opened fire immediately; one of us had a rifle, the other two had carbines. We fired as rapidly as possible into that mass of sprawling men. . . . It was difficult to distinguish between dead and living, and for one whole minute there was every sign of confusion and panic.

Then a curious thing happened. It seemed as if the whole division went into action against us. Small arms, heavy machine guns, mortars, small pieces of artillery, began plastering the woods on our side of the road over a space of at least five hundred yards, and although trees and bushes on our flanks and rear were churned up, nothing dropped near.

It was so typically German! They found it difficult to locate us, they

47. Ibid.
48. Ibid.

thought we were more numerous than we were, so they shot at anything moving—even a branch in the wind. They were using a sledge-hammer to crack a walnut—and missed the walnut!

. . . after a period of less than five minutes . . . we ourselves decamped. . . . I looked back once . . . two parties could already be seen fifty yards from the road coming up to encircle us and progressing by "movement and fire" alternately. . . . They continued to fire in our direction with all calibres, long after we left that wood behind. . . .[49]

Postwar writings frequently compared accomplishments of conventional and unconventional arms. Detractors of irregular warfare, usually professional soldiers, sometimes caused the proponents to indulge in unfair comparisons: Foot, for example, wrote that

. . . Bomber Command frequently lost in a night more men than F Section lost in the entire war; once it lost in a night more people than F Section ever sent to France. The command's total of dead (47,268 on operations) was more than four times as great as SOE's total strength. . . .[50]

This is an example of the numbers game that was to become increasingly popular in the irregular-warfare era. It fails to include the civil population. Bombings, particularly mass night attacks, may kill numerous civilians and may on a Dresden or Hiroshima or Nagasaki occasion wipe out populations, and bombers may suffer heavy casualties.

But this does not reduce costs, direct or indirect, of clandestine operations and guerrilla warfare. French resistance paid a premium price for each operational success whether a piece of vital intelligence, an escaped pilot or a blown-up train. The organizations lost over five hundred agents, generally ghastly deaths; the Germans arrested and tortured hundreds more. In addition, from October 1940 to December 1941, according to official French figures, the Germans arrested 4,500 French men and women suspected of being resistance workers; they arrested 37,609 in 1942 and about 50,000 in 1943.[51] General de Gaulle later wrote that:

. . . with the co-operation of a considerable number of officials and a mass of informers, 60,000 persons had been executed and more than 200,000 deported of whom a bare 50,000 survived. Further, 35,000 men and women had been condemned by Vichy tribunals; 70,000 "suspects" interned; 35,000 officials cashiered; 15,000 officers degraded under suspicion of being in the resistance.[52]

49. Foot, op. cit.
50. Ibid.
51. Hoover Institution on War, Revolution and Peace, *France During the German Occupation 1940–1944* (Stanford, Calif.: Stanford University Press, 1957). Tr. P. W. Whitcomb. 3 vols.
52. De Gaulle, op. cit. (Vol. 3).

FRANCE 1940-1945
• Towns and Cities

M.E.P.

According to Robert Aron, some twenty-four thousand maquisards were killed—a high percentage in view of their total strength of two hundred thousand. French headquarters in London distributed over 15 billion francs to resistance forces; the cost to SOE and OSS must have been astronomical. SOE and OSS dropped more than half a million small arms and four thousand larger weapons, many of which fell into enemy hands.[53]

53. Ibid.; see also F. O. Miksche, *Secret Forces—the Technique of Underground Movements* (London: Faber & Faber, 1950): ". . . During the war the following

France paid another internal price—that of revenge. Maquis units summarily executed an estimated 6,675 collaborators before the liberation, another 4,000 after. Tribunals subsequently condemned 2,071 persons to death (De Gaulle commuted 1,303 of the sentences); the courts also passed 39,900 prison sentences.[54]

Resistance is not an easy task.

---

arms supplies were parachuted into France: 198,000 Sten guns, 128,000 rifles, 20,-000 Bren guns, 10,000 carbines, 58,000 pistols, 595,000 kilograms of explosives, 723,000 hand grenades, 9,000 mines, 20,700 bazookas, 285 mortars."

54. De Gaulle, op. cit. (Vol. 3).

Chapter 34

German invasion of Russia • Ukrainian apathy • The Red army and guerrilla warfare • Stalin calls for guerrilla resistance • Early guerrilla operations • Guerrilla problems • Germany's extermination policy • German counterguerrilla tactics • Kaminski and Vlasov • German intransigence

FEW INVADING ARMIES in history have received the spontaneous welcome accorded to Hitler's powerful legions in some areas of the Ukraine in 1941. Instead of sniper fire or Molotov cocktails, Panzer commanders received floral bouquets from cheering civilians who greeted the Teutonic host as "liberators" from Soviet rule. Ukrainian nationalists in eastern Galicia actually rose against their Soviet masters, ". . . a revolt savagely repressed by the retreating Red Army and NKVD [secret police]. . . ."[1] If local reception was less enthusiastic in other areas, in general it was at first pacific, the population showing every desire to accommodate itself to the new masters.

This halcyon state of affairs sprang from a variety of reasons: general hostility of border peoples to the Soviet regime; Kremlin failure to plan effectively for partisan resistance; the surprise, speed, and weight of the

1. Alexander Dallin, *German Rule in Russia, 1941–1945* (New York: St. Martin's Press, 1957).

German advance, which in many areas temporarily neutralized small guerrilla groups that managed to form.

The touchy international political situation helped explain the Kremlin's reluctance to plan extensive guerrilla resistance. Red army planners obviously respected the potential. Shortly after the 1917 revolution, the father of the Red army, Frunze, demanded ". . . the spirit of offensive maneuver" but stressed need for ". . . preparation for conducting partisan warfare in the territories of possible theatres of military activities":

. . . Therefore one of the tasks of our General Staff must be working out the ideas of "little war" in its application to our future wars with an enemy technologically superior to us.

An important part will be played by partisan operations, which should be prepared for action on a large scale, and certain army units should be educated systematically in the spirit of such operations.[2]

Subsequent Red army planners stressed regular army operations, but did not exclude guerrilla warfare. Prior to World War II,

. . . military textbooks and courses in Red Army academies analyzed partisan operations of the Civil War period and occasionally referred to partisan activity in other periods or countries. . . . Historical and political journals, especially those concerned with the history of the Communist Party, printed lengthy articles on the Red partisans of the Civil War.[3]

Although the government organized and partially equipped small guerrilla bands in some border areas, lack of organization and official fears greatly restricted the project. The Kremlin had no wish to create a Frankenstein monster of armed peasants, any more than the Spanish Republican Government had wanted to arm workers in 1936. Civilian morale also entered: to prepare for partisan warfare bespoke retreat of regular forces, an admission of weakness which did not square with Kremlin infallibility.

In the event, the Kremlin tried to make up for lost time. Five days after the German invasion, the head of the Ukrainian Communist Party, Nikita Khrushchev, ". . . gave fairly detailed instructions on partisan organization to a provincial Party secretary. . . ."[4] In early July 1941,

2. R. L. Garthoff, *How Russia Makes War—Soviet Military Doctrine* (London: Allen & Unwin, 1954).

3. J. A. Armstrong and K. DeWitt, "Organization and Control of the Partisan Movement." In Armstrong, *supra*. The German use of the word *Partisanen* abruptly halted when authorities learned that the Russian word signified "fighters for freedom." Instead—shades of Chiang Kai-shek and Ngo Dinh Diem—they began to use *Banditen*.

4. Armstrong, op. cit.

in a backs-to-the-wall broadcast to the Russian people, Joseph Stalin ordered:

. . . In areas occupied by the enemy, guerrilla units, mounted and on foot, must be formed; diversionist groups must be organized to combat the enemy troops, to foment guerrilla war everywhere, to blow up bridges and roads, damage telephone and telegraph lines, set fire to forests, stores, transports. In the occupied regions conditions must be made unbearable for the enemy and all his accomplices. They must be hounded and annihilated at every step and all their measures frustrated.[5]

In early July, a new army command charged with partisan warfare ordered political leaders in combat areas to organize guerrilla units:

. . . Generally they were to operate only at night and from ambush. Their mission was to attack troop columns and assemblies, motorized infantry, camps, transports of fuel and ammunition, headquarters, air bases, and railroad trains previously halted by rail demolitions.[6]

Special diversionary units were to carry out sabotage, ". . . cutting telephone lines, firing fuel and ammunition dumps, railroad demolition, and attacks on individual or small groups of enemy vehicles."[7]

The army also began setting up guerrilla training camps to furnish small teams that would parachute behind German armies. Army Group South encountered these in late July and learned from interrogation that they had been charged with intelligence collection, sabotage and terror missions. Later, the camps trained persons to organize resistance and carry out various technical aspects of guerrilla activities.

The first guerrilla groups consisted of what one authority has well termed "shareholders" of the Soviet political system, mostly NKVD officials and party members from towns and cities.[8] But Red-army fugitives, at first officers and political commissars, followed civilians into forests and swamps, where ordinary soldiers and civilian refugees began joining them:

. . . before the first of July [1941] infantry units of *Army Group North* were harassed from all sides by bypassed Red elements. Numbers of Soviet troops were still roaming the swamps and forests, von Leeb reported to OKH [army high command], many in peasant clothes, and effective counter-

5. Armstrong and DeWitt, op. cit.
6. E. M. Howell, *The Soviet Partisan Movement, 1941–1944* (Washington: U. S. Government Printing Office, 1956).
7. Ibid.
8. Garthoff (op. cit.) has pointed out that ". . . according to former partisans now in the West, the majority of partisan units arose spontaneously and later were usually taken over by Party officials, since the latter were the only ones able to effect arrangements for supply (and guidance) from Moscow."

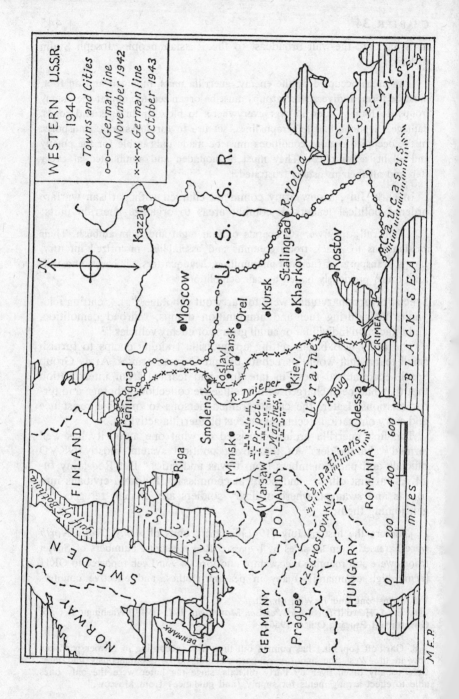

WESTERN U.S.S.R.
1940

● Towns and Cities
○–○–○ German line
     November 1942
×–×–× German line
     October 1943

NORWAY

SWEDEN

FINLAND

Gulf of Bothnia

DENMARK

GERMANY

Prague●

CZECHOSLOVAKIA

POLAND

Warsaw●

HUNGARY

Carpathians

ROMANIA

Odessa

R. Bug

Kiev

Ukraine

R. Dnieper

Pripet
Marshes

Minsk

Riga

Leningrad

Smolensk

Roslavl

Bryansk

Orel

Kursk

Kharkov

Rostov

Stalingrad

R. Volga

Moscow

Kazan

U. S. S. R.

CAUCASUS

CASPIAN SEA

BLACK SEA

CRIMEA

N

0   200   400   600
      miles

M.E.P.

measures were frustrated by the expanse and difficulty of the country and by manpower limitations. . . .[9]

Nowhere was this resistance serious. German weight had severely dislocated embryo partisan activity. The few guerrilla bands that managed to form became greatly segmented and devoid of central control. Although one German division operating in northeast Belorussia in late July 1941 spoke of "partisan regions" and reported ". . . that roads were mined daily,"[10] this was the exception. Also in 1941 in Belorussia, ". . . a single security division protected 250 miles of the main railroad."[11]

Most partisans were having too much difficulty keeping alive to worry about resistance. In the south, flat and treeless steppes broken only by isolated forests and swamps provided unsuitable sanctuary, and the bands here were early eliminated. In general, a hostile population hindered the guerrilla effort. Peasants and townspeople in numerous areas refused to give guerrillas food or information and did not hesitate to report their presence to the enemy. Primarily for this reason, the partisan movement in the mountain areas of the Caucasus, the Crimea, and western Ukraine never developed into a serious threat.

Guerrillas in the center and north found far more suitable terrain in wide belts of swamps, forests, and lakes encircling the Pripet Marshes. Not only did the land provide sanctuary, but, by channeling enemy communications to a few roads and railroads, it provided suitable targets for guerrillas. However, peasants and townspeople here and especially in Baltic areas, to the north, also proved hostile, and survival was not easy.

Finally, the first winter, of 1941–42, hurt the movement everywhere: forays to collect food and fuel meant tracks in the snow, and naked trees often meant naked guerrillas. In order to survive, various bands amalgamated into good sized camps, and some of these became vulnerable to German attacks. The more secure the camp, the farther it lay from profitable targets, thus complicating operations.

Three factors, however, saved incipient guerrilla groups at this crucial time, and even allowed them to expand: German occupation policy, German counterguerrilla methods, and Soviet organization and support of the guerrilla effort.

By far the most important of the three was the overriding German attitude toward the Russian population. First revealed by Soviet wartime propaganda, it was confirmed at the Nuremberg trials. But as schol-

9. Howell, op. cit.

10. R. Mavrogordato and E. Ziemke, "The Polotsk Lowland." In Armstrong, *supra*.

11. Armstrong and DeWitt, op. cit.

ars continue to sift millions of captured German documents, the whole story is slowly emerging. In addition to earlier official histories, outstanding work was done by Alexander Dallin in his book *German Rule in Russia, 1941–1945*.[12] More recently, Professor John Armstrong has edited a valuable symposium, *Soviet Partisans in World War II*.[13]

From Hitler down, the Nazi high command regarded Russians as *Untermenschen,* or subhuman beings, an attitude succinctly noted by Goebbels in his diary: the Russians ". . . are not people, but a conglomeration of animals. . . . Bolshevism has merely accentuated this racial propensity of the Russian people."[14]

Before the Wehrmacht marched, Hitler had decided that Russia must cease to exist as a nation. Expecting to accomplish her military destruction within four months, he foresaw a civil occupation and ultimate partition that would eliminate Bolshevism, the Russian nation, and most Soviet states, to provide a vast and rich area for German colonization and exploitation. Hitler decreed a civil occupation just as soon as possible and created a Ministry for the Occupied Eastern Territories (the *Ostministerium*), under Alfred Rosenberg, to accomplish it. Each of three army groups held responsibility for a Zone of Operations, which was divided into a Combat Zone and Army Rear Areas. The area behind this became the bailiwick of Rosenberg's civil commissars, who followed closely the army groups to take over territory as fast as the military forged ahead.

So far, so good.

But, sandwiched between army groups and civil functionaries and lapping over into each sphere, came Himmler's SS organization, ". . . charged with preparation for political administration in the military zone of operations."[15] And to confuse matters further, Hitler charged Goering with economic exploitation of occupied areas, which could not but lead to conflict with Rosenberg and even with Himmler and army group commanders.

Himmler's mission spelled evil. His was a murder function authorized by Hitler's Commissar Order, which called for elimination of all Communist Party officials and Red army commissars at ". . . not later than the transit prisoner of war camps."[16] To eliminate the Jewish-Bolshevik enemy, Himmler set up special action teams (*Einsatzgruppen*) composed of SS, SD, and Gestapo troops and agents who ". . . would move in behind the conquering army, comb the newly-won lands, and mercilessly exterminate ideological and racial enemies. . . ."[17]

12. Dallin, op. cit.
13. Armstrong, op. cit.
14. Dallin, op. cit.
15. Ibid.
16. Howell, op. cit.
17. Dallin, op. cit.

Each *Einsatzgruppe* was ". . . generally responsible for all political security tasks within the operational area of the Army and the rear areas so far as the latter did not fall under the civil administration."[18] They were not only operationally independent from army group commands, but their activities often spilled over into rear civil areas, which in any event eventually reacted adversely to their bestial activities.

The fragile and confused bodies of this organization would have had a difficult time instilling order even in victory. When the Wehrmacht failed to destroy the Red army, Hitler's jerry-built administrative house found itself in charge of an area of about four hundred thousand square miles holding some 65 million heterogeneous peoples. Within a few months, Hitler's basic premise had vanished, but the mission remained: exterminate and exploit.

This incredible policy immediately affected two important groups of Russians: prisoners of war and people of occupied Soviet areas.

Within six months of invasion, German armies had captured some 3 million Soviet soldiers, with hundreds of thousands of additional prisoners coming in each month. No particular arrangements existed to care for these unfortunates; very little food existed to feed them and very little humanity to serve them. Murder resulted:

. . . Testimony is eloquent and prolific on the abandonment of entire divisions under the open sky. Epidemics and endemic diseases decimated the camps. Beatings and abuse by the guards were commonplace. Millions spent weeks without food or shelter. Carloads of prisoners were dead when they arrived at their destination. Casualty figures varied considerably, but almost nowhere amounted to less than 30 per cent in the winter of 1941–42, and sometimes went as high as 95 per cent.[19]

The shocking conditions even filtered back to Berlin. Goering complained to Count Ciano that Soviet prisoners were not only eating their own boots but ". . . they have begun to eat each other, and what is more serious, have also eaten a German sentry."[20]

Inadequate security forces, particularly in forward prison camps, allowed thousands of Soviet prisoners to escape. Others, cut off by the German advance and learning of German treatment of their fellows, refused to surrender. Throughout autumn and winter, some of these fugitives reached woods and swamps to bring badly needed military skills to the hard-pressed guerrilla bands. By spring of 1942, three or four hundred thousand soldiers were roaming free, and many of these, from sheer necessity, drifted into the forest and joined the guerrillas.[21]

18. Howell, op. cit.
19. Dallin, op. cit.
20. Ibid.
21. E. Ziemke, "Composition and Morale of the Partisan Movement." In Armstrong, *supra.*

Meanwhile the first bloom on the German rose of occupation had vanished. Most senior army commanders had welcomed the relatively pacific reception that promised secure lines of communication—particularly important in view of voracious appetites of tanks, trucks, and aircraft for fuel and oil. But as their progress continued, initial victories seemed to validate Hitler's notion of a short war in the east. Nazi arrogance, never far below the surface, at once asserted itself, and the *Untermensch* philosophy captured many minds. Hitler himself instructed his commanders to spread ". . . that measure of terror which alone is apt to deprive the population of all desire to resist."[22]

As war continued into autumn and winter and no victory resulted and casualties continued to soar and Hitler's strategic incompetence became obvious, fear also began to capture military minds.[23] In partisan areas, ". . . military considerations and often a sense of physical danger, isolation, and self-defense on occupied soil, caused commanders to attempt to eliminate the partisans 'at all costs' "—to insist on "prophylaxis by terror."

"Collective measures of force" were to be applied promptly in any instance of even "passive resistance" in which the perpetrator could not be immediately identified. Soviet soldiers behind the lines who refused to turn themselves over to the Germans were to be considered insurgents ". . . and treated accordingly."[24]

In mid-September 1941, the Wehrmacht commander, General Keitel, ordered that ". . . in every instance of active opposition against the German occupation authorities, regardless of the specific circumstances, Communist origin must be assumed."

. . . Since "a deterrent effect can be attained only through unusual hardness," the High Command sanctioned brutal retaliation against the innocent population:

"As atonement for the life of a German soldier, a death sentence for from fifty to one hundred Communists must be generally deemed commensurate. The means of execution must increase the deterrent effect still further. . . ."[25]

In rear army areas, Himmler's special teams caused additional terror:

. . . One of the four *Einsatzgruppen* commanders, Otto Ohlendorf, stated [at the Nuremberg trials] that during the first year of the campaign, the group under his command liquidated about 90,000 men, women and chil-

---

22. Dallin, op. cit.
23. Ibid.: ". . . By the end of the year [1941] about one out of every four German soldiers in the East had been killed or wounded, and the Wehrmacht needed 2.5 million troops as replacements."
24. Ibid.
25. Ibid.; see also Howell, op. cit.

dren. The activities of these teams were dictated not by military necessity but purely by ideological considerations.[26]

The general policy of terror carried over into *Reich Commissariat Ostland* and *Reich Commissariat Ukraine,* vast areas that fell to German civil administration. Gauleiter Erich Koch ruled the Ukraine. Koch believed that his subjects ". . . stood [sic] far below us and should be grateful to God that we allow them to stay alive. We have liberated them; in return, they must know no other goal except to work for us. There can be no human companionship. . . ."[27] Though less blunt, Koch's colleague Lohse ruled the center and north with the same philosophy.

Part of their task was to siphon off agricultural production for relief of the homeland, just as Goering's people were attempting to exploit various industrial complexes. But part also was to siphon off skilled workers. By early spring of 1942, the *Ostarbeiter* program had sent fifty thousand persons to Germany, by that summer 1 million, and a year later 2 million.[28]

Meanwhile Himmler's people were happily conducting the extermination task: One *Einsatzgruppe,* in the spring of 1942, complained that only 42,000 out of 170,000 political undesirables (Bolsheviks and Jews) had been exterminated. The general commissar there, Wilhelm Kuhe, soon put matters right, announcing in July that ". . . in the past ten weeks we have liquidated about 50,000 Jews in Belorussia. In the rural areas of Minsk, Jewry has been eradicated without jeopardizing the labor situation."[29]

Exploitation and extermination could only create local hatreds. As the over-all German policy of genocide, direct or indirect, became clear, numerous peasants and workers preferred to risk life under the partisans. German failure to capture Moscow in late winter of 1941–42 also exercised a major psychological effect and tended to make the civil population more co-operative in supporting guerrilla units with recruits, food, and intelligence. As these grew stronger and their activities increased, German authorities had to expand security measures, which in turn added to the general climate of terror.

Each of the three German army commanders had to depend on an army-group rear-area headquarters and three "security divisions" to safeguard his immediate rear, ". . . maintaining the supply of the field armies and guaranteeing the exploitation of the land for the immediate use of the military."[30]

26. Dallin, op. cit.
27. Ibid.
28. Ibid.
29. Ibid.: Kuhe was killed by a bomb placed in his bed by a "trusted" chambermaid.
30. Howell, op. cit.

A security division only remotely resembled its combat brother. It consisted of two regiments, one of regular combat infantry whose three battalions would furnish "alert units" for mobile operations, and one of *Landesschützen,* or second-line battalions, to carry out static guard duties. Support units such as motorized military police, engineers, and signal troops fleshed out these jury-rigged divisions.

Although the regular infantry and motorized police were well trained, with many combat veterans, Landesschützen units consisted of older, often unfit men. Major Howell noted that, in general, security divisions ". . . were staffed with retired or overaged officers and inexperienced reservists."[31] Supply officers were "inadequately trained," and intelligence officers were ". . . admittedly inept in intelligence matters and generally had no knowledge of counter-intelligence methodology."[32] Transport was short, arms and equipment second rate, morale and discipline generally poor.

The primary task of security divisions centered on protecting supply depots, railheads, and airfields, and keeping open lines of communication to the front. As huge armies moved forward, security divisions followed to set up ". . . a series of strong points to protect the supply lines and insure control of the populace."[33] Since the war would be over in four months, the problem of pacification and thus counter-guerrilla warfare had not been studied: The German army did not even possess a standard operating procedure for counterguerrilla warfare, and only in October 1941 did the high command issue a *Directive for Anti-Partisan Warfare*—a rather innocuous work.[34]

When guerrilla attacks began, security divisions working with Himmler's SS security and police units replied with severe punitive measures that more often hurt the general population than guerrillas:

. . . Because of the expanse of country which had to be covered, they took positive measures against the partisans only when the supply lines and installations were openly threatened. Even then they stuck closely to the roads and rail lines and the urban areas, and avoided the more difficult terrain and back-country regions. Seeing little of the growing opposition, unaware of or indifferent to the possibility of a developing pattern of hostility in the rear, and victorious in a few insignificant incidents over small insurgent groups, the security units gained in confidence and foresaw an early advent of complete peace and quiet there. They felt they were winning their war and that their areas of responsibility would be completely under control in a matter of weeks or days.[35]

31. Ibid.
32. Ibid.
33. Ibid.
34. Ibid.
35. Ibid.

When guerrilla attacks continued and mounted in intensity, rear-area commanders responded by "logical" measures—by trying to tighten unit security, by offering bribes of money and food for accurate information on guerrilla activities, by weapons collection, by setting up intelligence nets of *Vertrauensleute,* or collaborators, by trying to streamline intelligence procedures—carrots that never totally replaced sticks of severe reprisals. More-imaginative commanders formed "counter" or "dummy" bands,

. . . made up of units from the security police and the security service and of the *Ordnungspolizei,* with a number of reliable natives, and committed in partisan-dominated areas in the manner of a genuine partisan unit. In this manner they would be able to keep a constant check on the sentiments of the population, make contact with irregular units, and often quietly eliminate partisan leaders.[36]

Commanders also strengthened strong points, added guards to bridges and railway lines, and developed small, mobile pursuit units (the *Jagdkommando*). As matters worsened for the Germans, measures became more extreme. In the Bryansk area, the local commander insisted on escorted motor convoys traveling by daylight and on armored trains; troops built special security zones up to nine miles wide on each side of major railroad lines:

. . . Brushwork and forests were cleared, all civilian residents registered, and movements of the people controlled day and night.[37]

In the center and north, harassed commanders began early to conduct counterguerrilla "sweeps," the intention being to uncover and destroy the bands.

These operations normally utilized combat units temporarily transferred from the front. The basic technique involved locating the general guerrilla area, surrounding it, and then "combing" through it with additional units.

One of the earliest counterguerrilla operations occurred in spring of 1942 north of Smolensk, where guerrillas controlled an impressive area of some two to three thousand square miles. For about a month, ". . . all or parts of nine German divisions mounted an attack which shattered the partisan movement." The German forces reported that out of fifteen to twenty thousand enemy, about two thousand broke out and another two to three thousand went into hiding, but that the remainder were killed or captured.[38]

36. Ibid.
37. K. DeWitt and W. Moll, "The Bryansk Area." In Armstrong, *supra.*
38. G. L. Weinberg, "The Yelna-Dorogobuzh Area of Smolensk Oblast." In Armstrong, *supra.*

The Germans may well have exaggerated their success. Certainly other "combing" operations did not similarly prosper. Also in spring of 1942, in the Bryansk area, Operation *Vogelsang* employed local troops reinforced by one armored and two infantry regiments. At small cost to the Germans, 58 dead and 138 wounded, the operation allegedly killed 1,193 guerrillas, wounded an estimated 1,400, and captured 498. Security forces arrested 2,249 men and evacuated 12,531 persons from the area.[39] These impressive figures did not impress the Second Panzer Army, which reported:

. . . The success did not measure up to expectations. The partisans continued their old tactics of evading [contact], withdrawing into the forests, or moving in larger groups into the areas south and south-west of the Roslavl-Bryansk highways and into the Kletnya area. Although no attacks were noted in the pacified section, mines continued to be planted and . . . several vehicles were damaged. . . .[40]

Two authorities who studied this operation, DeWitt and Moll, concluded that ". . . the later reappearance of these partisans suggests that a large proportion of the casualties reported by the Germans consisted in fact of non-partisan members of the local population." Subsequent counter-guerrilla "sweeps" in the same area tended to confirm this significant conclusion.[41] So did Operation *Kottbus,* a year later in northeastern Belorussia, which involved a prolonged attack by sixteen thousand German troops:

. . . Reporting to Rosenberg [Minister of Eastern Territories] on the first phase of this operation, the German Commissar General . . . for Belorussia pointed out that among the 5,000 people shot for suspicion of collaborating with the partisans, there were many women and children. He also argued that if for 4,500 enemy dead only 492 rifles were captured, the implication clearly was that the dead included many peasants who were not necessarily partisans. The effect of these operations on the partisans was negligible. Within a few weeks they reappeared as strong as ever. . . .[42]

Few military or political commanders at first protested, since extreme repression fitted Nazi political policy. Professor Armstrong concluded:

. . . Most of the time . . . the German counter-guerrillas took the position that the civilians, since they had supplied the partisans with food and information, ought to be punished. The Germans also imagined that by destroying agricultural production they would starve the partisans. Consequently, horrible atrocities were committed against the civilian population, including the

39. DeWitt and Moll, op. cit.
40. Ibid.
41. Ibid.; see also Howell, op. cit.
42. Mavrogordato and Ziemke, op. cit.

elderly, women and children. Village-burning was the main feature of the combing operations. In addition, the Germans rounded up all able-bodied younger men and women for the *Ostarbeiter* program of [forced] labor in Germany. The combined effect of these measures was to turn neutral elements of the population toward the partisans, and particularly to send them a constant flow of new recruits seeking to escape the *Ostarbeiter* program. . . .[43]

As Armstrong pointed out, theoretically the Germans might have isolated guerrilla units by evacuating specific areas, but the size of areas, the vast population, and partisan strength prevented this.

Even where combing operations broke up guerrilla activities, the effect was only temporary. Howell later wrote:

. . . they failed to even approach a permanent solution. In combing out these areas the Germans scattered a number of bands, but nowhere were they able to trap and annihilate any sizable groups. Under pressure, the partisans merely dispersed, slipped through the attacking lines, and reassembled elsewhere.[44]

The operations did break up the bands, however, and eliminated the immediate threat to communications by keeping them off balance. The Germans continued to employ the tactic almost to the end and would have used it more often had enough soldiers been available.

Security divisions, however, suffered constantly from manpower shortages. Once Soviet counteroffensives began, German army commanders did not hesitate to transfer regular infantry regiments away from security divisions to front-line duty. Conversely, only occasionally could security divisions obtain services of front-line units for counterguerrilla operations. At one point in 1942, in the north, thirty of thirty-four security battalions had been ordered to the front:

. . . Whereas previously all bridges behind the *Sixteenth Army* had been guarded, the security command there became so short of men that guard details were pulled off all spans less than 45 feet long, and 14 bridges totaling more than 500 yards, on which sentries were maintained, were covered with a total armament of but 14 light machine guns. The situation was equally pinching behind *Army Group Center*.[45]

Rear-area commanders attempted to solve the manpower problem in several ways. In addition to front-line troops, they used satellite security divisions, generally unreliable units. Sometimes they suborned German replacement units still in training, definitely an unsatisfactory arrangement. They also formed indigenous battalions called *Osttruppen,* but

43. Armstrong, op. cit.
44. Howell, op. cit.
45. Ibid.

Hitler's political policy and the sharp eyes of Nazi purists made this a disjointed, generally surreptitious effort (although eventually it recruited some five hundred thousand locals). Later, when German losses and Soviet battle successes caused Nazis to have second thoughts, theretofore-willing recruits changed their minds and if impressed into duty often deserted in droves to the partisans. Similar programs to enlist local peoples in various types of militias, village defense forces, and youth movements (to deprive partisans of recruits) encountered the same political obstruction.

Even when these measures materialized, most came too late and in too slight quantity to radically influence the counterguerrilla campaign. Had the Germans mobilized the generally anti-Soviet border populations in 1941 and early 1942, the whole tenor of the campaign would undoubtedly have changed. Even after this error, opportunity still remained. As one example, south of Bryansk German officials quietly supported an irregular group of anti-Soviet Russians, the Kaminski band, which eventually numbered some nine thousand irregulars and performed valuable counterguerrilla services.[46] On a bigger scale, more-imaginative German officials sponsored an anti-Soviet army recruited from prisoners of war and commanded by a prisoner, an anti-Soviet General, Vlasov. Although Vlasov could easily have raised an army of from ten to twenty divisions, he understandably demanded some postwar political guarantees, which ranking Nazis refused to give him. The program died, only to be revived at too late a date.

Some German officials and officers early recognized the stupidity of official policy. After ten weeks of battle, Field Marshal von Kluge

. . . issued an order sharply condemning plundering and wanton requisitions by German troops, and demanding the prompt and complete cessation of all abuse under threat of summary punishment.[47]

As early as December 1941, Goebbels expressed concern ". . . about the extent to which the occupation authorities were antagonizing the population."[48] That winter, a host of occupation authorities, civil and military, warned officials in Berlin of the disastrous policy. In August 1942, an OKW (Army High Command) report reflected the feelings of many officials in the Soviet Union:

. . . Time after time the population of the Ukraine shows itself grateful for every instance when it is dealt with humanely on the basis of equality, and reacts strongly against contemptuous treatment.[49]

46. Ibid.
47. Dallin, op. cit.
48. Ibid.
49. Ibid.

At a conference of military and civil occupation officials in October 1942,

. . . Colonel Claus von Stauffenberg, Hitler's would-be assassin, took the floor to flail German policy in an impassioned half-hour impromptu speech. The Reich, he exclaimed, was sowing a hatred that the next generation would reap; the key to victory was winning the sympathy and support of the people who lived in the East![50]

But dissenters already had lost their case. In late 1942, Hitler made counterguerrilla operations in combat areas a General Staff responsibility; in rear army areas and civil areas, ". . . the S.S. obtained overall command and responsibility for the extermination of partisans." Hitler left no doubt of his own attitude: ". . . the struggle against the partisans in the entire East is a life-and-death struggle in which one side or the other must be exterminated."[51]

50. Ibid.
51. Ibid.

Chapter 35

Stalin's reorganization of partisan units • Guerrilla hardships • Early guerrilla tactics • Long-range guerrilla operations • Over-all effectiveness of guerrilla warfare

GERMAN FAILURE to pacify, let alone mobilize, occupation areas immeasurably aided the Soviet high command's effort to harness diverse guerrilla forces, first to cause damage to the enemy, but also to prevent anti-Soviet forces from arising.

In spring of 1941, Stalin replaced earlier, makeshift partisan staff arrangements with the Central Staff of the Partisan Movement, headed by Marshal Voroshilov, soon replaced by a high-ranking party official, P. K. Ponomarenko, and operating directly under the Supreme Defense Council. The NKVD also formed a partisan section, as did army groups and armies a few months later.

Liaison teams trained and sent to the guerrilla units by these various headquarters did not fare well to start with, but, by summer of 1942, German brutality and Red army gains were causing passive acceptance by peasants and townspeople, and they were starting to give direction to the guerrilla movement. Simultaneously, the Soviets began to win local

air superiority, which greatly eased delivery of more teams, arms, and
equipment, increased liaison between guerrillas and operational headquarters, and provided evacuation for badly wounded fighters. *The
Partisan's Handbook* appeared in quantity from Moscow to offer
". . . guides on partisan tactics, Soviet and enemy weapons and explosives, German anti-partisan tactics, first aid," and other pertinent
subjects.[1] By mid-1942, fifteen guerrilla training centers existed *behind*
German lines around Voronezh alone; one of them taught a six-week
course to classes ranging from 170 to 250 guerrillas.[2] Larger units, in
the north, claimed a doctor and several nurses, also the ubiquitous political commissars. Arms began arriving in some quantity, and in addition
to rifles included light mortars, machine guns, automatic rifles, bazookas,
grenades, mines, and explosives. More airfields appeared in guerrilla
country. As early as August 1942, leading guerrilla officials flew to Moscow to receive Stalin's direct orders and return to their units![3]

Progress remained slow, however, and setbacks frequent. German
counteroperations kept many units on the run. By July 1942, Central
Headquarters ". . . was in radio contact with only ten per cent of the
partisan groups," and nowhere along the great battle line were guerrillas
really hindering the German military effort. Hunger and sickness
plagued many units. Guerrillas suffered badly from rheumatism, scurvy,
pellagra, boils, toothaches, stomach and intestinal disorders—one "regiment," of 737 men, in 1942 recorded 261 casualties from sickness, 52
from combat and 20 from desertion.[4] The few units that boasted doctors
suffered from lack of medicine. In September 1942, one guerrilla wrote
of the hard life shortly before his death:

. . . We are crossing the Lebyashka swamp. The villages round about are
in flames. In the distance the thunder of cannon can be heard. Every five
to six hundred yards we have to rest. We sit right down in the water, and,
after ten minutes, move on. Everyone is weak. The swamp sucks us down.
We sink in often, sometimes up to the hips. There is no end; the forest seems
to be moving away from us. Finally the order is given to rest until dawn.
. . . Camp fires are forbidden; the swamp-land is flat; and the Germans are
all around. . . .[5]

Although guerrillas would endure incredible hardships until the end
of the German presence, their lot began to improve in late 1942. By
mid-November, central headquarters was in radio contact with 20 per
cent of the guerrilla units; ". . . by the first of the year there were 424
radio transmitters in partisan groups, connecting the Central Staff with

1. Garthoff, op. cit.
2. Ziemke, op. cit.
3. Garthoff, op. cit.
4. Ziemke, op. cit.
5. Ibid.

1,131 detachments."[6] Where the movement numbered an estimated 30,000 at the beginning of 1942, the Germans reported some 150,000 by the summer of 1942 and about 200,000 in mid-1943.[7]

In the center and north, large partisan areas existed, some numbering between twelve thousand and twenty thousand. These comprised operational "brigades" of from three hundred fifty to two thousand guerrillas. Each brigade consisted of battalions, companies, and platoons which

. . . might be dispersed over ten or twenty square miles. Groups of brigades occasionally occupied areas of several hundred square miles.[8]

Units devoted a great deal of effort, particularly in early stages, to security and survival. In populated areas, this meant almost constant involvement with the civil population. Although partisan commanders forbade indiscriminate looting, in order to gain food and supply and to deny it to the enemy and also to assert the government's presence, they did not hesitate to burn collective farms and destroy farm machinery. Under direction of political commissars specifically assigned by the Central Staff, units barraged the people with propaganda. One partisan propaganda officer wrote of the early days:

. . . We wrote leaflets by hand. We had very little paper; we wrote on cardboard, on thin wooden boards, on glass, and we typed even on cloth and birch rind [sic]. In the morning our boys would distribute the leaflets in the villages, railroad stations, and even in Bryansk.[9]

The propaganda effort eventually became much more sophisticated and gained greatly because of enemy atrocities. Partisans also used selective terrorism, frequently killing German officials and Russian collaborators.

Small guerrilla units tried to become as self-sufficient as possible. Although air drops supplied essentials such as sugar, salt, and coffee, bands relied on the land and on raids of German dumps for food. A few isolated units tilled their own fields and kept herds of cattle.[10] One forest base of the time

. . . included a log encampment, with flour mills, vats for soap-making, forges and home-made lathes for the repair and alteration of weapons. In addition to a wireless transmitting and receiving station, there was the inevitable printing works for the production of propaganda material and news sheets.[11]

6. Armstrong, op. cit.

7. Ibid.; see also Garthoff, op. cit.

8. Ziemke, op. cit.

9. A. Dallin, R. Mavrogordato, and W. Moll, "Partisan Psychological Warfare and Popular Attitudes." In Armstrong, supra.

10. Howell, op. cit.

11. Blair, op. cit.

In addition to "natural" defense provided by distance, terrain, and civil co-operation, the partisans depended on fortified permanent camps. One German lieutenant later described the defenses he encountered:

. . . The bunker was solidly built. The walls were made of five to six inch logs, extending only about a foot above the level of the ground. The dugout was covered with earth, with only the entrance and window left uncovered. The roof was supported by two log beams and covered with a foot of ground. . . . The bunker on the inside measured about twenty-six feet in length, sixteen feet in width, and six feet in height. Nearby we found a supply of firewood, a kitchen dugout, and a well. The small stock of food was worthy of note.[12]

Partisan combat operations varied enormously. Some units worked out of base areas, returning after a specific operation. Others operated independently in German rear areas. One unit leader, Major General Sidor Kovpak, led a "roving band" on an eight-thousand-mile patrol over a twenty-six-month period. Moving mainly at night, Kovpak's people concentrated on attacking enemy lines of communication and isolated enemy detachments. Ironically the unit was nearly destroyed when it sought sanctuary in the northern Carpathians, where the people refused to support it.[13] A mounted brigade commanded by M. I. Naumov left Bryansk area in February 1943 to operate in the southwestern Ukrainian steppe. Attacked west of Kiev, the fourteen-hundred-man unit disintegrated. Only three hundred guerrillas escaped, but these managed to find sanctuary in woods in the northwest Ukraine, which eventually they made into a partisan stronghold.[14]

In the center and north, guerrilla units concentrated on destroying railroads and roads and on ambushing German detachments. At first, guerrillas struck targets of opportunity, but as units grew stronger and communications improved, they sometimes co-ordinated operations with the Red army. In the case of larger targets, for instance an enemy headquarters or an airfield,

. . . in general, three echelons formed a raiding party: a "combat group," a "demolition group," and a "reserve" (which often ambushed pursuers). All raids and ambushes were prepared in advance with meticulous care, which comprised detailed reconnaissance observation (often performed by girls), detailed planning and the allotment beforehand of specific individual tasks, and cautious execution.[15]

The Soviet high command constantly called for maximum performance. Order after order stressed the need to cut German communi-

12. Ziemke, op. cit.
13. Blair, op. cit.; see also Armstrong, op. cit.
14. Armstrong, op. cit.
15. Garthoff, op. cit.

462   WAR IN THE SHADOWS

cations. A captured document stated requirements for a partisan commander who wished to be awarded the coveted Order of Lenin:

. . . The destruction of a large railroad center with the result that it is put out of use for not less than 20 days; the demolition of 2 railroad bridges not less than 100 metres long with the result that they are out of use for not less than 20 days; rendering a railroad station unusable for a period of not less than 30 days, including the destruction of the water tower, the track and crossings, the depot and shops, and other installations; the capture of not less than 10 railroad trains involving the liberation of not less than 10,000 persons being shifted from the USSR to Germany as forced labor; the liberation of not less than 5,000 men from a prisoner-of-war camp; the destruction of not less than 10 railroad trains loaded with military equipment, supplies, men, fuel, food, and material of general military usefulness; the capture of an enemy supply point containing military equipment, motor fuel, food, or not less than 300 vehicles; the capture of not less than 500 horses belonging to the German Fascist army; the destruction of an armored train of the enemy; the destruction of 10 enemy trucks; the capture for use in the unit of 1,000 rifles, or 150 machine guns and submachine guns, or 15 heavy machine guns, or 20 company and battalion (sized) mortars, or 9 heavy mortars, or artillery of different calibers.[16]

How many Orders of Lenin were so earned has not been recorded. In February 1943, however, the Central Staff issued priority targets:

. . . At the top of the list were roads, rail lines, bridges, and enemy vehicles and rolling stock. Secondary targets comprised telephone and telegraph lines and supply depots. The bands were to take offensive action against German guard posts, patrols, and other small units only when they had a definite superiority in numbers.[17]

Authorities differ as to how much damage guerrillas inflicted. Lieutenant General Ponomarenko, chief of the Central Staff, later claimed that, up to mid-1943, partisans killed over 300,000 Germans, destroyed 1,191 tanks and armored cars, 476 airplanes, 378 guns, over 4,000 trucks, and 895 supply depots, and attacked and in some cases destroyed thousands of rail and road bridges.[18] At the Nuremberg trials, the German defense counsel claimed that partisans killed over 500,000 Germans.[19]

Nearly all Western authorities refute these figures as gross exaggeration. Professor Armstrong has argued that total German military casualties inflicted by partisans probably did not exceed thirty-five thousand

16. Armstrong and DeWitt, op. cit.
17. Howell, op. cit.
18. N. Galay, "The Partisan Forces." In B. H. Liddell Hart (ed.), *The Soviet Army* (London: Weidenfeld & Nicolson, 1956).
19. Ibid.

and that no more than half of these were German soldiers. Other authorities have pointed out that nowhere did guerrillas prevent the supply of German front-line troops and that in general they did not cause the high command to divert front-line troops to anti-partisan warfare. Captain Galay, however, has claimed that in late 1942 the German high command had committed fifteen field divisions to the rear area and that a year later was diverting twenty-five field divisions, about 10 per cent of the army's strength. Somewhat surprisingly, he concluded that ". . . there was not a single case in which partisan warfare . . . had any important influence on the operational situation of the German front," and more-recent scholars generally agree.[20]

"Important influence" must be defined in accepting this conclusion. Even the boldest German commander must have worried when an important rail line was knocked out for a day or two, and he must have fretted when he had to transfer battle-worn infantry units to the rear, where they tired themselves further by fruitless "combing" operations against guerrillas. With various and often-impressive guerrilla accomplishments in mind, Major Howell more sensibly concluded:

. . . Certainly the bands hurt the *Wehrmacht.* Every rail break, every piece of rolling stock damaged or destroyed, every German soldier killed, wounded, or diverted from other duties to guard against the bands hurt. But the damage was never decisive.[21]

This seems a reasonable conclusion, although it is based primarily on German reports by professional officers probably unwilling to give the guerrilla his complete due. These reports constantly stress quantitative measurement—so many thousands of demolitions, so many hundred raids, so many roads blown up. A quantitative approach does not always provide a fair judgment, for example raids against a modern railroad with efficient maintenance and repair organizations will not cause the damage and delay of raids against a worn and obsolete system such as the Germans had to employ.

The immense battle action also hindered objective measurement. A few trains or convoys blown up could not overly impress German commanders who in five days of Operation *Zitadelle,* for instance, lost 2,268 armored vehicles and suffered thousands of casualties.[22]

Nor do reports stress the guerrilla achievement of growth under extremely difficult circumstances. All units faced numerous operational disadvantages and obstructions. An apathetic and often hostile population coupled with rigorous climate spelled extreme hardship with high casualties and low morale. In general, units suffered from lack of train-

20. Armstrong, op. cit.; see also Dallin, op. cit.; Howell, op. cit.
21. Howell, op. cit.
22. Ibid.

ing, poor leadership, command confusion both internally and with various external headquarters, supply shortages, poor target selection, poor demolition techniques, and distance from target and from German counteroperations.

The guerrillas nonetheless plagued the enemy in a hundred ways and often caused him to commit troops that could better have used rest. They slowed and sometimes stopped important road and rail movements. During later offensives, they often operated effectively with regular army units. They supplied valuable intelligence from the beginning. They also played a passive role of a force in being—an effective psychological presence attested to by numerous German and Austrian survivors who, years later, shuddered when speaking to this writer of the dreaded *Partisanen*. As a force in being, they also formed a strong political influence in many areas and played a major role in preventing Germans from exploiting the civil population to maximum effectiveness.

Finally, many deficiencies that plagued the guerrilla movement were being repaired when the Red army began its vast series of offensives that eventually recovered Soviet territory and ended the guerrilla movement. Because of internal difficulties and German suppression, it had attained neither full growth nor full striking power, and had it been needed in case of battle reverses, its role might indeed have proved decisive. In the event, the Kremlin was delighted to pat it on the back and end its existence as soon as possible.

Ironically, German commanders could have been spared the guerrilla menace to a large degree. The trouble started when Hitler and his closest advisers, holding Russia in contempt, seriously underestimated her military strength and her national will to resist invasion. As Alexander Dallin wrote:

. . . No provision was made for the Führer's fallibility. If the campaign should last longer or if enemy defeats should be less than decisive, the Reich had no military reserves to throw into action, no plan for enlisting the Soviet population on its side, and no blueprint of political conduct except the eradication of "undesirables" in the occupied area.[23]

Had Hitler and his cohorts not combined arrogance of ignorance with arrogance of power, the Wehrmacht might well have won the war against Russia.

23. Dallin, op. cit.

Chapter 36

The Germans occupy Yugoslavia • Guerrilla units form • The Balkan guerrilla tradition • Scanderbeg • Heyduks *and* klefts *• Kosta Pečanac • World War II: Chetniks versus Partisans • Tito and the Yugoslav Communist Party • Early operations • SOE intervenes • German counterguerrilla offensives • Tito's growing strength • New German offensives • Fitzroy Maclean reports • Tito grows stronger • His near capture • Final guerrilla actions • German and Yugoslav losses*

ELEVEN DAYS after Germany invaded Yugoslavia in March 1941, King Peter and his government fled to England, and the Yugoslav army, not yet fully mobilized, surrendered. To eliminate what Hitler regarded as a threat to his southern flank, he divided Slovenia between Germany and Italy, fed chunks of border areas to his satellite hounds—Hungary, Albania, Bulgaria—and established an independent Croatia under titular rule of Ante Pavelić, boss of an extremist Croat party called the Ustasi. What was left of Serbia went to the quisling rule of General Nedić. German minions, following hard on the heels of the fast-moving Wehrmacht, soon introduced wholesale conscription of men for forced labor in Germany and exploitation of food and economic resources.

Numerous Yugoslavs already had escaped the Nazi juggernaut by fleeing to traditional refuge in the mountains, and now thousands more left villages to escape forced labor or deportation to Germany. By midsummer 1941, sources of guerrilla bands were roaming broad mountain ranges that stretch 450 miles through Slovenia and Montenegro—rugged terrain which continues inland from the coast and runs southeast through Macedonia to the Yugoslav-Greek border.

Had Adolf Hitler paid attention to history, he would have braced for trouble. Greek, Roman, and Byzantine armies at one time or another received bloody noses in the Balkans. Although the Slavs were dominated first by Avars and then by Greeks, their military reputation early became formidable. One authority, Professor Ferdinand Schevill, noted that

. . . the individual Slav was a brave and even an ingenious fighter of the guerrilla type. His ambuscades in forest and mountain were well managed, and when pursued his favorite device seems to have been to disappear under water, where, securely hidden, he breathed so deftly through a reed that he could only with great difficulty be detected.[1]

Passing centuries of conflict that saw the emergence of ethnic groups, of Slovenes, Croats, Serbs, and Bulgars, enhanced this reputation. Almost constant war between Arabs and Greeks frequently lapped over the Balkan Peninsula and nearly always proved cruel in the extreme. In 1014, for example, Basil II defeated Czar Samuel of Macedonia and earned the name Basil the Bulgar-killer in the following way:

. . . Basil's victory yielded some 15,000 Bulgar captives. These, incredible as it sounds, he caused to be blinded and divided into hundreds; then, appointing as leader of each hundred a man who, in order to act as guide, had in hideous mockery been deprived of only one eye, he set the blank, staring faces homeward to carry the message of his omnipotence to his beaten adversary. When the ghastly procession approached the tsar's capital the people crowded the walls to see, and the tsar, as though struck with a bolt, sank to the ground in a stupor and died without recovering consciousness.[2]

The rise of the Ottoman Empire brought no surcease to the Balkans. Defeat at Kosovo in 1389 cost Serbia her independence for more than four centuries. But Turkish rule was never secure. Montenegrins under George Balsha shut themselves up in the Black Mountain to wage guerrilla warfare against both Turks and Venetians. One of the subsequent Zupans, or chiefs, probably Ivan the Black, who came to the throne in 1466, enacted a decree

. . . to the effect that he who in the hour of battle should, on any pretext without the express order of the Zupan, leave the field and attempt to seek safety by flight, should as a mark of contempt and disgrace be dressed as a

1. F. Schevill, *History of the Balkan Peninsula* (New York: Harcourt, Brace, 1922).
2. Ibid.

woman, equipped with a spindle in place of a sword, turned out of his home, beaten with spindles by the women, and finally hounded over the frontier as a traitor to Montenegrin liberty.[3]

Meanwhile in Albania a natural leader arose to frustrate the splendid Turkish army. This was a tribal chief, George Castriotes whom the Turks named Scanderbeg and who fought guerrilla warfare so successfully that Mohammed II finally came to terms with him:

. . . The fame of Scanderbeg . . . went like wild-fire throughout Balkania and the West. Great states like Hungary and Venice sought his alliance; the pope hailed him in quaint and picturesque phrase as "the athlete of Christendom."[4]

Scanderbeg died in 1467, and the tribes he had welded together by his own charisma fell apart and soon submitted to Turkish rule. The Montenegrins continued to hold out. In 1484, they burned their capital and withdrew to the mountain village of Cetinje, which they held for another 150 years, their attitude best expressed by the words spoken over male infants at the baptismal font: "God save him from dying in his bed."[5] Their guerrilla tactics infuriated Napoleon, who swore to turn Monte Negro into Monte Rosso. Even their Austrian allies shied away:

. . . the Emperor of Austria desired to employ their assistance as little as possible, "as from their savage characters and the lawless ferocity of their manners they must spread terror among the peaceable inhabitants, and produce ill-will and hatred towards the troops of His Imperial Majesty."[6]

The rest of the Balkans meanwhile suffered under the Ottoman yoke. The Turks considered the peoples as "rayahs," or "conquered infidels," who held ". . . no rights or privileges, who paid to the Sultan 'haratch,' and a tenth of the product of their labor, and who were at the mercy of their Turkish landlords, Turkish officials and warriors."[7] Beginning about 1750, Turkish oppression brought guerrilla bands into being. Called *heyduks* by the Serbs and *klefts* by the Greeks, these bands

. . . moved through the Servian mountains and forests, hurrying from one point to another, where a specially brutal misdeed of Turks against the Christian men and women was to be avenged. The Hydooks were a sort of irregular national force, insurgents who were permanently leading a guerrilla war against the Turks. They were the original model of the Committadjis

3. Alex Devine, *Montenegro in History, Politics and War* (London: T. Fisher Unwin, 1918).
4. Schevill, op. cit.
5. Devine, op. cit.
6. Ibid.
7. Chedo Majatovich, *Servia of the Servians* (London: Putnam & Sons, 1911).

of our days, only without a central leadership and without committees. Fear of the Hydooks was the only consideration which restrained the Turkish lawlessness, rapacity and violence. The Turks called them "brigands," and whoever of them fell into their hands was mercilessly impaled alive.[8]

Professor Schevill noted that:

. . . they were looked on by the common people as avengers of their wrongs and as a species of national heroes. A popular ballad literature gathered around them and carried to every rajah fireside the stirring tale of the blood paid by the oppressor for his age-old crimes.[9]

The crimes continued despite the heyduks, but the Serbs had just about had enough. In 1804, four Turkish captains known as the *Dahees* murdered the ruling Vizier Mustapha and formed

. . . a peculiar political, military and commercial partnership, proclaimed themselves masters of the entire Pashalik of Belgrade. They covered the country with a net of wooden blockhouses (*Hans*), which were occupied by their armed agents, who lived there at the expense of the neighboring villages, and collected the increased taxes and new imposts introduced by the Dahees.[10]

Frightened by rising restlessness of the people, they reacted by repression—by trying to kill every native leader or potential leader in the country. One of these intended victims was a heyduk chief, George Petrovich, who escaped to organize guerrilla war against the Janissaries. Successful in this, he led a revolt against the Turks and became famous as Black George. In 1813, however, he panicked and fled. Serbia returned to Moslem rule but, two years later, Milosh Obrenovich led a new and successful revolt. Obrenovich subsequently arranged for Black George's murder, thus starting a dynastic feud that lasted over a century.[11]

Interminable quarrels that made the Balkans famous as "the cockpit of Europe" invariably involved border guerrilla actions and terrorist raids. World War I, however, at first brought conventional battle to Serbia. But when the weight of Austro-Hungarian and Bulgarian armies told, and the Serbs found themselves cut from the supply line to Salonika, they refused to surrender. Instead,

. . . hundreds of thousands of men, accompanied at the beginning by many thousands of women and children too, set out by two roads—one over the mountains of Montenegro to Skadar (Skutari), and the other from Prizren

8. Ibid.
9. Schevill, op. cit.
10. Majatovich, op. cit.
11. H. W. V. Temperley, *History of Servia* (London: G. Bell & Sons, 1917).

up the valley of the White Drin and over the very peaks of the almost impassable Albanian mountains—to reach the sea.[12]

Hungry and cold, beset by bands of outlaws and hostile Albanian tribesmen, the fugitives died by tens of thousands. But over a hundred thousand managed to reach the coast, where French ships evacuated them to training areas—an army that eventually joined the allies at Salonika.

Meanwhile the peasants who remained also refused to submit to Austrian rule. In 1916, the allies flew in from Salonika a famous guerrilla leader, Kosta Pečanac, who started irregular warfare against the enemy.

. . . Although this rising, like all the others, was suppressed with the utmost ferocity and cruelty, reprisals being taken against old men, women and children if the rebels themselves could not be caught, Kosta himself remained at liberty and fighting right to the end of the war.[13]

In summer of 1941, numerous guerrilla bands struggling to survive in Yugoslav mountains served one of two flags: Chetnik or Partisan. Division between the two was deep, for little unity had existed in this Balkan country since its optimistic creation at the Paris Peace Conference.

Kosta Pečanac, hero of Serbian resistance in World War I, headed the Chetniks, a Serbian nationalist organization.[14] In theory, Chetniks formed the guerrilla arm of the Royal Yugoslav Army and were properly organized on a country-wide basis. In fact, no such organization existed. Pečanac, obsessed by reprisals that followed the partisan rising in 1916, preferred to accommodate the enemy and took a number of Chetniks over to General Nedić's puppet government. This left the main body of Chetniks in the hands of a regular officer, Colonel Draža Mihailović, who set up guerrilla headquarters in the mountains near Valjevo, in western Serbia.

Cored by the Yugoslav Communist Party, the Partisans formed a much more homogeneous force than the Chetniks. Forced underground in 1921 because of terrorist activities, party members had led a clandestine life, depending on wits, courage, and discipline to survive a series of police states. Originally sixty thousand strong, the party succumbed to feuding factionalism until, by 1928, membership numbered only three thousand. Government repression further hurt it until, in 1934, it was falling apart at the seams.[15]

Meanwhile, however, a young Croat metalworker, Josip Brozovich,

---

12. H. D. Harrison, *The Soul of Yugoslavia* (London: Hodder & Stoughton, 1941); see also Rebecca West, *Black Lamb and Grey Falcon* (London: Macmillan, 1942), Vol. 1 of 2 vols.

13. Ibid.

14. Seton-Watson, op. cit.: "Literally . . . a member of a *Cheta,* which is the Serbian word for an armed band."

15. Fitzroy Maclean, *Disputed Barricades* (London: Jonathan Cape, 1957).

had been rising in party ranks. Born in 1892, the seventh of fifteen children in an impoverished home in a small village, Josip completed elementary school before leaving home to work as locksmith and mechanic. Enlisting in a Croat regiment to fight for Austria in World War I, he rose to warrant-officer rank, was badly wounded and captured by the Russians, learned the language, and, in 1917, joined the Bolsheviks. He married a Russian, fought with the Kirghiz nomads, who were Mongol horsemen, and in 1920 returned to what had become Yugoslavia, a state of 12 million persons.

Josip Broz, as he had become, worked as party organizer and agitator, slowly rising in the party while fathering a family and spending a good many years in jail. In 1935, he worked for the Comintern, then returned to Yugoslavia to set up a "rat-line" which fed some fifteen hundred volunteers to the fighting in Spain; many of his future generals fought with international brigades. In 1937, the Kremlin liquidated his boss and made him secretary-general of the Yugoslav party. Tito, as he was now known, reorganized the party, raising its membership to twelve thousand, a small but disciplined group dedicated to the Communist ideal.[16]

In 1941, the German invasion caught Yugoslav Communists off balance, mainly because of the existing German-Russian non-aggression pact. When Hitler's legions broke that by invading Russia, the Comintern cabled Tito: ". . . Organize partisan detachments without a moment's delay. Start a partisan war in the enemy's rear."[17] Out went word to take to the hills. Tito set up partisan headquarters near Užice, in western Serbia, not far from Mihailović's camp.

The German invasion of Russia brought partisan recruits to each camp:

. . . throughout Yugoslavia, and particularly in the Serbian provinces, sympathy for Russia was deep-rooted and traditional. The Serbs not only loved Russia, but greatly over-estimated her strength. The mood of the Serbian people now suddenly changed from bewildered despair to extravagant optimism. . . .[18]

Tito at once exploited the prevailing mood, insisting on offensive action against the enemy in order to disrupt his forces, hinder operations, and provide his own guerrilla bands with arms, equipment, food, and clothing. Mihailović, who considered himself legitimate representative of the government-in-exile, wanted to avoid enemy reprisals by taking no overt action but instead building a resistance movement for later cooperation with the allies and also for postwar political purposes.

Although Chetniks joined Communists in clearing the Užice area of enemy garrisons, the truce quickly disintegrated. The first British liaison

16. Ibid.
17. Ibid.
18. Seton-Watson, op. cit.

officer smuggled into the country, Captain Hudson, found some Chetnik and Communist units in open battle.[19] Hudson managed to bring the leaders together—a strange meeting: the slightly built eminently proper professional officer Mihailović, steel-rimmed spectacles, his beard trimmed, his words demanding cautious tactics; the *nouveau* Tito, the rebel, guest of royalist jails, big and tough, Slav features passive, blue eyes cold in rejection of all Mihailović stood for. The meeting accomplished nothing except to expose to Hudson the opposite, intransigent attitudes.

Hudson represented the main headquarters of the British organization devoted to covert operations, the Special Operations Executive, or SOE. At this stage, late 1941, SOE suffered a terrible ignorance of the true situation in most world battle areas. Lacking organization and communications, SOE could not repair its deficiencies overnight, nor did it yet own either supplies or delivery means to aid dissident groups. In the case of Yugoslavia, Hudson reported to the best of his ability. Poor communications and his own limitations—he was a young mining engineer—severely hindered his attempts to unravel the tangled skein of Yugoslav politics to his London superiors, and shortly after his arrival in the country he was forced off the air for nearly six months. SOE attempts to infiltrate other agents during this crucial period failed, primarily from want of satisfactory means. Meanwhile, Mihailović's optimistic reports to London of Chetnik resistance resulted in the Yugoslav government-in-exile promoting him to general and minister of war. SOE (London) also declared for the Chetniks, an understandable error in view of their ignorance of the true situation, and in any event an academic error, considering SOE's lack of resources.

During this confused period, the German army, in mid-November 1941, launched its first offensive against the guerrillas.[20] In two weeks, the Wehrmacht gained control of the Užice area. Tito's Partisans bore the brunt of this fighting, which ended with retreat to mountains in the Northwest. Some Chetnik units, disillusioned by Mihailović's refusal to fight, joined the Partisans, who also found new allies hiding in Bosnian mountains.

Mihailović's fears had proved correct:

. . . The suppression of the revolt in Serbia was followed by a massacre. Thousands of Serbs were shot or hanged, and thousands more were arrested, maltreated and imprisoned or deported to forced labor. The worst atrocities occurred in the industrial town of Kragujevac, where 8,000 people are be-

19. Blair, op. cit.
20. Fitzroy Maclean, *Eastern Approaches* (London: Jonathan Cape, 1949). The author offers an excellent description of both German and Partisan tactics in this excellent work; see also Department of the Army, *German Antiguerrilla Operations in the Balkans (1941–1944)* (Washington: U. S. Government Printing Office, 1954).

lieved to have been shot, including several hundred school-children. Bitter hatred was created against the Germans, but there was at the same time resentment against the partisans because they had failed to fulfil their high hopes, and had brought suffering on innocent people.[21]

Tito had just established new headquarters northeast of Sarajevo when a second German offensive forced him to retreat south to the rugged mountains of the Drina headwaters—a defeat caused in part by refusal of Chetnik units to fight. Hard on the heels of this disaster came another Communist defeat, in Montenegro, one partially brought on by savage reprisals of Communist guerrillas against anyone co-operating with Italian occupation forces. With Mihailović's blessing, Chetniks openly co-operated in an Italian offensive that drove Communist bands back into Herzegovina and Bosnia.

By mid-1942, an irreparable rift existed between Chetniks and Partisans. Chetnik groups in Herzegovina, Montenegro, and Dalmatia collaborated openly with Italians. In Serbia, Mihailović commanded about ten thousand Chetniks who, based on the countryside, maintained an armed truce with the Nedić quisling and German troop units. Ustasi militia in Croatia formed pro-Axis shock-troop units whose members, as with Darnand's *milice* in Vichy France, provided invaluable local knowledge to German commanders.

Tito, on the other hand, despite severe setbacks, never stopped fighting. Nor did he ever forget that he was fighting for a purpose, a political purpose. He early began building a political base by creating local administrations in liberated areas which he called OBDORs. In November 1942, at Bihać, in southern Bosnia, he and his followers unfurled the flag of the Anti-Fascist Council of National Liberation, or AVNOJ— a scene faintly reminiscent of Communists in southern China in 1928. AVNOJ at once publicized its dedication to freeing the country and forming a state along democratic and federal lines, welcome words that brought fresh recruits flocking in.

Simultaneously, Tito was developing a regular army. He began this effort during the retreat after the First German Offensive by creating the First Proletarian Brigade. By mid-1942, he claimed two "divisions" —unorthodox formations each about twenty-five hundred strong, but sufficient when combined with other Partisan units to regain the area vacated in the Second Offensive and to push on into Bosnia and Croatia. This led to the "People's Army of Liberation," or JANL, created in late 1942 and composed of seven "shock divisions." In addition to these, he developed an ever-growing guerrilla army, and he also relied on part-time Partisans, who lived and worked among the enemy—gentle farmers and civil folk by day, cut-throat assassins and saboteurs by night.

During mid-1942, SOE officers in London and Cairo began forming

21. Seton-Watson, op. cit.

a more accurate picture of Yugoslav resistance. Hudson again was transmitting, as was Radio Free Yugoslavia, a Russian-sponsored operation that supported Tito. Mihailović continued to flood London with reports, claims, demands, and protests—each increasingly scrutinized and questioned by SOE officers in view of Mihailović's inaction.

Toward the end of the year, SOE(London) sent in a new mission, under one Colonel Bailey. Shortly after his arrival, SOE(Cairo) infiltrated several liaison teams to Mihailović's units. Independent reports from Bailey and these new teams confirmed not only Mihailović's inaction but his collaboration with the enemy. SOE(London) now began to look more favorably on Tito's Partisans.

Tito's Partisans had their hands full. In January 1943, the Germans opened a Fourth Offensive: a two-prong thrust from the north intended to drive Tito's forces south to the river Neretva, strongly defended by Italian and Chetnik units. Learning of the German plan, Tito sent three divisions south to break through before the defenses hardened.[22] They were still attacking when the Germans struck from the north. Fighting hard, the Partisans slowly withdrew to the south, but suffered heavy casualties before punching through the Italo-Croat-Chetnik defense. On the credit side, the Partisans blasted Mihailović's Chetnik force, some twelve thousand irregulars, whom the Partisans, despite their own serious losses, chased into Montenegro.

At the end of May 1943, the enemy struck again. This, the Fifth Offensive, involved German, Ustasi, Bulgar, and Italian troops, an immense force of over one hundred thousand supported by tanks, artillery, and aircraft while encircling and closing on the Partisan stronghold. A captured German order revealed high hopes: ". . . Now that the ring is completely closed, the Communists will try to break through. You will ensure that no able-bodied man leaves the ring alive."[23]

The Partisans finally broke out, not to the east but to the northwest. General von Löhr later wrote: ". . . The Germans were too exhausted to stop them and there were no reserves."[24] The effort nonetheless cost Tito about ten thousand dead or missing.[25] Survivors found respite in the mountains north of Sarajevo. Here, joined by fresh guerrilla forces, Tito rested briefly. By August, he had considerably expanded his area of operations. Meanwhile the British had dropped a liaison officer, an Oxford historian, F. W. Deakin, who reached Tito at the height of the Fifth Offensive (and was wounded along with Tito). His favorable

22. Blair (op. cit.) has suggested that perhaps a ranking German officer who was a secret agent tipped off Tito.
23. Maclean, *Disputed Barricades, supra;* see also F. W. D. Deakin, *The Embattled Mountain* (London: Oxford University Press, 1971).
24. Maclean, *Disputed Barricades, supra.*
25. Otto Heilbronn, *Warfare in the Enemy's Rear* (New York: Frederick A. Praeger, 1963).

report prompted SOE(London) to send Tito an aid mission. Still hoping for maximum resistance, SOE(London) also reiterated willingness to aid Mihailović, but only if he ceased collaboration with the enemy and came to operational agreement with the Partisans.

Tito exploited Italy's collapse, in September, by establishing contact with Partisan units in Slovenia and by occupying a large portion of the Dalmatian coast and offshore islands. Although the Germans soon expelled the guerrillas from the coast, Tito retained the islands, his forces growing stronger in the process—tactical gains shortly to pale in comparison with a political victory.

For, also in September, a powerful SOE mission under Brigadier Fitzroy Maclean reached Tito's headquarters. Maclean was not a career officer. A testy Scot, at thirty-two years of age he had served eight years in diplomacy, felt at home in difficult political situations, and was a sufficient realist to appreciate the dimensions of Tito's past work and future potential. More important, he belonged to the British Establishment—a member of Parliament, he was a personal friend of Winston Churchill, who appointed him his personal representative much to the annoyance of SOE and the Cairo military command. Maclean did not take long to make up his mind: Tito must be supported to the maximum of SOE's ability.

In sorry contrast to Maclean's optimistic reports stood those from a regular British officer, Brigadier Armstrong, who headed a new mission to Mihailović. Colonel Bailey and Mihailović had long since fallen out, and Armstrong quickly suffered a similar disillusionment. He found Mihailović ". . . dominated by the single thought of how to overcome the Partisans, to whom he was bitterly and irreconcilably hostile. He appeared completely disinterested in attacks on communications. . . ."[26] Armstrong's blunt reports brought forth a series of SOE demands blithely ignored by Mihailović. After repeated warnings, SOE suspended further aid, in December 1943; with departure of the last liaison team, in spring of 1944, allied contact ceased.

While Mihailović's star declined in the allied sky, Tito's was rising, mainly due to the exuberant Maclean, who presented the Partisan case in most vigorous terms to his own government. In November, the Partisan government, the AVNOJ, met to proclaim ". . . a new federal Yugoslavia, having denounced the exiled King and Government, and promoted Tito to the rank of Marshal."[27] Almost simultaneously, Maclean's representations caused allied heads of state at Tehran to agree that ". . . the Partisans in Yugoslavia should be supported by supplies and equipment to the greatest possible extent. . . ."[28]

26. Blair, op. cit.
27. Ibid.
28. Ibid.; see also Maclean, *Disputed Barricades, supra.* An American OSS officer joined the British Mission in September; American OSS missions later worked with both Tito and Mihailović.

Maclean himself suffered no illusions concerning Tito's political bent. He reported that ". . . in any event, [allied] help or not, the partisans were going to be a decisive post-war influence in Jugoslavia." He went on: "Much will depend on Tito, and whether he sees himself in his former role of Comintern agent or as the potential ruler of an independent Jugoslav State." In Cairo he explained this to Mr. Churchill, and stressed the probability of Yugoslavia becoming a Communist state. Churchill's reaction underscored his priority concern for winning the war:

"Do you intend," he asked, "to make Yugoslavia your home after the war?"

"No, Sir," I replied.

"Neither do I," he said. "And, that being so, the less you and I worry about the form of Government they set up, the better. That is for them to decide. What interests me is, which of them [Partisans or Chetniks] is doing most harm to the Germans?"[29]

The allied decision to support Tito at first meant little. In summer of 1943, SOE had been talking grandly of supplying 500 tons a month to the Partisans; they actually delivered a meager 230 tons for *all* of 1943. And in December of that year, Tito once again was fighting for his life, in the Sixth Offensive, Operation *Kugelblitz* (Thunderbolt), a massive effort undertaken by over fourteen German divisions and five non-German divisions. Lasting several weeks, this effort forced Partisans out of all offshore islands except Vis, a major Partisan base, and it also penetrated into the mountains of Slovenia, Bosnia, and western Serbia before running out of steam. It left the Germans generally in command of towns and most communication centers, but it left Partisan forces relatively intact throughout the country.

With increased allied aid, the Partisan movement began to take off. In September 1943, Maclean estimated a total Partisan force of one hundred thousand. By spring of 1944, this had grown to over two hundred thousand and Tito was demanding tanks, artillery, and aircraft. Allied planes were also flying out wounded Partisans: ". . . During 1944 more than 10,000 military and 2,000 civilian casualties were thus evacuated."[30] Meanwhile, at allied request, Tito raised Partisan units in Serbia to interdict German communications through the Morava Valley, a successful effort that attracted thousands of Serbs to the Partisan banner. Again at allied request, Tito ordered units in Slovenia to prepare for Operation Bearskin: by cutting roads and railroads in the north, allied planners hoped to prevent German troop reinforcement either to northern Italy or to Normandy, where the allies would soon land.

29. Maclean, *Eastern Approaches, supra.*
30. Seton-Watson, op. cit.

At this point, Tito was riding high and perhaps grew complacent. Neither he nor his staff officers at the cave command post in Drvar seemed suspicious of a German airplane that ". . . spent half an hour or more flying slowly up and down at a height of about two thousand feet."[31] The British mission did not like it and moved off into surrounding hills. Four days later, at the end of May, with no warning, bombers plastered the area, then six JU-52s dropped paratroopers, who were followed by troops crash-landing in gliders while a three-column ground attack pressed in overland.

While Tito's "palace guard" held off German paratroopers, the Partisan leader escaped through a rear exit. After a furious pursuit, Tito, his principal staff officers, the British and Russian missions, and 118 wounded guerrillas were evacuated by a series of hastily improvised airlifts. Tito subsequently established himself on Vis, where his headquarters remained until war's end.

This interruption upset planning for Operation Bearskin, as did increased enemy security in target areas and poor weather, which hindered airdrops of vital demolitions. For all these reasons, Bearskin only partially succeeded. But, in September, Partisans brought off Operation Ratweek, by cutting roads and railroads from one end of the country to the other. In restricting German troop movements, this guerrilla ef-

31. Maclean, *Eastern Approaches, supra.*

fort primarily assisted the British-U.S. offensive in northern Italy; secondarily it assisted the Russians moving into Bulgaria.

The final major Partisan offensive concentrated on interdicting the German XXI Mountain Corps during withdrawal north. Although guerrillas, heavily supported by the allies, caused the enemy to abandon transport and heavy equipment, they did not prevent his main body from reaching the northern border. Maclean has pointed out, however, that in the last two months of the fighting, the Germans lost close to one hundred thousand killed and over two hundred thousand captured.[32] Captured German figures reported twenty-four thousand Germans killed and twelve thousand missing.[33] According to the Yugoslav Government, the Yugoslavian people lost over 10 per cent of its population and over 60 per cent of its national wealth: ". . . We lost 1,685,000 people, of whom over 75 per cent were shot or lost their lives in Fascist camps or death chambers. We lost over 90,000 skilled industrial workers and miners and 40,000 intellectuals. There are 425,000 wounded or disabled. . . ."[34]

By January 1945, what was left of Yugoslavia was virtually clear of enemy troops. Most Ustasi and Chetnik leaders had fled. Supported by the Russians, Tito easily expanded his power base, and by the end of the war had emerged incontestably as the new ruler of Yugoslavia.

32. Maclean, *Disputed Barricades, supra.*
33. Basil Davidson, *Partisan Picture* (London: Bedford Books, 1946).
34. Ibid.

Chapter 37

German strength in Yugoslavia • German operational problems
• Tito and Yugoslav nationalism • The Hauspartisanen *• Ti-*
to's guerrilla tactics • Kosta's operations • SOE's liaison prob-
lems • The Russian attitude

THE GERMAN EXPERIENCE in Yugoslavia emphasized the importance of a guerrilla force in being. Without Tito's Partisans, the Germans could have enjoyed an easy occupation with benefits the term
implies: total access to the country's manpower and economic resources,
a fertile ground for New Order propaganda—all for a minimum investment of occupation forces.

As it was, until autumn of 1943, the guerrilla threat forced Germany
to keep nine Wehrmacht divisions in Yugoslavia, a hefty force buttressed by ten Italian divisions and numerous Bulgarian and local quisling units. The value of the collaborators was questionable. Local
German commanders, in trying to exploit "sympathetic" resistance
groups, frequently conflicted not only with Italian policy but with ". . .
German military policy and German Nazi Party and Gestapo policy."[1]

1. Seton-Watson, op. cit.

Italy's collapse, in late 1943, forced Germany to raise her occupation troops to 14-plus divisions, a force augmented by five satellite divisions: an estimated total of 140,000 German troops and 66,000 satellite troops. In addition, Germany supported 150,000–170,000 Bulgar, Croat, and Chetnik troops. In 1943, establishing a new command in Belgrade, Army Group F, the German high command in effect changed an army of occupation to an operational fighting force.[2] Tito's force at this time numbered around 100,000 soon to climb to some 220,000.

This number ratio helps to validate Partisan operations, as do certain enemy testimonials: ". . . Field Marshal von Weichs, the German Commander-in-Chief South-east (Balkans), directed his formations to refer in their reports to Tito's partisans not any longer as bands but to brigades, divisions and so on, and expressed himself to the effect that they had to be considered as the equivalent of the regular forces of Germany's other enemies."[3] Final proof rests in the seven major German attempts to capture Tito and eliminate the Partisans. These were not slapdash affairs, but were carefully planned military operations. They suffered a host of problems: poor internal security, poor co-ordination among German, satellite and local forces, general ineptness of satellite and local-force commanders, failure of German commanders to adjust to the tactical problem, for example their insistence on night bivouacs while the Partisans marched. But ultimate failure stemmed not from these problems but from what history already should have taught the German high command: the seemingly uncanny ability of guerrillas to survive in home grounds. The lesson gains in importance when large areas of these home grounds, unlike vast forests of the Ukraine, held considerable hostile forces, in this case Croatian Ustasi, Serbian Chetniks, and Nedić quislings, not to mention German, Italian and Bulgarian occupation troops.

How to explain this?

The first factor was the fertile field of human feeling, a sort of patriotic anarchy best described in the controlled panic of a dispatch sent by a ranking German civil official, Dr. Thurner, from Belgrade, in August 1941:

. . . All our attempts to canalize these people in a constructive direction and separate them from the Communists have failed and had to be abandoned. We have argued with them, conferred with them, cajoled them and threatened them, but all to no purpose. We do not believe that it is possible to achieve anything in this country on the basis of authority. The people just do not recognize authority. A minority question cannot be created among the Serbs as it was with such success among the Croats. Practically

2. Maclean, *Disputed Barricades, supra;* see also Blair, op. cit.; Department of the Army, op. cit.
3. Heilbronn, op. cit.

nobody is interested in the old political parties. They do not believe in anyone any more and they follow the Communist bandits blindly. With their slogans the Communists have succeeded in rallying round them elements who in the past would never have dreamt of co-operating with them. Some go so far as to prefer Bolshevism to occupation by our troops. . . . My impression is that even the news of the capitulation of the Soviet Union would not cause these bandits to capitulate. They are tougher than anything you can imagine. What is more, their organization is excellent. It might serve as the classical example of a perfect secret organization.[4]

Thurner hit on the second factor, which was qualitative. In contrast to leaders of pro-German parties, Tito headed a small and disciplined organization, the Communist Party, whose members never questioned the Partisan mission of fighting the enemy and never forgot the party's political goal of constantly expanding to achieve postwar power. Tito constantly stressed the necessity of retaining support of the general population. Shortly after taking to the field in 1941, he issued an Order:

. . . Experience hitherto has shown that insufficient attention has been paid to the concept of a general uprising of the people. This mistake must be rectified without delay. There is a danger that otherwise the Partisans may lose touch with the masses who are ready to fight for the just cause. . . .[5]

About the same time, he ordered a Croatian leader:

. . . Do everything in your power to see that in future the conduct of operations is well organized and centralized under strong leadership. Form strong Partisan formations and see that they are constantly in action.[6]

This bellicose unity contrasted violently with that of other national groups such as the Chetniks—a splintered organization with important segments either remaining feckless in pathetic desire to let war wash harmlessly over them or waiting to see the probable result, sometimes secretly aiding Partisans, sometimes even coming over to them.

Tito exploited divisive national feeling in several ways. Partisan propaganda, particularly the promise of "a liberal and democratic" postwar government, appealed to a great many unaligned people who loathed the repressive prewar order represented by the government-in-exile through Mihailović's Chetniks. The harshness of German and Italian occupation policies further influenced the population in favor of the Partisans, who possessed much wider support than either western allied observers or Germans supposed.

Tito always respected the need for this support. When he was on the run after the First German Offensive, his meager supply train still in-

4. Maclean, *Disputed Barricades, supra.*
5. Ibid.
6. Ibid.

cluded twelve oxcarts that held a printing press and five thousand newly printed copies of *The Short History of the Communist Party*.[7] He insured discipline by attaching political commissars to Partisan units at all levels. He also harnessed national feeling by establishing local administrative units, or OBDORs, in "liberated" areas. When the enemy "captured" such an area, OBDOR became a "shadow" government and, as such, performed numerous valuable functions, for example acting as a deterrent to would-be collaborators and helping to establish and maintain one of the Partisans' most valuable adjuncts: small groups of volunteers who stayed in their own locality and ". . . lived as civilians among the population, followed their normal occupations and worked as part-time partisans."[8] In addition to furnishing food and intelligence, ". . . they killed sentries, threw hand-grenades into German barracks, burned down garages, mined village streets and house entrances, destroyed railway lines—in one night they blew up the rails of the Agram-Belgrade railway in eighty places—and did all the other jobs which partisans usually perform."[9] The Germans called them *Hauspartisanen,* or Home Partisans, and detested them. Colonel General Rendulic, commanding a German Panzer army, later stated that ". . . the life and tasks of the German troops would have been much easier if the opponent had had only closed formations. The Home Partisans were a much more dangerous enemy because it was from them that all the hostile acts emanated against which the troops could protect themselves only with the greatest difficulty and which caused them large losses. They could seldom, if ever, be caught."[10] In attempting to catch them, Germans killed and imprisoned thousands of innocent people, thus creating new Partisans. The effect of Home Partisans was beyond all proportion to their limited numbers—an estimated eight thousand in June 1944.[11]

Tito was also smart enough to keep his regular military organization simple. JANL, despite regular army trappings, remained essentially a guerrilla organization of small, semi-independent, and lightly armed bands. Tito could boast about "divisions"—but a Partisan division counted only about twenty-five to thirty-five hundred men divided into "brigades" consisting of several groups, or "battalions." These units lacked any sort of artillery or formal communications, but, singly or in unison, they fought extremely well under tough, self-reliant leaders of unquestioned loyalty. Moving often at night, guerrilla bands covered vast areas, often fighting against great odds with no doctors or medicines to treat their wounded. Allied observers remarked feelingly on Partisan resilience and the high state of morale, and this must have been the

7. Ibid.
8. Heilbronn, op. cit.
9. Ibid.
10. Ibid.
11. Ibid.

case in order for them to have survived numerous vicissitudes of war such as the 180-mile retreat with thousands of wounded during the Fourth Offensive.

Tito later offered Brigadier Maclean a remarkable analysis of his operational success, words as pertinent now as then:

. . . We sought to instil in our units the strictest possible discipline, not by extra drills, but by ceaseless political instruction with the object of improving both individual and collective morale and of securing a proper attitude towards the population. Our aim was to build up from our Partisan Detachments an army which would win the devotion of the civil population. Hence the severe sanctions inflicted on those who did anything to alienate the population. . . . Every defeat had at once to be made up for by a victory—anywhere—so that morale did not suffer. For this reason even our worst defeats, even the big enemy offensives had no effect on the morale of our men, for we ourselves at once went over to the offensive, choosing the place where the enemy least expected it. . . . It was vital also to impress upon our men that they must never allow the fact of being surrounded to demoralize them, but must regard it as the normal situation in our kind of war. By concentrating our efforts against one point, we could always break out of any encirclement. . . . Whenever the enemy launched an offensive, we sent out Partisan Detachments to destroy communications behind his lines. That had a demoralizing effect on our opponents and prevented them from bringing up the supplies they needed. Finally—and this, too, is important—we were always in dangerous and difficult situations; but our men never cursed us because we were always exposed to the same dangers they were.[12]

Tito was always careful to retain mobility. At the time of the Fourth Offensive, he wrote:

We must avoid fixed fronts. We must not let the enemy force us by clever tactics on to the defensive. On the contrary, the spirit of our troops must be offensive, not only in the attack, but in defense as well. During an enemy offensive the offensive spirit must find expression in vigorous and audacious guerrilla tactics, in operations behind the enemy's lines, in the destruction of his communications, in attacks on his supply centers, and on bases which are temporarily weakened. We must be no more afraid of being surrounded now than when we had fewer troops. We must make up for the loss of an area by the conquest of a larger and more important area.[13]

Brave words, these, and only partially carried out. The almost always precarious Partisan position greatly restricted offensive operations. Early in the war, guerrillas had to attack targets that would yield arms and

12. Maclean, *Disputed Barricades*, *supra*.
13. Ibid.

clothing, but even later, when allied supply started reaching them in some quantity, they were not strong enough to strike where they wished. Many sensitive targets such as communication centers lay beyond reach. Co-ordination of effort at times was very poor, the inevitable result of primitive communications: couriers often became lost or captured, and lack of satisfactory codes frequently endangered security. A security error almost led to Tito's demise in the Drvar raid, but such carelessness on his part was rare.

Partisan operations perforce were often decentralized, which meant that Tito had to rely on capable subordinate leaders. These men generally worked out their own tactics. Basil Davidson, who served as British liaison officer to one of Tito's chief guerrilla leaders, Kosta Nadj, later described Kosta's tactics for taking towns:

. . . to feint elsewhere whilst moving his assault units stage by stage into position under cover of darkness; and then to precede the final night assault by the infiltration of a picked unit whose job it was to get into the center of the town without firing a shot and to occupy one or two prominent buildings; as soon as the general assault began this panic unit would open rapid fire in all directions, and create conditions in the rear of the defenders which enabled those outside to open a breach, and then by street-fighting to link up and isolate the enemy for piecemeal destruction.[14]

Like many other unit commanders, Kosta started with almost no weapons, relying on militia forces to furnish them. His success caused German garrisons to change tactics by mid-1942, basing town defense on a system of central bunkers. Partisans replied by sneaking in grenadiers, or *bombashi,* to throw grenades through the bunker slits.

. . . The best bombashi were boys of twelve or fourteen, little chaps who could nip quickly over the hundred yards or so that might separate the bunker from the nearest cover to throw their bombs before the enemy knew what was happening. Many of them were killed in the course of this hazardous but necessary operation.[15]

Davidson accompanied Kosta's considerable force on operations east of Belgrade, where it fought virtually independently of Tito's headquarters. Once the guerrilla mastered his new surroundings, once he held "intimate" knowledge of terrain and enemy locations and habits, he was on top:

. . . This nearness gave rise to contempt for the enemy; he was slow, and inferior, and frightened of the dark, and he could move in large numbers and in broad daylight but almost never by himself. He was like a huge and overfed caterpillar, obese and horrible, many-legged, abominable. In com-

14. Davidson, op. cit.
15. Ibid.

parison with this stupid monstrosity the partisan felt himself to be a superman, alone perhaps, but self-reliant in his cunning and strong health, his existence rooted as deeply in the land as the long smooth timbers of the oaks of Fruska Gora, his survival guaranteed somehow by the very nature of things. The country belonged to him, not to the enemy.[16]

The guerrilla's lot could have been greatly eased by a more realistic allied aid policy. Tito's accomplishments loom considerably larger when we consider that, up to the end of 1943, he received the barest minimum of arms and equipment. Almost entirely on his own, he had organized an army and government while alternately harassing the enemy and escaping from him. An earlier supply effort would have solved many of his problems, besides saving thousands of lives.

The basic British difficulty stemmed from lack of area intelligence, surprising in view of Britain's political sophistication, and the failure of means to repair that deficiency. A more objective appraisal of the resistance movements was also hindered by natural sympathy for the Royal Yugoslav Government as exemplified by Mihailović and his Chetniks. But liaison officers, properly trained for the target country and possessing adequate communications, could have cleared the confusion in short order. SOE never overcame the liaison problem, and Blair concludes that, in general, Maclean's liaison officers ". . . knew nothing of guerrilla warfare and little of the Yugoslav language, history or politics, and their reports were of limited value. Very few actions were ever fought which would not have taken place without the missions, and as one description states, 'half a ton of ammunition and explosives would in most areas have been more effective than half a ton of BLOs [British liaison officers].' Their presence was also a source of suspicion to the Partisans."[17] An interesting side effect resulted from their reports, which the BBC used: Although broadcasts of world news by this august organization were renowned for accuracy, its Yugoslav coverage drew heavy criticism for inaccuracy, Maclean himself complaining, and the Germans making a propaganda field day out of patent errors.[18]

SOE operations also suffered from tortured command channels. This sometimes led to the ludicrous, as in the case of Bailey's mission to Mihailović. While Bailey at Mihailović's headquarters duly reported to SOE (London), his subordinates, liaison officers in the field with Chetnik units, *reported independently to SOE (Cairo)*. On at least one occasion, SOE (Cairo) acted under duress from the military high command and issued orders that had to be countermanded by SOE (London). Maclean wore three hats: SOE commander to Tito, personal

16. Ibid.
17. Blair, op. cit.
18. Ibid.

representative to Supreme Allied Commander, Middle East, and personal representative to the British Prime Minister. The latter appointment obfuscated the other two and, at best, meant that, should his nominal superiors tread at all, they would tread very lightly.

Command confusion grew along with the allied effort. SOE could handle a supply problem of a few hundred tons; it could not support large training programs, supply a small army, and co-ordinate required air, naval, and ground efforts. This difficulty led to drastic command reorganization, in spring of 1944.[19]

Despite these shortcomings, British and American military aid to Tito represented a distinct sacrifice, both in early stages, when arms and supply were measured in single tons and in delivery requirements of one or two aircraft, and later, when this aid measured thousands of tons delivered by squadrons of aircraft and ships. Military critics of the time, including some ranking officers, argued that this considerable investment in men and material could have been used more profitably in more orthodox operations.

This assessment depended on ultimate objectives. If the allied objective had been merely to sustain Tito in harassing the enemy—an objective incidentally defended by Dr. Heilbronn over more aggressive operations—then a great deal of aid and the concomitant machinery could have been eliminated in favor of "hard" supply of small arms. Allied planners, however, looked far beyond this mundane achievement. Until late 1943, their most distant horizon comprised a joint Chetnik-Partisan resistance, and one can argue that such a contingency either would have reduced the enemy to abject impotence or forced him from Yugoslavia, an interesting consideration in view of Winston Churchill's eagerness to extend orthodox military operations to the Balkans. The Chetnik default dimmed this glorious horizon but briefly, for now Maclean painted a glorious picture of an enormous Partisan army of combined arms, and indeed in some very valid colors. Nor did Tito hesitate to jump on the new band wagon: early in 1944, he was demanding tanks, artillery, and aircraft.

This was not as stupid as it sounds in retrospect, and for reasons already mentioned. No one knew in early 1944 when the war would end— the atomic-bomb situation was still far from clear. In the event, Tito's army became superfluous.

Superfluous, at least, to allied military operations. And hereby hangs a curious irony. Had Tito not built his Partisan army, in part with allied aid, a most uncomfortable vacuum would have existed in postwar Yugoslavia—a geographical entity traditionally in the Russian sphere of influence. Stalin did not wait for cannons to stop firing before asserting

19. Each service assumed command of its own operating forces, with the RAF appointed to co-ordinate operations and the supply function assigned to Special Operations, Middle East, at Cairo.

his dominance over Tito and the country. But Stalin had showed up badly compared to the West. Tito had begged the Soviets to send him arms beginning in August 1941. Stalin had paid no attention either to that or subsequent requests, and a Soviet military mission, which did not even reach Tito until February 1944, accomplished nothing. Tito had never been overly impressed with the Russian Communists, and his war experience did not endear them to him. Although he would have trouble with the West in postwar years, he still had to face the inescapable fact that the West had helped him when the chips were down.

So it was that Tito not only filled the Yugoslav vacuum left by World War II, but, shortly after doing so, proved to the world that communism and Moscow were not synonymous. Although his rule left much to be desired, it turned an area once riddled with factionalism into a reasonably stable country whose insistence on independent political status has more than once proved a healthy stabilizing factor in international diplomacy. To accomplish this, his people have paid the piper by sacrificing individual liberties in what remains still another totalitarian regime.

Chapter 38

German occupation of Greece • Political and military background • Initial resistance • Greek passivity to occupation • First SOE mission • Conflict among resistance groups • SOE difficulties, internal and external • Operation Animals • The ELAS guerrillas • German countertactics • The Russian mission • Operation Noah's Ark • Italian occupation of Albania • Albanian resistance • Enver Hoxha and the LNC • First SOE mission • Internal political conflicts • The Germans arrive • The Davies mission • Maclean's new mission • Hoxha's guerrilla operations • Assessment of guerrilla operations in Greece and Albania

I F RESISTANCE became confused in Yugoslavia, it grew positively chaotic in Greece—traditionally the home of violent politics.

In spring of 1941, the German invasion of this Mediterranean country sent King George II and the monarchist government into exile, first in Cairo, then in London. By June, the enemy held the entire country. As in the case of Yugoslavia, Hitler distributed large portions of it to his allies: Thrace and eastern Macedonia to Bulgaria, central and western Greece to Italy. The German army concentrated primarily on protecting main lines of communication running from Montenegro in the north through the Struma and Vardar valleys south to the trading center of Salonika and on to Athens and Piraeus (and across the Mediterranean to North Africa). As elsewhere in the Axis world, occupation proved harsh and brutal, and, in short order, resistance movements appeared.

Those readers who know Greece will remember the strong individualism of her peoples, a national characteristic of great charm but one that has helped to keep her politically splintered through the ages. The monarchy founded after the War of Independence, in 1821, ended in a shaky republic established in 1924. When King George II regained the throne eleven years later, his was a disputed mandate. Besides such non-royalist parties as republicans and socialists, the Communists had grown quite strong, a worker-oriented party founded in 1918 and affiliated to the Comintern in 1920 as the Communist Party of Greece, the KKE.[1]

Political anarchy followed restoration, and, in 1936, the prime minister, General Metaxas, established a dictatorship and forced the KKE underground. Metaxas continued to purge the army of republican and Communist officers, and he also treated Italy's occupation of Albania with restraint, quietly strengthening diplomatic ties with Turkey, France, and Britain while trying to strengthen his armed forces. When Mussolini demanded partial occupation of Greece, in October 1940, Metaxas refused and ordered general mobilization. Within weeks, the small but keen Greek army, ably commanded by Lieutenant General Alexander Papagos, reinforced by Royal Air Force squadrons, had smashed Italian attacks in the Pindus Mountains and driven thirty miles inside Albania.

Metaxas died in early 1941. Mussolini's failure meanwhile had caused Hitler to intervene, not so much to save Mussolini's reputation as to secure the Balkan flank prior to his invading Russia. In March, he sent troops into Hungary, Romania, and Bulgaria. The Greek Government, of Prime Minister Alexander Korizis, now accepted British reinforcements. By April, a British (mainly Australian-New Zealand)-Polish force of some seventy thousand men, constituting three divisions and two brigades hastily mobilized in Egypt, had landed and deployed along a line southwest of Salonika. Inadequate liaison between Greek and British high commands exposed the left flank of this force by leaving General Papagos and most of the Greek army isolated on the Albanian front. The Germans struck in early April, soon pushing the shattered British force from the country. Three weeks later, they marched into Athens; they went on to capture Crete, and, in June, the Greek Government fled to Cairo.

German occupation authorities working with Prime Minister Tsolakoglou's puppet government cracked down hard on some Communists, arresting and deporting such prominent leaders as Nikos Zakhariadhis, Secretary General of KKE. But, working on the principle of divide and conquer, the Germans released other Communists from prison.

1. C. M. Woodhouse, *The Story of Modern Greece* (London: Faber & Faber, 1968): A Greek scholar and historian, and an active participant in Greece with SOE(Cairo) during World War II, Mr. Woodhouse has written a splendid short history of this troubled land; see also, by the same author, *Apple of Discord* (London: Hutchinson, 1948): This excellent study of the Axis occupation and subsequent civil war contains a thoughtful defense of the Metaxas dictatorship.

Zakhariadhis' replacement, Yioryios Siantos, organized an underground labor movement, the EEAM, and, in September 1941, the Greek Liberation Front, or EAM, which gained some socialist support. In spring of 1942, EAM formed the National Popular Liberation Army, or ELAS, its agents recruiting in Roumeli, Thessaly, and Macedonia.

At about the same time, three republican resistance movements sprang up: EDES, headed by Colonel Zervas; a much smaller group, EKKA, whose military leader was Colonel Psaros; and the AAA, headed by Colonel Saraphis. A royalist organization also appeared, the Six Colonels, an operationally impotent group, as did a student organization under Professor Kanellopoulos.

Six more-disparate groups probably never existed; yet they possessed a common trait: a distinct preference to fight anyone but the enemy. By spring of 1942, Italian and German garrisons carried out duties generally unmolested, and since duties included supporting Rommel's armored forces in North Africa, guerrilla inactivity brought increasingly blue language to British military conferences at GHQ, Middle East, Cairo.

Resistance leaders were not altogether to blame. In 1941, the stuff of their armies was a generally inert mass of country people who expressed but slight desire to fight the Germans. Will to resist had to be imposed from without. Resistance had to be generated. As C. M. Woodhouse later wrote,

. . . it was not the easy-going peasant who started the resistance to the Germans in the mountains. That was the last thing they wanted: they had hardly seen a German, or noticed the slightest difference in their way of life, until the talkers from the towns arrived with exhortations to take arms against the invader. For them the resistance movement meant the loss of their livelihood, the burning of their homes, the looting of their property; all of which they endured as long as they believed the cause to be a good one; but none of which they would have inflicted upon themselves without prompting. . . .[2]

Primarily for this reason, Communist leaders of EAM spent a year in developing a clandestine network of cadres ". . . so efficiently woven and deployed that when, in the summer of 1942, the first guerrilla bands under the name of ELAS appeared in the mountains, they multiplied quickly. When they could they swept out of their way or absorbed all rival bands that they came across. . . ."[3]

Part of the difficulty also stemmed from ignorance of Greek politics on the part of British Foreign Office officials who supported Prime Minister Tsouderos' promonarchist government-in-exile.[4] The king, who had

2. Woodhouse, *Apple of Discord, supra.*
3. Ibid.
4. Ibid.; Korizis committed suicide during the retreat.

seriously violated the Greek constitution in 1936 by dissolving parliament and failing to hold a general election within the prescribed period, refused to admit his lack of popularity in Greece; in Cairo and later in London, he insisted that he would restore monarchical rule after the war. Meanwhile he did not want the British to aid other than *royalist* guerrilla groups. In view of the inability of royalist leaders in Greece to raise such groups, this meant guerrilla inactivity at an extremely crucial time.

GHQ Middle East found this unacceptable. Wanting support for a planned allied offensive in North Africa, it ordered SOE(Cairo) to contact and support any guerrillas willing to fight the enemy.

SOE's first attempt to contact resistance leaders met almost instant disaster. Landed by submarine on the island of Antiparos, the British party fell into Italian hands, as did ". . . complete lists of men they intended to meet in Athens, all of whom were promptly arrested. Many lost their lives. . . ."[5]

Despite this setback, an SOE mission parachuted into northern Greece in autumn of 1942. Colonel E. C. Myers, a thirty-six-year-old army engineer, commanded this effort, with Captain C. M. Woodhouse, a twenty-five-year-old scholar fluent in Greek, serving as deputy.[6] Myers and Woodhouse found considerable guerrilla, or *andarte,* activity. Strikes and other resistance efforts in cities had caused the Germans to make mass arrests, and in August they began organizing forced-labor transports—repressive measures that resulted in growth of guerrilla groups.

But the British officers also found a serious antagonism existing between ELAS and EDES, and only with a great deal of effort did Woodhouse persuade them to co-operate in destroying a vital rail viaduct.[7] After this success, which cut rail communications between Salonika and Athens for six weeks and thus helped deprive Rommel of much needed supply, Myers started back to Cairo, Woodhouse remaining to work with EDES. But the Cairo command, which could only have profited from Myers' return with accurate and up-to-date information, ordered him to remain in Greece. SOE(Cairo) also ordered Woodhouse to Athens, there to contact the organization known as Six Colonels, which Cairo, still influenced by the Greek government-in-exile, mistakenly thought would co-ordinate all guerrilla activities in Greece. At the same time, SOE(Cairo) decided to send in liaison teams to work with mountain guerrilla groups.

This plan only muddled an already confused situation. In spring of

5. Sweet-Escott, op. cit.
6. E. C. W. Myers, *Greek Entanglement* (London: Rupert Hart-Davis, 1955).
7. Ibid. The author gives an excellent account of this operation.

1943, Myers and Woodhouse, who held a reasonably realistic grasp of facts, pointed out that the Six Colonels organization was incapable of co-ordinating anything, that they could not repair the rift between ELAS and other guerrilla organizations, indeed that EAM/ELAS was Communist controlled. They sensibly concluded ". . . that the practical answer was to limit the guerrilla movement to a few small independent bands who by their very smallness would be able to operate on a hit-and-run basis when and where required in support of Allied strategy."[8]

Unfortunately, SOE(Cairo) refused to listen to common sense. In March, the Greek king and his exiled government had returned to Cairo, which meant additional pressure on SOE, both from Greek monarchists and British Foreign Office officials. A newly infiltrated British liaison officer attached to ELAS headquarters further distorted the picture. This man, who knew but little Greek, ". . . for some months continued to report on ELAS and EAM as a national uprising which must be given British support so that the democratic parties in the movement might be strengthened."[9] ELAS, he reported, had ". . . no political aims whatsoever" and was ". . . purely a military Resistance Movement."[10] Refusing to abandon dreams of a vast guerrilla army in Greece, SOE(Cairo) now attempted a compromise by organizing independent guerrilla areas, each commanded ". . . by a senior Greek officer" working with a British liaison team.

EAM/ELAS quickly scotched this plan by attempting to take over the entire resistance movement. An ELAS unit captured Colonel Saraphis, titular head of Six Colonels, and other units attacked EDES forces under Colonel Zervas. Myers answered this insubordination by requesting SOE(Cairo) to cut off aid to EAM/ELAS, but Cairo, unduly influenced by its liaison officer with ELAS, refused. To add to Myers' temper, Saraphis, whom Myers had saved, now went over to the Communists to become military commander of ELAS!

As a final straw, EAM/ELAS persuaded SOE(Cairo) to establish a joint guerrilla headquarters with representation so rigged as to leave EAM in control.

SOE's acquiescence stemmed from lack of concerted policy, from continued ignorance and confusion, the inevitable result of poor organization and communications and unreliable reporting.

Part of the trouble was divided responsibility: SOE(Cairo) not only answered to its parent, the Ministry of Economic Warfare, but to Foreign Office and military representatives, a triple responsibility that proved ". . . a source of confusion."[11] It also suffered from poor in-

8. Blair, op. cit.
9. Ibid.
10. Myers, op. cit.
11. Woodhouse, op. cit.

ternal organization, a sort of Topsy characteristic whereby in four years it carried eight different names:

. . . Each change of name corresponded to a change of structure and nature; often slight, but always real and significant. During the same period there were eight different heads of the same organization, sometimes concurrently; three of them were civilians who did not entirely trust soldiers, and five were senior officers who did not entirely trust politicians or diplomats. . . .[12]

Bickham Sweet-Escott, who served in the Cairo office, later wrote:

. . . Nobody who did not experience it can possibly imagine the atmosphere of jealousy, suspicion, and intrigue which embittered the relations between the various secret and semi-secret departments in Cairo during that summer of 1941, or for that matter for the next two years. It would be quite beyond my powers to describe it.[13]

Such internal flux hampered relations with the field, as did distance and communication problems. The above authority later noted that ". . . there was no coherent planning . . . all the emphasis in Force 133 had been getting parties with radio transmitters into the field as soon as possible. But no provision had been made to have enough people in Cairo to cipher and decipher the messages which would result."[14]

Poor agent preparation played a destructive role. Most British liaison officers

. . . entered Greece for the first time with no previous knowledge of the country, the people, or the language. . . . Few of them had political opinions, but their unconscious sympathies were rather to the left than the right. What formed their prejudices was not how they thought but whom they liked. In most cases, that meant whatever guerrillas they were with. . . . They had, in common with other irregular units operating in the Eastern Mediterranean, a levity of outlook upon their grim life, which at its best enchanted the common Greek population with a sense of sympathy, but at its worst inspired serious-minded Greeks with angry despair. . . . With the exception of two or three at the top, none of them received any political brief or was authorised to make any political pronouncement. From the day the first of them arrived in Greece on 1st October, 1942, their task was to fight the occupation: later, under pressure of political complications, it was enlarged to military liaison; but it was never specifically political. . . .[15]

Allied military pressures also influenced SOE representatives in Cairo and in the field. Foremost was the coming invasion of Sicily. Allied plan-

12. Ibid.
13. Sweet-Escott, op. cit.
14. Ibid.
15. Woodhouse, op. cit.

ners wanted guerrilla help in Greece in order to try to fool the Germans into believing that the invasion would occur there and thus tie down as many enemy troops as possible. This project, Operation Animals, required ELAS support, and Myers and Woodhouse gained it only by overlooking EAM/ELAS insolence and continued growth of EAM/-ELAS power. In the event, a small British team destroyed the key Asopos viaduct in a model operation.

Two British officers made a preliminary reconnaissance, noting that the only possible approach to the heavily guarded structure lay through a tortuous mountain gorge. A volunteer party, at great personal danger, then backpacked the necessary charges most of the way down the gorge. A small party, two SOE officers, two engineer officers, and two enlisted men, planted the charges at night. The explosion toppled a section of the viaduct into the deep gorge, which eliminated the single-line main railroad to Athens for four months. Myers later wrote:

. . . We learnt later that the viaduct had been guarded by about forty Germans, with six heavy machine guns and more light automatics. The whole defense [including searchlights] had been laid out in every direction except up the gorge. The Germans were so convinced that the viaduct had been blown up as a result of treachery that they shot the entire garrison guarding it.[16]

ELAS and EDES forces partially co-operated by ambushing German troops, cutting telephone communications, and making forty-four major cuts in road and rail communications—an effort that indicated their very considerable but never fully realized potential.[17]

Colonel Saraphis had greatly improved the fighting potential of ELAS, which now amounted to over fourteen thousand guerrillas, divided into six territorial commands.[18] Though not particularly subservient to Soviet doctrine, ELAS did employ the "three-man committee" command concept, whereby each unit had a military commander, an administrative officer, and a political officer who held considerable power. A guerrilla "band" varied from thirty to one hundred men, several bands forming a "battalion." These units received Communist political indoctrination, although this was not overly stressed in view of EAM claims to represent a broad front. Saraphis also developed ELAS reserve units in the villages, youth units (to provide couriers) known as EPON, and he even organized a small navy (ELAN).

By autumn of 1943, guerrillas controlled nearly two thirds of Greece, and EAM/ELAS controlled a large portion of that area. Their hold on

16. Myers, op. cit.
17. Ibid.; see also Woodhouse, op. cit.; Sweet-Escott, op. cit.
18. Edgar O'Ballance, *The Greek Civil War, 1944–1949* (London: Faber & Faber, 1966).

the new joint guerrilla headquarters, to which the British Foreign Office supplied a representative, Major Wallace, resulted in the Communists administering large areas, where they established food depots, communications, schools, courts, and newspapers. Tens of thousands of refugees streamed in from enemy-controlled areas, and, in feeding and caring for these generally illiterate mountain peoples, EAM/ELAS (financed by a British subsidy of about $120,000 per month) mixed a strong ration of Communist propaganda. Woodhouse, who was on hand, later wrote:

. . . EAM/ELAS set the pace in the creation of something that Governments of Greece had neglected: an organized state in the Greek mountains. All the virtues and vices of such an experiment could be seen; for when the people whom no one has ever helped started helping themselves, their methods are vigorous and not always nice. The words "liberation" and "popular democracy" filled the air with their peculiar connotations. Uneasy stirrings were breaking the surface everywhere, but only the KKE knew how to give them direction. . . .[19]

Although actual guerrilla attacks remained minimum, ELAS units did build a landing field and support other covert allied activities such as gathering intelligence and helping downed airmen to escape.[20]

In August, a joint guerrilla deputation flew to Cairo under Myers and Wallace's aegis. The ensuing confrontation with monarchists demonstrated the existing gulf between exiled and guerrilla forces, with everyone condemning everyone else. This resulted in a British command reorganization which transferred policy decision making from SOE(Cairo) to a newly formed "Special Operations Sub-Committee in the Middle East." But it scarcely solved internal Greek political problems.

Guerrilla leaders returned to Greece ". . . disappointed, angry and with the fixed idea that the British government intended to reimpose the monarchy."[21] Moreover, the men who wielded what little allied authority existed, Myers and Wallace, remained in Cairo. The junior Woodhouse now took command of what had become known, thanks to the addition of two OSS officers, as the Allied Military Mission (AMM).

Matters rapidly deteriorated. Woodhouse himself later questioned

. . . whether the military value of guerrilla movements in the Balkans justified their continued existence after August 1943 . . . by August 1943 the Allies had passed to the offensive; numerical and material superiority made

19. Woodhouse, op. cit.
20. Blair, op. cit.
21. Ibid.

victory in the long run certain; the value of guerrilla campaigns ceased to bear any proportion to the disasters which they brought upon the civilian population, and the political troubles which they laid up for the future. . . .[22]

He certainly had a point in the case of Greece. Already-strong ELAS forces had gained more arms and supply from Italy's collapse in September. Saraphis now converted his territorial commands into five "divisions," deployed in the most vital areas. A youth unit performed courier tasks for each division, which also featured engineer, communication, supply, and medical companies.[23]

Growth in ELAS strength, coupled with failure of the Cairo talks, increasingly hindered the allied effort. Although the Italian Pinerolo Division surrendered intact to the British, EAM persuaded the Allied Military Mission to break it into small detachments, which ELAS units promptly attacked to capture sufficient arms for two new divisions. In October, ELAS units opened new attacks against Zervas' EDES groups.

But Saraphis had been moving too rapidly, and these attacks generally failed. Moreover, German temper had been growing short and the high command now launched a series of strong offensives against ELAS mountain strongholds. Three months of operations scattered Communists and disintegrated their new "mountain state." Germans also allowed the Greek puppet government to form anti-Communist "security battalions" of about five hundred men each, an organization eventually numbering about fifteen thousand and active for the most part in the Peloponnese.[24]

Adversity forced EAM/ELAS to a more co-operative attitude, a development welcomed by British officers in Cairo trying to plan Noah's Ark, an operation designed to hinder German withdrawal from Greece. Renewed negotiations with disparate guerrilla units led to the "Plaka Agreement," of late February 1944. Designed to end civil war among guerrillas, this agreement provided only temporary postponement of hostilities. EAM now created the Political Committee of National Liberation, or PEEA, whose strong non-Communist representation was supposed to insure a national bias; in reality, PEEA formed a rival to the government-in-exile.

In April, an ELAS unit attacked the small EKKA group and murdered Colonel Psaros. Tempers flared into fighting between ELAS and EDES units. But, once again, the situation quieted, possibly due to the

22. Woodhouse, op. cit.
23. O'Ballance, op. cit.
24. Ibid.; see also Woodhouse, op. cit.: Prime Minister Rallis ". . . regarded the force as a bridge across which Greece would pass from German occupation to Allied liberation without an interval of chaos. . . ."

influence of a Russian mission that arrived secretly in EAM/ELAS headquarters. Woodhouse later wrote:

... ELAS, who had expected the Soviet Mission to bring manna from
heaven, found Colonel Popov unable even to supply his own party with
vodka, let alone ELAS with gold, arms and ammunition. On the other hand,
the Soviet Mission, which had expected to find an army of at least the same
kind, if not the same magnitude, as Tito's partisans, found a rabble thinly
veiled by an elaborately centralised command. . . . Neither on the military
nor on the political level does it seem likely that a favorable report on
EAM/ELAS went to Moscow. . . . Circumstantial evidence suggests that
EAM/ELAS suffered an abrupt shock as a result.[25]

Although infighting continued through summer and autumn, plans for
Noah's Ark moved slowly forward. EAM/ELAS agreed to participate
in phase one—guerrilla strikes scheduled to harass retreating Germans
in conjunction with allied air attacks. Phase two called for a British
landing in the Athens area, and both Saraphis and Zervas agreed to
keep their guerrillas in the country while the Greek Government landed.

Noah's Ark began in September 1944, the guerrilla units concentrating on cutting road and rail networks and attacking ponderous German
convoys. Neither ELAS nor EDES fought to maximum capability, but
Woodhouse and other observers nonetheless estimated that guerrilla action destroyed a hundred locomotives and five hundred trucks, besides
killing some five thousand enemy.

Phase two, the British landing and return of the Greek Government,
also occurred on schedule. But that begins another saga, to be narrated
in a later chapter.

The forces found in Greece displayed themselves simultaneously in
Albania, the tiny mountainous country (eleven thousand square miles)
tucked between Greece and Yugoslavia on the Adriatic Sea. In some
ways similar to Morocco, this feudal remnant of civilization consisted
of a long coastal plain that supported a peasant agricultural economy
and was backed by rugged mountains, the home of a welter of tribes
whose conflicting traditions, loyalties, and religions frequently flared into
serious feuds: Roman Catholics, Moslems, Greek Orthodox—perhaps
one million people divided roughly into the Ghegs of the North and
the Tosks of the South, but each division ruled by factionalism of centuries.

Long under Italian influence, the country offered but little resistance
when Mussolini's divisions landed, in April 1939. King Zog and his government fled, leaving the country at the mercy of some five Italian divi-

25. Woodhouse, op. cit.; see also O'Ballance, op. cit.: Neither before nor after
the visitation did ELAS receive military aid from the Soviet Union, nor, at this
time, was Tito furnishing aid to ELAS.

sions. These encountered resistance from guerrilla bands, or *chetas,* mainly in the mountains, but it was sporadic and unco-ordinated. Attempting to exploit the situation, in mid-1939 the British infiltrated an agent from Belgrade with orders to work up a guerrilla united front. The fall of Yugoslavia cut short this effort and led to the agent's capture.

Almost no information filtered from the country in the next two years. But as allies began planning for the invasion of Italy, interest revived in Albania. In spring of 1943, Bill Maclean, a young British SOE officer with guerrilla experience in Palestine and Abyssinia, led a small mission into the South. Maclean found a situation akin to those in neighboring countries. Three main groups had developed: the Royalist, or Zogist, movement, led by Abas Kupi, a promonarchist army officer, and confined largely to the North; the Republican, or Balli Kombetar (National Union) movement, which developed along the coast and central foothills and was strongly rightist; the Communist, or LNC, forces, led by Enver Hoxha, in the South.[26]

Hoxha's movement was by far the most active. As Julian Amery explained in his interesting book *Sons of the Eagle,* Italian influence had resulted in some youths being educated abroad. These young men, who neither owned land nor respected tribal tradition,

. . . could find no outlet for their energies within the narrow limits of independent Albania. . . . They were thus peculiarly susceptible to the influence of revolutionary ideas. In other countries such young men often inclined to Fascism, but in Albania Fascism was the creed of the overlord and, in their search for faith and discipline, they therefore turned to the Communists. It is unlikely that there were ever more than two, or at the most three, thousand of these young men, but they were to be the backbone of the Communist organization and the leaders under whom the landless peasants were organized. The combined discontent of these two classes— the youth of the towns and the landless peasants—produced a social revolutionary movement, which presently won the support of many of the richer peasants as well by its appeal to their patriotism or their land hunger. This, in turn, provoked the most conservative elements to combine for the defense of their own interests; and so the general unrest among the Tosks was increased.

The general poverty of the Albanians, their resentment of foreign rule, the anarchy and mercenary economy of the Ghegs, and a growth of a crisis in social relationships among the Tosks were thus the conditions out of which the Albanian resistance movement grew. . . .[27]

26. Julian Amery, *Sons of the Eagle—A Study in Guerrilla Warfare* (London: Macmillan, 1948); see also, Julian Amery, *Approach March* (London: Hutchinson, 1973).
27. Ibid.

Enver Hoxha himself stemmed from the bourgeoisie. He was a thirty-two-year-old professor of history who had been educated in France and Belgium, and many of his subordinate leaders came from the same middle-class background. In late 1942, he persuaded the most important royalist-Gheg guerrilla bands to joint the partisan movement under the banner of the National Liberation Movement, or LNC. The collaboration proved highly tenuous, with one of the strongest Gheg leaders, Abas Kupi, never a willing participant. Despite the LNC veil, Hoxha remained a hard-line Communist with Comintern connections to KKE in Greece and Tito in Yugoslavia.[28]

Albanian Communists, including some Gheg bands, were fighting the Italian enemy when Maclean's mission arrived. Impressed by their activity, Maclean arranged for delivery of arms and equipment and began training two shock brigades. Other SOE teams parachuted in to join the various groups. But as the Italians showed signs of surrendering, the question of a new government arose, and conflict developed between the partisans and the Balli guerrillas. The Italian surrender heightened tension, since Italian arms equipped more guerrillas, who also recruited Italian deserters.

Subsequent German occupation further hindered the resistance movement. Moving in about two and a half divisions, the Germans soon pressed various guerrilla bands back into the hills: ". . . within a fortnight the insurgents were everywhere on the defensive."[29] The Germans were essentially interested in coastal defense against an allied landing and contented themselves with occupying principal towns and keeping roads open. ". . . The rest of the country they determined to neutralize by policy rather than force."[30] They released political prisoners, announced that they would withdraw from Albania once war ended, and set up a puppet government.

This policy played into Enver Hoxha's hands. If Germans controlled cities and coastal communications, Hoxha would control the rest of Albania, and, in autumn of 1943, he ordered his people to begin attacking and destroying his rivals in the South, the Balli bands. The Ballis soon began falling back toward the coast, where, to survive, they collaborated with the Germans, who willingly fitted them out for counterguerrilla duties: ". . . The civil war in Southern Albania was thus indefinitely prolonged, to the exhaustion of the Albanians and the repose of the German army."[31]

At this critical point, SOE replaced Maclean with a more senior representative, Brigadier "Trotsky" Davies. A Sandhurst regular and twice-decorated veteran of the Mesopotamia campaign (1920) and the

28. Blair, op. cit.
29. Amery, op. cit.
30. Ibid.
31. Ibid.

Palestine fighting in 1938, Davies brought in a small staff, which he based at Biza, in the South. He also brought in nearly half a million dollars in gold to help him accomplish his major task: ". . . to back the political party, or parties, which gave evidence of fighting our enemies."[32]

Although he had some good men who subsequently performed well in the field and although he was a man of considerable charm and unquestioned personal courage, Davies erred in trying to implant regular army order in guerrilla warfare disorder:

. . . Our H.Q. [headquarters] was organized . . . as an orthodox H.Q., even down to the Italian defense platoon, and we all fitted into a detailed alarm scheme—action on air attack, drill for an air drop, and so on. . . .[33]

Where Maclean traveled light, Davies dug in and soon had an impressive but useless headquarters of ". . . interpreters, Italian cooks, servants, mulemen and others," all requiring food and quarters, and one calculated to attract the attention of even the most myopic enemy.[34]

Thus situated, Davies turned to the immense task of forging peace between Enver Hoxha and the Balli, a task that would have required a skillful diplomat armed with Jobian patience. The old boy simply wasn't up to the challenge. At his first conference with the Communist leader, he refused Hoxha's request to review the present world political situation:

. . . Enver said, very pointedly, "The military situation depends entirely on the political situation, so why will you not first give us your impression of world politics?"

I replied, "Because I am a soldier and not a politician."[35]

As Davies continued to argue, with both Hoxha and the Balli, the situation continued to deteriorate, the *chetas* merrily shifting sides, while almost no one fought the Germans. Davies himself grew increasingly frustrated and disgusted:

. . . I felt that we could bring the country to a standstill with two brigades of British troops acting as guerrillas, or with half a dozen *Commandos* [i.e., special operation units]. . . .[36]

That such a notion was never tried was just as well. After moving his ponderous headquarters two or three times in response to German pressure, he decided to break off the guerrilla campaign until spring and move his headquarters south in conjunction with Hoxha's forces. Al-

32. Brigadier Davies, *Illyrian Venture—The Story of the British Military Mission to Enemy-Occupied Albania 1943–1944* (London: Bodley Head, 1952).
33. Ibid.
34. Blair; see also Davies, op. cit.; Amery, op. cit.
35. Davies, op. cit.
36. Ibid.

though Hoxha and his guerrillas reached sanctuary, the Davies group never made it. Hotly pursued by Germans and turncoat Albanians, Davies was wounded and captured and his organization broken up. His field missions suffered various fates: Many were captured and their gold stolen; a few survivors escaped north to join Abas Kupi's guerrillas. As though to haunt the mission's failure, gold circulated by Davies caused severe inflation in the mountains, thus exercising an effect precisely opposite to the intention.[37]

In spring of 1944, SOE parachuted a new mission, again under Maclean, into the North, to try to build a resistance movement cored by Abas Kupi's group and even to bring Abas Kupi into joint effort with Enver Hoxha.

Maclean and two principal lieutenants, Smiley and Amery, found considerable potential in the northern mountains—Amery estimated a total fifteen thousand rifles with possibility of another ten thousand. But they found tribes ". . . very torn and divided, some pro-German, all suspicious. . . ."[38] Although they managed to bring off some small operations, they did not receive support necessary to bring about a general uprising—and very possibly they could not have accomplished this even with prodigal supply.

In contrast, Hoxha and his guerrillas in the South prospered, their numbers growing from an estimated five thousand in January 1944 to over twenty thousand by May. Allied supply, though still in limited quantities, began arriving by air and sea, and LNC units soon were striking German convoys and even garrisons throughout the area with operations expanding north to the other side of Tirana.

In June, the German high command brought in the 1st Mountain Division, a crack outfit which in a month ". . . succeeded in closing the Allied bridgehead north of Saranda, reopening communications with Greece and scattering Partisans into the mountains."[39]

But with transfer of this division to Yugoslavia and replacement by a second-rate outfit, LNC quickly reorganized and recommenced harassing activities. Its units now came into open conflict with royalist and republican movements, but, with SOE support, neutralized these organizations while spreading farther north.

Ensuing internecine fighting greatly helped the Germans to evacuate Albania. Although Partisans and Zogists harassed the German retreat, the former claiming to have killed between five and six thousand Germans, they expended their real energy in fighting civil war, a war the Partisans won. With the ignominious retreat of Abas Kupi and SOE advisers, LNC controlled the country, which became and has remained Communist.

37. Blair, op. cit.
38. Amery, op. cit.
39. Blair, op. cit.

What did guerrilla warfare accomplish in Greece and Albania?

It contributed to keeping enemy divisions from service in other theaters. The Albanian occupation tied up over five Italian divisions and, after the Italian surrender, about four German divisions; the occupation of Greece required six German and twelve Italian divisions. But we

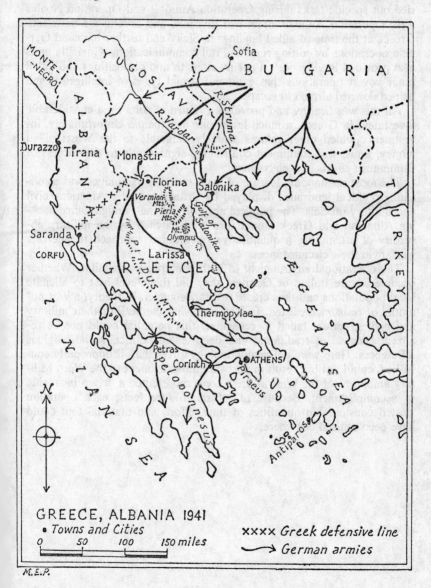

GREECE, ALBANIA 1941
• Towns and Cities   ×××× Greek defensive line
0   50   100   150 miles   ⟶ German armies

M.E.P.

should remember that some of these units would have been necessary without guerrilla resistance, and also that some of them were so second rate as to be useless in a combat zone.

The resistance in Albania was least impressive, although LNC reportedly did good work during the German withdrawal. Greek guerrillas carried out specific tasks during Operation Animals and Operation Noah's Ark. Operation Animals drew two divisions and several air units into Greece at the time of allied landings in Sicily and further harassed German operations by cutting road and rail communications. Guerrilla units also provided intelligence on enemy strength and dispositions and aided other covert operations that gathered special types of intelligence and helped downed airmen to escape.

All this was healthy and provided a return of sorts on a considerable investment in Greece, a much lesser one in Albania. Unfortunately, investment yielded other returns scarcely palatable to the West: allied money, arms, and equipment contributed significantly to the success of Communist efforts in each country.

The most outstanding feature of these guerrilla campaigns was astonishing political ignorance displayed by British and later American civil and military officials. The political absurdity of the Foreign Office backing Albanian and Greek monarchies was matched by the military absurdity of attempting a quantitative operational approach to guerrilla warfare in these circumstances.

The operational environment in both countries was similar. Whether occupiers were Italian or German, they did their level best to alienate local populations and thus create resistance nuclei. In theory, a vast potential of resistance existed. In fact, and what the SOE or their military and civil superiors failed to recognize, this potential could not be realized, because of traditional and deep-seated political-social-religious differences. Here were politically dubious forces that, if improperly controlled, could not but result in postwar embarrassment to the West. Military ambitions of the West in these areas represented a dream incapable of accomplishment. Because of refusal to face facts, each operation wasted considerable quantities of time, effort, and material that could have been utilized elsewhere.

Chapter 39

Japanese conquests • Australian coastwatchers • American marines on Guadalcanal • Japanese occupation of Timor • Australian independent companies • Callinan fights guerrilla warfare • Japanese countertactics • The native element • A summing up

THE READER may recall that, by spring of 1942, Japanese armies occupied all of Southeast Asia, the Philippines, and the Dutch East Indies—the so-called Co-Prosperity Sphere, whose eastern flank Japan protected by a string of newly occupied bases terminating in New Guinea and the Solomon Islands, the western flank by the conquest of Burma, which isolated China and posed a direct threat to India.

The rapidity of these conquests threw potential resistance movements into considerable confusion. With few exceptions, no real resistance organizations existed, although, as in European countries, local Communist parties converted quite easily into militant organizations.

But temporary defeat and immense distances prevented the allies from supplying essential arms and ammunition to, or even communicating with, much less controlling, dissident groups. In some areas, important segments of the population either welcomed Japanese as liberators or suffered them in preference to white colonial rule. Although harsh occupation policies usually changed such halcyon situations, delayed emergence of dissident groups again posed communications and supply problems.

Terrain also influenced the situation: Tiny Pacific islands such as Tarawa and Iwo Jima offered neither natives nor sanctuaries for infiltrated teams, nor did the American navy or marines dispose of specially trained groups for use in more likely target areas such as Guam. An inhibiting political factor also existed, particularly with the British, who did not want such empire possessions as Burma and Malaya promiscuously supplied with arms in the postwar era.

All these factors sharply delimited guerrilla movements, which, as in other theaters of war, greatly varied in motivation, composition, application, and effectiveness.

Almost alone in the vast area of conquest, the Australian high command had taken certain "stay behind" precautions against war with Japan. The original idea stemmed from 1919, when an Australian naval intelligence officer ". . . put forward a suggestion that Australia's vast coastal areas be policed by a network of 'watchers' to report any suspicious characters and happenings in isolated parts."[1]

Through the years, naval intelligence extended the system to New Guinea, Papua, and the Solomon Islands, an intelligence net supported by government officials, missionaries, pilots, and planters. Alarmed by the worsening international situation, in 1939 Commander Eric Feldt recruited small "stay behind" teams and equipped them with teleradios and codes. When war broke, these incredibly brave men, usually white district officers or plantation managers assisted by a few loyal natives, took to the hills, where, often living like animals, they reported enemy strength and dispositions to Port Moresby. Just such a report first disclosed Japanese presence on Guadalcanal and led to U. S. Marine Corps landings in August 1942.

The coastwatcher who reported this development was named Martin Clemens. About a week after marines landed, he presented himself to Major General Alexander Vandegrift. The marine commander found him ". . . a remarkable chap of medium height, well-built and apparently suffering no ill effects from self-imposed jungle exile."

. . . Clemens brought with him a small and loyal group of native scouts including Sergeant Major Vouza, a retired member of the Solomon Islands constabulary. At the outbreak of war Vouza, a black and bandy-legged little fellow, as were all the natives, reported to Clemens and accompanied him into the hills. There they recruited a goodly force of natives who hated the Japanese because of cruelty to the islanders. Clemens and Vouza trained

1. M. Murray, *Hunted—A Coastwatcher's Story* (London: Angus & Robertson, 1967).

these young men as scouts and when Clemens offered me his and their services I was delighted to accept. Vouza later rendered superb service as did all the scouts—of the entire coastwatcher organization I can say nothing too lavish in praise.[2]

The coastwatchers were neither trained nor equipped to generate native guerrilla movements, but their operations nonetheless profited immensely from Japanese occupation policy, which treated Solomon Islands natives as so much dirt. This was a gross error, for these natives possessed eyes and ears and swift jungle feet and the ability to jabber in pidgin English—and their words frequently sang through the ether to Port Moresby, often a siren song calling down air and naval attacks.

Their courage was as splendid as their loyalty. To confirm reports of enemy forces forming on the marine left flank, Vouza volunteered to scout behind Japanese lines. Vouza appeared back in marine lines during the battle of the Tenaru River. In Vandegrift's words:

. . . During the night's action Vouza, bleeding from a dozen wounds, crawled into Pollock's front-lines. Soon he was gasping out his story to Martin Clemens: the enemy had surprised his patrol, captured him, interrogated him without success, then tied him to a tree to torture him unmercifully and finally leave him for dead. His face a pulp from rifle butts smashed into it and bleeding from bayonet wounds in the throat, shoulders and chest, he chewed through his ropes and on hands and knees crawled through the battle to reach our lines and gasp out valuable information on the strength and dispositions of the attacking enemy.[3]

Guadalcanal offers the first tactical paradox in the Pacific war. Despite training that stressed extreme mobility and quasi-guerrilla jungle tactics, Japanese soldiers no more found themselves at home in Guadalcanal jungles than the Americans. Command jealousies, disease, and supply and communication problems combined to frustrate attacks against the marine perimeter guarding Henderson Field. Although supported by clear naval and air superiority, various attacking columns suffered thousands of casualties both from marine fire and from subsequent retreat through jungle rapidly becoming hostile as rations and medicines were consumed and not replaced.

The marines also suffered. At one point, most of Vandegrift's large command was down with dysentery or malaria or both. On several occasions, the jungle slowed, then halted, his limited offensive actions. But marines came to terms with the jungle, not only surviving but fighting and fighting well to invalidate forever the carefully inculcated myth of Japanese tactical invincibility. Part of the reason stemmed from Vande-

2. A. A. Vandegrift and R. B. Asprey, *Once a Marine, supra;* see also S. B. Griffith, *The Battle for Guadalcanal* (Philadelphia: J. B. Lippincott, 1963).
3. Ibid.; Vandegrift awarded him the Silver Star medal.

grift's personal leadership and his refusal to accept defeat, a charismatic performance of enormous importance, considering the long odds against him.

Nor was this sheer bravado. Vandegrift was no stranger to jungle, having campaigned for years in Nicaragua and Haiti. If jungle could hide Japanese, it could also hide marines. In early September, he learned that the American navy could no longer support operations on Guadalcanal—that, literally, he and his marines would have to fight on alone:

. . . I walked back to the CP [command post] with my operations officer [Lt. Col. G. C. Thomas]. "You know, Jerry," I told him, "when we landed in Tientsin, China, in 1927, old Colonel E. B. Miller ordered me to draw up three plans. Two concerned the accomplishment of our mission, the third a withdrawal from Tientsin in case we got pushed out." We walked a bit farther. "Jerry, we're going to defend this airfield until we no longer can. If that happens, we'll take what's left to the hills and fight guerrilla warfare. . . ."[4]

On the more positive side, Vandegrift used jungle later in the campaign when he sent Carlson's Raiders on a wide sweep intended to intercept a withdrawing Japanese column. Aided by native scouts and porters under Vouza and supplied by airdrop, Carlson extended the patrol far to the west. Although he missed the main body, he ambushed a number of rearguard units and cleaned out bothersome artillery positions—in all, killing some 450 enemy at a cost of seventeen killed and seventeen wounded.[5]

One wonders what would have resulted had Vandegrift possessed sufficient strength in the beginning to use Marine Raiders in this long-range penetration role instead of in the more orthodox fighting roles on Tulagi and Guadalcanal.

Another relatively simple action played itself out early in the war on Timor, a large island lying about five hundred miles northwest of Port Darwin, in northern Australia. Timor formed a natural protective flank for Japanese-held Java. Planes flying from its two airfields could neutralize Port Darwin, and it also furnished a staging-support area for operations in the Solomon Islands and New Guinea.

Timor is a large island, about three hundred miles long and an average forty miles wide; a central mountain range has produced terrain varying from scrub-covered slopes to open coastal areas interspersed by dense jungle. Before the war, the Netherlands owned its western half, Portugal its eastern half. In December 1941, a small contingent of Dutch and Australian troops known as Sparrow Force occupied the Dutch por-

---

4. Ibid.
5. H. S. Mirillat, *The Island* (Boston: Houghton Mifflin, 1944); see also Griffith, op. cit.; Vandegrift and Asprey, op. cit.

tion. When Portugal remained neutral, the Dutch and British persuaded her to allow "a friendly occupation" by Sparrow Force troops, in particular the Australian 2/2 Independent Company.

Britain had started the concept of independent raiding companies—forerunner of her famous Commandos—shortly after the fall of France in June 1940. With help of a small British military mission, Australian and New Zealand armies trained a total of eight such companies for independent harassing operations in the Middle East. A member of the British team, a thirty-three-year-old captain and former explorer and teacher, F. Spencer-Chapman, later described the operational thinking of the day:

. . . We talked vaguely of guerrilla and irregular warfare, of special and para-military operations, stay-behind parties, resistance movements, sabotage and incendiarism, and, darkly and still more vaguely, of "agents"; but the exact role of the Commandos and Independent Companies had never been made very clear. The recent Lofoten raid was much in people's minds, and some thought—and hoped—that the Companies would be used as shock troops for full-scale raids with air and sea support. . . .

Others believed that if the Japanese overran various islands,

. . . the role of the Companies would then be to stay behind, live off the country or be provisioned by air, and be a thorn in the flesh of the occupying enemy, emerging in true guerrilla style to attack vital points and then disappear again into the jungle. We also visualized long-range penetration of the enemy lines by parties so highly skilled in fieldcraft and in living off the country that they could attack their targets and get back again without being detected. . . .

Training conformed as much as possible to these various possibilities. The courses, lasting six weeks, concentrated on demolitions and fieldcraft. Spencer-Chapman

. . . taught them how to get a party from A to B and back by day or night in any sort of country and to arrive in a fit state to carry out their task. This included all sorts of sidelines—a new conception of fitness, knowledge of the night sky, what to wear, what to take and how to carry it, what to eat and how to cook it, how to live off the country, tracking, memorizing routes, and how to escape if caught by the enemy.[6]

The Japanese advance caused the high command to commit the newly trained companies to islands closer home. Australian 2/2 Independent Company went to Timor and subsequently to adventures beyond dreams of its hardy back-country-Australian members. The story is well told

6. F. Spencer-Chapman, *The Jungle Is Neutral* (London: Chatto & Windus, 1949).

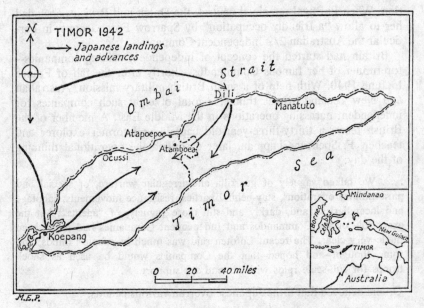

by the company commander, Major Bernard Callinan, in his book *Independent Company*,[7] which I have relied on in the following brief account.

Variously reinforced, 2/2 Independent Company comprised around 325 men totally unfamiliar with Timor. Sent to the Portuguese area of Dili, on the coast, the company completed what defenses it could before the Japanese onslaught in February 1942. Some fourteen thousand Japanese troops landed at Koepang, in Dutch Timor, and about six thousand at Dili. On Dutch Timor, the bulk of Sparrow Force fell back, only to encounter Japanese paratroopers fighting a guerrilla-style action in their rear. Inadequately trained and equipped, this force soon lost tactical cohesion, the units either surrendering or escaping to Portuguese Timor.

While 2/2 Company also fell back, its commander held no intention of surrendering. His situation was scarcely happy. The company was not supposed to be fighting independently on Timor, and logistically was anything but self-sufficient. It even lacked a radio transmitter capable of raising Port Darwin. It was well armed, however, for guerrilla warfare—its men carried the proportionately high number of sixty submachine guns and were splendidly trained for small-unit operations. Instead of surrendering, as the high command in Australia supposed had

7. Bernard Callinan, *Independent Company* (London: William Heinemann, 1953).

been the case, the company commander immediately chose defensive positions and began harassing the newly arrived enemy.

The Australians wisely refrained from complicating the relatively simple tactical problem of containing Japanese in the Dili area. To accomplish this, they set up a fluid defense in surrounding hills, from where small units ambushed roads and paths, besides raiding suitable enemy targets.

Wishing to push back the Australians so that their forces in the west could deliver the *coup de grâce,* the Japanese reinforced Dili units and began dispatching strong probing patrols into surrounding hills.

For combat veterans, they seemed surprisingly inept. They almost constantly telegraphed their movements. In Callinan's words,

. . . soon we saw some troops set up a mortar in the village square and fire off some bombs in our direction, to points which they thought we might be using as observation posts. It was slightly amusing to watch those marionettes loading the mortar, and then hear the bombs bursting hundreds of yards on our right. We had learnt not to use the highest peak, or even the most obvious spot.

Japanese patrols frequently walked through one ambush position to be attacked by a second; survivors were then struck from the rear. Small ambushes constantly hit enemy motor patrols, an activity that increased when the Japanese set up a base twenty miles inland from Dili. Australian roadblocks ". . . varied from rolling large rocks or felling trees across the roads, to blocking up culverts to cause the road to be washed away, and to blowing embankments away and then diverting creeks to continue the erosion." This facilitated successful ambushes,

. . . and our tally of enemy killed grew. To reduce the attacks the enemy established strong posts along the road, and from these patrols went out to keep the area clear. This was the culmination of all our efforts; we now had the enemy thoroughly worried, and his troops were being dispersed, and tired out on sentry and patrol duties. This system of posts also suited our capabilities as we were able to provide small parties which sat above these posts and observed them, and when the routine of the post was known a raid would be carried out. . . . One typical raid was carried out by Sergeant James, who with two sappers [engineers] sat less than one hundred yards from a Japanese post for two days. When he knew the routine of the post well, he decided that the best time to strike was just as the enemy were having breakfast. So the following morning there was a sharp burst of fire and twelve Japanese were killed, the raiders disappearing into the scrub.

Two or three such raids per week, each claiming from five to fifteen Japanese lives, worked an "enormous" effect on Japanese morale.

Australian morale meanwhile was none too good. By now, malaria claimed most of the company. Boots were wearing fast, weapons needed repair, ammunition was running low, money was needed to pay natives. So far as the world knew, 2/2 Company languished in some Japanese prison camp.

Imagine the surprise, then, of radio monitors one morning in Port Darwin picking up a faint signal from Timor. This came from a transmitter made by a radioman ingeniously working with two field radios and bits of variously acquired junk. According to Callinan,

. . . the set occupied a room about ten feet square, and there were bits and pieces spread around on benches and joined by wires trailing across the floor. Batteries were charged by a generator taken from an old car and driven by a rope which passed around a similar wheel about eighteen inches in diameter. Attached to this latter wheel was another small wheel around which a further rope passed on to a wheel about four feet or more in diameter, and to this large wheel were fixed handles by which four natives turned the machine.

New sets brought in from Darwin eventually replaced this Rube Goldberg contraption, which was just as well, considering the constant need for mobility!

Supply drops naturally increased 2/2 Company's effectiveness, to the astounding degree that the Japanese accepted the tactical status quo and began concentrating on raising natives against the Australians.

Timor natives give still another lie to the pleasant fiction of people everywhere wanting to die for what the West likes to call freedom. Timor natives did not know the meaning of freedom. To them, the white man represented oppression. At one point during the campaign, Callinan watched a two-hundred-man Portuguese force launch a punitive expedition against some rebel natives:

. . . Compared with this, the Japanese efforts at subjecting areas were just child's play. Every village and crop was burnt; every woman, child, and animal was driven off and fell as spoil to the victors. . . .

Was it any wonder that Japanese agents before the war had successfully implanted anti-white propaganda, not alone in Timor but throughout Pacific colonial areas?

After the landings, the Japanese continued to cultivate the native population by simple propaganda reinforced by strong physical presence. They also put a considerable price on each Australian head, and they tried to work up active native opposition *behind* the Australians.

. . . The steps they followed were, firstly, to threaten the natives in an area that if they assisted the Australians their villages and crops would be destroyed; then, if that was not successful, the Japanese would carry out their threat. The enemy was always able to mass many more troops and natives than we were, and although these expeditions were costly to him he was able to achieve his objective. The natives were materialists, with no great interest in a war between two almost mythical countries such as Australia and Japan, so gradually the areas through which we could move freely became restricted.

None of these measures deprived Australians of the initiative, though enemy caution forced them to drastic action. Patrols armed with three-inch mortars sent from Port Darwin sneaked close to Dili to launch surprise bombardments that caused Japanese patrols to issue forth (and frequently stumble into ambushes). Other brave souls relying on friendly native cover advanced to close range and eliminated enemy groups with submachine-gun fire.

To counter native treachery, Australians relied on friendly natives, who proved surprisingly loyal. A native servant, or *criado,* served each Australian, following him into combat and relieving him of gear, then helping him escape over difficult and unfamiliar terrain. Later in the campaign, 2/2 Company trained several native units in marksmanship and partially equipped them with rifles. Recruiting grew easier as occupation continued and Japanese cruelties multiplied. Natives particularly resented Japanese attacks on native women and girls. Australians also gained a psychological advantage over natives from their own air raids (by far the most important accomplishment of these raids). Finally, they relied on active patrol and area security and instant reprisal in case of native attack.

Mobility remained their best ally. Time and again, Japanese columns rushed from Dili only to encounter space. If they rushed too far, they found themselves cut off. If they did happen onto a few guerrillas, the latter quickly disappeared. It was as if guerrillas sprang from ground to disappear in sky. It seemed easy; in fact, it hinged on an extremely cunning organization whose disciplined members constantly utilized security measures.

The operational key was Force Headquarters, tucked away in the hills. This organization supported the active guerrilla groups and also administered a rear-area sanctuary in a mountain village, ". . . a remarkable achievement comprising a hospital, a convalescent depot, and a reinforcement training depot. . . ." Force Headquarters remained extremely mobile:

. . . Each little group of signal, administrative, transport, and cookhouse personnel was made responsible for its own mobility. There were regular practices at loading all their gear on to horses, taking them down a track for a few hundred yards and then back again; thus each group soon knew just how much they could carry, and where the best place was for each item.

This was not empty precaution. Although the signal section maintained careful radio discipline, the Japanese sometimes homed in on transmissions. On one occasion, they followed this with a raid in force. Callinan later recalled that ". . . although the signallers had been in the middle of a message to Australia, the sets and ciphers were on the track within fifteen minutes, and there was not a sign of their recent occupation left behind. . . ."

To maintain control over guerrilla groups, Force Headquarters relied on telephone and native runner to platoon headquarters. Whenever possible, the platoon leader placed himself in a safe position, where he would not be constantly forced to move. This gave a much needed continuity to the intelligence process, which flowed both ways. But if a platoon headquarters was attacked, damage was usually minimal. Good security normally warned the platoon leader, and excellent mobility usually provided escape. From the beginning, the Australians used a system of rallying points:

. . . Whether it was a two-man ambush, a sub-section, section or platoon action, we always had that rallying point where the troops reorganized, and it was this continual dispersing after an attack and rapid reforming which frustrated the Japanese efforts to exterminate us.

Far from exterminating the Australians, the Japanese seriously threatened their existence on only a few occasions. They could not prevent airdrops from reaching the guerrillas. A few ships also managed to bring in supply, an effort culminating by landing 2/4 Independent Company as much-needed reinforcement. In thirteen months, the Australians killed some fifteen hundred enemy troops at a cost of forty men.

But this was not their real accomplishment. Their supreme moment occurred when the Japanese high command, fearful of an allied landing on Timor, committed the 48th Infantry Division, fifteen thousand veterans of China, Philippines, and Java campaigns. As Nevil Shute pointed out in an introductory chapter to *Independent Company*, ". . . this at a time when their advance in Burma had been halted, when the American Marines were fighting on Guadalcanal, and bitter fighting was in progress in Papua [New Guinea]"—in other words, at a time when the Japanese had a dozen and one other uses for a good infantry division.

Australians on Timor undoubtedly could have insured a successful allied landing by temporarily protecting a beachhead. But, in 1943, the "withering on the vine" strategy, whereby allied forces bypassed island redoubts, leaving them to starve and eventually surrender, made pointless such a landing. Instead, one evacuated the Australians to leave the Japanese in uneasy occupation of the island.

This writer has been unable to determine if the allied high command explored the idea of increasing the guerrilla effort on Timor in order either to force the enemy to commit other troops badly needed elsewhere or to defeat the Japanese in detail for propaganda value.

Chapter 40

Guerrilla resistance in the Philippines • Area of operations • Kangleon's guerrillas on Leyte • Major missions • Japanese occupation policy • Japanese countertactics • Fertig's guerrillas on Mindanao • Major missions • Failure of Japanese counter- tactics • Communist resistance • Luis Taruc and the Huks • Volckmann's guerrillas on Luzon • His organization and growth • Major missions • The Japanese attitude

A MUCH LESS COHESIVE but no less instructive guerrilla re- sistance sprang up in the Philippine Islands after the fall of Corregidor, the island bastion lying off Bataan, in early 1942. Not all of the American-Philippine garrison surrendered to the Japanese. Although MacArthur's command was totally surprised, some commanders sent officers behind Japanese units with orders to raise guerrilla groups. Dur- ing retreat to the island bastion, a good many soldiers, cut off by the Japanese advance, had escaped to remote areas of Luzon, where willing Filipinos helped hide and feed them while they organized guerrilla units. (See map, Chapters 13–14.)

Elsewhere in the vast complex of islands, Filipino and American officers often refused to surrender, preferring instead to take to the hills to form resistance nuclei, which attracted fellow citizens, survivors of sunk American ships, and various American civilians who managed to elude the Japanese dragnet.

Still another guerrilla movement, and a potent one, centered around the Communist Party of the Philippines, which, like European Communist parties, was small but well organized.

About fifty guerrilla groups emerged in the islands before the Japanese had even consolidated their conquest, and a surprising number of these survived and prospered. In the vast archipelago, 7,100 islands with a land area of 114,830 square miles, they occupied in the main Luzon in the North, the Visayan Islands (particularly Leyte and Samar) in the center, and Mindanao in the South,[1] although small groups existed on many smaller islands, where they eventually lined the beaches to greet returning Americans.

At first, these units were out of touch with allied headquarters in Australia or even with each other. Nor were their aims always harmonious. While killing Japanese was the announced goal, some groups existed more to survive than to fight, some to prey as bandits on relatively helpless native barrios, some, particularly Communists, to fight but also to consolidate in so far as possible their power for postwar purposes, and some to fight as hard as they could until the Americans returned.

Whatever the goal, no one group enjoyed an easy existence, despite a good many natural sanctuaries. Some of the immense problems have been well presented by Ira Wolfert in his book *American Guerrilla in the Philippines,* which is the story of an American naval officer, Cliff Richardson, who joined a guerrilla force organized and commanded by a regular Philippine Army officer, Lieutenant Colonel Ruperto Kangleon.[2]

After escaping from a Japanese prisoner-of-war camp, Kangleon recruited a small guerrilla group in southern Leyte. At first, natives wanted to help the guerrillas, their motivation intense nationalism rather than particular ideology. About 70 per cent of the population, however, greatly feared the Japanese and did not hide their relief when guerrillas had vacated barrio or village areas. Initial enthusiasm later waned when a bandit group calling itself guerrillas "requisitioned" anything they could find, including women, with no notion of fighting the Japanese.[3]

Bandits provided but one difficulty to Kangleon's embryo army, which suffered from shortages of everything but spirit. The band owned few rifles and little ammunition. To keep rifles in repair and provide fresh ammunition, guerrillas rounded up ". . . a hand-forge, some

---

1. M. H. Cannon, *The War in the Pacific—Leyte: Return to the Philippines* (Washington: U. S. Government Printing Office, 1954).

2. Ira Wolfert, *American Guerrilla in the Philippines* (New York: Avon Books, 1945); see also S. E. Morison, *Leyte: June 1944–January 1945* (London: Oxford University Press, 1958), Vol. 12 of 15 vols.: After the war, Kangleon became Secretary of National Defense and a senator in the Philippine Government.

3. Wolfert, op. cit.

hacksaws, and a file. That was a small arms factory." Brass curtain rods taken from schoolhouses were cut and filed to make bullets.

. . . For the primer, we used sulphur mixed with coconut shell carbon. Later we were able to get hold of some antimony and add it to the mixture. . . . Our main source of powder was from Japanese sea mines that we would dismantle. We'd mix in pulverized wood to retard the burning because mine powder is too violent for a rifle bullet.[4]

The ordnance factory, which ". . . never filled more than a one-room house, about twenty feet by ten," boasted a staff of about sixty workers, but so laborious was filing down the curtain rods that "our production never got better than an average of 160 bullets a day."

Despite such disadvantages, the guerrilla force rapidly expanded. Almost all raw materials continued to come from the people—general requisitions carried out through local government. Guerrillas made their own ink, essential for news sheets and money; they made fuel for their few vehicles by distilling alcohol from tuba; they constructed 140 kilometers of telegraph lines by using nails made from barbed wire and insulators from old soda-pop bottles.[5]

Kangleon did not contact MacArthur's headquarters in Australia until spring of 1943, when an American naval commander, Charles Parsons, arrived by submarine to talk to guerrilla leaders and set up a chain of coastwatcher stations. After considerable confusion, during which Kangleon's guerrillas had to fight and defeat a rival guerrilla force, MacArthur recognized Kangleon as the official guerrilla commander on Leyte. Directed to concentrate on collecting and transmitting intelligence on enemy strength and dispositions, Kangleon continued to strengthen his forces, an effort helped by two American submarines, which began the hazardous task of bringing in arms and supply.[6]

Kangleon's early survival rested in part on a relatively light Japanese garrison in southern Leyte. Mainly for this reason, the Japanese

. . . tried to conciliate the guerrillas, offering, in return for their surrender, not only freedom from punishment but also jobs and the opportunity to resume their normal family life. A great many guerrillas took advantage of this offer of amnesty and surrendered. . . .[7]

Kangleon's force remained largely intact, however, and when guerrilla activity continued and as the Japanese experienced fresh reverses in the Pacific theater, they reinforced Leyte garrisons and attempted to clean out guerrilla bands.

4. Ibid.
5. Ibid.
6. Cannon, op. cit.; see also Morison, op. cit.
7. Cannon, op. cit.

By this time, Kangleon and his American officers had organized a quasi-regular army, whose companies maintained ". . . a guardhouse, barracks, mess hall, officers' quarters." The security of this army depended largely on the civil populace:

. . . a whole network of volunteer guards sprang up—civilians serving without pay, donating one day out of every four to act as sentinels or relay men for messages or lookouts. When Japanese approached, the civilians were warned, too, and in the hills and many coastal barrios patrols found only empty houses and vacant towns. . . .[8]

Beginning in late 1943, the Japanese increased size and frequency of patrols. Utilizing information supplied through collaborators belonging to "The Good Neighbor Association," they captured numerous guerrillas and guerrilla sympathizers, summarily executing each. Guerrillas replied by killing one collaborator for each victim:

. . . Cinco's [a unit leader] men developed the habit of killing Japan's "good neighbors," leaving their faces untouched so that they might be recognized but mincing up their bodies gruesomely, then floating them downstream to their home barrio where they could serve as an example to the others.[9]

Tactically the Japanese relied on large expeditions, or "sweeps," sometimes supported by aircraft whose bombs and machine-gun bullets proved virtually useless in heavy jungle. Richardson recalled watching an enemy force fan out

. . . into the hills. We watched their columns walking along staring curiously at our pop bottle telegraph system. Their columns converged on nothing. Their pincers clutched empty air. Not a shot was fired at them. They found nothing to shoot at. A fifth columnist would tell where a headquarters house was. The Japs would surround it stealthily at night. They would rush it at night. They would find a sleepy man and his sleepy wife and sleepy children.[10]

Once a patrol had worn itself out in a day of fruitless marching through difficult terrain, guerrillas frequently ambushed it on its way back to barrio.

Failure to eliminate guerrillas infuriated the Japanese, who resorted to harsher and harsher treatment of the civil populace. Suspect guerrillas or sympathizers often received the salt-water torture:

. . . they tied a man's hands and feet and ran the cord around his neck so that if he struggled he would strangle himself. Then they forced a wedge

8. Wolfert, op. cit.
9. Ibid.
10. Ibid.

into his mouth to hold it open, held his nose, and poured sea water into his mouth. He had to swallow to breathe.[11]

If he talked, they stopped the torture; if not, they continued until his death.

These and other punishments often caused people to leave villages for the hills, where the Japanese ruthlessly tried to ferret them out, often killing entire hill families and burning hill barrios in the process. To prevent this, guerrillas frequently attacked enemy units close to coastal towns rather than in more favorable ambush areas in the hills.

Hill people also reacted vigorously. The men began carrying a second, and smaller, bolo under the shirt, attacking Japanese soldiers as they closed in to tie their hands. When the Japanese learned this trick and made victims remove their shirt, ". . . the Filipinos took to carrying shards of glass in their mouths, razor blades if they found them and sharpened nails to strike enemy eyes—anything that would do damage and keep a man from feeling he was a dumb beast standing mutely to be killed." Hill natives also planted *suak,* or barbed pieces of tetanus-poisoned bamboo, along trails used by Japanese patrols. When a patrol passed, natives would ". . . fire a shot or . . . shout and the Japs would drop flat against the *suak.*"[12]

The combination of hill natives and guerrillas proved too much for the Japanese, who slowly yielded all but coastal towns, finally not daring even to send patrols to the hills. Nor did the Japanese commander dare to report failure. Instead, he insisted that, from January through August 1944, his troops fought 561 engagements with guerrillas:

. . . The Japanese declared that they had taken 2,300 prisoners of war, including 3 Americans; that 6 Americans and 23,077 Filipinos had surrendered; 1,984 guerrillas had been killed; and that the Japanese casualties amounted to 7 officers and 208 enlisted men killed; and 11 officers and 147 men wounded.[13]

Kangleon, on the other hand, reported minimum guerrilla casualties and significant Japanese losses. At the very least, his movement continued to grow. Armed with radios and new weapons landed from submarines, they continued to report valuable intelligence, and when American armies returned to the islands a few months later, they formed a potent and helpful force.

On Mindanao, the vast southern island, an American mining engineer and reserve officer, Colonel Wendell Fertig, built an impressive guer-

11. Ibid.
12. Ibid.
13. Cannon, op. cit.

rilla organization from a cadre of five officers and about 175 enlisted men.[14]

Although Mindanao proved ideal for guerrilla operations—it offered ample food, mountain sanctuary, and easy access to the sea and thus eventual supply by submarine—the movement did not immediately prosper. American defeat had caused important segments of the population to either support or submit to the Japanese presence. Japanese, not the guerrillas, soon changed this disadvantageous situation. Surfeited with superiority, they inflicted their boorish presence on the locals, frequently slapping men and molesting and raping women. As early as September 1942, forty-five uprisings occurred on Mindanao, and Fertig found himself heading a viable guerrilla movement.

The Japanese had intended to rule through the legal Philippine Government and native police, an intention voided by the army's stupid behavior. Instead, they organized a constabulary of native quislings brought in from other islands. These became the priority target of Fertig's guerrillas, who harassed them so effectively that they soon ceased patrolling and eventually confined themselves to two general areas.

Although the Japanese maintained about 150,000 troops on Mindanao, they held back in committing them to counterguerrilla actions. When they did so, they proved as inept as on the Visayan Islands, in general relying on "sweeps" that devastated "guerrilla areas" and accomplished little. In early 1943, the Japanese even introduced war dogs to track down guerrillas, a futile effort abandoned a few months later.

The Japanese failed to understand the nature of the target. Believing that they were fighting isolated groups of bandits, their various area headquarters refused to co-ordinate counterguerrilla operations, relying instead on local punitive actions.

They did not realize, or anyway would not admit, that they were fighting an entire population. A significant exception occurred in 1944, when one Japanese general chose a conciliatory approach to the people and nearly wrecked the guerrilla movement! More often, however, the enemy fell into the traditional trap: the more countermeasures failed to eliminate guerrilla activity, the more they persecuted the people and the stronger the movement became.

Fertig's substantial growth was recognized in early 1943, when allied headquarters designated Mindanao as the 10th Military District. Some escaped Australian army prisoners of war, including Major Rex Blow, arriving in June 1943, found a quasi-military organization of impressive proportions. Landing in northern Mindanao, in the Lianga area, they reported to Colonel Hedges, commanding 105th Regiment of guerrillas.[15]

14. S. T. Hosmer (Chairman), *Counterinsurgency: A Symposium—April 16–20, 1962* (Santa Monica, Calif.: Rand Corporation, 1963).

15. Rex Blow, "With the Filipino Guerrillas," *Australian Army Journal*, 1966.

Although Hedges, who had managed a timber company in the area before the war, commanded about ten thousand guerrillas, he was temporarily lying low as a result of vigorous Japanese punitive measures. Major Blow learned something of prevailing spirit, however, when he asked a young Filipino intelligence officer to type out some reports. "Sir," Lieutenant Villanueva replied, "I do not wish to work in an office, I want to kill Japs." He subsequently did so, only to lose his life while singlehandedly attacking some fifty Japanese soldiers.[16]

Hedges faced another problem in the form of confused religions. About two thousand Christians were fighting as guerrillas in coastal areas; the rest of his command consisted of fierce Mohammedan Moros, who fought under their old sultans. Moros not only fought Japanese and Christians but also each other, and Hedges and Blow spent a great deal of time trying to minimize their extracurricular wars.

The main guerrilla function in the north at this time was to survive while providing allied headquarters with intelligence. Each complemented the other. Major Blow later wrote:

. . . One of our agents was a young lady working in the Japanese Kempetai office in Iligan. She kept us supplied with all the latest information and was able to warn of us intended patrols. . . . We had several agents in all garrisons. . . .[17]

Guerrillas nonetheless practiced careful security precautions. Fertig himself frequently changed "headquarters"—the longest he ever stayed in one place was two months. They also used aggressive measures to throw the enemy off. The favorite was the small patrol to harass the usual two-hundred-man Japanese patrol. Filipinos knew every foot of the area, knew where to strike and where likely ambushes could occur —hill natives could actually *smell* the presence of Japanese.

But without the people's help, guerrillas would not have survived. For a long period, Fertig depended for interisland communication largely on a "bamboo telegraph," in which ten-year-olds played an integral role despite the blandishments of enemy, who, although offering candy one day, offered blows the next. Major Blow's fourteen-year-old houseboy and bodyguard, Sabu, had watched Japanese soldiers kill his father and rape his mother and sisters, an experience scarcely unique. As a result, people constantly risked their lives on behalf of guerrillas. Blow later wrote of an offensive that eventually forced the Japanese to evacuate Iligan:

. . . When out on patrol we never carried anything but a change of clothes, a toothbrush and our arms. Every house we passed would offer us something to eat, whether it was a piece of corn or a fat chicken. The Japs were now offering quite a large reward for my head, dead or alive—the price being

16. Ibid.
17. Ibid.

5,000 yards of West Point khaki drill, valued at about twenty pesos a yard then. But there was never the slightest suggestion of earning that prize. . . .

In the Lianga area, Blow continued:

. . . During these difficult days we were given great assistance by the Assemblyman, Mr. Lluch. He organized a body of young girls who cooked, sewed, and tended our wounds. They were a stout-hearted group and always back in town the day after the Japs had passed through, ready to organize a concert or dance, repair our clothes and feed us. . . .[18]

So effective were guerrillas in this area that, by the time of American landings, most of the considerable area of Lanao, including beaches, was devoid of Japanese. In the Malabang area, Blow's guerrillas seized and held an airstrip from which American marine fliers operated against Japanese for a week prior to actual landings. When this operation forced precipitate retreat of the Japanese garrison, General Eichelberger changed his landing plan to save about two days and a great deal of ammunition.

Still another movement centered on the Communist Party of the Philippines, itself in a transitional stage. In 1938, it had absorbed the Socialist Party—in some ways a shaky merger, with each party retaining ". . . its own organizations, even in the barrios [villages], and this arrangement continued until 1941 and, to a lesser extent, through the period of the Japanese occupation."[19]

Although differences between these radical parties in time would grow acute, the nationalist bias of each prevailed for the common purpose of fighting Japanese. In December 1941, Communists-Socialists published a twelve-point memorandum calling

. . . for all-out resistance to the Japanese. In forthright language it declared that anyone committing treason would do so at the cost of his life. It urged all patriotic Filipinos and anti-fascist organizations to organize squads of volunteers to begin training for guerrilla warfare while waiting for definite instructions on how and when to begin the fight.[20]

This movement naturally attracted its own followers, and it undoubtedly attracted other nationalists in areas lacking organized guerrilla units. At outbreak of war, Communists formed the *Hukbo ng Bayan so Hapon* (People's Army to Fight the Japanese), which we have come to know as the Hukbalahap, or Huks.

Organized on quasi-military lines and commanded by twenty-nine-

18. Ibid.; see also Morison, op. cit.
19. Luis Taruc, *He Who Rides the Tiger* (New York: Frederick A. Praeger, 1967).
20. Ibid.

year-old Luis Taruc, whom we shall again encounter in postwar years, these units formed regiments, battalions, companies, platoons, and squads. In time, leaders established semiliberated and liberated areas, from where they harassed Japanese to a far greater extent than has usually been admitted by anti-Communist postwar commentators.

One American fugitive, an army officer, came on a Huk camp in autumn of 1942. This was on Mount Arayat, about forty miles north of Manila:

. . . Early in the morning we arrived at the Huk headquarters. The approaches to it were well patrolled and guarded, as we were challenged at least a dozen times while climbing up Mount Arayat. . . .

We were well received at Huk headquarters, and I was much impressed by the order and the discipline that I observed. Upon learning where we were headed, they asked us to consider remaining with them as military advisors. . . .[21]

At this time, Huks were already active, regularly attacking Japanese units in order to gain arms and supply. Early successes produced an unhealthy overconfidence, however, and in 1943, Japanese troops attacked and practically destroyed the Mount Arayat stronghold—the only major counterguerrilla success during the occupation.[22]

The Huks recovered, however, to become a real menace to the Japanese, particularly in central Luzon but also on other islands. Captured Japanese files bulged with reports such as that of September 24, 1944, by the National Advisory Board on Public Safety to the puppet President Laurel: ". . . about 1,000 Hubkos armed with machine guns, automatic rifles and pistols struck Jaen in Nueva Ecija . . . looting, burning: 1 policeman dead; 2 Hubkos killed, 4 wounded. . . ." Three months later, the unhappy president learned ". . . that the mails coming from the Visayas and Mindanao are practically nil while those from Luzon are extremely limited."[23]

A variety of guerrilla movements took place on the northern island of Luzon. One of the most viable sprang from the efforts of a young West Pointer, thirty-year-old R. W. Volckmann, who began his Philippine experience a captain and ended a colonel—a remarkable saga well told in his book *We Remained.*[24] Promoted to regimental commander during the retreat down Bataan, Volckmann refused the final surrender order and took to the hills, where a number of small bands already had

21. R. W. Volckmann, *We Remained* (New York: W. W. Norton, 1954).

22. N. D. Valeriano and C. T. C. Bohannan, *Counter-Guerrilla Operations. The Philippine Experience* (New York: Frederick A. Praeger, 1962).

23. Mauro García, *Documents on the Japanese Occupation of the Philippines* (Manila: Philippines Historical Association, 1965).

24. Volckmann, op. cit.

formed, a disjointed effort, under two American army officers, Colonels Moses and Noble.

After a series of incredible adventures and hair-raising escapes, this latter-day Lawrence found himself in northern Luzon, a victorious trek that depended in part on his own incredible stamina and courage, in part on willingness of hundreds of natives to risk their lives and the lives of families and friends to hide, feed, and nurse him. Arriving more dead than alive, in September 1942, he recovered to organize and command one of the most valuable guerrilla nets in the archipelago.

Volckmann started nearly from scratch. He was not familiar with the history or philosophy of rebellion and guerrilla warfare, he probably had not read Lenin and certainly not Mao Tse-tung. Using common sense, he was aware that the first element essential to a resistance movement existed in the Philippines: a cause. Japanese invasion and occupation, he reasoned,

. . . were opposed in varying degrees by the vast majority of the people. Thus the underlying potential for resistance existed throughout the Islands. The major question was, Could the individuals who basically were opposed to the Japanese be organized and directed so as to express their opposition against the Japs actively by subversion and guerrilla warfare? The answer appeared to depend on an analysis of the human, psychological, and physical factors as they existed at the time.[25]

The history of the Philippines satisfied the human factor:

. . . A resistance movement and the culmination and active expression of a successful resistance movement, guerrilla warfare, can only be generated among people who have the courage and stamina to withstand privations, endure hardships, and face imminent death while fighting back against great odds. . . . To make use of these characteristics, I recognized that leaders must emerge to inspire, awaken, organize, and direct this potential. From the willingness of the Filipinos to trust and be guided by American leadership, I was confident that any lack of strong native leadership could be supplemented by a few determined Americans. . . .[26]

Psychologically, the situation was less apparent. Volckmann concluded that ambitions and aspirations implanted by the American experience would withstand Japanese propaganda up to a point. When he arrived in Ifugao, the Japanese were conducting an amnesty drive based on "Asia for the Asiatics." He did not find many natives impressed, and he believed, correctly, that Japanese brutality would swiftly supplant the velvet glove.

Physical factors ". . . included topography, enemy forces, friendly forces, space and time, and moral and material support." Mountains,

25. Ibid.
26. Ibid.

forests, and limited roads of northern Luzon favored guerrilla operations, as did numerous villages, ". . . a source of food and shelter":

. . . The Japs, to control such an area completely and effectively, without gaining the co-operation of the populace, would have to divert and maintain huge forces in North Luzon. But they were committed in force throughout Asia and the South-west Pacific.

They could, however (as they did in late 1942), concentrate sizable forces and conduct an extensive campaign against guerrilla forces and their supporting populace. They could be expected to continue to have this capability until Allied forces threatened or actually landed in Luzon. However, each Allied victory and the reduction of the time and space between the Allied forces and Luzon would reduce Japanese capabilities and in turn strengthen Filipino morale. I was certain also that reduction of the time and space factor would likewise mean material support, provided, of course, that contact could be established with friendly forces. To me, then, the time and space factor was the key.[27]

Volckmann thought that an earlier attempt to go into action had been a mistake. Lacking external pressure,

. . . the Japs retaliated in force and rushed thousands of troops into North Luzon. For eight months they conducted relentless mopping-up operations against the guerrilla forces and the loyal civilians supporting the resistance movement. Every town and city was garrisoned, and ten-day patrols which combed the surrounding country were kept out by each garrison. Entire civilian settlements suspected of supporting the "banditos" were destroyed.

. . . The entire civilian population was organized into "Neighborhood Associations" in which fifteen families were placed under a head, the "Presidente," who in turn was held directly responsible to the mayor of the municipality for the families under him. The mayor was answerable to the local Japanese garrison commander. The Neighborhood Associations were required to post around-the-clock guards on all trails and roads and to report all guerrilla activities.

As a check on their system the Japs hired spies and informers from among the natives who could be bought. These spies were paid large bonuses, in addition to their normal salaries, for information of particular value. Large rewards were placed on the heads of all Americans and of the better-known Filipino guerrilla leaders. To augment and strengthen their army the Japs organized and armed Filipino constabulary units and stationed them under close Jap supervision.[28]

These various measures severely impeded the guerrilla movement, which, in spring of 1943, numbered fewer than two thousand men dispersed throughout Luzon, a command known grandly as U. S. Army

27. Ibid.
28. Ibid.

Forces in the Philippines—North Luzon (USAFIP—N.L.). With the capture of Colonels Moses and Noble, Volckmann took command to carry out MacArthur's "Lay Low Order." This sensibly ordered guerrillas on Luzon to organize combat cadres and intelligence nets but avoid more active operations until arms and ammunition could be sent from Australia. To accomplish this, the young officer divided the vast area into six districts, each with its own commander and separate military and civilian organization. The reader will have to turn to his book to understand the dimensions of his remarkable achievement—I can only stress certain of his findings and conclusions.

Volckmann realized from the beginning the importance of civilian co-operation—his escape alone had constantly emphasized this:

. . . No resistance movement can flourish for long without mass civilian support. This support may be voluntary, induced, or imposed, but it is absolutely essential to the maintenance of large guerrilla forces for a prolonged period of time in a country overrun by the enemy. The ease with which this civilian co-operation was obtained varied between districts as well as between the various localities within the districts. It was generally found that areas which had no guerrilla forces for long periods were the hardest to bring back under control. In some instances severe measures had to be taken against individuals or groups who resisted the move to re-establish control.[29]

In this respect, the major enemy was not Japanese ". . . but rather the spies, informers and collaborators operating for them." Volckmann came up with an answer reflected in a simple order: eliminate them. After six months of often brutal countermeasures, the threat greatly diminished:

. . . The effect of this extermination program had more far-reaching results than those at first evident. Not only were the loyal and sympathetic civilians soon convinced that they could now safely support USAFIP, N.L., but the so-called "fence-sitters" began toppling in the right direction. Even those who had previously been opposed to the "misguided elements" realized that the Japanese could not guarantee protection, and they too when approached were willing to put their shoulders to the wheel. The Filipinos' fear of the Japs, created by their barbarous and inhuman acts, was overpowered by the quiet, sometimes ferocious, but always persistent methods of their own people.

The civilian support thus brought about was then organized and the civilian was made to feel that he was part of the resistance movement. Once fully committed to such a role, it was very unlikely that people will ever again turn to the enemy. . . .[30]

29. Ibid.
30. Ibid.

Despite any number of setbacks, the movement continued to grow. A year after he took command, Volckmann had established reliable communications with district commands. His combat units had grown from less than two thousand to about eight thousand in strength, with a reserve of another seven thousand plus about five thousand men organized into "bolo battalions," or service units. In August 1944, he gained radio contact with Australia, which meant direct transmission of intelligence as opposed to sending it via guerrilla commands to the south. It also meant some long-delayed help, and, in November, the first submarine reached the area.

With the influx of arms, radios, and other essential supply, Volckmann shifted from "lay low" to aggressive operations. Concurrently, he relayed a steady flow of intelligence to MacArthur's headquarters. Documents discovered in a crashed plane disclosed a major change in Japanese plans: General Yamashita had decided to withdraw from the Lingayen area into the northern hinterland. Such was Volckmann's flow of intelligence from the proposed allied landing area that, two days prior to D-Day, he sent a dispatch to MacArthur: ". . . There will be no repeat no opposition on the beaches." Simultaneously, his guerrillas throughout the area struck the Japanese:

. . . The numerous small enemy garrisons were quickly isolated and destroyed. Extensive demolitions, road-blocks, and continuous ambushing and destruction of transportation greatly reduced the mobility of large enemy concentrations and seriously aggravated their already difficult supply problems.[31]

When Sixth Army landed in January 1945, Volckmann reported for duty as commander of a force numbering nearly twenty thousand with its own service of supply—a force organized and in action *behind* enemy lines.

From January to June 1945, his five guerrilla regiments constantly disrupted Japanese lines of communication, intercepted and destroyed foraging and scouting parties, and ambushed troop units. Although official accounts later minimized the guerrilla contribution, Volckmann estimated that his people accounted for about fifty thousand Japanese casualties. When Sixth Army headquarters questioned casualty reports of one regimental commander, he showed a team of Rangers enemy bodies that his Igorot guerrillas had carefully stacked like cordwood for easier counting!

As Sixth Army units worked north to close with Volckmann's guerrilla strongholds, irregular units joined army divisions to furnish invaluable aid in the severe fighting ahead.

31. Ibid.; see also Morison, op. cit.: MacArthur's staff apparently ignored Volckmann's dispatch, to carry on with pointless prelanding bombardment.

Running threadlike through the resistance warp of Filipinos is the extraordinary behavior of the Japanese, who often resembled their Hitlerian counterparts. The innate arrogance of the Japanese military completely canceled the not inconsiderable advantages of the oriental-versus-white-man appeal as well as the natural desire of any civil population to live and let live. The Japanese attitude was stressed in a remarkable letter written by Claro M. Recto, the Minister of Foreign Affairs in the Laurel puppet government, to Lieutenant General T. Wati, the Japanese military commander in Manila. Dated June 20, 1944, it was designated "Personal and Confidential":

. . . I think you will agree with me that in spite of the best efforts of the Philippine Government, a considerable portion of the Filipino people have not rallied as they should to the common cause. It is deeply to be regretted that, notwithstanding the liberal policies laid down by the Tokyo Government and carried out in their larger aspects by its able representatives here, little has been accomplished, as a matter of fact, to eliminate the feeling of distrust and hostility which a considerable portion of our people continue to entertain towards the present regime. This fact requires a word of explanation lest the Japanese Government, unaware of the real reasons behind the present attitude of the Filipino people, should come to regard all of them, in general, as ungrateful, unwilling or unable to appreciate Tokyo's liberal policies towards the Philippines. For the Filipinos are an innately grateful people, and it would be unjust to accuse them of ingratitude simply because they have so far not shown the degree of co-operation which Japan had expected of them.

The explanation seems to be simple enough. It may be found in the first place, in the psychology of the common people, not only in this country but everywhere. Here as elsewhere the common man is less concerned with high policies, great issues or abstract principles than with matters that intimately affect him: his livelihood, his individual rights, the welfare of his family and of the small community to which he belongs. If he is treated with discrimination, arrogance and cruelty, if he is thrown out of his house without any other place of his own where to go, if his property is confiscated without what he believes to be just compensation, or if he is driven to desperation as a result of the present situation, he finds himself losing faith in the Republic and feeling aggrieved against Japan. It is then quite difficult to impress him with the display of his country's flag, with generous donations of clothing and medicines, or with such liberal policies as condonation of Army loans to the Republic, the restoration of public properties to his government, etc.

Minister Recto then removed the velvet glove of correspondence to get to the point:

. . . The practice, for instance, of slapping Filipinos in the face, of tying them to posts or making them kneel in public, at times in the heat of the sun, or beating them—this upon the slightest fault, mistake or provocation, or without any other reason than failure to understand each other's language . . . thousands of cases have been reported of people being either burned alive, killed at the point of bayonet, beheaded, beaten without mercy, or otherwise subjected to various methods of physical torture, without distinction as to age or sex. . . . Many [victims] have no fault at all except the fact that they have sons or brothers who are members of "guerrilla" bands, or that they have given food or temporary shelter to the latter, under threat of death or physical injuries. . . .

Another matter that needs to be mentioned is the practice of exacting collective responsibility for individual acts. If a "guerrilla" happens, for instance, to ride in a *carretela* with other peace-loving and law-abiding citizens who are completely unaware of the former's identity, and that "guerrilla" is arrested, all those who, by pure accident are riding with him, are also arrested and punished in the same way. Or, when a "guerrilla" is discovered and arrested in one of the small roadside eating places in the provinces, the owners of the place and all those who happen to be eating there at the time are also arrested and punished. Similarly, entire barrios and municipalities have been placed in concentration, or their inhabitants exterminated, because they have been unable to prevent "guerrillas" from ambushing and attacking Japanese soldiers passing there, or because some "guerrillas" happened to repair to the place and exacted food or other commodities of the innocent folk, who found themselves helpless because of the threats or coercion employed.

. . . The existence of "guerrilla" elements or of outright banditry, particularly in the provinces, is not, generally speaking, due in the main to any fundamental political motive. It is doubtful whether those who are engaged in such activities are pro-American by conviction. In the first place most of them, with the exception perhaps of some of their outstanding leaders, have no real understanding of the basic issues involved in the present war between the United States and Japan. Nor, it is believed, have they developed any feeling of real attachment to the Americans, not having closely mixed or associated with them, socially or otherwise. But many have turned "guerrillas" because of the sad and often tragic experiences which they or their relatives, friends and countrymen have undergone at the hands of the Japanese. . . .[32]

The war was to last well over another year, but the Japanese would never understand the subject of Minister Recto's long letter: a ruler's respect for common people.

32. García, op. cit.

Chapter 41

Japanese occupation of Indonesia • Historical background • Dutch overlords • Sporadic Indonesian resistance • Early nationalist movements • Sukarno and the PNI • Japanese exploitation and bestiality • Effects of the occupation • Indonesian independence • Dutch demands • Allied intervention

I N REFRESHING CONTRAST to its usual barbarous behavior, the Japanese army exploited the favorable political climate of the Dutch East Indies and, at first anyway, avoided local resistance. In February and March 1942, large numbers of Indonesians greeted invading Japanese soldiers more as liberators than as enemy[1]—not unlike Ukrainians welcoming Germans the previous year.

Indonesia's anti-European attitude had been building for nearly 350 years. Spain and Portugal began trade with the islands during the sixteenth century, a profitable commerce picked up by British and Dutch toward the end of the century. In 1602, the United Dutch East India Company began sending ships to establish Dutch presence throughout the archipelago. In 1618, Jan Pieterszoon Coen arrived as governor gen-

1. G. M. Kahin, *Nationalism and Revolution in Indonesia* (Ithaca, N.Y.: Cornell University Press, 1952).

eral of the East Indies and chased the British from the area. The following year, he captured and burned the old town of Jaharta, on Java,
and rebuilt it as Batavia. Within a century, early trade in spices expanded to coffee and indigo as Dutch control spread.[2]

Unlike explorers in the New World, early European arrivals in Indonesia found an ancient and established civilization. Like their counterparts in Indochina, Javanese guerrillas had driven Kublai Khan's
Mongols from the country. But such unity was rare, and internecine
dynastic warfare predominated. The Dutch exploited royal factionalism
to rule from a series of ports linked by sea power and supplied with
commodities by various sultans who, jealous of each other, proved relatively easy to dominate.

In eliminating foreign competition and holding chiefs to the mark,
Dutch rule slowly extended inland. By 1750, the Dutch had subdued
most minor princes and forced away colonial rivals such as Britain and
Portugal. But, in 1780, the Franco-British-American war cut communications between Holland and the Indies to end Dutch naval supremacy
in the archipelago. Holland's political eclipse during the Napoleonic era
opened Indonesia to the British East India Company. This reversal
ended in 1816, when the Dutch regained control. Earlier and immensely
profitable trade had steadily declined during the eighteenth century, and
this, coupled with ". . . widespread corruption in its administration in
the Indies and a reckless financial policy,"[3] brought demise of the Dutch
East India Company in 1799. Indonesia's future now rested in the hands
of the Dutch Government.

To the native, Dutch and British traders appeared about the same.
In his excellent book *Nationalism and Revolution in Indonesia*, Professor G. M. Kahin noted of the Dutch:

. . . The over-all system operated to exploit as much from the villages
as was possible. Their populations were compelled to make forced deliveries
of a large portion of their crops and to perform nonagricultural forced
labor on an extensive scale. Theoretically these deliveries in kind were paid
for, but actually they amounted to sustained tribute levies on an immense
scale, the village generally being allowed to keep just enough of its produce
to sustain its inhabitants as a labor force.

It must be emphasized that not only the Company but the native aristocracy upon which the functioning of the system was dependent likewise
benefited. . . .[4]

2. B. H. M. Vlekke, *Nusantara—A History of Indonesia* (The Hague: W. van
Hoeve, 1959); see also Kahin, op. cit.; Louis Fischer, *The Story of Indonesia*
(New York: Harper & Row, 1959); Leslie Palmier, *Indonesia and the Dutch*
(London: Oxford University Press, 1962).
3. Kahin, op. cit.
4. Ibid.

John Crawfurd, British Resident in Java from 1811 to 1816, took earlier Europeans sharply to task:

. . . The plunder of the east, for it did not deserve the name of commerce, was their object. . . . To give an equitable price for the commodity they purchased, or to demand no more than a reasonable profit, never entered into their minds. They considered the natives of those countries as fair game.

His own countrymen were no better than the "rapacious traders" of the Netherlands, and he found it ". . . difficult to say which party was *least* to blame. . . . On both sides the mean and bad passions which were excited by avarice, and by commercial and national rivalry, were carried to an unexampled extent." Royal families also showed badly:

. . . Their courts were centers of indolence, luxury, and profligacy. Their pageantry amused the white man and awed the brown. The evils of an aloof, foreign tyranny were compounded by an unfeeling feudalism. Native rulers, submissive to the company in effect owned the land, the villagers who tilled it, and the produce. . . .[5]

On occasion, Indonesians contested Dutch and even native rule. In mid-eighteenth century, the Dutch fought a five-year guerrilla war in Mataram, and, in 1770, Chinese miners in northwestern Borneo revolted and broke away from Dutch hegemony. In 1825, a disillusioned nobleman, Prince Diponegoro, prompted by "voices" which told him ". . . to rid the land of royal immorality, rural poverty, and Europeans," put together a guerrilla force mainly of peasants and started what the Dutch still refer to as the Java War. In Amsterdam, the Russian ambassador reported to St. Petersburg that the Dutch had sent out two thousand volunteer soldiers to meet the challenge. A year later, he reported

. . . that the seesaw war on Java continued. He described rebel strategy: "They avoid battle with the troops and have adopted a plan of undermining the strength of the Europeans with the help of the unhealthy climate and fatigue. Such a method of warfare may in the end give them superiority. . . ."

Military reverses soon caused the Dutch to send out an additional three thousand troops. The Russian ambassador duly reported this and added: ". . . When one thinks of the alarming growth of the insurgent mood, it is hard to say anything definite about the future of the colony."[6]

The Java war lasted five years. It cost the Dutch some fifteen thousand killed (including eight thousand Europeans) and an estimated 20 million florins; it cost the Javanese perhaps two hundred thousand dead

5. Fischer, op. cit.
6. Ibid.

(mostly from cholera).[7] Dutch victory surprised no one. Separated by geography, language, religion, and tradition, islanders were not able to unite against Dutch rule. With Diponegoro's exile, the Dutch settled down to exploitation uninterrupted until 1942.

The long guerrilla war, coupled with expenses of the Dutch-Belgian war in Europe, produced a particularly avaricious colonial policy. In 1825, an administrator named Van den Bosch introduced the "Forced Cultivation System," which was ". . . a new tax in the form of compulsory labor." In his excellent book *Indonesia,* Dr. Palmier has described this in detail. The new system ". . . resulted in the exploitation of Java as though it were a huge government plantation (or labor camp)." Between 1831 and 1877, this nefarious system yielded 823 million guilders from the Indies; ". . . annual budget of the Netherlands was not more than 60 million guilders; the Indies contribution averaged 18 million guilders a year."[8] The islands also provided enormous private trade and shipping fortunes. This brought a flow of investment capital and a stream of Western entrepreneurs, who continued to flourish after the pernicious system had ended.

The rape of Java brought expansion to Sumatra, the Celebes, western New Guinea, and most of Borneo—an empire rich in sugar, tobacco, rubber, and oil and other minerals, in addition to spices and coffee. Indonesians continued to resist these encroachments. Although Dutch arms generally put down protest movements with comparative ease, Bali did not submit to Dutch rule until the twentieth century. The kingdom of Atjeh, in northern Sumatra, fought a thirty-five-year war that lasted until 1908 and cost the Dutch an estimated 400 million florins.[9]

Throughout this period, the Dutch kept a tight rein on incipient nationalist desires. Although the government began to train Indonesians and Eurasians in modern administrative methods as early as 1848, the numbers were small enough. Financial milking permitted only minimum social services. The Dutch historian Vlekke later wrote:

. . . Once the System began to yield results, the human tendency to profiteer as much as possible revealed itself in the Netherlands Ministry of Colonies, and for nearly twenty years government expenses in the Indies were pared to the bone, without regard for their educational and political needs, in order to raise the figure of the remittances from Batavia to Europe.

Palmier concluded:

. . . There is no doubt that the system stunted Javanese social and political development; the country would not present the dejected picture it does now

7. Palmier, op. cit.
8. Ibid.; see also Vlekke, op. cit.; Kahin, op. cit.
9. Fischer, op. cit.

[1965] if some of the profits of the Forced Cultivation System had been ploughed back into the country *at the time*.[10]

Although land laws passed in 1875 resulted in wider individual ownership of land with some protection of small landholders, peasants nonetheless continued to pay income taxes which Dutch plantation owners avoided until 1908:

. . . Many peasants became debtors, borrowed money, thereby lost their farms, and became farm laborers or moved to the growing towns. The steeply rising birth rate likewise bred poverty and drove people away from the crowded countryside.[11]

The sordid story continued with the educational policy. Native village schools appeared only after 1854. These were of the rudest type, affording only primitive primary and secondary education. In 1903, an estimated 190,000 children were going to school—this out of an archipelago population of over 30 million! Those children fortunate enough to be educated in Dutch primary schools and thus learn the Dutch language —in 1900–4 they numbered just short of three thousand[12]—frequently could not obtain commensurate employment upon graduation, a difficulty also experienced by the handful of university graduates.

A few officials tried to change this restrictive policy. The majority, however, seemed convinced that Indonesians were not to be educated. One of the earliest nationalists, the young daughter of a nobleman, Kartini, wrote about this time: ". . . The Hollanders laugh and make fun of our stupidity, but if we strive for enlightenment, then they assume a defiant attitude towards us. . . ."[13]

Some long-overdue reforms appeared at the turn of the century. The so-called "Ethical Policy" did improve the peasant's lot, but government finances could not support most social services, and the few reforms that were introduced fell victim to constantly increasing population.

Moreover, these were largely carrot-and-stick reforms. At no time did the Dutch intend to prepare the people for ultimate independence. Again education figures are revealing:

. . . In 1930–1 there were only 178 Indonesians in institutions of university level, at a time when the population numbered some 59 millions. At the secondary level, both academic and vocational there were only 6,085 Indonesians being given instruction in Dutch. At the primary levels, the number of Indonesians given Western education amounted to only 83,655.[14]

10. Palmier, op. cit.
11. Fischer, op. cit.
12. Kahin, op. cit.
13. Palmier, op. cit.
14. Ibid.

Nor had employment opportunities significantly increased; Indonesian upper-school graduates generally could not compete with either Europeans or Chinese for the few jobs going.

This unhappy administration spawned a variety of nationalist movements beginning early in the century.[15] Ranging in bias from social to economic to religious to political, they assumed many shapes and colors. Some, such as the Budi Utomo (High Endeavor) and its religious counterpart, the Muhammadiyah, stemmed from Javanese aristocracy and remained essentially intellectual movements. Others, such as the Sarekat Islam (Muslim Society), offered a commercial-religious appeal; by 1918, Sarekat Islam numbered some 450,000. Only one year later, it had grown to 2.5 million members. Its radical section now broke away to establish the Partai Komunis Indonesia (PKI), which attracted numerous returning university graduates.

In partial answer to the nationalist trend, the Dutch formed a People's Council of Indonesia, which first met in 1918. Although natives constituted half its numbers, it held only two short sessions a year:

. . . Its members enjoyed parliamentary immunity but it was not a parliament. It had no legislative or executive functions. It could discuss and advise and thereby influence the Governor General. But it could decide nothing against his wishes. Many Indonesians consequently refused to collaborate with the Council.[16]

Communists also continued to pursue a disruptive policy, which exploded into a series of strikes and an uprising in 1927. As happened in the Middle East, the anti-religious element prevented widespread support, and government forces effectively suppressed the outbreak by arresting thirteen thousand, imprisoning forty-five hundred and interning another thirteen hundred.[17] Much of the Communist program, however, appeared in 1927 in the new Indonesian National Party (PNI), whose chairman was a twenty-five-year-old engineer, Dr. Achmed Sukarno. Although small, the party incorporated most of the student membership of the Indonesian Union and proved increasingly powerful. It wanted ". . . complete economic and political independence for Indonesia, with a government elected by and responsible to the people," a goal that could only be reached ". . . by non-cooperation with the Dutch."[18]

Henceforth this objective governed Indonesian nationalism. Not all Indonesians shared such a radical policy, yet world-wide depression,

15. Kahin, op. cit.; see also Vlekke, op. cit.; see also Special Operations Research Office (American University, Washington, D.C.), *Casebook on Insurgency and Revolutionary Warfare* (Washington: American University, 1962). Hereafter cited as SORO.

16. Fischer, op. cit.

17. SORO, op. cit.; see also Fischer, op. cit.

18. Palmier, op. cit.

which began in 1929, converted many, as did subsequent refusal of the Dutch to introduce long-overdue political and administrative reforms. Instead, government relied on oppression. Sukarno and many of his associates went to jail in 1929. A year after his release, 1932, he was arrested and exiled, a remedy that postponed without curing basic problems.

In 1939, per-capita annual income of the 70 per cent of the Javanese population dependent upon agriculture for a living ". . . was . . . estimated to be only $8.32, including the value of crops consumed as food, only $4.45 being actual cash income. . . ."[19] Using education as a guide, in 1940, 1,786 Indonesians attended high school and only 637 college.[20] At outbreak of war, 7 per cent of 70 million people were literate.[21] Europeans held 90 per cent of high administrative posts, and a Dutch governor general held veto power over any legislation passed by the Volksraad (People's Council). Discontent remained rife, the radical Greater Indonesian Party (PIR) vocal in demands for independence and socialist government.

The Japanese invasion struck Indonesia at a crucial time of internal development. Landing on Sumatra in February 1942, their army within a few days won a Dutch surrender, which forever dispelled the carefully nurtured myth of Western supremacy. As Louis Fischer later wrote: ". . . A power that had held sway over them for more than three centuries vanished in three weeks at the touch of fellow Asians."[22]

But what was to replace Dutch rule?

The Japanese never quite decided. In theory, they had won a great victory by seizing Sumatra, Java, Borneo, and the Celebes—some three thousand islands with a land area of nearly one and a half million square miles, almost half the size of Australia. Not only did the islands offer copious quantities of tin, bauxite, nickel, coal, oil, rice, cocoa, rubber, tobacco, sugar, coffee, tea, and copra, but nearly 70 million people, of whom 75 per cent were peasants, were available to work mines and estates.

The Japanese also found a nationalist movement that they thought to convert into a convenient puppet government. This, the Indonesian Educational Union, which kept the initials of Sukarno's earlier movement, the PNI, was run by Dr. Mohammed Hatta and Sutan Sjahrir. When the Japanese arrived, Hatta openly collaborated while Sjahrir remained underground in charge of the resistance movement. This was a clever precaution, because the Japanese completely misinterpreted the people's joyful mood, believing, as Professor Kahin wrote, ". . . that they could exploit the resources of Indonesia for the benefit of the war

19. Kahin, op. cit.
20. Fischer, op. cit.
21. SORO, op. cit.; see also Kahin, op. cit.
22. Fischer, op. cit.

effort without having to make concessions to Indonesian nationalism."[23]

The Japanese commander, Lieutenant General Imamura, disbanded all political parties and forbade discussion of independence. Still worse, Japanese brutality almost immediately asserted itself, the Indonesians, for example, having to bow low to every passing Japanese soldier. Completely carried away with their own conceit, the Japanese, in spring of 1942, launched the "Triple A" movement—Japan the Leader of Asia, Japan the Protector of Asia, Japan the Light of Asia—designed to increase production. When people failed to respond satisfactorily, the Japanese began a long series of concessions. At Mohammed Hatta's urging, they brought Sukarno back from exile in order to harness rampant nationalism to the war effort. In March 1943, the conquerors authorized limited government in the form of the Center of People's Power, or Poetera, with Sukarno appointed chairman and Hatta vice-chairman. A few months later, Japanese Prime Minister Tojo authorized limited self-government. To defend the islands in case of allied invasion, the Japanese permitted Sukarno to organize and train an army, the Peta, or Volunteer Army of Defenders of the Fatherland, which eventually numbered 120,000 men.

Although promising Indonesians eventual independence, the Japanese continued a harsh occupation. Years after the war, the *Times of Indonesia* published a pertinent editorial:

. . . As we who lived through the occupation can testify, the Japanese are probably the most stupid of all Asian peoples in their dealings with natives of other races, for, with that compound of arrogance and idiocy which is the make-up of the average Japanese, they have a genius for getting themselves thoroughly detested. That Japan was bound to lose the war is one of those self-evident facts any schoolboy should have known: that Japan lost the friendship of the whole of South-east Asia in a matter of some forty months is something of more than ordinary interest for the historian. What cost the Japanese the good will of the countries they raped was their brutality. . . .[24]

By 1944, Japanese brutality had turned most of occupied Indonesia against Japanese rule. Fearing the increasing nationalist bias of Poetera, the Japanese disbanded the movement in March 1944, establishing instead the People's Loyalty Organization. The war was now going very badly for the Japanese and they tended to panic. In October 1944, they again promised independence, and, in the remaining months of occupation, granted increased powers to what became the Sukarno government.

Despite unpleasant aspects, the total experience benefited Indonesians. Without intending to do so, Japanese occupation policy encour-

23. Kahin, op. cit.
24. Fischer, op. cit.

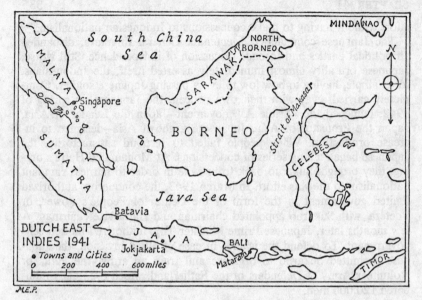

DUTCH EAST INDIES 1941
• Towns and Cities
0   200   400   600 miles

M.E.P.

aged nationalism: The Indonesian language, Bahasa Indonesia, spread among the people; the Japanese perforce used Indonesians in important civil service jobs, and people discovered, as their leaders had always insisted, that they could perform these jobs as well as, if not better than, Europeans. The Poetera offered a framework for self-government that survived the end of occupation and that the Peta protected. By war's end, ". . . Indonesia had provisional government, a national army, district administrations, a national flag and a national anthem."[25] Sukarno, in August 1945, proclaimed national independence.

The Dutch immediately protested. In Kandy, Ceylon, Dutch representatives at Lord Louis Mountbatten's South-East Asia Command headquarters ". . . demanded that the Japanese in Indonesia be ordered to suppress the new Republican government. . . . Mountbatten gave the instruction, but the Japanese parried it; the task, as events showed, would have been formidable. . . ."[26] The only available troops, British and American, made no move for six weeks. This gave Sukarno time to consolidate his new government and thus present the first Dutch troops with a *fait accompli.*

England meanwhile continued to display an ambivalent policy, on the one hand urging Dutch to negotiate with nationalists, on the other hand allowing Japanese to remain armed and eventually to fight against Indonesians.

25. SORO, op. cit.
26. Fischer, op. cit.

As the Dutch continued to refuse negotiations with Sukarno, incidents between nationalists and Dutch-British-Japanese troops multiplied. Having failed to protect her colony in adversity, Holland decided now to restore rule by force of arms. What she failed to realize was that Indonesians were equally determined to retain a new-found freedom.

Chapter 42

Japanese occupation of Thailand • Historical background • Exploitation of Thailand by great powers • Decline of monarchy • Dictatorship • The Japanese arrive • Limited OSS operations • The Japanese occupy Indochina • Historical background • Religion and the French conquest

GUERRILLA MOVEMENTS in Thailand and Indochina suffered from factors similar to those at work in other theaters of war: lack of allied organization, initial inability to overcome weather and distance, enemy countermeasures, and awkward internal political conflicts.

The kingdom of Siam, or Thailand, posed a unique problem to British and American planners in India and China. An independent country, it had slipped into the Japanese orbit and had even declared war on America and England, a bellicose posture that seemingly denied a tradition of diplomatic dexterity.

Like its neighbors, Thailand possesses an ancient and rich culture, probably reaching from the sixth century B.C. Some scholars believe that, in the seventh century A.D., a Thai kingdom, Nanchao, flourished in China's Yünnan province, only slowly becoming a vassal state. Migrating south, Thais intermingled with Laos and Shans of Burma while assimilating into the great Khmer Empire of Angkor (today's Cambodia). In 1238, two powerful Thai chieftains defeated Cambodians to establish the kingdom of Sukhothai, which, under King Ramkanheng (1275–1317), became the most powerful state in Indochina. The king and his successors wisely paid tribute to China, a pragmatic policy that enabled them not only to survive while wedged dangerously between Burma and the Khmer Empire, but to expand their lands into the kingdom of Ayutthaya, or Siam.[1]

The first Westerners to reach the kingdom, the Portuguese, arrived in 1518 and began trade. While Siam continued to fend off (and sometimes succumb to) rapacious neighbors Burma and Cambodia, she opened ports to Dutch and Japanese ships. The English followed. An overzealous Dutch presence caused Siam to court France, a short-lived romance ended by Louis XIV's persistent attempts to convert the country to Christianity. After a confrontation with an English fleet in 1687, Siam turned her back on Europe for the next 130 years.

Vietnam expansion and a series of weak kings hurt Siam, which, by 1767, was on verge of succumbing to Burma. But then China invaded Burma to relieve part of the pressure and help General Taksin defeat the Burmese army. As king, Taksin invaded and won Cambodia. A tyrant, he went insane and was deposed and executed in 1781. His successor, General Chakri, or Rama I (1782–1809), founded the present dynasty and, despite a series of Burmese invasions, made Siam the most powerful state in Southeast Asia.

Rama II continued to resist pressure from Burma, a threat greatly diminished when the British conquered the country, in 1826. But this proved a mixed blessing, since British presence in Malaya thwarted Siamese expansion in that direction, while expansion eastward brought her into conflict with Vietnam. The English presence also undermined Siam's policy of isolation. In 1826, she signed a limited trade agreement with Great Britain, another with America in 1833.

Britain's victory over China in 1842 caused Rama IV to open his country further. In 1855, he signed the Treaty of Friendship and Commerce with England, in Professor Nuechterlein's opinion, the ". . . turning point in Siamese history, not only in her relations with Western countries but also in her internal life." This lop-sided treaty, one of several imposed by England in Southeast Asia, limited duty on goods imported by British merchants in Bangkok, permitted opium to be imported duty free (subject to some restrictions), limited duties on goods exported by British merchants, and gave the British landowning privileges and extraterritorial rights. Burma signed similar treaties with

1. Donald E. Nuechterlein, *Thailand and the Struggle for Southeast Asia* (Ithaca, N.Y.: Cornell University Press, 1965); see also D. G. E. Hall, "Thailand (History)." In Encyclopaedia Britannica, 1968, Vol. 21.

France and America the following year. Townsend Harris, who negotiated for the United States,

. . . reported that most of his difficulties were the result of Siamese fear and
distrust of the British whom they characterized as "rapacious tyrants who
were seizing the whole of Asia."[2]

French presence in Vietnam soon added to Siamese woes. The French
began laying claim to the southern portion of the country in 1859 and
soon began pushing north and west. If British presence in Siam proved
irksome, it partially checked French designs. But, as the century spun
out, King Rama V (1868–1910) felt increasingly pinched between the
British in Burma and Malaya and the French in Indochina, an ugly period culminating, in 1893, when Siam, to avoid war with France, ceded
all territory east of the Mekong River and agreed to other humiliating
concessions.

At the turn of the century, Siam began looking to America and Japan
to offset European influence. In 1903, Professor E. H. Strobel of Harvard Law School became the first foreign-policy adviser to the Minister
of Foreign Affairs. After World War I, in which Siam fought on the
allied side, Woodrow Wilson's son-in-law, Francis Sayre, revised America's treaty with Siam, ending such privileges as limited export-import
duties and extraterritorial rights, and persuaded European nations to
similar reforms. Internal pressures, however, brought general decline in
Siam's prosperity.

In 1932, a bloodless coup established constitutional monarchy. Of
several causes, Nuechterlein cites as probably the most important

. . . the determination of a small group of foreign-trained young intellectuals to modernize Siam's political structure and to institute a program of
radical economic reform. These men, who had studied in Europe during the
nineteen-twenties were impressed with the ideas of liberal government and
political freedom that permeated Europe after World War I. . . .[3]

Two young men played dominant roles both in the coup and subsequently. The first, Pridi Phanomyong, better known in the West as
Luang Pradit Manutam, came from a well-to-do provincial family.[4]
After studying law in Paris, he returned to Bangkok, to become secretary of the bar association and play an active role as leader of the left
group of the dominant political force, the People's Party. Thirty years
old at the time of the coup, he tried to initiate state socialism, a radical
program that soon caused a break with the new rulers and, in 1933,
his exile to Europe.

2. Nuechterlein, op. cit.
3. Ibid.
4. D. Insor, *Thailand—A Political, Social and Economic Analysis* (London: Allen & Unwin, 1963).

Pridi's military counterpart, Pibul Songgram, had studied in France as a military officer. A thirty-five-year-old major at the time of the coup, he defeated a royalist rebellion the following year and became minister of defense. The government quickly turned to authoritarian rule; in four years, the military budget doubled. In 1935, the king abdicated in favor of his ten-year-old nephew. Three years later, Pibul became prime minister and Pridi returned to serve as minister of finance.

In 1939, the government adopted the name Thailand—land of the free. Although Pridi continued to press for economic reforms, the Pibul government remained authoritarian, with Pibul himself increasingly an admirer of Germany and Japan. In 1940, with Japanese support, he recovered Laotian and Cambodian territory ceded to France early in the century. On December 8, 1941, the day after the Japanese attacked Pearl Harbor, Pibul accepted a Japanese ultimatum and surrendered his country to Japan; he subsequently declared war on England and America.[5]

At first glance, the operational climate in Thailand for either SOE or OSS appeared unfavorable, particularly since some fifty thousand Japanese troops occupied the country. But Thailand had not forsaken her tradition of international opportunism. The Thai ambassador in Washington, Seni Pramoj, refused to deliver Pibul's declaration of war to Secretary of State Cordell Hull. As one result, America did not declare war on Thailand. As another, Seni rounded up various students and officials to establish a "Free Thai" movement sponsored by OSS.

Meanwhile in Thailand, a secret resistance movement was growing under Pridi, whom Pibul had appointed regent (the young king was studying in Switzerland). Some evidence suggests that Pibul and Pridi were playing a game similar to that of Sukarno-Hatta-Sjahrir in Indonesia. At very least, in Professor Nuechterlein's words, ". . . what seems clear is that Pibul apparently had no objection to Pridi's [underground] activities, because he certainly could have taken steps against the underground if he had wanted to do so."[6]

Early in 1943, Western agents learned of Pridi's double role. The OSS effort to exploit the situation has been told in part in Alsop and Braden's previously mentioned book *Sub Rosa*. Although Thailand is a large country, roughly the size of France, early attempts to infiltrate liaison teams proved unsuccessful. The situation grew more favorable from mid-1944, when Pibul resigned and Pridi became the real power behind the new government. But so unfavorable were operational conditions that not until early 1945 did OSS officers start sending valuable information from Bangkok.

The movement blossomed in the following months, with OSS and

5. Ibid.
6. Nuechterlein, op. cit.

SOE setting up guerrilla camps throughout the country. Such was their success that Pridi, though walking a dangerous tightrope with Japan, wanted to start a guerrilla war.

Fortunately, American and British officers of South-East Asia Command persuaded him to hold off until allied forces could strike simultaneously—a plan voided by Japan's sudden collapse. As one result, Thailand remained the least war-torn of Southeast Asian countries.

An even more complicated political situation influenced the resistance effort in French Indochina—the large land mass, some 285,000 square miles, that forms the eastern promontory of Asia and, in 1940, supported perhaps twenty-three million people.[7]

Such is the impact of recent history that we tend to think of this land in the relatively tidy, if split, geographical terms of today's Vietnam. Yet, only thirty years ago, Vietnam comprised three distinct entities: Annam, Cochin China, and Tonkin. French Indochina included not only Vietnam but the ancient kingdoms of Cambodia and Laos, an enormous and politically variegated land mass boasting old cultures and extremely bellicose histories—histories inextricably connected with the kingdom to the north, China, which intermittently had held much of the southern area in thrall. This helped to account for centuries of revolt, often abortive efforts impeded by bloody internecine wars that kept the land in a state of perpetual if lackadaisical ferment.

Internal divisions brought external penetration. As early as the seventeenth century, warring princes sought military help from abroad. But as Joseph Buttinger has pointed out in his comprehensive political history *Vietnam: A Dragon Embattled:*

. . . It was precisely during these periods of open warfare between the North and South that a few doors were opened to the West. Each party tried to gain an advantage over the other through help from abroad. But through the doors opened for Western arms and Western experts of modern warfare slipped Western explorers, missionaries, and traders as well. Accepting cannons from the Portuguese also meant accepting their missionaries—particularly since most of the technical experts imported from the West were Jesuit priests. And in accepting naval aid from the Dutch, they also had to be granted permission to trade.[8]

By 1627, a Jesuit missionary, Father Alexandre de Rhodes, was busy converting members of the Trinh court in Tonkin; ten years later, Dutch traders opened a factory there.[9] French missionaries joined the effort,

7. Ellen J. Hammer, *The Struggle for Indochina 1940–1955* (Stanford, Calif.: Stanford University Press, 1966).

8. Joseph Buttinger, op. cit.

9. Donald Lancaster, *The Emancipation of French Indochina* (London: Oxford University Press, 1961).

but Vietnamese rulers soon cooled to the new religion, which conflicted with so many basic Confucianist precepts. The region's limited wealth also inhibited trade, which slowed considerably during the eighteenth century. A dynastic war, the Tay Son revolt, further impeded the colonizing process. Ironically, intervention by a French missionary, Monseigneur Pigneau de Behaine, helped one Nguyen Anh to become Emperor Gia Long, the ruler of all Vietnam and voluntary vassal to China.

Although Gia Long and his successor, Minh Mang, improved and strengthened the empire, ". . . the country was not in fact to escape the intellectual and economic stagnation which paralyzed states ruled according to Confucian principles during the nineteenth century."[10]

But where Gia Long respected a sort of armed truce with French missionaries, Minh Mang tried to eradicate Christianity.

. . . by an edict promulgated in 1833 the profession of Christianity was declared a crime punishable by death, while orders were issued that buildings which had served either for the celebration of the mass, or to house Catholic priests should be demolished. The implementation of this edict was to result in the execution, imprisonment, or exile of a number of European missionaries.[11]

Three years later, having put down a revolt in Cochin China, Minh Mang ". . . closed Vietnamese ports, with the exception of Tourane, to European shipping, while the death penalty was decreed against foreign missionaries discovered in the country."[12]

Although Minh Mang later tried for *rapprochement* with France, the missionary's lot in Indochina was never a happy one, during either Minh's reign or those of his successors. Vietnamese excesses on several occasions led to French naval intervention; in turn, French excesses brought new anti-Christian measures. Having established the friction of a tiny Catholic population in a predominantly Confucianist-Buddhist country, the French scratched it into fire of intervention: in 1859, a French force occupied Saigon and, in 1861, claimed Cochin China as a colony. A treaty forced on the court at Hué in 1862 transferred three eastern provinces of Cochin China to the French, opened the hinterland to traders and missionaries, and even won the French a cash indemnity. The following year, the Cambodian king, Norodom, agreed to protectorate status in order to fend off Vietnamese and Siamese incursions.[13]

10. Ibid.
11. Ibid.
12. Ibid.
13. Hammer, op. cit.

Missionaries provided pretext for intervention. A French military officer-historian, Captain Gosselin, wrote in 1904:

. . . Our compatriots, not well informed on history, suppose that France came to intervene in Annam solely for the protection of missionaries, or to seek vengeance for acts of hostility committed against them and for persecutions against the Catholic religion. The missionaries, in reality, have only been the pretext for our action against *Annam*. The loss of India in the eighteenth century, the increasingly rapid extension in the Far East of our perpetual rival England imposed on us the obligation to set foot in the China seas, the only alternative being our falling into a state of contemptible inferiority. Annam gave us the opportunity, the massacre of Frenchmen who were there as missionaries gave us the pretext.[14]

The French soon expanded their presence. Five years after gaining eastern provinces, continued opposition from western provinces justified French authorities, or so they reasoned, in adding this area to their new colony. The insinuating process continued during the next two decades, both to the west, where France gained predominant influence in Cambodia, and to the north, which she explored for commercial possibilities.

In planting the flag ever farther from Saigon, French colonizers played on traditional regional rivalries, a process never far removed from troops and gunboats. By a treaty of 1884, the boy emperor Kien Phuc ceded all of Cochin China and the cities of Tourane, Haiphong, and Hanoi to France, which placed them in a colonial status; the treaty also reduced Annam and Tonkin to protectorate status. China protested, but, after fighting and losing a war with France, agreed to the acquisitions and signed the 1885 treaty of Tientsin. Two years later, France extended her protective presence to the kingdoms of Laos and Cambodia, the whole euphemistically termed the Indochinese Union, a heterogeneous administrative hodgepodge whose three peoples distrusted each other and were distrusted in turn by ethnic minorities such as the Thai of the Tonkinese mountains and the Montagnards in southern Annam.

14. Ibid.

Chapter 43

The French presence in Indochina • Fallacy of the "peace and security" argument • The French contribution • Fallacy of the "non-profit" argument • Failure of French colonial policy • Conditions inside Indochina: the double standard

WHAT TO MAKE of the French presence in Indochina?
Apologists generally argue along two lines. The first holds that France (along with other colonizing powers) brought peace and security to an area that had known only war. This argument has even been repeated by non-apologists; one such recently wrote: ". . . On the other hand, much of Vietnam was immediately pacified, and thus French rule brought peace and security for the first time to an important part of the population."[1] In her comprehensive work *The Struggle for Indochina 1940–1955,* Ellen Hammer noted: ". . . The population of Indochina more than doubled under the French, for they brought peace and security to the country"—but she correctly emphasized that this positive de-

1. Roy Jumper and M. W. Normand, "Vietnam: The Historical Background." In M. E. Gettleman (ed.), *Viet Nam* (New York: Fawcett, 1965).

velopment in no way compensated for the profoundly negative aspects of colonial rule.[2]

This argument presupposes that Indochina, either acting on her own or beneficently influenced by other powers, would not have found peace and security during the twentieth century. The argument hinges on the earlier historical record, certainly a dismal recital of revolts and dynastic wars—but scarcely a more dismal recital than that underlying the emergence of most states. The argument denies progress: it ignores the probability that peace ultimately comes to an area once people tire of war; this occurred after the Hundred Years' War and the Thirty Years' War in Europe, and the peoples of Indochina also enjoyed peaceful periods in their history. It also denies the ability of peoples to work out their own destinies by allowing dominant forces to assert themselves and thereby continue the natural civilizing process. Nor is it altogether an accurate argument: the French presence may have brought peace and security to some, but it brought wholesale misery to millions, because it continued to deprive a large portion of peoples of dignity and hope, not to mention basic subsistence, and where desperate ones challenged French rule, their blood ran deep.

In short, the "peace and security" argument is the height of conceit —the ultimate statement not only of the white man's burden but of the *Christian* white man's burden.

The second argument excuses France on grounds that she acquired these colonial holdings more for reasons of prestige than for economic reasons. In his well-known book *The Two Viet-Nams,* the late Bernard Fall quoted the French historian Henri Brunschwig:

. . . The colonies were not supposed to be sources of revenue. Their role consisted in disputing the mastery of the seas with Britain and affirming to the face of the world the *présence,* the *grandeur,* and the *rayonnement* of France. It was normal that all this was to be paid for, like all expenditures of sovereignty.[3]

In defense of this thesis, Fall and other writers have presented impressive facts documenting the financial burden of Indochina to the French Government. They point to the immense task of modernizing the nation—of curing tropical diseases, introducing hygiene and hospitals, improving dikes to irrigate hundreds of thousands of acres, draining thousands of new acres, introducing the rubber tree, building new roads and railroads, increasing exports. Such was the monumental task, that

2. Hammer, op. cit. I should point out that this work, in general, is critical of the French presence and policy; see also Dennis J. Duncanson, *Government and Revolution in Vietnam* (London: Oxford University Press, 1968).

3. Bernard Fall, *The Two Viet-Nams—A Political and Military Analysis* (New York: Frederick A. Praeger, 1967).

Fall concluded not only France but all colonizing powers suffered financially from such undertakings:

. . . thus, the myth of the economic advantages of colonies can be quietly laid to rest, no matter how temptingly simple it makes the explanation of a rather complex problem.[4]

For a scholar of Fall's pretensions, this is surprising naïveté. As we have seen, the Dutch Government profited enormously from its Indonesian colony. Even when home governments suffered budgetary losses in administering colonies, control of these colonies often meant control of more extensive trade areas, with immense economic advantages to the home country. France needed the Indochina base first to prevent Great Britain from dominating Southeast Asia, second to further her own incursions into southern China, whose resources she was exploiting as avidly as were Britain and Germany in the North. Finally, French individuals and companies amassed vast fortunes in Indochina, just as some of the largest British fortunes stemmed directly from opium trade between India and China—and this allowed further capital expansion at home and abroad.

The above arguments also ignore the *moral* responsibility of the colonizing power. Surely no nation has a God-given right to possess another nation, whether to enhance its own prestige (and gain indirect economic profit thereby) or for any other reason. If the distorted philosophy underlying the white man's burden, or what the French called *la mission civilisatrice,* denied assimilation, the favored policy of association none the less bespoke responsibility of enlightenment: the nineteenth-century colonizing power would be responsible for future development—social, political, economic—of the concerned area.

In abrogating this responsibility, in allowing colonizers to pervert what was feckless policy at best, colonizing powers fell flat on their respective faces—and of these powers, France fell the flattest, in Indochina. As Ellen Hammer has written:

. . . They opened the country to the West. To people bogged down in their own past they brought a new science and technology, new patterns of living and thinking. An alien rule and an alien civilization were intruded into the closed and backward-looking society of Viet Nam. The effect, of course, was highly disruptive. The Vietnamese felt the shock of it in every part of their life—socially, economically, culturally, and politically.

Thus the pattern of land distribution changed, and the gap between rich and poor grew wider. This development was certainly not deliberate on the part of the French, but it was none the less real. . . .[5]

4. Ibid.
5. Hammer, op. cit.; see also Buttinger, op. cit., for a detailed and masterly analysis of the process.

Part of the disaster stemmed from the distorted concept of the white man's burden, part from French national failure. From 1870 on, France was a defeated, humiliated, and politically disorganized nation incapable of effectually governing herself, much less an overseas empire. She had no colonial policy. Such was the state of affairs in the turbulent Third Republic that ". . . French colonial affairs became an almost private preoccupation of the Minister of Colonies [in Paris] and of the colonial governors."[6]

The governor general and his ancillary governors and ministers ruled through a French Indochinese civil service whose senior members found themselves subject to political whims of French politicians, just as did the governor general. Buttinger has pointed out that

. . . Between 1886 and 1926, counting regular and interim governors, the French administration of Indochina changed heads no less than fifty-two times. This fact alone would explain the constant fluctuations of Indochinese policy, as many of these men either arrived with their own ideas or inherited problems which they thought only new policies could solve.[7]

Some governors worked hard at the job. Paul Doumer, who became governor general in 1897,

. . . was to show that Indochina could be a source of profit to commercial and financial interests, without cost to the French taxpayer, by providing the country with a uniform administrative service, with ample public revenues, and with economic equipment which compared favorably with that of other countries in South East Asia.[8]

Doumer accomplished a great deal in five years, but, as Buttinger concluded:

. . . It is indeed not often that one man can so lastingly shape the destiny of a country in so short a time. But the Vietnamese people, his chief victims in Indochina, found little in his achievements for which to be grateful, and even less in his person to admire or praise. Doumer ruled Vietnam in the bold and hard manner of the proconsuls of old. He was not without concern for the people he called his "native charges," but his concern was largely nullified by his belief that what was good for France was also good for Vietnam. For the Vietnamese people, sound budgets meant crippling taxes, railroad construction meant conditions of forced labor, while the denial of industries and education meant that their living standard would at best remain as miserable as ever, and they were excluded from the general forward movement of mankind. . . .[9]

6. Fall, op. cit.
7. Buttinger, op. cit
8. Lancaster, op. cit.
9. Buttinger, op. cit.

Increasingly, however, real power rested in European colonials, or *colons,* who, almost without exception, devoted impressive efforts to milking area resources while almost totally ignoring the welfare of its peoples:

. . . The peasant labored under a grinding burden of debt. The French tried to alleviate his dependence on the usurer, but much of the credit which they made available went to line the pockets of the large landowners, who borrowed only to relend at exorbitant rates. Usury thrived, and the local Chinese and Indians joined wealthy Vietnamese in raking in the profits. . . .

The Cochin Chinese landlord often collected more in usury than he did in rent. Cochin China was the center of French economic activity in Indochina. The abundant benefits of usury, combined with the French practice of granting extensive concessions in undeveloped land to French companies and rich Vietnamese, led to the development of many large estates owned by absentee landlords. These estates were worked by tenant farmers and landless agricultural laborers. The *ta dien* or sharecropper worked between 60 to 80 percent of the Cochin Chinese farmland. He generally had to give far more than half his annual harvest to his landlord, partly as rent, partly as usurious interest.[10]

Europeans fought any reforms attempted by government, Fall noted,

. . . and much of what was done in education and social welfare—and in the fields of work conditions, child labor, and tuberculosis prevention particularly, it was a great deal more than any other colonial power had done—was done in the face of the fiercest opposition and counter-pressure from the Europeans.[11]

The record discloses the paucity of accomplishment. Despite such trappings as Pasteur health institutes and a *lycée* in Hanoi and roads and railways (built by the *corvée* system of compulsory labor), Indochina remained a grossly underdeveloped area. Primary and secondary schools were at a premium, as were hospitals, doctors, and nurses.[12] The few Vietnamese who graduated from the *lycée* or from foreign universities had the greatest difficulty in finding commensurate positions.

The French presence loomed generously. To administer India with her 320 millions, the British employed a civil service of forty-eight hundred Europeans; to administer Indochina with her 30 millions, France

10. Hammer, op. cit.
11. Fall, op. cit.
12. Buttinger, op. cit.: ". . . Precolonial Vietnam had been famous for its system of free general and higher education. At least 80 per cent of the people were literate to some degree . . ."; the author also quotes authoritative evidence that, in the 1930s, in the Philippines one doctor existed for every 3,200 natives; in Indochina one doctor existed for every 38,000.

employed five thousand Frenchmen.[13] Everywhere a double standard existed:

. . . at all echelons, even the most humble . . . [the Vietnamese] were confronted by Frenchmen holding exactly the same or lower jobs but being paid two or three times more. Thus, the French janitor at the University of Hanoi received a base pay that was slightly higher than that of a Vietnamese professor with a Ph. D. from the University of Paris.[14]

A leading Vietnamese nationalist wrote Governor General Beau in 1906:

. . . Whether in newspapers, or letters, or in conversation, the French always hold us in hatred and contempt. They consider us not merely as savages, but as dogs and swine. Not only do they not treat us as equals, but to them we are something dirty and stinking, to be avoided. In this era, any mandarin who dares to object to a French administrator, no matter how well-founded his objection, is insulted scornfully. More than a few people in the country-side have been beaten to death by Frenchmen. Everyone realizes that the French consider us as animals and brutes; everyone is angry, but who dares to voice his anger? . . . When a Vietnamese meets a Frenchman, whether a civilian or soldier, the Vietnamese is always ready to take flight lest the Frenchman kick or beat him.[15]

Despite the area's significant contribution to the allied cause in World War I—thousands of Vietnamese served in France—the Versailles con- ference all but ignored the colonial question and France blithely perse- vered in her incredible attitude.[16] Although France offered a few political sops such as representation in territorial assemblies and later in an area-wide Grand Council, the Vietnamese, Laotians, and Cam- bodians remained in servile status. Asians could not enter French clubs; Frenchmen addressed even ranking Asians with the informal pronoun *tu,* as opposed to the courteous *monsieur.* Asian inferiority was obvious to all but themselves. For once, neither nationalists nor Communists had to invent propaganda, for what their leaders said and wrote was also said and written by provincial leaders, and such was the dismal situation that hyperbole and invective became truth.

13. Ibid.
14. Fall, op. cit.
15. Buttinger, op. cit.
16. Hammer, op. cit.: ". . . Indochina provided more than half the wartime loans and gifts made to France by her colonies, more raw materials than any other part of the empire except West Africa; and more than 43,000 Indochinese soldiers and almost 49,000 workers were sent to Europe"; see also Virginia Thomp- son, *French Indo-China* (London: Allen & Unwin, 1937): In this comprehensive and pioneering historical survey, Dr. Thompson pointed out that the Vietnamese sent to France were forcibly recruited "by reprehensible methods and vio- lence. . . ."

Prewar social evils also continued: ". . . in 1924 only some 6,200 boys and 1,000 girls out of some 600,000 children of school age were receiving an education. . . ."[17] The few university graduates continued to find themselves shut off from economic opportunity. French administration continued to indulge in the pernicious but extremely profitable opium trade. Periodic famines swept through Tonkin and northern Annam:

. . . The majority of Tonkinese could afford only two meals a day during most of the year. They managed three around harvest time, when they had to work harder than usual, but this came after a period of privation. Almost every year there was a time before the harvest when the peasant could not afford to eat more than once a day. He did not even have enough rice for that, unless he boiled it so long that it became a soup which looked and tasted like a gluey paste.[18]

Herein lay the fallacy of increasing rice exports. As Buttinger has perspicaciously written:

. . . These rising exports, and the corresponding profits, would not have been possible if the great stretches of land made cultivable by the French had been given to landless peasants or to peasants with insufficient acreage. In full control of their crop, the peasants could have eaten all they wanted, and very little would have remained for export, unless measures were taken substantially to increase the yield. This was not done because it would have taken time and cost money, which the French in Vietnam wanted to make, not spend. And it could be made quickly only by growing large quantities of rice, and only if the new rice was not consumed but marketed. This is why the policy of creating large estates was adopted, and why landlordism, despite its disastrous social and political consequences, was preserved to the last day of French rule.[19]

The French also retained control of industry and finance, treating ". . . Indochina pre-eminently as a source of raw materials for France and as a market for French manufacturers. They kept the country inside the walls of the French tariff system, forcing the Indochinese to pay more to import from France the goods which they might have bought elsewhere at lower prices. . . ."[20] The highly vaunted rubber plantations and mines remained mostly under French ownership, which worked them with a labor system just short of slave labor.[21]

17. Lancaster, op. cit.
18. Hammer, op. cit.; see also Thompson, op. cit.
19. Buttinger, op. cit.
20. Hammer, op. cit.
21. Buttinger, op. cit.

Neither political representation nor protest righted matters:

. . . The protection of French interests remained the responsibility of an omnipresent Security Service. Vietnamese who wished to leave the region in which they were domiciled had to obtain a passport, while an exit visa was required to go abroad. Mail was censored, domiciliary visits were carried out by police or customs officials without a warrant, and the Governor-General was empowered to intern Vietnamese without trial and to sequestrate their property for a period of ten years. The allegation in clandestine Communist tracts that Indochina was a prison thus had some justification, and even moderate nationalists who were anxious to find a pacific solution to these difficulties complained that Vietnamese were treated like aliens in their own country.[22]

22. Lancaster, op. cit.

Chapter 44

Indochinese resistance to French suzerainty • Early guerrilla wars • Continued resistance • Vietnamese objectives • Rise of nationalism • Bao Dai and Ngo Dinh Diem • The Yen Bay mutiny • Enter Ho Chi Minh • The Vietnamese Communist movement • Ho's peregrinations • Further Vietnamese uprisings • The Cao Dai and the Hoa Hao

SOCIETY may condemn a man to hang, but the victim rarely agrees with the verdict, particularly if he is innocent. The Indochinese peoples did not gladly suffer French rule. Throughout the colonizing period, isolated groups fought what usually were guerrilla actions against French arms. When the boy emperor Ham Nghi rebelled, the French deposed him; in 1884, he and his regent fled to the mountains and fought a guerrilla war for three years, a widespread resistance that ended only with Ham Nghi's capture and exile. A few years later, another major insurrection sprang up and lasted for two years before its bloody repression. In the Tonkin Delta, partisan leaders such as Nguyen Thien Thuat, Doc Ngu and De Kieu led the French a merry chase until 1892, when they were subdued:

. . . Here and there, they "transformed villages into fortresses, surrounding them with deep ditches filled with water and protected by bamboo fences as well as enormous walls of earth crowned with battlements in stone." But as a rule, the war in the delta was fought by small and constantly moving groups of twenty to twenty-five guerrillas. These groups usually attacked by night and only when they were certain to take the enemy by surprise. They wasted no ammunition and promptly retreated when they met a superior force. Retreat, to the despair of the pursuing French, always meant that the guerrillas disappeared, either hiding in rice fields or resuming their original role of peaceful peasants, whom no other peasant or mandarin in the village in which they hid would betray. In the delta, says Isoart, these partisans "had the broadest popular support. Indeed, in a land of vast plains, only the support of the population could assure the existence of the rebellion."[1]

Resistance continued in northern Tonkin, where, as we have seen (Chapter 17), Gallieni and Lyautey had their hands full bringing local nationalist-bandit groups to submission. They were not altogether successful: French forces fought wily guerrilla leader De Tham, the "Tiger of Yen Tre," off and on until 1913, when they caught and executed him.[2]

. . . These men who fought the French in the late nineteenth and early twentieth centuries had no particular wish for social or political reform. Their one desire was to drive out the French so that the Nguyen Emperors and the mandarinal bureaucracy could rule in independence once again and the old order could be secured. They fought for independence from France as their ancestors had fought to oust the Chinese from Viet Nam since the first century A.D.

But as the years passed:

. . . Natural opposition gained stimulus from outside forces: In the early part of the twentieth century they [the Vietnamese rebels] were profoundly influenced by events in China and Japan. The Vietnamese had long been sensitive to political currents across the frontier, and China, so long a citadel of the past, yet crumbling with decadence, was in the midst of a new ferment as the rule of the Manchu emperors neared its close. The Vietnamese learned of reform and then of revolution from China. At the same time, they read in Chinese books about revolutionary nationalism in nineteenth century Europe and studied with interest the Italian struggle for unification and the careers of men like Mazzini, Garibaldi, and Cavour.[3]

Japan's emergence as an international power, in 1905, when she defeated Russia, also worked an important effect: ". . . if the Japanese could reorient themselves so successfully to the modern world, as Gia Long had tried to do many years before, surely other Asians could do

1. Buttinger, op. cit.
2. Ibid.
3. Hammer, op. cit.

the same. Vietnamese nationalists began to talk of 'modernizing' their country so that they would be powerful enough to oust the French."[4] A few even realized that failure of resistance rested on its negative quality: restoration of mandarin rule with all its evils as opposed to assimilation of Western technology and political institutions in order to build a politically viable Vietnam. One of the first far-seeing nationalists, Phan Boi Chau, by 1903 was trying to organize dissident elements into a national revolutionary party.

The work of Chau and others insured continued opposition to French rule. One group of nationalists cut their hair—the Vietnamese wore it traditionally long—and, known as the Hair-Cutters, demanded social reforms. In 1908, thousands of peasants demonstrated and one group of terrorists attempted to poison the French garrison at Hanoi. The famous guerrilla leader in northern Tonkin, De Tham, fought so successfully that the French agreed to a virtual "coexistence" policy with him. In 1912, Phan Boi Chau organized the Phuc Quoc in Canton and ". . . inspired and directed the underground revolutionary movement in Viet Nam."[5]

In 1916, Emperor Duy Tan supported a mandarin-inspired revolt. Its failure brought his exile, and death or imprisonment of leading rebels. Taken with the Vietnamese contribution to World War I, however, it helped cause the French to promise postwar reforms. But Duy Tan's successor, Khai Dinh, a French puppet, failed ". . . to persuade the French authorities to abandon coercive methods of government and to adopt a policy directed to securing the co-operation of the Vietnamese in the administration of the Protectorate." In 1925, the throne went to Khai Dinh's son, Bao Dai. Raised and educated in France from the age of nine, Bao Dai did not return to rule until 1932, when he

. . . proclaimed his desire to reign as a constitutional monarch. He also announced his intention of reforming the mandarinate and the administration of justice and reorganizing public education. . . .[6]

The young emperor appointed a province governor, Ngo Dinh Diem, his minister of interior and head of a reform commission. French and senior court officials frustrated the commission's work by playing regional power factions and individual leaders one against the other, a disruptive game eagerly embraced by the French commercial community, which also refused the notion of widespread reforms. Combined opposition proved too strong. Diem resigned to begin a life of contemplative protest. Bao Dai resigned himself to role of puppet ruler, his material extravagances paid for by the French. They will enter our story again in later chapters.

4. Ibid.
5. Ibid.; see also Thompson, op. cit.; Buttinger, op. cit.
6. Lancaster, op. cit.

As local rulers once contested the French colonizing process, new groups of dissidents contested French administration. In 1927, a young teacher, Nguyen Thai Hoc, founded the Viet Nam Quoc Dan Dang— the VNQDD, or National Party of Vietnam.[7] Adopting ". . . the methods, organizations, and political program of the Kuomintang," this nationalist group grew to about fifteen hundred members in two years:

. . . But the party's activities, which included blackmail, assassination and the manufacture of bombs, soon attracted the attention of the French authorities, and after the arrest and interrogation of some of its members the French Security Service discovered the revolutionary aims and extensive ramifications of the organization.[8]

The VNQDD continued to operate, however, and, in early 1930, took the lead in ordering a general rebellion. In the event, four companies of troops mutinied at Yen Bay and killed their officers; sporadic outbursts occurred elsewhere. The French replied quickly and brutally, and VNQDD leaders who survived fled to Yünnan, in southern China. Nguyen Thai Hoc and twelve comrades died on the guillotine. Hoc wrote in his last statement

. . . that if the French wanted to occupy Indochina peacefully and without revolution, they would have to call a halt to all brutal and inhumane methods, to behave not as cruel masters of the people but as friends. They would have to respect such rights of the individual as liberty of travel, education, association and press. They would have to end the corruption in official places, educate the people, and develop trade and native industries.[9]

Meanwhile, a more vigorous movement was under way. Beginning in 1925, a thirty-five-year-old Vietnamese expatriate and Comintern agent named Nguyen Ai Quoc was training a cadre of young Communists in the Chinese city of Canton. This man, who would one day become famous as Ho Chi Minh, was born in central Vietnam about 1890. Like Mao Tse-tung, his father was a relatively well-off peasant (some authorities describe him as a scholar), an ardent nationalist whose activities in anti-French organizations got him in periodic trouble with authorities. The youngster enjoyed a village education, an experience enlivened by acting as covert courier for his father's seditious letters. After attending the Lycée Quôc-hoc, at Hué, which taught in nationalist rather than French tradition, the student became teacher in a southern Vietnam fishing village.

In 1911, he studied briefly in Saigon, a trade-school course, perhaps in pastry cooking. He then signed on as kitchen boy aboard a French

7. Hammer, op. cit.
8. Lancaster, op. cit.
9. Hammer, op. cit.

ship which sailed to Africa, Europe, and North America. He spent most of World War I in London working as a school janitor and at night as pastry cook in the Carlton Hotel under the famous chef Escoffier. He also joined an Asian revolutionary organization, the Lao-Dong Hai-Ngoa, or Overseas Workers' Association. From London he sailed for America and may have worked for a time in New York's Harlem district.

In 1918, the young man lived in Paris, working as a photo retoucher and political agitator among Vietnamese expatriates. In the following year, he formed a one-man lobby at the Versailles Peace Conference. Announcing himself as representative of the Association of Vietnamese Patriots, he presented a memorandum

. . . based on Point Six of President Wilson's Fourteen-Point program invoking the interests of colonized peoples, omitted all reference to national independence and merely demanded that a stop should be put to the abuses caused by the arbitrary exercise of power in Indochina and that the Vietnamese should be accorded certain basic liberties including protection from arbitrary arrest and imprisonment.[10]

His attempt to enlist allied support failed—not surprising, in view of Great Power determination to avoid the awkward colonial question.

Now a member of the French Socialist Party, the twenty-nine-year-old rebel became increasingly active in politics and spent considerable time working with a large residue of Vietnamese soldiers waiting return from France to the Far East. When Socialists splintered over the colonial question, he joined the new French Communist Party, where he soon began making his mark as a colonial expert. At this time, he attacked French policy in a book, *French Colonization on Trial,* which, smuggled into Indochina, ". . . became the bible of nationalists."[11]

In 1922, he attended the Fourth Comintern Congress, in Moscow, met Lenin, and probably became a member of the Comintern's newly created Southeast Asia Bureau. Subsequently he became active in the Peasant International, or *Krestintern.* In 1924, he moved to Moscow for study at the University of the Toilers of the East and there impressed important party members as an intelligent and hard-working activist.

Posted to Canton in late 1924, he quickly and efficiently organized Vietnamese and other Asian nationalists into a League of Oppressed Peoples of Asia, which was nothing less than ". . . the Comintern front organization for the whole Far East and soon became the Nan-yang or South Seas Communist Party—the parent organization of later Communist parties in Korea, Indonesia, Malaya, India, China, and Vietnam."[12]

Under Ho's aegis, young Vietnamese students graduated from Wham-

10. Lancaster, op. cit.
11. Hammer, op. cit.
12. Fall, op. cit.

poa, the military academy established by Chiang Kai-shek; others received advanced political training in Moscow:

> . . . Ho himself ran an accelerated training course that graduated 20 to 30 Vietnamese political agitators every three months. Between January, 1925, and July, 1927 (when Chiang broke with the Communists), Ho formed 200 *can-bo* (cadres), which were infiltrated back to Indochina.[13]

This beehive of subversion burst into cells with Chiang Kai-shek's sudden crackdown on Communists. When Mao Tse-tung fled south, Ho escaped across the Gobi Desert to the Soviet Union, operated as a Comintern agent in Europe for two years, then returned to the Far East to reorganize the party effort.

Working in Hong Kong under the alias Tong Van So, Ho partially succeeded in restoring party unity and, in October 1930, forming an expanded Indochinese Communist Party.

All this meant swimming against strong repressionary currents. Failure of the Yen Bay mutiny and associated peasant uprisings, while hurting the burgeoning revolutionary movement, played into Communist hands. In September 1930, the party began to lead peasant demonstrations and uprisings in northern Annam (where the peasants ". . . sold their starving children for a couple of francs if they could find a buyer, hoping that they would be fed and that the proceeds from the sale of some of their children would enable them to keep the remaining ones alive").[14]

To reclaim control over peasant-administered local "soviets," the French rushed in troops and, in a chaotic few months, restored order at cost of some ten thousand civilian casualties.[15] Widespread arrests followed, with perhaps fifty thousand persons deported.[16] In the general roundup of the next two years, many of Ho's colleagues in Vietnam, names that one day would become only too familiar in the West—Pham Van Dong, Vo Nguyen Giap, Truong Chinh, Tran Phu—went to jail: ". . . in 1932 the number of political prisoners confined in Indochinese jails, penal settlements, and 'special camps' was estimated at 10,000."[17]

Meanwhile, British police in Hong Kong, acting on information supplied by a French Comintern agent, picked up Ho in June 1931. While serving a six-month sentence, he successfully fought extradition by the French in Vietnam (who had sentenced him to death *in absentia*). Released from jail, he slipped away to remote Amoy, then to Shanghai, and finally back to the Soviet Union, where, allegedly, he attended two senior party schools. Apparently untouched by Stalin's purges of this

13. Ibid.; see also Hammer, op. cit.
14. Buttinger, op. cit.
15. Lancaster, op. cit.; see also Hammer, op. cit.
16. Buttinger, op. cit.
17. Lancaster, op. cit.

period, he next appeared in Mao Tse-tung's new base, in northwestern China. After performing relatively menial jobs, he accompanied a Chinese Communist mission to Tonkin, where it trained Chinese Nationalist guerrillas—and where we shall leave Ho for the moment.

While Ho agitated and studied and organized, his Indochinese Communist Party continued in adversity. In the South, in Cochin China, a Trotskyist movement challenged party unity. Although the French broke this up in the late 1930s, general repression continued to hinder the movement. In November 1940, an important party leader in the South, Tran Van Giau, foolishly led a peasant uprising which the French crushed quickly and effectively; they squelched another insurrection in the Lang Son area, in the North, and executed the veteran revolutionary leader Tran Tung Lap.[18] As a result of these and other repressive measures, the party remained weak and divided at the outbreak of war.

In addition to nationalist and Communist movements, two other potential power groups appeared in these turbulent prewar years. These were the Cao Dai and the Hoa Hao quasi-religious sects.[19]

The Cao Dai originated in the Saigon area in 1925 and spread through Cochin China and into Cambodia, numbering some three hundred thousand members by 1940.

The Hoa Hao also functioned in Cochin China, particularly in western regions. Although neither group constituted an organized political force, each manifested the divisive nature of Vietnamese politics, and the French feared each sect as a potentially powerful political instrument.

Instead of fostering healthy political growth in Indochina, then, the French spawned only discord: a weak, ineffectual emperor; a squabbling, impotent court; a nationalist party with leaders mostly in exile; a torn and divided but still organized Communist party; two large but politically undeveloped sects—an altogether frustrated, fragmented, underdeveloped, impoverished country of strangely diverse national leaders whose only common ground consisted of an intensely emotional desire for national independence.

18. Hammer, op. cit.
19. Ibid.; see also Lancaster, op. cit.; Buttinger, op. cit.

Chapter 45

The Japanese threaten French Indochina • America's position • French capitulation • American reaction • Decoux's dictatorship • The French resistance plan • President Roosevelt's anticolonialism • Its effect on French resistance • Ho Chi Minh and the Viet Minh • Vo Nguyen Giap • Guerrilla operations in northern Vietnam • OSS support of Giap • Ho's strength grows • Allied postwar policy • British and Chinese occupation of Vietnam • Ho proclaims the Democratic Republic of Vietnam • Communist failure in the South

OUTBREAK OF WAR in Europe further diminished the unity of Vietnamese opposition to French rule. The Indochinese Communist Party, faithful to Moscow, denounced the French war against Germany and, in September 1939, was outlawed and forced underground.

But the French administration in Indochina had far more to worry about than the ICP, either above or underground. Her regular army garrison amounted to some eleven thousand troops, a force backed by fifteen modern aircraft and one light cruiser. Thailand's flanking army was a joke; British garrisons in Malaya and Burma, Dutch garrisons in the East Indies, and American garrisons in the Philippines were as unprepared for war as the French in Indochina. Yet each of these areas held a strong attraction for Japan, already moving south.

The fall of Holland and France, in spring of 1940, drastically changed the power picture in the Far East. The power hiatus could only have been filled by American naval forces, but America refused to become involved, a decision due partly to an isolationist foreign policy, to military weakness in general, and to her leaders, particularly Secretary of State Cordell Hull, who woefully miscalculated Japanese strength and intentions.

Japan, intent on cutting the railroad leading from the Tonkin port of Haiphong to Yünnan, in China, in order to deprive Chiang Kai-shek of a major supply line, already had demanded joint control of the Tonkin border. The Japanese ultimatum placed the French governor general, General Catroux, in a virtually impossible position. Isolated and alone, he yielded to Japanese demands, a move that cost him his job. His replacement, Vice Admiral Jean Decoux, fared no better. Washington not only refused to intervene, but actually blocked the sale of aircraft and anti-aircraft guns. In August 1940, the American State Department informed Vichy France that

. . . the United States was unable to come to the aid of Indochina but that it "appreciated the difficulties with which the French Government was faced and did not consider that it would be justified in reproaching France if certain military facilities were accorded Japan."[1]

England proved no more venturesome: in mid-August, Japanese threats caused her to close the Burma Road for three months, thus depriving China of much needed supply.[2] Lacking British or American support and strongly sympathetic to axis aims, the Vichy government recognized Japan's "pre-eminent position" in the Far East and instructed Decoux to come to an agreement that would retain French sovereignty over Indochina. When Decoux hesitated, the Japanese attacked French border forts and bombed Hanoi. These actions led to an agreement, in late September, whereby Japan occupied three airfields in Tonkin, her total occupation force not to exceed six thousand troops; in addition, she agreed not to send more than twenty-five thousand Japanese through Indochina at a time.[3]

Thus began French Indochina's capitulation, at first a relatively painless process:

. . . The Japanese seemed quite content to leave a framework of French control in Indochina. Decoux and the officials under him bore the burdens of government and kept order in the country, leaving the Japanese free to use Indochina more or less as they wished—to plug up a gap in the blockade of China, and to serve as a military base and a source of supply in the conquest of China and Southeast Asia. It was a profitable arrangement for

1. Fall, op. cit.; see also Hammer, op. cit.; Buttinger, op. cit.; Lancaster, op. cit.

2. Hammer, op. cit.

3. Ibid.; see also Lancaster, op. cit.

both French officialdom and the Japanese military, and it opened the door to Japanese domination of the country.[4]

The Japanese did not hesitate in asserting supremacy. In January 1941, Thailand sent an expeditionary force into Cambodia and a naval force to Hanoi. The French blew the Thai navy out of the water; Japan interceded, and in March forced the French to cede rich provinces in Cambodia and Laos to Thailand. A few months later, in July, the Vichy government accepted Japan as a defensive partner in Indochina, removed all restrictions as to the number of troops she could station there, and also made available ports and airfields, facilities which

. . . were exploited without loss of time in order to build up a forward base in Indochina for their plans for expansion in South East Asia.[5]

Japan's move caught Washington by surprise. President Roosevelt now proposed to the Japanese ambassador ". . . the complete neutralization of Indochina in exchange for a guarantee of Japan's 'right of acquisition . . . of supplies and raw materials therefrom on a basis of equality.' "[6] But, only two days later, the President issued his famous Executive Order that froze Japanese assets in America and placed an embargo on petroleum exports to Japan, an act that scarcely promoted favorable relations between the two countries. Japan ignored further proposals by President Roosevelt, including that of a neutral Indochina administered by a six-power protectorate; all discussions abruptly ceased with the surprise attack against Pearl Harbor on December 7, 1941.

The shock effect quickly rocked French forces in Indochina. In Fall's words,

. . . On the night of the strike against Pearl Harbor, Japanese troops surrounded all the French garrisons, and Decoux was faced with yet another ultimatum: to stay put and cooperate with the Greater East Asia Co-Prosperity Sphere or face the immediate destruction of his garrisons as well as the loss of even nominal French sovereignty. Decoux yielded, thus saving 40,000 of his countrymen from the immediate ordeal of Japanese concentration camps and saving for France at least the appearance of being in command of the local population.[7]

Fall tried hard to defend this abject surrender. The key question, in his opinion, ". . . in appraising the situation must be whether or not

4. Hammer, op. cit.

5. Lancaster, op. cit., points out that Japanese bombers flew from Saigon Airfield to sink the British battleships HMS *Prince of Wales* and HMS *Repulse* off the Malayan coast.

6. Fall, op. cit.; see also Robert E. Sherwood, *Roosevelt and Hopkins* (New York: Harper & Brothers, 1948).

7. Fall, op. cit.

the situation in Indochina hampered the Allied war effort." He has pointed out that no French units fought against Allied troops; further,

. . . the continued presence until March, 1945, of 50,000 armed French troops compelled the Japanese to maintain a far larger force "in being" in Indochina than would have been required had those forces been destroyed once and for all in September, 1940, when all the other allies were sitting on their hands. Those are the objective facts of the situation; they do not make the French attitude look particularly heroic or moral—but in eminently practical terms (and those were the terms under which the situation should have been considered at all times, instead of the high-level emotionalism that did prevail), it served the Allied cause in the Far East a great deal better than has been admitted.[8]

With due respect to this writer-scholar who was to meet his death in Vietnam, he failed to consider the effects had a guerrilla campaign been waged by this French force. Even a fighting withdrawal across Thailand into Burma would have proved preferable to capitulation. Had the French promised Vietnamese people postwar independence, they undoubtedly would have supported, in time, any resistance effort against the Japanese and would have proved valuable Asian partners in a postwar commonwealth arrangement.

Decoux wanted none of this. After brutally crushing Communist and nationalist peasant uprisings in 1940 and 1941,[9] he established a dictatorship modeled on Marshal Pétain's fascist National Revolution.[10] At first, life continued almost normally for the French. But, as Ellen Hammer has written,

. . . Having no responsibility for the conduct of the war, and scant hope, at least at first, of influencing its outcome, isolated from homes and families in France, the French in Indochina created for themselves an unreal world. . . .

They had their problems, too, but these were mostly difficulties of daily living which loomed disproportionately large because they had no others. They experienced shortages of European food when the transports stopped coming. They had few vegetables, no sugar. They lacked machine parts and tools, oils and gasoline, and textiles. Cars and machines began to run down, factories were destroyed by bombs, medicines were used up and could not be replaced.

This was not a heroic atmosphere in which to live. Pétainism thrived and Admiral Decoux sounded its keynote. He ruthlessly applied the laws of Vichy against Gaullists, against liberals, against Freemasons, against Jews. And to

8. Ibid.
9. Buttinger, op. cit.
10. Hammer, op. cit.

Vietnamese, whether nationalists or communists, he applied the same policy. Some eight to ten thousand Indochinese political prisoners, most of them Vietnamese were in French jails in Indochina in March 1945.[11]

In attempting to preserve a status quo that did not exist, Decoux was mounting his cannons in sand. The political threat of the Japanese Greater East Asia Co-Prosperity Sphere, which, as in Indonesia, held considerable appeal for already anti-Western peoples, prompted Decoux and his lieutenants to a counteroffensive. In reply to the popular Japanese appeal of "Asia for the Asiatics," the French began talking long and seemingly in earnest of an Indochinese Federation, ". . . a mutually beneficial organization of different peoples, each with their separate traditions, held together and directed by France."[12] Decoux's courtship extended to the people as well. The French opened new schools, encouraged teaching the Vietnamese language, sponsored public works, organized a youth program over a million strong, brought in more Indochinese to run civil services and promoted others, developed industries, and introduced new crops.[13]

At the same time, however, he made it abundantly clear that France would retain control of Indochina. He failed to understand that he had opened Pandora's box. By admitting and even encouraging forces of nationalism, he was yielding what artificial control he still exercised—a slow process that would culminate finally in total French surrender to the Japanese.

In a world at war, Decoux was attempting to preserve without fighting. In sacrificing honor for survival, he unwittingly was insuring eventual end of French hegemony in Indochina.[14]

Not all Frenchmen subscribed to Decoux's accommodation. As early as 1941, intelligence began filtering from the country, and American agents operating in southern China even established a few networks. A Free French mission that reached Kunming in 1943 enlarged the effort.

As allied victories became known and as allied naval blockade and aerial bombing made life in Indochina increasingly uncomfortable, a good many Frenchmen swung from the Vichy to the Gaullist camp to provide resistance nuclei which, taken with indigenous guerrilla groups, could have grown to considerable dimensions. Working with SOE

11. Ibid.
12. Ibid.
13. Ibid.
14. Ibid.; the Japanese jailed Decoux in March 1945. After the war, the Gaullist government arrested him and held him in jail for two years. Finally released because of ill health, he was formally cleared of charges in 1949—a decision that raised considerable protest in France.

Force 136 in Calcutta and later Ceylon, and with OSS officers in China, French dissidents conceived a general resistance plan that included a rising against Japanese in event of an allied landing in Indochina.

Several factors hampered the plan's growth and execution.

The first was President Roosevelt's anti-colonial attitude. Roosevelt regarded the humanitarian principles set forth in the Atlantic Charter more seriously than Winston Churchill, who held no intention of losing the British Empire. Of many crosses that Churchill bore as a poor relation, the colonial issue reigned supreme. Roosevelt frequently infuriated Churchill with his nagging concern for India's future, and he left no doubt in Churchill's mind that he would prevent a French return to Indochina.[15] Roosevelt deplored what he felt was indefensible exploitation of this land by French colonials, and he never forgave the French surrender to Japan. Evidence exists, however, that he was willing to recognize special interests of colonial powers so long as they guaranteed colonies eventual independence under separate plans, an attitude picked up and exploited by General de Gaulle at the Brazzaville Conference of December 1943.[16]

As early as March 1943, Roosevelt suggested to Anthony Eden, Britain's foreign secretary, a postwar trusteeship for Indochina, an idea later presented to Stalin and also discussed at the November 1943 Cairo Conference. Roosevelt pursued the topic at Tehran, where he found Stalin in general agreement. The trusteeship question again rose at Yalta, but this time Churchill proved obstructive and the matter quietly rested. Roosevelt died before it could be revived. But, at Tehran, the powers had agreed to immediate postwar occupation of the area by British forces up to the sixteenth parallel, by Chinese forces north of the parallel. The Potsdam conference confirmed this operational decision.

Roosevelt's intransigence dampened clandestine efforts inside the country. So far as the American command in China was concerned, the allied effort would confine itself to collecting intelligence and rescuing downed allied airmen.

The British labored under no such anti-colonial policy. Their attitude, taken with growing strength of the Free French and liberation of France in mid-1944, brought new and awkward forces into play. SOE Force 136, operating out of Lord Louis Mountbatten's South-East Asia Command in Ceylon, began setting up resistance groups that were supposed to work with French garrisons in Indochina. Despite various hindrances, the effort grew: ". . . By the beginning of 1945 an Allied ferry service was dropping men and equipment into Indochina on an average of twice a week."[17]

15. Sherwood, op. cit.
16. De Gaulle, op. cit. (Vol. 3); see also Buttinger, op. cit.
17. Hammer, op. cit.

Roosevelt refused to support the French. In October 1944, he wrote Hull ". . . that we should do nothing in regard to resistance groups or in any other way in relation to Indochina." His words reached American command headquarters in China in November along with an order enjoining American field commanders from giving ". . . American approval . . . to any French military mission being accredited to the South-East Asia Command."[18]

Other factors also hurt the effort. Dissension ruled French garrisons in Indochina. Although a great many Vichyites converted to Gaullism, treachery remained a major factor. So did military stupidity. Despite pleas of resistance agents such as Paul Mus to arm Vietnamese guerrillas, the army refused to release arms brought in by parachute for this purpose. The principal Vietnamese resistance group, the Viet Minh, repeatedly ". . . called upon the French to work with it against the Japanese. But the French authorities had chosen to regard its members as bandits, of which the Tonkinese countryside had seen many, and had started a clean-up drive against them, bottling them up in the forests."[19]

The principal Free French representative in Indochina, General Mordant, was unable to co-ordinate the work of various underground groups from headquarters in Hanoi. Apparently, all French officers were privy to plans for an uprising and were inclined to discuss them openly. As a result, Japanese counterintelligence agents became privy to most details.

In early 1945, the Japanese quietly moved troops from China to reinforce Indochinese garrisons. In March, they surrounded principal French garrisons and arrested senior French commanders. Some units managed to hold out and some to escape and fight as guerrillas in mountainous areas of the North. But despite impassioned pleas, Washington refused to reverse its policy and allow Chennault's 14th Air Force to drop vital supplies. By the time he received a green light, French resistance had virtually ended.[20]

The whole affair proved costly. The Japanese action caught perhaps thirteen thousand French troops outright. Another four thousand fell during the fighting and retreat. About fifty-five hundred soldiers, of whom some two thousand were Europeans, survived the eight-hundred-mile exodus to Yünnan.[21]

18. Cordell Hull, *Memoirs* (New York: Macmillan, 1948), Vol. 1.
19. Hammer, op. cit.
20. Ibid.
21. Fall, op. cit., has largely blamed American policy, but Buttinger, op. cit., points out that the attempts of the French ". . . to remain in the country as *maquis* failed, not so much because they did not receive the requested assistance from the American Air Force in China, but rather because of lack of support by the local population. They did not seek this support because they did not want it, for equally unsound political and military reasons. . . ."

CHINA

Red River

TONKIN

BURMA

Yen Bay
Hanoi
Haiphong

HAINAN

Mekong R.

VIETNAM

LAOS

Vientiane

THAILAND

Hué
Tourane

VIETNAM

Bangkok

CAMBODIA

Phnom
Penh

Mekong R.

COCHIN CHINA

Saigon

Gulf of Siam

N

THAILAND

SOUTHEAST ASIA 1941
• Towns and Cities
0   100   200   300 miles

M.E.P.

Adding insult to injury, the Japanese simultaneously bestowed their particular brand of "independence" on Vietnam. On March 10, 1945, the Japanese radio announced: ". . . The colonial status of French Indochina has ended."[22] Repudiating the 1885 treaty with France, Emperor Bao Dai affirmed the independence of Vietnam (the Japanese remaining in direct control of Cochin China), his words soon echoed by King Norodom Sihanouk of Cambodia and King Sisavang Vong of Luang Prabang, in Laos.[23]

In the Japanese mind, Indochina was to be a viable political entity in the Greater East Asia Co-Prosperity Sphere. This enterprise, however, survived but a few months. Scarcely had Bao Dai appointed a prime minister and necessary ministers and officials, than Japan surrendered.

An indigenous resistance movement had developed simultaneously with the French effort. This was largely the work of Ho Chi Minh, whom we left with a Chinese Communist mission in Tonkin early in the war. When this mission moved North, Ho apparently returned to Comintern activities, probably joining a group of Vietnamese nationalists and Communists at Liuchow, in Kwangsi province. He definitely attended the eighth meeting of the Central Committee of the Indochinese Communist Party, held in northern Vietnam in May 1941. As party charter member and important Comintern agent, he was instrumental in establishing a new front organization, the Viet Minh.[24]

Ho now returned to China, to the camp of a powerful war lord, Chiang Fa-kwei, who, with Chiang Kai-shek's blessing, was subsidizing a Vietnamese Special Training Camp outside Liuchow. Although details are contradictory, Ho apparently contested the war lord's own designs on Vietnam and was imprisoned for just over a year, a traumatic experience which he captured in haunting verse:

> . . . Four months leading a life in which there is
> nothing human
> Have aged me more than ten years.
> Yes: in a whole four months I have never eaten
> my fill,
> In four months I have never had a comfortable
> night's sleep,
> In four months I have never changed my
> clothes, and in four months
> I have never taken a bath.
> So: I have lost a tooth, my hair has grown grey,
> And, lean and black as a demon gnawed by hunger,
> I am covered with scabies. . . .

22. Hammer, op. cit.
23. Ibid.
24. Ibid.; see also, Lancaster, op. cit.

And again:

> . . . My body has been battered under the changing weather
> of China,
> My heart is sorely troubled by the misfortunes
> befallen Viet Nam. . . .[25]

While Ho scratched these painful verses in a Chinese jail, the Chinese
sponsored a coalition of Vietnamese revolutionary parties which
emerged as the Dong Minh Hoi, or Vietnam Revolutionary League.
From the resistance standpoint, the most valuable participant in the new
party was the Viet Minh. Probably at instigation of OSS representatives
attached to Chiang Kai-shek's headquarters in Kunming, the Chinese
released Ho and made him head of the Dong Minh Hoi.

Disorganization and internecine feuding of other Vietnamese nationalist units played into Viet Minh hands. Preaching nationalist gospel,
Ho had little trouble in winning Kuomintang and OSS support for active
Viet Minh guerrilla operations in Indochina. Nor did he fail to insinuate
himself and Communist cohorts into leadership of the Provisional Republican Government of Vietnam, organized in March 1944.

Guerrilla operations in northern Vietnam were in the hands of a
young history teacher and militant Communist, Vo Nguyen Giap, who
commanded some ten thousand irregulars by 1945. Not only did OSS
provide Giap's units with liaison teams, which in turn procured arms
and supply, but OSS missions operating in Vietnam came to rely on
Vietnamese interpreters, many of whom reported back to Giap and
Ho.[26]

The Viet Minh apparently performed various missions to OSS satisfaction. In accordance with Washington policy, these primarily concerned intelligence collection and evacuation of downed allied airmen.
In return, the Viet Minh consolidated its ranks and won numerous recruits to the Communist cause.

The Japanese take-over of Vietnam, in March 1945, brought further
action. The Viet Minh ordered the people to

> . . . Organize demonstrations, processions and strikes; close down all the
> markets and hinder, through boycott and other means, the enemy's last
> desperate effort. Destroy all communication and transport facilities; tear
> down all telegraph wires and destroy their ammunition dumps and food-
> stores; launch surprise attacks on their isolated outposts and ambush their
> patrol units in order to prevent them from turning against our population.[27]

In April, Viet Minh leaders proclaimed a liberated zone consisting
of seven northern provinces. At war's end, Ho and Giap commanded

25. Ho Chi Minh, *Prison Diary* (Hanoi: Foreign Languages Publishing House,
1962). Tr. Aileen Palmer.
26. R. H. Smith, op. cit.
27. Hammer, op. cit.

a powerful and cohesive guerrilla force whose disciplined organization contrasted strongly with the confused and divisive elements that constituted Bao Dai's government.

On August 13, 1945, the Indochinese Communist Party held a national conference. In a remote village in northern hills, the party, according to its secretary-general,

. . . advocated an extremely clear policy: to lead the masses in insurrection in order to disarm the Japanese before the arrival of the Allied forces in Indo-China; to wrest power from the Japanese and their puppet stooges and finally, as the people's power, to welcome the Allied forces coming to disarm the Japanese troops stationed in Indo-China.[28]

Three days later, the Viet Minh announced creation of the National Liberation Committee of Vietnam. Meanwhile, British forces had landed in the South, but they numbered a mere 1,400; several Chinese armies were inching down from the north, an aggregate 150,000 troops far more interested in what the occupation could do for them (food, women, loot) than in what they could do for the occupation. French forces either were shaking prison lice from clothes or were strung out in defensive mountain enclaves generally out of touch with each other. Bao Dai's officials, in any event ill-prepared to administer the country, were at each other's throats in the struggle for political pre-eminence. A severe famine developed in the ravaged country. Bao Dai's government fell.

Here was a power vacuum, and Ho's people set about to fill it. On August 19, Ho's main forces occupied Hanoi; a week later, Viet Minh forces moved into Saigon. In early September, Viet Minh leaders (accompanied by OSS officers) stood on the balcony of the Hanoi opera house to proclaim the new Democratic Republic of Vietnam (the DRV).

Ho's hold on this immense country was tenuous in the extreme. But bold action more than paid off. In the North, Viet Minh forces fell heir to French and Japanese weapon dumps—Fall gives the numbers as ". . . 31,000 rifles, 700 automatic weapons, 36 artillery pieces, and 18 tanks." In addition, the Viet Minh purchased ". . . 3,000 rifles, 50 automatic rifles, 600 submachine guns, and 100 mortars . . ." from newly arrived Chinese armies—weapons manufactured in America and supplied by America to Nationalist China.

Bold action did not similarly prosper in the South. Major General Gracey, commanding the small British occupation force, refused to acknowledge Viet Minh authority. Instead, in contravention of his orders, he allowed skeleton French forces to eject the self-proclaimed Viet Minh government from Saigon. He then released French prisoners

28. Fall, op. cit.

from Japanese stockades and allowed them to organize into military units.

Fighting soon broke out between occupation forces and the Viet Minh, fighting that would increase with arrival of Free French expeditionary forces in October.

Chapter 46

Japanese conquest of Malaya • Japan's surprise tactics • Prewar British attitude • Japanese army training • The SOE in Malaya • The historical background • British colonization • Origin of the Malayan Communist Party (MCP) • Its alliance with SOE • Early resistance to the Japanese • SOE problems • Japanese counterguerrilla operations • MCP organization, training, and tactics • Communist use of propaganda • SOE reinforcements • MCP strength at war's end

THE JAPANESE CONQUESTS of Malaya and Burma required considerably more planning than those to south and east. To achieve desired surprise against reasonably strong defending forces, the Japanese high command introduced a tactical concept that represented as radical a departure from orthodox tactics as the German *Blitzkrieg*. Paradoxically, the oriental version scorned the technological sophistication of its German ally by employing quasi-guerrilla tactics that enabled its forces to strike where the enemy least expected.

British commanders in Malaya and Burma long since had agreed with the Chinese philosopher-general Sun Tzu that jungle is "difficult ground" and no place to wage war. In Malaya, the British considered jungle country "out of bounds" for training:

. . . No specialized jungle technique or equipment had been evolved, and

M.E.P.

of all the troops stationed in Malaya only the 2nd Battalion of Argylls had had any serious training in jungle warfare. Nor had the natives of the country been in any way prepared to expect or resist invasion.[1]

The Singapore fortifications, built at a cost of £60 million, defended this vital base only against sea-borne attack.

1. Spencer-Chapman, op. cit.; see also John Smyth, *Percival and the Tragedy of Singapore* (London: MacDonald, 1971).

A veteran of Burma fighting, Major General (later Field Marshal Viscount) William Slim, wrote:

. . . to our men, British or Indian, the jungle was a strange, fearsome place; moving and fighting in it was a nightmare. We were too ready to classify jungle as "impenetrable," as indeed it was to us with our motor transport, bulky supplies, and inexperience. To us it appeared only as an obstacle to movement and to vision. . . .[2]

Deciding to exploit this allied weakness, the Japanese in the mid-1930s began training selected divisions for jungle warfare. The experience caused senior commanders to revise tactical and logistic concepts in favor of small and relatively self-sufficient tactical movements. By drastically trimming bulky supply lines and by exploiting jungle terrain, unit commanders soon achieved extraordinary mobility. Once troops learned to live in the jungle, keeping reasonably comfortable while avoiding sickness and disease, units achieved satisfactory staying power. This was not easily accomplished, nor did the Japanese ever totally master the jungle, but in coming to terms with its traditionally awesome environment, they acquired an invaluable ally which they fully exploited in 1941–42.

A large part of their strength derived from British ignorance. No less an authority than the official British war historian later wrote:

. . . An inadequate staff and neglect of training, partly accounted for the fact that no detailed study of the available information regarding the training and tactics of the Japanese army was made at Command level, despite the fact that Japan was the only possible enemy and that the danger of war in the Far East had greatly increased as a result of the outbreak of war in Europe.

Military attachés in Tokyo had for many years

. . . sent accurate reports to the War Office showing that the Japanese Army was a most efficient force. Yet Malaya Command consistently underrated the efficiency and skill of the Japanese. It may have been the fact that they appeared unable to subdue the poorly-equipped Chinese forces that led to the belief wide-spread throughout the Far East, that their armed forces were inefficient.

That two views of Japanese military prowess existed is seen in the fact that in 1940 Army Headquarters Australia, and Malaya Command held

2. William R. Slim, *Defeat into Victory* (London: Cassell, 1956). This is one of the liveliest command memoirs ever written, but, then, Viscount Slim was surely one of history's liveliest and most human commanders. Perhaps the ablest tactician of World War II, he accepted resounding and humiliating defeat (through no fault of his own)—but, with minimal means and relying largely on charisma and ability, turned it into ultimate victory.

almost opposite views on this vital matter. The 8th Australian Division, before it left its homeland, had been issued with training pamphlets which gave warning that the Japanese were ruthless, had a high standard of armament and technical training, great physical endurance, few bodily requirements compared with British troops, a talent for misleading their opponents, a large potential fifth column in Malaya, and ample experience of landing operations. This pamphlet stated that Japanese troops could move across country at great speed and could be self-supporting for several days; that, as the thick country did not favor static defense, offensive action should be taken against the enemy wherever he was met; and that there was a need for training all ranks in moving through jungle. . . .[3]

In the event, a British intelligence officer who observed diverse Japanese units working down the Malay Peninsula was not as impressed with their tactical performance as he was with the simplicity of their logistics:

. . . Their cooking gear was also of the lightest, and they were living off the country by collecting rice, fowls, and vegetables from the roadside villages. We saw several parties cooking their evening meal. Each man produced a cigarette tin with a loop of wire over the top and, cutting a stick, he hung his tin and boiled his rice over a communal fire. Some of those we watched produced a small tin of fish or other concentrated food, while others seemed to eat the rice alone. The whole meal only took a quarter of an hour to prepare and eat. All this was in very marked contrast to our own front-line soldiers, who were at this time equipped like Christmas trees with heavy boots, web equipment packs, haversacks, water-bottles, blankets, ground-sheets, and even great-coats and respirators [gas masks], so that they could hardly walk, much less fight.[4]

This courageous observer was F. Spencer-Chapman, whom we met earlier when he was training Australian independent companies. Transferred in September 1941, he joined the staff of Special Operations Executive (SOE), which had set up Number 101 Special Training School in Singapore.

Spencer-Chapman later wrote that the school wanted to train ". . . all types of personnel—military and civilian, European and native—in irregular warfare . . ." for special operations throughout Southeast Asia. The concept included training and equipping stay-behind parties, small guerrilla units of Asians commanded by British officers, that would supply intelligence and operate against Japanese lines of communication.

3. S. W. Kirby, *The War Against Japan—The Loss of Singapore* (London: HMSO, 1957).
4. Spencer-Chapman, op. cit.

But the commander-in-chief, Malaya, turned this down on the grounds that it

. . . would be too great a drain on European man-power, and that in any case white men would not be able to move freely in occupied territory. Objection was taken to the employment of Asiatics on the grounds that a scheme which admitted the possibility of enemy penetration would have a disastrous psychological effect on the Oriental mind. Nor might any Chinese be armed, since many of them belonged to an illegal organization, the Malayan Communist Party. . . .

The British attitude can best be explained by a brief look at Malayan history. An ancient empire like its neighbors, Malaya met the West in the form of Portuguese traders as early as 1511. Western nations, however, asserted only a peripheral trade interest in the peninsula until the end of the eighteenth century. At that time, Malaya consisted of a welter of kingdoms or sultanates, some small, some large, all generally feuding.[5]

Largely to counter Dutch presence in Indonesia, the English East India Company acquired the island of Penang by lease in 1786; in 1795, the British occupied Malacca, which they returned to the Dutch but gained permanently in 1824. Meanwhile, in 1819, Sir Thomas Stamford Raffles had left Indonesia to develop the island of Singapore, which he acquired from the sultan of Johore. British influence continued to spread, and, in 1867, the government proclaimed the three settlements a crown colony. A few years later, Great Britain, alarmed by an increasing German presence, began pushing inland, a process encouraged by the breakup of the Johore Empire and a series of fratricidal wars among the rajas.

British influence mounted in Perak, Selangor, Pahang, and the Negri Sembilan to the extent that in 1895 the four states accepted a federation status under British aegis. As the colonizing effort prospered, British capital flowed increasingly into the peninsula. In 1909, Britain won a treaty transfer of the northern states from Siam, and in 1914, the sultan of Johore, the last independent ruler, appointed a British "adviser" to administer the sultanate: ". . . All Malay states south of Siam were then under the protection of Great Britain."

By comparison to the French in Indochina and the Dutch in Indonesia, British colonial administration continued to claim positive gains. Apologists point out that, prior to World War II, Malayans enjoyed one of the highest standards of living in the Far East—a statement that would have provided the average rubber or tin worker with scant comfort. Here, as elsewhere, European colonists and indigenous royalty

5. R. O. Winstedt, "Malaysia (History)." In Encyclopaedia Britannica, 1968, Vol. 14. My historical introduction is taken from this excellent account.

profited immensely, as did sharp Chinese and Indian traders. Rather than train Malayans for self-government, Britain continued to exercise a paternalistic attitude that remained virtually unchallenged by rich and lazy sultans and resulted in fragmented and unhealthy political environment.

In the 1920s, the Malayan Communist Party (MCP) began emerging—the spawn of the Chinese Communist Party, established in 1921. Progress from the Marxist-study-group phase remained slow, the result of party setbacks in Indonesia and China. The MCP itself only emerged in 1930, under aegis of the Nan Yang, or South Seas Communist Party. Professor Lucian Pye, an expert in the field, has described the 1930 child as ". . . an ill-organized movement dedicated to conspiracy. . . ."[6]

The party enjoyed no spectacular growth during the 1930s, but it did train a large cadre of professional revolutionaries who fomented some serious strikes in the 1936–37 period. Foreign, rather than internal, developments, however, changed the MCP ". . . from a curious, at times annoying, but never profound movement into one of rising political power."[7]

The Japanese attack on China brought the MCP into collaboration with the Kuomintang in order to raise funds for Chiang Kai-shek. For this purpose, the MCP established a front group, the Anti-Enemy Backing-Up Society, or AEBUS. In August 1939, the German-Russian alliance turned the MCP and AEBUS away from the Kuomintang, but Hitler's invasion of Russia the following spring returned them to the fold.

Finally, Japanese landings in the north of Malaya in December 1941 brought the MCP into increased importance. Where the British command once refused to arm Asians, it now urgently sought help. But little time remained either to secure or train volunteers. In desperation, SOE officers with command blessing accepted an offer from the AEBUS. Early in 1942, SOE members hastily trained 165 Communists, mostly Chinese, supplied them with arms, demolitions, and food, and sent them north on the peninsula, where each was to raise a small guerrilla unit of ten to fifteen people. SOE officers also established a series of hidden supply dumps to support the guerrillas. Major Spencer-Chapman, who played an important role in this effort and who later took to the field in charge of a small guerrilla unit, has described his adventures in a book earlier cited, *The Jungle Is Neutral*.

Unfortunately, the fall of Singapore and evacuation of SOE headquarters to India vitiated the stay-behind effort. Spencer-Chapman's unit joined Communist groups that had been forming in the jungle. But

6. Lucian W. Pye, *Guerrilla Communism and Malaya—Its Social and Political Meaning* (Princeton, N.J.: Princeton University Press, 1956).
7. Ibid.

these units possessed no radio transmitters, and Spencer-Chapman's radio had been stolen. Moreover, his colleagues had hidden supply dumps so well that most of them were lost. Bandits stole other precious supplies. Out of touch with SOE(India) and reduced to minimum supply, Spencer-Chapman could do little more than strike at targets of opportunity while staying alive and trying to keep his organization intact until help arrived.

His isolation continued for two years. At times, he scored dramatic successes against the enemy. Early in this period, in one two-week flurry, he estimated that his small group of guerrillas

. . . derailed seven or eight trains, severely damaged at least fifteen bridges, cut the railway line in about sixty places, damaged or destroyed some forty motor vehicles, and killed or wounded somewhere between five and fifteen hundred Japs. Altogether we had used a thousand pounds of explosive and over a hundred grenades or home-made bombs.[8]

This effort convinced the Japanese that two hundred Australians were in the vicinity. The local commander detailed two thousand soldiers to hunt them down.

On a later occasion, Spencer-Chapman learned of a pending Japanese raid against a guerrilla camp. After evacuating the guerrillas, he prepared an observation post so that he could ". . . study the Jap methods of attack":

. . . At earliest dawn, about 5:45 A.M., without a sound to warn us of what was coming, two or possibly more mortars opened up from the rubber and plastered the whole area with bombs. . . . Apparently the Japs had nobody spotting for the later shots were no more accurate than the earlier ones but they systematically raked the whole area of the camp, and every hut was hit without actually being destroyed. After this there was silence for some time and then machine-gun fire broke out from the hill above the camp and continued for about ten minutes. Of course, there was no target other than the empty huts, and even if the camp had been occupied at the time of the attack, we should all have disappeared into the jungle after the first mortar bomb, and only the heavy baggage would have been lost. After this about a hundred Japanese soldiers and as many Malays and Indians charged down the hill with loud shouts and fixed bayonets. They then stood in a huddle on the parade-ground, gazing round them like a party of tourists, and I only wished I had a machine-gun with me. After shouting and talking excitedly for some time, they set fire to all the huts and retired hurriedly.

I later learned that at about four o'clock that morning the Japs had surrounded the Chinese *kampong* which lay a mile from the camp and had sent the 160 inhabitants—men, women, and children—away in the lorries which had brought the troops. When they had reached a deserted area of tin-tailing

8. Spencer-Chapman, op. cit.

ground on the way to Kuala Lumpur, they had made the men dig a trench and had then stood everybody in a row beside it and had tommy-gunned them to death.[9]

In ensuing months and years, the Japanese did not materially alter counterguerrilla operations. Although they enjoyed co-operation of a great many Malays and Indians, and some Chinese, they scored few successes.

After the British surrender at Singapore, the MCP established head-quarters in remote Johore and formed the Anti-Japanese Union and Forces (MPAJUF), which consisted of two main branches, the Anti-Japanese Union (MPAJU), and the Anti-Japanese Army (MPAJA). The party ordered AJU members to remain in villages and towns to endure rigors of occupation while secretly supporting the AJA, the rather grand title for the few guerrilla bands that existed in the jungle under leaders the British SOE had helped to organize and train. Chinese squatters along the jungle fringe acted as liaison between the two factions.[10]

The movement never proved a real threat to the Japanese. In August 1942, the *kempetai,* or secret police, arrested and executed top party leaders in Singapore, and, in the following month, eliminated a good portion of the Central Committee and top guerrilla leaders by a surprise raid in the Batu Caves area of Selangor.[11] The party's secretary-general, Lai Teck, survived, however (some authorities think he betrayed his comrades), as did his able and industrious assistant, Ch'en P'ing, and, under their leadership, the movement continued.

But, as Professor Pye later wrote:

. . . The great effort expended by the MCP in organizing the MPAJA did not mean that the party leaders contemplated engaging in extensive military operations against the Japanese. Rather, it was recognized that the function of the army was to provide an opportunity for individuals to feel that they were contributing something to the defeat of the hated Japanese without forcing them to expose themselves to the risks involved in fighting. Since the Japanese had introduced personal insecurity in Malayan society and the MCP sought to present itself as a sanctuary, it would have been foolhardy, in terms of the purposes of the party, to require the members of the MPAJA to face unnecessarily the insecurities of actual warfare. The leadership of the MCP had the task of effectively substituting indoctrination, propaganda, and camp life for actual military operations, thus ensuring that all members of the MPAJA felt they had gone through the rigors of combat without at the same time risking the organization in any serious test of battle. Not only

9. Ibid.
10. Pye, op. cit.; see also Blair, op. cit.
11. Pye, op. cit.

did the men have to believe that they were warriors who had proved themselves in a struggle of great violence, but the entire Chinese community had to be convinced that the MPAJA was a champion of all loyal Chinese and a powerful force striking against the Japanese enemy.[12]

To accomplish these goals, the Central Committee established eight regional guerrilla "groups." Each group controlled a number of "patrols." A patrol consisted of about one hundred men (and a few women) divided into sections of eight to ten that operated from a series of jungle camps.

Major Spencer-Chapman spent nearly a year with a guerrilla patrol operating in Pahang, east of the Main Range. This unique experience offered a splendid opportunity to study Communist guerrilla organization and operations at the working level.

Centralized command ruled in the best Marxist-Leninist-Maoist tradition:

. . . The control of guerrilla headquarters, in spite of its geographical vagueness, was absolute and all-embracing, being limited only by the difficulties of communication. Policy, discipline, routine, ethics, and above all political ideology were entirely regulated from above—and as the penalty for disobedience was death, opposition in word or spirit was practically unknown.[13]

The vertical administrative concept helped central headquarters to retain control:

. . . group and patrol leaders had complete power within their commands but none outside, nor would they ever dare to take the initiative. Even a patrol leader could not visit another camp in his group without permission from group headquarters, and there was no communication between groups except with the express permission of general headquarters. Every detail had to be referred above and the answer, if it came at all, would take several months to receive.[14]

Group headquarters consisted of four officers: the all-powerful political leader, a military commander, a quartermaster, and "a teacher-cum-propaganda worker who was invariably a Party member and probably the second most important officer of the four." In addition, however,

. . . Attached to group headquarters were usually one or more outside workers whose status depended on their own personality or their standing in the M.C.P. Their task, perhaps the most important of all, was to cultivate the minds of the outside people so that they would support the camps,

12. Ibid.
13. Spencer-Chapman, op. cit.
14. Ibid.

to allocate the areas of influence and the food lines between the various patrols, and to supervise the systematic discovery and eradication of traitors and informers. These men, who were usually the best educated and most intelligent of the guerrillas—and often most charming and delightful people —spent only a small proportion of their time in the camps and the rest in the *kampongs* or on tour.[15]

Patrol headquarters, where Spencer-Chapman spent most of his time,

. . . was a replica of group headquarters, but there was in addition a military second-in-command who supervised the guard and training. Its members were allowed very little initiative and would often go to any length to avoid responsibility. . . .[16]

Lack of arms and equipment constantly hindered the guerrilla effort, as did insufficient training and poor communications. Bad planning doomed most operations to failure, particularly if anything went wrong. Only a few guerrillas had received any training, and much of Spencer-Chapman's effort went to teaching them basic fundamentals of guerrilla warfare. Although, in general, he found keen and receptive students, he also noted a distinct morale problem:

. . . At this time [1942] many of the Chinese who had joined the guerrillas in a fit of enthusiasm were becoming disillusioned. They hated the rigorous camp discipline which even prevented them from visiting their *kampongs,* and found the food inferior to what they were used to in their own homes. In the early days there seemed every hope of keeping the Japanese out of Malaya, but now it looked as if they had come to stay. Consequently there were many desertions, either back to the *kampongs* or even to become informers to the Japanese. . . .

The facility with which the Chinese, otherwise so single-minded in their hatred of the Japanese, could turn informer was a perpetual source of astonishment to me. In the year that I spent with this patrol no less than six of its members were tried for treachery and summarily shot, and several others who had fled from the camp and turned informer were hunted down and dispatched outside. . . .[17]

Awkward as was the vertical command concept, it paid off in that defectors could offer only slight information to the Japanese, usually no more than the location of a jungle camp, which could be easily changed. Intense unit discipline and indoctrination resulting in *gung ho* psychology peculiar to the Communists also held down desertions, even

15. Ibid.
16. Ibid.
17. Ibid.

though only about 10–15 per cent of the group were Communists. In a guerrilla camp, according to another authority,

. . . all orders were discussed. Any man could bring a charge against another; the matter would then be debated in session and the sentence decided by majority vote, though this could be overridden by Headquarters. With the acute shortage of leaders these methods not only resulted in failure to take action but made junior and sometimes senior leaders frightened of giving definite orders. While punishments for minor offenses ranged from cutting down rations to depriving a man of his weapons, the death penalty was passed for what, by non-Communist standards, would appear to be comparatively minor crimes. These included stealing AJUF property or that of outside helpers, and in one case a man was sentenced to death for selling an AJA bicycle. . . .[18]

Deterrence and retaliation figured prominently in the Communist code. The Central Committee maintained special "traitor-killing" camps, one of which Spencer-Chapman later visited and whose twenty members claimed to have killed over a thousand informers. Armed with weapons captured from local police stations, they also liberated guerrilla prisoners, destroyed police records, intimidated Japanese work parties, and performed sabotage at will.[19]

Within camps, the rank and file impressed Spencer-Chapman as devoted and willing guerrillas. Indoctrination played a large role in training. Sections often operated on their own. A considerable part of their effort went to staying alive, no easy task in Malayan jungle, as Major Spencer-Chapman's frequent and severe illnesses emphasized. They also recruited wherever possible, the policy being ". . . to train at least as many reserves as there were men already in the camps." Training, by necessity, remained basic, as did ordinary camp routine. Propaganda played a constant role. Spencer-Chapman described a camp play in three acts:

. . . In the first act a Chinese family discussed the war; the son of the house asked his father for permission to join the guerrillas, but this was refused. In the next scene, the Japs—hideous and ridiculous little men with small black moustaches and huge spectacles—entered the house led by an informer. They ravished the daughter, tied up or killed the parents and, finding a bottle of *samsu*, became incapably drunk. In the final scene, the son of the house, who had run for aid into the jungle, reappeared with a band of guerrillas who overpowered the Japs and rescued any compatriots who were still alive. After two hours of this there was a short halt for sweet coffee and cakes made of grated coconut, palm sugar, and spices. Then the concert continued

18. Blair, op. cit.
19. Spencer-Chapman, op. cit.

in the same strain for another hour, to conclude at last with more speeches and the "Internationale" shouted by everybody into the still, starlit jungle night, and so to bed.[20]

Operational results varied considerably from patrol to patrol and from group to group. Although the Menchis group was too weak to take on the Japanese, the Kuantan guerrillas allegedly fought them quite often. Certainly the Japanese hated and feared the bands, as evidenced by brutal retaliations against various tribes suspected of supporting them.

Supply shortages greatly restricted operations. But once the British reorganized forces in India and opened the Burma front, the Malayan theater grew in importance, particularly since active guerrilla units could prepare the way for an allied landing. In May 1943, a small SOE liaison team reached the peninsula by submarine. Though other teams buttressed this effort, the distances were so great, supplies in such short quantity, delivery means so stringent, enemy troops so active, and the theater of operations so elongated and difficult to traverse that resistance continued to languish. The area remained out of air range from India and Ceylon until advent of the Liberator bomber, in 1944.

In November 1944, the MPAJA began to receive regular airdrops, and, in 1945, various shortages began to ease. In early February 1945, Spencer-Chapman transmitted his first radio message, and, by July, a number of SOE teams—something over three hundred men—were working with indigenous guerrilla units and had armed an estimated thirty-five hundred men.

Japanese surrender, in August, summarily terminated this effort. British troops landed in due course, and, within a few months, most guerrillas had turned in arms and been paid off.

Unfortunately this did not end the matter. Malayan Communists may not have fought the Japanese as actively as the allies desired—Pye credits them with killing only a few hundred Japanese—but they ended the war politically well organized:

. . . about 7,000 guerrillas came out of the jungle fully convinced that it was their might which had defeated the enemy, and they were welcomed by large elements of the civil population as heroes.[21]

Although a good many AJA members yielded arms (for a considerable sum of money), enough weapons remained hidden to constitute severe threat to internal security if utilized for improper purposes.

Nor did AJA's official demise, at the end of 1945, dispel threat of subversion. The MCP remained intact, with none of its virility sacrificed by temporary acceptance of British rule. What the British mistook for internal peace, unfortunately would prove little more than uneasy truce.

20. Ibid.
21. Pye, op. cit.

Chapter 47

The Japanese invade Burma • Allied defeat • Allied strategy • Stilwell versus British and Chinese • Historical background • British colonial administration • Saya San's rebellion • The Thakin movement • Aung San's collaboration with the Japanese • SOE organizes guerrilla units • SOE difficulties • The North Kachin Levy

WHEN THE DUST of Japanese conquest settled in Southeast Asia, the picture, in spring of 1942, looked something like this: Japanese armies occupied Malaya and Burma as well as Indochina (in alliance with Vichy-French civil and military forces) and Thailand, whose government had declared in favor of the Japanese. Remnants of the Burma army, hastily reinforced by reserve Indian army divisions, were defending some four to five hundred miles of India-Burma frontier. (See map, page 593.) This force belonged to British India Command, under General Wavell, soon to be replaced by General Auchinleck.

Up north, in Assam, about nine thousand Chinese troops who had escaped from Burma were being reorganized by an American officer, Lieutenant General Joseph "Vinegar Joe" Stilwell. By Combined Chiefs of Staff direction, Stilwell commanded the China-Burma-India theater; wearing a second hat, he served as chief of staff to Chiang Kai-shek. After his hasty appointment, he had flown into Burma titularly to command the two Chinese armies present; in reality, he accomplished little more than witnessing disorganized and costly retreat, an experience not without lessons, as Slim also discovered.

Still another Chinese force that had escaped from Burma was reorganizing in Yünnan province, bordering northeastern Burma. China herself stood on the defensive against strong Japanese armies. Loss of the Burma road irrevocably cut Chinese Nationalist armies from land communication with India, the single remaining supply life line being the hastily organized and still ineffectual American airlift over the Himalayas, the famous "Hump."

Allied reverses elsewhere meant continued supply shortages, with first claim exercised by the airlift to Kunming. India herself writhed with internal disorder, particularly in Bengal and Sind, where authorities had their hands full defeating local insurgencies.[1]

Dark days, indeed.

Dark days made darker still by national interests colliding with strategic thunder. Allied strategy, as determined by the Combined Chiefs of Staff, directed British-American-Chinese forces to exert maximum pressure against the Japanese in Burma in order to prevent reinforcements from being shifted to the Pacific theater and also to prepare the way for a future offensive designed to re-establish land communication with China.[2]

Stilwell ultimately envisaged a three-prong attack: the British from the west; his own Chinese-American force from the northwest; the Yünnan Chinese force from the northeast. The plan suffered British and Chinese disapproval. For political reasons, the British wanted to return to Rangoon, in the south, and then only when they held a preponderance of strength. Chiang Kai-shek, convinced that America would ultimately defeat the Japanese, wanted only to build and preserve military strength for the showdown he believed would come with Mao Tse-tung's Communists in northwestern China.

In short, during those dark months of 1942–43, three major allied commands headed in three different directions, a dispersion of effort that would adversely affect nearly every aspect of operations including those in enemy-held country.

As might be imagined, British exodus from Burma in spring of 1942 left a confused resistance situation, particularly since a late start had prevented Special Operations Executive (SOE) from establishing clandestine resistance groups.

Such was the state of the art and apathy of the regular military establishment regarding intelligence that the task could never have been

---

1. Philip Woodruff, *The Men Who Ruled India—The Guardians* (London: Jonathan Cape, 1954), Vol. 2 of 2 vols.
2. Slim, op. cit.

simple. Considering the country's internal state and the divisive forces at work, it could never prosper.

Burmese nationalist leaders, influenced by relatives and friends who were victims of pacification pogroms of 1885–90 (see Chapter 16), refused to be satisfied with British administration of what they regarded as their country, a country older, by far, than England.

As happened elsewhere in Southeast Asia, blatant exploitation of human and natural resources, coupled with the rise of Japan after 1905 as an international power, provided ample fuel to keep the grumbling pot of nationalism at a boil. In the century's early years, young Burmese students educated in Britain, many of them as lawyers, returned to practice in Rangoon and Mandalay and, almost from the beginning, exhibited an uncomfortable independence in relations with British magistrates and civil servants. A few Burmese newspapers appeared to rally further the forces of nationalism, which even prior to World War I inextricably mingled with Buddhism.[3]

The Great War weakened without destroying Britain's control of Burma. But nationalist opposition now became more vocal. One nationalist movement, the Wuntharnu, demanded with some success a boycott on British goods because of continued refusal to give the Burmese self-government. In 1920, a university strike spread to ". . . a nationwide movement of protest against British rule in general."[4]

Although the British offered palliative measures, for example introducing in 1923 a diarchy, or dual government, similar to that in India, Burmese extremists regarded the move as little more than a meaningless gesture. Defenders of imperialism have argued that such acts undoubtedly formed a necessary prelude to self-government, and there is much to be said for the argument. Certainly this particular reform signaled the rise of Burmese political parties and a parliamentary form of government, though whether this is good or bad is debatable in view of today's confused state of Burmese politics.

Unfortunately, reforms never outrun crises: the very word, reform, suggests previous neglect, and this was true of British colonial administration in Burma, where private Western interests frequently contravened Whitehall intentions. The world economic depression in 1930 raised numerous boils on an already irritated rice-paddy economy. A former monk and native quack, Saya San, felt called upon to cure the

3. Maung Htin Aung, *A History of Burma* (New York: Columbia University Press, 1967). A professor of history and veteran diplomat, the author enjoys advantages derived from personal experience. If the Westerner objects to a nationalist bias in this and similar revisionist works of history, the Easterner for long has been exposed to Western bias in traditional histories. Hopefully, another decade will provide a working synthesis for the oft-bewildered student.

4. Ibid.

disease. Jumping from boil to boil, he hit upon the Tharrawaddy district of Lower Burma, where

. . . the stocks of rice remained unsold, and although there was plenty of food there was nothing else. Many had lost their lands to the Indian money-lenders long before and, with the price of rice touching rock bottom, the Indian landlords would not engage labor to cultivate their fields. Those who still owned lands just sat on their stocks of rice, unable to find the cash to re-pay the interest on their debts. Their clothes had been worn out during the year, but without the cash to buy new supplies the men went about half naked and the women sat behind closed doors. Such dire poverty they had not even heard of before. To add to their troubles, the annual taxes were overdue. . . .[5]

Saya San's remedy proved worse than the disease. The Tharrawaddy rebellion soon spread to central and Upper Burma, involving the Shan states. In some ways reminiscent of the 1887 situation (see Chapter 16), it involved guerrilla bands led by natives such as Saya Nyan, a school-teacher, and a hermit, Bandaka. Lacking arms, outside support, and central leadership, the insurgents fought uncoordinated actions and, in 1932, succumbed to British arms. Professor Htin Aung claimed that the rebellion cost ten thousand rebel lives with nine thousand rebels captured and 128 ringleaders later hanged. He concluded that this rebellion ". . . was perhaps the nearest Asian counterpart of the peasants' rebellion in medieval England, and it was a rebellion born of sheer desperation."[6]

Neither rebellion nor suppression settled very much. Indigenous political ferment continued, but with a significant addition: an extremist university student movement. Adopting a nationalist cause, these young rebels expressed disapproval of British university administration (including a civil-servant faculty) ". . . by coming to classes in their shirt sleeves and walking noisily along corridors in wooden slippers. Dressed untidily in homespun clothes, they deliberately assumed an uncouth, obstinate, and stupid appearance. . . ."[7]

Meanwhile they were organizing a militant movement undreamed of by British officialdom. Charter members went so far as to take the prefix-name "Thakin"—this because British officials and officers since 1886 had called themselves *thakin* or "master." The Thakin movement was reinforced by a massive university-student strike in 1936, headed by Maung No and Maung Aung San, the latter's grandfather having been a prominent guerrilla leader in 1886. After the strike subsided, the two leaders joined the Thakin movement and greatly strengthened it.

5. Ibid.
6. Ibid.
7. Ibid.

The outbreak of World War II, in Europe, only aggravated matters in Burma. Political arrests by the British drove dissident parties such as the Thakins underground. Their leader, Aung San, escaped to Amoy, where he attempted to contact left-wing Chinese groups; meanwhile, in Rangoon, his followers contacted Japanese agents, who offered aid if they would rebel against the British.

For some time, Japanese agents had been active in the country, stirring up dissidence and collecting intelligence for two purposes: the first, to weaken British administration and force the government to close the Burma Road, by which arms and supply reached China; the second, to prepare the country for ultimate invasion by Japanese troops.

British weakness in general immensely aided the Japanese task, especially after Dunkerque when Britain, in Winston Churchill's words, stood ". . . naked before her foes." In July, she temporarily closed the road as a "friendly" gesture to Japan, but three months later, when that country failed to sheath its aggressive claws, Britain reopened the vital road.

Japanese agents meanwhile reached Aung San in Amoy and, with his agreement, hustled him off to Tokyo for special indoctrination in the Asia for the Asiatics concept. Returning to Rangoon in March 1941, Aung San selected a number of volunteers—known in Burmese history as the "Thirty Comrades"—and, with Japanese connivance, took them to Formosa "for intensive military training."[8] There they agreed to work with the Japanese army in the invasion of Burma.

In the event, they did this and, as will be seen, attracted numerous recruits to carry out various fifth-column activities. According to Professor Htin Aung,

. . . Aung San and his group genuinely believed that the Japanese would declare Burma to be an independent sovereign state the moment war broke out between Japan and the allies.[9]

Not everyone in Rangoon was so misled, and, in the country, the British retained some good friends, particularly among diverse mountain tribes. Beginning in late 1941, an SOE mission partially armed some fifteen hundred members of a loyal hill tribe, the Karens, and this irregular force screened the British army's left flank during the initial retreat.

When the British moved north up the Irrawaddy Valley, the Karens buried their arms and returned to their villages to await contact by SOE officers. As retreat continued, the British sent most regular Burmese soldiers home: ". . . Each man was given his rifle, fifty rounds [of ammunition], and three months' pay, told to go to his village, wait for our

8. Ibid.
9. Ibid.

return, and be ready to join any organization we should start to fight the Japanese in Burma."[10]

These men came mostly from hill tribes traditionally friendly to the British, and SOE officers on the way out of the country managed to organize a guerrilla unit from the Shans in the East and several units from the Kachins in the Northeast. Taken with the Nagas and the Chins along the western border, these hill tribes, each varying in strength from fifty thousand to over a million, represented a potential force of understandable interest to SOE, which spent the rest of the war trying to raise them against the Japanese.

A variety of operational factors frustrated this effort. Shattered remnants of the Burmese army consumed all available weapons and supplies, already scarce because of demands levied by Stilwell in the North and by Chiang's insatiable appetite in Kunming and Chungking.

A chronic shortage of delivery means also existed. Even when proper planes were available (late in the war), long distances, difficult weather, and rugged and unhealthy terrain made airdrops a costly and discouraging business.

SOE also lacked Burmese-speaking officers to head essential liaison teams, and though former planters and civil officials partially repaired this deficiency, the few early teams still had to work in a dangerous political climate. If a liaison party survived local political vicissitudes to contact a friendly tribe, it found little or no resistance organization among tribesmen, nor were radios technically up to sustained transmissions necessary to arrange essential supply drops.

In central and southern Burma, only a few intelligence-collection missions existed by end of 1944, mainly in Arakan. SOE experienced better luck in the Northeast, working with the Kachins. Here the British early had established an outpost at Fort Hertz that supported an organization called the North Kachin Levy, or NKL. Eventually amounting to six "companies" of guerrillas, the NKL provided intelligence essential for orthodox operations and, as will be seen, performed valuable work both on its own and in conjunction with those forces.

With these exceptions, the Burma resistance movement remained fairly stifled, although, in later stages, it picked up momentum. In the interim, however, other developments were proving of decided interest to guerrilla warfare: allied attempts to build armies suitable for fighting under the unorthodox tactical conditions imposed by the Japanese presence in Burma; and, an offshoot, the creation of special task forces to wage guerrilla warfare behind enemy "lines."

10. Slim, op. cit.

Chapter 48

A modern major general (I): William Slim • His analysis of Japanese tactics • He adapts to the tactical challenge • First Arakan offensive • A modern major general (II): Vinegar Joe Stilwell • His Chinese command • Retreat from Burma • Observations on the Chinese army • Stilwell's training programs • Orde Wingate and guerrilla warfare: Palestine and Ethiopia • His concept of "Long Range Penetration" operations • The first Chindit operation

Bᴿɪᴛɪsʜ-ᴄʜɪɴᴇsᴇ RETREAT from Burma left remnant survivors in a state of shock reminiscent of Roman legionaries who fell victim to Goth incursions in the third century. Fortunately for the allied cause, two military commanders of exceptional merit picked up fragments and formed them, eventually, into first-class fighting forces. One of these commanders was British, Major General William Slim, the other American, Major General Joseph Stilwell.

A supremely able and highly imaginative commander, the fifty-year-old Slim exercised that commodity too often lacking in his colleagues: professional objectivity. Wounded at Gallipoli in World War I and again in Mesopotamia shortly after the war, Slim served two extensive postwar tours in the Indian army in addition to normal staff and command assignments. Early in the war, he commanded a brigade in Major General Frank Messervy's famed Gazelle Force, which chased Italians out of East Africa. Again wounded, he recovered to command an Indian division in Syria-Persia-Iraq, from where he was rushed to the Far East.

Even while this stocky, jut-jawed Englishman chewed defeat in trying to hold his corps together during the nine-hundred-mile retreat through Burma, he was analyzing reasons for Japanese success.

Surprise headed the list, along with its corollary, British unpreparedness. But what impressed him most was Japanese use of the jungle. Slim later paid eloquent testimony to enemy quasi-guerrilla tactics:

. . . The Japanese obviously were able to move for several days at a time through jungle that we had regarded as impenetrable. This was not only because they had local Burmese guides, but they traveled lighter than we did and lived much more off the country. Nearly all our transport was mechanical, and this stretched our columns for miles along a single road through the jungle, vulnerable everywhere from air and ground.[1]

To exploit this supreme weakness, the Japanese employed the basic tactic of the hook:

. . . Their standard action was, while holding us in front, to send a mobile force, mainly infantry, on a wide turning movement round our flank through the jungle to come in on our lines of communications. Here, on the single road, up which all our supplies, ammunition, and reinforcements must come, they would establish a "road-block," sometimes with a battalion, sometimes with a regiment. We had few if any reserves in depth—all our troops were in the front line—and we had, therefore, when this happened, to turn about forces from the forward positions to clear the road-block. At this moment the enemy increased his pressure on our weakened front until it crumbled. Time and again the Japanese used these tactics, more often than not successfully, until our troops and commanders began to acquire a road-block mentality which often developed into an inferiority complex.[2]

Such tactics depended on an efficient intelligence organization, which the Japanese founded in part on British unpopularity in Burma. In contrast, the British intelligence system was practically non-existent. Slim later wrote:

. . . It is no exaggeration to say that we had practically no useful or reliable information of enemy strength, movements, or intentions. Our first intimation of a Japanese move was usually the stream of red tracer bullets and the animal yells that announced their arrival on our flank or rear.

In the early fighting,

. . . our only source of information was identification of enemy units by their dead and by documents found on them. Exploitation of even this source

1. Slim, op. cit.
2. Ibid.

was limited because in the whole corps there was only *one* officer who could speak and read Japanese reasonably well. . . .[3]

The Japanese not only depended on Burmese guides, informants and saboteurs (who cut telephone lines), but did not hesitate to employ guerrilla stratagems the more successful because of being outlawed by Western rules for land warfare—and therefore unexpected. Slim described one attack

. . . covered by numerous small parties of hostile Burmans and Japanese, disguised as peaceful villagers. These tactics were difficult to counter, as the countryside was covered by numbers of genuine refugees trying to escape from the battle area. It was always a toss-up for our men whether the group of Burmese men, women, and children, wandering past their positions with their creaking bullock carts, were what they seemed or Japanese with concealed machine-guns.[4]

On other occasions, the Japanese wore uniforms taken from dead soldiers of Burma Rifle regiments.

Only the monsoon halted this fantastic Japanese drive, which, by late spring 1942, had pushed British and Chinese from Burma. Fortunately for the allied cause, several strategic forces intervened to keep Japanese divisions poised on China-India borders, a respite used to reorganize defeated armies and begin the long road back.

Slim realized that a successful return would require tactics never taught in a Western staff college. A successful return demanded extraordinary command adaptability—an abandonment of orthodox thinking in favor of untried and sometimes even unknown tactical procedures.

Slim started putting his ideas to test as commander of 4 Corps. His soldiers, most of whom were Indian but who included Gurkhas, Burmese, and British, had to learn to live in jungle before being able to use it ". . . for concealment, covered movement, and surprise." All units, including medical sections, became responsible for their own security: ". . . there are no non-combatants in jungle warfare."

Unit commanders had to rely on patrols, for ". . . patrolling is the master key to jungle fighting." Commanders also had to practice fluid tactics: they had to get used to having Japanese parties in their rear, and, when this happened, regard not themselves, but the Japanese, as "surrounded."

Officers had to stop thinking in terms of frontal attacks; instead, ". . . attacks should follow hooks and come in from flank or rear, while pressure holds the enemy in front." In defense, ". . . no attempt should be made to hold long continuous lines. Avenues of approach must be covered and enemy penetration between our posts dealt with at once

3. Ibid.
4. Ibid.

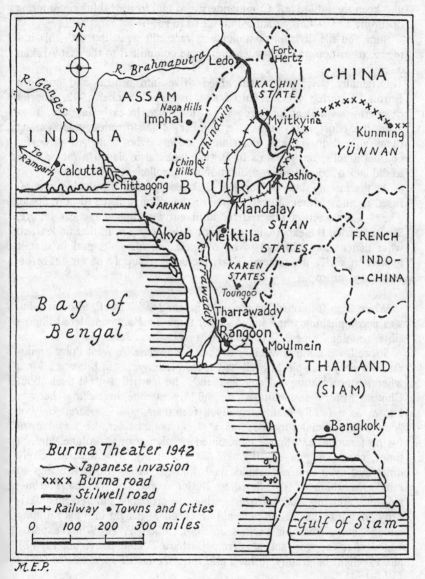

Burma Theater 1942
→ Japanese invasion
×××× Burma road
— Stilwell road
+―+ Railway   • Towns and Cities
0   100   200   300 miles

M.E.P.

by mobile local reserves who have completely reconnoitred the country."

Commanders had to acquire and retain mobility, for ". . . by mobility away from roads, surprise, and offensive action, we must regain

and keep the initiative." Commanders also had to start thinking in terms
of supply by air—bulky road columns had to go.[5]

Slim and his division commanders were still wrestling with this immense transition problem when they were committed to the first Arakan
offensive.

Originally envisaged as an allied drive into central and northern
Burma, it started 4 Corps into action in mid-December 1942, a series
of operations that at first progressed favorably. In early January, however, the effort fell victim to a number of misfortunes, chief among
them a well-dug-in and determined enemy who launched powerful
counterattacks; but sickness in British ranks also played a major role,
as did lack of command co-ordination and insufficient training.

At the last minute, Chiang Kai-shek also proved intractable and refused to allow either Stilwell's force or the Yünnan force to participate.
The 4 Corps action lingered on until early spring—a tactical failure.
Slim regarded the experience as worthwhile, however, in that he learned
what deficiencies still had to be overcome in his units and in that it
tended to verify his tactical ideas, including resupply of an entire division by airdrop.

While Slim fashioned his force, "Vinegar Joe" Stilwell, also in India,
was accomplishing what many Western commanders considered impossible: training Chinese divisions to fight modern warfare.

Stilwell was not a newcomer to the China scene. A West Point graduate, the sixty-year-old Stilwell had spent fifteen years in pre-war China,
where, concentrating on language study, he learned a great deal about
Chinese history and culture. As military attaché in Peking, he was
known as a family man, virtually a teetotaler, who appeared only at
"command" social functions; as a troop commander, he was known
for professional excellence punctuated by picturesque, profane, and, at
times, coarse language. Although tall and lanky, his eyes deceptively
quiet and even morose behind steel-rimmed glasses, Stilwell brings to
mind something of the Smedley Butler, something of the Patton—
vigorous and on occasion overbearing, he probably suffered an inferiority complex; the reader can gain an excellent insight into his thinking
and behavior from his various writings, which T. H. White expertly
edited after the war, and also from Barbara Tuchman's recent (1971)
and excellent biography, *Stilwell and the American Experience in China
1913–1945*.[6]

Although Stilwell was familiar with the Chinese army, he was not
prepared for the scene that greeted him in early 1942, when Chiang

5. Ibid.
6. Joseph W. Stilwell, *The Stilwell Papers* (New York: William Sloane, 1948).
Ed. T. H. White; Barbara Tuchman, *Stilwell and the American Experience in
China 1913–1945* (New York: Macmillan, 1971).

Kai-shek ordered him to take command of two Chinese armies fighting in northern Burma. Finding himself more onlooker than commander, due to jealous Chinese generals, he was appalled at the professional ineptitude and personal corruption that claimed commanders on every level. The experience convinced Stilwell that if the Japanese were to be driven from northern Burma, which was essential to reopen land communications between China and India, he would have to train and equip a new Chinese army.

Stilwell had studied the Chinese military problem before the Japanese invasion. Chiang's four million troops, he knew,

. . . were a starved, sickly, underarmed, misled mass of peasant soldiers whose control and administration was [sic] shot through and through with politics, personal jealousies and incompetence. It was a conscript army; for every soldier who died at the front, ten died of disease or deserted in the rear. The courage of its soldiery was never questioned; many of its individual officers were men of shining integrity—but as an instrument of war it had only a biological usefulness. It reacted, but could not act of itself.[7]

Stilwell realized the impossibility of retraining the entire army. Instead, he wanted to produce thirty "modern" divisions, a plan accepted by Chiang Kai-shek even before the Japanese invasion.

In summer of 1942, Stilwell vigorously pursued this plan. The American military mission in Kunming began to train and equip "Yoke Force," designed to strike into northeastern Burma from Yünnan. In India, Stilwell himself used the nine thousand Chinese survivors of the retreat from Burma as nucleus for a new army to be fleshed out by soldiers flown from Kunming over the Hump. In the event, he received about sixty-six thousand soldiers whom he turned into four divisions.

Stilwell was convinced, and Slim agreed with him, that if the Chinese soldier could be removed from control of corrupt and inefficient officers, he could be trained and equipped to perform as well as any other national, including the Japanese. The British co-operated in Stilwell's plan by furnishing an old Italian-prisoner-of-war camp, Ramgarh, in central India. As White later wrote:

. . . What Stilwell proposed to do was this: to take raw troops, divorce them from the possibility of retreat, abandon fixed supply lines as completely as did Sherman in Georgia, make them dependent on air drops alone, drive them two hundred miles through jungle, swamp, and mountain to conquer a skilful, entrenched and desperate enemy.

Stilwell's accomplishment, like Slim's, has never been fully appreciated in Western military circles. In White's words:

. . . Stilwell's insistence that the use of modern arms was not merely a matter of mechanical know-how, but a matter of discipline, training and military

7. Stilwell, op. cit.

organization, met Chiang's theory head on. It was impossible, felt Stilwell, to graft American instruments of war on the ancient doctrines of the Chinese army and government and win a modern war.[8]

Though close to the mark, White should have gone further. Stilwell's secret was to give the Chinese peasant something to fight for—pride in himself. Mao Tse-tung already had accomplished what Stilwell was trying to accomplish. This was no easy task when dealing with illiterate conscripts commanded by poorly trained and exceedingly corrupt officers, and Stilwell did not fully accomplish it. Chinese officers, in general, proved the most difficult. Feckless, ill-disciplined, and often venal, they forever hindered the best efforts of American instructors. Graft and inefficiency pervaded all levels—Major General Dorn, in charge of training Yoke Force, wrote in what Barbara Tuchman termed desperate jest: ". . . The obvious remedy is to clear out the Chinese Government and start afresh."[9]

Stilwell nonetheless accomplished considerable. Once American instructor teams cleaned up the troops, properly fed, clothed, equipped, and paid them, they offered the simplest possible instruction. Stilwell realistically envisaged less-sophisticated tactics than either Slim or Wingate. Wherever possible, he wished to avoid frontal attacks, both because the Chinese proved hopeless when it came to precise timing required for co-ordinated attacks and because they did not have adequate supporting weapons. Stilwell preferred the original Japanese tactic of establishing a roadblock behind the enemy, then engaging his front to hold him for a flank attack from the jungle. Integral to his plan were irregular units such as Wingate's.

Stilwell and his American training cadres worked swiftly and efficiently. By late 1942, the lanky general believed, perhaps optimistically, that Chinese forces in India and Yünnan could participate effectively in the Slim-Wingate offensive. He had reckoned without Chiang Kai-shek, however. Wanting to retain his forces intact to fight Communists once allies had won the war against Germany and Japan, Chiang refused to release divisions either in Yünnan or India. Failing to sway the Generalissimo, Stilwell could only swear—and keep on training.

Slim and Stilwell were not the only commanders with imagination and flair in India. If they professed a sort of bent military orthodoxy, Brigadier Orde Wingate preached tactical heterodoxy in the Lawrence tradition.

The eldest of seven children, Orde Wingate was the son of an Indian army officer. Raised in a deeply religious English household, he

8. Ibid.; see also F. Eldridge, *Wrath in Burma* (New York: Doubleday, 1946): The British also paid the Chinese and provided uniforms.
9. Tuchman, op. cit.

graduated from the Royal Military Academy in 1923 and became a regular-army artillery officer. After routine garrison service and a six-year stint in the eastern Sudan, Wingate was ordered to Palestine as a staff intelligence officer.[10]

Here he made a service reputation by introducing counterinsurgency tactics against Arab terrorists who were raiding Jewish settlements and blowing up oil lines. Noting the almost total failure of orthodox tactics, Wingate argued successfully for small unit patrol tactics at night. Against considerable opposition, he himself organized "Special Night Squads" composed of Jewish reserve constables commanded by British officers and NCOs—a concept that enjoyed impressive success under Wingate's undeniably charismatic leadership. Badly wounded during one action, Wingate was awarded the DSO and dubbed the Lawrence of Judea. From stubby beard to ancient tropical helmet to grease-stained uniform, he played the part—sometimes fulsomely.

While Wingate's tactics could scarcely be faulted—the reader will find the entire fascinating story in Christopher Sykes's comprehensive biography *Orde Wingate*—his means of achieving tactical success were highly suspect: He indulged in one tantrum after another, even against commanders favorable to his views; if a recruit misbehaved either in training or on patrol, Wingate was apt to strike him; when a *Kibbutz* leader walked on a terrorist mine and was killed, Wingate retaliated with a daylight raid in which innocent villagers were shot. Sykes has explained these actions as those of a highly strung, impulsive man of unquestionable talent.[11] Those readers with extensive military experience will reply that good leaders can obtain success with more-acceptable methods.

Even worse, however, Wingate early became an ardent Zionist, convinced that Palestine must become a state with its own national army. At times, his zeal for Zionism brought him uncomfortably close to treasonable disclosure of confidential information to Jewish leaders. Desirable as it might have been for these leaders to have the information, it surely was not the function of a captain, a junior staff officer, to provide it.

Wingate increased his reputation in the brief Ethiopian campaign in 1940–41 when he organized, trained, and commanded Gideon Force, an irregular unit of natives under British officers. Again, his tactical thinking could scarcely be faulted. But he erred operationally in trying to use camels where camels could not be used, and he also erred in insisting on an initial cross-country march:

. . . He owned after that he was wrong. He was too much under the influence of preconceived ideas formed in Palestine and he overlooked the fact

10. Christopher Sykes, *Orde Wingate* (London: Collins, 1959); see also L. Mosley, *Gideon Goes to War* (London: Arthur Barker, 1955).
11. Sykes, op. cit.

that marching on compass-bearing was one thing in well-mapped country and another in country for which the maps were unreliable. He wore out his men, beasts and machines unnecessarily.[12]

However, in subsequent operations against Italian garrisons, he displayed considerable tactical agility, relying largely on mobility and frequently deception to gain tactical surprise. He preached and wrote a qualitative approach to irregular warfare, for instance calling for small attacks: ". . . twenty men is a good number to work with, but fifteen is better than twenty, and at night ten is better than fifteen." He stressed psychological warfare and he again proved the charismatic leader who displayed unquestionable personal courage.

Two other factors entered, however, in assessment of Wingate's contribution to the campaign. The first was enemy weakness. Italian defenders did not provide a test of arms. The British advanced, the Italians retreated. While Gideon Force was running out of camels and otherwise suffering enormous hardships in cross-country advance, two orthodox British forces were making excellent progress with much less effort. General Cunningham's force of three divisions advanced over a thousand miles in thirty days, a feat not many guerrilla forces could equal.[13]

The second was personal weakness. In Cairo and Khartoum before the campaign, Wingate continued to behave strangely and often abominably:

. . . Among many extraordinary affectations he took to wearing a miniature alarm clock strapped to his wrist so that he could time his interviews exactly by the ringing of the bell. He took again to brushing his body instead of bathing and caused much amazement to some people with whom he had business by receiving them naked in his room in the Grand Hotel, brushing himself thoroughly the while. . . . His rudeness now went to grotesque lengths. . . .[14]

His temper continued short and with it physical cruelty appeared. An interpreter's mistake caused him to knock the man down with blows of a hide whip; he struck an Ethiopian soldier wrongly turned out. He fought almost constantly with colleagues, juniors or seniors. He fell out almost at once with the able Daniel Sandford, a man of extensive experience in Ethiopia who masterminded the campaign and who served during it as the emperor's political and military adviser. As had happened with Zionism, the emperor's cause became Wingate's cause, and he grew convinced that his own country was defeating the emperor's best interests.

In Cairo, after the campaign, bitter and ill from malaria, he wrote a

12. Ibid.
13. Ibid.
14. Ibid.

lengthy and vitriolic report that, according to his friend and protector, Wavell, ". . . would almost have justified my placing him under arrest for insubordination."[15] After detailing his qualitative theory of guerrilla warfare—which, he argued, contrasted with Lawrence's saturation theory—Wingate tore into authorities who, in his opinion, had sabotaged Gideon Force. Attacked from all sides, Wingate continued to nurse real and imagined grievances, a hideous period that ended with a serious attempt at suicide.[16]

After lengthy recuperation in England, he rewrote his report and expanded his thinking into a proposal for "Long Range Penetration" operations. Friends saw that this material reached Winston Churchill and the new Chief of the Imperial General Staff, Sir Alan Brooke. Their influence, in part, brought orders in early 1942 for Wingate to report to Wavell's staff in Burma ". . . for operational and liaison duty with the Chinese in Burma."[17]

Wingate was thirty-nine years old when he arrived, shortly after the fall of Rangoon. A stocky, powerful-looking man of medium height, he impressed most people with a sort of Old Testament melancholy and a professional intensity that at times bordered on the fanatic. Wavell appears to have backed Wingate's long-range penetration concept. A young major who became intimately associated with Wingate, a regular officer named Bernard Fergusson, later described the plan in his splendid book *Beyond the Chindwin:*

. . . Briefly, his [Wingate's] point was that the enemy was most vulnerable far beyond his lines, where his troops, if he had any at all, were of inferior quality. Here a small force could wreak havoc out of all proportion to its numbers. If it should be surprised, it could disintegrate into smaller prearranged parties to baffle pursuit, and meet again at a rendezvous fifteen to twenty miles farther on its route. Supply should be by air, communication by wireless: these two weapons had not yet been properly exploited. His proposal was to cut the enemy's supply line, destroy his dumps, tie up troops unprofitably far behind the line in the endeavor to protect these vulnerable areas, and generally to help the army proper on to its objectives.[18]

Wavell gave Wingate, as nucleus of a force, remnants of a guerrilla organization commanded by a brave and resourceful officer, Michael Calvert. Three battalions brought the new command to brigade strength: the 77th Indian Infantry Brigade, a heterogeneous force of about three thousand British, Gurkha, African, and Burmese soldiers that Wingate divided into seven lightly equipped mobile columns. Each column in-

15. Charles J. Rolo, *Wingate's Raiders* (London: G. G. Harrap, 1944).
16. Sykes, op. cit.
17. Ibid.
18. Bernard Fergusson, *Beyond the Chindwin* (London: Collins, 1962); see also Rolo, op. cit.; Michael Calvert, *Prisoners of Hope* (London: Jonathan Cape, 1952).

cluded a specialist guerrilla force, a signal section, and a small RAF section ". . . to direct, organize, and advise on supply by parachute."

Wingate's first operation was scheduled to complement the Arakan offensive earlier described. But when Chiang Kai-shek refused to let either Stilwell's force or the Yünnan force participate, Wavell, in early February 1943, canceled Wingate's part in the operation.

Wingate would not be put off. In vigorous prose, he offered Wavell what both believed were convincing arguments:

. . . if the expedition were cancelled, "the vast majority of Staff officers who denied the theory of Long Range Penetration would . . . continue to deny it"; the brigade stood in peak condition and could only decline if not committed to action; the British would remain ignorant of Japanese military methods unless Wingate provoked them to action; the Japanese were apt to overrun Fort Hertz in the north as well as to implant themselves on both sides of the Chindwin; without "the serious interruption of enemy plans and confusion in his military economy throughout Burma," such as 77 Brigade would bring about, the Japanese would be "free to develop offensive intentions."[19]

Wavell should have questioned Wingate's logic, which contradicted his tactical concept. The finest brigade in the world could scarcely prove a theory if the major operational ingredient—an attacking army—was missing. In addition, only two months earlier, Wingate had expressed serious doubt as to his brigade's readiness for what in anyone's tactical book was a major operational commitment.

So far as Japanese military methods went, Slim and other veterans of the Burma retreat were sufficiently familiar with the enemy to respect him—as we have seen, the experience converted Slim to a new tactical concept. If doubt still existed as to enemy fighting qualities, Wavell or Wingate only had to read U. S. Marine Corps operational reports from the Pacific war, or from their own 4 Corps in Arakan.

Wingate's fears concerning Fort Hertz were more imaginary than real, at least according to Ian Fellowes-Gordon, who commanded a guerrilla company to the south and who later wrote that the first enemy attempt to "clean out" the area, in December 1942, was easily defeated.[20] Subsequent attempts made but slight progress, and, from the enemy standpoint, the area remained of secondary priority until Stilwell's campaign to capture Myitkyina.

At this time, the Japanese were holding Burma with at least four divisions, battle-tested, dug in. The argument that a small brigade, not yet battle-tested (what military men call "blooded"), could divert and de-

19. Sykes, op. cit.
20. Ian Fellowes-Gordon, *Amiable Assassins—The Story of the Kachin Guerrillas of North Burma* (London: Robert Hale, 1957).

feat major units was a totally unjustified conceit, the more so since the brigade would operate in an area of but slight tactical importance.

Wavell nonetheless accepted Wingate's arguments and allowed the brigade to move out. Of subsequent accounts, my own favorite is Fergusson's, in *Beyond the Chindwin,* but Calvert's account is also worth while, as is Sykes's.

The columns crossed Chindwin River in two groups. Complete with bullocks, elephants, mules, horses, and a few messenger dogs, the men pushed through two hundred miles of some of the most difficult jungle terrain in the world. After numerous difficulties, including brushes with the enemy that scattered two columns, the remainder of the Chindits, as they would become known, reached the Mandalay-Myitkyina railroad. Here Calvert's and Fergusson's columns blew some bridges and cut the line in several places.

The columns then crossed the Irrawaddy in an attempt to cut the Mandalay-Lashio railroad. By now, however, a good many men were nearing the end of their strength; the columns had stirred up the enemy and were on the run, which hindered scheduled airdrops, already made difficult by terrain and weather. The sick and exhausted columns disintegrated into small parties that eventually struggled back across the Chindwin. Some eight hundred troops did not return. Of the 2,182 who reached India, only six hundred were sufficiently fit ". . . for active soldiering again."[21]

From the operational standpoint, Wingate's first raid was a supreme and expensive flop, but Slim, Fergusson, and others were correct in awarding it a psychological value reminiscent of that given Doolittle's expensive air raid on Tokyo in 1942. Blown up by army and press into major victory proportions, it flashed a beacon of hope at a very discouraging time for England, and even Slim concluded that it ". . . was worth all the hardship and sacrifice his men endured. . . ."[22]

Although this must be a debatable conclusion—it is difficult to believe that England would have *surrendered* without the Wingate "success" —it unquestionably improved national morale. That would have been all right, but, unfortunately, people who should have known better, including Alan Brooke, Winston Churchill, and Wingate himself, started believing their own propaganda. In making an operational mountain out of a mountebank, the British and eventually the Americans only threw more grit into an already groaning tactical machine.

21. Sykes, op. cit.; see also Bernard Fergusson, *Trumpet in the Hall* (London: Collins, 1970).

22. Slim, op. cit.

Chapter 49

Wingate's fame • South-East Asia Command • Slim inherits
Fourteenth Army • Slim's genius • Wingate's new "stronghold" concept • Slim's second Arakan offensive • Wingate's
second offensive • His death • Stilwell's northern command
• Merrill's Marauders • The Kachins • Japanese occupation
excesses • Aung San deserts the Japanese • The Karen guerrilla offensive • Japanese evacuation • The postwar political
situation

THANKS to cooked press reports and tired allies who embraced
them, Wingate's failure brought him considerable fame and even influence. He returned to England a hero. Already familiar to important members of the Establishment, he basked in strategic and tactical heterodoxy,
a fulsome period capped by Winston Churchill's taking him (and his
wife) to the Quebec Conference.

Already winged, Wingate's fortunes soared. As Christopher Sykes
has pointed out, he became ". . . a sort of point of agreement" between
Churchill and his discordant chiefs of staff, and also between British and
American chiefs. On the voyage to Canada, he persuaded Churchill and
the British chiefs to favor an offensive in Burma—a plan calling for a
second Chindit expedition of six brigades, or some 26,500 men. The
British chiefs went so far as to specifically allocate units, including
Slim's one jungle-trained division, to Wingate's command and to rec-
ommend to New Delhi that Wingate become the army commander in

Burma! Although Auchinleck firmly squashed the latter notion, at Quebec President Roosevelt and the Joint Chiefs of Staff embraced Wingate's operational proposals.[1] General Henry Arnold, chief of the U. S.
Air Force, personally promised him air support. After ordering special
arms and equipment in America and London, Wingate returned to
Delhi, an acting major general holding right of direct communication to
Churchill whenever necessary!—an unfortunate instruction on the prime
minister's part, an act that in effect belied trust in appointed commanders.

Wingate's cup was full, running over, for the Quebec Conference also
ordered a new South-East Asia Command (SEAC), headed by Admiral
Lord Louis Mountbatten, who knew and supported Wingate. In late
1943, Mountbatten took over, with Stilwell as deputy commander
(Stilwell remained Chiang Kai-shek's chief of staff as well as commander
of American forces), and SEAC became responsible for allied operations in Burma, Ceylon, Malaya, the Dutch East Indies, Siam, and Indochina.[2]

One of Mountbatten's early acts in autumn of 1943 created Fourteenth Army, with Slim in command. This was no particular plum:

. . . including Stilwell's Chinese, the greatest number of divisions I ever had
under my command in action at one time was eighteen. They fought on a
front of seven hundred miles, in four groups, separated by great distances,
with no lateral communications between them and beyond tactical support
of one another.[3]

Fourteenth Army units had known only defeat. Composed predominantly of Indian soldiers, most of its neglected divisions stood bewildered and confused, highly unsure of themselves. The army lacked
thousands of items needed to live and fight. Malaria, dysentery, and
other tropical diseases ravaged entire units.

Here was an army that, in Frederick the Great's words, was ". . . fit
only to be shown to the enemy at a distance." In converting it to a viable
offensive force, Slim's accomplishment ranks high in military annals.

1. Roosevelt loved the unorthodox, as did Churchill, possibly as one means of
deflating pompous admirals and generals, but undoubtedly also from standpoint
of political appeal. Inspired by his son James, a marine officer strongly influenced
by Evans Carlson (see Chapters 27 and 39) President Roosevelt foisted the Raider-
battalion concept on the Marine Corps, which did not want it, the argument being
that this was merely making elite units out of units already elite. Roosevelt won,
but when A. A. Vandegrift became commandant he soon disbanded such ancillary
units as the Raiders, Paratroopers, and Beach-Jumpers.
2. Vice-Admiral the Earl Mountbatten, *Report to the Combined Chiefs of Staff
by the Supreme Allied Commander South-East Asia, 1943–1945* (London: HMSO,
1951).
3. Slim, op. cit.

What was his secret?

In two words, leadership and simplicity. Like Scipio Aemilianus in Spain twenty-one centuries earlier, Slim splintered (and sometimes burned) the dead wood that invariably accumulates in large commands. What was left received massive doses of conditioning already injected into 4 Corps. Every man in Fourteenth Army was put through weapons training: ". . . the whole headquarters from the Corps Commander downwards went through qualifying courses in rifle, pistol, Bren gun, bayonet, mortar, and grenade. . . ." All units conditioned themselves to life in the jungle. Slim rightly charged unit commanders with responsibility for their men's health. In relatively short time, preventive medicine drastically lowered malaria incidence as well as other jungle diseases. To vary monotonous and not particularly healthful rations, corps and divisions started duck farms and fish saltings besides cultivating ". . . huge market gardens almost in the battle line."[4]

Slim emphasized patrolling as the key to jungle fighting. In time, training-patrols gave way to reconnaissance patrols, then small combat patrols, and finally unit offensives in such preponderant strength against minor targets as to guarantee victory and thus build a feeling of superiority. But training concentrated on the small unit:

. . . Companies, even platoons, under junior leaders became the basic units of the jungle. Out of sight of one another, often out of touch, their wireless blanketed by hills, they marched and fought on their own, often for days at a time. They frequently approached the battle in scattered columns, as they did for the crossings of the Irrawaddy, and concentrated on the battlefield. . . .[5]

To serve these units, Slim and his staff worked out greatly simplified supply procedures based on airdrops. Aircraft were never in generous supply, and unit commanders had to reorient their entire thinking in order to survive and fight well. Instead of relying on elaborate bridging units, for example, commanders taught men to swim and to make rafts from jungle materials; army engineers commandeered old boats and launches and built new ones to support infantry river crossings and to wage guerrilla warfare along waterways; airplanes used parachutes made out of jute to supply columns, and on occasion used such makeshift containers as old inner tubes to drop water. Resupply by air became standard operating procedure, and, in consequence, greatly increased ground mobility by drastically reducing supply columns and echelons.

Slim pared staffs to the bone, cut paper work to a minimum. At his own headquarters,

. . . every fortnight each section was ordered to sort its papers and destroy everything not essential. My order, rigidly enforced, was, "When in doubt,

4. Ibid.
5. Ibid.

burn." We constantly practised moving until the drill for it was thoroughly mastered; we could pack in a couple of hours and open up a properly camouflaged working headquarters in the bush in less. A large part of headquarters I kept permanently in tents and we frequently moved out into the jungle for several days at a time. . . .[6]

Applying a carefully thought-out formula of leadership based on spiritual, intellectual, and material factors, and on years of experience, Slim infused his army with unity of purpose, a sort of command osmosis absorbed by the most junior commander, who understood, respected, and acted upon the army commander's *intention:*

. . . this acting without orders, in anticipation of orders, or without waiting for approval, yet always within the overall intention, must become second nature in any form of warfare where formations do not fight closely *en cadre,* and must go down to the smallest units. It requires in the higher command a corresponding flexibility of mind, confidence in its subordinates, and the power to make its intentions clear right through the force.[7]

Slim was still training his army when the allied chiefs, meeting at Cairo in November 1943, agreed to an expanded Arakan offensive. But at the Tehran Conference immediately following, the grandiose scheme of multipronged invasion fell victim to various shortages. When the Combined Chiefs canceled part of the plan, Chiang Kai-shek immediately withdrew Chinese participation. Instead of the reconquest of Burma, Fourteenth Army, including Wingate's new force, undertook a limited offensive beginning early in 1944.

As with the earlier Arakan offensive, this change of plan pulled the rug out from under Wingate's long-range penetration concept. To save his operational skin, he now came to the surprising conclusion that his group, suitably reinforced, should provide the main effort by operating from a series of "strongholds" established miles behind enemy lines. A "stronghold" would serve two purposes: by defending an airfield, it would provide an administrative-supply base for his columns; by constituting a distinct threat, it would attract the enemy to attack a defended point. In Wingate's words, ". . . the stronghold is a machan overlooking a kid tied up to entice the Japanese tiger."[8]

Wingate's new concept was expensive in men and material. Primarily for this reason, Slim objected to it; the Combined Chiefs had not improved his temper by allocating his one ". . . completely jungle-trained division" to Wingate's command. Slim also argued that the Japanese were not going to be so easily drawn from their major defensive complex and that even if they were, Wingate's people ". . . were neither trained nor equipped to fight pitched battles, offensive or defensive."[9]

6. Ibid.
7. Ibid.
8. Otto Heilbronn, op. cit.
9. Slim, op. cit.

The forceful and politically powerful Wingate nonetheless sold the idea to Mountbatten, who authorized ". . . ever-increasing scales of defensive equipment, artillery, anti-aircraft guns, mines, machine-guns, sandbags, and the rest."[10] To transport and supply this miniature army, the U. S. Air Force provided Wingate with Philip Cochran's special unit ". . . containing not only fighters and light bombers for close support, but transport aircraft, gliders, light planes for inter-communication and evacuation of wounded." This caused added hard feeling in SEAC and in Tenth Air Force:

. . . It was represented very strongly by the air staffs, American and British, that it was uneconomical permanently to lock up what was an appreciable proportion of our total air strength in Burma in support of one subsidiary operation.[11]

Other responsible officers expressed certain misgivings. Bernard Fergusson logically feared ". . . the threatened repetition of the starvation conditions of the year before [the first Chindwin operation] and of renewed reprisals against our Kachin and other helpers within Burma." Wingate had to argue vigorously with Fergusson to keep him in command of 16th Brigade. Wingate's expansionist theories also alarmed Mountbatten—not surprising, since Wingate argued that if the present operation succeeded, he would need twenty to twenty-five brigades, or some one hundred thousand troops, not only to occupy Indochina but to join hands with the Americans in the Pacific![12]

Despite this infighting, which reached majestic proportions, Slim kicked off the second Arakan offensive with a series of probing efforts. These met only limited success and soon stung the Japanese into a counterinvasion of India. Although this surprised him, units that once had folded and fled now held and fought back. The enemy penetrated as far as Imphal. They paid heavily for their presumption. One major strike force lost almost its total of seven thousand. Slim himself later marked the Arakan battle as ". . . one of the historic successes of British arms. It was the turning-point of the Burma campaign. . . ."[13]

Wingate's force meanwhile had gone into action in early March, two brigades being airlifted and one marching into the interior of northern Burma. For the most part, the columns performed very well in this second offensive, Fergusson's 16th Brigade, for example, covering some 450 miles of incredibly difficult jungle terrain.[14] On March 12, Wingate wired an optimistic progress report directly to Churchill and concluded:

10. Ibid.
11. Ibid.
12. Sykes, op. cit.
13. Slim, op. cit.
14. Bernard Fergusson, *The Wild Green Earth* (London: Collins, 1946).

". . . Enemy completely surprised. Situation most promising if exploited."[15]

In the following days, the brigades continued to consolidate their strongholds. The operation was still in a crucial stage, however, when, on March 23, Wingate took off from Imphal in a Mitchell bomber which crashed with no survivors.

His successor, Major General W. D. A. Lentaigne, continued the operation, which, lacking the simultaneous advance of a regular army, deteriorated into a series of virtually independent actions. In early May, SEAC ordered the brigades to evacuate.

While Slim and Wingate were committing their forces, Stilwell was buzzing between Delhi, Ramgarh, and Chungking in desperate effort to launch an offensive from the north. Finally gaining Chiang Kai-shek's approbation, Stilwell started his divisions moving southeast from Ledo in April 1944. His Northern Combat Area Command comprised three brigades, each consisting of one American battalion and two Chinese battalions, supported by light tanks and aircraft. Integral to the operation was a U.S. medium-range penetration unit, Merrill's Marauders, trained to fight primarily in jungle. As the entire force moved south, it would also find itself fronted and flanked by friendly Kachin guerrillas.

Merrill's Marauders had started life as the 5307th Composite Unit Provisional, assigned to Orde Wingate's command. With considerable difficulty, Stilwell had brought about its transfer to his command. One veteran later described the unit in terms that belied its code-name "Galahad":

. . . It was 3,000 infantrymen so recruited as to ensure that they would exhibit the extremities of human character, the worst as well as the best, the best as well as the worst. It was a band of men who were unready and ill-prepared for the mission they had and who lived with fear. It was an organization that was never given time to organize, that was caught up in historical currents and crosscurrents far beyond its control or even understanding, that was mismanaged, that was driven until the accumulation of hardships and strain and the seeds of corruption it contained brought about its undoing.[16]

Colonel (later Major General) Frank Merrill, who had been Stilwell's G-3, or operations officer, commanded the unit, which attempted to snake behind the Japanese and strike from the flanks. As with Wingate's columns, American infantrymen soon began to tire and then flounder in difficult terrain and climate. Although they performed good work, the Marauders lasted only about a hundred days—and their life-span probably would have been shorter but for Kachin guerrillas.

15. Sykes, op. cit.
16. Charlton Ogburn, *The Marauders* (New York: Harper & Brothers, 1959).

Originally under British command, the Kachins had been operating out of Fort Hertz since early in the war. Known as Northern Kachin Levies, or NKL, the guerrilla companies, of about 125 men, fanned out quite far south, where each carved out a drop area and turned to performing a twofold mission: gathering intelligence and killing as many Japanese as possible. Although the factors that allowed them to survive —vastness of terrain coupled with general enemy weakness—adversely influenced their mission, they nevertheless performed well, soon becoming skillful practitioners of guerrilla warfare. One company commander, Ian Fellowes-Gordon, later recalled his experiences in a book, *Amiable Assassins.*[17] Working south of Sumprabum, a town occupied on and off by Japanese, his patrols frequently encountered the enemy. In fighting them, Fellowes-Gordon relied primarily on jungle ambushes and on a simple booby trap made by a grenade with a special instantaneous fuse cupped between a piece of split bamboo and tripped by a wire. He also noted that

. . . every N.K.L. position had, as a matter of course, a large number of sharp bamboo stakes projecting from the ground and concealed in the undergrowth round the position. When the Japs were fired on, they invariably flung themselves down at the side of the path or the road and the number transfixed by our *panjis* was often more than those killed by our firearms. . . .[18]

In December 1943, a theater reorganization placed NKL under Stilwell's Northern Combat Area Command. As Detachment 101 under OSS command, the companies performed invaluable service, during Stilwell's advance in spring of 1944, by harassing enemy units, dislocating communications, and by guiding Merrill's columns through the tortuous terrain. In the final push on Myitkyina, two Kachin groups working with Wingate's columns effectively prevented enemy reinforcement, while still another unit led the strike column almost to the airfield at Myitkyina without arousing the enemy.[19]

Detachment 101, according to two American writers, Alsop and Braden, in their earlier-cited work, *Sub Rosa,* continued to grow to a strength ". . . of more than 500 Americans, with organized guerrilla bands of 8,500 native Kachins." In the war's last stages, which saw retreat of the Japanese 56th Division, Kachins fell on enemy columns, killing and wounding thousands. Had Chinese Yoke Force moving down from Yünnan lived up to tactical expectations, the joint effort could have annihilated the Japanese division. In the event, Yoke Force, restrained by Chiang Kai-shek, who wanted to save it for postwar purposes, moved like molasses.

17. Fellowes-Gordon, *supra.*
18. Ibid.
19. Alsop and Braden, op. cit.; see also R. H. Smith, op. cit.

The primary secret of OSS success, according to Alsop and Braden, was the difference in attitude between OSS and SOE officers vis-à-vis the Kachins, who ". . . hated the Burmese, the Chinese, and the British, with varying degrees of intensity." According to Detachment 101 veterans,

. . . unlike the British, they did not treat them as "natives." The Americans were, they said, quite natural and open with the Kachins, asked their advice, which was frequently badly needed, and even on occasion slapped them affectionately on their bare backs. The Kachins, after their initial amazement, reacted highly favorably to this treatment, and took the Americans to their hearts.[20]

While no one can doubt the schism between American and British social behavior, including that exhibited toward aborigines, this is much too pat an explanation. British officers had worked with Kachins since mid-1942 and, as related, had built them into a formidable guerrilla force by the time Americans took over. The authors should also have pointed out the operational freedom and support accorded to OSS. SOE never enjoyed such financial and logistic benefits. Camaraderie is important, as long as it is sincere, but so is gold—and so, in some cases, is opium.

Desperately needing porters to carry supply from drop areas to ambush sites, the British had procured them by paying in strictly rationed quantities of opium—a disgusting and pernicious practice best forgotten by SOE. OSS not only picked up the practice but began to pay guerrillas as well as porters in opium[21]—a practice that undoubtedly proved more popular than even jocular American backslapping.

Political considerations also entered the picture. To the OSS, northern Burma was a place to punch a road through—one shudders at what our officers whispered to Kachin chiefs about postwar independence and other political goodies. To the British, Burma was a possession they would continue to govern after the war, so British officers could promise nothing to tribesmen.

Nor do the authors point out that the British enjoyed considerable success in working with other Burma tribes. Slim relied on intelligence provided by "V" force in Arakan, where British officers led small units of Chin tribesmen. Wingate also used "Dahforce," which consisted of Kachins led by British officers; the independent Lushai Brigade ". . . operated for six months . . . across two hundred miles of jungle mountains, against the enemy flank and rear," operations greatly aided by Shan tribesmen [22]

But the most important British guerrilla success occurred in the South

20. Alsop and Braden, op. cit.
21. Fellowes-Gordon, op. cit.
22. Slim, op. cit.

and not only involved Karens but also the Burmese puppet army, supposedly controlled by the Japanese.

The Japanese quickly disillusioned the Thakins, the Burmese dissidents led by Aung San. Not only did Tokyo refuse to declare Burmese independence, but it disbanded the Burmese Independence Army. In its place, the Japanese established the Burma Defense Army, a force of five to eight thousand, titularly headed by General Aung San but actually controlled by Japanese advisers backed by military forces.[23] Similarly, a puppet government under Dr. Ba Maw exercised no real civil power. This was held by a Japanese military government, which ". . . treated Burma as if it were an occupied enemy territory."[24]

But where Ba Maw and his followers accepted the status quo, Aung San again rebelled. As early as May 1942—shortly after the fall of Mandalay—he sent a lieutenant to India to ask British help in establishing an underground movement. Although this led to nothing except intense criticism from other nationalists, his judgment was vindicated as Japanese occupation continued. Professor Htin Aung, himself scarcely pro-British, wrote that three years of Japanese rule proved ". . . more irksome than some sixty years of British rule."[25]

As in the Philippines, Japanese behavior in Burma became so stupid as to defy credulity. Military police of a Gestapo type controlled major cities. A minor traffic violation by a cyclist earned a slap in the face; if a girl hesitated to show a cholera-inoculation card, a Japanese military policeman would pull up her skirt in full view of the public to search for inoculation marks on her buttocks. Arrests, beatings, tortures, and forced-labor camps became the order of the day. In Professor Htin Aung's words, ". . . the Japanese imposed a reign of terror."

Meanwhile, Aung San had organized a secret anti-Fascist league comprising most of his old followers but including nationalist and Communist components as well as a considerable number of Karen hill tribesmen, although the extent of Aung San's control of the latter is still obscure.[26] In late 1944, Aung San again contacted the British to ask for money and arms. Although SOE was actively at work organizing and arming Karen tribes, its officers wanted to help Aung San as much as possible. But civil-affairs staff officers, influenced by the Burmese government-in-exile, opposed giving aid on grounds that Aung San's organization ". . . especially after the liberation of Burma would be more trouble than use. . . ."[27] Mountbatten and Slim decided in favor of SOE, however. Slim later wrote:

23. Sweet-Escott, op. cit.
24. Htin Aung, op. cit.
25. Ibid.
26. Slim, op. cit., stated that he did not control the Karens; see also, Sweet-Escott, op. cit.; see also Mountbatten, op. cit.
27. Slim, op. cit.

. . . I did not expect the B.N.A. [Burmese National Army] to exert any serious influence on the campaign, but I hoped they would—as in fact they did—occasionally cut up stragglers, harass small parties, and ambush vehicles, but I made no changes in my plans because of any help expected from them.[28]

In the event, Slim received a great deal of intelligence from this secret force; according to one authority, Operation Nation

. . . provided some eighty percent of all the intelligence received from Japanese-occupied Burma, and played a worth while part in mopping up enemy units left behind in the rapid advance of the Fourteenth Army.[29]

Slim also received a great deal of help from Karens, who, contacted by British liaison teams, had been partially armed and equipped in early 1945. During Fourteenth Army's advance south from Meiktila, this guerrilla force prevented a Japanese division from reinforcing the key town of Toungoo. Once Slim controlled Toungoo, his Dakota planes supplied the guerrillas with over thirteen hundred tons of supplies, a miraculous figure when compared to aid previously furnished. Despite enemy pressures from all sides, Karen force continued to grow to about twelve thousand strong while effectively harassing Japanese who were trying to fall back on Moulmein. Blair estimated that this force killed about 12,500 Japanese while indirectly accounting for many more during final Japanese retreats.[30]

The Japanese left Burma in a terrible mess. Slim later wrote that

. . . insecurity and dacoity [brigandage] were rife. Great acreages had gone out of cultivation, while trade had vanished with the breakdown of communications and the loss of security. The almost complete absence of consumer goods had spun the Japanese paper currency into wild inflation. The whole population was short of clothing, necessities, and above all of food. Indeed, large sections of it were on the verge of starvation. Towns had been burnt and many were deserted, their inhabitants having taken to the jungle where they lived hazardously in miserable destitution. The Japanese throughout their occupation had done little or nothing to meet the essential needs of the civil population. Even where bombs and battles had spared them, public utilities, water supplies, and roads had, through Japanese indifference, deteriorated to a shocking degree.[31]

Nor was the political situation happy. At the approach of allied forces, Ba Maw and followers fled to the Japanese camp. For all practical purposes, Aung San, commanding general of the Burmese National Army,

28. Ibid.
29. Blair, op. cit.
30. Ibid.; see also Sweet-Escott, op. cit.
31. Slim, op. cit.

held real power. Wisely recognizing this, Slim soon sent for the young nationalist leader. At their first interview, Aung San ". . . began to take rather a high hand," an attitude eventually dispelled by Slim, who not only held powerful cards but evinced an obvious concern for the war-torn country.

Nor was the dialogue then and later one-sided. In Slim's words:

. . . I was impressed by Aung San. He was not the ambitious, unscrupulous guerrilla leader I had expected. He was certainly ambitious and meant to secure for himself a dominant position in post-war Burma, but I judged him to be a genuine patriot and a well-balanced realist. . . . I have always felt that, with proper treatment, Aung San would have proved a Burmese Smuts.[32]

With Mountbatten's blessing, Slim attempted to woo this important personality. Professor Htin Aung concluded that the British ". . . behaved as true liberators and treated the Burmese with sympathy and consideration. General Aung San and his Burmese troops were even absorbed into the British forces."[33] This arrangement continued under a British military governor, Major General Hubert Rance, who wisely recognized Burmese political aspirations and dealt reasonably with Aung San's new and powerful party, the Anti-Fascist People's Freedom League (AFPFL), which was rapidly becoming the core of a new national congress.

By the time of Japanese surrender, British and Burmese were working more or less together to put the country right. Htin Aung later wrote that, at this time, Aung San and his party were still aiming at dominion status ". . . rather than full independence."

Unfortunately, the policy of moderation and conciliation practiced by the British military soon gave way to a civil policy of vindictiveness and stubbornness. Although the British managed to avoid bloodshed, they quickly lost control and were soon forced to grant the unhappy country its independence.

32. Ibid.
33. Htin Aung, op. cit.

Chapter 50

China in World War II • Chiang Kai-shek's strategy • American aid • Continued Japanese gains • Chiang's government and army • Chiang and Roosevelt • Stilwell versus Chiang and Claire Chennault • The Miles mission • SACO operations • Miles's failure • Mao Tse-tung's strategy and tactics • The coalition problem • Patrick Hurley's mission • The Dixie Mission • Mao's increasing strength • Stilwell's relief • Wedemeyer takes over • The deteriorating Nationalist position • The Yalta conference and the "Far Eastern Agreement" • Mao prepares to strike

FROM THE STANDPOINT of guerrilla operations, China also proved disappointing—perhaps the inevitable result of conflicting interests both there and abroad. Western leaders regarded the war as an all-out battle against Germany and Japan, and naturally assumed that Chinese leaders would do everything in their power to defeat the common enemy.

But Chiang Kai-shek and Mao Tse-tung regarded World War II as but an interlude in civil war. Each believed that America ultimately would defeat Japan. They saw themselves, as Dr. Griffith has observed, ". . . in the situation of those ancient ministers who craftily 'used barbarians to control barbarians.' "[1]

Despite intensive American efforts, Chiang and Mao devoted far more effort to husbanding men and resources for the postwar showdown than in fighting Japanese. Although the veneer of rapprochement ap-

1. Griffith (CPLA), *supra*.

peared between Nationalist and Communist camps, civil war continued to manifest itself in a variety of divisive ways.

Failure of American officials from President Roosevelt on down to grasp this disappointing fact and take appropriate countermeasures led to a disastrous policy which indirectly played a significant role in Chiang's demise on the mainland of China.

To review briefly, Chiang faced real trouble by December 7, 1941. For two years, Japanese armies had controlled Manchuria, northern China, and important cities in the Southeast; Mao and the Communists controlled a large area in the Northwest. Nationalist strategy, as determined by Chiang and a newly created emergency body, the Supreme National Defense Council, ". . . was one of hoarding strength and waiting, keeping the army intact for one final smashing offensive."[2]

Considering the disorganized condition of government and military, this strategy might have been necessary. But it carried an immediate and costly price tag. As Professor Harrison has pointed out,

. . . the official defense of China depended upon the Chinese civil population, *without* the army, to take the blows and to act as the buffer between the enemy and the Nationalist forces. Thus, after 1939 the Kuomintang fought a siege warfare from South China and abandoned North China to the Communist forces, who were quite prepared to wage guerrilla warfare with the help of the Chinese civil population.[3]

Chiang's strategy seemed quite clear: to trade space for time, time to enable the army to rest and reorganize. His supply lines to the West remained open while his political piano tinkled louder and louder—tunes calculated to shame Washington and arouse American public opinion in his favor. Roosevelt already had tried to help him financially by purchasing Chinese silver in 1937; in 1941, he authorized Claire Chennault to organize the American Volunteer Group, the famous Flying Tigers, composed of American pilots—regular officers hastily resigned from their respective services—flying the latest pursuit aircraft.

Nonetheless, the situation continued to deteriorate. One by one, supply lines to the West were falling to enemy control. By mid-1941, Japan already dominated the greater part of Indochina, including the important railway from Haiphong to Kunming, and was exerting strong pressure in Thailand, whose government capitulated in December. Within a few months, the Japanese flag flew over Hong Kong, the Malay Peninsula, most of Indochina, and most of Burma. By spring of 1942, China was encircled, her only supply line being by air over the Hump.[4]

2. Harrison, op. cit.
3. Ibid.
4. Ibid.: One land route remained, through central Asia. The Russians refused to permit passage here for political reasons, namely fear that Western aid would be used against Communists in the Northwest.

America's entry into the war somewhat altered this dismal picture. A shower of gold, $500 million in 1942 alone (at the time an astronomical sum), filled Chiang's empty coffers, and when his associates and senior officials and generals made off with that, more was forthcoming. The trickle of supply over the Hump also continued to support Chennault's valorous effort. Meanwhile the militarily able Lieutenant General Stilwell and his task force of advisers arrived, vanguard of a small military and diplomatic army ready to help Chiang cure Nationalist China's ills while building strong forces that ultimately would expel the Japanese from China.

The newly arrived Americans found plenty of ills. A corrupt and ineffective government was sucking the country dry. The people daily experienced all the evils that Mao Tse-tung and his Communist agents so effectively exploited. Extortion, usury, police and army coercion, impossibly high taxes and rents, unfair prices for produce—Chinese peasants could have been living two centuries earlier. The army was even worse, a conscript mass commanded by corrupt and, in general, poorly trained and inefficient senior officers. Two astute observers, Theodore White and Annalee Jacoby, later wrote in their excellent, if controversial, book *Thunder Out of China,*

. . . the Chinese did not fear to fight for their country; there was no deficit in patriotism. But they knew what recruiting camps were like. Government regulations could be read with a mirror. Officers were forbidden to mix sand with the rice they fed the recruits; they were forbidden to seize any clothes, baggage, or personal possessions a conscript carried with him; they were forbidden to torture, tie up, or lock their recruits in barred rooms at night; they were forbidden to ask families of deserting recruits to pay for the uniforms and food the soldier got at the induction center. Conditions in combat units were horrible, but by comparison to conditions in induction centers they were idyllic. Recruits ate even less than the starving soldiers; sometimes they got no water. Many were whipped. Dead bodies were allowed to lie for days. In some areas less than 20 per cent lived to reach the front. . . . Near Chengtu one camp had received some 40,000 men for induction. Many had already died on the way; only 8,000 were still alive at the camp at the end of the drive. One batch of 1,000 inductees was reported to have lost 800 recruits through the negligence of its officers.[5]

Survivors fared badly. Division commanders received pay for their troops, passing on only what they judged fitting; unscrupulous commanders frequently sold unit rations; supplies, including arms and ammunition, disappeared into the vortex of greed to be sold to any buyers, Communists included. Armies lived off the countryside, robbing peas-

5. White and Jacoby, op. cit.

ants and raping their women, human locusts as perverted as the enemy. In January 1943, Stilwell vented private feelings in his journal:

. . . Cowardice, rampant, squeeze [bribery] paramount, smuggling above duty, colossal ignorance and stupidity of staff, total inability to control factions and cliques, continued oppression of masses. The only factor that saves them is the dumb compliance of the *lao pai hsing* [the common people]. The "intellectuals" and the rich send their precious brats to the States, and the farmer boys go out and get killed—without care, training, or leadership. And we are maneuvered into the position of having to support this rotten regime and glorify its figurehead, the all-wise great patriot and soldier— Peanut. My God.[6]

Stilwell, by this time, suffered no illusions concerning either mission or boss. To make the Chinese peasant a good fighter, drastic army reforms were necessary to ameliorate the fear and distrust that permeated feckless ranks. Although Stilwell forced Chiang to furnish over sixty thousand men for training in India, where he proved his thesis by fashioning them into four fairly efficient divisions, these were a drop in the bucket. And other training programs did not enjoy Ramgarh's success. As supplies continued to arrive over the Hump, other of Chiang's divisions received American arms, equipment, and training. But, without repair of basic and traditional abuses, this was like hanging tinsel on a dead Christmas tree.

The major villain was Chiang Kai-shek. Unable or unwilling to redress Kuomintang evils, he had come to deny existence of these evils. Time insulated him ever further from reality. Sun Yat-sen's ghost long since had fled his conscience; in its place ruled only the vain, cruel, contemptuous, and uncaring spirit of past Peking emperors. While he paraded himself to the West as China's savior, he was in reality a xenophobic dictator without real plan, a weak, not very bright man, a prisoner held in a life cell of vanity and fear. Dominated by his wife and her powerful family, wedded to venal and disloyal advisers, forced to bribe and otherwise coerce independent war lords and underworld leaders in order to survive, Chiang resembled a feudal ruler being driven mad by forces he could not identify. He therefore chose not to believe in their existence. In July 1942, General Stilwell exploded in a letter to his wife:

. . . This is the most dreary type of maneuvering I've ever done, trying to guide and influence a stubborn, ignorant, prejudiced conceited despot who never hears the truth except from me and finds it hard to believe. . . .[7]

6. Stilwell, op. cit.; see also C. F. Romanus and R. Sunderland, *The China-Burma-India Theater: Stilwell's Problems* (Washington: U. S. Government Printing Office, 1956); see also Tuchman, op. cit.

7. Stilwell, op. cit.

The situation fairly screamed for a prescient diplomat with a pipe-line to the President, a strong ambassador enjoined to present a policy of *quid pro quo*—we'll help you, Chiang, but, at the same time, you must clean your own house.

In the context of 1942, this approach perhaps was impossible. Roosevelt's China policy was based as much on romanticism as on reality, what Churchill liked to call "the great American illusion." We don't know the President's real feelings about Chiang—they met only once, in Cairo, briefly—but, as Barbara Tuchman has written, Roosevelt's admiration cooled considerably as war continued and Chiang remained intransigent regarding necessary internal reforms. Unfortunately, a powerful Nationalist China lobby existed (and still exists) in Washington; Roosevelt, consummate politician that he was, held no intention of antagonizing its members. Perhaps, had the President been fully briefed on Chiang's despotism, he, too, would have been disillusioned, as were so many American officials on the spot. Roosevelt, however, seems to have been fooled, perhaps willingly, by Chiang's flamboyantly advertised personal asceticism and his widely proclaimed and utterly meaningless New Life Movement.

By ennobling Chiang as a member of the Big Four, Roosevelt virtually placed him above reproach or, at very least, far from control either of a tired and embittered American ambassador, Clarence Gauss, or a spunky, not always tactful lieutenant general in the U. S. Army, Joseph Stilwell.

Stilwell's mission was primarily military, not political. Considering that he was checkmated before he started, he still played a pretty good game, frequently giving Chiang and his cohorts bad moments. He would have done much better, but for a divided American camp. For Stilwell not only had to fight entrenched Chinese bureaucracy at every turn, but he almost immediately collided with Major General Claire Chennault, and he also had to suffer Commander M. E. Miles, who headed the clandestine U. S. Naval Group, China, and later OSS-Far East.

Claire Chennault, airman, a short, stocky man of rugged features, a flier's piercing eyes, brown, and a stubborn chin, but soft of speech and pleasant enough until the name of Stilwell cropped up.[8]

Chennault, legendary boss of Flying Tigers, American champion of the Generalissimo and his clique. As commander of 14th U. S. Air Force he believed, as did many Air Corps brethren, that war could be won only in the air. Chennault's strategic beliefs, vigorously promoted by his aide, politically powerful Joseph Alsop, suited Chiang's position per-

8. A. C. Wedemeyer, *Wedemeyer Reports!* (New York: Henry Holt, 1958).

fectly: use of American air power would preserve the Nationalist army for postwar showdown with the Communists.

On Chennault's recommendation, Chiang obtained Combined Chiefs of Staff approval to construct a series of airfields in eastern China from where, so they argued, planes could interdict Japanese shipping and, in time, bring the air war to Japan proper. Stilwell fought this plan, arguing that the Chinese army could not possibly protect the fields and that the Japanese could move into the area at will. In spring of 1943, in Washington, Stilwell lost the argument to Chennault, and the fields were built.

A year later, the Japanese did open a major offensive and soon overran the airfields, stopping only at Kweilin. Chennault accused Stilwell of deliberately weakening Nationalist defenses to prove himself correct. Chiang Kai-shek echoed the charges and ordered Stilwell to transfer Chinese divisions from the Burma front. Stilwell refused, and the ensuing imbroglio led eventually to his dismissal.

That did not alter the ugly fact of the Japanese offensive. Not only did it cost Chiang a great many material resources, all in short supply, but it sent Nationalist and allied morale plunging. In retreating from Honan, one Nationalist army so ravaged the population that the people ". . . turned on them and destroyed them."[9] By yielding large areas to repressive Japanese occupation forces, the Nationalists only added to peasant disaffection, thereby enriching the ground for the Communist subversive effort.

Stilwell fared no better with the U. S. Navy. For an experienced naval officer, "Mary" Miles was painfully naïve, as is variously disclosed in a posthumously published book, *A Different Kind of War*.[10] An Annapolis graduate, the forty-two-year-old Miles arrived in Chungking in spring of 1942, his primary mission to establish a series of clandestine radio stations along the southern coast in order to transmit weather reports and Japanese shipping movements.[11] In carrying out this mission, Miles contributed satisfactorily to the war effort, but he also paid the piper by attaching himself, and thus the American flag, to one of the most sinister persons in the Far East: Lieutenant General Tai Li, head of Chiang's secret police.

The liaison could have been suffered had Miles remained limited in his operations. Unfortunately he saw himself as an oriental Lawrence, and, in attempting to set up a widespread guerrilla organization, he was soon rubbing elbows with a variety of cutthroats familiar to readers of *Terry and the Pirates*. In his later words,

. . . ultimately there were more than a thousand of us [Americans], working intimately with a hundred thousand guerrillas, with two or three hundred

9. Harrison, op. cit.

10. M. E. Miles, *A Different Kind of War* (New York: Doubleday, 1967).

11. Ibid.; see also Morison, op. cit.; R. H. Smith, op. cit.

thousand plainclothesmen, with fourteen active guerrilla columns and innumerable saboteurs who came to be adept at following our patient, cooperative tactics.[12]

A qualified superior at this point should have introduced the control question. Miles and the majority of his officers spoke very little Chinese. As he later wrote, ". . . When I arrived I soon saw how utterly dependent we were bound to be on our interpreters whom we correctly called 'liaison officers.'" One can suggest that these "liaison officers" were hand-picked by General Tai Li and that the Americans were told precisely what Tai Li wanted them to be told.

Miles perforce had to depend on information supplied by Tai Li. His early attempts to establish transmitting stations fell victim to Japanese counteraction. S. E. Morison later wrote:

. . . By the end of 1942 Miles realized that the weather-reporting network would have to be turned into a secret army to be really useful. Tai Li needed more guerrillas to protect the weather men, and more Americans to train the Chinese. On Commander Miles's recommendation an agreement was signed 15 April 1943, establishing the Sino-American Co-operative Organization (SACO), commanded by Tai Li with Miles as his deputy. Volunteers were carefully screened by the SACO office in Washington and put through a special training course before being sent out to China. No "old China hands" with preconceived ideas were wanted. . . .[13]

Later attempts to merge Miles's effort with OSS activities by making Miles director of OSS in China proved futile when Tai Li refused to carry out Washington's orders.[14]

SACO rapidly expanded. Miles's and Tai Li's headquarters, Happy Valley, outside of Chungking, supported five separate intelligence efforts as well as a number of guerrilla-training units headed by American officers. Later in the war, Miles commanded some 2,500 Americans, whose logistic appetite never ceased growing. From June to November 1944, American pilots flew in the incredible total of 869 tons to support SACO operations. This included 150 tons of ammunition, 60 tons of arms, 75 tons of explosives, 227 tons of gasoline [!], 51 tons of passenger baggage [!] and 185 tons of miscellaneous items such as trucks, office supplies, clothing, and mail—items hardly compatible with a mobile, hard-hitting guerrilla organization.

Considering SACO's size and impressive logistic support, operational results against the Japanese seem surprisingly mild. Although ". . . comprehensive weather maps were being broadcast daily to the Pacific Fleet" by October 1944, along with information on coastal shipping,[15] this activity scarcely justified SACO's expense. A less preten-

12. Miles, op. cit.
13. Morison, op. cit.
14. Ibid.
15. Ibid.

tious organization could have fielded small and select Chinese teams, much as Australian coastwatchers operated, and precisely as Mao's Communists were doing in Yenan. Colonel David Barrett, who commanded Dixie Mission, the American observer group sent to Yenan in 1944, later wrote:

. . . The Communists were also of great assistance to us in collecting weather reports of vital importance to our Navy and Air Force. With their cooperation, and under the supervision of our Signal Officer, Captain Domke, large numbers of small radios, with instructions concerning their operation, were sent to distant parts of the Communist-controlled area, and an astonishingly large number of useful reports, sent by means of these small radios, were received in Yenan.[16]

Regarding damage to the enemy from guerrilla operations, Miles's own claims probably err on the side of optimism, particularly the figure of seventy-one thousand Japanese killed. Although guerrillas, variously trained and commanded by American teams, at times scratched the enemy façade, their reports should not have been taken at face value. Chinese face is omnipresent. One Chinese guerrilla leader was not going to be outdone by another, a characteristic also familiar to most non-Chinese guerrillas. One fact is certain: the effort in no way prevented the Japanese army, itself greatly weakened, from carrying out the 1944 offensive against Chennault's exposed airfields.

As Miles developed his mission, he invariably collided with Stilwell, who, on one occasion, "held up all SACO's air shipments for six months."[17] Tai Li's intransigence also caused OSS to undertake an independent effort. As early as 1943, American military and civil officials wanted to arm Mao Tse-tung's guerrillas, a notion successfully fought by Chiang Kai-shek. During the successful Japanese offensive of 1944, the issue again grew dominant, and, as will be seen, played a role in Stilwell's dismissal.

But Miles and his group were also falling from official favor. When General Albert Wedemeyer replaced Stilwell, in late 1944, he dropped Tai Li in favor of General Chen Kai-ming. Miles later wrote that Wedemeyer apparently did not realize that Chen was Tai Li's number-two man—nor, apparently, did Miles see fit to tell him.[18] Wedemeyer suffered Miles's independent operations until spring of 1945, when Admiral King, Chief of Naval Operations, placed the naval group under Wedemeyer's command.[19]

16. David D. Barrett, *Dixie Mission: The United States Army Observer Group in Yenan, 1944* (Berkeley, Calif.: University of California Press, 1970).
17. Morison, op. cit.
18. Miles, op. cit.
19. Wedemeyer, op. cit.

Miles's supreme error lay in trusting Tai Li so completely, particularly in view of contrary evidence presented by older and more knowledgeable China hands than himself. As one result, Miles's reports forsook the realm of objectivity, when he was being paid to be objective. He later wrote, for example, ". . . over and over again I had sent in information that proved beyond a doubt that the Yenan Communists were being supported by Russia and supplied with Russian arms."[20] Leaving aside the dubious accuracy of such evidence—evidence undoubtedly supplied by Tai Li's agents and not confirmed by American observers in Yenan—this was not really Miles's mission, and certainly not his official worry.

Without doubt, Miles meant well, but, considering his rabid anti-Communist attitude, his all-out support of Tai Li and various mercenaries produced an ironic conclusion to his mission: God alone knows how many Chinese peasants became active Communists because of evils perpetrated by these men acting with American compliance and support!

In Yenan, to the northwest, Mao and his Communists were also dragging heels in the war against Japan. Mao allegedly had made his plans clear in October 1937, when he told his followers:

. . . The Sino-Japanese war affords our party an excellent opportunity for expansion. Our fixed policy should be seventy percent expansion, twenty percent dealing with the Kuomintang, and ten percent resisting Japan. There are three stages in carrying out this fixed policy: the first is a compromising stage, in which self-sacrifice should be made to show our outward obedience to the Central Government and adherence to the Three Principles of the People [nationality, democracy and livelihood, as outlined by Dr. Sun Yat-sen], but in reality this will serve as camouflage for the existence and development of our party.

The second is a contending stage, in which two or three years should be spent in laying the foundation of our party's political and military powers, and developing these until we can match and break the Kuomintang, and eliminate the influence of the latter north of the Yellow River. While waiting for an unusual turn of events, we should give the Japanese invader certain concessions.

The third is an offensive stage, in which our forces should penetrate deeply into Central China, sever the communications of the Central Government troops in various sectors, isolate and disperse them until we are ready for the

20. Miles, op. cit.; a former Naval Intelligence officer on Admiral Nimitz's staff has stated that the information passed by Naval Group China was not only useless but tainted, because it came from Tai Li and his people: letter in the author's private files.

counter-offensive and wrest the leadership from the hands of the Kuomin-tang.[21]

Even had Mao been inclined to wage more vigorous war, he would have found rough going. He was not strong enough to repeat the "Hundred Regiments Offensive" of 1940. General Okamura's policy of "Kill all, burn all, destroy all" continued to hurt Mao in 1941 and 1942. Okamura later claimed that his forces killed about a hundred thousand of Mao's guerrillas and that he would have eliminated them altogether except that, in late 1942, the Japanese high command began transferring seven of his best divisions to the Pacific theater.[22]

By late 1942, Japan had assumed the strategic defensive in China and Southeast Asia. In northern and central China, large garrisons defended major cities which were linked by strong points to keep open lines of communication. As Americans continued to press in from the Pacific, Japanese first-line strength diminished, with a corresponding reliance on Chinese puppet troops ". . . of negligible combat efficiency and questionable loyalty." According to Dr. Griffith,

. . . on rare occasions, Chinese Communist troops drove greatly inferior Japanese units from strong points in *hsien* towns or along the railways. But when the Japanese wished, they could invariably return in sufficient strength to force Communist withdrawals. . . . No authentic records support the proposition that Communist military operations succeeded in forcing the Japanese invaders from an extensive territory they physically occupied and wanted to hold. . . .[23]

Nor did Mao hold any such pretensions. Convinced that America would win the war, he devoted these years to consolidation and expansion. As Dr. Griffith concluded,

. . . the new policy put into effect in 1941, essentially political in nature, was to fill vacuums created by the withdrawal of Japanese garrison troops, to seep into rural areas administered by Chinese traitors and collaborators and "defended" by puppet ("bogus") troops . . . [who] speedily acquired the prudent habit of taking to their heels before the Communists fired a shot. When "bogus" troops were captured, they were indoctrinated and integrated.[24]

The reader will recognize these tactics as an extension of those employed against Nationalist forces prior to the war. Essentially, they were

21. Freda Utley, *Last Chance in China* (Indianapolis, Ind.: Bobbs-Merrill, 1947). This document was published by the Supreme National Defense Council, in Chungking, in 1944. While its authenticity can be challenged, it still presents an accurate enough blueprint for what happened; see also Wedemeyer, op. cit.
22. Griffith (CPLA), *supra*.
23. Ibid.
24. Ibid.

tactics of the poor. Although they resulted in steadily increasing Communist strength, Mao was never strong enough to undertake conventional operations against the Japanese. Like Tito in Yugoslavia, he needed arms and equipment, and, as attempts to gain these from either Russia or America failed, his frustrations grew.

Had he been supplied with arms, American observers reported, he might have constituted a significant threat to the Japanese presence.[25] As it was, he continued with nibbling guerrilla tactics while politically consolidating the area—and he also continued to tie up fifty thousand troops screening Chiang's two-hundred-thousand-man blocking force.

Unable to mount an offensive against the Japanese in China, Stilwell turned increasingly to the Burma front. By proving there that the Chinese, properly trained, equipped, and led, could win battles, he hoped to force Chiang's hand and bring about reforms necessary to produce a viable combat army. His star rose visibly in spring of 1944, when his predominantly Chinese force reached Myitkyina, the first major tactical success enjoyed by the Nationalists since 1937. (See maps, Chapters 24 and 48.)

Stilwell's success, however, meant absence from Chungking at a critical juncture. The Japanese meanwhile had launched an offensive against Chennault's forward airfields in eastern China, a move virtually uncontested by Chiang's divisions—precisely as Stilwell had warned. To Chiang's pleas for help in the form of divisions from the Burma front, Stilwell turned a deaf ear: the solution, he explained, lay in Chiang's making peace with the Communists, thus freeing some two hundred thousand Nationalist troops and fifty thousand of Mao's troops for operations against the Japanese. He also favored, as he had previously, arming the Communists, though this was probably as much to force Chiang to implement necessary reforms as it was to help Mao build a modern army.

The threat did make Chiang more pliant. In June 1944, Chiang told Vice-President Henry Wallace that he ". . . would welcome the assistance of the President in the settlement of the Communist problem, even though it was an internal one"; he also agreed to send a team of American military-civil observers to Mao's headquarters at Yenan, a move

25. U. S. Department of State, *United States Relations with China—With Special Reference to the Period 1944–1949* (Washington: U. S. Government Printing Office, 1949). Hereafter cited as USDS-China, this was subsequently published as *The China White Paper—August 1949* (Stanford, Calif.: Stanford University Press, 1967), 2 vols.; see also U. S. Department of State, *Foreign Relations of the United States—Diplomatic Papers 1944—Volume VI—China* (Washington: U. S. Government Printing Office, 1967). Hereafter cited as USDS-Foreign Relations China (1944); see also Barrett, op. cit.

previously recommended by Stilwell's headquarters but refused by Chiang.[26]

As enemy action continued through summer and threatened to cut China in two, Roosevelt took increasingly positive action. In July, he promoted Stilwell to four-star rank and told Chiang that he wanted him made commander-in-chief of the Chinese armies. He also sent two personal representatives to Chungking, Major General Patrick Hurley, to iron out existing problems between Chiang and Stilwell, and Donald Nelson, to work out a more generous aid program.

By the time Hurley and Nelson arrived in Delhi, Stilwell had announced the capture of Myitkyina and had started another offensive from Yünnan. The three traveled to Chungking in early September.

At sixty-one years of age, Patrick J. Hurley featured considerable experience in arbitration. A self-educated Oklahoma lawyer and decorated veteran of World War I, he had served government with the same unflagging zeal that had made him a fortune from representing private oil interests. A cabinet officer in the Hoover administration, he more recently had functioned as Roosevelt's ambassador to New Zealand and to Iran, besides representing the President to Stalin and other foreign figures.

Tall and lean, with a neat mustache and tailored uniform heavy with decorations, genial Pat Hurley looked the perfect diplomat. The look deceived. Hurley believed that ". . . contagious friendliness could be made a fundamentally effective part of diplomacy." If his Oklahoma drawl and fund of homespun stories amused President Roosevelt, they bored most people. This aside, in negotiations demanding the deepest knowledge and objectivity, Hurley preferred prejudice to fact. Basically an idealist, either unwilling or unable to differentiate between national ambitions and attainable objectives, he was becoming an increasingly embittered man, at odds with anyone who disagreed with him.

He was already convinced that Britain and Russia were fighting only for sinister imperialist purposes, as opposed to Atlantic Charter ideals, and in China his suspicions hardened into soul-destroying conviction that the U. S. Department of State consisted of two parts, half pro-British, half pro-Russian—the whole scheming to subvert the foreign policy of the United States, which he, Patrick J. Hurley, alone seemed intent on preserving. When his personal diplomacy failed disastrously, Hurley sought to blame others, whom he accused of disloyalty and subversion. Pat Hurley came to China to advance the American dream; he helped set the stage for the American nightmare.

Hurley's primary error consisted of oversimplification. The maze that

26. USDS-China, *supra*.

he walked into is well suggested by his later biographer. The directive that sent him to Chungking read in part:

. . . Your principal mission is to promote efficient and harmonious relations between the Generalissimo and General Stilwell and facilitate General Stilwell's exercise of command over the Chinese armies placed under his direction. . . .[27]

Harmonious relations between Chiang and Stilwell meant resolving the issue of aid to the Communists. According to Lohbeck, Roosevelt and Hurley agreed on a formula:

. . . The purpose of the armed Communists being the overthrow of the Government of the Republic of China, it would be futile for the United States to attempt to uphold the Republic while arming a force bent upon its destruction. The President therefore decided that lend-lease material could not be used to arm the Communists unless and until they acknowledged the National Government of the Republic of China, and the leadership of Generalissimo Chiang Kai-shek.[28]

It followed that Hurley's mission became that of making peace not only between Chiang and Stilwell, but between Nationalists and Communists —the latter already forming a divisive issue between Chiang and Stilwell.

By the time Hurley arrived in Chungking, in September, an American military-civil mission was working with Mao Tse-tung in Yenan. The Dixie Mission, as it was known, had arrived in July under command of an experienced China hand, Colonel David Barrett, American military attaché in Chungking.

Mao and his lieutenants welcomed the Barrett mission, in general cooperating with their fact-finding requirements. Old China hands, including Barrett, were favorably impressed with what they saw, but they almost immediately recognized a political military situation unfamiliar to Western warfare. Although Barrett and his army officers lectured on American training methods and tactics to Communist officers, Barrett later wrote:

. . . I doubt our talks meant much to the Communists, as their training methods were markedly different from ours. These methods were intended, moreover, for troops usually operating under conditions entirely unfamiliar to Americans. The Communists could almost always count on the cooperation and support of a local population which had excellent opportunities to acquire important information about the enemy and were eager to report

27. Don Lohbeck, *Patrick J. Hurley* (Chicago: Henry Regnery, 1956); see also Dean Acheson, *Present at the Creation—My Years in the State Department* (New York: W. W. Norton, 1969).
28. Lohbeck, op. cit.

it whenever they could. Thus their training, unlike ours, laid little stress on scouting, patrolling, air reconnaissance and other means of gathering enemy intelligence.[29]

In August 1944, an important civil member of the team, John Service,

. . . wrote the Department of State an objective summary reporting that the Communists were actively supporting the war "because this gives them an opportunity to mobilize, organize, and indoctrinate the people and to create and train an efficient army."[30]

In November, another diplomat on the team, John Paton Davies, told State Department seniors: ". . . The Chinese Communists are so strong between the Great Wall and the Yangtze that they can now look forward to the postwar control of at least North China. . . ."[31] Service complemented this unsettling fact with his own rational if blunt findings and conclusions:

. . . This total [Chinese Communist] mobilization is based upon and has been made possible by what amounts to an economic, political and social revolution. This revolution has been moderate and democratic. It has improved the economic condition of the peasants by rent and interest reduction, tax reform and good government. It has given them democratic self-government, political consciousness and a sense of their rights. It has freed them from feudalistic bonds and given them self-respect, self-reliance and a strong feeling of cooperative group interest. The common people, for the first time, have been given something to fight for. . . . Just as the Japanese Army cannot crush these militant people now, so also will Kuomintang force fail in the future. . . . With this great popular base, the Communists likewise cannot be eliminated. Kuomintang attempts to do so by force must mean a complete denial of democracy. This will strengthen the ties of the Communists with the people; a Communist victory will be inevitable . . . I suggest the future conclusion that unless the Kuomintang goes as far as the Communists in political and economic reform, and otherwise proves itself able to contest this leadership of the people (none of which it yet shows signs of being willing or able to do), the Communists will be the dominant force in China within a comparatively few years.[32]

While Barrett, Davies, and Service were so occupied, a storm of monumental proportions had broken in Chungking. A few days after Stilwell's return, in September, the continuing Japanese advance had forced him to order demolition of the large American base at Kweilin,

29. Barrett, op. cit.
30. Griffith (CPLA), *supra;* see also USDS-Foreign Relations China (1944), *supra.*
31. USDS-Foreign Relations China (1944), *supra.*
32. Lohbeck, op. cit.

an act that earned harsh words both from Chennault and Chiang Kai-shek. Hurley, meanwhile, continued to confer with Chiang, who finally agreed to recognize Stilwell as his new commander-in-chief, but in return demanded control of lend-lease supply. He also demanded return of Chinese divisions from Burma, which Stilwell refused to consider.

Stilwell at this point was a tired man, his normal irascibility honed razor-sharp. He had recently spent six active months in a jungle campaign that claimed as victim most men half his years. He had heard all Chiang's promises before, and, although he got on well enough with Hurley, he was hardly impressed with Hurley's optimistic forecasts of a favorable settlement with the Peanut.

The storm brewed throughout September. Hurley was convinced that he had persuaded Chiang to his way of thinking; Stilwell, from sad experience, pointed out that Chiang forever said yes and always did no. Stilwell's attitude is clear from a cable sent to General George Marshall on September 22:

. . . Chiang Kai-shek is following his usual policy. At first he readily agreed to the command arrangement and also by inference agreed to use the communist army under my command, then he began the delaying action, which still continues. He protests that there are many difficulties which have to be smoothed out and this takes time. Actually, he believes that our advance in the Pacific will be swift enough and effective enough to spare his further effort, and he would like to avoid the bitter pill of recognizing the communists and putting a foreigner in command of the army. . . .[33]

On September 26, he informed Marshall:

. . . Chiang Kai-shek has no intention of making further efforts to prosecute the war. Anyone who crowds him toward such action will be blocked or eliminated. . . . Chiang Kai-shek believes he can go on milking the United States for money and munitions by using the old gag about quitting if he is not supported. He believes the war in the Pacific is nearly over, and that by delaying tactics, he can throw the entire burden on us. He has no intention of instituting any real democratic regime or of forming a united front with the communists. He himself is the main obstacle to the unification of China and her cooperation in a real effort against Japan. . . . I am now convinced that, for the reasons stated, the United States will not get any real cooperation from China while Chiang Kai-shek is in power. I believe he will only continue his policy and delay, while grabbing for loans and postwar aid, for the purpose of maintaining his present position, based on one-party government, and reactionary policy, on the suppression of democratic ideas with the active aid of his Gestapo.[34]

33. USDA-China, *supra.*
34. Ibid.

Fired by such cables, the imbroglio, toward the end of the month, reached ultimatum proportions, inspired ironically by Roosevelt's intervention. Chiang now demanded Stilwell's recall. In October, the American general left Chungking, his job taken over by Major General (soon promoted to Lieutenant General) Albert Wedemeyer.

Wedemeyer might have been in a different army from Stilwell. Also a West Pointer, the forty-eight-year-old general had served in Washington before joining Mountbatten's staff in Ceylon. As he makes clear in his book *Wedemeyer Reports,* he fancied himself a global strategist of no mean talent. Unlike Stilwell (whom he disliked and who held him in genial contempt), the husky Nebraskan sympathized deeply with Chiang Kai-shek and set about to bail him out militarily.

Hurley meanwhile continued trying to bail Chiang out politically. In early November, Hurley flew to Mao's headquarters at Yenan. He brought a draft agreement from Chiang Kai-shek (probably drawn up by the U. S. Department of State), which would have incorporated Mao's forces into the Nationalist army in return for legalizing the Chinese Communist Party.[35] Despite considerable bonhomie—Hurley's habit of emitting Indian war whoops on the odd occasion appalled both American and Communist camps—the talks did not prosper. Mao believed that he was powerful enough to demand a coalition government, and this amounted to the main feature of his rebuttal to Chiang's draft. Hurley returned to Chungking with Mao's Five-Point Proposal; Mao's chief lieutenant, the young and bright Chou En-lai, accompanied him.

Subsequent talks with Nationalists and Chou dragged on inconclusively—not surprising, in view either of Chiang's intransigence or of Mao's relatively strong bargaining position. More to the point, neither side made any obvious effort to carry the war to the Japanese—a serious deficiency that was soon to exercise an important and harmful influence on American strategy.

When President Roosevelt flew to Yalta, in February 1945, the European war was approaching climax, but the Pacific war, though progressing well for the allies, was far from won. Although danger seemed slight of the enemy developing an atomic bomb, Hitler still spoke of new and secret weapons of great power. Question marks embraced the American-British atomic-bomb effort: scientists could not, in early 1945, promise a bomb that worked, let alone a delivery date.

Roosevelt met with Stalin before American marines landed on Iwo Jima. Despite Wedemeyer's military reforms and reorganization, Chiang seemed no more anxious than ever to fight the Japanese. Despite Hurley's ambassadorship, Chinese Nationalists and Communists remained

35. Barrett, op. cit., gives the draft treaty and also describes in detail the frustrating but always fascinating subsequent conferences and counterdrafts; see also USDS-Foreign Relations China (1944), *supra.*

at each other's throats, to the enemy's immense profit. Roosevelt and Churchill had been advised by their respective chiefs of staff ". . . that the war in the Pacific would last eighteen months after the end of hostilities in Europe."[36] According to military estimates, the invasion of Japanese home islands would cost perhaps one million American lives. Roosevelt's interpreter at Yalta, later Ambassador, Charles Bohlen, has recently pointed out that, according to American military estimates, it would have ". . . cost about 200,000 more in American casualties to assault the Japanese islands before rather than after Soviet entry into the Pacific war."[37]

The agreements made at Yalta aroused enormous controversy in postwar years. Leaving aside arrangements for Poland and the rest of Europe, Roosevelt was criticized and still is for negotiating Far Eastern questions without China's presence and in controverting certain clauses of the Cairo Declaration.

The document in question, the "Far Eastern Agreement"— ". . . negotiated by Roosevelt, Stalin, Harriman, and Molotov without the full knowledge of either the State Department or the Joint Chiefs of Staff and without Churchill's participation until the very end"— granted Stalin four major concessions, abridged by Professor Richard Leopold in his excellent work *The Growth of American Foreign Policy:*

. . . Stalin obtained four things exactly as he wished: the annexation of the Kuriles, the cession of southern Sakhalin, the naval base at Port Arthur, and the maintenance of the *status quo* in Outer Mongolia. His desire to lease [Port] Dairen and to control the Chinese Eastern and South Manchuria [railroad] lines did not fully materialize, the port being placed under international jurisdiction and the railways under joint operation.[38]

The agreement concerning Outer Mongolia and Manchuria would require concurrence of Generalissimo Chiang Kai-shek. In return for these concessions, Stalin promised to enter the war against Japan, once Germany had surrendered. Just as important, the final clause of this top-secret agreement read:

. . . For its part the Soviet Union expresses its readiness to conclude with the National Government of China a pact of friendship and alliance between the USSR and China in order to render assistance to China with its armed forces for the purpose of liberating China from the Japanese yoke.[39]

This document was neither as evil as postwar critics have made out, nor as sound as defenders have claimed. Two important considerations

36. C. E. Bohlen, *The Transformation of American Foreign Policy* (New York: W. W. Norton, 1969).
37. Ibid.
38. Richard Leopold, op. cit.
39. Ibid.

governed presidential thinking at Yalta (the claim that Roosevelt was feeble-minded, later advanced by Wedemeyer, Hurley, and others who were not present, and picked up by the right wing, must be discounted in view of overwhelming contrary evidence; ill he was, crazy he was not): One was the human and material cost to the United States of invading Japan, the other his belief that he could handle Stalin after the war, that, in William Bullitt's words, ". . . he could convert Stalin from Soviet imperialism to democratic collaboration."[40]

Roosevelt can scarcely be faulted for respecting the first consideration, and only a curious kind of American would suggest that the Joint Chiefs of Staff distorted their report in Stalin's favor. One of America's ablest wartime intelligence officers, Rear Admiral Ellis Zacharias, later wrote a fitting epitaph for the JCS report: ". . . It was an unfortunate and altogether wrong estimate, its authors being deceived by a purely military and quantitative evaluation of the enemy, a treacherous trap into which even the greatest military leaders are likely to fall occasionally."[41]

Roosevelt can be and has been heavily criticized for the ego inherent in his assumption of personal supremacy over Stalin. In the final analysis, however, it is what raises him above his predecessors or successors —the insistence on attempting to alter the great-power concept in favor of world government. In his desire for a free, peaceful, and prosperous world, Roosevelt embodied the real spirit of the American ideal.

Roosevelt recognized that the only hope for an ultimately peaceful world lay in a viable United Nations. Critics have condemned him for paying too much attention to military strategy and not enough to postwar politics. But at Yalta and elsewhere in intercourse with Stalin, Roosevelt acted with the knowledge, very realistic knowledge, that the United Nations or a similar organization could not function without Stalin's participation. Finally, such was deployment of forces, that Stalin had immediate access to the controversial areas which he would have occupied in any case. As Ambassador Bohlen concluded:

. . . It cannot be said that Yalta was a success, but, as I wrote earlier, there are no grounds for supposing that it was the folly or the weakness of the Western powers which made this true. The map of Europe would look exactly the same as it does today if there had never been a Yalta Conference.[42]

How many, if any, of the Yalta decisions were passed by Stalin to Mao Tse-tung is not known. Chiang Kai-shek was not consulted, only because his senior councils were so riddled with spies that Tokyo would

40. W. C. Bullitt, "A Report to the American People on China," *Life*, October 13, 1947.
41. Lohbeck, op. cit.
42. Bohlen, op. cit.

have learned all.[43] Ambassador Hurley informed Chiang of the agreement in June 1945. Chiang ". . . seemed disappointed but not upset"[44] and began planning for appropriate talks with Russia.

At this time, Nationalist-Communist talks were still in progress under Hurley's aegis. Whether Mao ever intended to join the Nationalist government is not known; he probably would have, had circumstances warranted this interim measure. But he was in no hurry to do so. In Chungking, his trusted and most able lieutenant, Chou En-lai, at once had recognized and defined divisive influences surrounding Chiang, news welcome to Mao. Stilwell's abrupt departure and Chiang's subsequent failure to cleanse his military stables (much less his house of government) also contrasted with Communist army strength, daily growing more powerful. In April 1945, General Chu Teh, its commander-in-chief, reported to the Seventh Party Congress, in Yenan, a regular army strength of nearly one million, augmented by a militia of well over two million, an organization devoted to bringing ". . . Mao's revolution to almost 100 million peasants living in the plains, valleys, and mountains of North China."[45]

43. USDS-China, *supra.*
44. Leopold, op. cit.; see also Wedemeyer, op. cit., who was present and who credits Chiang with a more severe reaction.
45. Griffith (CPLA), *supra.*

Chapter 51

Conflict in policy: the China question • Hurley and Stalin • Kennan's warning • Truman's inaction • The military position: Nationalists versus Reds • Postwar political situation • American marines land • Chiang occupies Manchuria • The Communist presence • Early clashes • Hurley's resignation • The Marshall mission • Fighting breaks out • Chiang's continued complacency • Marshall's warning • Limited Nationalist gains • Nationalist morale crumbles • Communist guerrilla offensives • The Wedemeyer mission • His analysis and recommendations • William Bullitt's accusations • His "domino" theory • Chiang's continued demands • Lin Piao's "Seventh Offensive" • Mao's guerrilla tactics • Chiang loses Manchuria • Mao moves south • The final debacle • American failure to analyze Chiang's defeat

PRESIDENT ROOSEVELT'S DEATH and ensuing confusion in Washington played directly into Chinese Communist hands by prolonging and even intensifying the divisive nature of American policy. When Harry Truman became President, in April 1945, three distinct schools of thought existed among concerned officials in China.

The first might be called the Stilwell syndrome: the continuing effort, mainly by Department of State representatives, both in the Chungking embassy and in Wedemeyer's headquarters, to make common cause with Mao's Communists for two reasons: first to more effectively fight the Japanese; second to force Chiang into political, economic, and military reforms by suggesting that the soft rug of American support could be pulled from under him to leave him standing on the cold floor of reality. Some powerful non-Communist Chinese political leaders agreed with this policy, as did many knowledgeable American military officers and most American journalists in the area.[1]

1. U. S. Department of State, *Foreign Relations of the United States—Diplomatic Papers 1945—Volume VII—The Far East—China* (Washington: U. S. Gov-

Ambassador Hurley did not agree, and succeeded in having leading proponents of military co-operation variously transferred and even persecuted. He emphasized his attitude in January 1945, when the Communist general, Chu Teh, asked for a loan of $20 million in U.S. currency in order to procure ". . . the defection of officers and men of the Chinese puppet government and for use in encouraging sabotage and demolition work by puppet troops behind the Japanese lines." Hurley turned this down: ". . . I am of the firm opinion that such help would be identical to supplying arms to the Communist armed Party [sic] and would, therefore, be a dangerous precedent. . . ." In Washington a month later, he vigorously opposed powerful arguments of his chargé d'affaires, George Atcheson, to furnish arms and supply to the Communists.[2]

Hurley himself was actively pursuing a conciliation policy that he believed was going to result in amalgamation of Nationalist and Communist forces. He had convinced himself that the Chinese problem was totally internal—this primarily the result of an earlier conference with Molotov, who promised to back Chiang Kai-shek's government—and that he, good fellow, could bring about a working conciliation between the two major power factions. A meeting with Stalin in April 1945 confirmed his belief. The Russian leader, as Hurley reported to Washington,

. . . wished us to know that we would have his complete support in immediate action for the unification of the armed forces of China with full recognition of the National Government under the leaderhip of Chiang Kai-shek. In short, Stalin agreed unqualifiedly to America's [Hurley's] policy in China as outlined to him during this conversation.[3]

Hurley's naïveté frightened among others the American chargé d'affaires in Moscow, George Kennan. Kennan had studied the Russians and their language for years and now cabled Ambassador Harriman, who had returned to Washington at President Roosevelt's death:

. . . There was, of course, nothing in Ambassador Hurley's account of what he told Stalin to which Stalin could not honestly subscribe, it being understood that to the Russians words mean different things than they do to us. Stalin is of course prepared to affirm the principle of unifying the armed forces of China. He knows that unification is feasible in a practical sense only on conditions which are acceptable to the Chinese Communist Party. . . .

Actually I am persuaded that in the future Soviet policy respecting China will continue what it has been in the recent past: a fluid resilient policy directed at the achievement of maximum power with minimum responsibility

ernment Printing Office, 1969). Hereafter cited as USDS-Foreign Relations China (1945); see also USDS-China, supra.

2. USDS-China, supra.
3. Lohbeck, op. cit.

on portions of the Asiatic continent lying beyond the Soviet border. This will involve the exertion of pressure in various areas in direct proportion to their strategic importance and their proximity to the Soviet frontier. . . .

After detailing what he believed to be specific Soviet aims, Kennan concluded:

. . . It would be tragic if our natural anxiety for the support of the Soviet Union at this juncture, coupled with Stalin's use of words which mean all things to all people and his cautious affability, were to lead us into an undue reliance on Soviet aid or even Soviet acquiescence in the achievement of our long-term objectives in China.[4]

Both Harriman and Secretary of State Edward Stettinius took this prescient warning to heart and attempted to impress Hurley with the complexity of the situation, including its perils:

. . . Mr. Harriman feared that Ambassador Hurley might give Chiang Kai-shek an "over-optimistic account of his conversations with Stalin" and he thought it might be advisable to suggest to General Hurley that he should be careful "not to arouse unfounded expectations. . . ."[5]

Albert Wedemeyer would have heartily applauded this advice. Unlike Hurley, with whom he had been quarreling for some time, the American general saw the greatest danger in postwar Russian moves and was convinced that the Kremlin ". . . sought from the outset to wreck the Nationalist Government" through its control of Chinese Communists. Primarily for this reason, he agreed with Hurley that America should not furnish arms and supply to the Communists (although on the occasion of a severe epidemic he did send Yenan eleven tons of medical supplies).[6] In March 1945, John Vincent of the Chungking embassy, tried to persuade Wedemeyer to supply the Communists with arms:

. . . General Wedemeyer refused to be a part of the State Department scheme—replying that while he did not have enough information to make a definite answer as to the possible usefulness of the Communist troops against Japan, he was against the idea of building up the Communists' strength. And General Wedemeyer, in helping to clarify the confusion over the actual military power of the Chinese Communists, "discussed the Chinese military problems with the Joint Chiefs of Staff on March 27, 1945. They were all of the opinion that the rebellion in China could be put down by comparatively small assistance to Chiang's Central Government."[7]

4. Ibid.; see also George F. Kennan, *Memoirs* (London: Hutchinson, 1968).
5. Lohbeck, op. cit.
6. Wedemeyer, op. cit.
7. Lohbeck, op. cit.

A very harassed President Truman bought bits and pieces from each of the three schools. While willing to accept the State Department's expressed long-range goal, ". . . the establishment of a strong and united China as a necessary principal stabilizing factor in the Far East," he also made it clear that if Nationalists wanted American help they would have to carry out overdue reforms, not to mention fighting the Japanese.

In essence, then, Truman merely continued an already unsatisfactory policy, whose pragmatism remained subservient to its poverty. Like Foch in 1918, he should have walked in his garden and asked himself: *De quoi s'agit-il* (Just what is the problem)? The problem obviously was an intractable Chiang Kai-shek, whose external power position derived in part from strategic factors, in part from conflicting American policy with a strong emotional bias.

The end of the war would solve the strategic aspect. The policy aspect was the difficult one, and such were the ponderous and complex factors that perhaps a complete solution did not exist. A partial solution could have resulted, however, by twisting loose threads of executive policy into a rope or even a noose with which to confront Chiang Kai-shek.

Truman did nothing of the kind. While summer months spun away, one branch of his power maintained diplomatic dalliance with Chinese Communists, whose strength was and remained space-time-will; another paid court to Chiang, who, also reassured by the powerful China lobby in Washington, remained confident of continuing American support; a third, in the form of Pat Hurley, kept buzzing from one camp to another like some kind of crazy bee gathering in meaningless political pollen.

The situation screamed for dynamic action; the administration replied by mediocrity, best expressed by one of Wedemeyer's reports in the final days of the war:

. . . Based on [my] limited knowledge, neither the Chinese Communist Party nor the Kuomintang is democratic in spirit, or in intentions. China is not prepared for a democratic form of government with 95 per cent of her people illiterate and for many other cogent reasons. The inarticulate masses of China desire peace and are not particularly interested in or aware of the various ideologies represented. An opportunity to work, to obtain food and clothing for their families and a happy peaceful environment are their primary concern.

Conditions here could best be handled by a benevolent despot or a military dictator, whether such dictator be a Communist or a Kuomintang matters very little. From my observation practically all Chinese officials are interested in their selfish aggrandizement. I retain the impression that the Generalissimo's friendship offers best opportunity at this time for stabilization in the area, political and economic.[8]

8. Harry S. Truman, *Year of Decisions 1945* (London: Hodder & Stoughton, 1955).

If astute American officials were not pleased with Chiang Kai-shek's inept government, very few, if any, thought in the confused summer and autumn of 1945 that China would ever fall under Mao Tse-tung's control. Most observers agreed that the talks engineered and steered by Ambassador Hurley between Nationalists and Communists would lead eventually to coalition government. When these talks terminated, in September, and the first military skirmishes developed in northern China and Manchuria, informed persons spoke in terms of temporary suspension, not war.

Nor did the first shooting incidents create panic. In numbers, Chiang held a comfortable military balance. By war's end, the Nationalist army numbered around three million men, and would soon increase. Despite deficiencies noted by Stilwell and others, this army included five divisions equipped and trained by Stilwell's India command, two of them having proved themselves in combat. In addition, Chiang's army included some twenty-five divisions trained and equipped by the American military mission at Kunming, and some of these were also battle tested.

Chiang's modern divisions contained artillery, armor, transport, and communication units, and, thanks to Stilwell's teachings and Wedemeyer's various reforms, had attained a degree of operational sophistication undreamed by either Nationalist or Communist commanders. Chiang also possessed an air force of about eight groups, with a pool of some five thousand American-trained pilots. Finally, Chiang knew that the Western horn of plenty would continue spewing forth dollars and airplanes and guns and tanks and bullets and food to help him achieve stable postwar government.

Mao Tse-tung, by comparison, was a poor relation. His army may have numbered around a million, but it remained essentially a guerrilla force that lacked small arms and supply in all categories, let alone supporting arms, such as armor, artillery, and aircraft. Nor did Mao's prospects for substantial aid seem great. In the treaty signed between Nationalist China and Russia in August, Stalin promised to support Chiang's government, and, at this stage, he did not seem to be going out of his way to help Mao. In refuting Kuomintang claims believed or at least reported by some American officials, Ambassador Hurley, as late as December 6, 1945, ". . . told the Foreign Relations Committee that the Chinese Communists were not getting help from Moscow."[9]

On paper, then, the numerical balance favored Chiang—a later State Department estimate suggested a ". . . five to one superiority in combat troops and in rifles. . . ."[10] In the minds of Chiang and his closest Kuomintang advisers, elimination of the Japanese threat had brought back the problem of the early thirties: suppression of Communist ban-

9. Leopold, op. cit.; see also Lohbeck, op. cit.: Hurley later changed his mind.
10. USDS-China, *supra*.

dits. That the problem's dimensions had drastically altered, Chiang refused to admit. And, despite Wedemeyer's warnings, he also refused
to repair deficiencies in government and army. In autumn of 1945, he
displayed even greater arrogance of ignorance than formerly. He fancied
himself much stronger than he was, the Communists much weaker than
they were. With considerable optimism, even elation, he insisted on occupying not only northern China but all of Manchuria as rapidly as
American planes and ships could move his armies.

The Japanese surrender had found Nationalists unprepared to move
forces rapidly to major cities in central and northern China, there to re-
assert governmental authority and to begin the immense task of repatri-
ating nearly four million Japanese soldiers and civilians.

After appealing successfully to the Americans for transportation,
Chiang forbade Chinese Communists to accept surrender of Japanese
arms. In turn, General Douglas MacArthur ordered Japanese units *not*
to surrender to Chinese Communists. Simultaneously, an impressive
American airlift carried three Nationalist armies to key points in eastern
and northern China, including Shanghai, Nanking, and Peiping. Wedemeyer asked the Joint Chiefs of Staff for seven U.S. divisions ". . . in
order to create a barrier through North China and Manchuria against
Soviet Russia."[11] Not having seven divisions available, the JCS sent a
U. S. Marine Corps task force of about fifty thousand troops, which
landed in October ". . . and occupied Peiping, Tientsin, and the coal
mines to the north, together with the essential railroads in the
area. . . ."[12] Ostensibly landed to accept surrender of Japan's North
China Army on behalf of Chiang Kai-shek and to start repatriation of
Japanese nationals, the marine force in reality attempted to deny the
area to Communist influence—an impossible task in view of its limited
numbers and of Communist organizational strength in the countryside.

The sad truth was that none of these measures had frightened Mao
Tse-tung, any more than had Chiang's paper strength. While peace talks
continued with Nationalists, Mao sent units by forced marches to northern China and Manchuria. Some Japanese units voluntarily surrendered
to these on-the-spot forces; others resisted in at least token fashion. In
northern China, Communists soon controlled most of the countryside
and, from that power position, began claiming control of most railroads.
Incidents, including quite serious skirmishes, now began between Communist forces and Nationalist-American forces.

Largely because of Chiang's weakness in northern China, Wedemeyer had vigorously objected to his occupation of Manchuria, arguing
that Chiang could not afford to move there until he had consolidated

11. Wedemeyer, op. cit.
12. USDS-China, *supra.*

his position in northern China. Wedemeyer argued primarily on logistic grounds. The problem of maintaining large forces a thousand miles north loomed enormous in its own right; add the possibility of Communist interdiction of vital lines of communication and, as Wedemeyer foresaw, a formula emerged for potential disaster. Instead, he wanted Chiang to arrange a five-power guardianship over Manchuria by the United States, Great Britain, France, China, and the Soviet Union, and send ". . . his best administrators as well as military leaders to North China, south of the Great Wall, to insure that his control there would be firmly established."[13]

Chiang's complacence forbade compliance. He insisted on sticking to his overly ambitious plan, and the American Government very foolishly acquiesced. After delay caused by procuring cold-weather clothing from Alaska and by inoculating troops, American planes and ships began lifting Chinese armies into Manchuria, an impressive effort that involved nearly half a million men.[14]

Meanwhile, under terms of the Yalta and Potsdam agreements and the Sino-Soviet treaty, Soviet troops had occupied Manchuria and had accepted the surrender there of Japanese forces. The agreement called for the Soviets to remain for three months. But such was the delay in deploying Nationalist armies, that, in November, Chiang asked Stalin to extend his occupation. Stalin gladly agreed—his locustlike minions were stripping Manchuria's industrial plants, nor did the Soviet dictator object to Chinese Communists rapidly infiltrating the area.

Whether the Chinese Communist move accorded with Stalin's wishes is a moot question, despite later assertions by a vociferous American faction who endeavored to paint a black-and-white picture of a scene fraught with nuance and subtlety. Some evidence exists that Mao acted independently and presented Stalin with a *fait accompli* which he may not have welcomed, but which he could not reverse.

Whatever the case, when the Japanese surrendered, Mao had sent an army to Manchuria by forced marches across Jehol. Commanded by capable Lin Piao, this force had two targets: one, the cities and all-important Japanese arms dumps; the other, the countryside and all-important peasants who would bear arms to make a new field army.

No question exists that Chinese Communists acquired Japanese arms. If the Russians tried to deny them access to dumps, they didn't try very hard. An American army officer, Lieutenant Colonel Robert Rigg, who was assistant military attaché in China, was in Manchuria at this time. In Changchun, a Soviet officer in charge of one of these depots told him that Chinese Communists had attacked. ". . . We shot at them, but our

13. Wedemeyer, op. cit.
14. USDS-China, *supra*.

guards were too few. They were overwhelmed and had to flee." Colonel Rigg ". . . found little variance to this pattern. The Soviets placed a few guards over arms depots; but they were always 'attacked.' . . . Whether the Chinese were invited to attack at a given time I cannot verify, but the results were always the same. The Reds of China got the arms. . . ."[15]

The Reds of China were getting more than arms. A large part of Lin Piao's effort went to recruiting peasants for his new army. This effort prospered for the same reasons as earlier Communist successes: a simple "pitch" that exploited existing grievances and offered immediate and visible reforms. Lin's soldiers also treated peasants with a consideration that contrasted, as in the past, with the rapacious performance of Nationalists, who soon began arriving in large numbers. Wedemeyer had feared precisely this development. One of his reasons for trying to steer Chiang away from Manchuria was

. . . his conviction that National Government abuses and malpractices had already created serious discontent among the local population in areas taken over from the Japanese, and even this soon after the end of the war against Japan had seriously alienated a considerable amount of sympathy for the National Government.[16]

As the build-up of Communist and Nationalist troops continued in Manchuria and northern China, serious clashes began to end Western hopes for coalition settlement. The Cassandra tone of Wedemeyer's final reports on Nationalist combat efficiency deepened Washington gloom. Although Hurley had succeeded in forging a Nationalist-Communist agreement that, in October, he told Truman ". . . promised to lead to true peace in China," his own behavior grew increasingly morbid. For months, he had been complaining of slights by State Department officials as well as impugning the loyalty of certain of his Chungking subordinates. Instead of returning to China, as he promised Truman, he suddenly resigned and, on November 27, delivered a speech at the National Press Club that, in Truman's words, attacked ". . . the administration, the State Department, our foreign policy and me personally."[17]

Truman now appointed a special representative with personal rank of ambassador, the recently retired and extremely able General of the Army George C. Marshall, to try to negotiate a peace.

Despite Wedemeyer's gloomy prognostications, Marshall succeeded in bringing both sides to the conference table, where Mao's representative, Chou En-lai, ". . . acknowledged the leadership of Chiang Kai-

15. Griffith (CPLA), *supra.*
16. USDS-China, *supra.*
17. Truman, op. cit.; see also Acheson, op. cit.

shek and disavowed any desire to establish a separate government."[18] This favorable beginning unfortunately meant very little. When it came to working out participation in a government, each side remained intransigent. Chiang, his confidence increased by a series of minor military victories in early 1946, demanded full control of Manchuria prior to initiating legislative reforms; Mao Tse-tung, aware that his own power was growing daily in the area, refused to accede.

While talks continued, clashes between the two armies grew more frequent and severe. In March, the Russians transferred garrison areas to Nationalists and withdrew their forces. Active fighting set in.

Although Marshall arranged another cease-fire, in spring of 1946, he was holding two tigers by the tail and finally had to let go. His failure did not surprise Wedemeyer, who had originally warned

. . . that he would never be able to effect a working arrangement between the Communists and Nationalists, since the Nationalists, who still had most of the power, were determined not to relinquish one iota of it, while the Communists for their part were equally determined to seize all power, with the aid of the Soviet Union.[19]

Wedemeyer returned to America in April 1946, critical of administration policy and scornful of Marshall's efforts. In July, Marshall received a rather more helpful associate in the person of Dr. J. Leighton Stuart, the newly appointed American ambassador.

At this stage, neither Stuart nor anyone else seemingly could disturb Chiang Kai-shek's complacency. On the military front, Marshall warned him that he was not winning in Manchuria, that, at best, Nationalists ". . . were holding their own while draining away those forces needed to hold China proper."[20] To a high-ranking government official,

. . . General Marshall emphasized that the tactics being followed by the Government were such that in its efforts to prevent communism the Government was creating conditions favorable for a Communist regime. He cited as an example the existing financial and economic situation which would be made more serious by continuation of military operations and added that civil war, accompanied by economic chaos, would provide fruitful breeding grounds for communism.[21]

Chiang refused to respect Marshall's views and also vigorously rebutted a strong warning by President Truman to settle the problem by negotiation and not force. When Chiang opened an offensive in northern China in the autumn, Truman placed a limited embargo on arms shipments to China. Despite these and other measures, the Communists

18. Leopold, op. cit.
19. Wedemeyer, op. cit.
20. Harrison, op. cit.
21. USDS-China, *supra*.

openly accused Marshall of belonging to Chiang's camp. In November, Chou En-lai returned to Yenan, and, in December, Marshall returned to America and, shortly after, became secretary of state.

Marshall delivered a final warning to Chiang Kai-shek: In his opinion, the Communists were too powerful to be eliminated by military force alone; in view of current Nationalist military expenditure—about 70 per cent of the total government budget—the country would face economic collapse before eliminating the Communists. Chiang replied that he would exterminate the Communists in from eight to ten months.[22]

For a time, Nationalist armies seemed to give the lie to Marshall's warnings. In winter of 1946–47, they incontestably held major cities of northern China and Manchuria; in March 1947, a Nationalist offensive in northern China captured a number of Communist-held towns, including the capital, Yenan.

But these gains proved dangerously illusory, as stated in a report by Ambassador Stuart:

. . . Although the Government claims it routed over 100,000 Communist troops, this appears to be a gross exaggeration since American observers during the return of Communist mediation personnel reported the virtual evacuation of Yenan. It has long been apparent that the Communists have prepared well for this eventuality and that they never had any real intention of defending Yenan should such action appear to be costly. Rather it is more in keeping with their long developed tactics to evacuate any given point in the face of enemy pressure, draw him into a pocket, and thereafter gradually sap his strength with guerrilla tactics. Furthermore, Government lines are seriously extended into territory which can be counted upon to be hostile in all respects.[23]

Sadly, Chiang and his principal advisers either would not or could not recognize the true nature of this war. Nationalist armies in Manchuria and northern China behaved like conquerors, looting and raping virtually at will. Local commanders used puppet troops and even Japanese troops in carrying out the occupation. Professor Harrison wrote that

. . . in the countryside the Kuomintang returned the land titles of the landlords and permitted them to demand impossible back rents and interests for the years they had been absent. In addition, returning officials attempted to collect back taxes for the years of Japanese occupation. No actions could

---

22. Ibid.: Widespread optimism infested the Chinese military high command. Chiang's chief of staff publicly claimed that the Communists would be defeated in six months; Chiang himself told Ambassador Stuart that ". . . by the end of August or the beginning of September the Communist forces would either be annihilated or driven into the far hinterland."

23. Ibid.

have been more calculated to enrage the peasants and throw them into the waiting arms of the Communists.[24]

Nepotism, corruption, and inefficiency continued to infest top-heavy officer ranks already torn with intense jealousy and internecine feuds. Dr. Griffith has pointed out that, in Manchuria, ". . . General Tu Yu-ming, commander in chief of the North-east Combat Command, did not speak, except officially, to General Hsiung Shih-hui, Chiang's administrator of this vast area." At a time when running the elusive enemy to ground called for most-carefully co-ordinated operations, the army was disintegrating into a welter of feuding factions, and American advisers could not persuade Chiang to relieve incompetent generals who were friends in favor of competent leaders whom he did not trust.[25] As early as spring of 1946, ". . . entire companies and battalions of provincial troops" had begun to defect to the Communists; in October an entire Nationalist division went over to the enemy.[26] Morale plunged further when Nationalist armies cooped themselves in the cities for winter—what Chiang called "sitting the enemy to death,"[27] but what proved to be the death warrant of his own armies.

On the other hand, and contrary to Kuomintang belief, attrition warfare suited the enemy, whose forces had grown remarkably strong in Manchuria, primarily the result of incessant political effort that exploited Nationalist weaknesses. In early 1947, Lin Piao assumed command of a new People's Liberation Army. In April, he began attacking small Nationalist garrisons throughout Manchuria; in May, his Fifth Offensive forced almost all Nationalist garrisons in Manchuria on the defensive. At month's end, the American consul general at Mukden reported that deteriorating Nationalist morale was a

. . . matter of wide public knowledge and talk. It is reflected in jumpy nerves of military garrisons, efforts to evade conscription, and reliable information from all sectors of Nationalist territory (including points distant from current fighting) indicating that Nationalists in a panicky state are feverishly building trench systems everywhere with only "Maginot" defense strategy in mind. There is good evidence that apathy, resentment, and defeatism are spreading fast in Nationalist ranks causing surrenders and desertions. . . .

This does not mean Manchurian collapse is necessarily imminent. It does mean, however, that Nationalist morale has reached a point where there is the possibility of a sudden debacle laying all Manchuria open to the Communists whenever they choose to take it. . . .[28]

24. Harrison, op. cit.
25. Griffith (CPLA), *supra;* see also USDS-China, *supra:* the reports of Major General Barr are particularly informative.
26. Griffith (CPLA), *supra.*
27. Schurmann, op. cit. (Vol. 2).
28. USDS-China, *supra.*

By autumn, Communists virtually controlled the area, with exception of isolated Nationalist garrisons in the big cities. Meanwhile, other Communist forces, in northern China, were striking at Chiang's lines of communication, primarily railways, as Wedemeyer had foreseen. The deteriorating situation had caused President Truman to send General Wedemeyer as his personal ambassador to make still another survey. The Wedemeyer Mission reached China in July 1947.

Wedemeyer did not like what he found, and he took the unusual step of saying so in an address the following month to Chiang Kai-shek, his ministers, and the State Council. Wedemeyer told his listeners that, due to inefficiency and corruption at all civil and military levels, they had lost the opportunity for military victory and now had to fight an insurgency situation with political and economic means. The American general laid his adverse conclusions on the line in terms of Stilwellian candor reinforced by chilling accuracy:

. . . I believe that the Chinese Communist movement cannot be defeated by the employment of force. Today China is being invaded by an idea instead of strong military forces from the outside. The only way in my opinion to combat this idea successfully is to do so with another idea that will have stronger appeal and win the support of the people. This means that politically and economically the Central Government will have to remove corruption and incompetence from its ranks in order to provide justice and equality and to protect the personal liberties of the Chinese people, particularly of the peasants. To recapitulate, the Central Government cannot defeat the Chinese Communists by the employment of force, but can only win the loyal, enthusiastic, and realistic support of the masses of the people by improving the political and economic situation immediately. The effectiveness and timeliness of these improvements will determine in my opinion whether or not the Central Government will stand or fall before the Communist onslaught.[29]

Since General Marshall had repeatedly warned Chiang of this eventuality, the Chinese president could not have been very surprised. His advisers were suitably insulted, however—all stage play, for they held no intention of putting matters right.

Wedemeyer privately advised Truman to end the fighting by United Nations intervention and work out some sort of international trustee arrangement in Manchuria—as he had recommended to Chiang in 1945. He also recommended ". . . a bold program of military and economic support, lasting at least five years . . . [and] contingent upon Chiang's promise to initiate sweeping political and social reforms."[30]

Scarcely had administration officials in Washington digested Wedemeyer's pessimism than a new crisis exploded in a government already

29. Ibid.
30. Leopold, op. cit.

shaken by Greek and European crises. In October 1947, *Life* magazine published a long and explosive article, "A Report to the American People on China." Its special correspondent was a fifty-six-year-old one-time American ambassador to the Soviet Union, William C. Bullitt.[31]

Bullitt's long article deserves considerable attention, because it reflected the thinking of the China lobby in Washington and because certain of its points scored with such Republican leaders as Senator Vandenberg and John Foster Dulles, who made China a prominent issue in the 1948 presidential campaign.

Bullitt followed a scare opening with a flattering account of Chiang's political acumen and a highly critical précis of Roosevelt's wartime diplomacy. To anyone familiar with the record, Bullitt's bias came as no surprise: A one-time intimate of Roosevelt, he had been dropped from 1940 onward to the extent that, in 1944, he became a major in the Free French army under De Gaulle. After the war, he unsuccessfully tried to reinsinuate himself into government. In 1947, the Republican party and Henry Luce found him a convenient device by which to break the pre-election storm.

They made a good choice. Writing of the Yalta agreements, Bullitt thundered: ". . . No more unnecessary, disgraceful, and potentially disastrous document has ever been signed by a President of the U.S." The clauses relating to Manchuria, the writer told his readers, represented a plot by Stalin to gain eventual control not only of Manchuria but of all China. General Marshall's postwar success in gaining a cease-fire, Bullitt went on, played into Soviet hands by giving Chinese Communists time to replace Soviet forces in Manchuria. Truman's embargo on further arms shipments to Chiang ". . . resulted in disarming our friends while the Soviet Union was arming our enemies." Unless America took prompt action, Chiang would lose Manchuria and ". . . a course of events fatal to China would follow."

Bullitt wanted Truman to release vast quantities of non-essential arms and supply, including aircraft, to Chiang and also to grant credits of $450 million a year for a minimum of three years ". . . to break the vicious circle of Chinese inflation. . . ." He then recommended an eighteen-point reform program (which would have warmed Stilwell's heart). Bullitt, who knew virtually nothing about China, told readers, ". . . A program of this sort would unquestionably be popular throughout China, and with some American assistance it can be carried out." In the past, wrote Bullitt:

. . . Too many Americans, clothed with a little brief authority, when they go to China confuse the might, majesty, power and dominion of the U.S. with their own personalities and talk down to Chinese who, in truth as men,

31. Bullitt, op. cit.

are their superiors. In the pages of history Generalissimo Chiang Kai-shek bulks larger than any living American. . . .

In Bullitt's opinion, the only American with sufficient ". . . military knowledge, political skill, and personal magnitude to organize such co-operation" was General MacArthur:

. . . The General would not have to abandon his work in Japan. He could divide his time between Tokyo and Nanking. . . . He could establish rapidly with the Generalissimo the relation of two comrades in a front-line trench. . . .

Bullitt ended his article with a "domino" prediction as frightening as it was inaccurate:

. . . If China falls into the hands of Stalin [!], all Asia, including Japan, sooner or later will fall into his hands. The manpower and resources of Asia will be mobilized against us. The independence of the U.S. will not live a generation longer than the independence of China.

Bullitt's understanding of the guerrilla problem was even more muddled, but it was particularly significant, since he stated that MacArthur's ". . . military, economic, and political proposals might well be those outlined in this report." Bullitt was plainly puzzled by actual fighting, which

. . . in no way resembles warfare of the sort that our troops experienced in Europe in either World War. The Communists use guerrilla tactics, moving swiftly and attacking at night, hiding in villages and resting in the daytime. An observer in a plane may fly low over hundreds of miles of territory in North China and Manchuria through which these guerrillas are scattered and never see a single soldier or the slightest evidence of troop movement. At dusk the Communists assemble, march fast towards their objective, often covering as much as twenty miles, and strike in the night. They are attempting to bring down the government not by destroying its armed forces [!] but by wrecking the economic life of the country. Hence they do not hesitate to burn towns and villages, destroy railroads, and blow up industrial installations, such as power plants, which they cannot carry away.

The government armies attempting to protect cities, towns and villages are for the most part tied down to fixed points. They move more slowly than the Communists and often when they attack they find that the Communists have quietly withdrawn in the night. . . .

In Bullitt's opinion, ". . . to drive out of Manchuria the 350,000 Communists will require the training and equipment in the American manner of ten new divisions." While proposed reforms were eliminating "all graft" from the Chinese army, ". . . American military men can and should run the service of supply in Manchuria." In northern China,

. . . where the Communists hold no large cities and are essentially raiders, the problem is one of cornering and capturing guerrillas. For this purpose light-armed, fast-moving troops are needed, equipped with jeeps, half-tracks, light trucks, small arms, machine guns, and 75s [75-mm. pack howitzers]. The estimates of the ablest American and Chinese officers who have studied this problem indicate that twenty divisions of such troops should be able to clean up North China. . . .

Both Bullitt's and Wedemeyer's suggestions for political, economic and military reforms read sensibly enough, except that they were all old hat. Stilwell had started citing them in 1942, his words repeated and embroidered by Hurley, Wedemeyer himself, and Marshall, not to mention their deputies, civil and military, as well as a host of important visiting firemen. All had told Chiang that he must ". . . initiate sweeping political and social [and military] reforms" and had been ceremoniously promised that this would happen.

But it never happened—and, in view of Chiang's severe limitations, possibly it never could have happened. President Truman, who has been severely criticized for inaction during this period, was being more realistic than his critics. American observers were reporting that lack of arms and supply was least of Chiang's problems. He was already receiving substantial financial aid—since Japan's surrender, he had received a good portion of what eventually would total two billion dollars, and this did not include another billion dollars' worth of arms.[32]

Although Truman refused to be stampeded, Chiang continued to demand increased aid; Republican voices such as Dewey's echoed Chiang, and, in December, Congress rebuked the President by voting a specific $338-million appropriation for China as part of the European aid bill.[33] In a new year's address to his country, Chiang promised that the "Communist bandits" would be eliminated within a year.

Neither money nor words provided the answer. Nothing short of dynamite could have blasted Nationalist armies from rotting to pieces in their city-islands. While Congress was voting dollars, Lin Piao, commanding an army of about 320,000, struck out in the "Seventh Offensive," designed to eliminate the few remaining connecting points between Nationalist-held cities. In northern China, Communist guerrilla units commanded by Nieh Jung-chen and P'eng Teh-huai, though outnumbered three to one, ". . . found ample opportunity to cut communications, attack weak detachments, and otherwise punish isolated Nationalist forces."[34] Farther south, Communist guerrillas were well on

32. Acheson, op. cit.
33. Leopold, op. cit.
34. Griffith (CPLA), *supra*.

their way to dominating railway lines essential to support of northern China and Manchuria garrisons.

Early in the new year, Lin Piao began the siege of Mukden. In March, Chiang's American military adviser, Major General David Barr, sensed disaster and recommended "progressive withdrawal" of Nationalist forces from Manchuria. Chiang refused to consider this, nor would he concentrate forces by evacuating the important northern garrisons into Mukden.[35] Throughout spring and summer, Communists continued encircling tactics. Nationalist morale continued to deteriorate, with Communists enjoying increasing defections from Nationalist garrisons. In final battles that autumn, entire regiments and divisions laid down arms. Chinchow fell in mid-October, Changchun and Mukden soon after. By early November, Communists controlled all of Manchuria. Chiang had lost some thirty-three divisions—over 320,000 men, in General Barr's words ". . . the finest soldiers the Government had. . . ."[36] Eighty-five per cent of these units were equipped with the best American weapons: Rifles, machine guns, mortars, artillery, radios—all went to Lin Piao's guerrillas.

Mao turned now to two tasks: the conquest of northern China and, simultaneously, a push into the Yangtze Valley. Each battle area favored his tactics. In the North, as in Manchuria, Nationalist city garrisons lent themselves to isolation and attack. Farther south, Chiang insisted on defending along the railway line east and west of Hsuchow. American advisers recommended the more natural line of the Hwai River, to the south. Chiang overruled them to deploy large army groups east and west of the city, itself defended by an enormous garrison that included Chiang's last major artillery and armor units.

Mao's commanders in the center and South had proved as adept as Lin Piao in applying standard Communist tactics. Beginning in late October, General Liu Po ch'eng applied pressure to the western force while his columns snaked between army groups and garrison to interdict communications between defenders as well as between the battle area and the Yangtze. Simultaneously, General Ch'en Yi's army struck the eastern defenders, the Seventh Army Group.

By early November, the situation was so serious that General Barr recommended a fighting withdrawal of the Hsuchow garrison to the line of the Hwai. A few days later, Seventh Army Group surrendered to Ch'en Yi—". . . almost 90,000 officers and men; 1,000 howitzers, cannon, and mortars; and vast stores of other weapons, ammunition, and assorted matériel."[37] Despite this disaster, the battle of Hwai-Hai, fought by Chiang's last real army and involving over a million troops,

35. USDS-China, *supra*.
36. Ibid.
37. Griffith (CPLA), *supra*.

lasted sixty-five days before final Nationalist defeat. Chiang lost sixty-six divisions surrendered or destroyed.

With Nationalist armies shattered and Communists in control of China north of the Yangtze, the end was clearly in sight. General Barr's final reports put one in mind of Kierkegaard's pessimistic thought: ". . . The individual cannot help his age, he can only express that it is doomed." Barr concluded that only massive U.S. aid would ". . . enable the Nationalist Government to maintain a foothold in southern China against a determined Communist advance. . . . The complete defeat of the Nationalist army . . . is inevitable."[38]

Washington correctly translated "massive U.S. aid" to mean direct intervention, which, for a variety of reasons, President Truman would not consider. Although remnant Nationalist forces held the line of the Yangtze during winter 1948–49, Chiang had almost run out of time. Mao's knowledge of the favorable political situation only added to the tidal crest of victory. In April 1949, when his call for unconditional surrender and the trial of Chiang Kai-shek as a war criminal went unanswered, he ordered Ch'en's and Liu's victorious armies to cross the Yangtze.

By autumn, resistance had virtually vanished. On the first day of October, 1949, Mao proclaimed the People's Republic of China. In early December, Chiang and the remnants of government and army slipped away to Formosa.

A number of factors hindered healthy analysis of the China disaster. The emotional and psychological impact of Nationalist China's defeat reverberated throughout the West. Coming on the heels of Soviet explosion of an atomic bomb, in September 1949, it seemed to many good citizens to portend disaster. Convictions of Alger Hiss for perjury and of Klaus Fuchs for atomic espionage, early in 1950, added to general gloom.

Fear began to fill otherwise-rational minds.

Instead of objective study of complex issues raised by the administration's White Paper on China, published in August 1949, influential portions of the American public turned to the deceptively simple but politically powerful thesis that a small group of diplomats and army officers was responsible for "the loss of China"—a thesis so successfully developed by that great American shame Senator Joseph McCarthy.

Minds that refused fear, cooler and calmer minds, which, under normal circumstances, would have examined Chiang's defeat analytically, continued to be burdened with domestic and international crises that culminated in the outbreak of the Korean War, in June 1950.

Thus it was that the fall of the House of Chiang produced a disastrous

38. USDS-China, *supra*.

rubble of conflicting and generally erroneous conclusions in American political and military circles. Although a few observers bravely insisted on the ingenuity of Mao Tse-tung's revolutionary strategy and tactics, almost no one probed beneath the wreckage to discover precisely what had happened in Mao's camp.

And such was the impact of the crash, such the emotional outbursts and almost panic-stricken air, that only a superficial correlation emerged between the civil war in China and guerrilla actions being fought in Greece, Indonesia, the Philippines, Malaya—and French Indochina.

Failure to study each of these actions in its own right and to identify common and peculiar characteristics, simply added to the general ignorance that traditionally had surrounded guerrilla war.

Works Cited in This Volume

Acheson, Dean. *Present at the Creation—My Years in the State Department.* New York: W. W. Norton, 1969.

Adcock, F. E. *The Roman Art of War Under the Republic.* Cambridge, Mass.: Harvard University Press, 1940.

Alba, Victor. *The Mexicans—The Making of a Nation.* London: Pall Mall Press, 1967.

Alden, J. R. *The American Revolution, 1775–1783.* New York: Harper & Brothers, 1954.

——. *A History of the American Revolution—Britain and the Loss of the Thirteen Colonies.* London: MacDonald, 1969.

——. *The South in the Revolution, 1763–1789.* Baton Rouge, La.: State University Press, 1957.

Aldington, R. *Lawrence of Arabia—A Biographical Enquiry.* London: Collins, 1955.

Alsop, S.; and Braden, T. *Sub Rosa—The OSS and American Espionage.* New York: Harcourt, Brace & World, 1963.

Altamira, Rafael. *A History of Spain.* New York: D. Van Nostrand, 1949.

Amery, Julian. *Approach March.* London: Hutchinson, 1973.

——. *Sons of the Eagle—A Study in Guerrilla Warfare.* London: Macmillan, 1948.

Amery, L. S. (ed.). *The Times History of the War in South Africa.* London: Sampson, Low, Marston, 1902. Vol. 2 (1902) of 5 vols.

Anders, W. *An Army in Exile.* London: Macmillan, 1949.

Anon. *An Historical Account of the Expedition Against the Ohio Indians in the Year MDCCLXIV Under the Command of Henry Bouquet, Esq.* London: n.p., 1766.

Appian. *Appian's Roman History.* London: William Heinemann, 1964. Vol. 1 of 4 vols. Tr. Horace White.

Armstrong, J. A. (ed.). *Soviet Partisans in World War II.* Madison, Wis.: University of Wisconsin Press, 1964.

Armstrong, J. A.; and DeWitt, K. "Organization and Control of the Partisan Movement." In Armstrong, *supra.*

Aron, Robert. *De Gaulle Before Paris—The Liberation of France June–August 1944.* London: Putnam, 1962. Tr. H. Hare.

Arrian. *Anabasis Alexandri.* London: William Heinemann, 1929. Vol. 1 of 2 vols. Tr. E. I. Robson.

Arthur, George. *Life of Lord Kitchener.* London: Macmillan, 1920. Vol. 1 of 3 vols.

Asprey, R. B. "Guerrilla Warfare." In Encyclopaedia Britannica, 1969.

——. "The Peninsular War" and "Wellington at Waterloo," *Army Quarterly*, Vols. 77–78, April and July 1959.

——. "Small Wars—1925–1962," *Leatherneck*, 1962.

——. "Waller of Samar," *Marine Corps Gazette*, May and June 1961.

Atkin, Ronald. *Revolution! Mexico 1910–1920*. New York: John Day, 1969.

Azan, Paul (ed.). *Par l'Épée et par la Charrue—Écrits et Discours de Bugeaud*. Paris: Presses Universitaires de France, 1948.

Badian, E. "Alexander the Great and the Unity of Mankind." In *Historia*. Wiesbaden: Franz Steiner Verlag, 1952. Vol. 7, pp. 425–44.

Baker, Carlos. *Hemingway: The Writer as Artist*. Princeton, N.J.: Princeton University Press, 1967.

Barclay, C. N. *Battle 1066*. London: J. M. Dent & Sons, 1966.

Barea, A. *The Track*. London: Faber & Faber, 1943. Tr. Ilsa Barea.

Barrett, David D. *Dixie Mission: The United States Army Observer Group in Yenan, 1944*. Berkeley, Calif.: University of California Press, 1970.

Bass, Robert D. *Swamp Fox—The Life and Campaigns of General Francis Marion*. London: Alvin Redman, 1959.

Beckett, J. C. *The Making of Modern Ireland 1603–1923*. London: Faber & Faber, 1966.

Beeler, John. *Warfare in England, 1066–1189*. Ithaca, N.Y.: Cornell University Press, 1966.

——. *Warfare in Feudal Europe, 730–1200*. Ithaca, N.Y.: Cornell University Press, 1971.

Behr, Edward. *The Algerian Problem*. London: Hodder & Stoughton, 1961.

Bennett, Richard. *The Black and Tans*. London: Hulton, 1959.

Bernard, Stéphane. *The Franco-Moroccan Conflict, 1943–1956*. New Haven, Conn.: Yale University Press, 1968.

Bertrand, L.; and Petrie, C. *The History of Spain*. London: Eyre & Spottiswoode, 1934.

Bigelow, John. *Principles of Strategy*. Philadelphia: J. B. Lippincott, 1894.

Billias, George A. (ed.). *George Washington's Opponents*. New York: William Morrow, 1969.

Bird, M. J. *The Secret Battalion*. London: Muller, 1965.

Blair, C. N. M. *Guerrilla Warfare*. London: Ministry of Defence, 1957.

Bleicher, Hugo. *Colonel Henri's Story*. London: William Kimber, 1954. Ed. Ian Colvin.

Blow, Rex. "With the Filipino Guerrillas," *Australian Army Journal*, 1966.

Bohlen, C. E. *The Transformation of American Foreign Policy*. New York: W. W. Norton, 1969.

Boswell, James. *The Journal of a Tour to Corsica; and Memoirs of Pascal Paoli*. London: Williams & Norgate, 1951. Ed. with an Introduction by Morchard Bishop.

Bouchier, E. S. *Spain Under the Roman Empire*. Oxford: Blackwell, 1914.

Boyle, Andrew. *Trenchard*. London: Collins, 1962.

Branche, Lesley. *The Sabres of Paradise*. London: John Murray, 1960.

Brett-James, Antony. *Wellington at War 1794–1815*. London: Macmillan, 1961.

Bullitt, W. C. "A Report to the American People on China," *Life*, October 13, 1947.

Burn, A. R. *Alexander the Great*. New York: Macmillan, 1947.

——. *Persia and the Greeks*. London: Edward Arnold, 1962.

Burne, A. H. *The Agincourt War*. London: Eyre & Spottiswoode, 1956.

——. *The Crecy War*. London: Eyre & Spottiswoode, 1955.

Bury, J. B. *A History of the Eastern Roman Empire*. London: Macmillan, 1912.

——. *A History of Greece—To the Death of Alexander the Great*. London: Macmillan, 1959. Rev. R. Meiggs.

——. *History of the Later Roman Empire*. London: Macmillan, 1923. 2 vols.

Butler, J. R. M. *History of the Second World War, Grand Strategy*. London: HMSO, 1957. Vol. 2.

Buttinger, Joseph. *Vietnam: A Dragon Embattled*. New York: Frederick A. Praeger, 1967. Vol. 1 of 2 vols.

Caesar, Julius. *Commentaries on the Gallic War*. London: Macmillan, 1908. Vol. 1 of 2 vols. Tr. T. Rice Holmes.

Caird, L. H. *The History of Corsica*. London: Unwin, 1899.

Callinan, Bernard. *Independent Company*. London: William Heinemann, 1953.

Callwell, C. E. *Small Wars—Their Principles and Practice*. London: HMSO, 1899.

——. *The Armed Strength of Roumania*. London: HMSO, 1888.

——. *Hints on Reconnaissances in Little Known Countries*. London: HMSO, 1890.

——. *Handbook of the Armies of the Minor Balkan States*. London: HMSO, 1891.

——. *Handbook of the Turkish Army*. London: HMSO, 1892.

Calvert, Michael. *Prisoners of Hope*. London: Jonathan Cape, 1952.

Calvert, Peter. *The Mexican Revolution, 1910–1914—The Diplomacy of Anglo-American Conflict*. London: Cambridge University Press, 1968.

Cannon, M. H. *The War in the Pacific—Leyte: Return to the Philippines*. Washington: U. S. Government Printing Office, 1954.

Carr, E. H. *Karl Marx—A Study in Fanaticism*. London: J. M. Dent & Sons, 1934.

——. *Studies in Revolution*. London: Macmillan, 1950.

Carr, Raymond. "Spain and Portugal—1793 to c. 1840." In *The New Cambridge Modern History*. London: Cambridge University Press, 1965. Vol. 9 of 12 vols.

Cate, James L. "The Crusade of 1101." In Setton, *infra*.

Caulaincourt, Duke of Vicenza. *Memoirs*. London: Cassell, 1935. 2 vols. Ed. Jean Hanoteau; tr. Hamish Miles.

Charles, First Marquis Cornwallis. *Correspondence*. London: John Murray, 1859. Ed. Charles Ross. Vol. 1 of 3 vols.

Cheetham, Sir Nicolas. *A History of Mexico*. London: Rupert Hart-Davis, 1970.

Cheshire, H. T. "The Great Tartar Invasion of Europe," *The Slavonic Review*. Vol. 5. London, 1926.

Christiansen, E. *The Origins of Military Power in Spain—1800–1854*. London: Oxford University Press, 1967.

Churchill, Peter. *Of Their Own Choice.* London: Hodder & Stoughton, 1952.

Churchill, Randolph S. *Winston S. Churchill.* London: William Heinemann, 1966. Vol. 1 of 2 vols.

Churchill, W. S. *Marlborough—His Life and Times.* London: G. C. Harrap, 1933. Vol. 2 of 4 vols.

——. *The World Crisis.* London: Thornton Butterworth, 1929. Vol. 5.

Clark, R. W. *The Birth of a Bomb.* London: Phoenix House, 1961.

Clarke, H. B. *Modern Spain 1815–1898.* London: Cambridge University Press, 1906.

Clausewitz, Carl von. *The Campaign of 1812 in Russia.* London: John Murray, 1843.

——. *On War.* London: Routledge & Kegan Paul, 1968. Vol. 2 of 3 vols. Tr. J. J. Graham.

Clery, C. F. *Minor Tactics.* London: Kegan Paul, Trench, 1887.

Cole, D. H.; and Priestley, E. C. *An Outline of British Military History, 1660–1936.* London: Sifton Praed, 1936.

Comnena, Anna. *The Alexiad.* London: Routledge & Kegan Paul, 1967. Tr. E. A. S. Dawes.

Cookridge, E. H. *Inside SOE—The Story of Special Operations in Western Europe 1940–45.* London: Arthur Barker, 1966.

Costigan, Giovanni. "The Anglo-Irish Conflict, 1919–1922," *University Review.* Dublin: Spring 1968.

Crosthwaite, Charles. *The Pacification of Burma.* London: Edward Arnold, 1912.

Cumberland, Charles C. *Mexico—The Struggle for Modernity.* New York: Oxford University Press, 1968.

Dallin, Alexander. *German Rule in Russia, 1941–1945.* New York: St. Martin's Press, 1957.

——; Mavrogordato, R.; and Moll, W. "Partisan Psychological Warfare and Popular Attitudes." In Armstrong, *supra.*

Dalton, H. *The Fateful Years.* London: Muller, 1957.

Davidson, Basil. *Partisan Picture.* London: Bedford Books, 1946.

Davies, Brigadier. *Illyrian Venture—The Story of the British Military Mission to Enemy-Occupied Albania 1943–1944.* London: Bodley Head, 1952.

Davies, J. D. G.; and Worts, F. R. *England in the Middle Ages—Its Problems and Legacies.* London: Alfred A. Knopf, 1928.

Deakin, F. W. D. *The Embattled Mountain.* London: Oxford University Press, 1971.

De Beer, Gavin. *Alps and Elephants—Hannibal's March.* London: Geoffrey Bles, 1955.

——. *The Struggle for Power in the Mediterranean.* London: Thames & Hudson, 1969.

de Gaulle, Charles. *War Memoirs.* London: Collins, 1955. Vol. 1 of 6 vols. Vol. 1 (Text and Documents) tr. J. Griffin; Vols. 2 and 3 (Text and Documents) tr. R. Howar.

Department of the Army. *German Antiguerrilla Operations in the Balkans (1941–1944).* Washington: U. S. Government Printing Office, 1954.

Deschamps, H.; and Chauvet, P. *Gallieni Pacificateur*. Paris: Presses Universitaires de France, 1949.

Devine, Alex. *Montenegro in History, Politics and War*. London: T. Fisher Unwin, 1918.

DeWitt, K.; and Moll, W. "The Bryansk Area." In Armstrong, *supra*.

Dictionary of National Biography 1922–30. London: Oxford University Press, 1937.

Dodge, T. A. *Hannibal*. Boston: Houghton Mifflin, 1891. Vol. 1 of 2 vols.

Duncalf, Frederic. "The First Crusade: Clermont to Constantinople." In Setton, *infra*.

Duncanson, Dennis J. *Government and Revolution in Vietnam*. London: Oxford University Press, 1968.

Earle, E. E. (ed.). *Makers of Modern Strategy*. Princeton, N.J.: Princeton University Press, 1941.

Eldridge, F. *Wrath in Burma*. New York: Doubleday, 1946.

Éditions G. P. *La Merveilleuse Histoire de l'Armée Française*. Paris, 1947.

Edmonds, James E. "Jomini and Clausewitz," *Army Quarterly*, April 1951.

Ehrlich, Blake. *The French Resistance*. London: Chapman & Hall, 1966.

Fall, Bernard. "Two Thousand Years of War in Viet-Nam," *Horizon*, Spring 1967.

———. *The Two Viet-Nams—A Political and Military Analysis*. New York: Frederick A. Praeger, 1967.

Fellowes-Gordon, Ian. *Amiable Assassins—The Story of the Kachin Guerrillas of North Burma*. London: Robert Hale, 1957.

Fergusson, Bernard. *Beyond the Chindwin*. London: Collins, 1962.

———. *Trumpet in the Hall*. London: Collins, 1970.

———. *The Wild Green Earth*. London: Collins, 1946.

Fink, Harold S. "The Foundation of the Latin States, 1099–1118." In Setton, *infra*.

Fischer, Louis. *The Story of Indonesia*. New York: Harper & Row, 1959.

Fisher, H. A. L. *Europe—Ancient and Medieval*. London: Eyre & Spottiswoode, 1938.

Fitzgibbon, Constantine. *Out of the Lion's Paw*. London: MacDonald, 1970.

Foot, M. R. D. *SOE in France*. London: HMSO, 1966.

Fortescue, John. *Wellington*. London: Ernest Benn, 1925.

Fox, Robin Lane. *Alexander the Great*. London: Allen Lane, 1973.

Franke, Wolfgang. "The Taiping Rebellion." In Schurmann, *infra*.

Frédéric II. *Oeuvres (Histoire de Mon Temps)*. Berlin: Decker, 1846. Vol. 2 of 30 vols. Ed. J. D. E. Preuss.

———. *Oeuvres (Militaires)*. Berlin: Decker, 1856. Vols. 28 and 30 of 30 vols. Ed. J. D. E. Preuss.

Fuller, J. F. C. *British Light Infantry in the Eighteenth Century*. London: Hutchinson, 1925.

———. *The Conduct of War, 1789–1961*. New Brunswick, N.J.: Rutgers University Press, 1961.

———. *The Decisive Battles of the Western World*. London: Eyre & Spottiswoode, 1956. Vols. 1 and 2 of 3 vols.

——. *The Generalship of Alexander the Great.* London: Eyre & Spottis-woode, 1958.

Furneaux, Rupert. *Abdel Krim—Emir of the Rif.* London: Secker & Warburg, 1967.

Galay, N. "The Partisan Forces." In Liddell Hart, B. (ed.), *The Soviet Army. Infra.*

Gallieni, General. *La Pacification de Madagascar (Opérations d'Octobre 1896 à Mars 1899).* Paris: Librairie Militaire R. Chapelot, 1900.

García, Mauro. *Documents on the Japanese Occupation of the Philippines.* Manila: Philippines Historical Association, 1965.

Gardner, Brian. *German East.* London: Cassell, 1963.

Garnett, David (ed.). *The Letters of T. E. Lawrence.* London: Jonathan Cape, 1927.

Garthoff, R. L. *How Russia Makes War—Soviet Military Doctrine.* London: Allen & Unwin, 1954.

Gaxotte, Pierre. *Frederick the Great.* London: G. Bell & Sons, 1941.

Gettleman, M. E. (ed.). *Viet Nam.* New York: Fawcett, 1965.

Gheusi, P. B. *Gallieni et Madagascar.* Paris: Éditions du Petit Parisien, n.d.

Gibb, H. A. R. "The Rise of Saladin 1169–1189." In Setton, *infra.*

Gilbert, Felix. "Machiavelli: The Renaissance of the Art of War." In Earle, *supra.*

Gillespie, Joan. *Algeria—Rebellion and Revolution.* London: Ernest Benn, 1960.

Giraldus Cambrensis. *The Autobiography of Giraldus Cambrensis.* London: Jonathan Cape, 1937. Ed. and tr. H. E. Butler.

Giskes, H. J. *London Calling North Pole.* London: Arthur Barker, 1966.

Goodrich, L. C. *A Short History of the Chinese People.* London: Allen & Unwin, 1969.

Gordon, C. D. *The Age of Attila.* Ann Arbor, Mich.: University of Michigan Press, 1960.

Graves, Robert. *Lawrence and the Arabs.* London: Jonathan Cape, 1927.

Griffith, S. B. *The Battle for Guadalcanal.* Philadelphia: J. B. Lippincott, 1963.

——. *The Chinese People's Liberation Army.* New York: McGraw-Hill, 1967.

——. "Guerrilla," *Marine Corps Gazette,* August 1950.

——. *Sun Tzu: The Art of War.* London: Oxford University Press, 1963.

Groves, Leslie. *Now It Can Be Told.* London: André Deutsch, 1963.

Gwynn, Sir Charles. *Imperial Policing.* New York: St. Martin's Press, 1934.

Hall, D. G. E. "Thailand (History)." Encyclopaedia Britannica, 1968, Vol. 21.

Hammer, Ellen J. *The Struggle for Indochina 1940–1955.* Stanford, Calif.: Stanford University Press, 1966.

Hargreaves, Reginald. *Beyond the Rubicon.* New York: New American Library, 1966.

Harrison, H. D. *The Soul of Yugoslavia.* London: Hodder & Stoughton, 1941.

Harrison, John A. *China Since 1800.* New York: Harcourt, Brace & World, 1967.

Hart, Sir Robert. *These from the Land of Sinim—Essays on the Chinese Question*. London: Chapman & Hall, 1903.

Haukelid, Knut. *Skis Against the Atom*. London: William Kimber, 1954.

Hayes-McCoy, G. A. *Irish Battles*. London: Longmans, Green, 1969.

Hearings Before the Commission on the Philippines of the United States Senate in Relation to Affairs in the Philippine Islands. Washington: U. S. Government Printing Office, 1902. Vol. 2 of 2 vols.

Heilbronn, Otto. *Warfare in the Enemy's Rear*. New York: Frederick A. Praeger, 1963.

Heinl, Robert D. *Soldiers of the Sea*. Annapolis, Md.: U. S. Naval Institute, 1962.

Hemingway, Ernest. *For Whom the Bell Tolls*. London: Penguin Books, 1955.

Henderson, G. F. R. *Stonewall Jackson and the American Civil War*. London: Longmans, Green, 1961.

Herodotus. *The History of Herodotus*. London: John Murray, 1897. Vol. 1 of 2 vols. Ed. A. J. Grant; tr. George Rawlinson.

Herring, Hubert. *A History of Latin America*. London: Jonathan Cape, 1955.

Heymann, Frederick G. *John Zizka and the Hussite Revolution*. Princeton, N.J.: Princeton University Press, 1955.

Hindus, Maurice. *The Cossacks*. New York: Doubleday, Doran, 1945.

Ho Chi Minh. *Prison Diary*. Hanoi: Foreign Languages Publishing House, 1962. Tr. Aileen Palmer.

Ho Kan-chih. "Rise of the Working Class Movement." In Schurmann, *infra*.

Holt, Edgar. *Protest in Arms—The Irish Troubles 1916–1923*. London: Putnam, 1960.

Hoover Institution on War, Revolution and Peace. *France During the German Occupation, 1940–1944*. Stanford, Calif.: Stanford University Press, 1957. Tr. P. W. Whitcomb. 3 vols.

Hordern, Charles. *Military Operations East Africa 1914–1916*. London: HMSO, 1941. Vol. 1.

Hosmer, S. T. (chairman). *Counterinsurgency: A Symposium—April 16–20, 1962*. Santa Monica, Calif.: Rand Corporation, 1963.

Howard, Michael. "Jomini and the Classical Tradition in Military Thought." In *Studies in War and Peace*. London: Maurice Temple Smith, 1970.

Howard-Johnston, James. "Studies in the Organization of the Byzantine Army in the Tenth and Eleventh Centuries." Oxford: Ph.D. thesis, 1971.

Howe, Sonia E. *Lyautey of Morocco*. London: Hodder & Stoughton, 1931.

Howell, E. M. *The Soviet Partisan Movement, 1941–1944*. Washington: U. S. Government Printing Office, 1956.

Hoyt, R. S. *Life and Thought in the Early Middle Ages*. Minneapolis: University of Minnesota Press, 1967.

Htin Aung, Maung. *A History of Burma*. New York: Columbia University Press, 1967.

———. *The Stricken Peacock—Anglo-Burmese Relations 1752–1948*. The Hague: Martinus Nijhoff, 1965.

Hull, Cordell. *Memoirs*. New York: Macmillan, 1948. Vol. 1.

Ibarruri, Dolores. *They Shall Not Pass*. London: Lawrence & Wishart, 1966.

Insor, D. *Thailand—A Political, Social and Economic Analysis*. London: Allen & Unwin, 1963.

Isaacs, Harold. *The Tragedy of the Chinese Revolution*. Stanford, Calif.: Stanford University Press, 1962.

Ivanov, Miroslav. *The Assassination of Heydrich*. London: Hart-Davis, Mac-Gibbon, 1974. Tr. Patrick O'Brian.

Jomini, Baron de. *The Art of War*. Philadelphia: J. B. Lippincott, 1879.

Jones, Gwyn. *A History of the Vikings*. London: Oxford University Press, 1968.

Jumper, Roy; and Normand, M. W. "Vietnam: The Historical Background." In Gettleman, *supra*.

Kahin, G. M. *Nationalism and Revolution in Indonesia*. Ithaca, N.Y.: Cornell University Press, 1952.

Kaminsky, Howard. *A History of the Hussite Revolution*. Berkeley, Calif.: University of California Press, 1967.

Kendall, P. *The Story of Land Warfare*. London: Hamish Hamilton, 1957.

Kennan, G. F. *American Diplomacy, 1900–1950*. London: Secker & Warburg, 1952.

———. *The Decision to Intervene*. London: Faber & Faber, 1958.

———. *Memoirs*. London: Hutchinson, 1968.

———. *Russia Leaves the War*. London: Faber & Faber, 1956.

Kirby, S. W. *The War Against Japan—The Loss of Singapore*. London: HMSO, 1957.

Kirkpatrick, F. A. *The Spanish Conquistadores*. London: Adam & Charles Black, 1934.

Knightly, P.; and Simpson, C. *The Secret Lives of Lawrence of Arabia*. London: Nelson, 1969.

Kochan, Lionel. *Russia in Revolution 1890–1918*. London: Weidenfeld & Nicolson, 1966.

Krausnick, H. *Anatomy of the SS State*. London: Collins, 1968.

Lacroix, Paul. *Military and Religious Life in the Middle Ages and the Renaissance*. New York: Frederick Ungar, 1874.

Laffan, R. G. D. *Select Documents of European History*. London: Methuen, 1930. Vol. 1 of 2 vols.

Lancaster, Donald. *The Emancipation of French Indochina*. London: Oxford University Press, 1961.

Lawrence, T. E. "Guerrilla Warfare." In Encyclopaedia Britannica, 1957, Vol. 10.

———. *Revolt in the Desert*. London: Jonathan Cape, 1927.

———. *Seven Pillars of Wisdom*. London: Jonathan Cape, 1973.

Lenin, V. I. *Selected Works*. Moscow: Foreign Languages Publishing House, c. 1961. Vol. 3 of 3 vols.

Leopold, Richard. *The Growth of American Foreign Policy*. New York: Alfred A. Knopf, 1965.

Leonard, R. A. *A Short Guide to Clausewitz on War*. London: Weidenfeld & Nicolson, 1967.

Lettow-Vorbeck, General von. *My Reminiscences of East Africa*. London: Hurst & Blackett, 1920.

———. *Mein Leben*. Munich: Koehlers, 1957.

Li, D. J. *The Ageless Chinese*. New York: Charles Scribner's Sons, 1965.

Liddell Hart, B. H. *The Decisive Wars of History—A Study in Strategy*. London: G. Bell & Sons, 1929.

———. *T. E. Lawrence*. London: Jonathan Cape, 1934.

——— (ed.). *The Soviet Army*. London: Weidenfeld & Nicolson, 1956.

Lloyd, E. M. *A Review of the History of Infantry*. London: Longmans, Green, 1908.

———. "The Third Coalition." In *The Cambridge Modern History*. London: Cambridge University Press, 1904. Vol. 9 of 13 vols.

Lohbeck, Don. *Patrick J. Hurley*. Chicago: Henry Regnery, 1956.

Longford, Elizabeth. *Wellington—The Years of the Sword*. London: Weidenfeld & Nicolson, 1969.

Luce, Siméon. *Histoire de Bertrand du Guesclin et de Son Époque*. Paris: Librairie Hachette, 1867.

Lyautey, H. "Du rôle social de l'officier" and "Du rôle colonial de l'Armée," *Revue des Deux Mondes* (1891 and 1900).

———. *Lettres du Sud de Madagascar (1900–1902)*. Paris: Librairie Armand Colin, 1935.

———. *Lettres du Tonkin*. Paris: Éditions Nationales, 1928. 2 vols.

———. *Lettres du Tonkin et de Madagascar (1894–1899)*. Paris: Librairie Armand Colin, 1933.

Lyautey, Pierre. *Lyautey L'Africain—Textes et Lettres du Maréchal Lyautey présentés par Pierre Lyautey*. Paris: Librairie Plon, 1953. 4 vols.

MacDonald, J. R. M. "The Terror." In *The Cambridge Modern History*. London: Cambridge University Press, 1904. Vol. 8 of 13 vols.

Mackenzie, A. M. *Robert Bruce King of Scots*. London: Oliver & Boyd, 1934.

Mackesy, Piers. *The War for America 1775–1783*. London: Longmans, Green, 1964.

McLaren, Moray. *Corsica Boswell*. London: Secker & Warburg, 1966.

Maclean, Fitzroy. *Disputed Barricades*. London: Jonathan Cape, 1957.

———. *Eastern Approaches*. London: Jonathan Cape, 1949.

MacMunn, G.; and Falls, C. *Military Operations, Egypt and Palestine*. London: HMSO, 1928 (Vol. 1) and 1930 (Vol. 2).

Madariaga, Salvador de. *The Fall of the Spanish American Empire*. London: Hollis & Carter, 1947.

Mahan, A. T. *The Influence of Sea Power upon the French Revolution and Empire 1783–1812*. London: Sampson, Low, Marston, 1892. 2 vols.

———. *The Influence of Sea Power upon History 1660–1783*. London: Sampson, Low, Marston, 1900.

———. *Sea Power in Its Relations to the War of 1812*. London: Sampson, Low, Marston, c. 1905.

Mahon, Lord. *The Life of Belisarius*. London: John Murray, 1829.

Majatovich, Chedo. *Servia of the Servians*. London: Putnam & Sons, 1911.

Malraux, André. *Days of Hope (L'Espoir)*. London: Penguin, 1970. Tr. S. Gilbert and A. MacDonald.

———. *Man's Estate (La Condition Humaine)*. London: Penguin, 1972. Tr. Alistair MacDonald.

Mao Tse-tung. *Basic Tactics*. New York: Frederick A. Praeger, 1966. Tr. and with an Introduction by Stuart R. Schram.

———. *On Guerrilla Warfare*. New York: Frederick A. Praeger, 1962. Tr. and with an Introduction by S. B. Griffith.

———. *Selected Works*. Peking: Foreign Languages Press, 1965. Vol. 1.

Markham, Felix. *Napoleon*. London: Weidenfeld & Nicolson, 1963.

Marshall, Bruce. *The White Rabbit*. London: Evans Brothers, 1964.

Masaryk, T. G. *The Spirit of Russia*. London: Allen & Unwin, 1919. Vol. 1 of 2 vols.

Matthews, Tanya. *Algerian ABC*. London: Geoffrey Chapman, 1961.

Maurois, André. *Marshal Lyautey*. London: John Lane, Bodley Head, 1931. Tr. H. Miles.

Mavrogordato, R.; and Ziemke, E. "The Polotsk Lowland." In Armstrong, *supra*.

May, E. S. *A Retrospect on the South African War*. London: Sampson, Low, Marston, 1901.

Mazour, A. G. *Russia—Tsarist and Communist*. New York: D. Van Nostrand, 1962.

Meinertzhagen, R. *Army Diary 1899–1926*. London: Oliver & Boyd, 1960.

Mende, Tibor. *The Chinese Revolution*. London: Thames & Hudson, 1961.

Miksche, F. O. *Secret Forces—The Technique of Underground Movements*. London: Faber & Faber, 1950.

Miles, M. E. *A Different Kind of War*. New York: Doubleday, 1967.

Millar, George. *Horned Pigeon*. London: William Heinemann, 1946.

———. *Maquis*. London: William Heinemann, 1945.

Mirillat, H. S. *The Island*. Boston: Houghton Mifflin, 1944.

Mommsen, Theodor. *The History of Rome*. London: J. S. Dent & Sons, 1911. Vol. 3. Tr. W. P. Dickson.

Moorehead, Alan. *The Russian Revolution*. New York: Harper & Brothers, 1958.

Morison, S. E. *Leyte: June 1944–January 1945*. London: Oxford University Press, 1958. Vol. 12 of 15 vols.

———. *The Oxford History of the United States 1783–1917*. London: Oxford University Press, 1928. Vol. 2 of 3 vols.

Morison, S. E.; and Commager, H. S. *The Growth of the American Republic*. New York: Oxford University Press, 1962. Vol. 2 of 2 vols.

Morison, S. E.; and Obregón, M. *The Caribbean as Columbus Saw It*. Boston: Little Brown, 1964.

Morris, J. E. *The Welsh Wars of Edward I*. London: Oxford University Press, 1901.

Mosley, Leonard. *Duel for Kilimanjaro*. London: Weidenfeld & Nicolson, 1963.

———. *Gideon Goes to War*. London: Arthur Barker, 1955.

Mountbatten, Vice-Admiral the Earl. *Report to the Combined Chiefs of Staff by the Supreme Allied Commander South-East Asia, 1943–1945*. London: HMSO, 1951.

Murray, M. *Hunted—A Coastwatcher's Story*. London: Angus & Robertson, 1967.

Myers, E. C. W. *Greek Entanglement*. London: Rupert Hart-Davis, 1955.

Neave, Airey. *Saturday at MI-9*. London: Hodder & Stoughton, 1969.

Nuechterlein, Donald E. *Thailand and the Struggle for Southeast Asia*. Ithaca, N.Y.: Cornell University Press, 1965.

Nutting, Anthony. *Lawrence of Arabia*. London: Hollis & Carter, 1961.

O'Ballance, Edgar. *The Greek Civil War, 1944–1949*. London: Faber & Faber, 1966.

———. *The Red Army*. London: Faber & Faber, 1964.

Ogburn, Charlton. *The Marauders*. New York: Harper & Brothers, 1959.

O'Hea, Patrick. *Reminiscences of the Mexican Revolution*. Mexico City: Editorial Fournier, 1966.

Olcott, C. S. *William McKinley*. New York: Houghton Mifflin, 1916. Vol. 2 of 2 vols.

Oldenbourg, Zoé. *Catherine the Great*. London: William Heinemann, 1965.

Oman, C. W. C. *A History of the Art of War in the Middle Ages*. London: Methuen, 1924. Vol. 1 of 2 vols.

———. *A History of the Peninsular War*. London: Oxford University Press, 1902. 6 vols.

Otway-Ruthven, A. J. *A History of Medieval Ireland*. London: Ernest Benn, 1968.

Painter, Sydney. "Western Europe on the Eve of the Crusades." In Setton, *infra*.

Palmier, Leslie. *Indonesia and the Dutch*. London: Oxford University Press, 1962.

Pares, Bernard. *A History of Russia*. London: Jonathan Cape, 1955.

Paret, Peter. *French Revolutionary Warfare from Indochina to Algeria—The Analysis of a Political and Military Doctrine*. New York: Frederick A. Praeger, 1964.

———. *Yorck and the Era of Prussian Reform*. Princeton, N.J.: Princeton University Press, 1966.

Paret, Peter; and Shy, John. *Guerrillas in the 1960s*. London: Pall Mall Press, 1962.

Parker, H. M. D. *The Roman Legions*. Cambridge, England: W. Heffer & Sons, 1958.

Paul, Elliott. *Life and Death of a Spanish Town*. London: Peter Davies, 1939.

Payne, Robert. *The Civil War in Spain*. London: Secker & Warburg, 1962.

———. *Lawrence of Arabia—A Triumph*. New York: Pyramid Books, 1963.

———. *Mao Tse-tung*. London: Abelard-Shuman, 1967.

Pearson, C. H. *History of England During the Early and Middle Ages*. London: Bell & Daldy, 1867.

Perroy, E. *The Hundred Years War*. London: Eyre & Spottiswoode, 1951. Tr. W. B. Wells.

Philippines Commission—1904, Fifth Annual Report of the. Washington: U. S. Government Printing Office, 1905. Vol. 1 of 2 vols.

Philippines Commission to the President, Report of the. Washington: U. S. Government Printing Office, 1900.

Philippines Commission (1900–1903), Report of the. Washington: U. S. Government Printing Office, 1904.

Piquet-Wicks, Eric. *Four in the Shadows*. London: Jarrolds, 1957.

Platonov, S. F. *History of Russia*. London: Macmillan, 1925. Tr. E. Aronsberg.

Plutarch. *Lives*. London: Macmillan, 1902. Vol. 3 of 5 vols. Tr. A. H. Clough.

Pokrovsky, M. N. *Brief History of Russia*. London: Martin Lawrence, 1933. 2 vols. Tr. D. S. Mirsky.

Polo, Marco. *The Travels of Marco Polo*. New York: New American Library, 1961. Ed. Milton Rugoff.

Polybius. *The Histories*. London: William Heinemann, 1922. Vol. 2 of 6 vols. Tr. W. R. Paton.

Ponteil, Félix. *L'Éveil des Nationalités et le Mouvement Libéral*. Paris: Presses Universitaires de France, 1968.

Poole, A. L. (ed.). *Medieval England*. London: Oxford University Press, 1958. Vol. 1 of 2 vols.

Pratt, Fletcher. *A Short History of the Civil War*. New York: Pocket Books, 1948.

Prescott, William H. *The History of the Conquest of Mexico*. Chicago, Ill.: University of Chicago Press, 1966.

Preston, R. A.; and others. *Men in Arms*. London: Thames & Hudson, 1962.

Pushkin, A. S. *The Captain's Daughter*. Moscow: Progress Publishers, 1954.

Pye, Lucian W. *Guerrilla Communism and Malaya—Its Social and Political Meaning*. Princeton, N.J.: Princeton University Press, 1956.

Rankin, Hugh F. "Charles Lord Cornwallis: Study in Frustration." In Billias, *supra*.

Rapoport, Anatol (ed.). *Clausewitz on War*. London: Penguin Books, 1968.

Roberts, Adam (ed.). *The Strategy of Civilian Defense*. London: Faber & Faber, 1967.

Roeder, Franz. *The Ordeal of Captain Roeder*. London: Methuen, 1960. Tr. and ed. Helen Roeder.

Rolo, Charles J. *Wingate's Raiders*. London: G. G. Harrap, 1944.

Romanus, C. F.; and Sunderland, R. *The China-Burma-India Theater: Stilwell's Problems*. Washington: U. S. Government Printing Office, 1956.

Rose, J. H. "The Second Coalition." In *The Cambridge Modern History*. London: Cambridge University Press, 1904. Vol. 8 of 13 vols.

Ross, Stanley K. *Francisco I. Madero—Apostle of Mexican Democracy*. New York: Columbia University Press, 1955.

Rostow, W. W. *The United States in the World Arena*. New York: Harper & Brothers, 1960.

Runciman, S. *A History of the Crusades*. New York: Penguin Books, 1965. 3 vols.

——. "The First Crusade: Constantinople to Antioch." In Setton, *infra*.

Schevill, F. *History of the Balkan Peninsula*. New York: Harcourt, Brace, 1922.

Schlesinger, A. M. *Political and Social History of the United States*. New York: Macmillan, 1926.

Schram, Stuart R. *Mao Tse-tung*. New York: Simon & Schuster, 1967.

Schulten, A. "The Romans in Spain." In *The Cambridge Ancient History*. London: Cambridge, England: The University Press, 1930. Chapter 10 of Vol. 8.

Schuman, F. L. *Russia Since 1917*. New York: Alfred A. Knopf, 1957.

Schurmann, Franz; and Schell, Orville (eds.). *China Readings 1 (Imperial China—The Eighteenth and Nineteenth Centuries)*. New York: Penguin Books, 1967.

———. *China Readings 2 (Republican China—Nationalism, War, and the Rise of Communism, 1911–49)*. New York: Penguin Books, 1968.

Scullard, H. H. *Scipio Africanus, Soldier and Politician*. London: Thames & Hudson, 1970.

Ségur, Philippe-Paul de, *Napoleon's Russian Campaign*. London: Michael Joseph, 1958. Tr. J. D. Townsend.

Seton-Watson, Hugh. *The Decline of Imperial Russia, 1855–1914*. London: Methuen, 1952.

———. *The East European Revolution*. London: Methuen, 1956.

Setton, Kenneth M. (ed.). *A History of the Crusades*. Madison, Wis.: University of Wisconsin Press, 1969. Vol. 1 of 2 vols.

Sheean, Vincent. *Personal History*. New York: Doubleday, Doran, 1936.

Sherwood, Robert E. *Roosevelt and Hopkins*. New York: Harper & Brothers, 1948.

Skeen, Sir Andrew. *Passing It On—Short Talks on Tribal Fighting on the North-West Frontier of India*. London: Gale & Polden, 1932.

Skobeleff, General. *Siege and Assault of Denghil-Tépé*. London: HMSO, 1881. Tr. J. J. Leverson.

Skodvin, Magne. "Norwegian Non-Violent Resistance During the German Occupation." In Roberts, *supra.*

Slessor, Sir John. *The Central Blue*. London: Cassell, 1956.

Slim, William R. *Defeat into Victory*. London: Cassell, 1956.

Smail, R. C. "Art of War." In Poole, *supra.*

———. *Crusading Warfare (1097–1193)*. London: Cambridge University Press, 1956.

Smith, R. Harris. *OSS—The Secret History of America's First Central Intelligence Agency*. London: University of California Press, 1972.

Smyth, John. *Percival and the Tragedy of Singapore*. London: MacDonald, 1971.

Snow, Edgar. *Random Notes on China 1936–1945*. Cambridge, Mass.: Harvard University Press, 1957.

———. *Red Star over China*. New York: Random House, 1938.

Special Operations Research Office (American University, Washington, D.C.). *Casebook on Insurgency and Revolutionary Warfare*. Washington: American University, 1962.

Spencer-Chapman, F. *The Jungle Is Neutral*. London: Chatto & Windus, 1949.

Standing, Percy Cross. *Guerrilla Leaders of the World: From Charette to Delvet*. London: Stanley Paul, 1912.

Stenton, F. M. *Anglo-Saxon England*. London: Oxford University Press, 1943.

Stilwell, Joseph W. *The Stilwell Papers*. New York: William Sloane, 1948. Ed. T. H. White.

Strauss, Lewis. *Men and Decisions*. New York: Macmillan, 1963.

Strayer, J. R.; and Munro, D. C. *Middle Ages, 395–1500*. New York: Appleton-Century, 1942.

Stschepkin, E. "Russia Under Alexander I, and the Invasion of 1812." In *The Cambridge Modern History*. London: Cambridge University Press, 1904. Vol. 9 of 13 vols.

Sukhanov, N. N. *The Russian Revolution, 1917*. London: Oxford University Press, 1955. Ed. and tr. Joel Carmichael.

Sutherland, C. H. V. *The Romans in Spain*. London: Methuen, 1939.

Sweet-Escott, Bickham. *Baker Street Irregular*. London: Methuen, 1965.

Sykes, Christopher. *Orde Wingate*. London: Collins, 1959.

Tanham, George. *Contribution à l'Histoire de la Résistance Belge*. Brussels: University of Brussels Press, 1971.

Tannenbaum, Frank. *Peace by Revolution: An Interpretation of Mexico*. New York: Columbia University Press, 1933.

Tarlé, Eugène. *Napoleon's Invasion of Russia, 1812*. London: Allen & Unwin, 1942. Tr. G. M.

Tarleton, Banastre. *A History of the Campaigns of 1780 and 1781, in the Southern Provinces of North America*. London: T. Cadell, 1787.

Tarn, W. W. *Alexander the Great and the Unity of Mankind*. London: Oxford University Press, 1933. Vol. 1 of 2 vols.

Taruc, Luis. *He Who Rides the Tiger*. New York: Frederick A. Praeger, 1967.

Taylor, L. A. *The Tragedy of an Army: La Vendée in 1793*. London: Hutchinson, 1913.

Temperley, H. W. V. *History of Servia*. London: G. Bell & Sons, 1917.

Thomas, Hugh. *Cuba or The Pursuit of Freedom*. New York: Harper & Row, 1971.

——. *The Spanish Civil War*. London: Eyre & Spottiswoode, 1961.

Thompson, Virginia. *French Indo-China*. London: Allen & Unwin, 1937.

Thucydides. *History of the Peloponnesian War*. Cambridge, Mass.: Harvard University Press, 1953. Vol. 2 of 4 vols. Tr. Charles F. Smith.

Toy, Sidney. *A History of Fortifications*. London: William Heinemann, 1955.

Trevelyan, George. *George the Third and Charles Fox*. London: Longmans, Green, 1914.

Truman, Harry S. *Year of Decisions 1945*. London: Hodder & Stoughton, 1955.

Tsiang Ting-fu. "The English and the Opium Trade." In Schurmann, *supra*.

Tuchman, Barbara W. *Stilwell and the American Experience in China—1913–45*. New York: Macmillan, 1971.

Urrutia Lleó, Manuel. *Fidel Castro and Company, Inc.: Communist Tyranny in Cuba*. New York: Frederick A. Praeger, 1964.

U. S. Department of State. *Foreign Relations of the United States—Diplomatic Papers 1944—Volume VI—China*. Washington: U. S. Government Printing Office, 1967.

——. *Foreign Relations of the United States—Diplomatic Papers 1945—Volume VII—The Far East—China*. Washington: U. S. Government Printing Office, 1969.

——. *United States Relations with China—With Special Reference to the Period 1944–1949.* Washington: U. S. Government Printing Office, 1949. Subsequently published as *The China White Paper—August 1949.* Stanford University Press, 1967. 2 vols.

Usborne, C. V. *The Conquest of Morocco.* London: Stanley Paul, 1936.

Utley, Freda. *Last Chance in China.* Indianapolis: Bobbs-Merrill, 1947.

Valeriano, N. D.; and Bohannan, C. T. C. *Counter-Guerrilla Operations. The Philippine Experience.* New York: Frederick A. Praeger, 1962.

Vandegrift, A. A.; and Asprey, R. B. *Once a Marine.* New York: W. W. Norton, 1964.

Vernadsky, George. *A History of Russia.* New Haven, Conn.: Yale University Press, 1945.

Vlekke, B. H. M. *Nusantara—A History of Indonesia.* The Hague: W. van Hoeve, 1959.

Volckmann, R. W. *We Remained.* New York: W. W. Norton, 1954.

Waley, Arthur. *The Book of Songs.* London: Allen & Unwin, 1937.

Wallace-Hadrill, J. M. *The Barbarian West, 400–1000.* London: Hutchinson, 1952.

Walsh, W. B. *Russia and the Soviet Union.* Ann Arbor, Mich.: University of Michigan Press, 1958.

Ward, Christopher. *The War of the Revolution.* New York: Macmillan, 1952. Ed. J. R. Alden. Vol. 2 of 2 vols.

Watteville, H. de. *Lord Kitchener.* London: Blackie & Son, 1939.

Webster, Graham. *The Roman Imperial Army of the First and Second Centuries A.D.* London: Adam & Charles Black, 1969.

Wedemeyer, A. C. *Wedemeyer Reports!* New York: Henry Holt, 1958.

Weigley, R. F. *History of the United States Army.* New York: Macmillan, 1967.

Weinberg, G. L. "The Yelna-Dorogobuzh Area of Smolensk Oblast." In Armstrong, *supra.*

West, Rebecca. *Black Lamb and Grey Falcon.* London: Macmillan, 1942. Vol. 1 of 2 vols.

White, Lynn, Jr. *Medieval Technology and Social Change.* London: Oxford University Press, 1962.

White, T. H.; and Jacoby, A. *Thunder Out of China.* New York: William Sloane, 1946.

Wickwire, Franklin; and Wickwire, Mary. *Cornwallis: The American Adventure.* Boston: Houghton Mifflin, 1969.

Wighton, Charles. *Heydrich—Hitler's Most Evil Henchman.* London: Odhams Press, 1962.

Wilcken, U. *Alexander the Great.* London: Chatto & Windus, 1932. Tr. G. C. Richards.

Willcox, William B. (ed.). *The American Rebellion—Sir Henry Clinton's Narrative of His Campaigns, 1775–1782,* with an Appendix of Original Documents. New Haven, Conn.: Yale University Press, 1954.

——. *Portrait of a General—Sir Henry Clinton in the War of Independence.* New York: Alfred A. Knopf, 1962.

——. "Sir Henry Clinton: Paralysis of Command." In Billias, *supra.*

Wingate, Ronald. *Wingate of the Sudan.* London: John Murray, 1935.

Winstedt, R. O. "Malaysia (History)." In Encyclopaedia Britannica, 1968, Vol. 14.

Wolfert, Ira. *American Guerrilla in the Philippines.* New York: Avon Books, 1945.

Wolff, Leon. *Little Brown Brother.* Garden City, N.Y.: Doubleday, 1961.

Womack, John. *Zapata and the Mexican Revolution.* London: Thames & Hudson, 1968.

Wood, Bryce. *The Making of the Good Neighbor Policy.* New York: Columbia University Press, 1961.

Woodhouse, C. M. *Apple of Discord.* London: Hutchinson, 1948.

———. *The Story of Modern Greece.* London: Faber & Faber, 1968.

Woodruff, Philip. *The Men Who Ruled India—The Guardians.* London: Jonathan Cape, 1954. Vol. 2 of 2 vols.

Woolman, David. *Rebels in the Rif.* Stanford, Calif.: Stanford University Press, 1969.

Wright, G. N. *Life and Campaigns of Arthur, Duke of Wellington.* London: Fisher, Son, n.d. 4 vols.

Ziemke, E. "Composition and Morale of the Partisan Movement." In Armstrong, *supra.*